Red Hat®

Linux® 7.2

Bill Ball, et al.

SAMS

Unleashed

Red Hat® Linux® 7.2 Unleashed

Copyright © 2002 by Sams

International Standard Book Number: 0-672-32282-X

Library of Congress Catalog Card Number: 2001093564

Printed in the United States of America

First Printing: December 2001

04   03   02   4   3   2

Trademarks

All terms mentioned in this book that are known to be trademarks or service marks have been appropriately capitalized. Sams cannot attest to the accuracy of this information. Use of a term in this book should not be regarded as affecting the validity of any trademark or service mark.

Warning and Disclaimer

Every effort has been made to make this book as complete and as accurate as possible, but no warranty or fitness is implied. The information provided is on an "as is" basis. The author and the publisher shall have neither liability nor responsibility to any person or entity with respect to any loss or damages aris-ing from the information contained in this book

ASSOCIATE PUBLISHER
Jeff Koch

ACQUISITIONS EDITOR
Katie Purdum

DEVELOPMENT EDITOR
Mark Renfrow
Brian Proffitt

MANAGING EDITOR
Matt Purcell

PROJECT EDITOR
Christina Smith

PRODUCTION EDITOR
Rhonda Tinch-Mize

INDEXER
Sharon Shock

PROOFREADER
Harvey Stanbrough

TECHNICAL EDITOR
Jason Byars

TEAM COORDINATOR
Denni Bannister

INTERIOR DESIGNER
Gary Adair

COVER DESIGNER
Aren Howell

PAGE LAYOUT
D&G Limited, LLC

Contents at a Glance

Contents

16 Apache Web Server Management 403

About the Lead Author

Bill Ball is the best-selling author of a dozen books about Linux, including several previous editions of *Red Hat Linux Unleashed*, Que's *Using Linux*, and Sams Publishing's *SuSE Linux Unleashed*. He is a technical writer, editor, and magazine journalist, and has been using computers for the past 26 years. He first edited books for Que in 1986, and wrote one of the first best-selling Linux books, *Teach Yourself Linux in 24 Hours*, in 1997. He has long been a fan of Linux and XFree86, and uses the software on Intel-based PCs, the Apple PowerMac, and MIPS platforms. He is an active member of the Northern Virginia Linux Users Group (NOVALUG), and lives in the Shirlington area of Arlington, Va. He can be contacted through `http://www.tux.org/~bball`.

About the Contributing Authors

Rich Blum has worked for the past 13 years as a network and systems administrator for the U.S. Department of Defense at the Defense Finance and Accounting Service. There, he has been using UNIX operating systems as an FTP server, TFTP server, e-mail server, mail list server, and network monitoring device in a large networking environment. Rich currently serves on the board of directors for Traders Point Christian Schools, and is active on the computer support team at the school, helping support a Microsoft network in the classrooms and computer lab of a small K-8 school. Rich has a Bachelor of Science degree in Electrical Engineering, and a Master of Science degree in Management, specializing in Management Information Systems, both from Purdue University. When Rich isn't being a computer nerd, he is either playing electric bass for the church worship band, or spending time with his wife Barbara and two daughters, Katie Jane and Jessica.

Tige D. Chastain (tigechastain@home.com) received his Bachelor's of Science in Computer Technology from Purdue University in West Lafayette, IN. He has contributed to the GNOME project, working on the Procman application that will be incorporated into the GNOME 2.0 Desktop. He has previously been published by Tech Republic (http://www.techrepublic.com) for an article on the Network+ Exam, a certification he also holds. Tige is currently working as an Oracle DBA for a small consulting firm in Indianapolis, where he is also a Network Administrator and instructor for Linux and Oracle classes. An avid Linux fan, Tige is constantly reconfiguring his seven servers to experiment with toys that he's not allowed to play with at work. He lives with his wife, Misty, and dog, Cheyenne, in Anderson, IN.

Hoyt Duff (www.maximumhoyt.com) plays cocktail piano on the weekends and tends to a family-owned sport fishing pier during the week. Currently writing the "Desktop" column for *Linux Format* magazine in the UK, he has enjoyed Linux for the past three years because he can "fix it until it breaks" again and again and again.

David B. Horvath, CCP is a Senior Consultant in the Philadelphia Pennsylvania area. He has been in the field for more than fifteen years and is also a part-time adjunct professor at local colleges, teaching topics that include C++ Programming, UNIX, and Database Techniques. He completed his Master's of Science degree in Organizational Dynamics at the University of Pennsylvania in 1998. He has provided seminars and workshops to professional societies and corporations on an international basis. David is the author of *UNIX for the Mainframer* (Prentice-Hall/PTR), coauthor of *SAMS Teach*

Yourself C++ for Linux in 21 Days, contributing author to *UNIX Unleashed Second Edition* (with cover credit), *Red Hat Linux Unleashed* (various editions), *Using UNIX Second Edition* (Que), *UNIX Unleashed Third Edition*, *Learn Shell Programming in 24 Hours*, *Linux Unleashed Fourth Edition*, and has written numerous magazine articles.

When not at the keyboard working or writing, he can be found working in the garden or soaking in the hot tub. He has been married for more than fourteen years and has several dogs and cats (the number of which is always changing). David can be reached at `rhlinux7@cobs.com`. No Spam please!

John Kennedy started his computer career in the United States Air Force in early 1987. After nine years of working mostly in mainframe environments, he left the military to shift his career toward computer networking. Since then he has worked as a LAN technician, doing almost everything one can do to install a new computer network plus PC hardware repair. The last four years he has worked as a UNIX System Administrator. Most of this has been with Solaris and Linux, with a brief stint on HP-UX. He has a wife named Michele and two children, Denise, 11, and Kieran, 9 1/2 months old. He is currently serving as librarian for the Lehigh Valley Linux Users Group (`http://thelinuxlink.net/lvlinux`) in Allentown, Pennsylvania.

Abhijit Menon-Sen occasionally writes for magazines and books to direct attention away from his more dubious activities, including the development of free crypto software, toxicology research, and the maintenance of Perl. He and his dog Bertie live in New Delhi, India.

Michael Urban has been working with various forms of UNIX for about seven years, including Linux, Solaris, and FreeBSD. He is a biology student at the University of Minnesota, where he works with the Lion Research Center and does Web site design, Linux administration, database programming, and software development. His previous writing projects include *FreeBSD Unleashed* from Sams Publishing. His primary interest is African lions, and he can usually be found immersed in research material on them when he has free time available.

Dedication

To the citizens of the world who advocate, support, and uphold the values of personal freedom, liberty, fair use, and free software.—Bill Ball

This is dedicated to my wife, Barbara, and daughters, Katie Jane and Jessica. Thanks as always for your love, faith, and support.—Rich Blum

I'd like to dedicate my work to my father, Daniel, for being a partner that I can always share my knowledge of computers with, my mother, Carolyn, for always reminding me to enjoy the human side of life, and to my loving wife, Misty, for enduring the long nights and days I spent away from her writing this book.—Tige D. Chastain

To my wife of 28 years, Bobbie Lou, whose love, support, and understanding have made me a better person. And thanks to Bryan Del Rizzo who provided my first opportunity to write about Linux as well as copious thanks and gratitude to the editors of this book, who obviously enjoy their work.—Hoyt Duff

I would like to dedicate my portion of this book to my brother Paul and his fiancée Erin. By the time this book actually hits the shelves, they should be husband and wife. I wish them many happy and healthy years together!—David B. Horvath

To my wife Michele, daughter Denise, and son Kieran. Surprise! All my love.—John C. Kennedy

To Jon Postel and W. Richard Stevens.—Abhijit Menon-Sen

To the lions at Ngorongoro. Hopefully I will be dropping by for a visit sometime soon. —Michael Urban

Acknowledgments

First, many thanks to the readers of *Red Hat Linux Unleashed*. I have received numerous comments, criticisms, and critiques from all over the world and cherish your thoughts. Many thanks to my acquisitions editor, Katie Purdum, whose calm and deliberate approach to publishing (and handling of authors) has helped to make this book one of the best guides to Red Hat Linux on the market. She is, without a doubt, one of the most capable and professional editors in the business. Thanks to Jason Byars for technical edits and helping me to not look like an idiot. No acknowledgment would be complete without a big nod to the thousands of programmers around the world who freely give their time and talent towards helping to produce software such as Linux, XFree86, the GNU Project, and the many commands and clients created or ported to Linux. Kind words are also needed for my fellow friends and comrades-in-arms at the Northern Virginia Linux Users Group (NOVALUG), especially its founder Greg Pryzby. NOVALUG has been and continues to be a communal source of inspiration for ideas, hardware hacks, and software fixes. Acknowledgment must be given Richard M. Stallman for the GNU GPL and to Linus B. Torvalds for sharing Linux with the world. And finally, a big vote of thanks to Microsoft Corporation; without its software, licensing schemes, and lawyers, fewer consumers and companies would have the impetus to migrate to Linux.

—Bill Ball

I want to acknowledge all the good folks at Sams Publishing and the other authors. As always, my wife deserves acknowledgement: she's the one who suffers when I'm sitting at the keyboard writing (or as she says, "playing around with the computer"). Of course, it is usually after a long day at work that I finally get a chance to write.

—David B. Horvath

Many thanks to Nicolai Langfeldt for teaching me nearly everything I know about the DNS, and to the many people who helped me to write and improve this chapter.

—Abhijit Menon-Sen

I would like to thank the people at Sams Publishing for giving me the opportunity to work on another writing project with them. Also, I'd like to thank Linus Torvalds. Had it not been for a single newsgroup posting by him many years ago, this book would not exist.

—Michael Urban

About the Technical Editor

Jason Byars(darth@purdue.edu) is a graduate student at Purdue University. He has a Bachelor of Science in Computer Engineering and enjoys both the hardware and software aspects of the field. His interests draw him to robotics, 3D graphics, software development, and IT work. He has been a fan of Linux since going to Purdue in the fall of 1996.

Tell Us What You Think!

As the reader of this book, *you* are our most important critic and commentator. We value your opinion and want to know what we're doing right, what we could do better, what areas you'd like to see us publish in, and any other words of wisdom you're willing to pass our way.

As an associate publisher for Sams, I welcome your comments. You can fax, email, or write me directly to let me know what you did or didn't like about this book—as well as what we can do to make our books stronger.

Please note that I cannot help you with technical problems related to the topic of this book, and that due to the high volume of mail I receive, I might not be able to reply to every message.

When you write, please be sure to include this book's title and author as well as your name and phone or fax number. I will carefully review your comments and share them with the author and editors who worked on the book.

Fax: 317-581-4770
E-mail: feedback@samspublishing.com
Mail: Jeff Koch
          Associate Publisher
          Sams Publishing
          201 West 103rd Street
          Indianapolis, IN 46290 USA

Introduction

Welcome to *Red Hat Linux Unleashed*! This is an all-new edition of one of the best-selling books about Red Hat, Inc.'s distribution of Linux, known as Red Hat Linux. If you're familiar with computers and computer operating systems, but new to Red Hat Linux, you've made the right choice in choosing one of the best Linux distributions available. If you're a new reader of Red Hat Linux Unleashed, congratulations again—you've picked one of the best books on the market about Red Hat Linux.

This edition has been completely updated to match the very latest developments found in Red Hat Linux, and as always, includes a free copy of the Publisher's Edition of Red Hat Linux on CD-ROM. Veteran readers will find that every chapter has been rewritten to include new topics, cover new features, and add additional information, such as security tips and a listing of Internet resources.

Red Hat Linux Unleashed is the best choice if you're looking for the right book for the best computer operating system in the world. We've taken the gloves off with this edition—Linux is no longer the new kid on the block, but a mature contender for all levels of computing. From embedded devices to laptops, desktops to servers, and mainframes to new Itanium CPUs, Red Hat Linux continues to be in the vanguard and a major force in the free software marketplace.

This book contains everything you need to plan, install, configure, maintain, administer, rebuild, and use Red Hat Linux to its fullest capabilities. You'll first see to how to set up and plan for an install. You'll then get step-by-step directions on how to install Linux in a variety of ways. Following directions on configuration, you'll be introduced to basic system administration, followed by instructions on advanced administration techniques and concepts. A section on programming and productivity rounds out the host of skills you'll acquire and learn when you use this book.

What Is Linux?

Linux is the core, or *kernel,* of a free operating system first developed and released to the world by Linus Benedict Torvalds in 1991. Torvalds, then a graduate student at the University of Helsinki, Finland, and now an engineer with the CPU design and fabrication company Transmeta, Inc., fortuitously chose to distribute Linux under a free software license named the GNU *General Public License (GPL).*

The GNU GPL is the brainchild of Richard M. Stallman, the founder of the Free Software Foundation. Stallman, the famous author of the emacs editing environment and gcc compiler system, crafted the GPL to ensure that covered software would always be free and available in source code form. The GPL is the guiding document for Linux and its ownership, distribution, and copyright. Torvalds holds the rights to the Linux trademark, but thanks to a combination of his generosity, the Internet, thousands of programmers around the world, GNU software, and the GNU GPL, Linux will remain forever free and unencumbered by licensing issues.

Linux, pronounced "lih-nucks," is free software. Combining the Linux kernel with GNU software tools, and other non-GPL'd software such as The XFree86 Project Inc.'s XFree86 X Window System, creates a Linux *distribution*. There are many different Linux distributions from different vendors, but many are derived from or closely mimic Red Hat Inc.'s distribution of Linux, Red Hat Linux.

What Is Red Hat Linux?

Red Hat Linux is the product of Red Hat, Inc. In 1994 Marc Ewing and Bob Young combined forces to create Red Hat (named after a Cornell University lacrosse team hat) in order to develop, release, and market an easily installed, easily managed, and easy-to-use Linux distribution. Five years later, Durham, N.C.–based Red Hat, Inc. would have one of the most successful Initial Public Offering (IPO) on the stock market. Today, the company has grown from a handful of employees to more than 500 in 20 locations around the world.

Red Hat, Inc. was one of the first companies to adopt, promote, and use open source as a business model for supporting development, technical service, support, and sales of free software to the computer industry. Its business practices have spawned a shift in paradigm of proprietary attitudes prevalent in the monopolistic software industry, and the company is a role model and business leader in the open source movement. For more details about Red Hat, Inc. and Red Hat Linux, see Chapter 1, "Introducing Red Hat Linux."

However, it is important to understand that not all software packages included on your Red Hat Linux CD-ROMs are free software. Only software in the public domain or covered by the GNU GPL or compatible license is free; the remaining software, such as the X Window System, various utilities, and other programs can be considered Open Source (available with source code) or even shareware. There are many different licensing schemes! If you purchase the official Red Hat Linux distribution from Red Hat, Inc., you might also find commercial software included on the distribution's CD-ROMs. These software packages are often included as an enticement to purchase more feature-laden or corporate versions.

Why Use Linux?

Using Linux is a good idea for a number of reasons, especially if you ignore the Fear, Uncertainty, and Doubt (FUD) being sown by an increasingly paranoid software industry monopoly. These reasons include

- There is little or no cost on a "per seat" basis. Unlike commercial operating systems Linux has no royalty or licensing fees, and a single Linux distribution on CD-ROM can form the basis of an enterprisewide software distribution, replete with applications and productivity software. Custom corporate CD-ROMs can be easily crafted to provide specific installs on enterprisewide hardware. This feature alone can save hundreds of thousands, if not millions of dollars in Information Service/Information Technology costs—all without the threat of a software audit from the commercial software monopoly, or the need for licensing accounting and controls.

- Linux, in conjunction with its graphical interface, the X Window System, has worked well as a consumer UNIX-like desktop operating system since the mid-1990s. The fact that UNIX is ready for the consumer desktop is now confirmed with the introduction of Apple Computer's BSD UNIX-based MacOS X—the only difference is that more applications are available for Linux than Mac OS X. Your Red Hat Linux CD-ROMs contain nearly 3,000 clients, including Internet connection utilities, games, a choice of three different office suites, thousands of fonts, and hundreds of graphics applications.

- Linux is fast, stable, scalable, and robust. Latest versions of the Linux kernel easily support multiple-processor computers (optimized for eight CPUs), large amounts of system memory (up to 64GB RAM), individual file sizes in excess of hundreds of gigabytes, a choice of journaling filesystems, hundreds of process monitoring and control utilities, and the (theoretical) ability to simultaneously support more than four billion users.

- Linux works well on a variety of PCs, including legacy hardware, such as Intel-based 486 CPUs. Although programs might be recompiled and optimized for Pentium-class CPUs, full base installs can be performed on lower-end computers with at least 8MB of RAM. This feature provides for a much wider user base, extends the life of older working hardware, and can help save money for home, small business, and even corporate users.

- There are versions of Linux for nearly every CPU. Embedded systems developers now turn to Linux when crafting custom solutions using ARM, MIPS, and other low-power processors. Linux is the first full operating system available for Intel's new Itanium CPU, and ports are available for Compaq's Alpha and Sun

Microsystem's SPARC CPUs. PowerPC users regularly use the PPC port of Linux on IBM and Apple hardware.

- Linux provides a royalty free development platform for cross-platform development. Because of the Open Source development model and availability of free high-quality development tools, Linux provides a low-cost entry point to budding developers and tech industry startups.

- Big-player support in the computer hardware industry from such titans as IBM now lends credibility to Linux as a viable platform. IBM has pledged to enable Linux on the company's entire line of computers, from low-end laptops through "Big Iron" mainframes. New corporate customers are lining up and using Linux as part of enterprise-level computing solutions.

Look forward to even more support as usage spreads worldwide throughout all levels of business in search of lower costs, better performance, and stable and secure implementations.

Who This Book Is For

This book is for anyone searching for guidance on using Red Hat Linux, with an emphasis on Red Hat's distribution for Intel-based PC platforms. Although the contents are aimed at intermediate to advanced users, even new users with a bit of computer savvy will benefit from the advice, tips, tricks, and techniques presented in each chapter. Pointers to more detailed or related information are also provided at the end of each chapter.

What This Book Contains

Red Hat Linux Unleashed is organized into five parts, covering installation and configuration, system administration, system services administration, programming and productivity, and a reference section. A complete set of the Publisher's Edition of Red Hat Linux CD-ROMs (including documentation) is included, so you'll have everything you need to get started. This book starts by covering the initial and essential tasks required to get Red Hat Linux installing and running on a target system.

If you're new to Linux, and more specifically, Red Hat Linux, first read the chapters under Part I, "Installation and Configuration." You'll get valuable information on

- An overview of Red Hat Linux and its role in various computing environments.
- Planning for an installation by examining hardware requirements and the need for organizing how the system is installed.

- Detailed steps that take you by the hand on different types of installations.
- Critical advice on key configuration steps to fully install and configure Linux to work with your system's sub-systems or peripherals, such as pointers, keyboards, modems, USB devices, power management and for laptop users, PCMCIA devices.
- Initial steps needed by new users transitioning from other computing environments.
- Configuration and use of the X Window System, the graphical interface for Linux.

Part II, "System Administration," is aimed at users familiar with Linux, but targets information specific to Red Hat Linux. Using the information in this part's five chapters, intermediate users will find out how to

- Control and track down problems during the boot process.
- Manage software, processes, and other system resources.
- Manage users and groups.
- Work with a new journaling filesystem, and craft remote filesystem mounting strategies.
- Ensure high-availability and reduce data loss through proper choice of backup media and strategies.

More advanced users integrating Red Hat Linux with the Internet and networking will want to read Part III, "System Services Administration." These chapters provide critical information related to

- Establishing local and remote printing services.
- Connecting a Red Hat Linux system to a network using a variety of hardware, such as serial, Ethernet, and wireless connections.
- Managing a domain name server.
- Connecting to the Internet, firewalling for security, and offering Internet connection services to remote users.
- Managing a Web server.
- Crafting database systems and managing databases.
- Providing secure FTP service.
- Handling Electronic Mail.
- Providing Network News service.

Part IV, "Programming and Productivity," expands on the capabilities provided by every Red Hat Linux system by covering:

- Basic development tools used for native Linux program and cross-platform development.
- Using Perl scripts for a variety of administrative tasks.
- Crafting new Linux kernels and managing kernel modules.
- Productivity applications included with Red Hat Linux, including various office suites, scheduling, graphics and scanner manipulation clients, and Personal Digital Assistant (PDA) connectivity.
- Using Linux to emulate other operating systems, or offering Linux services to other operating systems.

Part V, "Reference," provides a list of Internet resources, such as top Linux Web sites, a detailed listing of the Red Hat Package Manager (RPM) archives included with this book, and a quick reference guide to commonly used Linux commands.

Conventions Used in This Book

A lot of documentation is included with every Linux distribution, and Red Hat Linux is certainly no exception. In fact, Red Hat Linux includes so much documentation that it is included on a separate CD-ROM!

Although the intent of *Red Hat Linux Unleashed* is to be as complete as possible, it is impossible to cover every option of every command included in the distribution. However, where possible, tables of various options, commands, or keystrokes will be included to help condense, organize, and present information about a subject.

Screenshots will be included to cover nearly all Red Hat Linux specific graphical utilities, especially those related to system administration, or configuration and administration of various system and network services.

In order to help you better understand example code listings and sample command lines, several formatting techniques are used to show input and ownership. For example, if the example command or code listing shows typed input, the input will be formatted in boldface like this:

```
$ ls
```

If typed input is required, as in response to a prompt, the example typed input will also be in boldface, like so:

```
Delete files? [Y/n] y
```

This approach will also be used in all statements, variables, and text that is supposed to appear on your display. Additionally, command lines that require root or superuser access are prefaced with a pound sign like this:

```
# printtool &
```

Example command lines that can be run by any user will be prefaced with a dollar sign ($) like so:

```
$ ls
```

Other formatting techniques used to increase readability include the use of italics for placeholders in computer command syntax, and italicizing of computer terms or concepts upon first introduction in text.

Finally, you should know that all text, example code, and screenshots in *Red Hat Linux Unleashed* was developed using Red Hat Linux and open source tools.

Read on to start learning about the latest version of Red Hat Linux. Experienced users will want to consider the new information presented in this edition when planning or considering upgrades. New users, or users new to Red Hat Linux will benefit from the details presented in this book.

Installation and Configuration

PART

I

Introducing Red Hat Linux

CHAPTER 1

Welcome to Red Hat Linux Unleashed! It might be hard to imagine, but you're holding nearly $1 billion worth of software in your hands. That's one estimate of what it would cost to develop as complete an operating system, graphical interface, and related software to equal your copy of the latest Red Hat Linux included with this book.

This book is about Red Hat Linux, the best-known Linux distribution on the market, and is for intermediate to advanced Linux users. Red Hat Linux, provided by Red Hat, Inc. of Durham, N.C., is the Linux distribution against which all other Linux distributions are compared. Red Hat Linux has spawned more legions of imitators than any other Linux distribution, and is the distribution of choice for many computer hardware manufacturers, software shops, and Value-Added Resellers (VARS)—with good reason.

As you'll learn in this chapter, Red Hat Linux is one of the most up-to-date and mimicked distributions of Linux. You'll soon see why Red Hat Linux is a good choice in a variety of computing environments, and when combined with advances provided by the latest stable 2.4-series Linux kernel, provides multitiered support for the home, small office, traveler, small business, and even enterprise class corporate user.

What Is Red Hat Linux?

Red Hat Linux is a brand of Linux developed and distributed by Red Hat, Inc. This book includes a copy of the latest Red Hat Linux for Intel-based PCs, although there are versions of Red Hat Linux for other CPUs, such as Intel's Itanium and Compaq's (soon to be Intel's) Alpha CPU.

A free base version of Red Hat Linux will be found on the CD-ROMs included with this book. The distribution comprises the Linux kernel, installation utilities, thousands of pages of documentation, several thousand fonts, a comprehensive graphical networking interface, and several thousand individual commands and clients. Full source code, in the form of more than 21 million lines of C and nearly 5 million lines of C++ code is included. A comprehensive suite of programming tools, including compilers, interpreters, and report-generation utilities are also included in the base distribution.

However, Red Hat, Inc. also markets commercial Linux distributions, such as its Deluxe Workstation version, Professional Server version, Enterprise Edition (used for deploying Oracle 8i on the Linux platform), High-Availability Server, along with various update CD-ROMs. Differences between the commercial versions center on the amount and type of software included, along with the duration and type of technical support structure, ranging from 30 days to one year via the Web, networking, or phone.

> **Caution**
>
> Do NOT contact Red Hat, Inc. for any type of support when using or attempting to install the software included with this book. Although every effort has been made to ensure that information in this book matches the included software, you should instead contact Sams Publishing for any problems related to the CD-ROMs contained in this book. Only users who purchase the "official" Red Hat Linux from Red Hat, Inc. are entitled to support from Red Hat.

In July 2001, Red Hat also released the first commercial version of Linux for Intel's new 64-bit Itanium processor (a developer's edition had been available since the previous year). An Alpha Deluxe distribution is also available for the Alpha CPU. Unfortunately, Red Hat, Inc. stopped distribution of Red Hat Linux for the SPARC after version 6.2 (although bug fixes and security updates are available).

The Advantages of Using Red Hat Linux

Red Hat, Inc. has spent more than seven years developing and marketing its brand of Linux. Admittedly, although underneath all distributions are the same (they all use the Linux kernel), Red Hat continues to hold a market lead by selling a distribution that is easy to install and use, provides a host of features, and is backed by extensive bug fixes and security updates. Red Hat, Inc. is also one of the world's foremost open source development houses, and returns nearly all of its development efforts back to the Linux development community.

Some of these open source and GNU GPL projects include the Apache Web server, the glibc software libraries, the GNU Network Object Model Environment (GNOME), various GNU software tools and packages, the Linux kernel and device drivers, the PostgresSQL database system, and the Red Hat Package Manager (RPM). Other clients recognized by users familiar with Linux include the AbiWord word processor, programming tools such as `autoconf` and `automake`, the K Desktop Environment (KDE), the open source Web browser Mozilla, XFree86, `bzip2`, and Tcl/Tk.

Red Hat also supports many other projects by providing FTP service and Web hosting. It is also one of the few companies that actively promotes and uses the open source business development model. This means that although many of its products are also available for free, Red Hat pursues revenue streams associated with spin-off and related technologies and services. These include

- Embedded Solutions—Red Hat, Inc. sponsors an Embedded Tech Center and develops, supports, and markets the open source eCos embedded operating system. The company also maintains the EL/IX embedded Linux compatibility interface, markets embedded Linux solutions to Original Equipment Manufacturers (OEMs), developers and chip fabricators, and develops and releases RedBoot, an embedded firmware debugger and bootstrap for CPUs such as the ARM, MIPS, MN10300, PowerPC, Hitachi SHx, v850, and x86 series. Red Hat, Inc. also supports the uClinux distribution and provides embedded engineering services and development tools.

- Global Learning Services—Red Hat, Inc. was one of the first open source companies to provide Linux training and certification; current education and certification programs include the Red Hat Certified Engineer (RHCE) track, developer courses covering advanced programming applications, online courses, such as e-learning for Internet-based interactive course training, e-business courses covering e-commerce services and applications, embedded systems engineering courses, and various Linux skills courses.

- GNU Developer Tools—Even though nearly every Linux distribution includes the GNU gcc compiler system, Red Hat, Inc. also markets a commercial software development suite named GNUPro. This product provides embedded and cross-platform developers a suite of development tools, such as the gcc and g++ compilers, the gdb debugger, the gas assembler, ld linker, along with graphical interfaces for development, debugging and source-code management, and an Internet-based subscription service. For developers migrating applications to the software monopoly's commercial operating system, Red Hat also offers Cygwin, a set of software tools that provides a UNIX/Linux development environment on Windows.

- Red Hat Network—Red Hat, Inc. offers fee-based up-to-date bug fixes, security patches, software updates, technical support and documentation via an Internet-based subscription service known as Red Hat Network. Information service and information technology shops using Red Hat Linux can use this network for custom software management solutions as the network uses "dynamic system profiles" to only update installed services or software.

- Red Hat Professional Consulting—Building on the incredible growth of the installed base of Linux systems, Red Hat, Inc. also offers network business, open source, internetworking and security consulting, along with enterprise systems management and e-commerce solutions for today's online corporations and retailers.

- Software—Perhaps the best known of Red Hat products, these software distributions include various Red Hat Linux distributions, professional server solutions, and application bundles (such as IBM's DB2, Oracle's Oracle 8i, an IBM small business suite, Lotus Domino, and IBM WebSphere). Red Hat also develops and distributes an e-commerce suite, interchange e-commerce platform, secure Web server, credit card verification system (CCVS), and the Red Hat Database.

- Support and Development Services—When you buy a copy of Red Hat Linux, you'll receive some form of technical support and installation assistance. Other support programs include corporate support, scalable support solutions, Web server and e-commerce services, engineering support, and support for hardware and software certification.

You can't go wrong when choosing Red Hat Linux. This Linux distribution forms the basis for more than half the currently available Linux distributions, and is used in many of the newer embedded appliances appearing on the market, such as the GigaDrive, a network-attached storage device from Linksys, Inc. Although distributions can differ in file system layout, boot configuration and startup, software locations, and configuration file schemes, you'll be at home with most Linux distributions if you choose to start with Red Hat Linux.

What's New with Red Hat Linux?

New versions of Red Hat Linux are generally released every six months. Versions starting with a whole number (such as 6 or 7) generally indicate a major new release, with version numbers (such as .0, .1, or .2) indicating updates, fixes, or minor new features.

Recent features added to Red Hat Linux include choices of type of installation (such as server, workstation, or laptop), the choice of a text-based or graphical install, adoption of the 2.4 series of the Linux kernel, updated support for Universal Serial Bus (USB) devices, adoption of a new Internet superserver, xinetd, inclusion of the most recent stable version of the Mozilla Web browser, movement toward a multi–CD-ROM install, inclusion of support for KDE client development, a separate CD-ROM for documentation, minor changes to program and Linux documentation location in the installed file system (such as from /usr/doc to /usr/share/doc), and an update to RPM version 4 and newer.

The latest version of Red Hat Linux includes support for the ext3 journaling filesystem. Although other filesystems have similar features (such as Reiser, IBM's JFS, and SGI's XFS), ext3 offers the advantage of performance, safety, and ease of use and implementation. In other words, ext3 not only offers enterprise-level features desperately needed to propel Red Hat Linux into the corporate marketplace, but also makes migration of existing data much easier.

Red Hat Linux in the Enterprise

As Linux has matured over the last 10 years, additional features that are essential to its placement and success in enterprise-level environments have been added. Besides the addition of virtual memory (the ability to swap portions of RAM to disk), one of the first features was a copyright-free implementation of the TCP/IP stack (mainly due to BSD UNIX being tied up in legal entanglements at the time), followed by support for a variety of network protocols. Closely on the heels of network support, developers added the ability to read and write a variety of popular *filesystems*, or low-level data structures used on read-write and read-only media.

The next important feature, introduced with the 2.0 series of Linux kernels, was the ability to support multiple processors. This allowed Linux to be deployed in more advanced computing environments with greater demands on CPU power. With the advent of the 2.4 series of the Linux kernel, support has been added for at least eight CPUs, enabling Linux to run on ever more powerful hardware.

The 2.4 series of kernels also provides support for system RAM sizes up to 64GB, individual file sizes in excess of 2GB (extremely important for database operations), and support for many millions—and theoretically, billions—of users. And thanks to the efforts of IBM, SGI and individual programmers, the ability to use the JFS, XFS or ReiserFS journaling filesystem arrived on the scene. More than any other feature, the ability to safely and quickly recover from a catastrophic system event (such as loss of power) vaulted Linux (and Red Hat Linux) into the enterprise-class computing environment.

Corporations that depend on large-scale, high-volume, and high-availability systems can now turn to Red Hat Linux as a stable, robust, scalable, and inexpensive solution for various platform hosting. This means that bringing up a system with storage in the terabyte range following a powerdown no longer requires lengthy filesystem checks. Downtime is reduced to a minimum in the instance of power problems, and with enterprise solutions, services can be maintained without interruption.

Red Hat Linux is in use in a variety of environments by different customers with widely disparate computing needs. For example, Red Hat's Web Server is used by Ameritrade; the now ubiquitous Google Web search engine uses more than 8,000 Red Hat Linux systems; the New Jersey State Police uses a Red Hat-based Oracle system; and Kenwood America adopted Red Hat Linux as a network solution. Red Hat Linux is used around the world in a variety of systems and computing environments.

Red Hat Linux for Small Business

Using Red Hat Linux in small- and medium-sized business environments also makes good sense. Compared to the usurious licensing fees and per-seat charges of the software monopoly, small business owners can earn great rewards by stepping off the software licensing and upgrade treadmill when adopting a Linux-based solution. Using Red Hat Linux not only avoids the need for licensing accounting and the threat of software audits, but provides viable alternatives to many different types of commercial productivity software.

> **Note**
>
> Taxpayers of Virginia Beach, Va. were probably dismayed when the city sent Microsoft Corp. a check for nearly $129,000 in November 2000, and spent an estimated $81,000 in staff time on a month-long software audit. In all, the audit, a result of a threatening letter from Microsoft earlier in the month concerning software licenses, cost the city nearly $210,000—all of which could have been avoided had the city used Linux and open source software for its computing needs.
>
> On a happier note, in June 2001 the U.S. Dept. of Defense (DoD) ordered 25,000 of Sun Microsystems' StarOffice, a free office suite for Linux, UNIX, and other operating systems. This act alone will save U.S. taxpayers millions of dollars in costs for commercial software. One can only hope that the impetus will spread throughout the U.S. federal government, academia, and governments throughout the world.

Red Hat and Linux Documentation

Every commercial Linux distribution includes manuals and documentation covering installation and configuration. You'll find documentation from Red Hat, Inc. included on one of the CD-ROMs included with this book. You can also get copies of the Red Hat manuals online through `http://www.redhat.com/apps/support/documentation.html`. There you'll find Red Hat's official manuals and guides (specific to Intel-based PC Linux systems):

- The Official Red Hat Linux x86 Installation Guide
- The Official Red Hat Linux Getting Started Guide
- The Official Red Hat Linux Reference Guide
- The Official Red Hat Linux Customization Guide

These guides are available in Portable Document Format (PDF) and can be read using Adobe's Acrobat Reader for Linux or the xpdf client. The guides are also available as bundled HTML files for reading with a Web browser such as lynx, Netscape Navigator, or Mozilla. Along with these guides, Red Hat, Inc. provides various tips, Frequently Asked Questions (FAQs), and HOWTO documents.

For information regarding software management using the Red Hat Package Manager (RPM), you can also download a free copy of Ed Bailey's classic *Maximum RPM*. Developers interesting in writing or porting programs to Linux can also get a copy of *Linux Application Development* by Michael K. Johnson and Erik W. Troan.

Along with the guides and books, new users might also want to check Red Hat's listing of certified hardware and hardware compatibility list. For more technical information, a series of "white papers" are also available online. Red Hat also provides a series of mailing lists you can subscribe to. The following is a partial listing of the available mailings:

- *redhat-announce-list*—General announcements about Red Hat Linux
- *redhat-devel-list*—Information for developers
- *redhat-install-list*—Discussions regarding installation
- *redhat-list*—General Red Hat Linux discussions
- *redhat-ppp-list*—Discussions regarding Internet connectivity
- *redhat-secure-server*—Discussions about Red Hat's Secure Web Server
- *redhat-watch-list*—Announcements of updates, and security and bug fixes
- *rpm-list*—Discussions regarding use of RPM
- *under-the-brim*—The Red Hat Linux newsletter

Savvy Red Hat Linux users will turn to some of these discussions, which are archived online, for answers when searching for troubleshooting information.

If you choose to perform a full installation of Red Hat Linux, you'll find traditional Linux software package documentation under the /usr/share/doc directory. Red Hat Linux includes hundreds of separate documents known as HOWTOs that contain information regarding specific subjects. If the HOWTO documents are in compressed form (with filenames ending in .gz), you can easily read the document by using the zless command, which is a text *pager* that allows you to scroll back and forth through documents (use the less command to read plain text files). You can start the command by using less, followed by the complete directory specification and name of the file, or *pathname*, like this:

```
$ less /usr/share/doc/ipchains-1.3.10/HOWTO.txt
```

After you press Enter, you can scroll through the document using your cursor keys. Press the q key to quit.

Reference

Each chapter in this book includes a Reference section listing links to additional or related information covered in the text. You can use these links to learn more about Red Hat Linux and related technologies. You can also use the Reference section material to build custom sets of bookmarks to use while browsing or researching for more information about Linux.

`http://www.dwheeler.com/sloc`—David A. Wheeler's amazing white paper covering the current state of GNU/Linux, its size, worth, components, market penetration.

`http://www.redhat.com`—Home page of Red Hat, Inc., and your starting point for learning more about Red Hat Linux.

`http://www.redhat.com/support/docs/gotchas/7.1/gotchas-71.html`—Key information related to problem-solving with Red Hat Linux 7.1 release. You'll find similar information regarding current Red Hat Linux releases in the same support area.

`http://www.redhat.com/about/success/`—A listing of government and corporate Red Hat, Inc. customers.

`http://www.freerepublic.com/forum/a3a0569e96e74.htm`—Virginian-Pilot news story regarding Microsoft's demand for license accounting by the Virginia Beach, Va. city government.

`http://www.pilotonline.com/archives/`—Information regarding Virginia Beach, Va.'s licensing follies in November 2000.

`http://www.redhat.com/apps/support/documentation.html`—Web page with links to current Red Hat Linux documentation, guides, technical papers, and free online books.

`http://www.redhat.com/mailing-lists/`—The entry point to many different archived, online mailing list contents concerning Linux and Red Hat Linux.

`http://www.linuxdoc.org`—The definitive starting point for the latest updates to generic Linux FAQs and HOWTO documents.

Preparing to
Install Red Hat
Linux

Proper preparation and planning before considering a Red Hat Linux installation can pay big dividends later on. After choosing to deploy Linux, it's time to take a hard look at how to deploy the new operating system.

Installing Red Hat Linux for the first time can seem daunting to inexperienced users or system administrators. A whole generation of computer users have grown up without the need to worry about partitioning a hard drive to support multiple operating systems because little choice existed on Intel-based platforms. Other operating systems, such as Mac OS, ran on radically different computer hardware, with little interoperability between the systems.

Computer users now have a choice of operating systems, and many different types of users are now choosing to jump ship to Linux in the hopes of breaking the software monopoly's stranglehold on their desktops while at the same time reaping rewards in better performance and price. As you'll see in this chapter, Red Hat Linux is a flexible Linux distribution that can adapt to a variety of hardware configurations and can be installed in a number of ways.

This chapter outlines some of the basic hardware requirements for using Red Hat Linux, provides a general overview of the installation process, and covers planning for partitioning to support different configurations.

Obviously, before even planning an installation, considerations have been made concerning the type of deployment and how Red Hat Linux will be used in the installation. Computing needs will dictate the type of hardware and software solutions required for success, but before making the plunge, some hard questions need to have been asked and answered, such as why use Linux, or more specifically, why use Red Hat Linux?

Table 2.1 provides a minimal checklist you can use to help plan a deployment.

TABLE 2.1 Deploying Red Hat Linux

Consideration	*Description*
Applicability	How is Red Hat Linux going to be used?
Boot Management	Will remote booting be required?
Connectivity Wireless?	Will the system be an intranet? Bandwidth requirements? Mobile?
Context	How does this install fit in with academic, business, or corporate needs?
Consensus	Are managers and potential users on board with the project?

TABLE 2.1 continued

Consideration	Description
Comparison	Is this install part of platform comparison or benchmarking?
Development Platform	Will development tools be used?
Embedded Device	Is it an embedded device project?
Hardware	Are there any special hardware or device interfacing requirements?
Finance	How much is in the budget? Will cost comparison be required?
Marketing	Will a product or service be offered as a result?
Networking	What type of networking will be required?
Objective	Is there a specific objective of the install?
Power Management	Any special power or energy requirements?
Prototype Project	Is this a prototype or test install?
Public Relations	Does the public need to know?
Quality of Service	Is high-availability or data integrity an issue?
Roadmap	What other steps might precede or follow the install?
Reporting	Are follow-up reports required?
Security	What level or type of security will be required?
Server	Is this a server installation?
Siting	Does the location provide needed temperature, security, or even matter?
Software	Are any special device drivers needed for success?
Storage	Size or integrity needs? Back up plan devised?
Time Line	Are there time constraints or deadlines to the install?
Training	Will special training be required for users or administrators?
Users	How many and what type of users are expected?
Workstation	Is this a workstation install? Is the workstation portable?

There are many factors in favor of using Red Hat Linux as a computing solution. The current distribution can fill many different roles on various tiers and hardware platforms because Red Hat Linux offers preconfigured installation scripts to fit development, workstation, e-commerce, server, and mobile platform needs—only the required software will be installed.

Addressing concerns beforehand can help quell any worries or fears felt by new users. Some key factors include preparation, pre-configuration, correct installation, and choosing the right hardware to do the job.

Hardware Requirements

Red Hat Linux can be installed on and will run on a wide variety of Intel-based hardware. This includes legacy platforms up to the latest workstations, rack-mounted systems, and multi-processor servers available from the entire tier of computer hardware vendors. Small, medium-sized, and even large-scale deployments of Red Hat Linux are available through a number of companies such as IBM, which offers hardware, software, and service solutions (with more than 200 software solutions for clustering application alone). However, it is always a good idea to check for compatibility and extensively explore options before jumping on board with a specific vendor.

Obviously the type of deployment and how you're going to use Linux will determine the hardware required for the task at hand or program satisfaction. The range of requirements and hardware type is quite wide, especially when you consider that Red Hat Linux can also be used for embedded device development, and even runs on SODIMM or PC-104 form factor hardware.

Whether you're building a Web server the size of a matchbox, or installing 12,000 Red Hat Linux servers on an IBM S/390, understanding the basic requirements can save time and money. However, understanding the basic requirements for Red Hat Linux won't mean a thing unless you have a thorough understanding of the designated hardware, potential limitations, and potential expenses. Buying a turn-key Linux solution is one way to avoid hardware problems, and many vendors are standing by, ready to prescribe solutions. However, managing deployments aimed at using existing hardware requires some information collection.

Using an Installation Checklist

Small business and individual users would be well advised to prepare detailed checklists of existing hardware before attempting or even expecting a move to Red Hat Linux. Not only will you benefit from the collected information, but you might also be able to sidestep or anticipate problems before, during, or after installation. Problems are most likely to occur with newer hardware, cutting-edge hardware such as new motherboard chipsets, video cards, or extraneous hardware such as operating system-specific scanners, printers, or wireless devices.

Table 2.2 provides a comprehensive checklist you can use to take inventory of target hardware, such as the computer and any peripherals. Veteran Red Hat Linux users can take the collected information to build custom systems by adding known hardware or substituting cheaper, but par-level hardware.

TABLE 2.2   System and Peripheral Inventory Checklist

Item	Errata
Audio Devices	Microphone:
	Line out:
	Line in:
BIOS	Type:
	Revision:
CDROM Drive	Brand:
	Type:
CDRW Drive	Brand:
	Type:
	CDR Write Speed:
	CD Re-Write Speed:
	CD-ROM Read Speed:
DVD Drive	Brand:
	Type:
Digital Camera	Brand:
	Model:
	Interface:
CPU	Brand:
	Socket Type:
	Speed:
Firewire (IEEE 1394)	Chipset:
	Device(s):
IrDA Port	Device number:
	Port IRQ:

TABLE 2.2 continued

Item	Errata
Keyboard	Brand:
	Type:
Laptop	Brand:
	Model:
	Hibernation partition:
Legacy Ports	Parallel type:
	Parallel IRQ:
	RS-232 number(s):
	RS-232 IRQ(s):
Mice	Brand:
	Type:
Modem	Brand:
	Type:
Motherboard	Brand:
	Type:
	Chipset:
Monitor(s)	Brand:
	Model:
	Horizontal freq:
	Vertical freq:
	Max. Resolution:
Network Card	Wireless:
	Brand:
	Type:
	Speed:
PCI Adapter	Brand:
	Model:
	Type:
PCMCIA	Controller:
	Cardbus:
	Brand:
	Type:

TABLE 2.2 continued

Item	Errata
Printer(s)	Brand:
	Model:
System RAM	Amount:
	Type:
	Speed:
S-Video Port	X Support:
Scanner	Brand:
	Model:
	Interface type:
Sound Card	Chipset:
	Type:
	I/O Addr:
	IRQ:
	DMA:
	MPU Addr:
Storage Device(s)	Removable:
	Size:
	Brand:
	Model:
	Controller(s):
	Rotational Speed:
Storage Device Controller	Type:
Tablet	Brand:
	Model:
	Interface:
Universal Serial Bus	Controller:
	BIOS MPS Setting:
	BIOS Plug-n-Play Setting:
	Device(s):

2

PREPARING TO
INSTALL RED HAT
LINUX

TABLE 2.2   continued

Item	Errata
Video Device(s)	Brand:
	Model:
	Chipset:
	VRAM:

You'll be much better prepared for your Red Hat Linux installation after you know why you're going to use the system and after conducting an inventory of your computer's subsystems and peripherals. The largest hurdles in getting Linux properly installed and running on a system are

- Making room for Red Hat Linux on the storage medium, known as *partitioning*, and then installing Linux and the distribution's software.
- Configuring X to work at the greatest resolution and color depth available using a combination of the computer's graphics card and monitor.
- Configuring Linux to work with the system's sound card.
- Getting connected (configuring networking or an Internet connection).
- Configuring a printer, scanner, or other devices.

Choosing an Installation Class

Making room for Red Hat Linux requires you to decide on how to use existing hard drive space—perhaps replace existing hard drives—or decide to use only one operating system on your computer. The Red Hat Linux installer offers a choice of installation types or *classes*, and each has its own hard drive storage requirements:

- Workstation—You'll need more than at least 2GB hard drive storage, or even more if you choose to install everything. This installation is intended for developers and other users who want to use the entire spectrum of Linux software offered by the Red Hat distribution.
- Server—You'll need less storage for the software (ranging from 650MB to more than 1GB), but you should take into consideration other storage requirements. For example, if you plan to run a Web site with a lot of graphics or serve other files, you might need to add storage to your system, or accommodate remotely mounted storage locally.
- Laptop—This new class of installation, introduced with Red Hat Linux 7.1, is just for laptops but will still require at least 1.5GB of hard drive space.

- Custom—For a minimal installation, choose the 300MB custom install; however, you can also choose to install every package in the distribution, in which case you'll need 3.6GB more of storage, along with several hundred megabytes of free space for temporary files.

The storage requirements for each of these classes can be revised somewhat, depending on the X desktop environment you choose (such as KDE or GNOME). Choosing the "expert" mode when installing Red Hat Linux will also let you choose specific software packages from the group package categories. It is possible to pare down a system, especially if you choose not to install documentation, the X Window system, graphics utilities, or any development software or libraries.

Hardware Specifics

Red Hat Linux software for Intel-based PCs is compiled for the minimum x86 platform supported by the Linux kernel, the x386 CPU family. Note that other distributions, such as SuSE Linux (which requires an x486) and Red Hat–based Mandrake Linux (which requires a Pentium-class CPU) might have different storage and CPU requirements.

Specific issues regarding hardware compatibility can be researched online through Red Hat, Inc.'s hardware compatibility database at `http://hardware.redhat.com/hcl/gen-page2.cgi`. You can enter the name or type of computer, video card, hard drive, printer, or other hardware device to check for compatibility or see if there are any issues. Click in the Quick Search field, and then click the Search button, as shown in Figure 2.1.

FIGURE 2.1

Enter search queries to research hardware compatibility issues before purchasing hardware or installing Red Hat Linux.

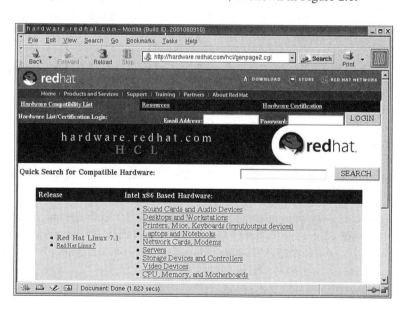

2

PREPARING TO
INSTALL RED HAT
LINUX

After you press Enter, matching returns with a compatibility graphic and any issues will be appended and displayed on the Web page. This is a great research resource to use before purchasing equipment to use with Red Hat Linux or before installing potentially problematic hardware. Hardware categories covered in the database include

- Controller cards—Such as SCSI, IDE, Firewire
- CPUs—Intel, AMD, and others
- Input devices—Keyboards
- Modems—External, PCMCIA, PCI, and controllerless workarounds
- Network cards—ISA, PCI, USB and others
- Pointing devices—Mice, tablets, and possibly touchscreens
- Printers—Various printer models
- RAM—Issues regarding types of system memory
- Sound cards—Issues regarding support
- Specific motherboard models—Compatibility or other issues
- Specific PCs, servers, and laptop models—Compatibility reports
- Storage devices—Removables, fixed, and others
- Video cards—Console issues (X compatibility depends on version of XFree86 or vendor-based X distribution used)

If you have a particular laptop or PC model, you should also check with its manufacturer. Some enlightened manufacturers now offer Red Hat Linux pre-installed, or have in-house Linux hardware certification programs.

Overview of the Install Process

Installing Red Hat Linux can be as simple as inserting the first Red Hat Linux CD-ROM and rebooting the computer. But if you choose this method, you should first make sure that your system's BIOS is set to boot from CD-ROM. Entering the BIOS to make this change is usually accomplished by depressing a particular key immediately after turning on the computer. After entering the BIOS, navigate to the BIOS Boot menu, such as that shown in Figure 2.2.

There are many other methods of installing Red Hat Linux. Some installation methods will require the use of a boot and auxiliary driver disk. These disks can be created using the DOS RAWRITE.EXE command or the Linux dd command using disk images included on the first Red Hat Linux CD-ROM.

FIGURE 2.2

In order to boot to an install using your Red Hat Linux CD-ROM, set your BIOS to have your computer boot using its CD drive.

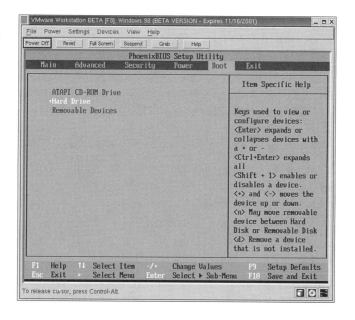

For example, to create a boot disk using dd, insert and mount the CD-ROM, and then insert a blank floppy diskette in drive A: of your PC. You can then use the dd command like this:

```
# dd if=/mnt/cdrom/images/boot.img of=/dev/fd0 bs=1440k
```

After you press Enter, the floppy image will be copied from CD-ROM to the floppy diskette. You can also use this method (or RAWRITE.EXE) to create any other needed diskettes.

Selecting a type of installation method might depend on the equipment on hand, existing bandwidth, or equipment limitations. In general, you can install Red Hat Linux using a variety of methods, including

- A hard drive partition—By copying the Red Hat Linux installation files from the first and second CD-ROMs, you can then boot to an install using a boot disk or the DOS LOADLIN command.

- CD-ROM—Using a compatible CD-ROM drive attached to the computer. Laptop users with an external CD-ROM drive will need PCMCIA support.

- DOS—By using LOADLIN, you can boot to a Linux install by pointing LOADLIN to use a Red Hat Linux installation kernel and ramdisk.

- File Transfer Protocol (FTP)—As with an NFS install, installation via FTP will require that the Red Hat Linux software from CD-ROM one and two be available on a public FTP server. You'll also need an installed and supported network interface card, along with a boot floppy with network support.

- Hypertext Transport Protocol (HTTP)—As with the FTP and NFS installs, installation via HTTP will require that the Red Hat Linux software from CD-ROM one and two be available on an accessible Web site. You'll also need an installed and supported network interface card, along with a boot floppy with network support.

- Installation via the Internet—If you have the bandwidth, it is also possible to install Red Hat Linux via the Internet; however, this method may not be as reliable as using a Local Area Network (LAN).

- Network File System (NFS)—A remotely mounted hard drive containing the Red Hat Linux software can be used, but you'll need to have an installed and supported network interface card, along with a boot floppy with network support.

- Pre-installed media—It is also possible to install Linux on another hard drive and then transfer the hard drive to your computer. This is handy, especially if your site uses removable hard drives or other media.

Installations are also possible using software via an Iomega Zip drive, via the Parallel Port Internet Protocol (PLIP), and even a null-modem cable supporting the Serial Line Internet Protocol (SLIP) or Point-to-Point Protocol (PPP).

Once you've selected the type of installation and then boot to the install, the procedure will be nearly the same for each type of install. Red Hat Linux also supports the ability to monitor the background processes running during an installation. You can watch the progress of an install by navigating to a different console display or *virtual* console by pressing Ctrl+Alt+ a designated Fn key, such as F1 through F5. This way you can via the installation, access a shell prompt, view a log of the install, or watch for any kernel messages.

Partitioning Before and During Installation

Partitioning your hard drive for Linux can be done before or during installation. If you have a running Linux system, adding a new hard drive will also involve partitioning (and formatting with a new filesystem), but this can be accomplished while running Linux. If you plan to prepare your partitions before installing Linux, you'll need to use either commercial partitioning software, the free FIPS.EXE command, or boot your system using a live Linux distribution (such as Linuxcare's Bootable Business Card) and then use a native Linux utility such as `fdisk`.

Some of the popular commercial software you can use to create Linux partitions include PowerQuest's PartitionMagic or VCOM Products' Partition Commander. The GNU `parted` command can be used under Linux, and can handle (at the time of this writing) Linux ext2, FAT, FAT32, and Linux swap partitions, with support planned for HFS, NTFS, and ReiserFS.

Like deployment and installation of Linux, partitioning your hard drive to accept Red Hat Linux requires some forethought, especially if the target computer is going to be used other than as a home PC on which to learn Linux. At the very least, Linux requires a native Linux partition and a swap partition. Notebook users might find an existing "save-to-disk" or hibernation partition slightly larger than installed memory—this partition should be left untouched unless you want to lose that power-saving function.

The Red Hat Linux installer will automatically create and use a partition scheme according to the type of installation selected during the install if Linux will be the only resident operating system. If you plan to have a dual-boot system, in which you can boot Linux or another operating system, you'll need to manually partition your hard drive before and possibly during the install. The order in which operating systems are installed might also be important because the software monopoly's operating systems typically disregard previously installed software and will overwrite the primary hard drive's Master Boot Record.

The simplest partitioning scheme would be, as previously mentioned, a single Linux native root partition and swap partition. A single-drive system with 10GB storage and 128MB RAM, the scheme might look like this:

```
Hard Drive Partition     Mount Point     Size
/dev/hda1        /          9.74GB
/dev/hda2        swap       256MB
```

On a system running Windows 9/x, the scheme might look like this:

```
Hard Drive Partition     Mount Point     Size
/dev/hda1        /mnt/dos    2GB
/dev/hda2        /           7.74GB
/dev/hda3        swap        256MB
```

However, on a system that is being designed for expansion, greater capacity, or the capability to host additional software or users, additional partitions can be used to host various parts of the Linux file system. Some candidates that should be separate partitions or even filesystems include

- /home—Users will store hundreds upon hundreds of megabytes of data under their directories. This is important data, perhaps even more so than the system itself. Using a separate partition (on a different volume) can make sense.

- /opt—As the home directory for additional software packages, this directory can have its own partition or remote filesystem.

- /tmp—This directory can be used as temporary storage by users, especially if disk quotas are enforced; as such, it could be placed on its own partition.

- /usr—This directory can become quite large if additional software is added, especially on a workstation configuration. Using a separate partition can make sense.

- /var—Placing this directory (or perhaps some of its subdirectories) on a separate partition can be a good idea, especially because security logs, mail, and print spooling takes place under this tree.

Other areas of the Red Hat Linux filesystem that are good candidates include storage of FTP files, active Web pages, and other data that might be in continuous use.

Using Red Hat's `kickstart` Installation Method

Installation of Red Hat Linux can also be automated through the use of Red Hat's kickstart installation method. This type of automatic installation uses a single configuration file with a special, extensive syntax on a server, boot floppy, or other medium to install Red Hat Linux via a network connection. In turn, the complex configuration file, used as an installation profile, can itself be automatically configured by using Red Hat's Kickstart Configurator. To start the configuration, log in as the root operator, and then run the ksconfig command like so:

```
# /usr/sbin/ksconfig
```

After you press Enter, you'll see a dialog box, as shown in Figure 2.3.

Click to select various options, and then enter the specifics desired for the target system. Of course, automated installations work best when installing to similar equipment. When finished, click the Save to File button, and the configuration will be saved with the name ks.cfg.

FIGURE 2.3

Red Hat's kickstart *configuration tool,* ksconfig, *can be used to quickly and easily create installation profiles for use in automated installations.*

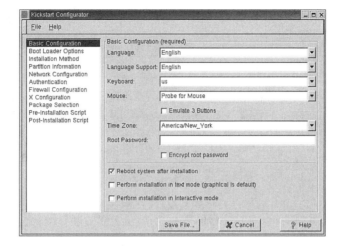

The kickstart file will be read by computers booting to the install. The kickstart language covers nearly every aspect of an install with the exception of sound card, printer or modem setup. Using kickstart is fairly easy and involves passing a kernel argument to the Red Hat Linux boot kernel. The various arguments tell the boot kernel to look for the configuration file on floppy, a designated server, via a network, specific file, or CD-ROM.

A companion program, mkkickstart, can be used to generate a ks.cfg file using the current workstation as a model. Information regarding the system's setup is gathered and then saved in a model file. Specifics concerning using kickstart and its configuration language are available online in Red Hat's support area.

Automating the installation process can save system administrators a lot of time and effort during an initial Red Hat Linux deployment, upgrade, or maintenance cycle, by managing multiple computers at one time.

Reference

The following is a list of references you can use to learn a bit more about partitioning, installation tools, and installing Red Hat Linux and Linux variants on a variety of hardware. You'll also find information about installation on hardware employed for embedded and mainframe solutions.

http://www.yale.edu/pclt/BOOT/DEFAULT.HTM—A basic primer to partitioning that is operating system non-specific `http://www-1.ibm.com/linux/`—Home page for Linux at IBM, with links to products, services, and downloads

`http://oss.software.ibm.com/developerworks/opensource/linux390/index.html` —Home page for IBM S/390 Linux solutions

`http://www.esrf.fr/computing/cs/sysadmin/rtk/pc104project/howto/linux/ master_hw.htm`—One approach to installing and using Linux on a PC-104 single board computer (SBC)

`http://www.dell.com/us/en/biz/topics/linux_aacraid.htm`—Dell Computer's server lineup running Red Hat Linux

`http://www.dell.com/us/en/bsd/topics/linux_000_linux_products.htm`—Links to Dell computers available with Red Hat Linux

`http://www.redhat.com/support/hardware/`—Entry point to Red Hat's hardware compatibility database

`http://linux1394.sourceforge.net/`—Home page for the Linux Firewire Project, with information regarding the status of drivers and devices for this port

`http://www.linux-usb.org`—Home page for the Linux USB Project, with lists of supported devices and links to drivers

`http://www.schirmacher.de/arne/dvgrab/dvgrab_features_e.html`—Digital video grab software (via Firewire) for Linux

`http://www.elks.ecs.soton.ac.uk/`—Home page for Linux for x286 and below CPUs, ELKS Linux

`http://open-projects.linuxcare.com/BBC/`—Home page for the Bootable Business Card, a 50MB compressed Linux distribution that offers hundreds of networking clients, a live X session, Web browsing, PDA backup, wireless networking, rescue sessions, and file recovery

`http://www.gnu.org/software/parted/parted.html#introduction`—Home page for the GNU `parted` utility

`http://www.linux.org/vendors/systems.html`—One place to check for a vendor near you selling Linux pre-installed on a PC, laptop, server, or hard drive

Installing Red Hat Linux

CHAPTER 3

This chapter provides a basic guide to installing Red Hat Linux through a short step-by-step installation. Before installing Red Hat Linux, you should have a basic understanding of your system's hardware. This will help ensure that the process of creating a new Linux system is done quickly and efficiently with a minimum of problems. Arm yourself with information about your system beforehand in order to head off potential problems such as choosing partition sizes that are too small or hardware mis-configuration.

It is your job to properly allocate your system's resources, and create a working, stable install. You should know the type of installation to perform beforehand (such as a workstation, server, firewall, gateway, router, development system, and so on). Servers that are designed for a single purpose, such as serving or managing electronic mail will have software, storage, and system requirements different from a simple gateway. Installing and configuring a workstation or development workstation will have different software and storage requirements, which can either lighten the load of or tax CPU, RAM, and storage resources.

Most new users with standalone Red Hat Linux computers will install all the software included with Red Hat Linux and depend on Red Hat's RPM technology to sort out and handle software dependencies (see Chapter 8, "Managing Software and System Resources" for more details about using RPM). Using Linux isn't like living in a house built with a pack of playing cards where one misplaced or missing piece of software can bring down the computer. But crafting an efficient, stable, and working system will require some consideration about the type of software to use.

Planning Partition Strategies

Part of planning a custom system involves implementing a partitioning strategy based on the knowledge of existing hardware before the install. And in corporate or enterprise-level environments, part of the planning should also take into consideration future expansion or evolution of the system. The idea can be to craft a flexible system that might possibly evolve as it is used. Knowing how to allocate software on your hard drive for Linux involves knowing how Red Hat Linux organizes its *file system*, or layout of directories on storage media. This knowledge will help you make the most out of hard drive space, and in some instances, such as planning to have user directories mounted via NFS or other means, can help head off data loss, increase security, and accommodate future needs. Create a great system, and you'll be the hero of information services. Create a house of cards, and you'll be looking for a new job.

Some questions you should have the best possible (or correct) answers to before installing Red Hat Linux include "How much disk space is required now or in the future?" "Will the system boot just Red Hat Linux or another operating system?" or "How much data needs to be backed up, and how will it be backed up?"

Choosing a Boot Loader

You will also need to know how the system will be booted. Various software packages and schemes can be used. For example, will you use the Linux Loader, LILO, or the GRand Unified Bootloader, known as GRUB? LILO is a small boot loader usually installed in the Master Boot Record of an IDE hard drive, the root Linux partition, or on a floppy disk. This loader (like others) can be used to pass essential kernel arguments to the Linux kernel for use during the boot process. Some arguments include disk geometry, additional network interfaces, or perhaps installed RAM values. LILO uses a configuration file named /etc/lilo.conf. Other boot loaders, such as GRUB, might support boot read-only memory (ROM) or flashed memory chips containing boot-loading code. Yet other approaches supported by some, but not all, PC hardware BIOS include booting via a network. And Linux can also be booted via removable media or a floppy disk.

> **Note**
>
> Red Hat's mkbootdisk command can be used to create boot media while using Linux by using the Linux kernel release number (returned by using the uname -r command) and a specified device, such as: **mkbootdisk --device /dev/ fd0 2.4.7-2**

Red Hat Linux can also be booted from a DOS session using the LOADLIN program, a DOS PATH to the Linux kernel, and the location of Linux kernel, such as:

```
LOADLIN c:\KERNEL\VMLINUZ root=/dev/hda2 ro
```

In this example, the kernel named VMLINUZ is loaded, and the second primary partition of the first IDE hard drive is specified at the root (\) partition of the Red Hat Linux system.

> **Note**
>
> If you find that LOADLIN fails to boot Linux and complains about a large kernel size, you can either try using make bzimage to build a smaller kernel, or rebuild a kernel that relies less on built-in features and more on loadable modules. See Chapter 23, "Kernel and Module Management," for more information.

A good boot loader will support multiple operating systems, the ability to boot different Linux kernels (in order to change the characteristics of a system or easily accommodate new hardware), password protection, custom boot displays, and sane defaults.

Another consideration in using a system hosting one or more operating systems is that some operating systems "don't play well with others" (such as later versions of Windows from Microsoft), and might wipe out MBR settings or might not use the MBR. If you find yourself in this situation, it might be best to turn to commercial boot loader software. If you run into trouble after installing Red Hat Linux, make sure to read the documentation for your boot loader to acquire any diagnostic information. Most boot loaders will report on any problems and the solution might be commonly fixed.

Choosing How to Install Red Hat Linux

Red Hat Linux can be installed in a variety of ways using different techniques and hardware. You should also know how you plan to install Linux before starting in order to devise a policy or perhaps foil subsequent installs for security. For example, installing via a network onto workstations lacking removable media can help increase security to some degree.

Red Hat Linux is typically installed by booting to the install directly from a CD-ROM. Other options include

- Booting to an install using a floppy diskette
- Using a hard drive partition to hold the installation software
- Booting from a DOS command line
- Booting to an install and installing software over a network using FTP or HTTP protocols
- Booting to an install and installing software from an NFS-mounted hard drive

How you choose to install (and use) Red Hat Linux depends on your system's hardware, corporate information service policy, or personal preference.

Installing from CD-ROM

Most PCs' BIOS supports booting directly from a CD-ROM drive, and offers an ordering of devices to search for bootable software. Set your PC's BIOS if required, and then insert the CD-ROM and turn on or reboot the PC to install Red Hat Linux. Problems can arise if the CD-ROM isn't recognized by the Linux kernel, but trouble shouldn't occur unless there is hardware failure. (In the past, some CD-ROM drives required a kernel patch, this should no longer be a problem; see Table 3.1 in this chapter, which lists a driver disk image used to support older drives.)

Booting to an Install from DOS

As previously mentioned, a DOS utility such as LOADLIN (or BOOTLIN) can be used to either boot to an install directly from CD-ROM or to load the Red Hat Linux install kernel. See the `dosutils` directory on the first Red Hat Linux CD-ROM included with this book, and read the README file under the `dosutils` directory for an overview of the DOS utilities. The directory contains a one-line DOS batch file (`.bat` file) that can help boot to an install:

```
loadlin autoboot\vmlinuz initrd=autoboot\initrd.img
```

In this example, the LOADLIN command will boot the Red Hat Linux install kernel residing under the `dosutils/autoboot` directory, and then load the installation software to launch an install.

Making an Installation Boot Diskette

Your Red Hat Linux installation can also be started using a boot floppy. Floppy images (`.img` files) are contained in the images directory on the first Red Hat Linux CD-ROM. Red Hat, Inc. provides a number of images, as listed in Table 3.1.

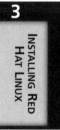

3

INSTALLING RED
HAT LINUX

TABLE 3.1   Red Hat Linux Boot Images

Name	*Description*
boot.img	Enable booting using CD-ROM or hard drive partition
bootnet.img	Install via FTP, HTTP, or NFS
pcmicia.img	Boot install using PCMCIA hardware (requires the pcmciadd.img)
drivers.img	Utility image containing various hardware drivers
oldcdrom.img	Support image for booting using old CD-ROM drives
imageo/pxeboot	Directory containing a PXE-enabled Linux kernel

Most of the images listed in Table 3.1 support booting to an install using either local hardware or using local hardware to install using a network. The `pxeboot` directory contains a kernel that supports a remote booting protocol named PXE that enables installation or upgrades of network-only PCs. Use of this software requires a properly configured server and local PCs BIOS settings.

The diskettes images can be created using the DOS RAWRITE command or the Linux dd command to create the floppy. The RAWRITE command is used after starting DOS like this:

D:\dosutils\rawrite

You'll need one or more blank diskettes. Follow the prompts to create the images, entering a source filename and a target drive (such as A or B). To create a boot diskette dd, mount the first Red Hat Linux CD-ROM and use the dd command like so:

 # dd if=/mnt/cdrom/images/*nameofimage*.img of=/dev/fd0

This will create a diskette in the DOS drive A. Use /dev/fd1 if you want to use an installed secondary floppy drive. PC notebook users installing via a network or external CD-ROM drive using a PCMCIA adapter might need the pcmcia.img and pcmciadd.img diskettes.

Hard Drive Partition Installation

A hard partition can be used to either boot the Red Hat Linux install or hold the software required from an install. The partition must be large enough to hold .iso images (binary images of a CD-ROM). Copy the images of the first and second Red Hat Linux CD-ROMs in a directory on the local hard drive. If you use this type of install and don't need the required hard drive space later on, a system can be quickly reinstalled from the partition.

The .iso images can be downloaded from Red Hat, Inc. or a mirror FTP site. Images can also be created using Linux utilities such as mkisofs, dd, and the mount command.

To perform this installation, you will need to know the hard drive's device name (such as /dev/hdb), along with the partition number and the name of directory containing the images (such as /dev/hdb1 and /redhat/images; if you simply copy the images to the formatted DOS or Linux partition, you don't need the directory information).

Installing Using a Network

Red Hat Linux can be installed using a local network (or even over the Internet if you have broadband access). Boot your PC to the install, and then choose the type of installation. Installing Red Hat Linux using the File Transfer Protocol (FTP) will require access to an FTP server. You'll need to know the hostname or IP address of the server, along with the path (directory) holding the Red Hat Linux software. Installing Red Hat Linux using a remotely mounted Network File System (NFS) is similar to a hard drive installation, but requires access to an NFS server. You'll need access permission, a permitted IP address or hostname for your computer, the hostname or IP address of the NFS server, and the path to the Red Hat Linux software.

To install Red Hat Linux using HTTP, you will need the hostname or IP address of the remote Web server, along with the directory containing Red Hat Linux. Other installation methods might be variations on network installation or the installation and subsequent use of an alternative Linux distribution (such as a floppy based distribution) to bootstrap to an install.

Step-by-Step Installation

This section provides a basic step-by-step installation of Red Hat Linux from a CD-ROM. There are many different ways to proceed with an install, and the Red Hat Linux installer can provide a graphical or text-based interface in a variety of modes. The example approach outlined here should work with any PC and can be used as a starting point for learning more about installing Red Hat Linux.

To get started, insert the first Red Hat Linux CD-ROM and reboot your computer. You'll first see a boot screen that offers a variety of options for booting. These options (shown in Figure 3.1) are

- <ENTER>—Start the install using a graphical interface
- text—Start the install using a graphical text interface
- lowres—Start the install using a 640x480 resolution
- nofb—Start the install avoiding use of a video framebuffer
- expert—Offer manual installation and configuration during the install, and disable autoprobing of hardware by the installer
- linux rescue—Boot to single-user mode with a root operator prompt, disabling X, multitasking and networking
- linux dd—Use a driver disk and possibly one or more kernel arguments (such as linux mem=512M expert) to enable certain types of hardware, such as networking cards

3

INSTALLING RED
HAT LINUX

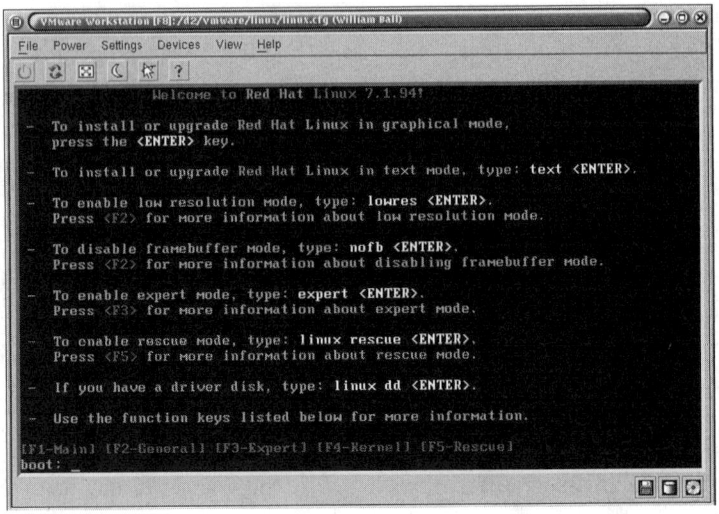

FIGURE 3.1

Select a type of installation, installation mode, or rescue installation when first installing Red Hat Linux.

Other options that can be used at the boot prompt include setting a specific resolution and color depth for the installation. This is done by typing **vga=** at the boot prompt, along with a number such as

- 773—use 256 colors at 1024x768
- 775—use 256 colors at 1280x1024
- 791—use thousands of colors at 1024x768
- 794—use thousands of colors at 1280x1024

Function keys can be used at the boot prompt to get more information about an installation mode or to enable a mode. Pressing F2 provides a single screen of help text. Pressing F3 gives information about the expert mode. Pressing F4 describes how to pass kernel arguments. Pressing F5 describes Red Hat's rescue mode.

Press the spacebar to halt an automatic boot to the install. Type the word text at the boot prompt and press Enter to continue. The installer's kernel will load, and you'll be asked to select a language for the installation, as shown in Figure 3.2.

Use the Tab key to navigate to scrolling lists or buttons in the graphical dialog box. Scroll through the list to highlight a language, and then use the Tab key to highlight the OK button and press Enter. You'll then be asked to select a keyboard for the install, as shown in Figure 3.3.

FIGURE 3.2

Select a language to use when installing Red Hat Linux.

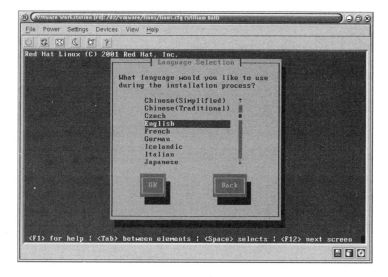

FIGURE 3.3

Select a default keyboard to use when installing and using Red Hat Linux.

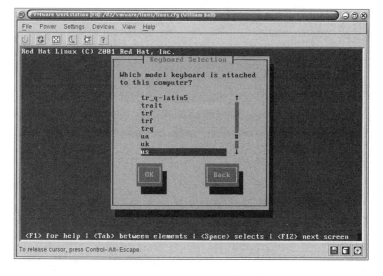

3

INSTALLING RED
HAT LINUX

Again, select a keyboard, and then highlight the OK button and press Enter. You'll next be asked to select a pointing device, as shown in Figure 3.4.

FIGURE 3.4

Select a pointing device to use when installing and using Red Hat Linux.

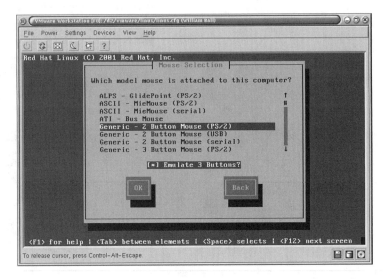

Select a mouse type to use for Red Hat Linux sessions. Note that Red Hat Linux supports USB devices, including USB mice. If you have a two-button mouse, select it by scrolling through the list. Note that three-button emulation will be automatically selected. (This emulation enables a middle-mouse button to be simulated when both the left and right mouse buttons are pressed simultaneously.) Highlight OK to continue. You'll see a splash screen and will be offered the opportunity to go back to change the previous settings. If the settings are correct, highlight the OK button and press Enter. You'll be asked to select a type of installation, as shown in Figure 3.5.

FIGURE 3.5

Select a type of Red Hat Linux installation.

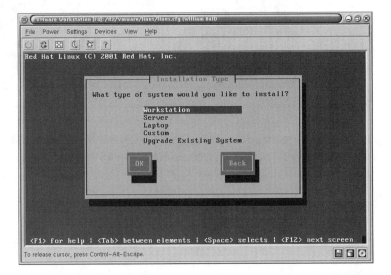

Select a type of installation using your cursor keys and the Tab key. The Workstation, Server, and Laptop installations offer a unique set of preselected software libraries and packages. The Custom installation allows selection of individual software packages with the ability to resolve any *dependency* issues automatically. Software dependencies should be resolved in order to have a stable system because some software packages depend on other software packages to function properly.

> **Note**
>
> You can use Linux virtual consoles during installation to monitor the hardware detection, gain access to a single-user shell, and view progress of the installer script. When using a graphical installer, press Ctrl+Alt+F1+4 to navigate to the various screens. Press Alt+F7 to jump back to the installer. When performing a text-based installation, use Alt+F1+4; use Alt+F1 to jump back to a text-based install, and Alt+F5 to jump back to the install screen if you use a graphical install.

In this example, select a Server install and press Enter to continue. You'll then see a screen, as shown in Figure 3.6, that offers a choice of partitioning schemes and tools.

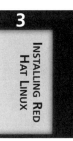

FIGURE **3.6**

Select a partitioning scheme or tool.

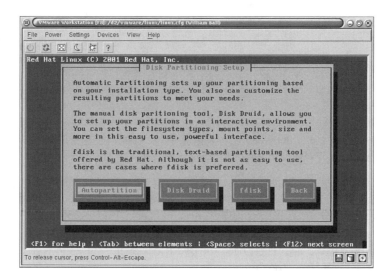

The Autopartition button will partition your hard drive according to the type of selected installation, and automatically configure the partitions for use with Linux. The Disk

Druid button will launch a graphical partition editor. The fdisk button will launch the Linux fdisk utility. The fdisk command offers the ability to create (not format) nearly 60 different types of partitions, but has a text-based interface.

Click the Disk Druid button. If you are using a new hard drive that hasn't previously been partitioned, you'll be asked if you would like to create new partitions on the drive. Click the Yes button to initialize the drive. If you are using a hard drive that has been previously partitioned or formatted and the partitions are recognized, Disk Druid will present a graphical interface. Figure 3.7 shows a hard drive with nearly 1.5GB of free space that hasn't been partitioned.

FIGURE 3.7

Partition your drive before installing Red Hat Linux.

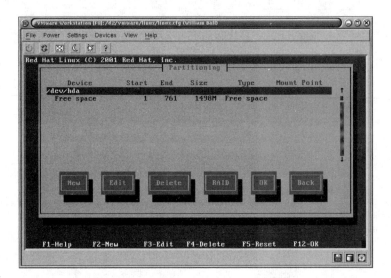

To use Disk Druid, select any listed free space, and then press the New button. To create free space, scroll to an existing partition and use the Delete button to delete the partition. If you use the New button, you'll see a dialog box as shown in Figure 3.8.

The Add Partition dialog box is used to select a hard drive, assign a mount point (such as /boot or /), assign a filesystem (such as ext2, ext3, RAID, swap, or vfat), assign the size of the partition, and assign a filesystem check. The size of the partition can be fixed, or if you press the spacebar when selecting the Fill All Available Space field, will use all remaining free space. The Check for Bad Blocks item is used to verify low-level formatting (and will take a long time on a hard drive with a capacity larger than 1GB). Use the OK button when finished.

FIGURE 3.8

*Set partition infor-
mation about a
selected or new
partition on a
hard drive.*

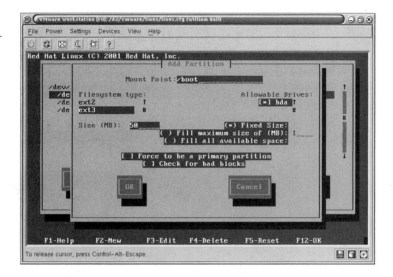

Red Hat Linux requires at least a root (/) and swap partition. The swap partition should
be more than twice as large as the amount of installed memory, and perhaps three times
as large because of new memory requirements of the Linux 2.4–series kernel. Figure 3.9
shows a completed partitioning scheme for a server with an initial 1.5GB hard drive.
Note that you can assign other schemes, such as a remote /home partition, but this can be
accomplished after installation.

FIGURE 3.9

*Review your parti-
tioning scheme for
your hard drive.*

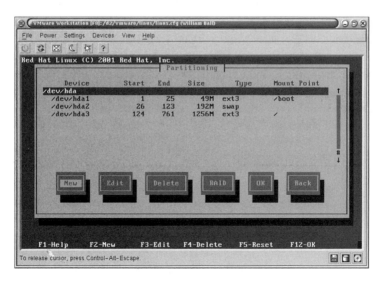

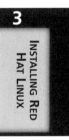

3

INSTALLING RED
HAT LINUX

Take a moment to review your partitioning scheme. Changes can be made by selecting a desired partition, and then using the Edit or Delete button, followed by use of the New button to use any free space. When satisfied, use the OK button to continue the install. You'll then be asked (as shown in Figure 3.10) to select a boot loader for booting Red Hat Linux, or whether you'd prefer not to use a boot loader (when booting from floppy, a DOS partition, or over a network).

FIGURE 3.10

Select whether you want to use a boot loader, and if so, which type.

Using GRUB or LILO depends on your need for a particular feature, familiarity or preference. The GRUB loader works with all BSD UNIX variants and many proprietary operating systems. The utility also supports menuing, command lines, installed RAM detection, and diskless and remote network booting. On the other hand, LILO has a much longer Linux history and might be more familiar to long-time Linux users. Select the desired boot loader, and then use the OK button, and you'll be asked where you want to install the boot loader, as shown in Figure 3.11.

GRUB and LILO are typically installed in the MBR of the first IDE hard drive in a PC. However, the boot loader can also be installed in the first sector of the Linux boot partition. Note that you can also backtrack through the install process to change any settings. Select a location and use the OK button to continue. You'll then be asked (as shown in Figure 3.12) if you'd like to pass any kernel arguments before booting Linux.

FIGURE 3.11

Select where you'd like to install the boot loader.

FIGURE 3.12

Enter any desired kernel arguments to be passed by the boot loader.

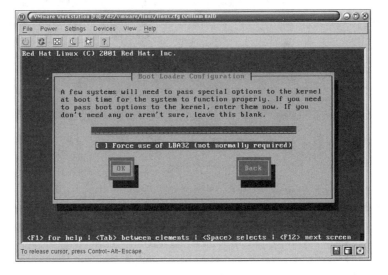

Enter the arguments in the dialog box or use the OK button to continue. After you press Enter, you can graphically edit the loader's configuration file to add or remove choices of booting other operating systems. The default operating system to boot will be Red Hat Linux, but if you are configuring a dual-boot system, you can configure the boot loader, either now or later on when using Red Hat Linux, to support booting another installed operating system residing on a different partition. When finished, click the OK button, and you'll be asked to select a firewall configuration, as shown in Figure 3.13.

3

INSTALLING RED
HAT LINUX

> **Note**
>
> You'll be asked to configure network settings if your computer's installed network adapter is recognized by the Red Hat installer. If you install a recognizable network adapter after installation, Red Hat Linux will ask during the boot process if you'd like to configure the adapter. Network adapters can also be configured by using the `netconf` command.

FIGURE 3.13

Selected a desired security level.

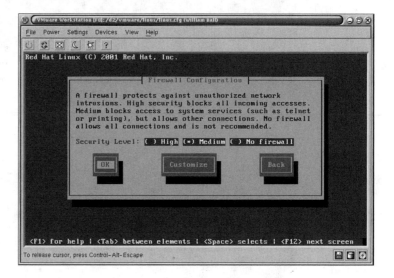

Use the dialog box shown in Figure 3.13 to set a security level. Although the No firewall setting isn't recommended, this setting can be used if you're using Red Hat Linux as a non-networked workstation. The Medium setting might be acceptable for use on an intranet protected by a firewall and served by an Internet gateway. Certainly use a high security level if your computer is attached directly to the Internet. Note that you can also manually configure security settings after installing Red Hat Linux. Use the Customize button to choose allowable services, as shown in Figure 3.14.

The dialog box in Figure 3.14 should be used to set allowable incoming service requests. This is important if you want to allow requests immediately following installation and the start of Red Hat Linux. For some servers, HTTP, FTP and Simple Mail Transport Protocol (SMTP) requests are acceptable and reasonable. Use the OK button when you finished selecting services. You'll then be asked to select any additional languages you'd like supported by the installed Red Hat Linux system. You'll then see a Time Zone Selection dialog box, as shown in Figure 3.15.

FIGURE 3.14

Select allowable incoming service requests for your custom security setting.

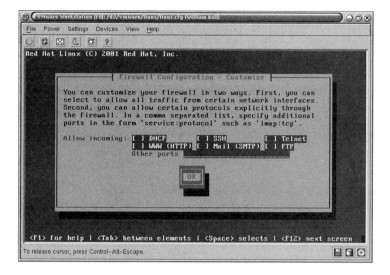

FIGURE 3.15

Select your time zone.

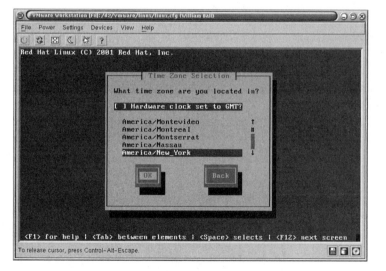

There are two "clocks" or times when using a PC: the hardware clock, maintained by chips in the computer and a backup battery; and the system time, set upon booting and used by the Linux kernel. It is important to keep the two times accurate and in synchronization because automated system administration might need to take place at critical times. Many computer installations use computers with hardware clocks set to Greenwich Mean Time (a misnomer because the correct designation is UTC or Coordinated Universal Time). The Linux system time is then set relative to this time and the current time zone, such as Eastern Standard Time, which is -5 hours of UTC. Setting the computer's hardware clock to UTC (GMT) has the advantage of allowing the Linux system time to be easily set relative to the geographic position of the computer and resident time zone. (Such as a Linux laptop user who would like to create files or send electronic mail with correct time stamps, and who has traveled from New York to Tokyo).

> **Tip**
>
> Read the manual page for the `hwclock` command to learn how to keep a running Linux system synchronized with a PC's hardware clock.

Choose your time configuration, and then press the OK button. You'll then be asked to enter a root operator password. Type in a password, press Enter, and then type it again to make sure that it is verified. The password, which is case sensitive, should be at least six characters (or more) and consist of letters and numbers. Note that the password isn't echoed back to the display. When finished, use the OK button to continue. You can then create a normal user account, as shown in Figure 3.16.

FIGURE 3.16

Create a user account for use with Red Hat Linux.

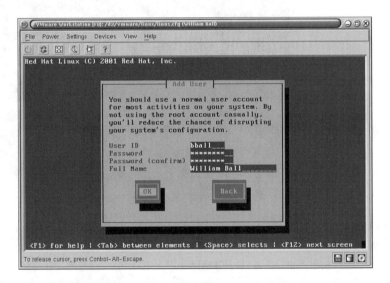

Create a user account for yourself and any additional users of the system. Users are assigned a username, password, shell, and home directory. The default home directories reside under the /home directory. When finished, use the OK button to continue. You can then add additional users if you created a user for your system. (Even if you use Red Hat Linux on a standalone workstation, you should create a user for yourself, and then use the su or sudo commands to perform root tasks.)

In the Package Group Selection dialog box, shown in Figure 3.17, are select software groups, each of which contains many different software packages.

FIGURE 3.17

Select software package groups for installation.

3

INSTALLING RED HAT LINUX

Use the spacebar to select various groups of software packages. Note that the size of the installed software will dynamically reflect your choices. Use the Select Individual Packages item to choose individual software packages. This can allow fine-tuning of the software installation to only installing desired commands or clients, and to prune unwanted software. Use the OK button when finished. You'll then be asked to configure a video card for the X Window System (if selected for installation) as shown in Figure 3.18.

You won't be asked to select a video card if you don't install the X software. Note that you can select and choose X software for installation, and then skip the configuration step and configure X for Red Hat Linux after installing. See Chapter 6, "The X Window System," for details on configuring X to work with a PC's graphics card. If you select a graphical or text-based install and don't use the Expert mode to install Red Hat Linux, your graphics hardware will be automatically probed.

FIGURE 3.18

Select a video card for use with X11 or skip the configuration.

After X configuration or skipping the configuration, the installer will then format your partitions using your settings. Next, an install image will be transferred to the formatted partition for use during the install. The installer will then check your software selection for any package dependencies and begin copying software from the CD-ROM (or a selected source) onto the new Linux partitions, as shown in Figure 3.19.

FIGURE 3.19

Monitor your installation and packages.

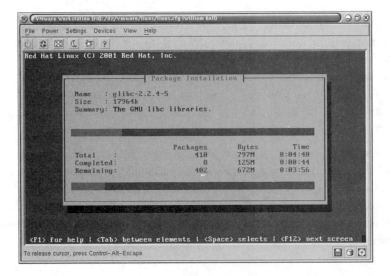

The installer, shown in Figure 3.19, reports on the name of the current package being installed, the total number of packages, time remaining for the installation, and number of completed and remaining packages. At some point during the installation, you will be asked to remove the first CD-ROM and insert the second. When the installation finished, the installer will perform some temporary file cleanup, install the boot loader and then ask if you'd like to create a boot diskette for possible use later, as shown in Figure 3.20.

FIGURE 3.20

You can create a boot disk for later use.

You can create this book disk now, or you can use Red Hat's `mkbootdisk` command later on while using Red Hat Linux. Select Yes or No. If you choose to create a boot disk, you'll need to have a blank diskette on hand. Having a boot disk can be handy, especially if the boot loader fails to boot Linux.

After this portion of the install, you're done! Press the OK button and Red Hat Linux will eject any inserted CD-ROM and reboot. If you choose to use the LILO boot loader, you'll then be presented with a graphical boot prompt as shown in Figure 3.21. (The GRUB boot loader will look similar.)

If you do nothing for five seconds or press Enter, the boot loader will boot Red Hat Linux. To use a text-based boot prompt, press Ctrl+x and press Enter. You'll then see the boot: prompt if you use LILO. Both LILO and GRUB offer the chance to pass any required kernel arguments.

FIGURE 3.21
*Boot Red Hat
Linux by pressing
the Enter key
or waiting five
seconds.*

Login and Shutdown

After rebooting your PC, you'll be able to log in to a Linux session. If X11 wasn't configured during the installation, you'll log in at a text-based login prompt. If you configured X and enabled a graphical login, the screen will clear after Red Hat Linux boots, and you'll be presented with a graphical login screen.

To log in, type **root** and press Enter. Next, type in your root password and press Enter to start using Linux as the system administrator. If you use a graphical login, you can use the shutdown or reboot menus in the dialog box to shut down or reboot your system. To shut down your system from the command line of a text-based session, use the shutdown command with its -h or halt option and the keyword now or the numeral 0 like this:

```
# shutdown -h now
```

You can also use

```
# shutdown -h 0
```

You can also use the shutdown command halt to reboot your computer like this:

```
# shutdown -r now
```

Or you can use

```
# shutdown -r 0
```

For new users, installing Red Hat Linux is just the beginning of a new and highly rewarding journey on the path to learning Linux. For Red Hat Linux system administrators, the task ahead is to fine-tune the installation and to customize the server or user environment.

Reference

`http://www.redhat.com/support`—The place to start when looking for information and FAQs about installing and configuring Red Hat Linux.

`http://www.redhat.com/apps/support/resources/`—Links to online Red Hat Installation manuals.

`http://www.nwc.com/columnists/1101colron.html`—How to use the PXE protocol to remote boot workstations.

`http://www.gnu.org/software/grub/`—Home page for the GRUB boot loader.

`http://elserv.ffm.fgan.de/~lermen/HOME.html`—Home of the LOADLIN Linux loader.

`http://www.linuxdoc.org/HOWTO/BootPrompt-HOWTO.html`—Link for obtaining BootPrompt-HOWTO, a guide to using the boot prompt for passing kernel arguments.

`/usr/share/doc/lilo*/doc/User_Guide.ps`—A guide to using LILO with Linux and other operating systems.

`http://www.linuxdoc.org/HOWTO/Installation-HOWTO/index.html`—Link for obtaining Linux Installation-HOWTO, a guide to installing Linux by Eric S. Raymond.

3

INSTALLING RED
HAT LINUX

Post-Installation Configuration

CHAPTER 4

Perhaps the hardest task facing a Red Hat Linux system administrator (or user of a stand-alone workstation) is performing post-installation configuration of various hardware devices, or adding and configuring new devices attached to a system. This chapter addresses just some of these issues regarding changes and customizations.

With the exception of installing a new kernel and insertion or removal of critical PC components, a Red Hat Linux system administrator can perform many post-installation tasks without rebooting or downtime. Given some thought and consideration beforehand, it is also possible to create a server or workstation configuration that allows "hot-swapping" of storage and other components without the need for any downtime. (Most newer and mission-critical servers come with redundant power supplies and other components that can be replaced while the system is in use.)

Pointer and Keyboard Configuration

This section provides guidance on using Red Hat Linux tools to configure a computer's keyboard or pointing device. Although devices can be configured manually by editing system configuration files, using a graphical tool can be a lot faster and reduce the chances for errors.

Red Hat Linux supports many different types of keyboards. Whereas Intel-based PCs have traditionally used keyboards using the PS/2 protocol, newer computers use USB devices for user input with PS/2 devices slowly headed for legacy hardware status. Although the majority of today's PCs (and notebooks) continue to provide PS/2 ports, some manufacturers are introducing "legacy free" computers without PS/2 support.

The majority of Red Hat Linux (and X, KDE, or GNOME) keyboard utilities and clients will normally support any properly configured input device. Text-base (console) keyboard commands include the dumpkeys, kbd_mode, and loadkeys commands, used to display translation tables, get or set a keyboard mode, or reconfigure a keyboard's key set.

X11 keyboard clients include xkbcomp, xkbprint, xset and xmodmap. These clients can be used to input a keyboard description into a running X server, show current keyboard character translations, change a keyboard map and other keyboard (and pointer) preferences. Although X11 settings are generally contained in a system's XF86Config-4 file (see Chapter 6, "The X Window System" for more information), console keymaps will be found in various directories under the /lib/kbd/keymaps/i386 directory.

Use Red Hat's kbdconfig command (as root) to configure or reconfigure a keyboard. This command can be used with or without an active X session like this:

```
# kbdconfig
```

After you press Enter, you'll see a dialog box as shown in Figure 4.1.

FIGURE 4.1

The kbdconfig command can be used to reconfigure a keyboard for Red Hat Linux.

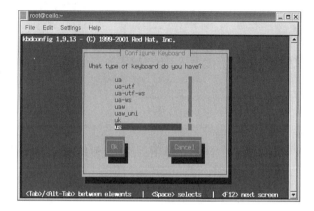

Scroll through the list of keyboards to highlight a desired type, and then use the Tab key to highlight the OK button and press Enter. (The keyboards represent entries under the /lib/kbd/keymaps/i386 directory.) The keyboard configuration is stored in the file /etc/sysconfig/keyboard, which might look like this:

```
KEYBOARDTYPE="pc"
KEYTABLE="us"
```

There are many different types of pointing devices. And although a pointing device might not be needed or necessary when administering a server, most users will want to use a pointing device (especially for X sessions). Configuring pointing devices, such as the IBM Trackpoint (found in several versions of IBM non-notebook keyboards), a trackball, a joystick, the Synaptics TouchPad, the Cirque GlidePoint, and wireless or infrared (IrDA) pointers can require the installation and configuration of additional drivers.

The Linux General Purpose Mouse driver (gpm) is a daemon mouse server that supports copy-and-paste operations while using Red Hat Linux in console mode (and is started by the /etc/rc.d/init.d/gpm script). Whether this service starts when Red Hat Linux boots can be controlled using the ntsysv command as root, like this:

```
# ntsysv
```

After you press Enter, you'll see a dialog box as shown in Figure 4.2.

FIGURE 4.2

The ntsysv *command is used to control services, such as the gpm driver, at boot time.*

Note

You can also use the linuxconf command (as root) to configure your keyboard or mouse. Use linuxconf's Config menu to access the Peripherals menu items. However, you might need to first enable these configuration modes by using the Control menu's Linuxconf management menu item (click on the Modules entry and check the modules you want to use).

Your system's users will benefit by using a three-button mouse during X sessions. The left mouse button is most often used for clicking and selection, whereas the right mouse button is generally used for configuration or property display. The middle mouse button is used for scrolling and pasting of text (or graphics). The Red Hat Linux installer generally recognizes and correctly configures a computer's pointing device, but changing a pointer will require reconfiguration for immediate use.

If you have enabled Red Hat's kudzu service, Red Hat Linux will automatically detect new hardware upon rebooting, and you (or the user) will be offered the opportunity to configure the newly found device. When using a PS/2 pointing device, the symbolic link /dev/mouse will point to /dev/psaux; when using a USB pointing device, /dev/mouse will point to /dev/input/mice. A serial mouse will have /dev/mouse point to a specific serial port, perhaps /dev/ttyS0.

USB service (most likely initially configured by the installer) is started during the boot process by an entry in the system's module configuration file, /etc/modules.conf:

```
alias usb-controller usb-uhci
```

In this example, the PC platform uses a Universal Host Controller Interface (uhci), and the uhci.o kernel module will be loaded from the /lib/modules/2.4-X/kernel/drivers/usb directory when Red Hat Linux boots. Another USB controller commonly in use is the Open Host Controller Interface (ohci), requiring loading of the ohci.o module to enable USB service.

Many other types of input devices can be used with Red Hat Linux and XFree86. For information about using a mouse with XFree86, read the file README.mouse under the /usr/X11R6/lib/X11/doc directory. If you're having trouble with a pointing device, the dmesg command can be used to get some information, especially if the Linux or the driver (perhaps a module) output diagnostic information:

```
...
usb-uhci.c: USB UHCI at I/O 0xfce0, IRQ 9
usb-uhci.c: Detected 2 ports
usb.c: new USB bus registered, assigned bus number 1
hub.c: USB hub found
hub.c: 2 ports detected
usb-uhci.c: v1.251:USB Universal Host Controller Interface driver
hub.c: USB new device connect on bus1/1, assigned device number 2
usb.c: USB device 2 (vend/prod 0x5e3/0x1205) is not claimed by any \
active driver.usb.c: registered new driver hid
input0: USB HID v1.00 Mouse [05e3:1205] on usb1:2.0
usb.c: registered new driver hiddev
hid-core.c: v1.8 Andreas Gal, Vojtech Pavlik <vojtech@suse.cz>
hid-core.c: USB HID support drivers
...
```

In this example, Red Hat Linux has recognized a generic USB mouse. Following this, the following modules will be loaded (note that you might see different memory size values, depending on your computer and module version):

```
mousedev            4064   1
hid                19056   0 (unused)
input               3424   0 [mousedev hid]
usb-uhci           20512   0 (unused)
usbcore            48896   1 [hid usb-uhci]
```

As you can see, USB support involves a chain of modules rather than a single driver. However, once your hardware is recognized, you can use the mouseconfig command to configure a new pointer. Start the command like this:

mouseconfig

After you press Enter, you'll see a dialog box as shown in Figure 4.3.

FIGURE 4.3

The mouseconfig *command can be used to configure a new pointing device.*

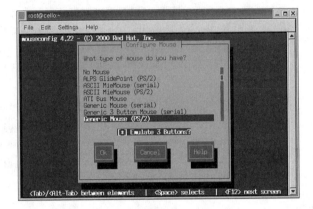

Scroll through the list of pointers. If a two-button pointer is recognized, the mouseconfig command should automatically select three-button emulation (a simultaneous depress of both buttons will send a middle-button click). Pointer configuration entries are stored in the file /etc/sysconfig/mouse, and can be examined like this:

```
# cd /etc/sysconfig; cat mouse
MOUSETYPE="ps/2"
XMOUSETYPE="PS/2"
FULLNAME="Generic Mouse (USB)"
XEMU3=yes
DEVICE=/dev/mouse
```

In this example, a two-button USB pointer emulates a PS/2 pointing device. The corresponding configuration for XFree86 looks like

```
Section "InputDevice"
        Identifier      "Mouse0"
        # Modified by mouseconfig
        Driver          "mouse"
        Option          "Device"            "/dev/mouse"
        Option          "Protocol"          "PS/2"
        Option          "Emulate3Buttons"   "yes"
        #Option          "ZAxisMapping"      "4 5"
EndSection
```

This entry, taken from /etc/X11/XF86Config-4, allows use of the pointing device during X sessions. The ZAxisMapping entry (disabled in the preceding example) enables scrolling via a mouse with a combination scroll-wheel and middle button.

Adding or Changing Display Graphics

Adding or changing the display adapter for a workstation or server can be as simple as swapping out the monitor or removal and addition of a new display adapter. For Intel-based PCs, this most likely means switching from the use of the motherboard's built-in display adapter (if available) by inserting a graphics card in the Accelerated Graphics Port (AGP) slot, or perhaps adding a second display adapter to support the use of multiple display monitors for X sessions.

These issues usually won't affect server operations because many servers are managed in a "headless" mode (where no display adapter is used and management is conducted via HTTP, SSH, telnet sessions, or keyboard, video and monitor switches, known as *KVM* hardware). Though a display monitor can be easily disconnected or reattached to a running Red Hat Linux system, insertion or removal of a graphics display adapter will require downtime, the bane of academic, enterprise, corporate or small-business operations.

Red Hat Linux and KVM

KVM hardware provides the ability to quickly switch display and control between banks of individual computers using a single monitor, keyboard, and pointer. This provides efficient organization, diagnostics and use of computers in larger installations, and allows a single operator to perform system administration tasks without physically moving to each computer.

Other savings are realized in economics and energy consumption. Less hardware is required for the computing environment (such as furniture) and fewer hardware items are running (such as monitors); savings are also realized in related energy costs such as lighting and air conditioning.

Red Hat Linux system administrators should be careful to research any hardware compatibility issues beforehand. Many switches work regardless of the operating system and application used; however, keyboard and pointer protocols should be taken into consideration (such as whether serial I/O, PS/2, or USB devices are required). Some KVM switches are devices with some form of an embedded operating system (even Linux) providing hardware emulation, and will have power requirements.

Other issues to consider included cable construction, compatibility, and distance limitations, hardware or software switch configuration, use (such as providing push-button or key-combination switching), security, and scalability.

continues

Smaller Red Hat Linux–based operations can avoid the use of KVM switching hardware by instead leveraging the graphical networking features of X11, multiple terminal sessions, and virtual desktops. Text-based virtual consoles can also be used to manage multiple computers or to receive logging messages from various services (such as e-mail or Web servers and the kernel). Linux supports up to 63 virtual consoles. If you are limited to a single remote session window, use the `screen` command, a text-based window manager that allows a single terminal session to manage several shells.

The increasing popularity and use of LCD monitors can help reduce air conditioning problems at computer sites with a large number of workstations. Improved manufacturing techniques and better yields (of screens with few or no so-called "dead" pixels) allow the purchase of displays in ever-increasing sizes—even up to 52-inches diagonal. These improvements are most evident in notebook manufacturing, and today it is possible to purchase a portable computer with a display resolution of up to 1600x1200.

Fortunately, creating a working `XF86Config-4` file (found in the directory `/etc/X11`) is usually easily accomplished when installing Red Hat Linux. If a new video card or monitor is put in use, it will most likely work because XFree86 supports many families and types of graphics chipsets. Although newer graphics chipsets might cause some display compatibility problems, it is usually possible to configure a basic working display using existing software. The XFree86 Project, Inc. and contributing developers do a great job of providing software that works with nearly every product on the market. However, if your equipment is problematic, you can also pursue a commercial alternative X11 distribution from a vendor such as Xi-Graphics.

If you are experiencing X11 configuration problems during installation, skip the configuration. Boot Red Hat Linux, and then look for a pertinent document under the `/usr/X11R6/lib/X11/doc` directory. Various README files with specifics about a particular chipset are included with XFree86. You can also check the XFree86 Web site (see the "Reference" section at the end of this chapter) for any errata, changes, updates, or new releases.

Tip

Before running any X configuration tool, make sure to make a copy or back up any working `XF86Config-4` configuration file.

The details about configuring XFree86 for Red Hat Linux are covered in Chapter 6, "The X Window System," but the basic utilities you can use to configure a new XF86Config file are

- `xf86config`—A text-based X configuration tool
- `Xconfigurator`—Red Hat's graphical X configuration tool
- `xf86cfg`—XFree86's graphical X configuration tool
- `XFree86`—The XFree86 server, which can be used to generate an `XF86Config` file by probing installed hardware

Sound Configuration Issues

A wide variety of sound systems are in use by PC manufacturers. Sound might not be an important issue in server operations (unless you're in charge of a streaming audio or video operation), but most workstation users will want to have a configured sound card working with Red Hat Linux. Sound support is generally configured when Red Hat Linux first boots (or during the install process if the sound card is recognized). Although support can be compiled directly in the Linux kernel, loadable kernel modules are most often used to start sound service, enabled by entries in `/etc/ modules.conf`, perhaps like this:

```
alias sound-slot-0 sb
options sound dmabuf=1
alias synth0 opl3
options opl3 io=0x388
options sb io=0x220 irq=5 dma=0 mpu_io=0x330
```

This example, for a SoundBlaster-compatible chipset, specifies the kernel sound modules to load, along with proper options passed to required modules before loading. Sound service, started by the the `/etc/rc.d/rc.sysinit` boot script, is specified in the file named `soundcard` under the `/etc/sysconfig` directory, which might look like this (and will only exist if your have used the `sndconfig` command):

```
# THIS FILE IS WRITTEN BY SNDCONFIG
# PLEASE USE SNDCONFIG TO MODIFY
# TO CHANGE THIS FILE!
# There should be no spaces at the start of a line
# or around the '=' sign
CARDTYPE=SB16
```

As the example shows, this file is generated by the `sndconfig` command. You'll need to use this command if you install a new or different sound card in your PC. Start this command (as root) like this:

```
# sndconfig
```

After you press Enter, sndconfig will probe for any installed sound hardware (note that you can also launch sndconfig using Red Hat's setup command). Installing a sound card in a PC with built-in sound on the motherboard will usually disable the built-in sound chipset; however, you might need to specifically disable built-in sound hardware by changing the PC's BIOS setting. Probing of sound hardware can be disabled by using the --noprobe command-line option. You can manually select and then configure your sound hardware (when either the hardware is not automatically recognized or if you use the --noautoconfig or --noprobe option) as shown in Figure 4.4.

FIGURE 4.4

The sndconfig *command can be used to configure a new sound card.*

You'll find some documentation about the Linux kernel's sound support under the /usr/src/linux-2.4/Documentation/sound directory. Red Hat Linux supports many types of sound cards, but you can also turn to software from the Advanced Linux Sound Architecture (ALSA) project. Truly problematic configuration problems might also call for commercial sound drivers from 4Front Technologies. These drivers support more than 350 sound systems, and are installed, configured, and controlled using shell scripts.

Detecting and Configuring a Modem

Many Red Hat Linux users continue to use dial-up modems for access to the Internet (and other computers) despite the recent explosion and growth in the use of broadband access. Services requiring cable or DSL modems now account for more than 7 million users in the U.S., but for many users a modem is the standard way to connect with an Internet service provider (ISP) using the Point-to-Point Protocol (PPP).

Other common tasks for modems include sending and receiving faxes. Red Hat Linux includes several tools you can use to configure and use an internal or external modem in your notebook or PC. Chapter 15, "Internet Connectivity," contains the details about configuring Red Hat Linux to connect to the Internet using different modems. This section covers recognition and configuration of legacy and newer modems using serial ports (using a standard formerly known as RS232, but now termed EIA232) or USB.

A legacy external phone-based modem is attached to a desktop PC's serial port, whereas newer USB modems are becoming increasingly popular. Linux uses /dev/ttySX, /dev/ttyUSBX, or /dev/usb/ttyUSBX for serial ports, where X can range from 0 to 15. Many additional ports can be added to a system using multi-port cards or chained USB devices. A PC's integral serial ports are generally recognized at boot time. Pipe the dmesg command output through the fgrep command to check and make sure a PC's serial ports are recognized, like so:

```
# dmesg | fgrep tty
ttyS00 at 0x03f8 (irq = 4) is a 16550A
ttyS01 at 0x02f8 (irq = 3) is a 16550A
```

In this example, Linux reports that two serial ports have been recognized. The PC's external modem can be attached (most likely using a male DB9 adapter) to either port. Under Red Hat Linux, nearly all modem-based software can use a symbolic link named /dev/modem that points to the desired device. As root, you can create this device manually by using the ln command like this:

```
# ln -s /dev/ttyS0 /dev/modem
```

In this example, /dev/modem will point to the 'first' serial port. Another tool that can be used is modemconf, although Internet connection software such as Red Hat's rp3-config client (shown in Figure 4.5) will try to probe the system for an available modem. If a modem isn't found, you can manually enter modem data.

> **Note**
>
> The linuxconf command can be used to create the /dev/modem symbolic link, but you might need to first enable the modem module using the Linuxconf management menu under linuxconf's Control tab.

KDE provides the kppp client (shown in Figure 4.6) that can also be used to look for and set up a modem. This client, along with Red Hat's rp3-config, is covered in more detail in Chapter 15.

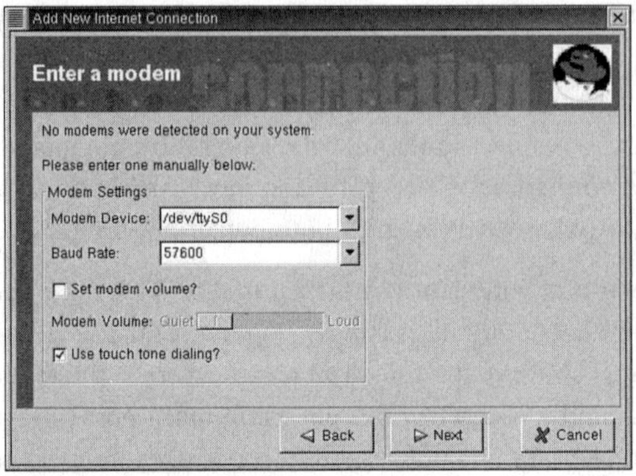

FIGURE 4.5

The Red Hat Linux rp3-config *client will probe for an available modem.*

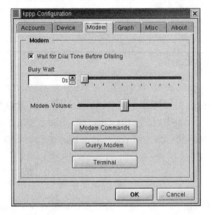

FIGURE 4.6

KDE's kppp *client can be used to find and configure an available modem.*

Red Hat Linux includes command-line–based diagnostic and serial-port configuration tools for the system administrator. For example, to get more information about a specific port, you can use the statserial command, along with a designated device like this:

```
# statserial /dev/ttyS0
Device: /dev/ttyS0

Signal  Pin  Pin  Direction  Status  Full
Name    (25) (9)  (computer)         Name
-----   ---  ---  ---------  ------  -----
FG       1    -       -         -    Frame Ground
TxD      2    3      out        -    Transmit Data
RxD      3    2      in         -    Receive  Data
RTS      4    7      out        1    Request To Send
CTS      5    8      in         0    Clear To Send
DSR      6    6      in         0    Data Set Ready
GND      7    5       -         -    Signal Ground
```

```
DCD     8    1     in      0    Data Carrier Detect
DTR     20   4     out     1    Data Terminal Ready
RI      22   9     in      0    Ring Indicator
```

The example output is a display of the associated device's port signals. Another tool is the `setserial` command that can be used to display port statistics and reconfigure a serial port's system interrupt or speed. To get information about a specific port, use `setserial` along with the device name like this:

```
# setserial -a /dev/ttyS0
/dev/ttyS0, Line 0, UART: 16550A, Port: 0x03f8, IRQ: 4
        Baud_base: 115200, close_delay: 50, divisor: 0
        closing_wait: 3000
        Flags: spd_normal skip_test
```

In this example, the characteristics of /dev/ttyS0 are displayed. The `setserial` command can also be used to configure or fine-tune a port's characteristics using 32 different command-line options and values.

One option for using a legacy serial device such as a modem on PC that doesn't have a serial port but supports USB is to use a USB-to-serial converter. These devices provide a serial-port dongle and plug in to a USB hub or port. Red Hat Linux should recognize and configure a designated serial port (such as /dev/ttyUSB*X*) when the device is plugged in.

Red Hat Linux also comes with a number of fax utilities that can be used to configure a system to send or receive phone faxes. One of the easier to configure fax utilities is the fax command. As root you can configure the software by editing a few entries in the /usr/bin/fax shell script:

```
DEV=modem
FROM="1 555 555-1212"
NAME="Company Name"
```

The most important entry is DEV=, which won't need to be changed as long as /dev/modem points to an active fax-capable modem. You can also edit /usr/bin/fax to customize other entries, such as the fax viewing command. Use the `test` command-line option to check the settings like this:

```
# fax test
```

Sending a fax using the fax command is straightforward:

```
# fax send 5551212 document.txt
```

Use the `minicom` or `xminicom` script (used for launching `minicom` in a terminal window during an X session) for dial-up connections and terminal sessions to remote Red Hat

4

INSTALLATION
CONFIGURATION

Linux systems. To configure this terminal program for use with an attached modem, start the client as root with its -s or setup option like this:

```
# minicom -s
```

After you press Enter you'll see a setup dialog box. Select serial-port configuration and press Enter. You'll then see a configuration settings dialog box as shown in Figure 4.7 that you can use to configure the program to work with an attached modem.

FIGURE 4.7

Use minicom's *setup dialog box to configure the program to work with an attached modem.*

Other issues regarding modems focus on Red Hat Linux notebook users with laptops using "controllerless" modems. These modems use proprietary software to emulate a hardware modem. Despite the release of binary-only drivers to enable use of some of these modems, these devices remain the bane of Linux notebook and some desktop users. You might find some support for Lucent (but not Lucent AMR), Motorola SM56-type, the IBM Mwave, and Conexant HSF (not HCF) controllers. At the time of this writing, there was no support for any 3COM or U.S. Robotics controllerless modems. For links to drivers and more information, browse to the Linux Winmodem Web page at http://www.linmodems.org.

Power-Management Issues

Advanced Power Management (APM) allows workstations and servers to automatically turn off when instructed to shut down. Most often used by Red Hat Linux mobile users, APM can help extend battery sessions through the use of intelligent storage-cell circuitry, CPU "throttling" (similar to, but not the same as safety thermal throttling incorporated by Intel in Pentium III and IV CPUs), and control of displays and hard drives.

Most PCs support APM (via the BIOS and hardware). APM support is configured, enabled, and then incorporated into the Linux kernel during the preliminary make config (or `menuconfig` or `xconfig`) step and a rebuild. APM information is constantly updated in the file /proc/apm, which can look like this:

```
# cat /proc/apm
1.14 1.2 0x03 0x01 0x03 0x09 100% 10800 sec
```

This example provides information such as battery charge, along with time and percentage of time remaining. Each of the eight different fields represents different information. From left to right in the example, this is the driver version, BIOS version, status, AC status, battery status, battery state, remaining battery life, and number of seconds of life remaining. Some X11 clients parse this file and display icons or graphical power LEDs to present the information in a easier to digest form.

APM might or might not be enabled in the installed uni-processor (UP) or Symmetric Multi-processor (SMP) kernel. If you use a notebook, you will find APM support. However, problematic hardware or APM mis-configuration can cause kernel panics with some hardware, requiring the need to reconfigure APM, and then build and install a new Linux kernel. (Refer to Chapter 23, "Kernel and Module Management" for more information.) Basic Linux kernel APM configuration options include

- `CONFIG_APM`—Whether or not to configure APM support
- `CONFIG_APM_IGNORE_USER_SUSPEND`—Ignore keyboard suspend instruction
- `CONFIG_APM_DO_ENABLE`—Enable APM at boot
- `CONFIG_APM_CPU_IDLE`—Idle CPU when not used
- `CONFIG_APM_DISPLAY_BLANK`—Enable monitor or LCD panel blanking
- `CONFIG_APM_RTC_IS_GMT`—Determine clock setting
- `CONFIG_APM_ALLOW_INTS`—Allow interrupts during APM use (such as serial-port activity)
- `CONFIG_APM_REAL_MODE_POWER_OFF`—Enable powering down

Red Hat Linux includes several APM-related commands, such as `apm` that prints APM information, and `apmsleep`, used to suspend and then possible re-awake notebook hardware at a specific time. Normal Red Hat Linux notebook users can use the `apm` command like this:

```
$ apm -v
APM BIOS 1.2 (kernel driver 1.14)
AC on-line, battery status high: 95%
```

Other power management incorporated in the kernel includes control of Peripheral Control Interface (PCI) devices and Display Power Management Signaling (DPMS) for enabled monitors, which can help energy costs by placing devices in a low-power state

4

POST-
INSTALLATION
CONFIGURATION

after a preset time. Screen-saving, as most astute Red Hat Linux system administrators and users know, is no longer necessary to protect displays from image "burn-in." And password protection enabled by the screensaver only provides a modicum of physical security.

Hardware health monitoring is supported by the `lm_sensors` software package, which acquired some notoriety when early versions allegedly caused IBM Thinkpad notebooks to suffer permanent damage. However, system administrators managing desktop PCs can benefit from using applications, such as the `sensors` command that takes advantage of the hardware monitoring features of the `lm_sensors` libraries.

Managing PCMCIA

Red Hat Linux notebook users take advantage of PCMCIA slots to add 70-pin, credit-card sized devices to support Ethernet LAN connectivity, wireless operations, Firewire devices, Compact Flash hard drives, external storage devices, serial ports, and modems. Many different types of PCMCIA cards and Compact Flash form-factor cards in a PCMCIA caddy are supported by the Linux kernel and David Hinds' Card Services software.

Power is provided to PCMCIA devices and adapters directly through the card slot, although some external hardware might require an additional power source. PCMCIA support is enabled and configured at boot time according to the `/etc/sysconfig/pcmcia` file and `/etc/rc.d/init.d/pcmcia` startup script. The `/etc/sysconfig/pcmcia` file might look something like:

```
PCMCIA=yes
PCIC=yenta_socket
PCIC_OPTS=
CORE_OPTS=
```

Previous incarnations of Red Hat Linux and PCMCIA used specific controller information in this file. With the newer Linux kernels however, support is provided by kernel modules or direct Linux kernel support. The PCMCIA Card Services software provides diagnostic information by one or more high or low beeps upon card insertion. One high and one low beep might indicate that a card is recognized, but failed to be configured. Only one beep might indicate that the card was only recognized. Two high beeps indicate that a card was recognized and configured.

Troubleshooting problems, especially with the explosion in popularity and type of 802.11b wireless networking cards, can be difficult. Driver configuration for some types of cards can be involved and complicated, requiring downloading, building, and installing new drivers. Fortunately however, nearly all serial, modem, and Compact Flash storage cards are easily recognized and configured. Many Ethernet cards are also supported. To check on the current support status for many cards, read the file SUPPORTED.CARDS. You'll find a copy under the `/usr/share/doc/kernel-pcmcia-cs-3.X.XX/` directory (where *X.XX* is the version of the package) if you install the `pcmcia-cs` RPM package.

Use the `cardctl` command to control PCMCIA service to one or more card slots on a notebook or desktop PC with a PCMCIA adapter. The `cardctl` command is used to get and print information about an inserted card, suspend or resume power to a card, reset a card, perform a software insertion or removal, or to configure a card according to a particular, predefined "scheme" (such as using a network in the office or at home). The format of the command is `cardctl command slot_number` (such as 0 or 1).

Performing post-installation configuration on a computer can involve many steps and can be somewhat labor intensive. Fortunately Red Hat Linux provides the system administrator a wealth of software tools to ease the task, and the inherent design of Linux enables nearly all software configuration (with the exception of using a new kernel) to be done without down time or rebooting.

Reference

The Linux Keyboard and Console HOWTO—Andries Brouwer's tome on keyboard and console issues; includes many troubleshooting tips.

`http://www.avocent.com/Cybex/PublicW2.nsf/gwMain?OpenFrameset`—Product details for a KVM switch running Linux.

`http://www.luv.asn.au/overheads/virtualconsoles.html`—Using virtual consoles with Linux.

`http://www.synaptics.com/products/touchpad.cfm`—Information about TouchPad pointing devices.

`http://www.compass.com/synaptics/`—Site for a Linux TouchPad driver.

`http://www.alsa-project.org`—Home page for the ALSA project, an alternative set of sound drivers for Linux.

`http://www.opensound.com`—Commercial sound drivers for Linux.

`/usr/src/linux-2.4/Documentation/power/pci.txt`—Patrick Mochel's document regarding PCI power-management routes for Linux kernel and PCI hardware support programmers.

`http://www.ibiblio.org/pub/Linux/docs/HOWTO/Modem-HOWTO`—One of the newest HOWTOs on using modems with Linux.

`http://www.ibiblio.org/pub/Linux/docs/HOWTO/Serial-HOWTO`—David S. Lawyer's Serial HOWTO, with additional information about Linux and serial port use.

`http://www2.lm-sensors.nu/~lm78/cvs/lm_sensors2/doc/FAQ`—Information regarding the `lm-sensors` software for Linux.

`http://pcmcia-cs.sourceforge.net/`—Source for the latest PCMCIA drivers for Linux.

`http://www.camiresearch.com/Data_Com_Basics/RS232_standard.html`—A description and tutorial on the EIA232 (formerly RS232) standard.

`http://www.qbik.ch/usb/devices/`—The place to check for compatibility of USB devices for Linux.

`http://www.linmodems.org`—This site provides links to several drivers for controller-less modem use under Linux.

First Steps with Linux

CHAPTER 5

This chapter is a short introduction to some of the basic concepts about using Linux and how Linux works. The information presented here, although generally applying to all Linux distributions, will be particularly helpful to users and system administrators migrating from other computer platforms. And, as Linux spreads and continues to grow in popularity, more and more system administrators might find themselves in the unfortunate position of having to educate one or more important users, such as a VP or PHB (pointy-haired boss). Hopefully the information presented here might make such short presentations a bit easier.

Understanding Linux

Linux is a UNIX clone, written from scratch, that contains no propriety code from the original AT&T UNIX software distributions. However, Linux aims to adhere to the ever-changing IEEE Portable Operating System Interface (POSIX) guidelines (it's about "... 90 percent there," according to Red Hat), and provides a stable and secure platform for many different types of computer operations.

New users should be reminded that Linux is the kernel, or core of the operating system, whereas Linux combined with the FSF's GNU utilities and other software, such as XFree86, denotes a Linux distribution—Red Hat Linux is one such distribution. After installing Linux, users are assigned a name, known as a *username*, which traditionally takes the form of one's first initial and last name in lowercase. For example, Beth Sullivan would have a username of *bsullivan*. A password will also be assigned, and is used with the username either at a graphical login or at a text-based prompt. After logging in, a user will either use the graphical networking interface known as the X Window System, or an interactive command prompt, known as a *shell* in the Linux text-based or *console* mode.

How Red Hat Linux Is Organized

When installed, Red Hat Linux, like most modern operating systems, uses a layout of hierarchical directories. One nice thing about the current state of Linux and its various distributions is that vendors have *generally* agreed on the naming and location of critical Linux files and directories, hopefully aiming for a modicum of compliance with the *FSSTND* (also known as *FHS*), or Linux Filesystem Hierarchy Standard.

This standard, which aims to dictate a universal layout of directories and file locations for UNIX and Linux, is extremely helpful when creating system distributions, packaging applications, and crafting system administration utilities. For example, knowing that the useradd command is always found under the /usr/sbin directory can simplify the creation of administrative shell scripts designed to be used by system administrators (even though the command can also be found in some distributions as a symbolic link under the same directory, but with the name adduser).

You can quickly examine the layout of a Red Hat Linux system by using the list directory contents command, ls, like this:

```
$ ls /
```

```
bin   dev  home    lib         misc  opt   root  tftpboot  usr
boot  etc  initrd  lost+found  mnt   proc  sbin  tmp       var
```

However, a more helpful command, named tree, can be used to show the *root* or base directory layout, along with associated subdirectories, like this (note that your system's /usr/src directory might be somewhat different):

```
$ tree -dx /
/
|-- bin
|-- boot
|-- dev
|-- etc
|   |-- X11
|   |-- ppp
|   |-- rc.d
|   |-- sane.d
|   |-- skel
|   |-- sysconfig
|   `-- xinetd.d
|-- home
|   |-- bball
|   `-- fsmith
|-- lib
|   |-- modules
|       `-- 2.4.2-2
|-- lost+found
|-- misc
|-- mnt
|   |-- cdrom
|   |-- dos
|   `-- floppy
|-- opt
|-- proc
|-- root
|-- sbin
|-- tmp
|-- usr
|   |-- X11R6
|   |-- bin
```

```
|    |-- dict
|    |-- games
|    |-- include
|    |-- lib
|    |-- local
|    |-- man
|    |-- sbin
|    |-- share
|    |-- src
|    |    |-- linux -> /usr/src/linux-2.4.7-2
|    |    |-- linux-2.4 -> linux-2.4.7-2
|    |    |-- linux-2.4.7-2
|    |    `-- redhat
|    `-- tmp -> ../var/tmp
`-- var
     |-- log
     |-- mail -> spool/mail
     |-- spool
     `-- tmp
```

This example, pruned to show the most pertinent directories, corresponds to the directories and descriptions in Table 5.1.

TABLE 5.1 Basic Linux Directories

Name	Description
/	The root directory
/bin	Essential commands
/boot	Boot loader files
/dev	Device files
/etc	System configuration files
/home	User home directories
/lib	Shared libraries, kernel modules
/mnt	Mount point for local, remote filesystems
/opt	Add-on software packages
/root	Superuser (root home)
/sbin	System commands (mostly root only)
/tmp	Temporary files
/usr	Secondary software file hierarchy
/var	Variable data (such as logs)

When a Red Hat Linux system administrator creates a user, by default a directory under the /home directory will be created with the user's username. Therefore, after logging in, *bsullivan*'s home directory (and current working directory) will be /home/bsullivan. However, user home directories and naming schemes are flexible and can be changed according to policy.

Using the Console

Users interact with the Linux kernel at the console by using a program known as a shell. This shell, assigned by a field in the user's entry in the system's /etc/passwd file, is an interactive command prompt that might have many different features, such as input and output redirection, background processing, job control, history editing, command-line completion, and command-line editing. The default shell for most Linux distributions, including Red Hat Linux, is the GNU bash or Bourne Again Shell.

The shell interprets keyboard commands and is generally used to launch other commands or programs, using the shell's interpreter language known as *shell scripts*. Default in-memory variables assigned and loaded when logging in are known as shell *environment variables*, and are used by the shell for a number of reasons.

These variables include the name of the current working directory, the user's name, the default language, the name and location of the current shell, the default location of executable files, location of important software libraries (as most, but not all, Linux commands use shared resources), the type of terminal in use, possible color assignments, system type, system architecture, and so on.

> **Note**
>
> Red Hat Linux system administrators maintain a list of valid system shells in a file named shells under the /etc directory. Each shell included with Linux might have a different feature set and language syntax, but you can use your shell to craft your own administrative, diagnostic, or productivity tools. To learn more about creating your own shell scripts, see Chapter 21, "Introduction to Basic Development Tools."

At the command line, you can use the env or printenv commands to display these environment variables, like so:

```
$ env
PWD=/home/bball
HOSTNAME=thinkpad.home.org
```

```
USER=bball
MACHTYPE=i386-redhat-linux-gnu
MAIL=/var/spool/mail/bball
BASH_ENV=/home/bball/.bashrc
LANG=en_US
DISPLAY=titanium:0
LOGNAME=bball
SHLVL=1
PATH=/usr/kerberos/bin:/usr/local/bin:/bin:/usr/bin: \
/usr/X11R6/bin:/home/bball/bin
SHELL=/bin/bash
HOSTTYPE=i386
OSTYPE=linux-gnu
HISTSIZE=1000
TERM=xterm
HOME=/home/bball
```

This abbreviated list shows a few common variables. These variables are set by configuration or *resource* files found under the /etc, /etc/skel, or user /home directory. For example, default settings for bash can be found in /etc/profile, /etc/bashrc, .bashrc, or .bash_profile.

Using the Keyboard

Red Hat Linux also supports the use of *virtual* consoles or terminals. This means that you can log in, run a program, and then jump to another login prompt, login, and start another session. By default, Red Hat Linux supports six virtual consoles, although the Linux kernel might be recompiled to support as many as 63 individual consoles!

To jump to another console while using Linux in text-based mode, log in and then press Alt+F2 (you'll be using the first virtual console, or vt1 by default). You should then see another login prompt. Log in, and you are then using vt2, the second Linux console. Jump back and forth between sessions by using the Alt key plus the F key number of the desired session. A related command named screen can be used if only one console is available during the session (such as when connecting and logging in via a shell account or telnet session). The only caveat when using virtual consoles is that there is a default limit on the available number (usually six) and there might be one or more active X Window sessions (occupying vt7 by default or vt8).

In addition to virtual console keystrokes, the Linux console might also recognize the three-fingered salute (or Vulcan neck pinch) Ctrl+Alt+Del. This behavior can be controlled by the system administrator by editing the system's *initialization table*, /etc/inittab. And while using the console, you can also get the screen to scroll. This is down by using Shift+PageUp or Shift+PageDown.

The Linux console also supports an available pointing device for copy and paste operations. This support is through the gpm or general purpose mouse server, which must be enabled or started while booting Linux. To copy a section of text, click and drag text with the left mouse button (button 1) held down. To paste text, click an insertion point, and then press the middle mouse button (button 2). To aid users with a two-button mouse, Linux supports three-button *emulation*, or the ability to simulate a press of the middle mouse button. This feature can be enabled during installation or by using the mouseconfig command. Afterward, press the right and left mouse buttons simultaneously to click the middle mouse button.

The gpm server provides the ability to reboot or shut down the system by holding down either the left or right mouse button (button 3), triple-clicking the opposite button, and then pressing a mouse button:

- left—Immediately reboot using the init command
- middle—Reboot the system using the shutdown command
- right—Immediately shut down the system using the shutdown command

Keyboard layouts can be changed by using the loadkeys command. To use a different font for the console, try the setfont command. Red Hat Linux comes with nearly 150 different fonts, found under the /lib/kbd/consolefonts directory. Some PCs also support different numbers of characters for line and lines per screen (80x25 is considered traditional). However, you can see a list of different console modes by passing the 'vga=ask' kernel argument when at the Linux boot prompt.

Navigation and Searching

Use the cd command (built into the shell) to navigate through the Red Hat Linux file system. This command is generally used with a specific directory location, or *pathname* like this:

```
$ cd /usr/X11R6/lib/X11/doc
```

Under Red Hat Linux, the cd command can also be used with several shortcuts. For example to quickly move up a directory, use the cd command like this:

```
$ cd ..
```

To return to one's home directory from anywhere in the Linux file system, use the cd command like this:

```
$ cd
```

You can also use the $HOME variable to accomplish the same thing like so:

```
$ cd $HOME
```

After you press Enter, you'll be back at your home directory. Linux also includes a number of GNU commands you can use to search the file system. These include

- whereis *command*—Returns the location of the *command* and its man page
- whatis *command*—Returns a one-line synopsis from the *command*'s man page
- locate *file*—Returns locations of all matching *file*(s)
- apropos *subject*—Returns a list of commands related to *subject*

File Management

Managing files in your home directory involves using one or more easily remembered commands. New Red Hat Linux users with some familiarity with now-ancient DOS will recognize some of these commands (but with different names). Basic file management operations include paging (reading) moving, renaming, copying, searching, and deleting files and directories. These commands include

- cat *filename*—Outputs contents of *filename* to display
- less *filename*—Allows scrolling while reading contents of *filename*
- mv *file1 file2*—Renames *file1* to *file2*
- mv *file dir*—Moves *file* to specified directory
- cp *file1 file2*—Copies *file1* and creates *file2*
- rm *file*—Deletes *file*
- rmdir *dir*—Deletes directory (if empty)
- grep *string file(s)*—Searches through *files(s)* and displays lines containing matching *string*

Note that each of these commands can be used with pattern-matching strings known as wildcards or *expressions*. For example, to delete all files beginning with the letters abc, you can use the rm command like this:

```
$ rm abc*
```

Linux shells recognize many types of expressions, which might be *regular* or *extended regular*. Extended regular expressions tend to be more complex than regular expressions. Both types allow for sophisticated searching.

Another file management operation is compression and decompression of files, or the creation, listing, and expansion of file and directory archives. Red Hat Linux includes several compression utilities that can be used to create, compress, expand, or list the contents of compressed files and archives. These commands include

- bunzip2—Expands a compressed file
- bzip2—Compresses or expands files and directories
- gunzip *compressedfile*—Expands a compressed file
- gzip—Compresses or expands files and directories
- shar *file*—Creates a shell archive of file
- tar—Creates, expands, or lists the contents of compressed or uncompressed file or directory archives known as *tape archives* or "tarballs"
- unshar *shellarchive*—Reassembles files from shell archive
- uudecode file.uu—Decodes an uuencoded text file to its binary form
- uuencode file—Encodes a binary file to text file form for transmission via e-mail

Most of these commands are fairly easy to use. However, the tar command has a somewhat complex and capable set of command-line options and syntax. But even tar can be used quickly and easily by remembering a few simple invocations on the command line. For example, to create a compressed archive of a directory, use tar's czf options like this:

```
$ tar czf dirname.tgz dirname
```

The result will be a compressed archive (a file ending in .tgz) of the specified directory. Add the letter v to the preceding options to view the list of files being added during compression and archiving. To list the contents of the compressed archive, substitute the c option with the letter t like this:

```
$ tar tzf archive
```

Of course if there are a lot of files in the archive, a better invocation is

```
$ tar tzf archive | less
```

To expand the contents of a compressed archive, use tar's xzf options like so:

```
$ tar xzf archive
```

The contents of the specified archive will then be expanded in the current directory.

Introduction to Text Editors

Red Hat Linux includes a number commands known as text editors that you can use to create text files or edit system configuration files. These commands range in features and ease of use, but are found on nearly every Linux distribution. Text editors differ from word processors in that text editors generally have fewer features, only work with text files, and might or might not support spell checking or formatting.

Some of the text editors included with Red Hat Linux are

- ed—A simple line editor
- emacs—The GNU emacs editing environment
- gedit—GUI text editor for GNOME
- jed—A programmer's text editor
- joe—Joe's Own Editor, a text editor
- kedit—A simple KDE text editor
- kwrite—A simple KDE text editor
- mcedit—A text editor for UNIX-like systems
- pico—A simple text editor included with the pine email program
- sed—A stream editor
- vim—An improved version of the vi text editor

Note that not all the text editors described here are *screen-oriented*; editors such as ed and sed work on a line-by-line basis or a stream of text. Other editors, such as those for GNOME or KDE, require an active X Window session and feature a graphical user interface with menus, toolbars, dialogs, and buttons.

Introduction to vi

The editor found on nearly every UNIX and Linux system is, without a doubt, the vi editor, originally by Bill Joy. This simple editor features a somewhat initially cryptic command set, but can be put to use with only a few commands. While older, more experienced UNIX and Red Hat Linux users continue to use vi extensively during computing sessions, many newer users might prefer learning an easier to use text editor such as pico. Die-hard GNU fans and programmers definitely use emacs!

One good reason to learn how to use a text-based editor such as vi is that system maintenance and recovery operations generally never take place during X Window sessions (negating the use of a GUI editor), and many larger, more complex and capable editors will not work when Linux is booted to its single-user or maintenance mode (See Chapter 7, "Managing Services," for more information about how Red Hat Linux boots). Another reason to learn a text-based editor, especially a text-based editor that works under the Linux console mode, is that you'll be able to edit text files through dial-up shell connections.

You can start an editing session by using the `vi` editor like this:

```
$ vi file.txt
```

The `vi` command (actually named `vim`) works by using an insert, or editing mode, and a viewing mode. The Esc key is used to toggle modes. Although `vi` supports many complex editing operations and have numerous commands, you can accomplish work by using a few basic commands. These basic `vi` commands are

- Cursor movement—`h`, `j`, `k`, `l` (left, down, up, and right)
- Delete character—`x`
- Delete line—`dd`
- Mode toggle—`ESC`, `Insert` (or `i`)
- Quit—`:q`
- Quit without saving—`:q!`
- Run a shell command—`:sh` (use `'exit'` to return)
- Save file—`:w`
- Text search—`/`

Introduction to `emacs`

Richard M. Stallman's `emacs` editor, like `vi`, will be found with nearly every Linux distribution, including Red Hat Linux. Unlike other UNIX and Linux text editors, `emacs` is much more than a simple text editor—it is an editing environment and can be used to compile and build programs, act as an electronic diary, appointment book and calendar, compose and send electronic mail, read Usenet news, and even play games. The reason for this capability is the `emacs` contains a built-in language interpreter that uses the Lisp programming language. The editor is easily extensible by including extra snippets of Lisp code when the editor starts or during editing sessions.

The GNU version of this editor requires quite a bit of hard drive space—more than 30MB. However, there are versions with less resource requirements, and at least one other text editor included with Red Hat Linux, named `joe`, can be used as a `emacs` clone (albeit with fewer features).

Like `vi`, you can start an editing session like this:

```
$ emacs file.txt
```

Tip

If you start `emacs` when using X11, the editor will launch in its own floating window. To force `emacs` to display inside a terminal window instead of its own window, use the -nw command-line option like this: `emacs -nw file.txt`

The `emacs` editor uses an un-Godly extensive set of keystroke and named commands, but like `vi` can be put to work right away by learning a basic subset from its feature-laden list. Many of these basic commands require you to hold down the Ctrl key, or to first press a *meta* key (generally mapped to the Alt key). The basic commands are listed in Table 5.2.

TABLE 5.2   Emacs Editing Commands

Action	*Command*
Abort	Ctrl+g
Cursor left	Ctrl+b
Cursor down	Ctrl+n
Cursor right	Ctrl+f
Cursor up	Ctrl+p
Delete character	Ctrl+d
Delete line	Ctrl+k
Go to start of line	Ctrl+a
Go to end of line	Ctrl+e
Help	Ctrl+h
Quit	Ctrl+x Ctrl+c
Save As	Ctrl+x Ctrl+w
Save file	Ctrl+x Ctrl+s
Search backward	Ctrl+r
Search forward	Ctrl+s
Start tutorial	Ctrl+h t
Undo	Ctrl+x u

One of the best reasons to learn how to use emacs is that you can use nearly all the same keystrokes to edit commands on the bash shell command line. Another reason is that like vi, emacs is universally available on nearly every UNIX and Linux system. You'll be right at home whether you're using Red Hat Linux or IBM's AIX environment.

Working as root

The root, or superuser account is a special account and user on UNIX and Red Hat Linux systems. When logged in as root, you have total control over your system. This includes the ability to destroy a running system with a simple invocation of the rm command like this:

```
# rm -fr /
```

This command line will not only delete locate files and directories, but could also wipe out file systems on other partitions and even remote computers. This alone is reason enough to take precautions when using root access. Red Hat Linux comes with a command named su that allows you to run one or more commands as root and then quickly return you to normal user status. For example, if you'd like to edit your system's filesystem table (a simple text file that describes local or remote storage devices, their type, and location), you can use the su command like this:

```
$ su -c "pico -w /etc/fstab"
Password:
```

After you press Enter, you'll be prompted for a password. This extra step can also help you "think before you leap" into the command. Enter the root password, and you'll then be editing /etc/fstab using the pico editor with line-wrapping disabled.

Note

When editing any system configuration file, make sure to launch your text editor with line-wrapping disabled! By convention, nearly all configuration files are formatted for 80-character text width, but this isn't always the case. If you edit a configuration file without disabling line-wrapping, you could insert spurious carriage returns and line feeds, causing the configured service to fail when restarting. By default the vi and emacs editors don't use line wrap (although they can be configured to do so).

Another command Red Hat Linux system administrators can use is sudo. This command might be used to assign permission to perform specific tasks to specific users (similar to

BSD UNIX and its "wheel" group of users). The sudo command works by first examining the file named sudoers under the /etc directory. (This file is modified by the visudo command.)

The only time you should run Red Hat Linux as the superuser is when booting to run-level 1, or system maintenance mode. This is most often done for filesystem or system configuration repair and maintenance. Logging in and using Linux as the root operator isn't a good idea, and defeats the entire concept of file permissions, discussed next.

Permissions

Under Red Hat Linux (and UNIX), everything in the file system, including directories and devices, is a file. And every file has a set of permissions. These permissions form the basis for security under Linux and consist of a series of fields designating read, write, and execute permission assigned to every file. You can examine the permissions for a particular file (if you have read access) by using the ls command's long-format listing like this:

```
$ touch file
$ ls -l file
-rw-rw-r--   1 bball    bball          0 Jul 23 12:28 file
```

In this example, the touch command is used to quickly create a file. The ls command then reports on the file showing permissions, owner, group, size, and create (or modification) date. Under Linux, permissions are grouped by owner, group and others, with read, write, and execute permission assigned to each, like so:

```
Owner    Group    Others
rwx      rwx      rxw
```

These permissions can also be represented by base 8, or octal values, with read permission=4, write permission=2, and execute permission=1. In the previous example for the file named file, the owner, bball, has read and write permission, as does any member of the group named bball. All other users may only read the file. In octal notation, the file has a permission setting of 664 (read+write, read+write, read-only).

Directories are also files under Linux. For example, again use the ls command to show permissions like this:

```
$ mkdir foo
$ ls -ld foo
drwxrwxr-x   2 bball    bball       4096 Jul 23 12:37 foo
```

In this example, the mkdir command is used to create a directory. The ls command and its -ld option is used to show the permissions and other information about the directory (not its contents). Here you can see that the directory has permission values of 775 (read+write+execute, read+write+execute, read+execute). This shows that the owner and group members can read and write to the directory and, because of execute permission, also list the directory's contents. All other users can only list the directory contents. (Directories require execute permission in order for anyone to be able to view their contents.)

You should also notice that the `ls` command's output shows a leading d in the permissions field. This is a letter that specifies the type of file (in this case, a directory). Normal files will have a blank field in place. Other files, such as those specifying a block or character device, will have a different letter. For example, if you examine the device file for a Linux serial port, you'll see:

```
$ ls -l /dev/ttyS0
crw-rw----   1 root      uucp       4,  64 Mar 23 23:38 /dev/ttyS0
```

Here you can see that `/dev/ttyS0` is a character device (designated by a c), owned by root, and available to anyone in the uucp group. The device has permissions of 660 (read+write, read+write, no permission). On the other hand, if you examine the device file for an IDE hard drive, you'll see:

```
$ ls -l /dev/hda
brw-rw----   1 root      disk       3,   0 Mar 23 23:37 /dev/hda
```

In this example, b designates a block device with similar permissions. Other device entries you might run across on your Red Hat Linux system include symbolic links (s).

The `chmod` command is used to alter a file's permissions, and uses various forms of command syntax, such as octal or a mnemonic form (such as u, g, o, or a and rwx, and so on) to specify a desired change. Although either form can be used, octal is easy to use quickly after you visualize and understand how permissions are numbered.

For example, to modify a file's permissions so that only you, the owner, can read and write, use the `chmod` command and a file permission of 600, like this:

```
$ chmod 600 file
```

By using various combinations of permission settings, you can quickly and easily set up a more secure environment, even as a normal user in your home directory. Files might be hidden inside directories that might not be listed or accessed by anyone else (except the root operator, of course, who has access to any file on your system).

Another type of permission available for use under Linux is set user ID, known as *suid*, and set group ID (*sgid*) permissions. These settings allow programs to be run as if owned by other users or groups. One commonly used program with a special user ID is the passwd command:

```
$ ls -l /usr/bin/passwd
-r-s--x--x    1 root     root           13536 Jul 12  2000 /usr/bin/passwd
```

This setting allows normal users to execute the command (as root) in order to make changes to a root-only accessible file, /etc/passwd (another such command is chfn, which allows users to update or change finger information in /etc/passwd). This permission modification is accomplished by using a leading 4 (or the mnemonic s) in front of the three octal values.

> **Note**
>
> Other files that might have suid or guid permissions include at, rcp, rlogin, rsh, chage, chsh, ssh, crontab, sudo, sendmail, ping, mount, and several UNIX-to-UNIX Copy (UUCP) utilities.

Files that are suid or guid can present security holes because normal permissions are bypassed. This problem is especially compounded if the permission extends to an executable binary with inherent security flaws. Savvy Red Hat Linux system administrators will keep the number of suid or guid files present on a system to a minimum.

Reading Documentation

Although learning the basics of Red Hat Linux can be accomplished quickly and easily, mastering or troubleshooting more complex aspects of the operating system and distribution can take some time. The best place to first turn to for help is the documentation included with your system. You'll often find more detailed information about a particular distribution on the vendor's Web site. Occasionally perusing Red Hat's Web site for security updates and bug fixes is also a good idea.

Linux, like UNIX, is also a self-documenting system. To learn more about a command or program, use the man command, followed by the name of the command. Manual pages for Linux and X Window commands are found under the /usr/share/man, /usr/local/man, and /usr/X11R6/man directories. For example, to read the rm command's man page, use the man command like this:

```
$ man rm
```

After you press Enter, the command's manual page will be displayed by a text browser, such as `less`. You can then scroll back and forth through the document to learn more about the command. Type the letter **h** to get help, use the forward slash to enter a search string, or press q to quit.

Documentation for various software packages will be found under the `/usr/share/doc` directory in a directory with a package's name. Other documentation, known as HOWTOs and FAQs will be found in documents under the `/usr/share/doc` directory. HOWTO documents contain specific information related a particular subject, such as using PCMCIA services or programming a serial port. These documents can be read by using a pager such as `less` or `more`. If the documents are in compressed form, use the `zless` pager, which will decompress a document first.

Reference

The migration to a new computer operating system doesn't have to be painful to management and users. Providing easy-to-understand directions, some background information, and pre-configuration of an installed system can help the transition. This section lists some additional points of reference with background information on the standards and commands discussed in this chapter.

`http://www.winntmag.com/Articles/Index.cfm?ArticleID=7420`—A typical article by a miscreant Windows NT user who, when experimenting with Linux, blithely confesses rebooting the system after not knowing how to read a text file at the Linux console.

`http://standards.ieee.org/regauth/posix/`—IEEE's POSIX information page.

`http://www.itworld.com/Comp/2362/lw-01-government/#sidebar`—Discussion of Linux and POSIX compliance.

`http://www.pathname.com/fhs/`—Home page for the Linux FSSTND, Linux File System Standard.

`http://www.linuxdoc.org`—Browse the HOWTO section to find and read The Linux Keyboard and Console HOWTO—Andries Brouwer's somewhat dated but eminently useful guide to using the Linux keyboard and console.

`http://www.gnu.org/software/emacs/emacs.html`—Home page for the FSF's GNU emacs editing environment; you'll find additional documentation and links to the source code for the latest version here.

`http://www.washington.edu/pine/`—Home page for the pine email (and pico editor) programs.

`http://www.vim.org/`—Home page for the vim (vi clone) editor included with Red Hat Linux. Check here for updates, bug fixes, and news about this editor.

`http://www.courtesan.com/sudo/`—Home page for the sudo command. Check here for the latest updates, security features, and bug fixes.

The X Window System

CHAPTER 6

The X Window System, also known as X11 or more simply X, is a graphical networking interface used with Red Hat Linux. Approaching the age of 20, X is more than just a pretty face however. X started as a consortium-based project at the Massachusetts Institute of Technology in the mid-1980s, and over the years has gone through several major revisions.

The current version of X is X11R6.6. Its overall development and evolution in open source form is managed by an organization named X.org. An open-source version of X from The XFree86 Project, Inc. is included with Red Hat Linux, and is based on X11R6.5.1. There have been four major versions of XFree86 for Linux since 1994, with the current version at 4.1.0. X plays a major role for many users of Red Hat Linux by providing a stable, versatile, and viable support platform for using advanced graphical applications.

X is popular with UNIX and Linux users, system administrators, and network engineers for a number of reasons. X is extremely portable and works with nearly every hardware-based graphics system on the market. This allows X to be deployed and used with high-end workstations or diminutive embedded devices. X also provides portable and multi-platform programming standards that truly allow write-once, cross-platform development.

Another attractive feature of X is its networking capabilities, which easily allow management of thousands of workstations, deployment of thin client desktops, remote launching of applications, and standardization of installations—all working over a variety of media, such as Ethernet or wireless network connections.

Although early releases of X supported only a handful of display architectures, subsequent versions enable the use of compressed fonts, *shaped* (non-rectangular) windows, and a login manager or *display manager*. X also provides a mechanism for customizing how X programs, or *clients* appear by editing text files containing window or button appearance settings. These settings, known as *resources* are available for nearly every X11 client.

The XFree86 Project, Inc. was started in 1992, and today provides an XFree86 distribution for many different platforms. This chapter focuses on the version of XFree86 for Intel-based Linux distributions.

Basic X Concepts

The underlying engine of X11 is the X Protocol, which provides a system of managing displays on local and remote desktops. The protocol uses a client and server model that allows an abstraction of drawing locally and over a network. The drawing of a client's windows, dialog boxes, or buttons is handled locally by an X server, specific to the local hardware, and in response to client requests. The client however, doesn't have to be specific to the local hardware. This means that system administrators can set up a network with a large server and clients and enable users to view and use those clients on workstations with a totally different CPU and graphics display.

Note

For example, the text of this chapter was written using Sun Microsystem's StarOffice office suite, but the keyboard and display used for writing was attached to an Apple G4 Cube running PPC Linux and a PowerPC version of XFree86; StarOffice was launched from an Intel-based PC running the Red Hat Linux distribution included with this book.

This form of distributed processing means that Red Hat Linux, along with XFree86, can be used as a stable, cost-efficient desktop PC platform for using clients launched from a more powerful server, minicomputer, or mainframe. The X model provides a way to continue to use legacy PCs when more powerful systems are put in place, and can help centralize the job of system management.

Many home and hobbyist computer users can run Red Hat Linux and X locally on a non-networked PC, but small business, academic, corporate, and enterprise-class environments can also quickly benefit by using and adopting X as a computing solution. By using X, administrative staff, users and in-house developers can enjoy custom or standardized desktops.

Overview of XFree86

The current version of X for Red Hat Linux is the result of several years work by The XFree86 Project to incorporate new features to an older internal architecture. Some of these new features include a new, modular X server named XFree86 (which replaces 10 hardware-specific X servers provided by previous distributions by using loadable support modules) and support for multiple monitors (a feature known as *Xinerama*).

The base XFree86 distribution for Red Hat Linux consists of nearly two dozen RPM packages containing the X server named XFree86, along with support and development libraries, fonts, various clients, and documentation. Depending on your system, you might find a framebuffer-based X server, additional fonts, and perhaps another package of contributed clients. This of course, doesn't include 1,000 or more additional X clients, fonts, and documentation included with Red Hat Linux.

A full installation of X and related files can take up nearly 150MB of hard drive space and most likely much more because Red Hat chose to place additional clients, configurations files and graphics (such as icons) under the /usr/bin and /usr/share directory trees instead of the traditional /usr/X11R6 directory. System administrators can pare excessive disk requirements by judiciously choosing which packages to install on workstations. However, with the increased capacity of most desktop PC hard drives nowadays, this is rarely a consideration except when configuring thin-client desktops or embedded systems.

The /usr/X11R6 directory and its subdirectories contain the majority of XFree86's software. Some important subdirectories are

- /usr/X11R6/bin—Location of your X server and various X clients (note that not all X clients require an active X session).

- /usr/X11R6/include—Path to necessary files for developing X clients and graphics such as icons.

- /usr/X11R6/lib—This directory contains required software libraries to support the X server and clients.

- /usr/X11R6/lib/X11—This directory contains fonts, default client resources, system resources, documentation, and other files used during X sessions and for various X clients. You'll also find a symbolic link to this directory named X11 under the /usr/lib directory.

- /usr/X11R6/lib/modules—The path to drivers and X server modules used by the X server to enable use of various graphics cards.

- /usr/X11R6/man—Directory containing directories of manual pages for X11 programming and clients.

The main components generally required for an active local X session are the X server, miscellaneous fonts, a terminal client (for access to a shell prompt), and a client known as a *window manager*. Window managers, discussed later in this chapter (see "X Window Managers" later), handle the drawing and management of windows, such as overlapping or tiling, and window decorations, such as button outlines and titlebars.

The `XF86Config-4` File

The single most important file required to launch X on your desktop is the `XF86Config-4` configuration file. This text file, usually found under the `/etc/X11` directory (and hopefully configured during installation of Red Hat Linux on the PC), contains file locations, hardware descriptions, and specifications needed by the `XFree86` server in order to work with your computer's graphics card and display monitor.

It is important for Red Hat Linux system administrators to understand the contents of this file in order to troubleshoot configuration problems or perhaps add or remove features of the X session. The components of `XF86Config-4` specify the X session, or *server layout*, along with paths for files used by the server, server options, optional support modules to load, descriptions of the mouse and keyboard, the graphics device, monitor, screen layout, and video modes to use.

An typical `ServerLayout` section from an automatically configured `XF86Config-4` might look like this:

```
Section "ServerLayout"
        Identifier      "Anaconda Configured"
        Screen      0   "Screen0" 0 0
        InputDevice     "Mouse0" "CorePointer"
        InputDevice     "Keyboard0" "CoreKeyboard"
EndSection
```

In this example, a single display is used (the numbers designate position of a screen), and two default input devices, `Mouse0` and `Keyboard0` will be used for the session. The files section might look like this:

```
Section "Files"
    RgbPath     "/usr/X11R6/lib/X11/rgb"
    FontPath    "unix/:7100"
EndSection
```

Here, the path to a list of available session colors (in the text file `rgb`) and the port number to the X font server are listed. The font server, `xfs`, is started at boot time and doesn't require an active X session. If a font server isn't used, the `FontPath` entry could instead list each font directory under the `/usr/X11R6/lib/X11/fonts` directory, such as

```
FontPath "/usr/X11R6/lib/X11/fonts/100dpi"
FontPath "/usr/X11R6/lib/X11/fonts/misc"
FontPath "/usr/X11R6/lib/X11/fonts/75dpi"
FontPath "/usr/X11R6/lib/X11/fonts/PEX"
FontPath "/usr/X11R6/lib/X11/fonts/Speedo"
...
```

These directories contain the default compressed fonts available for use during the X session. The font server is configured using the file named `config` under the `/etc/X11/fs` directory. This file contains a listing, or catalog of fonts for use by the font server. By adding an `alternate-server` entry in this file and restarting the font server, system administrators can specify remote font servers for use during X sessions. This can help centralize font support and reduce local storage requirements (even though only 25MB are required for the more than 4,800 fonts installed with Red Hat Linux and X).

The Module section of the `XF86Config-4` file specifies loadable modules or drivers to load for the X session. This section might look like this:

```
Section "Module"
        Load   "GLcore"
        Load   "dbe"
        Load   "extmod"
        Load "fbdevhw"
        Load "pex5"
        Load   "glx"
        Load   "pex5"
        Load   "record"
        Load   "xie"
EndSection
```

These modules can range from special video card support to font rasterizers. The `InputDevice` section configures a specific device, such as a keyboard or mouse:

```
Section "InputDevice"
        Identifier   "Keyboard0"
        Driver       "keyboard"
        Option   "XkbRules"       "xfree86"
        Option   "XkbModel"       "pc104"
        Option   "XkbLayout"      "us"
        Option   "XkbVariant"     "basic"
EndSection
Section "InputDevice"
        Identifier   "Mouse0"
        Driver       "mouse"
        Option       "Protocol" "PS/2"
        Option       "Device" "/dev/psaux"
        Option       "ZAxisMapping" "4 5"
        Option       "Emulate3Buttons" "no"
EndSection
```

System administrators can configure multiple devices and there may be multiple `InputDevice` sections. The preceding example specifies a basic keyboard and a three-button PS/2 mouse (actually a ThinkPad TrackPoint pointer). Next, the `Monitor` section configures the designated display device as declared in the `ServerLayout` section:

```
Section "Monitor"
        Identifier    "Monitor0"
        VendorName    "Monitor Vendor"
        ModelName     "Monitor Model"
        HorizSync   31.5-48.5
        VertRefresh 50-70
        Option "dpms"
EndSection
```

Note that the X server will automatically determine the best video timings according to horizontal and vertical sync and refresh values in this section. If required, old-style mod-eline entries (used by pre-XFree86 4.0 distributions and servers) might still be used. The `Device` section provides details about the video graphics chipset used by the computer:

```
Section "Device"
    Option      "externDisp"
    Option      "internDisp"
        Identifier    "NeoMagic (laptop/notebook)"
        Driver        "neomagic"
        VendorName    "NeoMagic (laptop/notebook)"
        BoardName     "NeoMagic (laptop/notebook)"
EndSection
```

In this example (for a NeoMagic video chipset), two chipset options are enabled to allow display on a laptop's LCD screen and an attached monitor. Various chipset might have other options, and are generally documented in README files under the `/usr/X11R6/lib/X11/doc` directory. These files contain hints about optimizations and troubleshooting.

The `Screen` section ties the previous information together (using the `Screen0`, `Device`, and `Monitor Identifier` entries), and also specifies one or more color depths and resolutions for the session:

```
Section "Screen"
        Identifier    "Screen0"
        Device        "NeoMagic (laptop/notebook)"
        Monitor       "Monitor0"
        Subsection "Display"
                Depth       16
                Modes     "1024x768"
        EndSubsection
EndSection
```

Here a color depth of thousands of colors and a resolution of 1024x768 is the default (and only available setting). Multiple `Display` subsection entries with different color depths and resolutions can be used if supported by the graphics card and monitor combination. System administrators can also use a `DefaultDepth` entry, along with a specific color depth to standardize display depths in installations.

The XF86Config-4 file can be created manually or automatically by using the XFree86 server or configuration utilities (discussed next). As the root operator, you can create a test configuration file by using the server like this:

```
# XFree86 -configure
```

After you press Enter, a file named XF86Config.new will be created in the /root directory. This file can then be used for a test session like this:

```
# XFree86 -xf86config /root/XF86Config.new
```

Configuring X

This section covers the use of two configuration utilities for XFree86. Although the Red Hat installer will generally configure X during installation, problems can arise. If you are unable to configure X during installation, don't specify booting to a graphical configuration and skip the X configuration section. (Many installations, such as a server, don't require an active X session, but do require installed X clients.)

At least three configuration tools can be used by a system administrator to create a working XF86Config-4 file:

- xf86cfg—This XFree86 client provides graphical configuration, launches a base X session, and may be used to create an XF86Config file.

- xf86config—This is a text-based configuration tool that does not require an X session.

- Xconfigurator—Red Hat's console-based configuration tool that provides a GUI and does not require an X session.

If you want to create your own file manually, you'll find a template file named XF86Config.eg under the /usr/X11R6/lib/X11 directory.

Using the `xf86cfg` Client

The xf86cfg client can be used to create or update an XF86Config-4 file. Start the client from the command line (as root) like this:

```
# xf86fg
```

The screen will clear, and xf86cfg will attempt to start an X session. If you start this client during an X session, it's main window will appear as shown in Figure 6.1.

FIGURE 6.1

The xf86cfg *client provides a graphical configuration interface to creating or updating a system's* XF86Config-4 *file.*

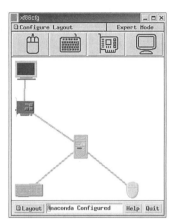

This client will display icons representing defined components or sections of an existing XF86Config-4 file. You can use its window to add or remove additional devices or configure existing devices by right-clicking on a device icon in the window. For example, to add or configure a pointer, click the mouse icon at the top of the window. You'll see a drop-down menu as shown in Figure 6.2.

FIGURE 6.2

Use xf86cfg's *icon menus to create or update a device for X.*

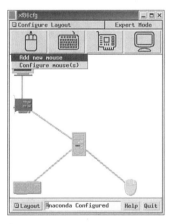

Click to select the Add New Mouse button to add a new pointing device to your X session. You can also right-click an existing device to re-configure or remove the device. You'll see a menu appear as shown in Figure 6.3.

If you select the Configure menu option (perhaps if you've changed the device or want to add a feature), you'll see a configuration dialog box appear, as shown in Figure 6.4.

FIGURE 6.3

Configure or remove an existing pointing device by right-clicking its icon.

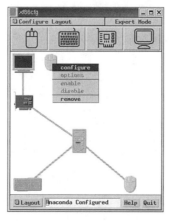

FIGURE 6.4

Select a device and protocol to re-configure an existing device.

The Identifier field shown in Figure 6.4 corresponds to the device's definition in XF86Config-4. To re-configure the device (or define a new device), select an appropriate Linux device and protocol. Changes can be made right away, or you can save the entry for the next X session.

Use this same technique when using xf86cfg to change the existing keyboard, display and graphics card, or to craft your XF86Config-4 file.

Using Xconfigurator

To make the job of creating an X configuration file easier, Red Hat Linux provides the Xconfigurator command. This program can be used from the console or command line of an X11 terminal window, and is started (as root) like so:

```
# Xconfigurator
```

After you press Enter, the screen will clear, and you'll see a Welcome screen. Press Enter, and you'll see a dialog box as shown in Figure 6.5.

FIGURE 6.5

The Xconfigurator *command creates an* XF86Config-4 *and will probe your video hardware.*

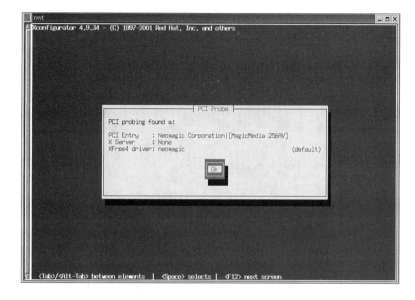

Use the Tab key and spacebar when using this command to navigate the dialogs. Press Enter, and you'll be asked to select your monitor, as shown in Figure 6.6.

FIGURE 6.6

Select your monitor by scrolling or press Enter to specify custom settings.

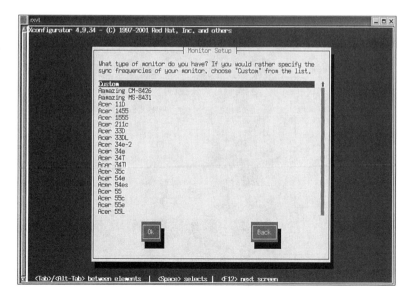

Scroll through the list of monitor makes and models until your model is highlighted, and then press Enter. Select and use the Custom entry if your monitor isn't listed. If you choose a custom entry, you'll see a list of basic types, as shown in Figure 6.7.

FIGURE 6.7

Select a type of monitor or select Custom to enter specific settings.

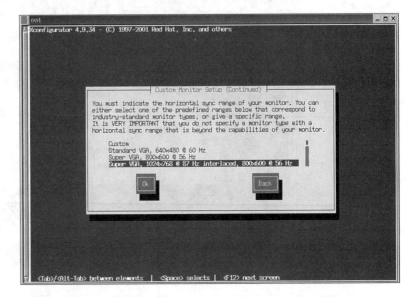

If you select Custom settings, you'll see a dialog box as shown in Figure 6.8.

FIGURE 6.8

Choose a range of horizontal frequencies when using Custom settings.

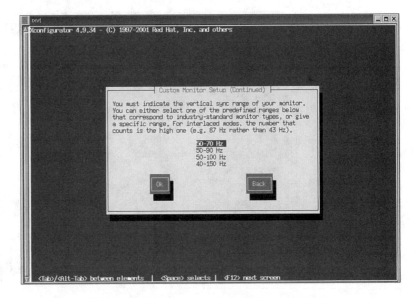

Select a horizontal frequency range that matches the capabilities of your display. Select Custom if you want to use a specific range. (You'll need to type in the numbers.) After entering your ranges or selecting a range or monitor, you might then be asked if you want the X server to probe your computer's graphics system, as shown in Figure 6.9.

FIGURE 6.9

Choose whether you'd like XFree86 *to probe your graphics hardware.*

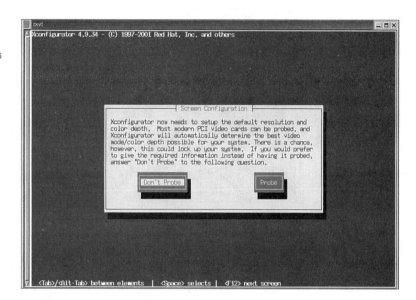

The X server can determine settings such as the amount of video memory, the video chipset, and clock chip frequencies. If you don't have your hardware probed, you'll be then asked to select your card's video memory, as shown in Figure 6.10.

Scroll through the values to select the correct amount of video memory. You'll then be asked to select a clockchip setting (if used), as shown in Figure 6.11.

Do not select a clockchip setting unless required. Press Enter to continue. Depending on your graphics hardware, you might be asked to allow another probe; if not, you'll be asked to select one or more sets of color depths and resolutions to use with X, as shown in Figure 6.12.

FIGURE 6.10
FIGURE 6.10

Select the amount of video memory installed.

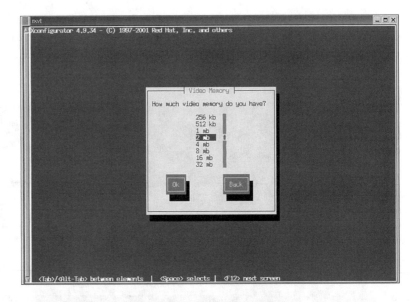

FIGURE 6.11

Use Xconfigurator *to select a clockchip setting if required.*

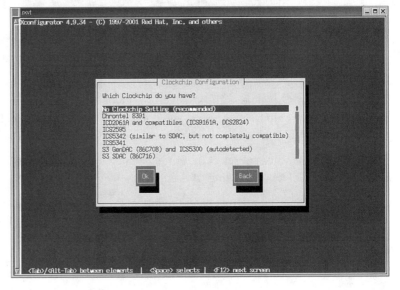

This dialog box allows you to select one or more modes for use during your X session. To toggle a mode selection, press the spacebar. Navigate through the modes using the Tab key. Selected modes are marked with an asterisk (*). The resolutions within each color depth (if available, depending on your card and monitor's capability) can be used during an X session. To switch resolutions after starting X at a selected color depth, use

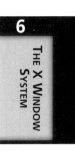

Ctrl+Alt+numeric keyboard's plus (+) and minus (-) keys. After choosing the modes, highlight the OK button and press Enter.

FIGURE 6.12

Select one or more video modes for your X sessions.

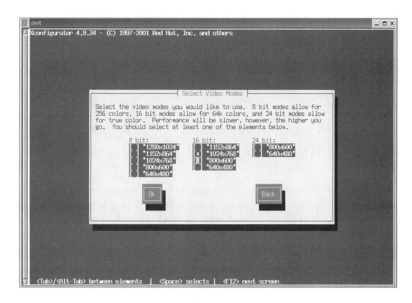

You'll then be asked if you'd like to test your configuration, as shown in Figure 6.13.

FIGURE 6.13

You can test your configuration before creating a new XF86Config-4 *file.*

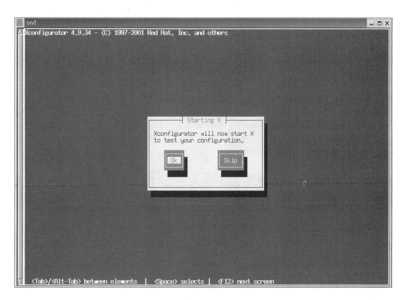

If you choose to test the configuration and the test fails, you'll be asked to go back and enter new settings. If the test succeeds or you skip the test, your new XF86Config-4 will be saved under the /etc/X11 directory.

Using `xf86config`

The xf86config command is part of the XFree86 and works through the console or inside an X11 terminal. Start xf86config (as root) like this:

```
# xf86config
```

After you press Enter, you'll see introductory text like this:

```
This program will create a basic XF86Config file, based on menu selections you
make.

The XF86Config file usually resides in /usr/X11R6/etc/X11 or /etc/X11. A sample
XF86Config file is supplied with XFree86; it is configured for a standard
VGA card and monitor with 640x480 resolution. This program will ask for a
pathname when it is ready to write the file.

You can either take the sample XF86Config as a base and edit it for your
configuration, or let this program produce a base XF86Config file for your
configuration and fine-tune it.

Before continuing with this program, make sure you know what video card
you have, and preferably also the chipset it uses and the amount of video
memory on your video card. SuperProbe may be able to help with this.

Press enter to continue, or ctrl-c to abort.
```

Press Enter to start the configuration process. You'll be asked to select your pointer's protocol:

```
First specify a mouse protocol type. Choose one from the following list:

 1.   Microsoft compatible (2-button protocol)
 2.   Mouse Systems (3-button protocol)
 3.   Bus Mouse
 4.   PS/2 Mouse
 5.   Logitech Mouse (serial, old type, Logitech protocol)
 6.   Logitech MouseMan (Microsoft compatible)
 7.   MM Series
 8.   MM HitTablet
 9.   Microsoft IntelliMouse

If you have a two-button mouse, it is most likely of type 1, and if you have
a three-button mouse, it can probably support both protocol 1 and 2. There are
two main varieties of the latter type: mice with a switch to select the
protocol, and mice that default to 1 and require a button to be held at
```

```
boot-time to select protocol 2. Some mice can be convinced to do 2 by sending
a special sequence to the serial port (see the ClearDTR/ClearRTS options).

Enter a protocol number:
```

Most Intel-based PCs use PS/2 mouse, although USB pointing devices are very popular. If you have a USB device, go ahead and make a selection; however, you'll need to go back and manually editing the resulting configuration file. Here's an entry for a three-button USB mouse with a scrollwheel:

```
Section "Pointer"
  Device         "/dev/input/mice"
  Protocol       "IMPS/2"
  ZAxisMapping   4 5
EndSection
```

Note that the device might be different for your system.

> **Note**
>
> You can also use a PS/2 definition in your configuration file, even if you have a two-button USB mouse. Just ensure that /dev/mouse is a symbolic link to /dev/input/mice and that the mouse is configured properly for the console.

Type a number that matches your system's pointing device, and press Enter. You'll then be asked if you want three-button emulation:

```
If your mouse has only two buttons, it is recommended that you enable
Emulate3Buttons.

Please answer the following question with either 'y' or 'n'.
Do you want to enable Emulate3Buttons?
```

Three-button emulation is extremely important because the middle mouse button (emulated by simultaneously depressing the left and right buttons) is used for pasting text or graphics. The choice of mouse to use for X is also a hardware purchase consideration, especially if you are ordering hundreds of workstations. The best approach is to order three-button or two-button scrollwheel pointers for your users.

You'll then be asked to choose your mouse device:

```
Now give the full device name that the mouse is connected to, for example
/dev/tty00. Just pressing enter will use the default, /dev/mouse.

Mouse device:
```

Press Enter to continue because the Red Hat installer has most likely already chosen and configured your pointing device and created /dev/mouse as a symbolic link pointing to the correct device (such as /dev/psaux, /dev/ttyS*, or /dev/input/mice for a PS/2, serial, or USB pointer). You'll next be asked to select a keyboard:

```
Please select one of the following keyboard types that is the better
description of your keyboard. If nothing really matches,
choose 1 (Generic 101-key PC)

  1  Generic 101-key PC
  2  Generic 102-key (Intl) PC
  3  Generic 104-key PC
  4  Generic 105-key (Intl) PC
  5  Dell 101-key PC
  6  Everex STEPnote
  7  Keytronic FlexPro
  8  Microsoft Natural
  9  Northgate OmniKey 101
 10  Winbook Model XP5
 11  Japanese 106-key
 12  PC-98xx Series
 13  Brazilian ABNT2
 14  HP Internet
 15  Logitech iTouch
 16  Logitech Cordless Desktop Pro
 17  Logitech Internet Keyboard
 18  Compaq Internet
 19  Microsoft Natural Pro
 20  Genius Comfy KB-16M
 21  IBM Rapid Access
 22  IBM Rapid Access II
 23  Chicony Internet Keyboard

Enter a number to choose the keyboard.
```

Type a number corresponding to your model keyboard. Enter the number one (1) if you're unsure of your model. You'll then need to specify the language for the keyboard:

```
  1  U.S. English
  2  U.S. English w/ISO9995-3
  3  U.S. English w/ deadkeys
  4  Armenian
  5  Azerbaidjani
  6  Belarusian
  7  Belgian
  8  Brazilian
  9  Bulgarian
 10  Canadian
 11  Czech
 12  Czech (qwerty)
```

```
13   Danish
14   Dvorak
15   Estonian
16   Finnish
17   French
18   Swiss French

Enter a number to choose the country.
Press enter for the next page
```

Press Enter to see additional language keyboards, and then enter a number for your language and press Enter. You'll then be asked to select a variant keyboard:

```
Please enter a variant name for 'us' layout. Or just press enter
for default variant
```

If unsure about using a variant (which enables the use or more than one keyboard for X), just press Enter. You'll now be asked about keyboard options:

```
Please answer the following question with either 'y' or 'n'.
Do you want to select additional XKB options (group switcher,
group indicator, etc.)?
```

Type an **n** if you don't want to use any options. If you do want to use options, type a **y** and press Enter.

```
   Group Shift/Lock behavior

 1   R-Alt switches group while pressed
 2   Right Alt key changes group
 3   Caps Lock key changes group
 4   Menu key changes group
 5   Both Shift keys together change group
 6   Control+Shift changes group
 7   Alt+Control changes group
 8   Alt+Shift changes group

Please select the option or just press enter if none
```

If you press Enter (or make a selection and then press Enter) again, you'll be presented options regarding your keyboard's Ctrl keys:

```
   Control Key Position

 1   Make CapsLock an additional Control
 2   Swap Control and Caps Lock
 3   Control key at left of 'A'
 4   Control key at bottom left

Please select the option or just press enter if none
```

Again, if you press Enter (or make a selection and then press Enter), you'll see an introduction to monitor configuration:

```
Now we want to set the specifications of the monitor. The two critical
parameters are the vertical refresh rate, which is the rate at which the
the whole screen is refreshed, and most importantly the horizontal sync rate,
which is the rate at which scanlines are displayed.

The valid range for horizontal sync and vertical sync should be documented
in the manual of your monitor. If in doubt, check the monitor database
/usr/X11R6/lib/X11/doc/Monitors to see if your monitor is there.

Press enter to continue, or ctrl-c to abort.
```

Press Enter to begin configuring your monitor:

```
You must indicate the horizontal sync range of your monitor. You can either
select one of the predefined ranges below that correspond to industry-
standard monitor types, or give a specific range.

It is VERY IMPORTANT that you do not specify a monitor type with a horizontal
sync range that is beyond the capabilities of your monitor. If in doubt,
choose a conservative setting.

    hsync in kHz; monitor type with characteristic modes
 1   31.5; Standard VGA, 640x480 @ 60 Hz
 2   31.5 - 35.1; Super VGA, 800x600 @ 56 Hz
 3   31.5, 35.5; 8514 Compatible, 1024x768 @ 87 Hz interlaced (no 800x600)
 4   31.5, 35.15, 35.5; Super VGA, 1024x768 @ 87 Hz interlaced, 800x600 @ 56 Hz
 5   31.5 - 37.9; Extended Super VGA, 800x600 @ 60 Hz, 640x480 @ 72 Hz
 6   31.5 - 48.5; Non-Interlaced SVGA, 1024x768 @ 60 Hz, 800x600 @ 72 Hz
 7   31.5 - 57.0; High Frequency SVGA, 1024x768 @ 70 Hz
 8   31.5 - 64.3; Monitor that can do 1280x1024 @ 60 Hz
 9   31.5 - 79.0; Monitor that can do 1280x1024 @ 74 Hz
10   31.5 - 82.0; Monitor that can do 1280x1024 @ 76 Hz
11   Enter your own horizontal sync range

Enter your choice (1-11):
```

Type in a number that matches the range of frequencies available by your monitor and
press Enter. Enter specific values by typing **11** and pressing Enter. You'll then be asked
about your monitor's vertical sync ranges:

```
You must indicate the vertical sync range of your monitor. You can either
select one of the predefined ranges below that correspond to industry-
standard monitor types, or give a specific range. For interlaced modes,
the number that counts is the high one (e.g. 87 Hz rather than 43 Hz).

 1   50-70
 2   50-90
 3   50-100
```

```
 4  40-150
 5  Enter your own vertical sync range

Enter your choice:
```

Enter a number for a range or enter your own range values by typing **5**, and then press Enter. You can now enter a description of the monitor:

```
You must now enter a few identification/description strings, namely an
identifier, a vendor name, and a model name. Just pressing enter will fill
in default names.

The strings are free-form, spaces are allowed.
Enter an identifier for your monitor definition:
```

If you just press Enter, you'll be asked if you want to look at XFree86's card database (it is OK to not enter a monitor definition because a default will be used in the configuration file):

```
Now we must configure video card specific settings. At this point you can
choose to make a selection out of a database of video card definitions.
Because there can be variation in Ramdacs and clock generators even
between cards of the same model, it is not sensible to blindly copy
the settings (e.g. a Device section). For this reason, after you make a
selection, you will still be asked about the components of the card, with
the settings from the chosen database entry presented as a strong hint.

The database entries include information about the chipset, what driver to
run, the Ramdac and ClockChip, and comments that will be included in the
Device section. However, a lot of definitions only hint about what driver
to run (based on the chipset the card uses) and are untested.

If you can't find your card in the database, there's nothing to worry about.
You should only choose a database entry that is exactly the same model as
your card; choosing one that looks similar is just a bad idea (e.g. a
GemStone Snail 64 may be as different from a GemStone Snail 64+ in terms of
hardware as can be).

Do you want to look at the card database?
```

Type a **y** and press Enter to view the XFree 700-card database found in the /usr/X11R6/lib/X11/Cards. Select your system's card from the database:

```
0  2 the Max MAXColor S3 Trio64V+          S3 Trio64V+
1  2-the-Max MAXColor 6000                 ET6000
2  3DLabs Oxygen GMX                       PERMEDIA 2
3  3DVision-i740 AGP                       Intel 740
4  3Dlabs Permedia2 (generic)             PERMEDIA 2
5  928Movie                                S3 928
6  ABIT G740 8MB SDRAM                     Intel 740
7  AGP 2D/3D V. 1N, AGP-740D               Intel 740
```

```
 8  AGX (generic)                      AGX-014/15/16
 9  ALG-5434                           CL-GD5434
10  AOpen AGP 2X 3D Navigator PA740    Intel 740
11  AOpen PA2010                       Voodoo Banshee
12  AOpen PA45                         SiS6326
13  AOpen PA50D                        SiS6326
14  AOpen PA50E                        SiS6326
15  AOpen PA50V                        SiS6326
16  AOpen PA80/DVD                     SiS6326
17  AOpen PG128                        S3 Trio3D
```

```
Enter a number to choose the corresponding card definition.
Press enter for the next page, q to continue configuration.
```

Press the Enter key to page through the file, and then type the number corresponding to
your video card and press Enter. For example, after entering the number 410, xf86config
reports

```
Your selected card definition:

Identifier: NeoMagic (laptop/notebook)
Chipset:    (null)
Driver:     neomagic
Do NOT probe clocks or use any Clocks line.

Press enter to continue, or ctrl-c to abort.
```

In this example, a NeoMagic graphics chipset has been selected. After pressing Enter,
you might be asked to enter the amount of video memory for your card:

```
Now you must give information about your video card. This will be used for
the "Device" section of your video card in XF86Config.

You must indicate how much video memory you have. It is probably a good
idea to use the same approximate amount as that detected by the server you
intend to use. If you encounter problems that are due to the used server
not supporting the amount memory you have (e.g. ATI Mach64 is limited to
1024K with the SVGA server), specify the maximum amount supported by the
server.

How much video memory do you have on your video card:

1  256K
2  512K
3  1024K
4  2048K
5  4096K
6  Other

Enter your choice:
```

For example, if you have a video card with 2MB video RAM, type in the number **2** and press Enter. Use the Other option if you have more than 4MB video RAM. After entering the amount of video RAM amount, enter information about your card:

```
You must now enter a few identification/description strings, namely an
identifier, a vendor name, and a model name. Just pressing enter will fill
in default names (possibly from a card definition).

Your card definition is NeoMagic (laptop/notebook).

The strings are free-form, spaces are allowed.
Enter an identifier for your video card definition:
```

You can again just press Enter. Next, select one or more resolutions and color depths for your monitor and card:

```
For each depth, a list of modes (resolutions) is defined. The default
resolution that the server will start-up with will be the first listed
mode that can be supported by the monitor and card.
Currently it is set to:

"640x480" "800x600" "1024x768" "1280x1024" for 8-bit
"640x480" "800x600" "1024x768" for 16-bit
"640x480" "800x600" for 24-bit

Modes that cannot be supported due to monitor or clock constraints will
be automatically skipped by the server.

1  Change the modes for 8-bit (256 colors)
2  Change the modes for 16-bit (32K/64K colors)
3  Change the modes for 24-bit (24-bit color)
4  The modes are OK, continue.

Enter your choice:
```

Type **1**, **2**, or **3** to change the modes. Use **4** if the modes are OK. To change the modes for thousands of colors type a **2**, and you'll see this:

```
Select modes from the following list:

1  "640x400"
2  "640x480"
3  "800x600"
4  "1024x768"
5  "1280x1024"
6  "320x200"
7  "320x240"
8  "400x300"
9  "1152x864"
a  "1600x1200"
b  "1800x1400"
```

```
c   "512x384"
```

```
Please type the digits corresponding to the modes that you want to select.
For example, 432 selects "1024x768" "800x600" "640x480", with a
default mode of 1024x768.
```

```
Which modes?
```

Enter one or more numbers to select the modes, and then press Enter. You'll then be asked about virtual resolution:

```
You can have a virtual screen (desktop), which is screen area that is larger
than the physical screen and which is panned by moving the mouse to the edge
of the screen. If you don't want virtual desktop at a certain resolution,
you cannot have modes listed that are larger. Each color depth can have a
differently-sized virtual screen
```

```
Please answer the following question with either 'y' or 'n'.
Do you want a virtual screen that is larger than the physical screen?
```

Using an X desktop with virtual resolution is necessary if you need to run a client that requires a 1024x768 resolution, but your hardware is limited to 800x600. Fortunately, most monitors (and even laptops) now support the almost required X session resolution of 1024x768. To set a virtual screen, type **y** and follow the prompts. After finishing the configuration, select resolutions for each color depth:

```
For each depth, a list of modes (resolutions) is defined. The default
resolution that the server will start-up with will be the first listed
mode that can be supported by the monitor and card.
Currently it is set to:
```

```
"640x480" "800x600" "1024x768" "1280x1024" for 8-bit
"1024x768" for 16-bit
"640x480" "800x600" for 24-bit
```

```
Modes that cannot be supported due to monitor or clock constraints will
be automatically skipped by the server.
```

```
1   Change the modes for 8-bit (256 colors)
2   Change the modes for 16-bit (32K/64K colors)
3   Change the modes for 24-bit (24-bit color)
4   The modes are OK, continue.
```

```
Enter your choice:
```

Use a number that provides a 16-bit value if possible because most Linux clients and X sessions work well at a color depth of thousands of colors. You can also choose a 24-bit setting (providing millions of colors) if supported by your hardware. Next, select a default color depth:

```
Please specify which color depth you want to use by default:

   1   1 bit (monochrome)
   2   4 bits (16 colors)
   3   8 bits (256 colors)
   4  16 bits (65536 colors)
   5  24 bits (16 million colors)

Enter a number to choose the default depth.
```

After selecting a depth, press Enter to finish the configuration:

```
I am going to write the XF86Config file now. Make sure you don't accidently
overwrite a previously configured one.

Shall I write it to /etc/X11/XF86Config?
```

Save the file by entering **y**. Enter an **n** to write the file elsewhere or to write it with a different name. This concludes configuration of file; however, you might want to examine or edit the file before use and test it by launching XFree86 and using its -xf86config option. Regardless of the configuration tool used, when you start or boot to an X session, the X server will look for your XF86Config-4 file in the following locations:

```
/etc/X11
/usr/X11R6/etc/X11
/etc
/usr/X11R6/lib/X11
/root
```

Note that the server will only be able to use a configuration file found under the /root directory if you start an X session as root.

Starting X

X sessions can be started in a variety of ways. Normally the Red Hat Linux installer will set up the system's initialization table /etc/inittab to have Linux boot directly to an X session using a *display manager*, an X client that provides a graphical login. After logging in, the user will either boot to a local session, or if the system is properly configured to an X session running on a remote computer on your network.

Display manager use is generally controlled by a *runlevel* or system state entry in /etc/inittab. Red Hat Linux defines the following runlevels:

```
# 0 - halt (Do NOT set initdefault to this)
# 1 - Single user mode
# 2 - Multiuser, without NFS (The same as 3, if you do not have networking)
# 3 - Full multiuser mode
# 4 - unused
```

```
# 5 - X11
# 6 - reboot (Do NOT set initdefault to this)
```

Runlevel 5 is used for multiuser mode with a graphical X login using a display manager; booting to runlevel 3 provides a console, or text-base login. The `initdefault` setting in the `/etc/inittab` file determines the default runlevel:

```
id:5:initdefault:
```

In this example, Red Hat Linux will boot directly to X. The default display manager might also be specified in `/etc/inittab` like this:

```
x:5:respawn:/usr/bin/xdm -nodaemon
```

However, Red Hat Linux uses a shell script named `prefdm`, found under the `/etc/X11` directory to set the display manager:

```
x:5:respawn:/etc/X11/prefdm -nodaemon
```

According to this script, the display manager is based on the file named `desktop` under the `/etc/sysconfig` directory. The words GNOME, KDE, or AnotherLevel following a `DESKTOP=` entry determine the display manager used for login (such as `xdm`, `gdm`, or `kdm`). Logging via a display manager requires a user to enter a username and password.

Configuring `gdm`

The `gdm` display manager is part of the GNOME library and client distribution included with Red Hat Linux, and provides a graphical login when booting directly to X. Its login (actually displayed by the `gdmlogin` client) hosts drop-down menus of window managers, languages, and system options for shutting down (halting) or rebooting the workstation. Edit (as root) `gdm.conf` under the `/etc/X11/gdm` directory to configure `gdm`.

Another way to configure `gdm` is to use the `gdmconfig` client. This client, shown in Figure 6.14, can be used by the system administrator to configure many aspects and features of the login display. Launch this client from the GNOME desktop panel or from the command line like this:

```
# gdmconfig &
```

After you press Enter, you'll see its window as shown in Figure 6.14.

Settings for security, remote network logins, the X server, and session and session chooser setup can be made by clicking on a designated tab in `gdmconfig`'s dialog. Settings can be made available immediately or when X restarts.

FIGURE 6.14

Use gdmconfig *to configure the* gdm-login *screen when using* gdm *as a display manager.*

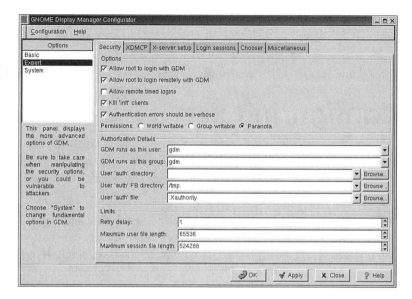

Configuring kdm

The kdm client, part of the KDE X desktop suite, offers a similar graphical login. Configure kdm by clicking on the KDE Control Center menu item in KDE's desktop panel. When the Control Center appears, click the System menu list and then the Login Manager menu item. You'll then see the kdm configuration dialog box as shown in Figure 6.15.

FIGURE 6.15

Configure kdm *by choosing option tabs and settings in the Control Center dialog box.*

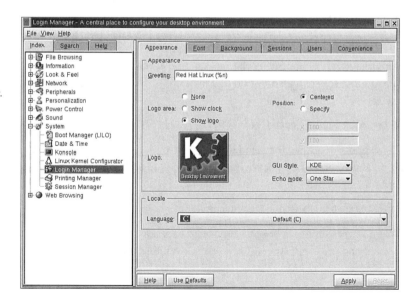

Click on a tab at the top of the dialog box to set configuration options. This dialog box offers control of the login display, prompts, setting user icons, session management, and configuration of system options (for shutting down or rebooting). Changes can be applied immediately or delayed until the X server restarts.

Configuring xdm

The xdm display manager is part of the XFree86 distribution and offers a bare-bones login for using X. Configure xdm by editing various files under the /etc/X11/xdm directory. The default login screen can be customized by editing the file Xsetup_0 in that directory.

You can also configure xdm to provide a remote login from another workstation or server on your network (if firewalling isn't enabled on the server). The basic steps are to first edit a workstation's Xaccess file under the /etc/X11/xdm directory, commenting out the CHOOSER BROADCAST line, and then uncomment the hostlist and CHOOSER line. Then insert the name or names of your servers in the hostlist line, perhaps like this:

```
%hostlist       green.home.org
```

These steps should be repeated for each workstation on the network. On the server (green.home.org in this example), uncomment the following line in the Xaccess file:

```
*                          #any host can get a login window
```

Start the xdm client on the server, and then use the Xwrapper command with XFree86's -broadcast option like this:

```
$ Xwrapper -broadcast
```

An xdm login will appear on the workstation from the server. Multiple servers can be specified. Users can also log on to a specific server using the -query option, followed by the server's name, like this:

```
$ Xwrapper -query green.home.org
```

This approach allows for standardized distributions and hard drive installs for workstations while centralizing services on one or more servers. You can also edit /etc/passwd and replace the shell entry with the name of a script that looks like this:

```
/usr/X11R6/bin/Xwrapper -broadcast
```

When a workstation is booted, a generic username and password is used at the xdm screen, and the login screen for the first available server will appear.

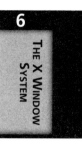

Using startx

To start X from the command line, use the `startx` command. This command (actually a shell script) can be used to pass a number of command-line options to the X server before launching an X session. `startx` will first look in a user's home directory for a file named `.xinitrc`. The default system `.xinitrc` is found in the `/etc/X11/xinit` directory, but a local file can be used to customize an X session and launch default clients. This is unnecessary when using a GNOME-aware window manager or KDE as these desktop environments offer *session management*, or the ability to save the state of a desktop session and restart clients that were active when logging out.

Launch the X server and an X session by using `startx` like this:

```
$ startx
```

You can also use `startx` to specify a color depth for an X session by using the `-depth` option, followed by an number such as 8, 16, 24, or 32 for 256, thousands, or millions of colors (as defined in your X configuration file and if supported). For example, to start a session with thousands of colors, use the command like this:

```
$ startx -- -depth 16
```

Another option that can be passed is a specific dots-per-inch (dpi) resolution to be used for the X session. For example, to use 100-dpi, use the `-dpi` option followed by `100`, like this:

```
$ startx -- -dpi 100
```

`startx` can also be used to launch multiple X sessions. This feature is due to Linux's support for *virtual consoles*, or multiple text-based displays. To start the first X session, use the `startx` command followed by a *display number* or X server instance (the first is 0, using screen 0), and a number representing a virtual console. The default console used for X is number 7, so the session can be started like this:

```
$ startx -- :0 vt7
```

After X starts and the window manager appears, press Ctrl+Alt+F2, and then log in again at the prompt. Next, start another X session like this, specifying a different display number and virtual console:

```
$ startx -- :1 vt8
```

Another X session will start. To jump to the first X session, press Ctrl+Alt+F7. Use Ctrl+Alt+F8 to return to the second session. `startx` is a flexible way to launch X sessions, but multiple sessions can be confusing, especially to new users, and are a horrific resource drain on the system without enough CPU horsepower and memory.

X Window Managers

A window manager is an essential client generally launched immediately after the X server starts. Many different window managers are available for Red Hat Linux. This wealth of choice in how one can make the graphical desktop appear and work forms part of the incredible attraction many users experience when using Linux and X.

A window manager provides an X display and customized desktop by handling many tasks, such as window decoration, movement, placement, and resizing operations. A window manager can also handle icons, support docking of icons, and other window operations such as tiling, and overlays. Another important task is *focus policy*, or how and when a window becomes active. Depending on settings, a window can become active when your pointer is over a window, or might require a mouse click for activation.

A window manager might also provide menuing on the root desktop or after clicking on a button in a client's window titlebar. Some window managers support the use of special keyboard keys to move the pointer and emulate mouse button clicks. Another feature is the *virtual desktop*, which isn't the same as the virtual screen (a desktop larger than the display), but two, four, or eight additional complete workspaces. Some window managers support advanced features, such as drag and drop of icons representing files or system devices. This allows the user to easily copy, print, delete, link, or move files.

Use Red Hat's `switchdesk` client to choose a default window or in the case of GNOME or KDE, a default desktop *environment*. Desktop environments not only use a window manager, but also include a entire suite of related clients, such as productivity or utility applications. The switchdesk utility can be use at a text-based console, along with a keyword (such as GNOME or KDE) to set the default X desktop before launching X. For example, to specify KDE, use `switchdesk` like this:

```
$ switchdesk KDE
Red Hat Linux switchdesk 3.9
Copyright  1999-2001 Red Hat, Inc
Redistributable under the terms of the GNU General Public License
Desktop now set up to run KDE.
For system defaults, remove /home/bball/.Xclients
```

If launched during an X session from the command line of an X11 terminal, `switchdesk` appears as a graphical dialog:

```
$ switchdesk &
```

After you press Enter, you'll be given a choice of window managers for your X sessions, as shown in Figure 6.16.

FIGURE 6.16

Use switchdesk *to set the default window manager for X sessions.*

Choosing a window manager is a matter of preference, necessity, or policy. For legacy PC hardware, some of the older window managers (such as twm or fvwm2) will have fewer system resource requirements (less hard drive space and system memory). Newer desktop environments will require 64MB and even more memory for better performance.

The twm Window Manager

The twm window manager included with XFree86 is a legacy client that provides modest but essential features in a small (less than 1MB) memory footprint. Window decorations, menus, icons, and other features are supported, but virtual desktops aren't. (For a similar window manager, but with virtual desktops, try the tvtwm window manager.)

This window manager is used as a fallback or *failsafe* window manager because it is included with XFree86, the default resource file; system.twmrc, is located under the /etc/X11/twm directory. System administrators can configure this file to provide a default desktop with an application menu. Custom user settings can be to a file named .twmrc in a user's home directory.

The twm desktop is shown in Figure 6.17.

The desktop menu is accessed by left-clicking in a blank area of the root window.

FIGURE 6.17

twm is included with XFree86 and offers basic window and icon management.

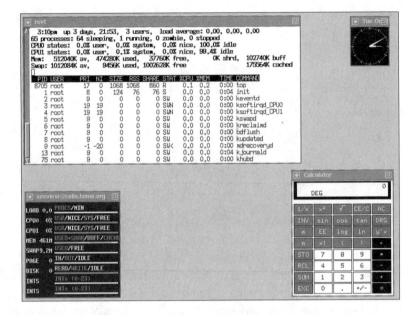

The FVWM2 Window Manager

The FVWM2 window manager is based on `twm` and offers virtual desktops navigated by clicking on a *pager*, a client that offers a grid of tiny windows on the desktop. Using virtual desktops allows related tasks to be grouped by desktop, such as relegating software development on one desktop with e-mail applications in another.

FVWM2's default resource file is located in `/etc/X11/fvwm2/system.fvwm2rc` and can be edited to provide custom settings when located in a user's home directory in a file named `.fvwm2rc`.

The FVWM2 desktop as shown in Figure 6.18.

The Enlightenment Window Manager

The Enlightenment window manager, also known as E, has a large number of features and is also a GNOME-aware window manager. This means that Enlightenment can be used as the window manager during a GNOME X session, and it supports GNOME clients. Some of the features include virtual desktops, icon docking, taskbars, and a complete set of preference menus. Systemwide defaults are in a series of files under `/usr/share/enlightenment` directory, whereas individual settings can be contained in a directory named `.enlightenment` in a home directory.

FIGURE 6.18

The FVWM2 window manager provides virtual desktops.

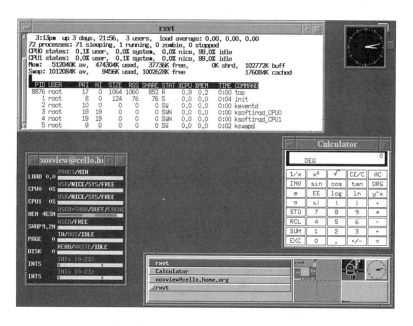

The Enlightenment desktop is shown in Figure 6.19.

FIGURE 6.19

The Enlightenment window manager supports GNOME libraries.

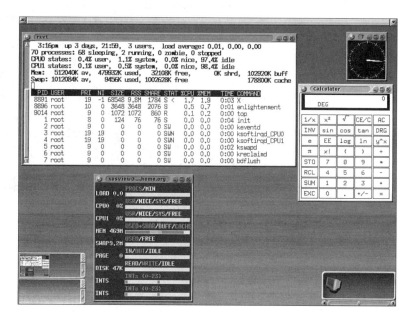

This window manager also supports *themes*, or sets of related settings that can radically change the appearance of the desktop. These settings are installed under the /usr/share/enlightenment/themes directory and become active after a restart and after selecting a new theme from the Themes menu item (accessed by clicking in a blank area of the desktop).

The Window Maker Window Manager

The Window Maker window manager mimics the legacy NeXT computer interface, and provides a wharf, or application dock, desktop menus, themes, and virtual desktops. Default configuration files are located under the /usr/X11R6/share/wmakerconf directory, whereas user defaults are located in the home directory in GNUstep/Defaults.

The Window Maker desktop is shown in Figure 6.20.

FIGURE 6.20

The Window Maker window manager mimics a well-known graphical interface for X.

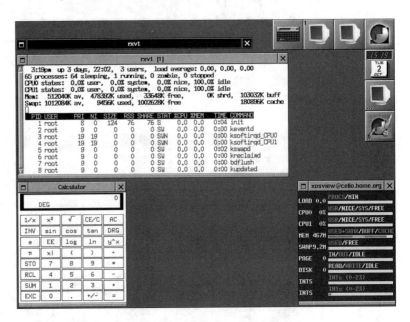

The mwm Window Manager

The mwm window manager, or the Motif window manager, is a clone window manager that closely mimics the original mwm window manager that was part of the OSF/Motif distribution from The Open Group. The mwm window manager is part of a Motif 1.2–compatible set of programming libraries and development files named LessTif. (Although it works like the Motif mwm, is actually based on fvwm.)

mwm can even use the same configuration files as the OSF/Motif version; its default configuration file, system.mwmrc, is located in /usr/X11R6/lib/X11/mwm. Like other window managers, user settings can reside in a file named .mwmrc in the home directory.

The mwm desktop is shown in Figure 6.21.

FIGURE 6.21

The mwm window manager mimics the OSF/Motif mwm window manager.

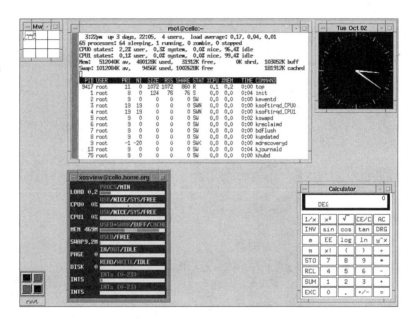

The GNOME and KDE Desktop Environments

Desktop environments for X provide one or more window managers and a suite of clients that conform to a standard graphical interface based on a common set of software libraries. When used to develop associated clients, these libraries provide graphical consistency for the client windows, menus, buttons, and other decorations, along with commonality in keyboard controls and client dialogs.

The GNU Network Object Model Environment

The GNU Network Object Model Environment, or GNOME, is the brain-child of Miguel de Icaza. GNOME was started in 1997 and has matured to provide a complete set of software libraries and clients. GNOME depends on a cognizant window manager to provide the desktop. Some compliant window managers that are GNOME-aware include Enlightenment, WindowMaker, IceWM, and sawfish, and they are included with Red Hat Linux.

GNOME user-friendly suite of clients provide a consistent and user-friendly desktop. GNOME is a staple feature of Red Hat Linux because Red Hat, Inc. actively supports its development. GNOME clients are found under the /usr/bin directory, and its configuration files are stored under the /etc/gnome and /usr/share/gnome directories with user settings stored in the home directory under .gnome.

A representative GNOME desktop is shown in Figure 6.22.

FIGURE 6.22

Red Hat's GNOME desktop uses the Nautilus graphical shell from the now-defunct Eazel.

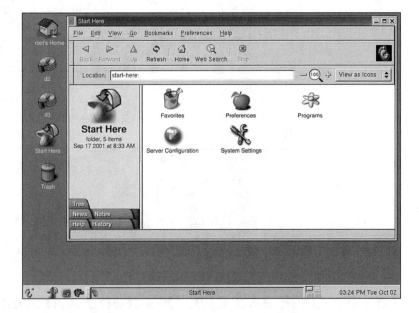

Red Hat's GNOME desktop includes Nautilus, a graphical shell originally developed by Eazel (which ceased operations shortly before Summer 2001). The Nautilus shell will require additional system resources, such as hard drive space and memory.

GNOME and the current window manager in use can be configured by clicking the Preferences icon in the Nautilus window, and then clicking on the current window manager's icon (such as sawfish). You'll then see a window of icons (as shown in Figure 6.23) to launch dialog boxes used to change the appearance, focus behavior, window behavior, placement, sound, and workspace settings.

FIGURE 6.23

Uses the Nautilus graphical shell's Settings icon to access a window manager's preferences when using GNOME.

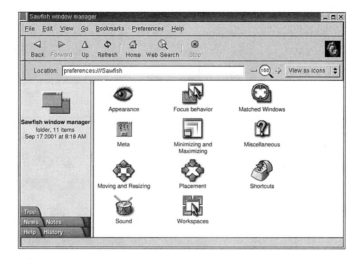

The K Desktop Environment

The K Desktop Environment (KDE) has been available for Linux and XFree86 since 1996. KDE was started by a German Linux software developer named Matthias Ettrich, and has gone through several major revisions. KDE is a graphical desktop environment that includes a huge suite of clients, including a free office suite named KOffice. When KDE first starts, the user will see a desktop as shown in Figure 6.24. The KDE Desktop Settings Wizard is used to personalize the desktop.

FIGURE 6.24

KDE is a graphical desktop and suite of clients for Red Hat Linux and X.

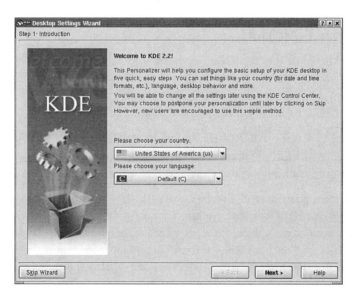

KDE clients are located under the /usr/bin directory, and the directory .kde in a user's home directory contains custom settings and session information. After using the Desktop Settings Wizard, additional changes can be made by using the KDE control panel or KDE Control Center dialog box (shown in Figure 6.25) to control additional window behavior, screen saving, and other features.

FIGURE 6.25

Use the KDE Control Center to manage nearly every aspect of the your desktop sessions.

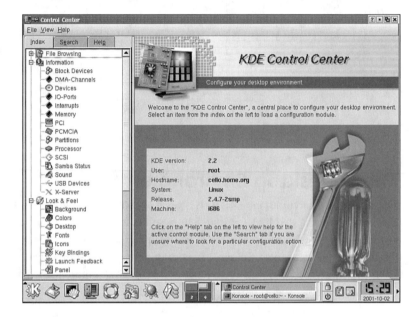

Ximian GNOME

In 1999, Miguel de Icaza and Nat Friedman, original GNOME developers, created a company now known as Ximian. Ximian is a polished GNOME environment that not only offers an updated suite of GNOME clients, but also groupware software providing integrated mail, calendar, addressing, and instant messaging.

Ximian isn't included with Red Hat Linux, but can be installed via CD-ROM, or if you have broadband access, in about an hour or less over the Internet. Versions are available for many different Linux distributions (even those on non-Intel platforms).

To get started, go to Ximian's Web site at http://www.ximian.com/download and select the current Red Hat Linux distribution. The text-only lynx Web browser is first used to quickly download a graphical installer, which is then used to select a download site, selected files, and the base Ximian distribution. Download and installation is an automatic process, and Ximian will replace your default Red Hat Linux GNOME software with its own GNOME distribution. After installation, you can quickly installs updates and bug fixes by using an update icon on the Ximian desktop.

Reference

`http://www.x.org`—Curators of the X Window System.

`http://www.x.org/xdownload.htm`—Want to download the source to the latest revision of X? Start at this site with a short registration.

`http://www.xfree86.org`—Home of The XFree86 Project, Inc., which has provided a graphical interface for Linux for nearly 10 years.

`http://www.kde.org`—The place to get started when learning about KDE and the latest developments.

`http://www.gnome.org`—The launch point for more information about GNOME, links to new clients, and GNOME development projects.

`http://sawmill.sourceforge.net`—Home page for the `sawmill` window manager.

`http://enlightenment.org`—Enlightenment's home page, where you can download the latest version for Red Hat Linux and other Linux distributions.

`http://www.windowmaker.org`—The source for the latest version of WindowMaker.

`http://www.icewm.org`—IceWM's home page.

`http://www.lesstif.org`—Home page of the LessTif project, which aims to provide GNU GPL versions of OSF/Motif-compatible software libraries.

`http://scwm.sourceforge.net`—Home page of a lightweight, yet virtual desktop-enabled window manager

`http://www.fvwm.org`—Home page for FVWM2, where you can download the latest version.

`http://nautilus.eazel.com/`—The current Nautilus graphical shell home page.

`http://www.ximian.com/download/`—The place to get started with Ximian GNOME.

System Administration

PART

II

IN THIS PART

Managing Services

CHAPTER

7

This chapter explores in detail how Red Hat Linux boots, and how system states or *run-levels* can control what system services are started upon boot up. As a system administrator, you'll also learn how you can control your system's services and manage system states on your computer. This information is essential to understanding how Linux works, and can help untangle some of the mysteries of your Red Hat Linux system's configuration files.

Nearly every aspect of your computer and how it behaves after booting can be managed through pre-configuration of boot scripts, ordering of these scripts, and by using various system administration utilities included with Red Hat Linux. Using the information presented in this chapter can help you troubleshoot and fix problems that might arise with software configuration or the introduction or removal of various types of hardware from your system.

Note that this chapter covers the basics and gives an overview of managing various services from the system's point of view—the details about managing specific services, such as File Transfer Protocol (FTP), or the Apache Web server, are contained in separate chapters.

How Red Hat Linux Boots

Although the actual boot loading mechanism will vary for Linux on different hardware platforms, such as the SPARC, Alpha, or PowerPC CPU, Intel-based PCs running Red Hat Linux most often use the same pre-boot mechanism throughout product lines. This homogenous characteristic is accomplished through a (mostly) standard BIOS, which will first check the basic subsystems of your computer, such as the amount and validity of RAM, CPU type and speed, the presence of a boot volume (such as a floppy, CD-ROM, or hard drive), keyboard, and other characteristics.

Problems with booting can arise at this stage, if for example, the BIOS detects a hardware failure, missing hardware, or hardware mis-configuration. Other problems included some legacy PCs and early BIOS distributions that not only failed to allow the PC to boot Linux without a keyboard but also failed to provide a way around this problem.

If all goes well, the BIOS will then look for a bootable volume, in the order established by its settings (such as the floppy first, followed by a CD-ROM, and then a hard drive). Next, the BIOS will look for boot code in the partition boot sector, also known as the *Master Boot Record (MBR)* of the first hard disk. This area of the disk usually contains a boot sector, which then loads the boot loader, such as LILO, Grub, or BootMagic.

Alternatively, the entire MBR might be replaced with a boot loader. In turn, the boot loader then loads the Linux kernel according to how the boot loader is configured.

Details about the specific sequence of events or what happens when the Linux kernel is loaded can be found in the file `/usr/src/linux/init/main.c` if you have installed the Linux kernel. In general, the kernel will,

1. Initialize and load a RAM disk image (if designated)

2. Pause, and then perform some timing (speed) tests.

3. Parse for any boot-time kernel arguments. Note that `main.c` is a good place to look for the specific vocabulary of various kernel arguments.

4. Recognize, set up, and initialize (activate) the CPU(s).

5. Set up kernel memory and process handling.

6. Open a console for displaying kernel boot messages.

7. Initialize configured system devices.

8. Start memory handling (paging, and so on).

9. Set up and mount the filesystem.

10. Start the `init` command.

After the kernel has detected your computer's hardware and loaded the correct device drivers, the main job of finishing the boot process and then starting appropriate and configured services falls on the `init` command, also known as the father or parent of all processes.

Red Hat Linux Runlevels

The `init` command then uses the Linux *system initialization table*, or `/etc/inittab` to boot Red Hat Linux to a specific system state or runlevel. These runlevels, in which various services might be in effect or not, are defined in `/etc/inittab`. The Red Hat Linux runlevels are defined as

```
# Default runlevel. The runlevels used by RHS are:
#   0 - halt (Do NOT set initdefault to this)
#   1 - Single user mode
#   2 - Multiuser, without NFS (The same as 3, if you do not have networking)
#   3 - Full multiuser mode
#   4 - unused
#   5 - X11
#   6 - reboot (Do NOT set initdefault to this)
```

> **Note**
>
> Not all Linux distributions use the same runlevel configurations or runlevel definitions! As a system administrator, you should be aware of this issue, especially if you've devised any administrative scripts or tools that deal with system states. For example, although Red Hat Linux uses runlevel 3 for a full, console-based multiuser mode, SuSE Linux defines this system state as runlevel 2.

Each runlevel is defined in /etc/inittab, and in turn, tells the init command what services (software) to start or stop. Although runlevels might have custom definitions, runlevel 0 and runlevel 6 are used to shut down or reboot the system. Runlevel 3 dictates that Red Hat Linux be booted to a console, or text-based mode, with networking and multiuser access. Runlevel 5 will boot Red Hat Linux to a networking, multiuser state with an active X session.

A special runlevel, defined as 1, 'S,' or *single*, boots Red Hat Linux to a root access shell prompt with networking, X, and multiuser access turned off. This is a maintenance or rescue mode, and allows the system administrator to perform work on the system, make backups, or repair configuration or other files. Runlevel 4 is undefined, but can be configured to boot Red Hat Linux to a custom system state.

Entries in /etc/inittab use a field-based notation that determines the runlevel—when to execute the process, whether or not the process is executed when booting, whether or not to wait for the process to complete, and when to execute the process during booting.

> **Note**
>
> Details about the fields used in the Red Hat Linux system initialization table are contained in the inittab manual page.

The default entry, or initdefault line in /etc/inittab determines what system state to boot Red Hat Linux to. For example,

```
id:5:initdefault:
```

In this example, Red Hat Linux will be booted to a networking, multiuser mode with an active X session and a graphical login. The value 5 is forwarded to the script named rc under the /etc/rc.d directory. (This script is used when booting or changing runlevels, and also acts as an interpreter when booting Red Hat Linux in its Interactive mode, accessed by pressing 'i' when booting.) In turn, `rc` will then execute all the scripts (actually symbolic links) under the `/etc/rc.d/rc.5` directory after executing `/etc/rc.d/rc.sysinit` (discussed next). The graphical login's definition will be found toward the end of `/etc/inittab` and looks like this:

```
# Run xdm in runlevel 5
# xdm is now a separate service
x:5:respawn:/etc/X11/prefdm -nodaemon
```

This example shows that the shell script named `prefdm` executes the proper X11 display manager when Red Hat Linux is booted to runlevel 5.

If you use LILO as a bootloader for launching Red Hat Linux, you can boot directly to a specific runlevel through the LILO `boot:` prompt. This method is similar to passing a kernel argument through LILO's `/etc/lilo.conf` file, and can work like this:

```
boot: linux 3
```

In this example, after accessing LILO's boot prompt (by pressing Ctrl+X at the graphical LILO boot screen), Red Hat Linux will boot to runlevel 3. To boot to a rescue or maintenance mode, use a boot prompt like this:

```
boot: linux single
```

How Runlevels Work

Runlevels are defined in `/etc/inittab`, and although `/etc/rc.d/rc` performs master control of which scripts to execute, a lot of work is first done by the file `/etc/rc.d/rc.sysinit`. This file is interpreted by `init` once at boot time, and contains `bash` shell script logic to perform some the following:

- Sets the system hostname.
- Reads in network configuration data.
- Prints welcome banner for login.
- Sets up the process directory.
- Configures the kernel.
- Sets the system time (usually from the computer's hardware clock).
- Sets the console and keyboard mapping.
- Loads the default console font (character set).
- Activates virtual memory (swapping).
- Initializes USB services and devices.
- Checks the root filesystem.

- Processes any quota settings.

- Sets up and initializes any plug-and-play devices.

- Sets up and initializes the Logical Volume Manager (if configured).

- Turns on IDE hard drive optimizations (if configured).

- Loads required or configured kernel modules.

- Sets up, turns on, and uses sound and sound mixer settings (if configured).

- Starts RAID service (if configured).

- Mounts any required filesystems (according to the system *filesystem initialization table*, /etc/fstab).

- Turns on process accounting.

- Performs other configurations, such as password settings, networking, or time.

- Performs backup file, temporary file, or log file cleanup.

- Initializes serial ports.

- Sets up SCSI devices.

After /etc/rc.d/rc.sysinit has finished, init then will use the corresponding /etc/inittab entry that matches to a designated default runlevel. Using our previous example, the line in /etc/inittab would then be

```
15:5:wait:/etc/rc.d/rc 5
```

Under the /etc/rc.d directory are a series of directories that correspond to each runlevel:

```
$ ls /etc/rc.d
init.d  rc0.d  rc2.d  rc4.d  rc6.d      rc.sysinit
rc      rc1.d  rc3.d  rc5.d  rc.local
```

If Red Hat Linux is booted to runlevel 5 for example, scripts beginning with the letter K followed by scripts beginning with the letter S under the /etc/rc.d/rc5.d directory are then executed:

```
$ ls /etc/rc.d/rc5.d
K03rhnsd         K34yppasswdd   K65krb524    S05kudzu        S56rawdevices
K05innd          K35dhcpd       K65krb5kdc   S06reconfig     S56xinetd
K09junkbuster    K35smb         K74ntpd      S08ipchains     S60lpd
K12mysqld        K35vncserver   K74ups       S08iptables     S80sendmail
K15httpd         K40mars-nwe    K74ypserv    S10network      S83iscsi
K15postgresql    K45arpwatch    K74ypxfrd    S12syslog       S85gpm
K16rarpd         K45named       K75gated     S13portmap      S90crond
K20bootparamd    K46radvd       K84bgpd      S14nfslock      S90xfs
K20nfs           K50snmpd       K84ospf6d    S17keytable     S95anacron
K20rstatd        K50tux         K84ospfd     S20random       S95atd
```

```
K20rusersd    K54pxe       K84ripd      S24isdn    S99linuxconf
K20rwalld     K55routed    K84ripngd    S25netfs   S99local
K20rwhod      K61ldap      K85zebra     S26apmd    S99wine
K25squid      K65identd    K89bcm5820   S28autofs
K28amd        K65kadmin    K92ipvsadm   S45pcmcia
K30mcserv     K65kprop     K96irda      S55sshd
```

These scripts are actually symbolic links to system service scripts under the
`/etc/rc.d/init.d` directory:

$ ls /etc/rc.d/init.d
```
amd          gated        junkbuster   mars-nwe   pcmcia       routed     tux
anacron      gpm          kadmin       mcserv     portmap      rstatd     ups
apmd         halt         kdcrotate    mysqld     postgresql   rusersd    vmware
arpwatch     httpd        keytable     named      pxe          rwalld     vncserver
atd          identd       killall      netfs      radvd        rwhod      wine
autofs       innd         kprop        network    random       sendmail   xfs
bcm5820      ipchains     krb524       nfs        rarpd        single     xinetd
bgpd         iptables     krb5kdc      nfslock    rawdevices   smb        ypbind
bootparamd   ipvsadm      kudzu        nscd       reconfig     snmpd      yppasswdd
crond        irda         ldap         ntpd       rhnsd        squid      ypserv
dhcpd        iscsi        linuxconf    ospf6d     ripd         sshd       ypxfrd
functions    isdn         lpd          ospfd      ripngd       syslog     zebra
```

The `rc5.d` links (yours might look different, depending on the type of installation, such
as workstation or server, and the services or software packages installed on your system)
are prefaced with a letter and number, such as `K15` or `S10`. These prefixes indicate
whether or not a particular service should be stopped (`K`), or started (`S`), and pass a value
of `stop` or `start` to the appropriate `/etc/rc.d/init.d` script. The numbering executes
the specific `/etc/rc.d/init.d` script in a particular order. This is important because you
certainly wouldn't want your Red Hat Linux system to attempt to mount a remote
Network File System (NFS) directory without first starting networking and NFS services.

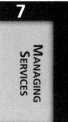

7

MANAGING SERVICES

Note

The naming, numbering, and number of the symbolic links to these scripts
under each `/etc/rc.d/rc*` directory can be (and are often) changed. Red Hat
Linux includes several command-line and graphical system administration utilities you can use to start, stop, reorder, or restart various services in different
runlevels. These commands (discussed next in this chapter) work by renaming
(reordering), removing, or creating symbolic links from `/etc/rc.d/init.d` to
`/etc/rc.d/rc.*` as appropriate.

Each `/etc/rc.d/init.d` contains logic that determines what to do when receiving a `start` or `stop` value. The logic might be a simple switch statement for execution, as in this example:

```
case "$1" in
  start)
        start
        ;;
  stop)
        stop
        ;;
  restart)
        restart
        ;;
  reload)
        reload
        ;;
  status)
        rhstatus
        ;;
  condrestart)
        [ -f /var/lock/subsys/smb ] && restart || :
        ;;
  *)
        echo $"Usage: $0 {start|stop|restart|status|condrestart}"
        exit 1
esac
```

Note that not all scripts will use this approach, and that other messages might be passed to the service script, such as `restart`, `reload`, or `status`. Also, not all scripts will respond to the same set of messages (with the exception of `start` and `stop`).

Following these actions, the `init` command may use the `/etc/rc.d/rc.local` script (which, in previous releases, created the `/etc/issue` file as a login banner; see the `mingetty` manual page for banner display options for this file). The user login prompt is presented by the `mingetty` command (as defined in `/etc/inittab`).

Tip

Although the `/etc/rc.d/rc.local` script can be used for local initialization of software services, such as sound or pointer device drivers, it isn't a good place to enable or start firewalling or security services because `rc.local` is executed after all the other system initialization scripts. If networking is enabled on your computer and security software initialization takes place in `rc.local`, your computer will be vulnerable, in some instances, for up to 30 seconds. The `rc.local` script should only be used for non-critical driver initialization or other services.

Controlling Boot Services

As the master control file for system startup, /etc/inittab and its corresponding system of symbolic links used to control system services can be managed by various graphical and non-graphic administrative tools. Although the legacy Red Hat Linux graphical tool ntsysv can be used to control which services are started when Linux boots, the linux-conf command can be used to control the actions of a service at a particular runlevel. In this fashion, linuxconf is a graphical interface to the actual command-line control utility, chkconfig.

Controlling system services and their actions is an important part of crafting a properly configured system. When and how services are started on a Red Hat Linux system is just as important, if not more so, than the presence or absence of a service when using Linux. For example, it makes no sense to have PCMCIA or networking services enabled after attempting to configure a non-existent Ethernet interface during the boot process.

Use the ntsysv command to control what services are started when Red Hat Linux boots. One way to access ntsysv is by launching the setup command as root from the console or command line of an X11 terminal window, like this:

```
# setup
```

After you press Enter, you'll see its main dialog box, as shown in Figure 7.1.

FIGURE 7.1

Use the setup *command's System Services item to access the* ntsysv *command.*

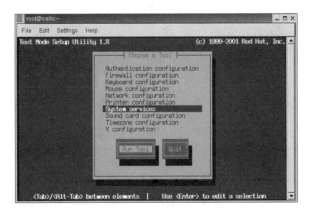

Scroll through the list of administrative tasks to highlight the System Services item; then use the Tab key to navigate to the Run Tool button and press Enter. This will launch the ntsysv command, as shown in Figure 7.2. You can also launch ntsysv at the console command line (or during an active X session at the command line of a terminal window) like this:

ntsysv

After you press Enter, you'll see its main dialog box, as shown in Figure 7.2.

FIGURE 7.2

The ntsysv *utility*
only manages
which services are
started when Red
Hat Linux boots,
but is a graphical
interface to the
command-line
chkconfig
command.

Scroll through the list of services (determined by the contents and scripts of the /etc/ rc.d/init.d directory). Toggle a service on or off by pressing the spacebar. When finished, use the Tab key to highlight the OK or Cancel button. Your changes will be saved and used the next time Red Hat Linux is booted.

Red Hat Linux also offers a manual configuration of boot services. Use the chkconfig command to display, diagnose, or change the starting or stopping of system services (as available under /etc/rc.d/init.d) in each runlevel. For example, to list all services that will be turned on in runlevel 5, you can pipe the output of chkconfig through the fgrep command like this:

```
$ /sbin/chkconfig – list | fgrep '5:on'
atd             0:off   1:off   2:off   3:on    4:on    5:on    6:off
keytable        0:off   1:on    2:on    3:on    4:on    5:on    6:off
syslog          0:off   1:off   2:on    3:on    4:on    5:on    6:off
gpm             0:off   1:off   2:on    3:off   4:on    5:on    6:off
kudzu           0:off   1:off   2:off   3:on    4:on    5:on    6:off
lpd             0:off   1:off   2:on    3:on    4:on    5:on    6:off
sendmail        0:off   1:off   2:on    3:on    4:on    5:on    6:off
autofs          0:off   1:off   2:off   3:off   4:on    5:on    6:off
rawdevices      0:off   1:off   2:off   3:on    4:on    5:on    6:off
netfs           0:off   1:off   2:off   3:on    4:on    5:on    6:off
network         0:off   1:off   2:on    3:on    4:on    5:on    6:off
random          0:off   1:off   2:on    3:on    4:on    5:on    6:off
ipchains        0:off   1:off   2:on    3:on    4:on    5:on    6:off
pcmcia          0:off   1:off   2:on    3:off   4:on    5:on    6:off
```

apmd	0:off	1:off	2:on	3:off	4:on	5:on	6:off
iptables	0:off	1:off	2:on	3:on	4:on	5:on	6:off
isdn	0:off	1:off	2:on	3:off	4:on	5:on	6:off
portmap	0:off	1:off	2:off	3:on	4:on	5:on	6:off
nfslock	0:off	1:off	2:off	3:on	4:on	5:on	6:off
crond	0:off	1:off	2:on	3:on	4:on	5:on	6:off
anacron	0:off	1:off	2:on	3:on	4:on	5:on	6:off
xfs	0:off	1:off	2:on	3:on	4:on	5:on	6:off
xinetd	0:off	1:off	2:off	3:on	4:on	5:on	6:off
sshd	0:off	1:off	2:on	3:on	4:on	5:on	6:off
wine	0:off	1:off	2:on	3:on	4:on	5:on	6:off
reconfig	0:off	1:off	2:off	3:on	4:on	5:on	6:off
iscsi	0:off	1:off	2:on	3:on	4:off	5:on	6:off
linuxconf	0:off	1:off	2:on	3:on	4:on	5:on	6:off

As you can see, chkconfig displays the value of 0 or 1 (off/on or stop/start) for each service and each runlevel. The example output only shows those services that will be started in runlevel 5. The chkconfig command can be used to reassign start or stop values for each runlevel and each service. However, this feature should only be used cautiously because it is possible to render a system temporarily unusable. (You can boot Red Hat Linux to single-user mode, or use the Red Hat Linux rescue mode to attempt a fix.) For example, to stop power management (controlled by the apmd script under /etc/rc.d/ init.d) when using Red Hat Linux during runlevel 5, use chkconfig like this:

```
# chkconfig – level 5 apmd off
```

You can then verify this action by again grepping chkconfig's output like so:

```
# chkconfig – list | fgrep apmd
apmd               0:off   1:off   2:on    3:on    4:on    5:off   6:off
```

Starting and Stopping Services

There are several ways to manually start or stop services or to change runlevels while using Red Hat Linux. To quickly manage a service (as root), call the service's /etc/rc.d/init.d name on the command line with an appropriate keyword, such as start or stop. For example, to start automated power management, call the /etc/rc.d/init.d/apmd script like this:

```
# /etc/rc.d/init.d/apmd start
Starting up APM daemon:                              [  OK  ]
```

The script will execute the proper program(s) and report on its status. Stopping services is equally easy, and in fact, you can also check some services by using the status keyword like this:

```
# /etc/rc.d/init.d/apmd status
apmd (pid 3156) is running...
```

In this example, the `apmd` script reports that the daemon is running and displays the daemon's process ID.

Using `linuxconf`

Another graphical utility you can use to control services is the `linuxconf` command. This command must be run by the root operator, and provides a convenient way to monitor and control running services. Start the command like this:

```
# linuxconf &
```

After you press Enter, you'll see the `linuxconf` main dialog box. Click the Control tab, and then click the Control Panel drop-down menu. Next, click the Control Service Activity menu item. You'll see a dialog box as shown in Figure 7.3.

FIGURE 7.3

The `linuxconf` *utility can graphically manage your system services.*

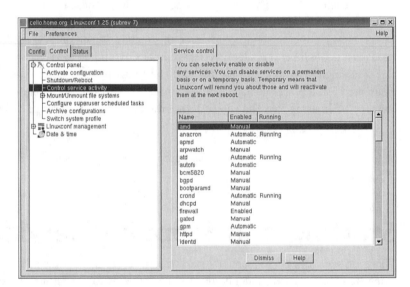

To use `linuxconf` to manage a particular service, scroll through the right side of the dialog box, click on a particular service, and click the Run levels tab. You'll then see a dialog box, as shown in Figure 7.4.

The `linuxconf` utility will display the current runlevel information about the service using check marks. Check or un-check a runlevel and then click the Basic info tab. You can then choose to set the service's status during booting, or use the Accept, Cancel, Start, Stop, or Restart buttons to control the service. This provides for one-click management of system services on your Red Hat Linux system.

FIGURE 7.4

The linuxconf utility will display information about a specific service and offers the ability to start, stop, restart or reassign a service's status during a particular Red Hat Linux system state.

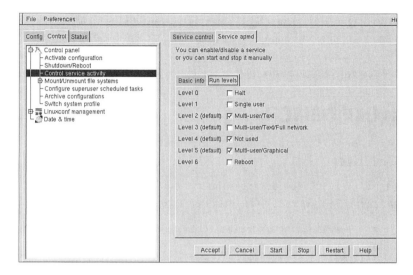

Changing Runlevels

After making changes to system services and runlevels, you can use the telinit command to change runlevels on-the-fly on a running Red Hat Linux system. For example, a system administrator can quickly change the system to maintenance or single-user mode by using the telinit command with its S option like this:

```
# telinit S
```

The telinit command will use the init command to change runlevels, and currently running services will be shut down. Services for the specified runlevel will then be started. This allows system administrators to alter selected parts of a running system in order to make or effect changes that might have been made (such as reassignment of IP addresses for a networking interface).

After booting to single-user mode, you can then return to multiuser mode without X like this:

```
# telinit 3
```

If you have made changes to the system initialization table, /etc/inittab, use the telinit command's q command-line option to force init to re-examine the table.

Re-ordering or changing system services during a particular runlevel is rarely necessary when using Red Hat Linux. But system administrators should have a basic understanding of how Linux boots and how services are controlled in order to perform troubleshooting or to diagnose problems. By using additional utilities such as the `dmesg` command to read kernel output after booting, or by examining system logging in the `/var/log/messages` file, it is possible to gain a bit more detail about what is going on when faced with troublesome drivers or service failure.

Reference

`http://www.linuxplanet.com/linuxplanet/reports/213/1/`—A basic article on how Linux boots.

`http://www-106.ibm.com/developerworks/linux/library/l-slack.html`—A link through IBM's Web site to an article on booting Slackware Linux.

`http://www.linux.com/newsitem.phtml?sid=82&aid=6316`—A short article on booting Linux.

`/usr/src/linux/init/main.c`—The best place to learn about how Linux boots.

`http://sunsite.dk/linux-newbie/`—Home page for the Linux Newbie Administrator Guide—a gentle introduction to Linux system administration.

"LILO User's Guide"—Werner Almesberger's definitive technical tome on the LInux LOader, or LILO, and how it works on Intel-based PCs. Look under the `/usr/share/doc/lilo*/doc` directory for the file `User_Guide.ps`, which can be viewed using the gv client, or browse to `http://www.ibiblio.org/pub/Linux/system/boot/lilo` for the latest `lilo` manual.

`http://os.inf.tu-dresden.de/L4/LinuxOnL4/overview.html`—Overview of an alternative kernel (Fiasco) for the L4 Linux distribution—a micro-kernel approach vs. the Linux monolithic kernel design.

"Managing Initscripts with Red Hat's chkconfig"—by Jimmy Ball, *Linux Journal*, April 2001, pp. 128-132.

`http://www.solucorp.qc.ca/linuxconf/`—Home page for the `linuxconf` utility.

Managing Software and System Resources

CHAPTER 8

This chapter introduces concepts, procedures, and software used to manage installed system resources on a Red Hat Linux system. Managing the software, storage, and memory resources of your workstation, server, or laptop is an important task, and can help maintain efficient, productive sessions, satisfied users, and a stable system. Knowing how to install, remove, upgrade, or rebuild software packages can be a vital task, especially when performed for security reasons.

As a Red Hat Linux system administrator, you should also know how to maximize your system's resources; this includes managing memory and storage to bring about the most efficient use of your system. Properly managing your system will ensure that you won't run out of room for new software, will be able to expand the system to fit changing needs and new projects, and will be able to provide the best possible computing experience for your users.

The following sections introduce the Red Hat Package Manager, along with command-line and graphical software-management tools. You'll also learn about monitoring and managing memory and disk storage on your system.

Using RPM

The Red Hat Package Manager (RPM) was derived (in part) from early Linux package management software named RPP, PMS, and PM that were written in Perl. RPM was first used with Red Hat Linux 2.0 in late 1995, and then rewritten in C for the Red Hat Linux 3.0.3 (Picasso) release in 1996. Since then, the rpm command has been the prime feature of Red Hat's unique software management system, which is based on the concept of *pristine* sources, or the ability to use a single, initial archive of program's source code not only to build packages for different systems, but also to track versions.

In addition to improving the package management of early software management scripts, RPM introduced software features that could ease the task of building software for different platforms from this single set of source-code files. Changes could be tracked and kept outside of a developer's initial source, and multiple packages could be built from scratch and installed at the same time, all while verifying installation dependencies. Additional features, such as the inclusion of a checksum and now, GNU Privacy Guard signatures, also means that binary software packages can be safely distributed without the fear of virus infection or inclusion of Trojan code.

The rpm command uses the RPM system to install, remove (erase), upgrade, verify, and build software archives known as .rpm files. These archives, or *packages*, contain package identification (a *signature*), checksums, and an archive of the software, either in source or binary form. An .rpm package also contains quite a bit of additional

information, such as a name, version, and basic description, and can even include pre-
and post-installation scripts used for installation, erasure, or upgrading.

RPM uses your system's /var/lib/rpm directory to store various files (actually *databases*) containing information about the software installed on your system. For example,
you can use the ls command to view these files (you might see file sizes different from
those shown here, depending on the amount of software you have installed):

```
$ ls -l /var/lib/rpm
total 35012
-rw-r--r--    1 rpm      rpm       5525504 Aug 13 07:19 Basenames
-rw-r--r--    1 rpm      rpm         12288 Aug 13 07:16 Conflictname
-rw-r--r--    1 rpm      rpm       1073152 Aug 13 07:19 Dirnames
-rw-r--r--    1 rpm      rpm         24576 Aug 13 07:19 Group
-rw-r--r--    1 rpm      rpm         20480 Aug 13 07:19 Installtid
-rw-r--r--    1 rpm      rpm         45056 Aug 13 07:19 Name
-rw-r--r--    1 rpm      rpm      28536832 Aug 13 07:19 Packages
-rw-r--r--    1 rpm      rpm        167936 Aug 13 07:19 Providename
-rw-r--r--    1 rpm      rpm         69632 Aug 13 07:19 Provideversion
-rw-r--r--    1 rpm      rpm          8192 Aug 13 05:54 Removetid
-rw-r--r--    1 rpm      rpm        245760 Aug 13 07:19 Requirename
-rw-r--r--    1 rpm      rpm        159744 Aug 13 07:19 Requireversion
-rw-r--r--    1 rpm      rpm         12288 Aug 13 06:49 Triggername
```

The primary database of installed software is contained in the file named Packages. As
you can see from the preceding example, this database can grow as large as (and perhaps
larger) 30MB if you perform a full installation of Red Hat Linux. After installing Red
Hat Linux, rpm and related commands will use this directory during software management operations.

8

SOFTWARE AND
SYSTEM
RESOURCES

Command-Line and Graphical RPM Clients

As a Red Hat Linux system administrator, you'll use the rpm command or one of its
graphical clients to perform one of five basic tasks. These operations, which must be
conducted by the root operator, include the following:

- Installing new software
- Erasing or removing outdated or unneeded packages
- Upgrading an installed software package
- Querying to get information about a software package
- Verifying the installation or integrity of a package installation

The rpm command has more than 60 different command-line options, but its administrative functions can be grouped according to the previous five types of action. Graphical RPM clients provide easy to use interfaces to these operations. As a system administrator, you'll have a choice between using a graphical interface and using rpm's various command-line options. The general format of an rpm command is

```
# rpm option packagename
```

The basic options look like this:

- -i—Install the selected package or packages.
- -e—Erase (remove) the selected package or packages.
- -U—Remove the currently installed package, and then install software with the contents of the selected package or packages.
- -q—Query the system or selected package or packages.
- -V—Verify installed or selected package or packages.

Many additional options can also be added to or used in conjunction with these options.

RPM Is for Programmers, too!

Remember that RPM was created not only to provide an easy to use administrative tool, but also as a developer's tool for use in multi-platform source-code package management. Programmers using rpm for development and distribution will use its -b or build option, along with a myriad of additional command-line flags. RPM can be used to build binaries, execute programs, test installations, verify and sign packages, build source packages, track versions, and target builds for specific architectures. Details can be found at the RPM home page (listed in the section "Reference" at the end of this chapter).

Using rpm on the Command Line

This section provides a quick introduction to the five basic operations when using the rpm command. You'll read examples of how to install, verify, query, remove, and upgrade a software package. The most common operation used is software installation. Using rpm is an easy way to keep track of installed software, and may be used to quickly remove undesired packages.

Use the -i option, along with the full or partial name (using expressions) of a software package to install software with rpm. For example, to install the pine e-mail package, use the rpm command like this:

```
# rpm -ivh pine-4.21-23.i386.rpm
Preparing...                  ######################################### [100%]
    1:pine                    ######################################### [100%]
```

This example also uses the v and h options, which provide a more verbose output and display of hash marks to show the progress of the installation. You can also use rpm to query its database after installing packages to verify an installation. Use the -V option, along with the name of a software package to verify installation your system. For example, to verify the pine email package, use the rpm command like this:

```
# rpm -V pine
```

Note

Note that if everything is fine, nothing will be displayed on your system.

You can get additional information about a package by adding additional verification options (such as two more vs) to the -V option. To get more information about an installed package, use one or more forms of the rpm query options. For example, to display concise information about an installed package, use the -q option, along with the i option and the installed package name, like this (note that your version will be different from that shown here):

```
# rpm -qi pine
Name        : pine                    Relocations: (not relocateable)
Version     : 4.21                          Vendor: Red Hat, Inc.
Release     : 23                         Build Date: Thu 24 Aug 2000 \
03:53:32 AM EDT
Install date: Mon 13 Aug 2001 06:29:06 PM EDT      Build Host: \
porky.devel.redhat.com
Group       : Applications/Internet      Source RPM: pine-4.21-23.src.rpm
Size        : 4206185                       License: Freely Distributable
Packager    : Red Hat, Inc. <http://bugzilla.redhat.com/bugzilla>
URL         : http://www.washington.edu/pine/
Summary     : A commonly used, MIME compliant mail and news reader.
Description :
Pine is a very popular, easy to use, full-featured email user agent
that includes a simple text editor called pico. Pine supports MIME
extensions and can also be used to read news.  Pine also supports
IMAP, mail, and MH style folders.
```

This form of the rpm query (you can also query packages *before* installation) provides quite a bit of information about the software package! However, if this package isn't up-to-date, you can easily and quickly upgrade the package by downloading a newer version and then using rpm's -U or upgrade option like this:

8

SOFTWARE AND
SYSTEM
RESOURCES

```
# rpm -Uvh pine-4.33-8.i386.rpm
Preparing...              ########################################### [100%]
   1:pine                 ########################################### [100%]
```

Note that it wasn't necessary to remove the currently installed software package—the new software is automatically installed following removal of the existing files. You can also upgrade your system software by using the rpm command's -F or "freshen" option, which will fetch a designated package from a remote FTP or HTTP server. For example, to upgrade using the previous example, use rpm like this (the FTP URL has been shortened in this example):

```
# rpm -Fv ftp://ftp.tux.org/redhat-7.1/os/i386/RedHat/RPMS/pine-4.33-8.i386.rpm
Retrieving ftp://ftp.tux.org/redhat-7.1/os/i386/RedHat/RPMS/pine-4.33-8.i386.rpm
Preparing packages for installation...
pine-4.33-8
```

If you have broadband access, upgrading a system in place can be accomplished fairly quickly (a primary feature of Ximian's version of GNOME). The rpm command will retrieve the designated package, and then upgrade the software on your system. Use the -e option, along with the name of a software package to remove or erase software from your system with rpm. For example, to remove the pine e-mail package, use the rpm command like this:

```
# rpm -e pine
```

Note that if the operation succeeds, nothing will be displayed on your system.

> **Note**
>
> Another essential and hopefully rarely used feature of the rpm command is its --rebuilddb option. If your system's RPM database becomes corrupted, this is your first (and perhaps only) option to try to restore software management services. When in doubt, always back up!

Package Organization

Software packages on your Red Hat Linux system are organized into various groups. Using a group organization helps to keep software organized by category, and provides for hierarchical listings of software when using graphical RPM clients. You can quickly view and save a list of the various groups used by Red Hat Linux and RPM by using the rpm command's query option like this (your output might look different):

```
#  rpm -qa --queryformat '%{GROUP}\n' | sort | uniq
```

Major package categories, along with sub-group categories are listed in Table 8.1.

TABLE 8.1   RPM Group Categories

Top-level	*Sub-categories*
Amusements	Games, Graphics
Applications	Archiving, Communications, Databases, Editors, Emulators, Engineering, File, Internet, Multimedia, Productivity, Publishing, Science, System, Text
Development	Debuggers, Languages, Libraries, System, Tools
Documentation	none
System Environment	Base, Daemons, Kernel, Libraries, Shells
User Interface	Desktops, X, X Hardware Support

Linux and UNIX Software Management

The Red Hat RPM system is used by a number of other Linux distributions, such as Mandrake and OpenLinux. RPM is also used by SuSE Linux (but managed by SuSE's yast command). Other Linux distributions such as Debian use a different software management model (using the app-get command). Open source UNIX variants, such as FreeBSD, OpenBSD, and NetBSD also have different software management systems, based on package utilities such as pkg_add, pkg_delete, and a centralized software database.

However, efforts are underway at http://www.openpackages.org to unify software delivery and management for BSD UNIX variants and other systems, including Linux. This could ease open source software distribution problems, increase security, and bridge differences between distributions and systems. The new software package design will involve a new package format, but aims to make the job of building, installing, and maintaining software much easier. The project is initially aimed at FreeBSD, NetBSD, OpenBSD, BSD/OS, and Darwin users, with planned support for Solaris, BeOs, and Red Hat Linux.

8

SOFTWARE AND SYSTEM RESOURCES

Graphical RPM Clients

Using the command-line form of the rpm command is fast, easy, and convenient, especially when crafting shell scripts in order to automate repetitive software management tasks. But many Red Hat Linux system administrators might prefer to use a point-and-click interface when administering a system's software. This section introduces two graphical clients you can use to manage your system's software: GNOME's gnorpm and KDE's kpackage clients. (There is also the xrpm client, but it isn't as popular, though just as useful.) These programs require an active X session and root access in order to be used for system maintenance.

Using the gnorpm Client

The gnorpm client, by James Henstridge, is included as part of the GNOME desktop environment and libraries for Red Hat Linux. Many Red Hat system administrators use this client during X11 sessions after installing Linux to fine-tune a software install by adding or removing software packages. Although one would suspect that this client is simply a graphical interface to the rpm command, the truth is that gnorpm doesn't use rpm for all of its operations, including software installation, making gnorpm somewhat faster for installing software.

However, all RPM-related commands will require access to your system's RPM database, especially for verification and installed query operations. gnorpm requires an active X session and might be launched through a panel menu item or from the command line of an X terminal window like this:

```
# gnorpm &
```

After you press Enter, you'll see a display as shown in Figure 8.1.

FIGURE 8.1

The GNOME RPM client, gnorpm, can be used to maintain your Red Hat Linux system's software.

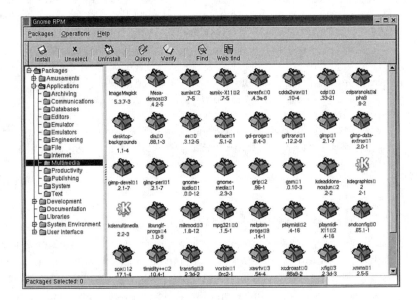

Use gnorpm's menu items or toolbar icons to perform installation, selection, query, verification, or removal of software packages. Installed software is displayed in a graphical cascading tree on the left side of this client's window. When you click on a group or subgroup folder, the assigned packages are displayed in the client's main window. To get information about a package or to remove a package, click to select the package, and then select Query, Verify, or Uninstall. Use the Operations menu or the toolbar's Install button to load and install a package.

You'll need to launch this client as root, but with an active Internet connection, you'll also be able to retrieve and perform software installs using packages on a remote server.

Use this client's Preferences menu item under the Operations menu to configure behaviors (such as dependency checking), display of listings, color selections, or network settings.

Using KDE's kpackage Client

The kpackage client, distributed with KDE, is another graphical interface to the rpm command and your system's package database. Similar to nearly all KDE clients, kpackage depends on Trolltech's Qt software libraries, along with KDE libraries, but offers some unique features, such as international language support, support for foreign packages, such as those for Slackware or Debian Linux and FreeBSD, and on-the-fly key configuration (use of *accelerators*).

> **Note**
>
> KDE's karchiveur is a related client you can use to easily display, browse, read, and extract contents of compressed files, including legacy archives such as *tarballs*, or compressed tar archives. These archives are recognized by their .gz or .tgz extensions. Other compressed files, such as those created with the compress command (ending in .Z) or bzip2 files (ending in .bz2), are also supported, and karchiveur will also convert compressed archives between gzip and bzip2 formats. This client is generally included with the KDE distribution, but can be found through its home page at: http://david.bieder.free.fr/karchiveur_en.shtml.

As with gnorpm, you'll need root permission to use this client to install or remove software. You can start kpackage from the desktop panel or command line of a terminal window like this:

```
# kpackage &
```

After you press Enter, you'll see a display as shown in Figure 8.2.

FIGURE 8.2

KDE's kpackage *client is an alternative software package maintenance tool you can use to manage your Red Hat Linux system's software.*

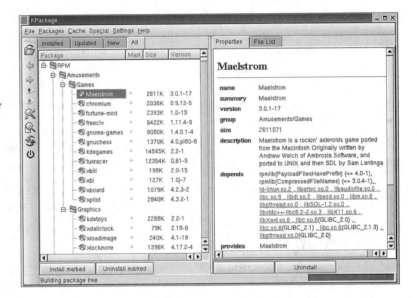

Note that you can get information about a specific package by navigating through the group listings menu on the left side of the client's screen. If you click on a particular package, essential information about the package is displayed on the right side of the screen. Use kpackage's menu items and toolbar to manage your system's packages. You'll need to install the Debian DPKG package manager and BSD UNIX package utilities (pkg_add, pkg_delete, and pkg_info) in order to use or manage "foreign" package formats.

Debian Package Tools

The Debian Package Manager consists of a number of software tools used for package management. Just as rpm contains quite a few features, under Debian Linux software management is provided the dpkg command, along with a handful of other utilities, such as dpkg-name, dpkg-buildpackage, dpkg-genchanges, dpkg-scanpackages, dpkg-gencontrol, dpkg-distaddfile, dpkg-source, dpkg-parsechangelog, dpkg-shlibdeps, dpkg-deb, and dpkg-split. Browse to http:// www.debian.org for more information.

System Monitoring Tools

Monitoring your server or workstation is an important task, especially in a commercial or corporate environment. Whether you're working on critical application programming or conducting e-commerce on the Internet, you'll want to track your system's health signs while it's running. Red Hat Linux system administrators are also quite vigilant about watching running processes on their systems, even though the task isn't strictly part of standard security operations such as examining system logs and network traffic.

The next sections introduce just a few of the basic tools and approaches used to monitor a running Linux system. Some of the tools focus on in-memory processes, whereas others aim to be more comprehensive and include filesystem reporting (disk usage) or network traffic. You'll also see how to control some system processes using various command-line and graphical tools included with Red Hat Linux.

Console-Based Monitoring

Traditional UNIX systems have always included the ps or process display command. Due to the architecture of the Linux kernel and its memory management, which basically models the UNIX application space, Linux also provides process reporting and control via the command line through the shell.

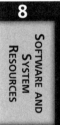

Whenever a program or command is launched on your Red Hat Linux system, the process started by the kernel is assigned an identification number, or *process ID*. This number is (generally) displayed by the shell if the program is launched in the background like this:

```
$ xosview &
[1] 11670
```

In this example, the xosview client has been launched in the background, and the (bash) shell first reports a shell *job number* ([1]). A job number or *job control* is a shell-specific feature that allows a different form of process control (such as sending or suspending programs to the background and retrieved background jobs to the foreground; see your shell's manual pages for more information).

The second number displayed (11670 in this example) represents the process ID. You can get a quick list of your process IDs by using the ps command like this:

```
$ ps
  PID TTY          TIME CMD
  736 tty1     00:00:00 bash
  743 tty1     00:00:00 startx
```

```
  744 tty1      00:00:00 tee
  752 tty1      00:00:00 xinit
  756 tty1      00:00:09 kwm
  ...
11670 pts/3     00:00:00 xosview
11671 pts/3     00:00:00 ps
```

Note that not all output from the display is shown here. But as you can see, the output includes the process ID, abbreviated as PID, along with other information, such as the name of the running program. You can get more detailed output or see all of your systems processes by using various command-line options, such as aux. You should also know that ps works not by polling memory, but through interrogation of the Linux /proc or process directory.

The /proc directory contains quite a few files, some of which include constantly updated hardware information (such as battery power levels and so on). Linux administrators will often pipe the output of ps through a member of the grep family of commands in order to display information about a specific program, perhaps like this:

```
# ps aux | fgrep xosview
bball    11670  0.3  1.1  2940 1412 pts/0   S    14:04   0:00 xosview
```

This example returns the *owner* (user who launched the program) and the PID, along with other information, such as the percentage of CPU and memory usage, size of the command (code, data, and stack), time (or date) the command was launched, and name of the command. Processes can also be queried by PID like this:

```
$ ps 11670
  PID TTY      STAT   TIME COMMAND
11670 pts/0    S      0:00 xosview
```

You can use the PID to stop a running process by using the shell's built-in KILL command. This command will ask the kernel to stop a running process and reclaim system memory. For example, to stop the xosview client in the example, use the KILL command like this:

```
$ kill 11670
```

After you press Enter (or perhaps press again), the shell might report

```
[1]+  Terminated              xosview
```

Note that users can only kill owned processes. Controlling any other running process requires root permission, which should be used judiciously (especially when forcing a kill by using the -9 option); by inadvertently killing the wrong process through a typo on the command, you could bring down an active system.

Using Priority Scheduling and Control

Priority scheduling can be an important tool in managing a system supporting critical applications or in a situation in which CPU and RAM usage must be reserved or allocated for a specific task. Two legacy applications included with Red Linux include the nice and renice commands. (nice is part of the GNU sh-utils package, whereas renice is inherited from BSD UNIX.)

The nice command is used with its -n option, along with an argument in range of -20 to 19, in order from highest to lowest priority. For example, to run the xosview client with a low priority, use the nice command like this:

```
$ nice -n 12 xosview &
```

The nice command is typically used for disk or CPU-intensive tasks that might be obtrusive or cause system slow down. The renice command can be used to reset the scheduling of running processes or control the priority and scheduling of all processes owned by a user. Users can only increase process priorities using this command, but the root operator can use the full nice range of scheduling (20 to -19).

System administrators can also use the time command to get an idea about how long and how much of a system's resources will be required for a task (such as shell script). This command is used with the name of a command (or script) as an argument like this:

```
# time -p find / -name core -print
/dev/core
/proc/sys/net/core

real 1.20
user 0.14
sys 0.71
```

Output of the command displays the time from start to finish, along with user and system time required. Other factors you can query include variations of time, memory, CPU usage, and filesystem statistics. See the time command's manual page for more details.

Graphical Monitoring Tools

Many different graphical process monitoring tools exist, and nearly all include some form of process control or management. Many of the early tools ported to Linux were legacy clones of UNIX utilities. One familiar monitoring (and control) program is top, originally by Roger Binns and based on the ps command. The top command provides a graphical, constantly update console-based output and can be started like this:

```
# top
```

8

SOFTWARE AND
SYSTEM
RESOURCES

After you press Enter, you'll see a display as shown in Figure 8.3.

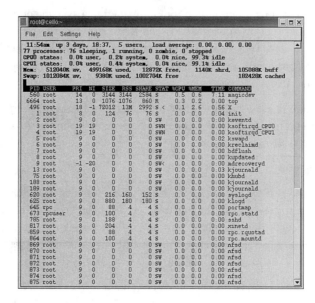

The top command displays quite a bit of information about your system. Processes can be sorted by PID, age, CPU or memory usage, time, or user. This command also provides process management, and system administrators can use its k or r keypress commands to kill or reschedule running tasks.

Another legacy tool included with Red Hat Linux is the xosview client, originally by Mike Romberg. This client provides load, CPU, memory and swap usage, disk I/O usage and activity, page swapping information, network activity, I/O activity, I/O rates, serial port status, and if APM is enabled, the battery level (such as for a laptop).

For example, to see most of these options, start the client like this:

```
# xosview -geometry 406x488 -font 8x16 +load +cpu +mem +swap \
  +page +disk +int +net +battery &
```

After you press Enter, you'll see a display as shown in Figure 8.4.

The display can be customized for a variety of hardware and information, and the xosview client (like most well-behaved X clients) obeys geometry settings such as size, placement, or font. If you have similar monitoring requirements, but want to try a similar but different client from xosview, try xcpustate, which has features that allow it to monitor network CPU statistics foreign to Linux.

FIGURE 8.4

The xosview
*client displays
basic system stats
in a small window.*

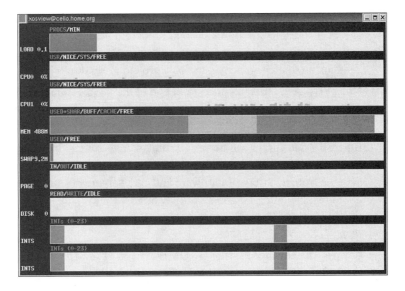

FIGURE 8.4

The xosview
*client displays
basic system stats
in a small window.*

Graphical Process and System Management Tools

The GNOME and KDE desktop environments offer a rich set of network and system monitoring tools. One advantage of using these tools is the use of a graphical interface, such as menus and buttons, along with graphical output such as metering, real-time load charts, and other visual aids you can use as an indicator of system status. These clients, which require an active X session and in some cases (but not all) root permission, are included with Red Hat Linux.

The graphical advantage of using these clients can also a disadvantage if you use the tools locally on a server; you must have X properly installed and configured, or at least have X installed and available. Although some tools can be used to remotely monitor systems or locally mounted remote filesystems, you'll need to also properly configure pertinent X11 environment variables, such as $DISPLAY, in order to use the software.

GNOME Monitoring Tools

GNOME has come a long way, and now includes a rich and diverse set of clients for X. Some of the monitoring tools included with Red Hat Linux and GNOME include the following:

- vncviewer—AT&T's open source remote session manager (part of the Xvnc package), which can be used to view and run a remote desktop session locally. This software (discussed in more detail in Chapter 25, "Emulators and Other Operating Systems") requires an active, but background X session on the remote computer.

- NmapFE—A GTK+ graphical front end to the nmap command. This client provides system administrators the ability to scan networks to monitor availability of hosts and services.

- Ethereal—This graphical network protocol analyzer can be used to save or display packet data in real time, and has intelligent filtering to recognize data *signatures* or patterns from a variety of hardware and data captures from third-party data-capture programs, including compressed files. Some protocols include AppleTalk, Andrew File System (AFS), AOL's Instant Messenger, various Cisco protocols, and many more.

- GTop—The advanced visual GNOME version of the top command (shown in Figure 8.5 and discussed next). This graphical client uses fewer system resources than the top command and has the advantage of displaying filesystem statistics (disk usage).

The gtop client provides a graphical system monitoring interface, along with process control. Start the client from the command line of an X terminal (or through GNOME's desktop panel under the System menu) like this:

```
# gtop &
```

After you press Enter, you'll see a display as shown in Figure 8.5.

Control processes by right-clicking on a process name in the main display window. You'll then see a menu that allows you to set the processes priority or send a kernel *signal* or message to the process. For example, sending the SIGKILL message is equivalent to using:

```
# kill -9 PID
```

You can also use gtop to show a usage map of memory and to discover how much memory various processes are using on your system. This display can be customized for a variety of hardware and can come in handy if your system is experiencing performance problems related to memory.

FIGURE 8.5

The GNOME gtop *client displays a list of processes, along with graphical meters regarding system load, memory, and filesystem usage.*

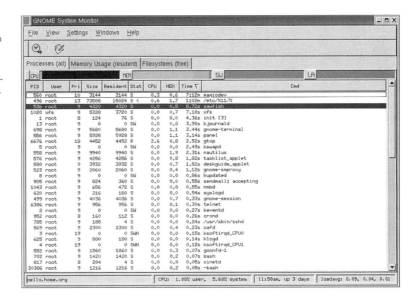

KDE Process and System Monitoring Tools

KDE includes a variety of process and system monitoring clients similar in scope and capability as those for GNOME. One advantage of using GNOME and KDE graphical clients is the consistency in design, window appearance, and menu behavior; for example, help is nearly always available via a Help menu item on each client's menu bar. These include the following:

- kcpumon—A small KDE client that *docks*, or places, an animated graph of CPU activity in your desktop's panel.

- kcpuload—Another docking monitor client that displays a tiny running graph of system load.

- kdiskfree—A graphical interface to your system's filesystem table, displaying free disk space, and offering the ability to mount and un-mount filesystems using a pointing device.

- kdirstat—A handy disk usage client that generates disk usage statistics, and then builds and displays graphic usage of your system based on your selection, such as by files, directories, or both.

- kimon—This client is used to monitor ISDN connections.

- kcron—A graphical interface to your system's /etc/crontab file.

- ktop—A KDE client with functionality similar to the gtop client for GNOME.

The `ktop` client provides a graphical system monitoring interface, along with process control just like GNOME's `gtop` client. Start the client from the command line of an X terminal (or through KDE's desktop panel) like this:

```
# ktop &
```

After you press Enter, you'll see a display as shown in Figure 8.6.

FIGURE 8.6

KDE's `ktop` *client displays a list of processes, along with graphical meters regarding system load and memory.*

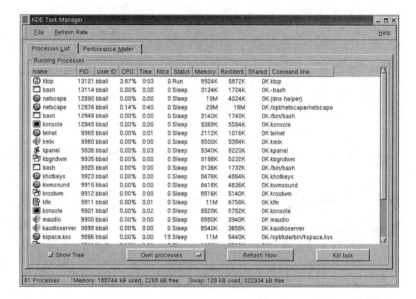

As with `gtop`, you can use `ktop` to control processes by right-clicking on a process name in its main display window and using one of the signals in the pop-up menu. A pop-up dialog box with a slider control also allows the root operator to set a new priority for the task. One unique feature is the ability to display two large running graphs of your system's CPU load and memory usage. If you don't find a copy of `ktop` on your system, you can download a version from `ftp.kde.org/pub/kde`.

Using Quotas

Quotas, although rarely used on a local or standalone workstation, are definitely a way of life at the enterprise level of computing. Usage limits on disk space not only conserve resources, but also provide a measure of operational safety. (You wouldn't want your users to index or model the Internet's collection of Web pages on your company's hardware, right?) Disk quotas are most commonly used by larger installations or *Internet service providers (ISPs)*. But whether you're managing 10, 10,000, or 100,000 users, quotas can come in handy and can be necessary.

Quota management with Red Hat Linux has traditionally been enabled and configured manually by system administrators using the family of quota commands, such as edquota to set and edit user quotas, and setquota to configure disk quotas, and quotaon or quotaoff to control the service. (Other utilities include warnquota for automatically sending mail to users over their diskspace usage limit.)

Manual configuration involves the use of the system editor (vi by default, unless you change the EDITOR environment variable), which will be launched when the root operator edits a user's quota. However, newer versions of the linuxconf client offer configuration and control of many different aspects of a Red Hat Linux system, including quotas.

To get started, make sure that you're logged in as root (using the su or sudo commands), and then launch linuxconf like this:

```
# linuxconf &
```

After you press Enter, the main dialog box will appear. (You'll get a greeting splash screen when you run it for the first time.) Click on the Config tab, and then click the Access local drive item under the File systems menu. You'll then see a display as shown in Figure 8.7.

FIGURE 8.7

The linuxconf graphical system administration tool can be used for a myriad of essential tasks, including configuration of disk quotas for users and groups.

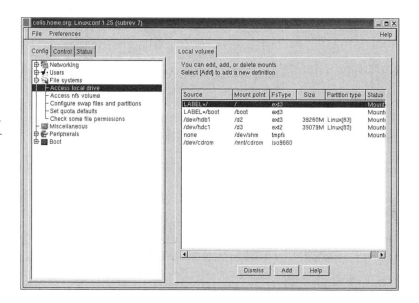

This dialog is used to enable disk quota usage for a specified filesystem, with settings generally saved in your system's filesystem table. Double-click on an existing partition, and then click the Options tab. By scrolling through a list of options, you can then enable or disable user and group quotas for the specified filesystem. (Don't forget to use the Accept button and activate the changes to ensure that quota support is enabled.) Next, click on the Set quota defaults list item on the left menu, and then set *hard*, or specific limits on disk usage concerning maximum number of files or sizes. You can also set *soft* limits that warn users about diminishing disk space when the limit is reached (a kinder, nicer way to enforce limits), as shown in Figure 8.8.

FIGURE 8.8

Use linuxconf *to configure specific quota limits for users and groups.*

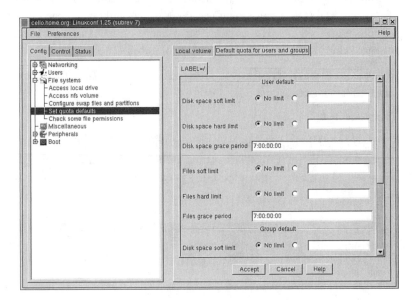

Managing software and hardware resources is an essential task, especially when supporting multiple users working on critical projects. By properly managing your system, you can provide a more efficient work environment to safely allocate CPU, memory, and storage requirements to get the job done.

Reference

http://www.rpm.org—Home page for Red Hat Package Manager technology. This site provides essential links to the latest version of RPM software for Linux and X desktop environments, such as GNOME.

http://www.rpm.org/max-rpm/—Link to the start of an update to Ed Bailey's classic tome and RPM reference book, *Maximum RPM*.

http://www.rpmdp.org/rpmbook/node3.html—History of the Red Hat Package Manager.

`http://www.ximian.com`—Ximian's version of GNOME, which can be installed remotely using a unique installer based on RPM technology.

`http://www.smoogespace.com/documents/behind_the_names.html`—A history of Red Hat Linux releases, and a good place to learn about the connection between the names of the releases.

`http://www.gnupg.org/`—Home page for GNU Privacy Guard, an unencumbered free replacement for Pretty Good Privacy.

`http://www.uow.edu.au/~andrewm/linux/ext3/ext3-usage.html`—Using the `ext3` filesystem with 2.4 Linux kernels.

`http://www.debian.org/doc/manuals/project-history/ch4.html`—History of the Debian Linux package system.

`http://www.daa.com.au/~james/gnome/`—The `gnorpm` client's home page, with technical information and details about related software libraries for GNOME and Linux.

`http://www.general.uwa.edu.au/u/toivo/kpackage/`—Screenshots of `kpackage` in action at its maintainer's home page.

`http://www.trolltech.com/`—Home page for Trolltech, developers of the essential QT libraries required for KDE and its clients.

`http://and.sourceforge.net/`—Home page of the and auto nice daemon, which can be used to prioritze and reschedule processes automatically.

`http://sourceforge.net/projects/schedutils/`—Home page for various projects offering scheduling utilities for real-time scheduling.

`http://www.ethereal.com`—Home page for the Ethereal client.

`http://www.uk.research.att.com/vnc/`—AT&T's home page for the Virtual Network Computing remote desktop software, available for a variety of platforms, including Red Hat Linux. This software has become so popular that it is now included with nearly every Linux distribution.

8

SOFTWARE AND SYSTEM RESOURCES

Managing Users

CHAPTER 9

A computer without users is a computer that isn't doing useful work. However, allowing others access to a computer is more than just allowing them to sit at a terminal and type. Several issues arise, not the least of which is security. All users have various needs and present differing problems to the system administrator; all users need not be treated the same. To begin examining how users are managed, let's reflect on both the needs of the user and the needs of the system administrator. The following list is suggested as a beginning framework for your own specific circumstances:

Users' Needs

- Users should be segregated from one another so that they won't interfere with one another.
- Users should be able to secure their own work from unauthorized access.
- Users should be allowed to work together in groups to share information and files.
- Users should be kept away from the system files and system commands so that they don't accidentally or maliciously break something.

System Administrators' Needs

- User account is easily created, modified, and terminated.
- User has access to directories, files, and devices only on a need-to-use basis.
- Delegated sysadmin authority shouldn't be across the board, but controlled as well.

In this chapter, we'll examine what's involved in the administration of users. The administration of users can be incredibly complex or amazingly simple. The best tool for the administration of users isn't some shell command of a fancy GUI tool—it's the skill, knowledge, and talent of the superuser that accomplishes the most. The proper administration of users separates the accomplishment of useful work from chaos.

Users Defined

There are three kinds of users in this world: the superuser, the regular user, and the luser. The superuser is also known by the name *root*. Although they might appear the same to you when you meet them, to Linux the superuser and the regular user are entirely different people. And, although there might be many system administrators on a large system, there is only one superuser and that superuser has all (and grants all) privileges on the system. This means that the superuser can use any program, manipulate any file, go anywhere, and do anything. For reasons of security, that kind of raw, mind-numbing power should only be given to a single, trusted individual.

Stereotypes

As is often the case in many professions, exaggerated characterizations known as *stereotypes* have emerged for typical users and system administrators (sysadmins). Many stereotypes contain elements of truth mixed with hyperbole and serve to help us understand the characteristics of and differences in users. They also serve as cautionary tales describing what behavior is acceptable and unacceptable in the community. In the UNIX community, the stereotypical sysadmin is known as the BOFH and the stereotypical user is irreverently referred to as a luser. Understanding these stereotypes allows you to more clearly define the appropriate and inappropriate roles of these individuals. The canonical reference to these terms is found in the alt.sysadmin.recovery FAQ.

Regular Users Serve a Vital Purpose

As a practical matter for reasons of identification and accountability, regular users exist. Each user has his own username, password, and permissions that can only be assigned by the superuser .(For security reasons, the user should later change his password after he has been "brought to life" by the superuser god.) The ability to run programs and access files can be restricted for regular users, and the access is again being determined solely by the superuser. All users have a *user ID (uid)* and a *group ID (gid)*. The superuser can assign access rights to both a particular user and a group, allowing for flexibility in the assignment of rights. The general rule of thumb is that no more rights should be given than those actually necessary to accomplish the task assigned to a user. The uid and gid of root are both 0, which is why there can only be one superuser. Assigning both those IDs to any user makes that user the superuser; contrary to popular belief, the superuser name doesn't have to be root, although that is the common practice.

Running as Root on a Regular Basis

On your home system, you are both the superuser and a regular user at the same time (you can be logged on as multiple users or logged on multiple times as the same user if you have the need). The traditional cautionary advice usually goes like this: Because of the potential for making a catastrophic error as the superuser (`rm -rf /*` comes to mind), it is generally suggested that you always use your system as a regular user and become root only temporarily to do sysadmin duties. While you are on a multiuser system, this is good, solid advice to follow always; on your home system, you can do as you please.

9

MANAGING USERS

As a general rule, it is never a good idea to do work that can be accomplished as a regular user when logged in as the superuser, a caveat commonly heard as "Don't run as root!" On a non-networked home or personal system, this rule is generally ignored. But on a multiuser system used for business, if root were to delete the wrong file or kill the wrong process, the results could be disastrous.

> **Note**
>
> Because some programmers are deeply invested in the "DON'T RUN AS ROOT!" mindset, there are programs that restrict your ability to run them as root for no good reason (the Bluefish HTML editor is one), or allow you do it after being told how bad you are. (The file browser for GNOME, gmc, is one). When running MS Windows emulators, that is another thing entirely, and it is never a good idea to run them as root (Win4Lin, a commercial emulator application, specifically prohibits this) because the MS Windows operating system, running on your Red Hat Linux system as root itself, will wreak havoc with your system by deleting and altering files.

Granting Root Privileges to Regular Users

On occasion, it is necessary for regular users to run a command as if they were root. They usually don't need these powers extensively, perhaps just on special occasions or to access certain devices.

There are two ways to run commands with root privileges: The first is useful if you are both the superuser and the user, the second if you aren't the regular user (as on a large, multiuser network).

The su Command

What if you are the superuser, logged on as a regular user because that's what you choose to do, and you need to do something that only the superuser can do? The su command is available for this. Contrary to popular belief, su means *substitute user*, not superuser; you can substitute the identity of any user for the one you are currently using as long as you know the password. The su command changes both the uid and gid of the existing user and automatically changes the environmental variables associated with that user, known as *inheriting* the environment.

The syntax for the su command is this:

```
su option  - username   arguments
```

The man page for su gives more details, but some highlights of the su command are

```
-c,  —command COMMAND
     pass a single COMMAND to the shell with -c

-m,  —preserve-environment
     do not reset environment variables

-p   same as -m
```

You can invoke the su command in different ways that yield diverse results. By using su alone, you can become root, but you keep your regular user environment. This can be verified by using the printenv command before and after the change. Note that the PWD (the current working directory) hasn't changed from where you started. By executing the following, you become root and inherit root's environment (again note the PWD):

```
$ su -
```

By executing the following, you become that user and inherit his environment—a pretty handy tool:

```
$ su - <some other user>
```

When leaving an identity to return to your normal self, use the exit command. For example, while logged on as a regular user,

```
$ su root
```

the system prompts for a password:

```
Password:
```

When the password is entered correctly, the root users' prompt appears:

```
#
```

To return to the regular users' identity, just type

```
# exit
```

This takes you to regular users' prompt:

```
$
```

If you need to allow other users access to certain commands with root privileges, it is necessary to give them the root password so that they can use su—that definitely isn't a very secure solution.

Granting Root Privileges on Occasion—The sudo Command

If it is desirable to give certain users only a few superuser permissions (to create an assistant system administrator, for example), the sudo (superuser do) command is used. sudo allows a regular user, after having been given permission, the ability to use a superuser command. To use sudo, the user must authenticate himself with his password and can re-use the command for several minutes (usually five minutes by default) without further re-authentication. The list of authorized users is kept in /etc/sudoers, a file accessible only by root. If a user attempts to use a sudo command without authorization, that event is logged and a warning mail message could optionally be sent to the administrator.

To use sudo as a regular user, you prepend the command you are authorized to use to the sudo command, for example,

```
$ sudo fdisk -l /dev/hda1
```

sudo will prompt you for a password and then check /etc/sudoers to see if you have permission to use that particular command. It issues a *ticket* that lasts for a short period of time (so that repeated use of the command can be made without additional hassle as long as the ticket is valid. The time limit can be determined by the superuser, otherwise the default time is used. Extensive logging of sudo use and misuse is maintained as a security measure.

If you desire customized use of sudo, extensive options are available during the compilation process, and the available options to use in the configuration file are extensive as well. Alias support makes configuration easier.

The configuration file is at /etc/sudoers; it should only be edited with the visudo command, so you should know how to use the vi editor. The sudo man page provides information on how to edit the sudoers file and is required reading; the information on sudo is somewhat dense.

Briefly, a line in the sudoers file to grant root privileges to user hoyt to examine any file on the system (and using aliases to extend this power to others easily if needed) would look like this:

```
User_Alias    GURU=hoyt
Cmd_Alias     FILE_TOOLS=/bin/ls,/bin/cat,/usr/bin/less

GURU    ALL=FILE_TOOLS
```

Now, the regular user hoyt can use ls, cat, and less with superuser privileges. It is easy to add additional users to the alias GURU as well as additional commands to FILE_TOOLS if their use was authorized. Note that ALL= permits these privileges over the same network; it is possible to limit the privileges to the local machine or to subnets.

> **Note**
>
> The use of sudo is recommended to extend certain privileges to users other than the superuser because of the ease of administration and the security logging that is done.

About Group IDs

As a general rule, the gid can be any integer. The custom is to use gids of 100 or more for regular users (Red Hat starts at 500) and gids of 99 or less for administrators or special programs. The groups are identified in /etc/group. A list of a sample /etc/group file reveals the following:

```
# cat /etc/group
root:x:0:root
bin:x:1:root,bin,daemon
daemon:x:2:root,bin,daemon
sys:x:3:root,bin,adm
adm:x:4:root,adm,daemon
tty:x:5:
disk:x:6:root
lp:x:7:daemon,lp
mem:x:8:
kmem:x:9:
wheel:x:10:root
mail:x:12:mail
news:x:13:news
uucp:x:14:uucp
man:x:15:
games:x:20:
gopher:x:30:
dip:x:40:
ftp:x:50:
lock:x:54:
nobody:x:99:
users:x:100:
slocate:x:21:
floppy:x:19:
utmp:x:22:
nscd:x:28:
```

9

MANAGING USERS

```
mailnull:x:47:
rpm:x:37:
ident:x:98:
rpc:x:32:
rpcuser:x:29:
radvd:x:75:
xfs:x:43:
gdm:x:42:
postgres:x:26:
apache:x:48:
squid:x:23:
named:x:25:
wine:x:101:
pcap:x:77:
junkbust:x:73:
pppusers:x:44:
popusers:x:45:
slipusers:x:46:
mailman:x:41:
mysql:x:27:
ldap:x:55:
pvm:x:24:
hoyt:x:500:
```

There are a number of groups, mostly for services (named, ftp, mail, news, and so on) and devices (floppy, tdfx, cdwriter, disk, and so on) as well as some special users (root, nobody, wheel).

What Are Those Special Groups?

If you examine the names of the groups, the purpose of many is very clear. Some are named after specific services and allow these services to manage their own files with permissions that restrict other users from them. Some, such as the wheel group, are even historical.

Note

In the days before su and sudo, the superuser anointed the chosen few with membership in a special group with access to superuser authority; they became big wheels. The name of this group became wheel. It works like this:

The regular user is added to the wheel group. The attributes of certain system commands are modified to change them from user:root/group:root to user:root, group:wheel. The wheel group can now execute the command with the same privilege as the owner, root.

This practice has been replaced (referred to as *deprecated* in UNIX jargon) by the su and sudo commands, which allow more control (especially with more logging when using sudo) so that it makes little sense to use the wheel group any more. It is kept for old system administrators who refuse to change and, of course, for sentimental historical reasons as well as backward compatibility.

Security and Passwords

Passwords are an integral part of Linux security and they are the most visible part to the user. An effective password policy is a fundamental part of a good system administration plan. The policy should cover

- Allowed and forbidden passwords
- The frequency of mandated password changes
- The retrieval or replacement of lost or forgotten passwords
- Password handling by users

Red Hat Linux 7.2 provides a password system using *Pluggable Access Modules (PAM)* to make the administration of passwords flexible and secure.

The Password File

The password file is /etc/passwd, and it is the database file for all users on the system. The format of each line is as follows:

```
username:password:uid:gid:gecos:homedir:shell
```

The fields are self-explanatory except for the gecos field. This field is for miscellaneous information about the user and is used for programs such as finger and mail. The data in this field is comma delimited. The reason it is called the gecos field is left as an exercise for the interested reader. (Hint: It's a holdover from another operating system—think General Electric.)

Note that a colon separates all fields. If no information is available for a field, that field is empty, but all the colons remain.

If an asterisk appears in the password field, that user won't be permitted to log on. Why does this feature exist? So a user can be easily disabled and (possibly) reinstated at a later date without having to be created all over again.

Several services run as pseudo-users, usually with root permissions. You wouldn't want these accounts available for general login for security reasons:

```
A list of /etc/passwd reveals;
# cat /etc/passwd
root:x:0:0:root:/root:/bin/bash
bin:x:1:1:bin:/bin:/sbin/nologin
daemon:x:2:2:daemon:/sbin:/sbin/nologin
adm:x:3:4:adm:/var/adm:/sbin/nologin
lp:x:4:7:lp:/var/spool/lpd:/sbin/nologin
sync:x:5:0:sync:/sbin:/bin/sync
shutdown:x:6:0:shutdown:/sbin:/sbin/shutdown
halt:x:7:0:halt:/sbin:/sbin/halt
mail:x:8:12:mail:/var/spool/mail:/sbin/nologin
news:x:9:13:news:/var/spool/news:
uucp:x:10:14:uucp:/var/spool/uucp:/sbin/nologin
operator:x:11:0:operator:/root:/sbin/nologin
games:x:12:100:games:/usr/games:/sbin/nologin
gopher:x:13:30:gopher:/usr/lib/gopher-data:/sbin/nologin
ftp:x:14:50:FTP User:/var/ftp:/sbin/nologin
nobody:x:99:99:Nobody:/:/sbin/nologin
nscd:x:28:28:NSCD Daemon:/:/bin/false
mailnull:x:47:47::/var/spool/mqueue:/dev/null
rpm:x:37:37::/var/lib/rpm:/bin/bash
ident:x:98:98:pident user:/:/sbin/nologin
rpc:x:32:32:Portmapper RPC user:/:/bin/false
rpcuser:x:29:29:RPC Service User:/var/lib/nfs:/sbin/nologin
radvd:x:75:75:radvd user:/:/bin/false
xfs:x:43:43:X Font Server:/etc/X11/fs:/bin/false
gdm:x:42:42::/var/gdm:/sbin/nologin
postgres:x:26:26:PostgreSQL Server:/var/lib/pgsql:/bin/bash
apache:x:48:48:Apache:/var/www:/bin/false
squid:x:23:23::/var/spool/squid:/dev/null
named:x:25:25:Named:/var/named:/bin/false
pcap:x:77:77::/var/arpwatch:/bin/nologin
amanda:x:33:6:Amanda user:/var/lib/amanda:/bin/bash
junkbust:x:73:73::/etc/junkbuster:/bin/bash
mailman:x:41:41:GNU Mailing List Manager:/var/mailman:/bin/false
mysql:x:27:27:MySQL Server:/var/lib/mysql:/bin/bash
ldap:x:55:55:LDAP User:/var/lib/ldap:/bin/false
pvm:x:24:24::/usr/share/pvm3:/bin/bash
hoyt:x:500:500:Hoyt Duff:/home/hoyt:/bin/bash
```

Note that all the password fields don't show a password, but contain an *x* because they are shadow passwords, which are discussed next.

Shadow Passwords

It is considered a security risk to use the encrypted passwords found in /etc/passwd; anyone with read access can run a cracking program on the file and obtain the passwords with little trouble. To deal with this, shadow passwords are used so that only and *x* or an * appears in the password field of /etc/passwd; the real passwords are kept in /etc/ shadow, a file that can only be read by the superuser (and PAM). Special versions of password and login programs must be used to enable shadow passwords. This feature is typically enabled during the installation phase of the operating system on Red Hat 7.2 systems. A system that doesn't use shadow passwords can be converted after the fact using the utilities that come with shadow passwords.

Let's look at the shadow companion to /etc/passwd, the /etc/shadow file:

```
# cat /etc/shadow
root:a3mUhgkEFmmBM:11577:0:99999:7:::
bin:*:11577:0:99999:7:::
daemon:*:11577:0:99999:7:::
adm:*:11577:0:99999:7:::
lp:*:11577:0:99999:7:::
sync:*:11577:0:99999:7:::
shutdown:*:11577:0:99999:7:::
halt:*:11577:0:99999:7:::
mail:*:11577:0:99999:7:::
news:*:11577:0:99999:7:::
uucp:*:11577:0:99999:7:::
operator:*:11577:0:99999:7:::
games:*:11577:0:99999:7:::
gopher:*:11577:0:99999:7:::
ftp:*:11577:0:99999:7:::
nobody:*:11577:0:99999:7:::
nscd:!!:11577:0:99999:7:::
mailnull:!!:11577:0:99999:7:::
rpm:!!:11577:0:99999:7:::
ident:!!:11577:0:99999:7:::
rpc:!!:11577:0:99999:7:::
rpcuser:!!:11577:0:99999:7:::
radvd:!!:11577:0:99999:7:::
xfs:!!:11577:0:99999:7:::
gdm:!!:11577:0:99999:7:::
postgres:!!:11577:0:99999:7:::
apache:!!:11577:0:99999:7:::
squid:!!:11577:0:99999:7:::
named:!!:11577:0:99999:7:::
pcap:!!:11577:0:99999:7:::
amanda:!!:11577:0:99999:7:::
junkbust:!!:11577:0:99999:7:::
mailman:!!:11577:0:99999:7:::
```

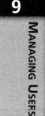

9

MANAGING USERS

```
mysql:!!:11577:0:99999:7:::
ldap:!!:11577:0:99999:7:::
pvm:!!:11577:0:99999:7:::
hoyt:cHzkMp3/14yV2:11577:0:99999:7:::
```

The fields are separated by colons and are, in order:

> The user's login name.
>
> The encrypted password.
>
> The number of days since Jan 1, 1970 that the password was last changed. This date is know in UNIX circles as the epoch. Just so you'll know, the billionth second since the epoch passed in September 2001.
>
> The number of days before the password can be changed (prevents changing a password and then changing it back to the old password right away—a dangerous security practice).
>
> The number of days after which the password *must* be changed. This can be set to force the change of a newly issued password that is known to the system administrator.
>
> The number of days before the password is to expire that the user is warned it will expire.
>
> The number of days after the password expires that the account is disabled (for security).
>
> The number of days since Jan 1, 1970 that account has been disabled.

The final field is a reserved field.

The permissions on the files /etc/shadow should be set so that it isn't writeable or readable by regular users.

Password Security

Selecting appropriate user passwords is always an exercise in tradeoffs. A password such as password (don't laugh, it's been used too often before in the real world) is just too easy to guess by an intruder as are simple words or number combinations (your street address, for example). A security auditor for one of my former employers would take the cover sheet from the employees' personnel file (which contained the usual personal information of name, address, birth date and so on) and would then attempt to log on to their terminal with passwords constructed from that information—and often succeeded in logging on.

On the other hand, although a password such as
256u'"F($84u&#^Hiu44Ik%$([#EJDndo68s(*Z might present great difficulty to an intruder (or an auditor), the password is so difficult to remember that it would be very

likely that the password owner would write that password down and tape it next to his keyboard. I worked for a business in which the safe combination was written on the ceiling tile over the safe because the manager couldn't remember it and was told he shouldn't keep it on piece of paper in his wallet, an example of poor but frequently encountered security.

The superuser has control, with settings in the /etc/shadow file, over how often the password must be changed. The settings can be changed using a text editor or a configuration tool such as linuxconf as shown in Figure 9.1.

FIGURE 9.1

Linuxconf is a powerful and versatile configuration tool, here being used to set the password length.

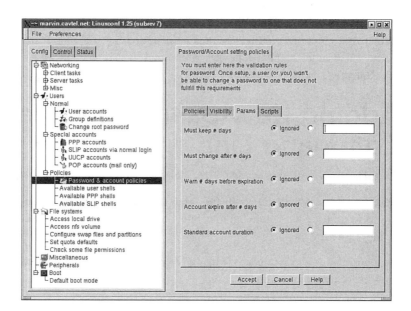

The Source of the Users' Home Files

When each new user is created, a home directory is also created for him, most commonly in /home/<username>, although it can be located anywhere it suits the system administrator. The set of files that initially are used to populate this home directory are kept in /etc/skel. This is very convenient for the system administrator because any special files, links, or directories can be placed in /etc/skel and will be duplicated automatically with appropriate permissions for each new user.

```
# ls -al /etc/skel
```

```
total 44
drwxr-xr-x    3 root      root          4096 Sep 15 03:34 .
drwxr-xr-x   71 root      root          8192 Sep 15 02:35 ..
-rw-r--r--    1 root      root            24 Jul  9 08:56 .bash_logout
-rw-r--r--    1 root      root           191 Jul  9 08:56 .bash_profile
-rw-r--r--    1 root      root           124 Jul  9 08:56 .bashrc
-rw-r--r--    1 root      root           820 Jul 30 06:03 .emacs
-rw-r--r--    1 root      root           118 Aug  9 20:15 .gtkrc
drwxr-xr-x    3 root      root          4096 Feb 28  2001 .kde
-rw-r--r--    1 root      root          3511 Aug  3 12:53 .screenrc
```

As you can see, root owns everything here, but the adduser command copies everything in /etc/skel to the new home directory and sets appropriate file permissions. If there are certain configurations that the system administrator doesn't want changed, the file in /home/<username> can have the permissions set so that he can read it but can't write to it, effectively locking him out of it.

Adding New Users from the Command Line

Command-line tools are easy to use, especially if you bother reading the man pages first.

Adding new users with the commands adduser and passwd (to change passwords) is simple to do from the command line, and you can make it even more elaborate to make it do more for you.

As root, running the adduser command (a symbolic link to useradd) by itself shows a brief list of possible options to it:

```
# man adduser

        useradd [-c comment] [-d home_dir]
                [-e expire_date] [-f inactive_time]
                [-g initial_group] [-G group[,...]]
                [-m [-k skeleton_dir] | -M] [-p passwd]
                [-s shell] [-u uid [ -o]] [-n] [-r] login

        useradd -D [-g default_group] [-b default_home]
                [-f default_inactive] [-e default_expire_date]
                [-s default_shell]
```

Most of the options are self-explanatory. We will use a simple approach. Add the user newguy with the password imanewuser:

```
# adduser -p imanewuser newguy
```

The new entry in /etc/passwd now shows this:

```
newguy:x:501:501::/home/newguy:/bin/bash
```

The system automatically assigned a uid, gid, home directory, and a default shell; newguy's home directory was created at /home/newguy. Of course, all these things could be explicitly assigned (or defaults changed) through the appropriate arguments in adduser.

This line could have been added, using an editor such as vi, directly to /etc/passwd, but then the appropriate gid and uid would need to be determined, a password set using passwd, a home directory created, and the contents of /etc/skel copied to it with the permissions appropriately set. The adduser command is so much easier.

If you have a number of new accounts to create, you could write a shell script to prompt you for information and then send that information to adduser. Two graphical user management tools are available if that is your preference.

The passwd command can be used to change the password tokens (encrypted password) of any user on the system. When using the passwd command as root, the username is given as an argument. Note that the old password isn't disclosed to the superuser, but a new password is easily entered. The regular user can then access his account and use passwd to change his password, keeping his new password confidential as a result.

The passwd command is configured in Red Hat 7.2 to use Pluggable Authentication Modules (PAM).

```
# passwd newguy
Changing password for user newguy
New UNIX password:
Retype new UNIX password:
Sorry, passwords do not match
New UNIX password:
```

In this case, the second typing of the password (passwords are not written to the display, so nothing will be seen) didn't match. Linux checks this as a security measure of sorts against having typos in passwords.

If you aren't familiar with the process, go ahead and create a few fictional users and experiment with different settings and options. Just remember to delete all these users when you are done; the presence of inactive user accounts represents a security hole that a malicious user can exploit to penetrate the system security.

Changing Passwords in a Batch

The superuser can change passwords in a batch by using the chpasswd command, which accepts input as a name/password pair per line in the following form:

```
username:password
```

Passwords can be changed en masse by redirecting a list of name and password pairs to the command.

PAM Explained

Pluggable Authentication Modules (PAM) is a system of libraries that handle the tasks of authentication on your computer system. It uses four management groups: account management, authentication management, password management, and session management. This allows the system administrator to choose how individual applications will authenticate users. Installing from source code and configuring PAM from scratch is a daunting task. Red Hat has pre-installed and pre-configured all the necessary files for you.

The configuration files in Red Hat 7.2 are found in /etc/pam.d. These files are named for the service they control and the format is this:

```
type control module-path module-arguments
```

The type field is the management group that the rule corresponds to. The control field tells PAM what to do if authentication fails; this can be done in a simple or elaborate manner and executed depending on the effect desired by the system administrator. The final two items deal with the PAM module that is used and any arguments it needs. Programs that use PAM typically come packaged with appropriate entries for the /etc/pam.d directory. To achieve greater security, the superuser can modify the default entries. (As long as the superuser knows what he is doing—misconfiguration can have predictably bad results.)

As an example of a PAM configuration file, here are the contents of /etc/pam.d/ linuxconf:

```
#%PAM-1.0
auth      required     /lib/security/pam_stack.so service=system-auth
account   required     /lib/security/pam_stack.so service=system-auth
session   required     /lib/security/pam_stack.so service=system-auth
session   optional     /lib/security/pam_xauth.so
```

PAM is more complex than can be explained in the context of this chapter. For more details, PAM has three guides:

- System Administrators Guide
- Module Developers Guide
- Application Developers Guide

You'll likely only need the system administrators guide. Even the PAM documents hint that you don't really need (or want) to know a lot about PAM to use it effectively.

Other User Administration Console Programs

The `adduser` and `passwd` commands aren't the only commands available for system administrators to use. The following commands have man pages from which the descriptions are taken:

> `shadow`—Manipulates the contents of the shadow password file, /etc/shadow.
>
> `groupadd`—Creates a new group account using the values specified on the command line and the default values from the system. The new group will be entered into the system files as needed.
>
> `groupdel`—Modifies the system account files, deleting all entries that refer to group. The named group must already exist.
>
> `groupmod`—Modifies the system account files to reflect the changes that are specified on the command line.
>
> `userdel`—Modifies the system account files, deleting all entries that refer to login. The named user must already exist.
>
> `usermod`—Modifies the system account files to reflect the changes that are specified on the command line.
>
> `newgrp`—Changes the group identification of its caller. The same person remains logged in, and the current directory is unchanged, but calculations of access permissions to files are performed with respect to the new group ID.
>
> `grpck`—verifies the integrity of the system authentication information. All entries in the /etc/group and /etc/gshadow are checked to see that the entry has the proper format and valid data in each field. The user is prompted to delete entries that are improperly formatted or that have other uncorrectable errors.

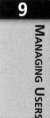

9

MANAGING USERS

The User Login Process

It's useful to know what happens when a user attempts to log in, if for nothing else than troubleshooting that user in the accounting department who can't get logged on to run the payroll program.

The man page for login states that "…login is used when signing onto a system. It can also be used to switch from one user to another at any time (most modern shells have support for this feature built into them, however)."

The login process is summarized as follows:

1. Login prompts for a username.

2. If the /etc/nologin files exists and the user isn't root, a warning message is issued and the login process is halted. The /etc/nologin file is typically used when the system will be shut down shortly.

3. The file /etc/usertty is examined to see if any restrictions are specified for the user. As a security measure, root logons can be restricted to specific terminals, and regular users can have the same restrictions placed on them as necessary.

4. The system prompts for a password; it is checked against the encrypted password kept in /etc/shadow. Unsuccessful attempts are logged via the syslog facility.

5. The uid and the gid of the tty (terminal) being used are set.

6. The TERM environment, if it has been set, is preserved.

7. The HOME, PATH, SHELL, TERM, MAIL, and LOGNAME environment variables are set. (If the -p option is used, all pre-existing environmental variables are preserved.)

8. The PATH defaults to /usr/local/bin:/bin:/usr/bin: for normal users, and to /sbin:/bin:/usr/sbin:/usr/bin for root.

9. Normal greeting messages and mail checking are disabled if the file .hushlogin exists; otherwise, those messages are displayed at the end of the logon process.

10. The user's command shell is started at this point, presenting the user with a command prompt. If no shell is specified for the user in /etc/passwd, /bin/sh is used by default. If there is no home directory specified in /etc/passwd, / is used.

When you log in as a regular user, the files that control your environment are found in your /home/username directory. These configuration files are normally hidden from view since their filename is preceded by a period (as in .bashrc—these are known as 'dot files').

The name of the file indicates which program it is associated with. The files .bash_ logout, .bash_profile, and .bashrc all determine how the bash shell is used by the user (These files can, of course, be preset by the system administrator and the user given only read access so they can't be changed. Other shells have their own associated files.)

The file .screenrc determines the console screen environment and the .Xdefaults file determines much the same thing for X11.

Other files might be present depending on the system and the system administrator. The point is that the environment of each user can be set globally through the use of files in /etc/skel and individually by allowing user modification of the files in their /home directory (or not depending on the system administration policies).

User Logging

Remember, the system administrator logs all the logins for review as well as uses of su and sudo. Modern security monitoring programs (or simple scripts you create) can scan these files for anomalies and signal possible security violations.

GUI Administration Tools

Red Hat 7.2 provides GUI tools for user administration. Their use is one of preference for the sysadmin because they accomplish the same thing as the console tools described previously.

Creating Users with the GUI Tools

To navigate to the Kuser application (see Figure 9.2), go to

KDE: K, System, User Manager (Kuser)

Gnome: Main Menu, KDE menus, System, User Manager (Kuser)

The KDE-provided tool allows the superuser to manage users and groups. To add the user bob, click on the Add icon or choose User, Add from the drop-down list. After entering the user name, a box appears, as shown in Figure 9.3.

As you can see in Figure 9.4, the program has selected the next available uid, selected the default login shell (it can be changed), and listed the location of the proposed home directory (a standard default value). With the boxes checked as shown, the proposed home directory will be created, and it will be populated with the files found in /etc/skel (where the system administrator is free to add or modify files as he sees fit).

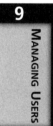

9

MANAGING USERS

FIGURE 9.2

The Kuser graphical tool.

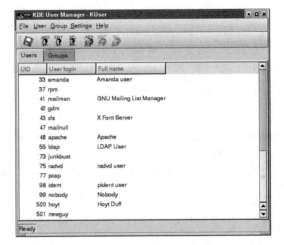

FIGURE 9.3

Click on the Add icon and a dialog box pops up to enter the new user's username. Here, we add "bob."

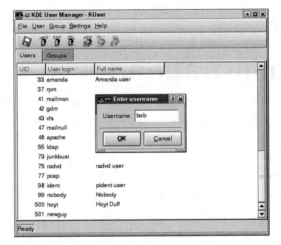

The Set Password button allows the standard double-entry-for-confirmation password. The Password Management screen allows for password expiration settings. By default, the as-installed Red Hat system allows passwords to be valid forever and requires that no change ever be made. If the system were used in a business environment, these fields would be set to accommodate the system security policy requirements.

Because each user is set up in his own private group by default, the Groups tab (see Figure 9.5) can be used to add the new user to groups that will allow the new user certain file access and privileges.

FIGURE 9.4

Although default values are automatically provided, this dialog box allows for customization.

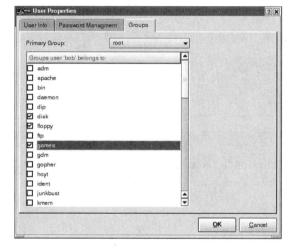

FIGURE 9.5

Adding a user to a group is as easy a checking a box. Note that groups can't be members of other groups.

The Groups tab allows the viewing of all the groups that have been set up, but clicking on Edit a Group brings up a dialog box that allows the system administrator to easily click on usernames to add them to a group. In Linux, a group cannot be the member of another group.

To exit Kuser, select Save. If the directory already exists, the program will ask if you want to change the ownership to the new user. Unless you are certain that is what you want—that is, if this isn't what you expected to happen—you should quit without saving and investigate that existing user.

9

MANAGING USERS

The Red Hat User Manager

KDE: K, System, User Manager (Red Hat)

Gnome: Main Menu, Programs, System, User Manager (Red Hat)

Red Hat 7.2 supplies its own administration tool (see Figure 9.6) for managing users. This tool presents (in a more useful format) additional information to that presented in the KDE utility, and it works in essentially the same way as the KDE tool.

FIGURE 9.6

The Red Hat version of the GUI user manager

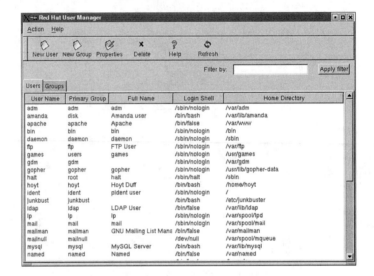

To create a new user, click on the New User icon and enter the information required in the single window. The Help files are accessed through the Mozilla browser.

Red Hat Change Password

KDE: K, System, Change Password

Gnome: Main menu, Programs, System, Change Password

A simple dialog box intended especially for regular users is provided. Although root can change his own password with it, he can't change a regular user's password with the tool shown in Figure 9.7

FIGURE 9.7

A simple dialog box to change a password of the current user; very convenient for the regular users.

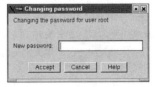

linuxconf

The most useful tool provided by Red Hat for managing users on a system is still linux-conf (see Figure 9.8). With no menu or desktop icon, it is accessible from one place: launched from a command line as root. It is menu driven—the menu appears slightly different when launched in either an X window or from the console. Linuxconf also allows for more detailed configuration than the KDE or Red Hat GUI tools. Its online help is somewhat lacking in places, But, if it isn't automatically installed on your system, linux-conf is only a short `rpm  -ivh` away. You'll find it useful.

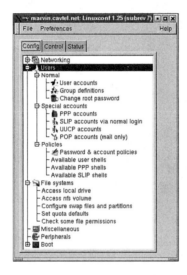

FIGURE 9.8

The main menu of the linuxconf configuration tool as displayed in an X window on your desktop.

The main menu offers, among other things, access to managing user accounts.

In Figure 9.9, under Normal Users, the options include

- User accounts
- Group definitions
- Change root password

Under Special Accounts, the options include

- PPP accounts
- SLIP accounts

9

MANAGING USERS

- UUCP accounts
- POP accounts (mail only)

Figure 9.9

Groups can be edited, added to, or deleted from this tab.

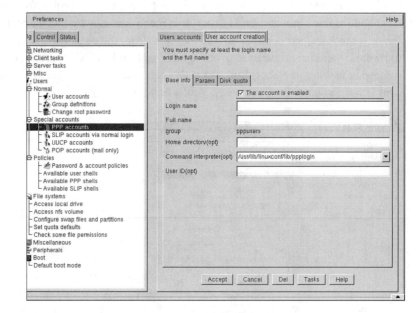

In Figure 9.10, under Policies, the options include

- Password & account policies
- Available user shells
- Available PPP shells
- Available SLIP shells

Using linuxconf in this way is relatively straightforward. If the Help menu is lacking in information, use this book or the appropriate man page to help you understand the options. Using a GUI tool is much easier once you understand what it does in the background.

FIGURE 9.10

Further global restrictions and accesses can be granted from this tab.

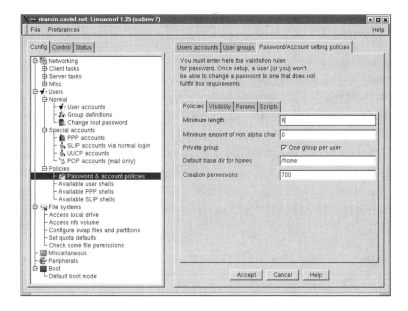

Disk Quotas

Sometimes, one of the things that you need to control is the amount of disk space a user has access to. Disk quotas are designed for this purpose.

Linuxconf (see Figure 9.11) is also handy for setting disk quotas that limit the amount of disk space a user can use. After all, disk space is a finite commodity, and you will want to ensure that all users have enough to meet their legitimate needs.

FIGURE 9.11

Although not always necessary, disk quotas are easy to establish using the linux-conf tool.

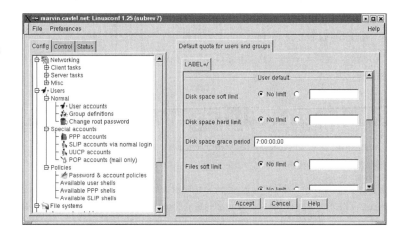

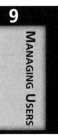

9

MANAGING USERS

The Help files for linuxconf with regard to quotas are excellent and go into great detail on how quotas work and how they are configured.

Quotas, managed by each partition, can be set both for individual users as well as groups; quotas for the group need not be as large as the quotas for the individuals in the groups. When files are created, both a user and a group own them; ownership of the files is always part of the metadata about the files. This makes quotas based on both users *and* groups easy to manage.

If you are curious where the actual quota files and information reside and quotas are already enabled on your system, you can see which partitions have either user quotas, group quotas, or both by looking at the fourth files in the file /etc/fstab. For example, one line in /etc/fstab shows that quotas are enabled for the /home partition:

```
/dev/hda5     /home    ext3         defaults,usrquota,grpquota 1 1
```

The root of the partition will have the files quota.user or quota.group in them (or both files if both types of quotas are enabled) and the files will contain the actual quotas. The permissions of these files should be 600 so that users cannot read or write to them (otherwise, they would change them to allow ample space for their music files and Internet art collections). In order to initialize disk quotas, the partitions must be remounted. This is easily accomplished with the following:

```
# mount mount -o ro,remount /<partition to be remounted>
```

For the curious or the command-line obsessed, the underlying console tools (complete with man pages) are

- quotaon, quotaoff—Toggles quotas on a partition.
- repquota—A summary status report on users and groups.
- quotacheck—Updates the status of quotas (compares new and old tables of disk usage); is run after fsck.
- edquota—A very basic management utility that is, unfortunately, incompatible with linuxconf.

Communicating with Users

On occasion, it is necessary for the sysadmin to speak with the users. Several time-tested applications (complete with man pages) are available for that purpose.

The wall command sends a message to the terminals of all users connected to the system. The message can be given as an argument to wall as in the following:

```
$ wall "I'm going to lunch!"
```

which displays that same message on the terminal or desktop over every user logged on at the moment. This can be quite annoying, but using wall is great for simple one-way communication.

The `talk` command is more sophisticated and allows two-way communication between any two users on the network over a split screen; it is the precursor to the instant messaging client. Received `talk` messages can be blocked by a user, and certain programs will block `talk` to keep it from interfering with their screen output.

How is that blocking done? The `mesg` command is used to control write access to your own terminal. In other words, you would use it to block others from contacting you with the `talk` command (by writing to your display).

If the file /etc/motd exists, its content are used as the "message of the day" to greet users as they log in. Creative system administrators automate the rotation of cheerful, puzzling, and occasionally useful sayings to greet the users every time they log in. The overriding rationale for motd is that it requires much less disk space than mail to all users, according to the man page.

Seeing Who's Doing What

The `w` command will tell you who is logged in, where they are logged in, and what they are doing. No one can hide from the superuser. The `w` command has a few useful options detailed in the man page.

Extreme Control Via Restricted Shells

If you have a desire to severely restrict what a user can do, you can provide him with a restricted shell. To run a restricted bash shell, you would use the `-r` option. It's easy to try yourself, just enter the following at your prompt:

```
$ bash -r
```

Then try to do something that you could do before as a regular user, such as listing the files in your home directory:

```
$ ls -a
```

You then see:

```
bash: ls: No such file or directory
```

Also, the cd command, redirection, using / in command names, and several other commands and options are disabled as well. The man page for bash goes into more details. (The appropriate information is buried at the end of a very long page.). Suffice it to say that control can be pretty tight, and a very determined user might find a way to confound the restrictions.

The chroot Command

Another way to deal with a misbehaving user, but more commonly used with programs, is to use the chroot command, which runs another command (given as the argument) with a superuser-specified root directory. On a normal system, files and directories all flow from the root (the "/") directory, and programs expect to be able to navigate to their configuration files from it. The chroot command alters the behavior by telling the program that your choice of directories will be the root directory. Of course, you must provide all the libraries, binaries, configuration files, and data files where the chrooted program expects to find them. The info page for chroot contains some worthwhile reading to begin configuring programs to run in this manner.

Why bother with restricted shells and chroot at all? Essentially, it's a security matter. If a user or an application might present a security threat, you might want to chroot them into an area where they can't affect the system if they misbehave or are made to misbehave. BIND, FTP, and Apache are all candidates for a "chroot jail."

Reference

http://www.linuxdoc.org/HOWTO/User-Authentication-HOWTO/index.html—The User-Authentication-HOWTO describes how user and group information is stored and used for authentication.

http://www.linuxdoc.org/HOWTO/Shadow-Password-HOWTO.html—The Shadow-Password-HOWTO delves into the murky depths of shadow passwords and even discusses why you might not want to use them.

http://www.linuxdoc.org/HOWTO/Security-HOWTO.html—A "must read" HOWTO, the Security-HOWTO is a good overview of security issues. Especially applicable to this chapter are sections on creating accounts, file permissions, and password security.

http://www.linuxdoc.org/LDP/lasg/—A general guide, the Linux System Administrator's Security Guide has interesting sections on limiting and monitoring users.

`http://www.linuxdoc.org/LDP/lasg/administration/index.html`—The LSAG Administration Tools Index is a good place to look at some administrative tools, but it is by no means an exhaustive list.

`http://www.linuxdoc.org/HOWTO/Config-HOWTO-4.html#config`—How can you customize some user-specific settings? The Config HOWTO Software Configuration gives some advice.

`http://www.linuxdoc.org/HOWTO/mini/Path.html`—How can one know the true path? The Path HOWTO sheds light on this issue. You need to understand paths if you want to guide the users to their data and applications.

`http://www.courtesan.com/sudo/`—The SUperuser DO command is a powerful and elegant way to delegate authority to regular users for specific commands..

`http://www.kernel.org/pub/linux/libs/pam/index.html`—The Pluggable Authentication Modules are complex and highly useful applications that provide additional security and logging for passwords. PAM is installed by default in Red Hat 7.2. It isn't necessary to understand the intricacies of PAM in order to use it effectively.

`http://www.toxiclinux.org/security.html`—"Armoring" a Linux box; modifying Pam config files to use MD5 passwords, creating and using the mysterious wheel group.

`http://localhost/localdomain`—Your Red Hat system contains man and info pages on just about everything covered here. Use man `-k` to search on a keyword.

9

MANAGING USERS

CHAPTER 10

Managing the Filesystems

The word *filesystem* is misunderstood and likely one of the most misused of any of the technical terms used in Linux. Understanding what a filesystem is will bring you enlightenment.

A filesystem is more than just a format for your hard drive or floppy disk and more than just the disk itself or the formatting process. We will define it as the structure and organization of data on a data storage device. In other words, it's how your files are stored and organized on your disk (or tape, CD-ROM, or other storage medium). A UNIX filesystem, the kind we are most concerned with, is used for storing not only data, but also metadata (information about the files, such as who the file owner is, what permissions are associated with the file, and other file attributes).

People who design filesystems always seem to have a better idea of just what constitutes a good filesystem. Some filesystems are developed to advance the state of the art, whereas some are developed as proprietary systems to provide a competitive advantage or provide features unique to that operating system. Typical, users of a specific operating system are locked into using the filesystem supplied with the operating system, called the *native* filesystem; even commercial Unix systems have proprietary filesystems and also employ proprietary partition table schemes. That's so unfriendly and incompatible, but might have made business sense at the time. Another, perhaps more familiar example, is that users of Windows 98 can only use the DOS/FAT filesystems supplied by Microsoft. You can obtain third-party drivers to access other filesystems when using MS Windows, but Windows must boot from a MS–supplied filesystem. Linux users are fortunate in that they have several filesystems to choose from, some providing backward compatibility, some providing interoperability with other operating systems, and some providing state-of-the-art filesystem features commonly found in Enterprise-class operating systems. The ability to access other filesystems (referred to as non-native) is a great strength of Linux.

The Linux filesystem is a lot more complex than most people care to know about, but all those features are patterned after features founds on commercial UNIX systems or believed by the Linux developers to be useful. Fortunately, the native Linux filesystem is robust and works well with the default settings. Red Hat has conveniently provided an easy-to-use setup tool for use during the installation, but dealing with the filesystem afterward is done largely by hand (or not at all). If you are curious, you certainly do have plethora of options at your disposal.

History of the Native Linux Filesystems

Linux was cross developed with a UNIX-like operating system named *minix* (in other words, Linus Torvalds used minix to compile Linux), so Linux used the minix filesystem for convenience. It didn't stay convenient for long when the needs of the Linux operating system outgrew the limitations and capabilities of the borrowed filesystem. For minix filesystems, the largest file size was 64MB, directories contained fixed-size entries, and the maximum filename length was only 14 characters long.

These shortcomings were addressed as the Virtual File System (VFS) layer was added to the Linux kernel. The VFS allowed the kernel to access different file systems by loading a kernel module. This ability to load modules for different types of filesystems makes any filesystem on the physical disk look the same to the operating system. By loading the correct module, the system can read and write files that have been written to a disk using almost any filesystem.

A sampling of the Red Hat 7.2 kernel modules for filesystems is as follows:

adfs—Acorn Disk filing system

bfs—SCO Unixware Boot filesystem

coda—Carnegie Mellon University network filesystem

cms—IBM mainframe mini-disk filesystem

cramfs—Compressed ROM filesystem

efs—non-iso9660 CD-ROMS and older SGI IRIX

ext2—Linux Extended Filesystem 2 (still the current universal standard)

ext3—Linux Extended Filesystem 3 (adds journaling to ext2)

fat—Microsoft File Allocation Table filesystem: FAT 12 and FAT 16

ffs—Amiga Fast filesystem

freevxfs—Free version of the Veritas VxFS filesystem used by SCO: Unixware, Sun Solaris, HP-UX

hfs—Macintosh: Hierarchial filesystem

hpfs—OS/2 High Performance filesystem

minix—Minix filesystem

msdos—Microsoft File Allocation Table -16

10

MANAGING THE FILESYSTEMS

ncfps—Novell Corporation protocol filesystem

nfs—Network filesystem

ntfs—Microsoft New Technology filesystem

ramfs—Memory-based RAM filesystem

reiserFS—Reiser filesystem

romfs—ROM filesystem

qnx—QNX4 filesystem

smbfs—Samba filesystem

sysv—System V Coherent filesystem: Xenix, System V, Coherent

udf—Universal Disk Format (DVD-ROM filesystem)

ufs—UNIX filesystem used on BSD and Sun

umsdos—MS-DOS filesystem with Linux permissions

vfat—Microsoft File Allocation Table filesystem: 32

There isn't an exact correlation between the filesystem source code and the modules compiled for the default kernel. The usage of some of these filesystem modules is mentioned in the man page for mount. Support for ext2 and iso9660 filesystems are compiled into the kernel.

As was mentioned previously, there is no single universal partition format. In addition to the commonly used DOS partition format (used by Linux as well), Red Hat 7.2 also provides support for the following partition types:

- Acorn
- Alpha OS
- Amiga
- Atari
- Macintosh
- BSD
- SunOS/Solaris
- Unixware
- SGI
- Ultrix

NOTE

Ultrix may not sound familiar to you. It became DEC, and then COMPAQ, and is now HP.

Other modules and support are likely available if you care to look about the Internet for them. As is always the case with Open Source Operating Systems, any skilled and enterprising soul can write their own filesystem modules.

The Disk Defined

Because our definition of a filesystem includes mention of the data storage device, let's look at the most common data storage device—the hard disk drive. Floppy disks are similar, as are removable disk drives.

Mechanically, the hard drive is a metal box that encloses disks, also known as platters, which have a magnetic coating on each side. There are typically multiple disks connected to the same spindle and rotated by motor. The read and write heads for each side of the disk are moved by a second motor to position them over the area of the disk where the data you are looking for is stored. Each platter is organized into cylinders (the default size is 512 bytes) and sectors, and each platter has a head. Each drive has some electronics on a controller card that, along with the disk controller card on the motherboard of the computer, are able to place the heads at the correct space to retrieve the data.

The three components, cylinders, heads, and sectors (CHS), are used to identify the geometry of the drive. The geometry is usually detected by the system BIOS and passed on to the operating system. Linux can ignore the BIOS-provided geometry and use geometry that you provide when loading the kernel. The geometry information helps the bootloader program know where on the disk the kernel is and helps the kernel understand how the data on the drive is organized.

If you examine the partition table and can do the math, you'll find that with only 10 bits in which to store the partition's cylinder offset, no disk can have any more than 1024 cylinders (the famous "1024 cylinder limit"). One creative way to get around that is to increase the number of heads so that the number of cylinders can remain small enough to fit the partition table. This scheme is known as *Logical Block Addressing*, or LBA. Modern BIOSes (post-1998 or so) support it, but older ones do not. But, because Linux is capable of being told about the drive geometry at boot time, it isn't as big a problem to Linux users as it is to users of other operating systems. For more detailed information,

10

MANAGING THE
FILESYSTEMS

you can look at the Large Disk HOWTO and the BootPrompt HOWTO if you have problems with large hard disks.

The first sector of the disk is the most important because it contains two things: the boot-loader code and the partition table. The bootloader code is executed after the system BIOS performs its task of getting the hardware ready. When that's done, the BIOS passes control to the bootloader and the bootloader program loads the kernel and turns over control of the system to the kernel, and Linux as we know it is on its way to providing us with one of the best operating system experiences in the world.

The name given to that special first sector is the *MBR*, or *Master Boot record*. It is 512 bytes long, and the first 446 bytes contain the bootloader code—the next 64 bytes containing the partition table and the final two bytes containing a special code (the hexadecimal values of 55 and AA) to identify that sector as the MBR. More details about the MBR can be found Chapter 11, "Backing Up, Restoring, and Recovery." (If you want to see a hexadecimal dump of your MBR, run fdisk on the drive, select x (extra functionality), and then select d to dump the partition to the screen. (We'll discuss more about fdisk in a moment.)

In order to create a filesystem on a disk, we must first create the partition table. The bootloader is created later by LILO, GRUB, or another bootloader program run in the operating system; no bootloader is necessary to create a filesystem and store data on a disk. In fact, IDE disks physically installed as something other than /dev/hda (such as /dev/hdc, the secondary master drive) won't have a bootloader written to them; the space will likely be blank. For SCSI disks, the drive designated in the BIOS as the bootable drive will have the bootloader written to it.

The partition table only has enough room for four partitions. (When the format was first created, it must have been assumed that four would be plenty!) To get around this problem, one of the four (historically, partition number four) can be used as an *extended* partition. In other words, in the partition table, it looks like a big partition taking up the rest of your disk. Actually, it's a link to a table that contains the offsets to as many as 63 partitions for IDE disks and 15 for SCSI disks. One extended partition is chained to the next one in this manner.

How to Access and Manipulate the Partition Table

Red Hat 7.2 provides several tools to create, examine, and modify the partition table. You used one of them when you installed Red Hat. The choice of utilities to work with partition tables is a matter of personal preference: Some people prefer command-line utilities, and some prefer a graphical interface. Because not all the tools we review can be installed on your system (or other system you might be working on for now), we'll start with the most commonly available tools and end with the graphical tools that Red Hat provides.

fdisk

The Linux fdisk counterpart in DOS edits the partition table, creates the disk structure (also known as a *low-level* format), and writes the bootloader to the MBR all in one operation. Linux fdisk, in the UNIX tradition of simple tools doing one job extremely well, performs only one task: editing the partition table. This has some powerful implications for disk recovery as discussed in Chapter 11.

You must be the superuser (root) before you can run the console tool fdisk (also said in shorthand as "run fdisk as root"). Only hard drives (IDE and SCSI) can be accessed with fdisk, and you must use the device name as an argument. USB hard drives are accessed under SCSI emulation and are treated just as if they were SCSI devices. For example, to open fdisk and use it on the first IDE hard drive on the system, you would type this

```
# fdisk /dev/hda
```

and you would see something like this:

```
# fdisk /dev/hda
```

The number of cylinders for this disk is set to 4982. There is nothing wrong with that, but this is larger than 1024, and in certain setups could cause problems with software that runs at boot time:

```
1) software that runs at boot time (e.g., old versions of LILO)
2) booting and partitioning software from other OSes (e.g., DOS FDISK
➥or the OS/2 FDISK)
```

Pressing the m key displays the help screen as follows:

```
Command (m for help): m
Command action
   a   toggle a bootable flag
   b   edit bsd disklabel
   c   toggle the dos compatibility flag
   d   delete a partition
   l   list known partition types
   m   print this menu
   n   add a new partition
   o   create a new empty DOS partition table
```

10

MANAGING THE
FILESYSTEMS

```
p    print the partition table
q    quit without saving changes
s    create a new empty Sun disklabel
t    change a partition's system id
u    change display/entry units
v    verify the partition table
w    write table to disk and exit
x    extra functionality (experts only)
```

Pressing the p key displays the partiton information as follows:

```
Command (m for help): p

Disk /dev/hda: 255 heads, 63 sectors, 4982 cylinders
Units = cylinders of 16065 * 512 bytes

   Device Boot    Start      End     Blocks  Id  System
/dev/hda1    *        1      383    3076416   b  Win95 FAT32
/dev/hda2           384      387      32130  83  Linux
/dev/hda3           388     1025    5124735  83  Linux
/dev/hda4          1026     4982  31784602+   5  Extended
/dev/hda5          1026     1042     136521  82  Linux swap
/dev/hda6          1043     1552    4096543+ 83  Linux
/dev/hda7          1553     4102   20482843+ 83  Linux
/dev/hda8          4103     4500    3196903+ 83  Linux
/dev/hda9          4501     4982    3871633+ 83  Linux
```

Older versions of `fdisk` would default to `/dev/hda`. The author of `fdisk` decided that wasn't a good thing, so now you must always type the device name.

`fdisk` can be dangerous to play around with only if you write the changes to the partition table. Because you are specifically asked whether you want to do this, poke around to satisfy you curiosity and avoid pressing the w key when you're done; just use q to quit. Armed with this knowledge, don't feel too shy if you're curious about the partition table. But if you really don't want to take a chance on messing it up, play it safe and use the -l (that's L, not the numeral 1) as in

```
# fdisk -l /dev/hda
```

`fdisk` happily prints the contents of the partition table to the screen (often referred to as *stdout*, or *standard output*) and exits without placing you in the edit mode.

Would you like to keep a hard copy of the partition table? That's always a good idea. You can redirect the output of `fdisk` -l to a file

```
# fdisk -l > mypartitiontable.txt
```

or send it to the printer with

```
# fdisk -l | lpr
```

Note that in the first example, a redirector symbol (>) is used to redirect the listing from stdout to a file and in the second example, we used a pipe (|) to send the output directly to the printer (assuming that you have one connected).

cfdisk

The console utility cfdisk can accomplish the same thing as fdisk, but it gives you a graphical interface at the console and just looks prettier. It's also menu driven, so you use the cursor keys and Tab key to navigate the screen. There is a man page for cfdisk. Many people prefer it to fdisk because of its menu-driven nature. You will find the cfdisk commands similar to those of fdisk (see Figure 10.1).

FIGURE 10.1

The cfdisk *command presents an easy-to-navigate graphical interface.*

sfdisk

The command-line utility sfdisk is described in the man page as powerful tool for hackers only. This is probably an attempt at programmer humor since sfdisk has a number of safeguards built in to it to prevent accidents. For example, running the command alone generates only a listing of commands. Although the command syntax is much different than that for fdisk, it is straightforward and accomplishes much the same thing.

sfdisk can be a little awkward to use. Figure 10.2 shows the help screen.

10

MANAGING THE FILESYSTEMS

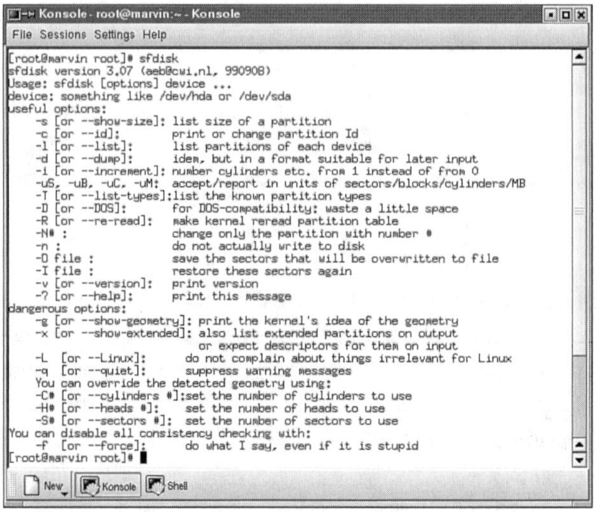

FIGURE 10.2

*A list of options
and some gentle
warnings from a
safe version of
fdisk; you'll need
to work harder to
make a mistake.*

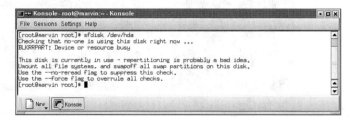

Running it with a device name for an argument as follows,

```
#sfdisk /dev/hda
```

results in a warning as shown in Figure 10.3.

FIGURE 10.3

*Even giving the
device name is
futile. You must
deliberately use
the -f option to
force *sfdisk* to
open the partition
table. Then, expect
more warnings. It
takes a concerted
effort to make a
mistake.*

The real power of sfdisk over fdisk and cfdisk is that its actions can be scripted, so
you can write scripts that force sfdisk to do what you want it to do without having it
tell you no. Otherwise, just start it with the -f argument as was done in Figure 10.4.

sfdisk contains some useful security precautions when manipulating the partition table.
It would be a good choice for use on a networked, multiuser system.

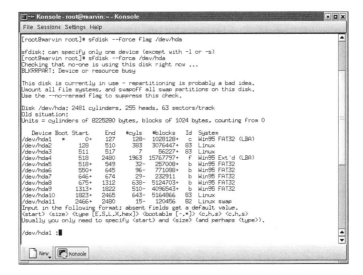

FIGURE 10.4

Finally, success with sfdisk.

GNUparted

Red Hat used to use a partition editor during its installation process called Disk Druid; you might have used it before back in Red Hat's earlier days. The underlying code for Disk Druid has been replaced by GNUparted (also known simply as parted, the name of the command itself), the GNU partition editor, a very powerful utility. The current GUI interface displayed during the installation process looks pretty much the same as the old one, but parted is really a console utility. parted can create, delete, move, resize, and copy ext2 and FAT32 partitions. It can be used interactively or scripted. The man page or info system offers more detailed information on its usage.

The Files

If you learn nothing else from this chapter, learn this: Everything is a File. That is "The Big Concept" for UNIX filesystems.

Although there are several different types of files, for the filesystem we are concerned primarily with two types: character special files and block special files. These are used for character devices and blocks devices, respectively, and are used to write and read data from devices. Just so you'll know, the other types are regular, named pipe, directory, symbolic link, and socket.

If you have installed the kernel documentation, it will contain a text file named devices.txt, an excerpt of which reads

10

MANAGING THE
FILESYSTEMS

```
3 char     Pseudo-TTY slaves
           0 = /dev/ttyp0     First PTY slave
           1 = /dev/ttyp1     Second PTY slave
           ...
         255 = /dev/ttyef     256th PTY slave

       These are the old-style (BSD) PTY devices; Unix98
       devices are on major 136 and above.

   block     First MFM, RLL and IDE hard disk/CD-ROM interface
           0 = /dev/hda          Master: whole disk (or CD-ROM)
          64 = /dev/hdb          Slave: whole disk (or CD-ROM)

       For partitions, add to the whole disk device number:
           0 = /dev/hd?          Whole disk
           1 = /dev/hd?1          First partition
           2 = /dev/hd?2          Second partition
           ...
          63 = /dev/hd?63       63rd partition

       For Linux/i386, partitions 1-4 are the primary
       partitions, and 5 and above are logical partitions.
       Other versions of Linux use partitioning schemes
       appropriate to their respective architectures.
```

The number 3 at the upper left of the listing represents the major number that identifies a class of device. In this case, major 3 identifies both character devices (Pseudo-TTY slaves) and block devices (IDE drives). The columns of numbers that follow under the device types are called the *minor* numbers; any device can be identified uniquely by its major and minor number. You might see error messages that supply only the major and minor number. This can be frustrating unless you know that devices.txt can help you figure out what the device actually is. Take some time to browse the entire file because it contains some interesting information that answers many FAQs others have had and you might have as well.

If you want to look at all the files in dev, use this command:

```
# ls -l --sort=none | less
```

The --sort=none argument keeps the devices mostly grouped by major numbers for your viewing pleasure; piping to the less command allows you to use the PageUp and PageDown keys to navigate the long list.

The Replacement Device Filesystem—DEVFS

A new, alternative device filesystem known as the Device Filesystem (DEVFS) will soon come into more common use. It only has entries for devices that you have attached to your system and the naming convention is different from the traditional system. It can be used in parallel with the traditional system.

For example, /dev/hda1 is named /dev/ide/hd/c0b0t0u0p1 and is a symbolic link to /dev/ide/host0/bus0/target0/lun0/part1.

It seems more complicated only because you are not yet familiar with it.

DEVFS is similar to the /proc filesystem in that it is a virtual filesystem; the devices exist in memory and not as actual files on the drive. Why use DEVFS? There are some limitations to the use of major and minor numbers (there are 128 maximum available), which is why H. Peter Anvin maintains devices.txt, and access to new device numbers is limited. The address space could be enlarged, but this creates some performance issues. It also gets around the requirement that the /dev directory be on the root filesystem, so read-only root filesystems are difficult to unrealistic. You can't share a root filesystem using NFS, and you can't embed it in a ROM filesystem. The workarounds require creating a ramdisk and copying the contents of /dev there.

Non-UNIX filesystems can't be mounted as the root filesystem because they don't support the special characteristics of UNIX filesystems. The devfs can solve these types of problems and provide even more flexibility to Linux. FreeBSD, BeOS, Plan9 and QNX use devfs, so it's not a new concept, just new to Linux.

For additional details, read the Linux DEVFS FAQ at `http://www.atnf.csiro.au/~rgooch/linux/docs/devfs.html`.

Naming Conventions Used for Block and Character Devices

The traditional naming system for block devices has been in use for a while. In the preceding excerpt from devices.txt, you can see that the device name for the first partition of the first IDE disk would be /dev/hda1. If it were a SCSI disk, it would be /dev/sda1 (shown elsewhere in devices.txt). All the names can be found in devices.txt, and all the devices that have been created on your system can be found in the /dev directory. There can also be links there; for example, /dev/cdrom can actually be a link back to the actual device that is your CD-ROM (perhaps /dev/hdc? or /dev/scd0?), and /dev/mouse and /dev/modem are commonly used links in the /dev/directory.

Using mknod to Create Devices

Did you notice that devices are listed in /dev/ that you don't have? That's because they need to exist in /dev before the system can use the actual device if you happen to actually install the hardware at some point in the future; the system won't create the device files on-the-fly. If you need a file in /dev that's not already there for some reason, these special files are created with the mknod command. The process is pretty straightforward as long as you know what type of device you are creating and what the major and minor numbers are. From the man page, the syntax is

```
#  mknod [OPTION]... NAME TYPE [MAJOR MINOR]
```

The useful option -m allows you to set the mode (like with chmod) at file creation instead of doing it separately.

The NAME, TYPE, MAJOR, and MINOR number can all be obtained from devices.txt, which even has a block of experimental numbers if you are inclined to experiment.

What Are Character Devices, Block Devices, and Special Devices?

A *character device* is a file that handles data one character at a time and processes them in order. Examples include TTY devices, SCSI tape drives, the keyboard, audio devices, the Coda network filesystem, and many more.

Block devices have a beginning, an end, and a fixed size; data can be written and read from anywhere inside them. Because a block device can be much larger than the data it contains, special utilities such as tar and cpio work with the files' data rather than the files' size, so they can store and retrieve the data directly on the block device rather than require a formatted file on a block device. This works especially well with tape devices because they are character devices rather than block devices and aren't formatted in the way that block devices are formatted.

Some special devices of interest are as follows:

/dev/null—This is the null device, also called the *bit bucket*. Any output written to it is discarded. It is useful to redirect messages to it when you don't want them displayed on the standard output or written to a file.

/dev/zero—This device has an inexhaustible supply of zeros; use all you want—it makes more. It's very useful for writing strings of zeros to a device or file.

What Filesystems Are Available on Your Red Hat 7.2 System?

You will likely be working with local filesystems—those on the computer you are using. What do you have? Although the output will vary from system to system because of hardware and kernel settings, the test system used for this chapter, when examined by

```
# cat /proc/filesystems
```

tells us what we are dealing with on our local computer:

```
nodev       proc
nodev       sockfs
nodev       tmpfs
nodev       shm
nodev       pipefs
            ext2
            iso9660
nodev       devfs
nodev       devpts
            ext3
            vfat
nodev       autofs
nodev     binfmt_misc
```

The entries *not* preceded by nodev are of interest to us.

What Kinds of Filesystems Are Available to Linux?

We can separate filesystems into two broad categories: network and disk filesystems, discussed in the following sections.

> **NOTE**
>
> Although there are encrypted filesystem for Linux, none are included in Red Hat 7.2. You can see more information at http://www.linuxdoc.org/HOWTO/Loopback-Encrypted-Filesystem-HOWTO.html.

10

MANAGING THE FILESYSTEMS

Network Filesystems

Network filesystems are physically somewhere else, but appear as if they are mounted on your local computer. Some common types are

- NFS—The Network File systems was developed by Sun and is in common use. It has no built-in security because it was originally designed to run over friendly networks. While considered problematic by some, it is easy to implement. It is typically used between UNIX peers.

- SMB—The network-focused System Message Block protocol was developed by Microsoft. The Linux implementation is known as Samba and can work quite well until Microsoft again changes the protocol slightly. It is typically used between Linux and Microsoft Windows peers.

Disk Filesystems

Disk filesystems are what you will find on a physical device, such as the hard drive in a desktop computer.

- FAT is a disk-oriented, table based (a linked list) filesystem used by Microsoft. It has been regularly extended to add functionality. Microsoft's Enterprise-level filesystem is known as NTFS.

- ext2, ext3, and reiserFS are inode-based (as are other UNIX filesystems).

Examining the ext2 Filesystem

In recent times, the ext2 filesystem has been the standard filesystem for Linux, although other filesystems have been used and are currently in use. For Red Hat 7.2 users, the current state of the art is the ext3 filesystem. Because it shares so much in common with the ext2 filesystem, we'll look at the ext2 filesystem and then at the ext3 filesystem.

ext2 Characteristics

The original Extended File System filesystem was named ext, and the second version was named, curiously, ext2. The filesystem native to Linux continues to be improved, so you can see where the ext3 filesystem name came from. The ext2 filesystem can accommodate files as large as 2GB, directories as large as 2TB, and a maximum filename length of 255 characters. (With special kernel patches, this limit can be increased to 1024 characters if the standard length is insufficient for your use.) One of the significant improvements in the ext2 filesystem was the capability of the filesystem itself to allocate and use empty space in a very efficient manner.

The usage of space is so efficient that ext2 filesystems typically don't need de-fragmenting. (This, then, is the answer to a FAQ: A defragmentation program for the ext2 filesystem does exist, but it is infrequently used, isn't typically included with standard Linux distributions such as Red Hat Linux 7.2, and isn't recommended for general use. So there you have it.) The dynamic allocation of resources is also the source of one Achilles heel for the ext2 file system. When a file is deleted, its inode is erased and the data blocks associated with it are freed; they might very well be re-allocated immediately and the old data lost forever. File undeletion utilities are available for the ext2 filesystem, but they aren't likely to be successful on a busy, multiuser system. On a home system, the chance of success is much greater, although not guaranteed by any means.

Synchronizing the Filesystem with sync

Because Linux uses buffers when writing to devices, the write won't occur until the buffer is full, until the kernel tells it to, or if you tell it to by using the sync command. Traditionally, the command is given twice, as in the following:

```
# sync ; sync
```

It's unnecessary overkill to do it twice.

---

ext2 Structure

Every filesystem varies in structure. Different structures are used for various purposes that are concerned with efficiency, security, and even proprietary designs to deliberately limit cross-compatibility. The ext2 filesystem was designed to follow UNIX design concepts, particularly "everything is a file." For example, a directory in the ext2 filesystem is simply a file containing the names of the files to be found in that directory in addition to the locations of those files. The list of names is linked so that space isn't wasted because of varying filename lengths.

What Is an Inode?

A file in the ext2 filesystem begins with the inode, which contains the following description of the file: the file type, its access rights, its owners, several timestamps, the file size, and pointers to data blocks that hold the information that is in the file. When you want to access a file, the kernel uses those pointers to calculate where the data resides physically on the disk.

What Are Symbolic Links?

Because of the structure of the ext2 filesystem, several names can be associated with a single file, allowing the use of symbolic links. In effect, you create another inode that references already existing data. The link appears in a directory listing as if it were a file, and standard I/O functions are used by accessing either the link name or the original name. The primary benefit of links is the reduction of space necessary to store duplicate files.

Physical Structure on the Disk

If you were to visualize the ext2 filesystem on the physical disk, it would resemble a series of boxes known as *blocks*. The first block on the disk is a special block that contains the boot sector; each subsequent block contains the operating system, applications, and your data.

Each individual block is made up of smaller groups of data: a *superblock* (called by that name because it contains redundant information about the overall filesystem), redundant filesystem descriptors, a bitmap of the block, a bitmap of the inode table, information from the inode table, and the data blocks. The redundant information is useful for reliability and recoverability from disasters and errors.

How big are these blocks? The default size is 1024 bytes, but the size can be made smaller or larger when the filesystem is first created. The optimum size is determined by the application of the particular machine. If you typically use very large files, a larger block size can speed up disk I/O operations at the expense of slower I/O for smaller files; the reverse is also true. For an individual system, it might require monitoring over time and benchmarking before an optimal value is determined. Block sizes can be selected when the partition is initially formatted.

Verifying File Integrity with the `fsck` Utility

ext2 filesystem integrity is assured through the use of the `fsck` program, one of five commands in the ext2 library that are use to maintain and modify the ext2 filesystem.

The filesystem state is tracked in the ext2 filesystem. A special field in the superblock tells the kernel that, after the filesystem is mounted read/write, it is marked as `not clean`; when it is property unmounted, it is marked as `clean`. If a filesystem isn't unmounted properly, it could contain corrupt data because all the file data might not have been written to it. (This is what the journaling filesystems such as ext3 strive to eliminate.) When the system is booted, this flag is checked and if it is `not clean`, the program `fsck` is run. (Actually, `fsck` is a wrapper program that runs the appropriate version of `fsck`: `fsck.minix`, `fsck.ext2`, `fsck.ext3`, `fsck.reiserfs`, `fsck.msdos`, and fsck.vfat.) If the kernel detects an inconsistency in the superblock field, the filesystem is marked erroneous, and the filesystem check is forced even if other indicators suggest that fsck doesn't need to be run.

By default, the system will run fsck on a filesystem after a periodic number of reboots regardless of the status of the clean flag, triggered by a mount counter kept in the superblock or after a predetermined amount of time has elapsed since the last reboot (information also kept in the superblock). These parameters can be adjusted through the tune2fs command, and this command can also be used to modify how the kernel handles the erroneous flag and, interestingly, the number of blocks reserved for the superuser, also known as root. This latter option is useful on very large or very small disks to make more disk space available to the user.

How fsck Works

When fsck is run, it performs a number of evaluations of the information available in the filesystem if it detects a directory that cannot be traced back to the root or an undeleted file with a zero link count. It places these directories and files in the /lost+found directory that is created on each physical partition by the filesystem formatting process. Some blocks are reserved for this and other uses of the superuser. It is possible to reduce this allocation to free additional space for regular users by special arguments to the formatting program mke2fs.

Examining the ext2 Filesystem

To examine the structure of your ext2 filesystem, the program dumpe2fs is provided in Red Hat 7.2. A list of typical program output is shown later in the chapter.

The syntax for the command is

```
dumpe2fs [ -bfhixV ] [ -ob superblock ] [ -oB blocksize ] device
```

Two useful options from the man page are as follows:

-b—Prints the blocks that are reserved as bad in the filesystem.

-f—Forces dumpe2fs to display a filesystem even though it might have some filesystem feature flags that dumpe2fs might not understand (and that can cause some of dumpe2fs's display to be suspect).

The next two options might be useful in recovering lost data. The stressed out and desperate system administrator (you) would be the "filesystem wizard" referred to.

-ob superblock—Use a specific alternate superblock when examining the file system. This option isn't usually needed except by a filesystem wizard who is examining the remains of a very badly corrupted filesystem.

10

MANAGING THE
FILESYSTEMS

-oB blocksize—Use blocks of "blocksize" bytes when examining the filesystem. This option isn't usually needed except by a filesystem wizard who is examining the remains of a very badly corrupted filesystem.

Another program, debugfs, can also be used to manipulate an ext2 filesystem as well as repair and recover a damaged filesystem. Because it is such a powerful command, it doesn't run by default with the capability to write any changes to the filesystem; that functionality must be explicitly enabled when the command is run. By entering the help command at the debugfs prompt, a menu of command options is displayed.

Alternative Filesystems for Linux

Because of the design of the Virtual File System, it is a comparatively easy to use alternative filesystem with Linux.

Most recently, there has been development of *journaling* filesystems for Linux. In general for a journaling system, metadata is written to a journal on the disk before it is actually used to modify the file. This way, if a system crashes, there is enough uncorrupted data available to finish writing to the original file. Several different schemes are employed using different combinations of real data and metadata—the intent being to make the file system consistent with what it would have been had the unplanned shutdown not occurred. A tradeoff always exists between speed and the amount of data written to the journal; the ext3 filesystem provides options to the system administrator (detailed later in this chapter) that deal with these choices. The problem with an ext2 filesystem is that, if the system crashes, an fsck of even a moderately large system can take a lot of time. On large systems, this time could account for hours of down time.

Commercial UNIX systems use some form of journaling filesystem, and XFS from SGI is being ported to Linux as well as IBM's JFS (based on the JFS from OS/2, not their AIX operating system). There is continued work on the ext3 filesystem, but currently the Reiser filesystem (reiserFS) is slightly more developed. Even though ext3 is stable enough for use as the default filesystem in Red Hat 7.2 and has been tested on production systems by Red Hat and others, it and all other journaling filesystems are still considered beta quality for mission critical machines even though they are currently in widespread use. For now, the ext2 filesystem remains the de facto filesystem for Linux although it is expected that a successor standard filesystem will emerge in early 2002. With Red Hat support for ext3, that is the likely candidate, but the choice of so many filesystems for Linux is nice to have.

Ext3

Red Hat has chosen to support the ext3 filesystem as the journaling filesystem for its distribution. Other distributions such as SuSE and Mandrake support the Reiser file system. At this writing, JFS and XFS are available for limited mainstream use, but it is more likely that they will be primarily used to allow existing JFS and XFS users to migrate their existing filesystems to Linux.

Red Hat's rational for choosing ext3 is compelling. Although it does provide the availability, data integrity, and speed similar to the other journaling filesystem choices, it has one unique advantage: it's an easy transition from ext2 to ext3, and the transition is forgiving of mistakes along the way.

You can choose to use the ext3 filesystem during a fresh install, or convert an ext2 filesystem after the fact when you upgrade your present system to Red Hat 7.2.

Converting an Existing ext2 Filesystem to ext3

You will use the tune2fs utility to add the journal to an existing ext2 filesystem. In our example, we will be changing /dev/hda2, an already formatted ext2 partition.

```
# tune2fs -j /dev/hda2
```

It doesn't matter if hda2 is mounted or unmounted at the time, the only difference being that if it is mounted, you will see a new file, .journal, in the directory.

Next, edit the appropriate line for /dev/hda2 in /etc/fstab and change the value from ext2 to ext3. It will be mounted as an ext3 filesystem the next time you reboot.

If you decide to migrate your root filesystem, it cannot be unmounted to run tune2fs -j on it, but that won't matter. You'll just see the .journal file on it when you're done. But you do need to create an initrd file (an initial ramdisk that contains a small kernel and enough of the Linux OS to load drivers so that the real kernel and the rest of the operating system can load) in order to load the ext3 driver so that the root partition will be mounted as an ext3 partition. (Even if you forget that, however, your system will still boot, but it will mount the root partition as ext2. That's very clever—none of the other journaling filesystems are as forgiving.)

NOTE

When compiling a new kernel, make certain to include ext3 filesystem support in your new kernel.

Making an Initial Ramdisk

Before you reboot, you should run the `mkinitrd` utility:

```
# mkinitrd 2.4.8-12 initrd-2.4.8.12.img
```

The first argument after the `mkinitrd` command is the version of the kernel you want to use. It doesn't have to be the version you are currently using, but it must match the version you use when you boot. The second argument is the name of the initrd file that will be placed in the /boot directory. The name can be anything; what is shown is just the usual naming convention. Other options are explained in the man page.

Then edit /etc/lilo.conf or /boot/grub.conf to change the `initrd` loaded at boot time. You would add the following line

```
initrd=/boot/initrd-2.4.8-12.img
```

in our example to the appropriate LILO stanza. For GRUB, you would add the same line beneath the kernel line in the section that references your kernel.

As an additional benefit, any other operating system, such as BeOS or Windows (with the appropriate drivers) and other Unix systems that have drivers to access ext2 partitions, can also access ext3 partitions because, to them (and their drivers) it looks just like an ext2 filesystem.

Let's examine the other claims that Red Hat makes for ext3 in support of its choice.

Availability

Like all journaling filesystems, the traditional filesystem check (`fsck`) isn't necessary. Although only mildly annoying on a 20GB drive on your machine at home, imagine the seemingly endless hours that a `fsck` would take to run on a terabyte of data. This feature is shared in common with the other journaling filesystems. The time needed to recover from an improper shutdown of a journaled filesystem isn't dependent on the filesystem size, but the amount of data in the journal. The ext3 filesystem has several options that, depending on your needs, allow you to select how much information is journaled. According to Red Hat, the typical journal requires a second or so to be read and recovered.

Data Integrity Versus Speed

You can trade off data integrity for speed. You can choose to expose some of your data to potential damage in the case of an improper shutdown in exchange for faster data handling, or sacrifice some speed to keep the state of the filesystem consistent with the state of the operating system.

Three modes are available:

Writeback—Allows old data to stay in the filesystem, attaining the fastest speed possible. It doesn't schedule any data writes; it just allows the kernel's 30-second writeback code to flush the buffer.

Ordered—Keeps the data consistent, but with some sacrifice in speed (the default mode for Red Hat).

Journal—Requires more disk space to journal more data. You might see slower performance because data is written twice, but there are some speed benefits if you are doing synchronous data writes as in database operations.

For most of us, the default selection represents a good tradeoff. Red Hat supports booting from an ext3 formatted root filesystem with the proper drivers loaded in the initrd image.

The mode is selected by using the appropriate mount option in /etc/fstab.

The Reiser Filesystem (reiserFS)

The other popular journaling filesystem is the written-from-scratch Reiser Filesystem, reiserFS. It is supported primarily in the SuSE and Mandrake distributions that support booting from a reiserFS root filesystem. ReiserFS offers similar features to ext3, but there is no easy migration path from an already existing ext2 partition (all data must be backed up, the partition reformatted, and the data restored), and reiserFS doesn't work well over NFS mounts. File recovery is impossible on a reiserFS filesystem.

Red Hat does offer reiserFS, but doesn't offer support for booting from it as the root partition filesystem, nor does it offer the choice to format non-root partitions as reiserFS during the installation process. It is offered primarily for compatibility with existing reiserFS partitions you might want to access.

JFS and XFS

Both SGI with XFS and IBM with its JFS are contributing these filesystems to Linux. Because these filesystems are generally suited for Enterprise systems rather than home or small office systems, it seems likely that they are being offered to ease the transition of IRIX and AIX users to Linux without having to reformat their very large filesystems.

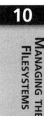

10

MANAGING THE
FILESYSTEMS

Neither are offered with Red Hat 7.2, but the adventurous can patch the kernel and obtain the filesystem tools. SGI has offered a CD that allows a recent version of Red Hat to be installed with XFS support; it is likely that they will offer one to support Red Hat 7.2.

DOS Filesystems

The extent of DOS filesystem support in Linux is often surprising to newcomers, but the DOS filesystem proved to be a viable option in the early years of Linux. Because Microsoft has been the dominant operating system on Intel computers, Linux has always worked toward co-existence.

vfat, FAT12, FAT16, and FAT32

Microsoft DOS and the consumer-oriented Windows operating systems use a filesystem known as *FAT (File Allocation Table)*. The number following the FAT name indicates the size of the space for naming address pointers; the more space, the larger a section of contiguous space can be identified and accessed. Early versions of FAT were designed for floppy use and couldn't address a large storage medium without using inefficient large blocks; FAT12 (the type used on floppy disks) is still used by default for floppy disks, however. (Linux commonly and easily uses FAT12 for floppy disks, although minix and ext2 have their uses with the biggest concern being how much usable space is left after formatting the disk). Filenames longer than 11 characters cannot be accommodated on older versions of FAT. The most recent version of FAT is known as FAT32 and is backward compatible with other versions of FAT; older versions aren't forward compatible.

The Red Hat 7.2 Linux kernel can access all versions of FAT formatted partitions (including floppy disks) using the vfat kernel module.

umsdos

First of all, the umsdos filesystem exists for the same reason that Linux first used the minix filesystem. It was commonly available, and it worked. Using a umsdos filesystem, Linux could be installed on the same partition as DOS or Windows without having to re-partition a disk that already had the other OS on it. Dual booting (two or more operating systems on a single computer) was the norm for early users and experimenters of Linux. Also, reliable and safe partition resizing applications have only recently become available. The use of umsdos was a useful convenience and a good example of ingenuity. In order for Linux to use files on a DOS or FAT partition in a multiuser environment, the inode information relating to file permissions must be available. Unfortunately, there is no provision in DOS or FAT filesystems for storing this information. The design of those filesystems never anticipated a need for that kind of information; it was designed for a single-user system.

A modification to FAT that permits it to be used in the multiuser Linux environment is called umsdos. A special file named --linux-.--- is added to each directory that contains the additional information used by Linux. These files are synchronized with the current state using the /sbin/umssync command. When initializing an existing DOS directory, this is known as *promoting* the directory, and it can be done manually. It can also be done automatically on mounting.

> **NOTE**
>
> Because umsdos support is increasingly less desirable and useful given more modern options, umssync is no longer provided with Red Hat. The umsdos tools can still be obtained independently, and then compiled and installed if you need them.

If you want to mount an existing DOS partition as a DOS partition, use vfat as the type (you might need to insmod vfat.o to load the module) to be able to view long filenames if the version of FAT you are accessing allows this. If you need to use restrictive permissions for the DOS partition, you can set some permissions globally using special options with the mount command. If you need to use file permissions selectively, use umsdos as the type, promote the filesystem, and set permissions as needed.

CD-ROM Filesystems

To the average user, the filesystem of a CD-ROM looks just like a native Linux filesystem. It's really not the native filesystem, but the features of the Virtual File System make it possible for it to appear that way. The CD-ROM filesystem standards continue to evolve to accommodate new technology.

iso9660

The filesystem typically used on a CD-ROM is known as iso9660, the name of the standard that defines the format. Each operating system translates the iso9660 filesystem into the native filesystem of the operating system (with some restrictions). Several extensions have been created to address certain special needs. The Rock Ridge extension allows long filenames and Unix-like symbolic links. The Joliet extension allows Unicode characters and long filenames, useful when dealing with non-English languages. El Torito

CDs contain a bootable image and, with a suitable BIOS, can boot an operating system from the CD.

UDF

This is the filesystem that is used on DVD-ROMs, and is known as the Universal Disk Format. It has a number of built-in features that the iso9660 filesystem would need extensions to accommodate.

Creating Filesystems

Once a disk has been partitioned for a specific filesystem, it is necessary to create a filesystem on it. The first process in the DOS world is known as *low-level formatting* and the latter as simple *formatting* In the UNIX world, the latter is known as *creating a filesystem*.

An unformatted disk storage device (a floppy disk, hard disk drive, or removable media) typically arrives to you with a low-level format (usually handled by a tool such as `fdisk` or `superformat`) already done. Although it might have a boot block and (possibly) partition information, it typically lacks the file structure needed for a filesystem. If it's something other than a floppy disk, examine it with `fdisk` or another utility of your choice and modify the partition table accordingly.

Zip disks are typically delivered with a single partition numbered 4. This has some arcane relevance to Apple computer users, but none of any importance to Linux users. Most of the advice you see about Zip disks simply notes that you use partition 4 in mounting the disk and leaves it at that. If it really bothers you, change it.

To create the filesystem structure, we need to do what is referred to as a high-level format. For FAT filesystems, this is accomplished by the `format` command. In Linux, the `mke2fs` command is used to create an ext2 and an ext3 filesystem, the `mkreiserfs` command is used to make a Reiser filesystem, and the `mkdosfs` command is used to create a DOS filesystem.

Other commands are available for other filesystems if you need them. They are as follows:

- `mkdosfs`
- `mke2fs`
- `mkfs`
- `mkfs.bfs`

- mkfs.ext2

- mkfs.minix

- mkfs.msdos

- mkfs.reiserfs

- mkfs.vfat

- mkreiserfs

mke2fs

A complete review of all the options and syntax for mke2fs can be found in man mke2fs. Some useful arguments from the man page are as follows:

To check for bad blocks during filesystem creation, use the -c option.

Using the -N option will allow you to override the default number of inodes created, typically to allow additional usable disk space; the default is usually a good choice.

By default, the system allocates 5% of the blocks to the superuser to be used in file recovery during fsck; lower this value with the -m option at your peril if you want to free up some space on the disk.

The -L option is used to give the volume a label, useful if you need to be reminded of the use of that filesystem and have many filesystems to work with or providing some flexibility in identifying volumes in /etc/fstab.

As a last-ditch effort for recovering a munged filesystem, use the -s option to write the superblock and escriptors only, leaving the information in the inodes unchanged; run fsck afterward.

As you can see, there are several options to make more space available for the regular users at the expense of the superuser, who would be using that space to recover damaged files. Although being wasteful isn't a positive attribute, the default settings accommodate most users and hard disks are getting less expensive all the time.

mk3fs

There is no mk3fs, although logically it would seem as if it would exist (and it is even mentioned on the Red Hat ext3 beta Web page). To make a new ext3 filesystem, you use the mke2fs command with the -j or -J option. Use the tune2fs command on an existing ext2 filesystem to add journaling.

```
# tune2fs /dev/hdxn -j
```

10

MANAGING THE
FILESYSTEMS

The appropriate arguments from the man page are

-j—Adds an ext3 journal to the filesystem. If the -J option isn't specified, the default journal parameters will be used to create an appropriately sized journal (given the size of the filesystem) stored within the filesystem. Note that you must be using a kernel, which has ext3 support in order to actually make use of the journal.

-J journal-options—Overrides the default ext3 journal parameters. Journal options are comma separated, and can take an argument using the equal (=) sign. The following journal option is supported:

size=journal-size—Creates a journal stored in the filesystem of size journal-size megabytes. The size of the journal must be at least 1024 filesystem blocks (that is, 1MB if using 1k blocks, 4MB if using 4k blocks, and so on) and can be no more than 102,400 filesystem blocks. There must be enough free space in the filesystem to create a journal of that size.

device=external-journal—This option will attach the filesystem to an external journal that must have already been created with the command mke2fs -O journal_dev external journal; the journal and the data files don't have to be on the same device.

> **NOTE**
>
> These two options are mutually exclusive.

In order to select the ext3 journaling mode, you must add the appropriate entry in /etc/fstab. Here is an excerpt from the man page for mount that describes the mounting options for ext3 partitions:

The ext3 filesystem is new version of the ext2 file system, which has been enhanced with journaling. It supports the same options as ext2, as well as the following additions:

journal=update—Updates the ext3 file system's journal to the current format.

journal=inum—When a journal already exists, this option is ignored. Otherwise, it specifies the number of the inode that will represent the ext3 file system's journal file; ext3 will create a new journal, overwriting the old contents of the file whose inode number is inum.

noload—Does not load the ext3 file system's journal on mounting.

data=journal / data=ordered / data=writeback—Specifies the journaling mode for file data. Metadata is always journaled.

journal—All data is committed into the journal prior to being written into the main filesystem.

ordered—This is the default mode. All data is forced directly out to the main file system prior to its metadata being committed to the journal.

writeback—Data ordering isn't preserved. Data can be written into the main file system after its metadata has been committed to the journal. This is rumored to be the highest-throughput option. It guarantees internal file system integrity; however, it can allow old data to appear in files after a crash and journal recovery.

mkreiserfs

A complete review of all the argument options and syntax for creating a Reiser file-system can be found in man mkreiserfs. The syntax and arguments are

```
mkreiserfs [ -h r5 | tea | rupasov ] [ -v 1 | 2 ] [ -q ] device
[ size-in-blocks ]
```

-h r5 | tea | rupasov—This specifies the name of the hash function filenames in directories that will be sorted with. Choose one of the preceding. r5 is default.

-v 1 | 2—This specifies the format that a new filesystem has to be.

-q—This makes the progress bar much less verbose. Useful when logged in via a slow link.

If you are logged in to a system remotely over a slow link and are formatting the partition with reiserFS, the -q option makes the progress bar less verbose. The man page provides more details, but the default values for reiserFS work well.

mkdosfs

It's possible to create DOS filesystems without owning any Microsoft software. A complete review of all the argument options and syntax for creating a DOS filesystem can be found in man mkdosfs.

Some useful arguments are as follows:

Use the -c option to check for bad blocks during filesystem creation.

If you want an image file with a FAT filesystem for testing, the -C option will do it for you followed by the name of the file to be created plus the block count desired. This would be a nice option for the other mkfs commands as well.

Mkdosfs is smart enough to select the best fit when choosing the appropriate version of FAT, but -F followed by 12, 16, or 32 will force a choice.

If you want a volume name of up to 11 characters, precede it with the -n option.

10

MANAGING THE
FILESYSTEMS

The `-v` option causes the command to execute in verbose mode, providing additional information to you if needed.

The command `dosfsck` can be used to check a FAT filesystem.

Mounting Filesystems

Filesystems in UNIX are very flexible in that they need not be physically present on your computer if you have network access to other filesystems on other machines. The Linux filesystem makes it appear as if all the filesystems are local and mounted somewhere on the root filesystem. As the system administrator, you must decide what filesystems are to be made available and where they will be attached, or mounted, to the root filesystem.

Why Filesystems Need to be Mounted

In Linux (and its UNIX cousins) all filesystems—whether local, remote, images on a disk, or in memory—are mounted on a single point known as *root* (which isn't the same as the root operator also known as the superuser). This mount point is written as a forward slash, `/`, which is read and pronounced root. The resulting file directory hierarchy all starts from `/`. Once mounted, the physical location of the files is unimportant.

Where Are They Mounted?

Any filesystem can be mounted anywhere, but some places are more useful than others. Even if the filesystems are different (FAT, ext2, HPFS, ntfs, and so on), the Linux kernel modules and the VFS make them all appear as part of the directory tree as native files.

The `mount` Command

Filesystems are mounted with the `mount` command and unmounted, curiously enough, with the `umount` command. Why the command isn't named unmount probably has an origin in UNIX lore, but because that's its name, just learn it whether it makes sense to you or not. The `mount` command looks at the file /etc/fstab, which is the Filesystem Table and has useful information about how the system administrator wants the filesystems to be mounted. The syntax for `mount` is

```
mount -t type filesystem_to_be mounted      mount_point
```

An explanation of the components of the `mount` command is as follows:

type—Always preceded by the `-t` argument, followed by a space and the type of filesystem you are mounting. Typical filesystems available are: ext2, vfat, iso9660, umsdos, msdos, hpfs, hfs, ntfs, and others. For many filesystems, `mount` can detect what type they are, and this argument is superfluous.

`filesystem_to_be` mounted (as represented by the partition on which it resides)—This is typically in the form of `/dev/hdxn`, `/dev/scxn`, `/dev/fdx` and is the device name of the filesystem you want to `mount`.

`mount_point`—The place in the directory tree where you want to `mount` the filesystem. Temporary mount points are usually under `/mnt`; you can create a special, serendipitous `mount` point anywhere you have permission to do so. Curiously, you can `mount` a filesystem over part of an existing filesystem. For example, if you have an existing directory at /foo with a single file named bar and `mount` a filesystem at /foo that includes a file named snafu, a listing of the directory /foo won't show the file bar, but only the file snafu. To show both files is a feature called *transparency*, which unfortunately isn't in the current Linux repertoire.

The only real restriction to "mount anything anywhere" is that the critical system files in /bin, /etc, /lib ,/dev, /proc, and /tmp need to be accessed at bootup, which typically means that they need to be on the same physical disk. If they can't be accessed at bootup, Linux won't load and run.

umount

To unmount a filesystem, the `umount` command is used with the syntax:

`umount mount_point`

You can also unmount by device name:

`umount /dev/<device name>`

Caution

You can `unmount` everything that the system doesn't require to run (or isn't currently using) with `umount -a`, but this is a very bad idea on a multiuser, networked system because your users will undoubtedly lose access to some or all of their files. So, as any good sysadmin will tell you, don't do that.

Numerous mount options exist that are invoked by preceding them (or a comma-delimited string of them) with the `-o` switch. These are used primarily in the /etc/fstab file and are listed in the man page for `mount` as well as the `fstab` section of this chapter.

10

MANAGING THE FILESYSTEMS

Mounting Automatically with `fstab`

A special file, /etc/fstab, exists to provide the system with predetermined options and mountpoints so that the filesystems can be automatically mounted or manually mounted with minimal typing and without having to recall arcane Linux syntax. Special options exist for specific filesystems, particularly FAT filesystems, so file permissions can be set globally (because the FAT filesystems don't provide for that functionality).

The /etc/fstab file can only be written to by the superuser. The commands `fsck`, `mount`, and `umount` all read information from /etc/fstab. Each filesystem gets its own line with the information separated by tabs.

A full description of `fstab` can be found in man `fstab`. A brief description follows:

On each line, the first field indicates the block device or remote filesystem that will be mounted.

The second field identifies the mount point on the local system where the filesystem will be mounted.

The third field is the filesystem type.

The forth field is a comma-delimited list of `mount` options. General options include `noauto` (the filesystem is never automatically mounted) and `user` (indicates that a regular user can mount the device, typically used with CD-ROM drives that regular users are allowed to access).

Options, as taken from the man pages, include

> `exec`—Permits execution of binaries.
>
> `noauto`—Can only be mounted explicitly (this means that the `-a` option won't cause the filesystem to be mounted).
>
> `noexec`—Doesn't allow execution of any binaries on the mounted filesystem. This option might be useful for a server that has filesystems containing binaries for architectures other than its own.
>
> `nosuid`—Doesn't allow set-user-identifier or set-group-identifier bits to take effect. (This seems safe, but is in fact rather unsafe if you have suidperl(1) installed.)
>
> `ro`—Mounts the filesystem read-only.
>
> `rw`—Mounts the filesystem read-write.

sync—All I/O to the filesystem should be done synchronously.

user—Allows an ordinary user to mount the filesystem. This option implies the options noexec, nosuid, and nodev (unless overridden by subsequent options, as in the option line: user,exec,dev,suid).

For FAT filesystems, the options are

umask=value—Sets the umask (the bitmask of the permissions that aren't present). The default is the umask of the current process. The value is given in octal.

conv=b[inary] / conv=t[ext] / conv=a[uto]—The FAT file system can perform CRLF<—>NL (MS-DOS text format to UNIX text format) conversion in the kernel. The following conversion modes are available:

•binary—No translation is performed. This is the default.

•text—A CRLF<—>NL translation is performed on all files.

•auto—A CRLF<—>NL translation is performed on all files that don't have a "well-known binary" extension. The list of known extensions can be found at the beginning of fs/fat/misc.c (as of 2.0, the list is exe, com, bin, app, sys, drv, ovl, ovr, obj, lib, dll, pif, arc, zip, lha, lzh, zoo, tar, z, arj, tz, taz, tzp, tpz, gz, tgz, deb, gif, bmp, tif, gl, jpg, pcx, tfm, vf, gf, pk, pxl, dvi).

For iso9660, the interesting option is un-hide, which shows hidden and associated files.

Remaining Fields

The fifth field is used by dump (a backup program) to determine whether the filesystem should be *dumped* (backed up); 1 is yes, and 0 is no.

The sixth field is used by fsck to determine how fsck needs to interact the filesystem— 0 means that fsck is never run on the filesystem (a FAT32 filesystem, for example); 1 means that fsck will be run on the drive at predetermined time. 2 is recommended for non root filesystems so that fsck isn't run on them as frequently.

fstab Example

Here is a simple fstab file from a system with a RAID0 ext3 root partition and dual-booted with MS Windows.

```
LABEL=/12        /                ext3    defaults        1 1
none             /dev/pts         devpts  gid=5,mode=620  0 0
none             /proc            proc    defaults        0 0
none             /dev/shm         tmpfs   defaults        0 0
/dev/hda11       swap             swap    defaults        0 0
```

```
/dev/cdrom        /mnt/cdrom        iso9660 noauto,owner,kudzu,ro 0 0
/dev/fd0          /mnt/floppy         auto    noauto,owner,kudzu 0 0
/dev/hda1         /mnt/win_c          vfat        auto,quiet,exec 0 0
```

Notice the two entries marked with the `kudzu` option. This is the result of the actions of `updfstab`, which keeps `fstab` consistent with removable devices on the system like CD-ROMs, floppy drives, Zip and Jaz drives, LS-120 drives and some digital cameras. The `quiet` option for the Windows partition will suppress error messages and is recommended if you use the WINE program.

Editing `fstab`

As long as you understand the syntax and options of the fstab file, the superuser can edit the file with any text editor or with a tool such as linuxconf from the consoles or from the desktop.

Configuring RAID

Software RAID is surprisingly easy to implement in Red Hat 7.2 either during the initial installation of the system or after the fact. The effective use of software RAID requires both an understanding of what it does and some pre-planning before it is configured.

Hardware RAID, using a separate or on-board RAID controller is becoming increasingly affordable as hard drive prices are declining and IDE drive speeds are increasing. With improved driver support for more hardware RAID devices, hardware RAID is rapidly becoming a viable option as well for users who desire the benefits of RAID performance.

RAID Defined

RAID is not a way to guarantee against data corruption. (It will write corrupt data to the disk in the same manner as valid data.) However, some RAID levels can be used to help guaranty against data loss, improve performance, or combine several disks into one large virtual disk. The average home users will likely never use RAID because their systems aren't really mission critical. (Although once your files for work or school have been lost, you might feel differently.) Performance benefits of RAID aren't really an issue (most hardware works well enough out of the box for home use), and the cost of very large hard drives has dropped so low, so there is really no need to combine smaller disks into larger ones (unless your MP3 or .jpg collections have gotten out of hand). One of the useful RAID levels, linear, seems to be better handled with Logical Volume Management.

The RAID levels are

- linear mode—Multiple disks are combined into one physical device. The disks are appended to each other, so the first disk is filled first, and so on.
- RAID 0—Also know as *striped mode*, writes are done in parallel to approximately equal-sized devices. You will see some performance increase, but there is no data protection.
- RAID 1—Also know as *RAID mirroring*, this two or more equal-sized disks with none or additional spare disks. Write performance is slower than a single disk, but this version of software RAID offers some data protection. If data is damaged and a spare disk is available, the system seamlessly repairs itself.
- RAID 4—Similar to a RAID 0 array, but needs three or more disks and keeps parity information to protect data. Every data write creates a write to the parity disk as well, so that disk should be the fastest one on the system.
- RAID 5—Similar to RAID 4, but the parity data is distributed among the disks, improving performance and spare drives can be used; RAID 5 can't survive simultaneous multiple disk failures.
- RAID 10—A RAID-1 array of two RAID-0 arrays.
- RAID swap partitions—This has been a kernel feature for a while. Just create swap partitions on all the drives, add them appropriately to /etc/fstab, and manually give them all the same priority by adding the `pri=1 mount` option to each one.

If you want to use RAID, some preplanning is necessary for your hardware as well as a thorough read of the HOWTO so that you can better understand your options. The drive partitioning section of the Red Hat installation program, Ananconda, will allow you to easily configure software RAID arrays during the install process if you desire.

Moving a Filesystem

Many home users start with a single disk partition that mounts not only the root filesystem, but also all the other filesystems. Although this might work quite well for most home users, there might come a time when the disk becomes full. Adding another drive and moving part of the filesystem there isn't difficult, but is the source of many questions from new Linux users. For our example, we will install a new IDE hard drive to /dev/hdb (the primary slave drive), create a single partition on it, format it as an ext3 filesystem, and move all the user files located in /home to it. Once done, we will make it mount at the /home mountpoint.

First, physically install the drive, making certain that the master/slave jumpers are set correctly (it will be a slave drive) and checking that the jumpers are set correctly on the existing master drive. (Some drives require a different jumper setting for being a single master drive or a master drive with a slave drive.) This is a common error made even by people who are familiar with computer hardware. Once installed, the drive must be correctly detected by the BIOS. Many modern BIOSes have an autodetect feature, or you can manually enter the drive geometry by hand (the CHS information found on the drive label or documentation).

Most all modern large drives use the LBA setting (Logical Block Addressing) to deal with the BIOS size limitations. If the drive isn't detected, check 1) the power connection, 2) the IDE cable connection (the red stripe usually goes next to the power connector, but always double check), and 3) the master/slave jumpers. If all these are fine, you might have a bad drive, or the two hard drives (if made by different manufactures) might not be playing nice with each other. To check further, reset the jumper of the new drive to make it the master drive, disconnect the old drive and plug in the new one in its place. If the new drive is now correctly detected, suspect some incompatibility between the drives. Always make cable changes to the drives with the power off or you will damage the drive.

Once installed and recognized by the BIOS, a partition table needs to be created. Use `fdisk` (or the program of your choice) to create a single partition on the drive, remembering to write the changes to the MBR before you exit the program.

Formatting the drive is next. Because we are creating a new ext3 filesystem, we use this:

```
# mke2fs -c -j /dev/hdb1
```

Notice that we are checking the drive for bad blocks as we format. The program will identify those blocks and not use them; they would only corrupt our data if we didn't ignore them. Even though it adds considerable time to formatting the drive, an initial bad block check is always a good idea.

Next, we create a temporary mount point and mount the new partition:

```
# mkdir /mnt/newpartition
```

```
# mount -t ext3 /dev/hdb1 /mnt/newpartition
```

It's now time to copy all the files from /home to /mnt/newpartition. It's important that we preserve the time and date stamps for the files and the permissions. We're copying entire directories and subdirectories, so we use one of our three basic copying methods (`tar`, `cpio`, or `cp`) that best accommodates this:

```
# cp -a /home/* /mnt/newpartition
```

We need to modify /etc/fstab so that our new ext3 partition will be mounted correctly:

```
/dev/hdb3      /home ext3    defaults        1 1
```

Here, we have chosen to use the default `mount` options for the ext3 partition. The defaults are identical to those for the ext2 filesystem, as well as additionally selecting the default `data=ordered` journaling mode.

When we reboot, the new partition containing the copied files will be mounted at /home. But before we do that, cd to /home and enter this:

```
# touch thisistheoldhomepartition
```

Now we can mount the new partition:

```
# umount /mnt/newpartition
```

```
# mount /dev/hdb1 /home
```

Note that if you do an

```
# ls -al /home
```

you will not see the thisistheoldhomepartition file we created with the `touch` command. So what happened to the old files? They are still there, just hidden because we mounted a directory over them. When we are satisfied that all is well, we can unmount our newly created home partition and delete the files in the partition that contains the thisistheold-homepartition file. You can use this technique as a placeholder or warning for any temporarily mounted filesystem so that you don't mistakenly think the filesystem is mounted when it isn't.

Something New—LVM

It's time to start getting used to something different. The previous example used traditional concepts of running out of disk space and adding new drives. But what if this could be done transparently? That's where Logical Volume Management comes in: Disk space from multiple drives can be pooled into a single *logical volume*.

As with any new technology, there is a steep learning curve, not the least of which is the vocabulary. Our former understanding of partitions is now known as *physical volumes*, or *pv*. We add pv's to a volume group that defines a logical volume upon which we can create our filesystem.

LVM can also make *snapshots* of the LV that can then be mounted and backed up. "Big deal," you say. On a heavily used system, the files being backed up can change during the backup, and the restored files might be in an unstable condition.

Red Hat 7.2 doesn't yet implement LVM. A source at Red Hat stated that "LVM is unlikely to be included until a stable LVM implementation is integrated into the mainstream kernel." If you are adventurous, the LVM homepage at `http://www.sistina.com/products_lvm.htm` offers info, help, and downloadable files via FTP.

GUI Tools To Mount Filesystems

KDiskFree (KDE) displays all the filesystems noted in the /etc/fstab file, presents information about them, and allows you to easily mount and unmount them (see Figure 10.5). *KWickDisk (KDE)* allows mounts and unmounts from a panel applet. (It is the panel applet for KDiskFree.)

FIGURE 10.5

KDiskFree.

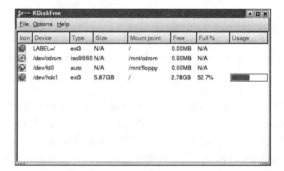

The User Mount Tool, accessed from the System menu as Disk Management, is a convenient way to mount and unmount filesystems (see Figure 10.6). It also allows you to format disks.

FIGURE 10.6

The User Mount Tool.

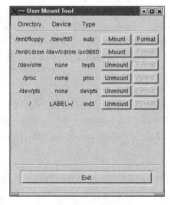

Floppy Formatter is a KDE tool to easily format a floppy in ext2 or Fat format. A comparable Gnome tool is Format A Floppy, which can also format ext2 and DOS floppy disks in 3.5" and 5.25" high and low density formats (see Figure 10.7).

FIGURE 10.7

Point and click for floppy formatting makes it easy. A large choice of formatting options (like a 1.7MB 3.5" floppy) would be nicer.

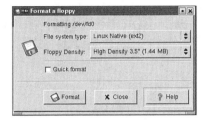

Other Console Tools

fsconf

The `fsconf` tool (see Figure 10.8) provides access to configuring `fstab`, configuring `nfs` mounts, setting user filesystem quotas, and automatically checking permissions on some important files. The interface looks slightly different when `fsconf` is started from a console.

FIGURE 10.8

Part of `linuxconf`, `fsconf` *can be used from the command line or as an X client. Shown here is the command line version of the interface.*

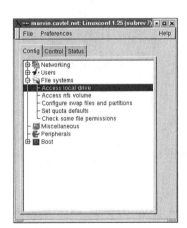

Figure 10.9 displays the contents of /etc/fstab and allows you to add additional entries. This presentation of information is more organized than what the traditional cat /etc/fstab command provides.

FIGURE **10.9**

If you highlight a particular partition and press the Enter key, you can then mount or unmount that partition.

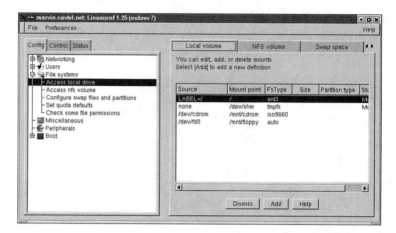

You must know the proper information that has to be entered (no GUI browsing or autodetection), but the input form structure (see Figure 10.10) is helpful.

FIGURE **10.10**

It might seem daunting, but the context-sensitive Help information for this screen is very good.

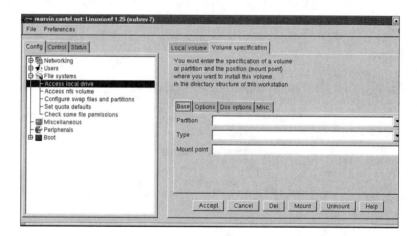

Red Hat used to provide a GUI interface to `linuxconf` called the Control Panel utility, but sadly, `linuxconf` seems to have fallen by the wayside as far as Red Hat is concerned.

e2label

The utility `e2label` can display or change the label of a device. (This can also be done with `tune2fs -L`.) For example, to change the label of /dev/hda4 to Storage:

```
# e2label /dev/hda4 Storage
```

Why label the device? You can use the label in /etc/fstab and if you have many devices, it can keep them organized in your mind if they have labels rather than names. You can also shuffle around partitions just by changing their label without editing `fstab`. The `e2label` command is easier to remember than the analogous `tune2fs` command (as if any Unix commands are really that easy to remember).

Examples

Education researchers postulate that different people have different learning styles. For those of you who prefer examples rather than lectures, here are a few.

Creating a Test Filesystem

Because most of us don't have a spare computer or spare hard drive upon which to experiment and practice, we can make one of our own by creating an image file containing the filesystem of our choice and using the loopback filesystem to mount it. That way, we don't run the risk of accidentally wreaking havoc on the system itself. Although you could also use a floppy drive for these same exercises, their small size limits your flexibility.

Step 1—Make a Blank Image File

Use `dd` to create a file. We'll use a block size of 1024 bytes (a megabyte) and create a file that is 10MB in size. (You need to have enough free space on your hard drive to hold a file this big, so adjust the size accordingly.) We want 10,000 1KB (1024-byte) blocks, so we select a count of `10000`.

If we wanted a floppy-sized image, we would have selected a block size of `512` and a count of `2880` for a 1.4M floppy and a count of `5760` for a 2.88M floppy.

```
# dd if=/dev/zero of=/tmp/rhlutest.img bs=1024 count=10000
```

We see the computer respond with the following:

```
10000+0 records in
10000+0 records out
```

If we check our new file with the `files` command, we see this:

```
# file /tmp/rhlutest.img
/tmp/rhlutest.img: ASCII text, with no line terminators
```

Step 2—Make a Filesystem

So it's just a file full of zeros. Now we need to make the system think that the file is a block device instead of an ASCII file, so we use `losetup`, a utility that associates loop devices with regular files or block devices; we will be using the loopback device.

```
# losetup /dev/loop0 /tmp/rhlutest.img
```

Now we can format the file as a filesystem:

```
# mke2fs /dev/loop0
```

We see the computer respond as follows:

```
mke2fs 1.22, 22-Jun-2001 for EXT@ FS 0.5b, 95/08/09
Filesystem label=
OS type: Linux
Block size=1024 (log=0)
Fragment size=1024 (log=0)
2512 inodes, 10000 blocks
500 blocks (5.00%) reserved for the super user
First data block=1
2 block groups
8192 blocks per group, 8192 fragments per group
1256 inodes per group

Writing inode tables: done
Writing superblocks and filesystem accounting information: done
```

Step 3—Mounting Our Test Filesystem

Once you have your test filesystem created, you can experiment with the different options to the formatting commands you will be using. It will be useful to make a mount point for our image file

```
# mkdir /mnt/image
```

and then mount it

```
# mount /dev/loop0 /mnt/image
```

We can do this now because we already have the loopback filesystem associated with the image file. Later on if we remount it, we must use the following format to use the loopback option:

```
# mount -o loop /tmp/rhlutest.img /mnt/image
```

After mounting the new filesystem, we can look at it and see that the lost+found directory has been created on it and that the `df` command returns:

```
# df -h /mnt/image
Filesystem          Size  Used Avail Use% Mounted on
/dev/loop0          9.5M   13k  8.9M    1% /mnt/image
```

To unmount it, use this:

```
# umount /mnt/image
Make a backup of the image just in case we break the original:
# cp /tmp/rhlutest.img *.bak
```

Once the test filesystem is created, you can create directories, copy files to it, delete them, attempt to recover them, and, in general, create controlled chaos on your computer while you are learning and practicing valuable skills. If you damage the filesystem on the image beyond repair, unmount it, delete it, and create a new one.

Using dumpe2fs

To examine our image filesystem using dumpe2fs, first unmount it, and then use this:

```
# dumpe2fs /tmp/rhlutest.img
```

```
Filesystem volume name:   <none>
Last mounted on:          <not available>
Filesystem UUID:          90f33ea6-76b2-4d12-adb7-3bf7bd0ad114
Filesystem magic number:  0xEF53
Filesystem revision #:    1 (dynamic)
Filesystem features:      filetype sparse_super
Filesystem state:         clean
Errors behavior:          Continue
Filesystem OS type:       Linux
Inode count:              2512
Block count:              10000
Reserved block count:     500
Free blocks:              9664
Free inodes:              2501
First block:              1
Block size:               1024
Fragment size:            1024
Blocks per group:         8192
Fragments per group:      8192
Inodes per group:         1256
Inode blocks per group:   157
Last mount time:          Sat Sep  8 12:26:03 2001
Last write time:          Sat Sep  8 12:26:04 2001
Mount count:              1
Maximum mount count:      36
Last checked:             Sat Sep  8 12:18:45 2001
Check interval:           15552000 (6 months)
Next check after:         Thu Mar  7 11:18:45 2002
Reserved blocks uid:      0 (user root)
```

```
Reserved blocks gid:      0 (group root)
First inode:             11
Inode size:       128


Group 0: (Blocks 1 -- 8192)
  Primary Superblock at 1,  Group Descriptors at 2-2
  Block bitmap at 3 (+2), Inode bitmap at 4 (+3)
  Inode table at 5-161 (+4)
  8018 free blocks, 1245 free inodes, 2 directories
  Free blocks: 175-8192
  Free inodes: 12-1256
Group 1: (Blocks 8193 -- 9999)
  Backup Superblock at 8193,  Group Descriptors at 8194-8194
  Block bitmap at 8195 (+2), Inode bitmap at 8196 (+3)
  Inode table at 8197-8353 (+4)
  1646 free blocks, 1256 free inodes, 0 directories
  Free blocks: 8354-9999
  Free inodes: 1257-2512
```

A lot of information is there. Match up the information shown with the filesystem characteristics presented previously in this chapter to get a better picture of how it all fits together.

Mounting a Partition as Read-Only on a Running System

Remember that to do most any filesystem manipulation (formatting, checking, and so on), the filesystem should be unmounted. How do you remount partitions on a running system? For example, to remount the /home partition (assuming that it's on a separate physical partition from root) as read-only to run fsck on it and the remount it as read-write, we use the remount option for mount:

```
#  mount -o ro,remount /home
```

> **NOTE**
>
> This won't work if a normal user is logged in because /home will be busy.

Now we can run fsck on the partition. When done,

```
# mount -o rw,remount /home
```

puts it back in service. If you reboot your system to mount the root filesystem read-only for maintenance,

```
#mount -o rw,remount /
```

will remount it read-write and you can continue on. That's easier that unmounting and remounting the device.

Examine a Floppy Image File

If you are curious to know what's in any of the boot floppy images that are on the install CD, mount the image using the mount command as follows:

```
# mount -o loop /<image> /mnt/image
```

Examine an initrd Image File

Curious about the initrd.img file? It's just a gzipped ext2 filesystem. Copy it to the /tmp directory and add the .gz suffix to it:

```
# cp /boot/initrd-2.4.7-2.img /tmp/initrd-2.4.7-2.img.gz
```

If your system doesn't have an initrd file in /boot, mount the boot floppy and see if it has one. If not, create one with initrd and examine that one.

Then uncompress it as follows,

```
# gunzip /tmp/initrd-2.4.7-2.img.gz
```

mount it as follows,

```
mount -o loop /tmp/initrd-2.4.7-2.img /mnt/image
```

and browse to your heart's content.

Not every system will have an initrd file. It's typically used to load device drivers for filesystems (like Reiser) or hardware (like the Promise controller) that must be in place before the system can continue booting. Some floppy-based Linux distributions use the initrd to load a small operating system that can then uncompress and load the working file system from the floppy.

You can also mount .iso images in the same way, but remember that they are always read-only because of the nature of the underlying iso9660 filesystem; you can write to the other images unless you explicitly mount them as read-only. If you want to read and write to the iso filesystem, you must first copy the files to a device that is mounted read-write, make your changes, and then use mkisofs to create a new .iso image.

10

MANAGING THE FILESYSTEMS

Disk Tuning

It seems that many of us love to tinker under the hood to increase the performance of our computers, and Linux gives us some great tools to do just that. Whereas my mother used to tell me, "Don't fix what's not broken," my Dad always said, "Fix it until it breaks." I have two suggestions for you, though. First, perform a benchmark on your system before you begin; the program `bonnie` (home page of `http://www.coker.com.au/bonnie++/`) is a useful disk performance-measuring tool (it's not installed by default). Second, tweak only one thing at a time, so you can tell what works, what doesn't work, and what breaks. Some of these tweaks might not work or might lock up your machine.

Always have a working boot floppy handy, and remember that you are personally assuming all risks for attempting these tweaks. Additional systemwide tuning tips can be found at the Tune Linux Web site at `http://www.tunelinux.com/`.

Using the BIOS and Kernel to Tune the Disk Drives

Read your motherboard manual for better possible settings and make certain that all the drives are detected correctly by the BIOS. Change only one setting at a time.

Linux uses both `hd.c` and `ide.c` as IDE driver code. One or both can be compiled into the kernel; `ide` might likely be a module. The `hd.c` code is used for compatibility with older IDE controllers and is used by default on ide0. If you have more modern hardware, force the use of the newer code by using the LILO command line parameter `ide0=0x1f0`. This can be entered at the initial LILO prompt, added by editing the GRUB boot menu, or be placed in the `append=` line of /etc/lilo.conf or at the end of the kernel line in /boot/grub/grub.conf.

Other options are in the following list, as outlined in the BOOTPROMPT HOWTO and the kernel documentation, and they can be used to force the IDE controllers and drives to be optimally configured. Of course, *YMMV (Your Mileage May Vary)* because these don't work for everyone.

> `idex=dma`—This turns on dma support.
>
> `idex=autotune`—This attempts to tune the interface for optimal performance.
>
> `idex=ata66`—If you have ATA66 drives and controllers, this will enable it.
>
> `hdx=ide-scsi`—This enables SCSI emulation. Required for CD-RW drives, and might provide some performance improvements for regular CD-R drives as well.

idebus=xx—This can be any number from 20 to 66; autodetection is attempted, but this can set it manually if `dmesg` says it isn't autodetected correctly or if you have it set in the BIOS to a different value (overclocked). Most PCI controllers will be happy with 33.

pci=biosirq—Some motherboards generate an error message saying that you should use this. Look in `dmesg` for it; if you don't see it, don't use it.

These options can be entered in the same way as the `ide0=0x1f0` tweak.

The `hdparm` Command

The `hdparm` utility can be used by root to set and tune the settings for IDE (but *not* for SCSI) hard drives.

Once a kernel patch and associated support programs, the program is included with Red Hat 7.2. You should experiment with the drives mounted read-only. It also works with CD-ROM drives and some SCSI drives.

The general format of the command is this:

```
hdparm <command> <device>
```

The man entry for `hdparm` is extensive and contains useful detailed information, but here are some of the most useful options from it:

-a—Gets/sets sector count for filesystem read-ahead. This is used to improve performance in sequential reads of large files by prefetching additional blocks in anticipation of them being needed by the running task.

-c—Queries/enables IDE 32-bit I/O support. A numeric parameter can be used to enable/disable 32-bit I/O support: Currently supported values include 0 to disable 32-bit I/O support, 1 to enable 32-bit data transfers, and 3 to enable 32-bit data transfers with a special sync sequence required by many chipsets. The value 3 works with nearly all 32-bit IDE chipsets, but incurs slightly more overhead. Note that 32-bit refers to data transfers across a PCI or VLB bus to the interface card only; all IDE drives still have only a 16-bit connection over the ribbon cable from the interface card.

-d—Disables/enables the `using_dma` flag for this drive. This option only works with a few combinations of drives and interfaces that support DMA and that are known to the IDE driver (and with all supported XT interfaces). In particular, the Intel Triton chipset is supported for bus-mastered DMA operation with many drives (experimental). It is also a good idea to use the -X34 option in combination with -d1 to ensure that the drive itself is programmed for multiword DMA mode2. Using DMA doesn't necessarily provide any improvement in throughput or system performance, but many folks swear by it. Your mileage might vary.

10

MANAGING THE
FILESYSTEMS

-i—Displays the identification info that was obtained from the drive at boot time, if available. This is a feature of modern IDE drives, and might not be supported by older devices. The data returned might or might not be current, depending on activity since booting the system. However, the current multiple sector mode count is always shown. For a more detailed interpretation of the identification info, refer to AT Attachment Interface for Disk Drives (ANSI AS X3T9.2 working draft, revision 4a, April 19/93).

-I—Requests identification info directly from the drive, which is displayed in its raw form with no endian changes or corrections. Text strings might appear mangled when using -I but that isn't a bug. Otherwise, similar to the -i option.

-k—Gets/sets the keep_settings_over_reset flag for the drive.

-K—Sets the drive's keep_features_over_reset flag. Setting this enables the drive to retain the settings for -APSWXZ over a soft reset (as done during the error recovery sequence). Not all drives support this feature.

-m—Gets/sets sector count for multiple sector I/O on the drive. A setting of 0 disables this feature. Multiple sector mode (also known as IDE Block Mode), is a feature of most modern IDE hard drives, permitting the transfer of multiple sectors per I/O interrupt, rather than the usual one sector per interrupt. When this feature is enabled, it typically reduces operating system overhead for disk I/O by 30-50%. On many systems, it also provides increased data throughput of anywhere from 5% to 50%. Some drives, however (most notably the WD Caviar series), seem to run slower with multiple mode enabled.

-p—Attempts to reprogram the IDE interface chipset for the specified PIO mode, or attempts to autotune for the best PIO mode supported by the drive. This feature is supported in the kernel for only a few known chipsets, and even then the support is iffy at best. Some IDE chipsets are unable to alter the PIO mode for a single drive, in which case this flag might cause the PIO mode for both drives to be set. Many IDE chipsets support either fewer or more than the standard six (0 to 5) PIO modes, so the exact speed setting actually implemented will vary by chipset/driver sophistication. Use with extreme caution! This feature includes zero protection for the unwary, and an unsuccessful outcome can result in severe filesystem corruption!

-q—Handles the next flag quietly, suppressing normal output. This is useful for reducing screen clutter when running from /etc/rc.c/rc.local. Not applicable to the -i, -v, -t, or -T flags.

-r—Gets/sets read-only flag for device. When set, write operations aren't permitted on the device.

-T—Performs timings of cache reads for benchmark and comparison purposes. For meaningful results, this operation should be repeated two or three times on an otherwise inactive system (no other active processes) with at least a couple of megabytes of free memory. This displays the speed of reading directly from the Linux buffer cache without disk access. This measurement is essentially an indication of the throughput of the processor, cache, and memory of the system under test. If the -t flag is also specified, a correction factor based on the outcome of -T will be incorporated into the result reported for the -t operation.

-t—Performs timings of device reads for benchmark and comparison purposes. For meaningful results, this operation should be repeated two or three times on an otherwise inactive system (no other active processes) with at least a couple of megabytes of free memory. This displays the speed of reading through the buffer cache to the disk without any prior caching of data. This measurement is an indication of how fast the drive can sustain sequential data reads under Linux, without any filesystem overhead. To ensure accurate measurements, the buffer cache is flushed during the processing of -t using the BLKFLSBUF ioctl. If the -T flag is also specified, a correction factor based on the outcome of -T will be incorporated into the result reported for the -t operation.

-u—Gets/sets the interrupt-unmask flag for the drive. A setting of 1 permits the driver to unmask other interrupts during processing of a disk interrupt, which greatly improves Linux's responsiveness and eliminates "serial port overrun" errors. Use this feature with caution: some drive/controller combinations don't tolerate the increased I/O latencies possible when this feature is enabled, resulting in massive filesystem corruption. In particular, CMD-640B and RZ1000 IDE interfaces can be unreliable (because of a hardware flaw) when this option is used with kernel versions earlier than 2.0.13. Disabling the IDE prefetch feature of these interfaces (usually a BIOS/CMOS setting) provides a safe fix for the problem for use with earlier kernels.

-W—Disables/enables the IDE drive's write-caching feature (usually off by default).

-X—Sets the IDE transfer mode for newer IDE/ATA2 drives. This is typically used in combination with -d1 when enabling DMA to/from a drive on a supported interface chipset (such as the Intel 430FX Triton), where -X34 is used to select multiword DMA mode2 transfers. With systems that support UltraDMA burst timings, -X66 is used to select UltraDMA mode2 transfers. (You'll need to prepare the chipset for UltraDMA beforehand.) Apart from that, use of this flag is seldom necessary because most/all modern IDE drives default to their fastest PIO transfer mode at power on. Fiddling with this can be both needless and risky. On drives that support alternate transfer modes, -X can be used to switch the mode of the drive only. Prior to changing the transfer mode, the IDE interface should be jumpered or programmed (see the `-p` flag) for the new mode setting to prevent loss or corruption of data. Use this with extreme caution! For the PIO (Programmed Input/Output) transfer modes used by Linux, this value is simply the desired PIO mode number plus eight. Thus, a value of `09` sets PIO mode1, `10` enables PIO mode2, and `11` selects PIO mode3. Setting `00` restores the drive's default PIO mode, and `01` disables IORDY. For multiword DMA, the value used is the desired DMA mode number plus 32. For UltraDMA, the value is the desired UltraDMA mode number plus 64.

Filesystem Tuning

Never content to leave things alone, Linux provides several tools to adjust and customize the filesystem settings. The belief is that hardware manufacturers and distribution creators tend to select conservation settings that will work well all the time, leaving some of the potential of your system unleashed—that's why you have this book to help you.

The Linux filesystem designers have done an excellent job of selecting default values used for filesystem creation. Although these values work well for most users, some server applications of Linux benefit from filesystem tuning. As always, observe and benchmark your changes.

The `mke2fs` Command

`mke2fs -O sparse_super` will create a filesystem with sparse superblocks, reducing the space allocated to root. This isn't a performance enhancement per se, but it will free up additional space on a drive. This command only works on pre-2.2 kernels and is included here because a number of existing references don't make that distinction. With kernel version 2.2, the sparse superblock option has been moved to tune2fs.

`mke2fs -b blocksize` will set the block size. The block size chosen can also have an effect on the performance of the filesystem, A larger block size works better with large files and vice versa. There doesn't seem to be any hard and fast rule about this, and most advice is to accept the default block size of 1024k unless you want to spend some time running benchmarks.

The `tune2fs` Command

With `tune2fs`, you can adjust the tunable filesystem parameters on an ext2 or ext3 filesystem. A few performance-related items of note are as follows:

To disable filesystem checking, the -c 0 option sets the maximal mount count to zero.

The interval between forced checks can be adjusted with the -I option.

The -m option will set the reserved blocks percentage with a lower value freeing more space at the expense of fsck having space to write any recovered files.

Decrease the number of superblocks to save space with the -O sparse_super option (modern filesystems use this by default). Always run e2fsck after you change this value.

More space can be freed with the -r option that sets the number of reserved (for root) blocks.

Note that most of these uses of tune2fs free up space on the drive at the expense of the capability of fsck to recover data. Unless you really need the space and can deal with the consequences, just accept the defaults; large drives are now relatively inexpensive.

The e2fsck Command

This utility checks an ext3 filesystem as well as an ext2 filesystem. Some useful arguments taken from man e2fsck are as follows:

-b superblock—Instead of using the normal superblock, use an alternative superblock specified by superblock. This option is normally used when the primary superblock has been corrupted. The location of the backup superblock is dependent on the filesystem's block size. For filesystems with 1k-block sizes, a backup superblock can be found at block 8193; for filesystems with 2KB block sizes, at block 16384; and for 4KB block sizes, at block 32768.

Additional backup superblocks can be determined by using the mke2fs program using the -n option to print out where the superblocks were created. The -b option to mke2fs, which specifies blocksize of the filesystem, must be specified in order for the superblock locations that are printed out to be accurate.

If an alternative superblock is specified and the filesystem isn't opened read-only, e2fsck will make sure that the primary superblock is updated appropriately upon completion of the filesystem check.

-c—This option causes e2fsck to run the badblocks(8) program to find any blocks that are bad on the filesystem, and then marks them as bad by adding them to the bad block inode.

-f—Forces checking even if the file system seems clean.

-l filename—Adds the blocks listed in the file specified by filename to the list of bad blocks. The format of this file is the same as the one generated by the bad-blocks(8) program.

-L filename—Sets the bad blocks list to be the list of blocks specified by filename. (This option is the same as the -l option, except that the bad blocks list is cleared before the blocks listed in the file are added to the bad blocks list.)

-n—Opens the filesystem read-only, and assumes an answer of no to all questions. Allows e2fsck to be used non-interactively.

-p—Automatically repairs (*preens*) the file system without any questions.

-v—Verbose mode.

The badblocks Command

Although not a performance tuning program per se, the utility badblocks checks a (preferably) unmounted partition for bad blocks.

Some detailed and useful arguments from man badblocks are as follows:

-f—Normally, badblocks will refuse to do a read/write or a non-destructive test on a device that is mounted because this can cause the system to potentially crash. This can be overridden using the -f flag, but this shouldn't be done under normal circumstances. The only time when this option might be safe is if the /etc/mtab file is incorrect, and the device really isn't mounted.

-i input_file—Reads a list of already existing known bad blocks. badblocks will skip testing these blocks because they are known to be bad. If input_file is specified as -, the list will be read from the standard input. Blocks in this list will be omitted from the list of new bad blocks produced on the standard output or in the output file. The -b option of dumpe2fs(8) can be used to retrieve the list of blocks currently marked bad on an existing filesystem, in a format suitable for use with this option.

-o output_file—Writes the list of bad blocks to the specified file. Without this option, badblocks displays the list on its standard output. The format of this file is suitable for use by the -l option in e2fsck(8) or mke2fs(8).

-n—Uses non-destructive read-write mode. By default, only a non-destructive read-only test is done. This option must not be combined with the -w option because they are mutually exclusive.

-s—Shows the progress of the scan by writing out the block numbers as they are checked.

-v—Verbose mode.

-w—Uses write-mode test. With this option, badblocks scans for bad blocks by writing some patterns (0xaa, 0x55, 0xff, 0x00) on every block of the device, reading every block, and comparing the contents. This option cannot be compiled with the -n option because they are mutually exclusive.

The `noatime` mount Option

This is an option for `fstab`. It doesn't update inode access times on this filesystem, which results in faster access if the files are frequently accessed and you aren't concerned about the last access time information.

Reference

`http://www.linuxdoc.org/HOWTO/Filesystems-HOWTO.html`—In the Filesystems HOWTO, you'll find extensive information on native Linux filesystems as well as more exotic filesystems.

`http://www.linuxdoc.org/HOWTO/mini/Partition/index.html`—A lot of detailed information is contained in the Linux Partition HOWTO on partitions and their requirements.

`http://people.spoiled.org/jha/ext3-faq.html`—The Linux EXT3 FAQ is an unofficial FAQ with some useful info.

`http://www.linuxdoc.org/HOWTO/mini/Ext2fs-Undeletion.html`—You deleted a file on your ext2/3 partition? The Linux Ext2fs Undeletion mini-HOWTO is there to help you out, as is Chapter 11 of this book.

`http://www.linuxdoc.org/HOWTO/mini/Ext2fs-Undeletion-Dir-Struct/index.html`—You deleted a directory on your ext2/3 partition? Read the Ext2fs Undeletion of Directory Structures HOWTO to see how to rescue your data.

`http://www.linuxdoc.org/HOWTO/mini/Loopback-Root-FS.html`—Here's the concept: not only can we have a traditional filesystem, but also we can have a filesystem inside a large file located on some other filesystem. The Loopback Root Filesystem HOWTO examines how this is done.

`http://www.linuxdoc.org/HOWTO/Loopback-Encrypted-Filesystem-HOWTO.html`—The Loopback Encrypted Filesystem HOWTO; making your data secure with encryption.

`http://www.linuxdoc.org/HOWTO/LVM-HOWTO.html`—Throw away those concepts that marry physical disks to finite-sized filesystem; the Logical Volume Manager HOWTO explains how to overcome that kind of thinking.

`http://www.sistina.com/products_lvm.htm`—The LVM homepage and the source of downloadable files via FTP.

`http://www.linuxdoc.org/HOWTO/UMSDOS-HOWTO.html`—If you are interested in using the umsdos filesystem, The UMSDOS HOWTO provides ample information to you.

10

MANAGING THE
FILESYSTEMS

`http://www.linuxdoc.org/HOWTO/mini/NFS-Root.html`—The NFS-Root mini-HOWTO, along with the NFS-Root-Client-mini-HOWTO, NFS-Root-Client Mini-HOWTO (`http://www.linuxdoc.org/HOWTO/mini/NFS-Root-Client-mini-HOWTO/index.html`) explain in detail how to set up and use NFS for exporting root filesystems.

`http://www.nyx.net/~sgjoen/disk.html`—The Multi Disk System Tuning HOWTO contains explanations of the drive and controller hardware that are useful, as well as discussion of filesystems. It has an interesting section on optimizing multi-disk setups.

`http://www.linuxdoc.org/HOWTO/Software-RAID-HOWTO.html`—The Software-RAID HOWTO is an excellent tour de force of software RAID.

`http://www.linuxdoc.org/HOWTO/mini/DPT-Hardware-RAID.html`—The Linux DPT Hardware RAID mini-HOWTO tells you how to set up hardware RAID for your Linux box. DPT is the manufacturer of a well-supported RAID controller.

`http://www.linuxdoc.org/HOWTO/Tips-HOWTO.html`—The Linux Tips HOWTO provides some useful tips that make it worth the time to read because it addresses some filesystem problem such as "Is there enough freespace?" and "How do I move directories between filesystems?"

`http://www.linuxdoc.org/HOWTO/Large-Disk-HOWTO.html`—Still unsure about drive geometry, the limits to LILO and GRUB, and those monster-sized disks? The Large Disk HOWTO goes into useful detail about that. It also tells you how to handle disks that use disk managers such as OnTrack and EZ_Drive.

`http://www.linuxdoc.org/HOWTO/BootPrompt-HOWTO.html`—The BootPrompt HOWTO informs you of boot time arguments that can be passed to the kernel to deal with misbehaving hardware, configure non-PNP devices and so on. For this chapter, Section 7, "Hard Disks," is most useful.

`http://www.atnf.csiro.au/~rgooch/linux/docs/devfs.html`—It's coming. It's coming and you should start to learn about it from the Linux Devfs (Device File System) FAQ.

`http://www.linux-usb.org/USB-guide/x498.html`—The USB Guide for mass storage and other USB devices. If you have a USB device and need to know if it's supported and how to access it, check here.

`http://www.tunelinux.com/`— The TuneLinux site offers great systemwide tuning tips.

`http://www.coker.com.au/bonnie++/`—The homepage of bonnie, a disk benchmaking tool.

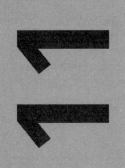

Backing Up, Restoring, and Recovery

CHAPTER 11

No matter what the pundits say, there are really only two kinds of backups: the kind that are useful and the kind that are useless.

Unfortunately, many backups fall into the latter category because many people don't care enough about their data and only perform backups out of some sense of guilt. Even when they do back up data, they ultimately fail at the task of backing up because they don't do it properly and, worse, have never attempted to recover data from backups (errata: data is a plural noun; the singular form is datum—almost everyone gets this wrong except, now, you).

Linus Torvalds has a testosterone-infused approach to backups, having said "Backups are for wimps." He prefers to store all his files on a remote server and let the system administrators (sysadmins) be responsible for it. Because few of us are fortunate to have someone else safeguard our data, we need to learn how to do it ourselves.

Backups are always tradeoffs. Any backup will consume time, money, and effort on an ongoing basis; backups must be monitored, validated, indexed, stored, and new media continuously purchased. Sound expensive? The cost of not having backups is the loss of your critical data. Recreating the data from scratch will cost time and money, and if the cost of doing it all again is greater than the cost associated with backing up, you should be performing backups. At the where-the-rubber-meets-the-road level, backups are nothing more than insurance against financial loss for you or your business. Putting it in money terms usually helps with motivation.

Still, you might find that it's not worth it for you to back up any data on an organized basis; the occasional file or two on a floppy thrown in the desk drawer is OK for you. If that's the case for you, you should still read this chapter and, if you think as Linus does on this subject, come back and re-read it after your files disappear.

Why Do We Need Backups at All?

Files disappear for any number of reasons, but they can be lost because the hardware fails and causes data loss, your attention might fail and you accidentally delete or overwrite a file, or because of circumstances beyond your control. And it all *will* fail at some time, most likely when it is extremely important for it not to fail.

As an example, during the writing of this chapter, a thunderstorm caused the electricity to fail. After the power was restored, the computer was turned back on automatically and experienced a head crash on the hard drive. Because this text was saved frequently to a floppy disk, repairing the computer and reinstalling Red Hat Linux 7.2 was time-consuming, but the difficult to re-create work was saved. The important configuration files in /etc and in /home were restored from an earlier backup.

Data can also be lost because the software being used misbehaves and corrupts the data as it attempts to write to the disk. Some applications, utilities, and drivers are not well written (the descriptive phrase most often heard is "still beta quality") or might suffer some corruption and fail to correctly write that all-important data you have just created. What you now have in the data file is indecipherable garbage of no use to anyone.

A natural disaster such as a tornado, flood, or earthquake could occur; perhaps the water pipes could burst or the building could catch on fire. Your data, as well as the hardware, would likely be destroyed in such a disaster. A disgruntled employee might destroy files or hardware in an attempt at retribution. No one likes to think that these events occur, but they do. If your data is important, you should be prepared.

However, the most frequent reason files get lost is from something we all share in common: universal human error. Who among us hasn't overwritten a new file with an older version or unintentionally deleted a needed file? This applies not only to data files, but also to configuration files and binaries as well. While perusing the mail lists or the Usenet postings, stories about deleting entire directories such as /usr or /lib seem all too common. Also occurring with great frequency is the incidence of incorrectly changing a configuration file and not saving the original in case it has to be restored (which it usually does because the person re-configured it incorrectly).

Proper backups can help you recover from these problems with a minimum of hassle, but you have to put in the effort to keep backups current, verify their intactness, and practice restoring the data in different disaster scenarios.

Doing It the Right Way

If you're going to back up your data, you need to do it the right way, and you do it the right way simply by implementing the steps discussed in the following sections.

1. Have a Plan

Having a plan means having a plan that is right for your needs and having equipment appropriate to the task. A plan that doesn't work is worth less than no plan at all; your data will be lost forever if you have no plan!

2. Follow the Plan

Following the plan also means verifying the data in the backups. Backups with corrupt data are of no use to anyone. If you think that all backups are perfect, think again: Hardware and software will fail and, according to our old friend Murphy, it will occur at the worst possible time.

3. Practice Your Skills

Practicing your skills means that you are able to restore the data easily and quickly, often appearing to be a miracle worker to those whose data you recover (please, don't delete data on purpose just to restore it and be a hero).

If you are a system administrator serving other users (as opposed to being both the system administrator and the sole user), your insistence on following system policies and adhering to backup procedures might make you the object of cruel jokes or cause you to be shunned at the annual office party. But when you recover a file for those same people, you will become their best friend (for the moment, at least).

Sound Practices

You should always

- Maintain more than one copy of critical data.
- Label the backups.
- Store the backups in a climate-controlled and secure area.
- Use secure off-site storage of critical data.
- Establish a backup policy that makes sense and can be followed religiously.
- Routinely verify backups and practice restoring data from them.
- Routinely inspect backup media for defects and regularly replace them (after destroying the data on them if it is sensitive).

Backup Strategies

Now that you're convinced you need backups, you need a strategy. If you are a new sysadmin, you might be inheriting an existing strategy. Take some time to examine it and see if it meets the current needs of the organization. Think about what is really needed and determine if the current strategy meets that need. If it doesn't, change it.

The frequency of backups should be determined by how quickly the important data changes. On a home system, most files never change and a few change daily, some weekly. No elaborate strategy needs to be created to deal with that. A good strategy for home use is to back up critical data frequently and back up configuration and other files weekly. At the enterprise level on a larger system with multiple users, a different approach is called for. Some critical data is changing constantly and could be expensive to recreate; this typically involves expensive solutions. Most of us are somewhere in between.

UNIX Backup Levels

UNIX uses the simple concept of backup levels as a shorthand way of referring to how much data is backed up in relation to another level. It works this way:

A level 0 backup is a full backup.

Backups at the other numbered levels will back up everything that has changed since the last backup at that level or a higher level (dump offers 10 levels). For example, a level 3 followed by a level 4 will generate an incremental backup from the full backup, whereas a level 4 followed by a level 3 will generate a differential backup between the two.

Let's examine a few of the many strategies that are in use today; many of the others are variations of these basic schemes.

Simple Strategy

If you just have a few configuration files and some small data files, copy them to a floppy disk, engage the write-protect tab, and keep them someplace safe. If you have a few more files, perhaps a ZIP disk (100 and 250MB in size) is more appropriate. Experts believe that if you've more data than that, you really need a formal backup strategy. You can also archive each user's home directory as well as the entire /etc directory. Between the two, that backup would contain most of the important files for a small system. Those can be easily restored after a complete reinstall of Red Hat if necessary.

Full Backup on a Periodic Basis

If you have the storage space, a backup of the complete filesystem every so often is easy. This is viable with the swappable disk drives discussed later on in the chapter. If you are connected to a network, it is possible to mirror the data on another machine (preferably off-site); the rsync tool is particularly well suited to this task. Recognize that this doesn't address the need for archives of the recent state of files; it only presents a snapshot of the system at the time the update is done.

Note

Two good rules of thumb for backup strategies are as follows:

If the backup strategy and policy is too complicated (and this holds true for most security issues), it will eventually be disregarded and fall into disuse.

The best scheme is often a combination of strategies.

Full Backups with Incremental Backups

This scheme begins to resemble what an sysadmin of a larger system would traditionally use. Once a week, a full backup is made, and then every day after that an incremental backup is made, backing up only those files that have changed so far that week.

This scheme can fork in two ways. In one way, each incremental backup can be made with reference to the original full backup. In other words, a level 0 backup is followed by a series of level 1 backups. A restoration requires only two tapes, but each incremental backup might be large (and grow ever larger) on a changing system. Alternatively, each incremental backup could reference the previous incremental backup. This would be a level 0 backup followed by a level 1, followed by a level 2, and so on. Backups are quicker (less data each time), but require multiple tapes to restore a full system. Again, it is a classic tradeoff decision.

Don't think that backups can only be performed on a daily basis. It might be necessary to backup some files hourly.

Rotating Media Along with Full Backups with Incremental Backups

Here, multiple sets of media are used so that the archives reach back several weeks. Four examples are discussed in the following sections.

Daily Backups

One tape is left in the machine and a script performs the backups every day or so. Believe it or not, this is a commonly used scheme chosen for its simplicity. It's also incredibly short-sighted and likely a waste of time because at no time is anyone verifying that the backed up data is good and can be restored. Many a sysadmin has lulled himself into a false sense of security with this scheme. The most you can say about it is that it is better than nothing, but even that's wrong: the regular users won't bother to make quick backups of their own data because they think it's being done for them. Wrong thinking such as this is usually punished with the irretrievable loss of data.

Grandfather-Father-Son Backups

Also known as GSF and as Monthly-Weekly-Daily backups in one iteration, this popular scheme attempts to save some time (full backups are only done weekly) and requires only two tapes to restore a totally destroyed system. It works like this:

Each week, a full backup (level 0) is made; this is the Father. The other days of the week, a differential backup is made, a tape for each day; these are the Sons (level 1). Once a month, a full backup is made using a fresh tape; this is the Grandfather. Restoring a full system can be done from a Father and its Son; The Grandfather tape becomes the historical archive and is typically stored off site. If multiple sets of tapes are used, many weeks' work can be archived, so the system can be restored to just about any state in the past. If the occasional tape malfunctions, the loss is minimized.

As alluded to, there are various permutations to this strategy, all designed to meet that individual's need. That means that there is no perfect strategy and no silver-bullet solution for the masses.

Tower of Hanoi Backups

Named after a puzzle game in which the completed puzzle resembles a tower, this approach resembles a tower when mapped out over its 15-day span. On the bottom level of the tower, the same tape (we'll call it tape A) is used for a backup every other day, leaving a one day gap to be filled. In the first gap, a new tape (called tape B) is used. It is reused every four days. This leaves an empty gap on day 4 that is filled by using tape C that is reused in eight days. All three tapes now cover each day of the cycle except day 8, covered by tape D, that is only used once a cycle. This method generates more full backups to ensure that something will be there to restore.

The dump man page suggests that the backup levels be as follows:

The D tape should be a level 0 backup, The A tapes begin a cycle of 3, 5, 7, 9, and 9, whereas the B tapes follow a cycle of 2, 4, 6, 8, and 9. The cycle could be repeated with a second set of tapes. The purpose is to generate a series of differential and incremental backups so that a minimum number of tapes will be necessary for a full restore and the amount of data actually transferred will be as small (and as fast) as possible. As well, the double set of tapes captures and retains a longer history of the filesystem, allowing older files to be recovered if that is a need of your system.

As you can see, this scheme can get quite complex, especially when you have to rotate the tapes through different levels to equalize wear and tear on them, not to mention keeping track of all those tapes.

Mirroring Data or RAID Arrays

Given adequate (and often expensive) hardware resources, you can always mirror the data somewhere else, essentially a real-time copy on hand. The use of RAID arrays (in some of their incarnations) provide for recovery if a disk fails, but remember that RAID arrays and mirroring systems will just as happily write corrupt data as valid data. If a file is deleted, a RAID array won't save it.

What Scheme Is Best for You?

Only you can decide what is best for your situation. It's a good idea to examine incidents of data loss in the past and decide if your chosen scheme will adequately address that loss. Then run through a few likely scenarios and assess the effectiveness of your choice. Finally, examine what effect a total disaster might have. In each case, ask yourself: What data am I protecting? How will it be safe? How will it be restored and how long will that take? The answers to all these questions should help you form your plan.

Many people also fail to consider the element of time when formulating their plan. Some backup devices are faster than others, and some recovery methods are faster than others. You need to take that into account when making choices.

What Hardware and Media Are at Our Disposal?

Many consumer grade workstations have a floppy drive and possibly a CD-RW drive if you're lucky; they typically don't have an overabundance of free disk space either. These are the same machines used in small offices, so the backup hardware options are limited unless additional equipment is purchased.

Floppy drives are commonplace today and useful for simple, quick backups of a few files by the user. Floppy disks are easily damaged, lost, and accidentally overwritten. They also unexpectedly fail at times. Floppies are good for a few files for the short term. Cheap and disposable, these are the low-rent district for data storage. At one time, 1.4MB was a lot of data.

Removable or portable drives can be used. Of all the removable hard drive manufacturers, Iomega seems to have acquired some staying power with its Zip (100 and 250MB) and Jaz (1GB and 2GB) drives. Although these drives now have good support in Red Hat Linux, in the past they have been plagued with mechanical problems that have rendered data unretrievable.

USB hard drives are the new kid on the block with big price tags to match. The advantages are large capacity and portability. Support under Linux is somewhat better than experimental, but not much more at the present time. Watch for better support and falling prices in the future.

Firewire (IEEE1394) drives are similar to USB drives, just much faster. Kernel support is available if you are fortunate enough to have this hardware. Found mostly on the Mac, controller and drive hardware exists for the PC platform as well.

Compared to floppy drives and some removable drives, CD-RW drives and their cousins, DVD-R drives, can store large amounts of data and are useful for a home or small business. Once very expensive, now CD burners and media are relatively inexpensive, although automated CD changing machines, necessary for automatically backing up large amounts of data, are still quite expensive. Each CD-RW disk can hold 650MB to 700MB of data (the media comes in both capacities), larger chunks of data can be split to fit on multiple disks. Some commercial backup programs support this method of storage. Once burned and verified, the shelf life for the media is at least a decade or longer.

DVD-R is similar to CD-RW, but its more expensive and can store up to 9.4Gb (double-sided) and 4.7GB (single-sided) of data per disk. Arrays of devices are available to increase the total storage that can be accessed. A benefit of CD and DVD storage over tape devices is that the archives can be mounted and accessed just like a hard drive, making the recovery of individual files easier.

If you are lucky to be on a network, another option might be useful: Arrays of hard drives can be used as storage devices for a network. Several hardware vendors offer such products in varying sizes. With the declining cost of mass storage devices and the increasing need for larger storage space, network storage (*NAS, or Network Attached Storage*) is available and supported in Linux. More modest and simple network storage can be done on a remote machine that has adequate storage space, but then that machine has to deal with all the problems of backing up, preserving, and restoring data, doesn't it? Networked systems also offer the advantage of centralizing the backup process.

With the drop in price of very large hard disks (in the 80+GB range), they are now inexpensive enough that it is possible to mirror individual systems if you only have a few. This might be a viable option for small offices or home use in which a large amount of data is important enough to protect, but the cost of elaborate tape drives, DVD-R drives, or enough media to hold all the data is prohibitive. Nowadays, a spare 20GB drive is cheaper than a CD-RW drive and 20GB of disks.

The Tried and True Backup Medium

Traditionally, tape has been the backup medium of professional choice. You might recall seeing old movies in which refrigerator-sized boxes held large spools of tape, constantly winding, stopping, and rewinding in an attempt to add some interest to the otherwise dull movie. They used mechanical Teletype machines in movies a generation prior to that for the same reason—those machines are the source of the name tty to describe a terminal.

Modern tape drives are cartridge based and can hold, compared to older tape drives, large amounts of data (70MB or more in compressed format), so a full backup of a system can be contained on as few cartridges as possible. Tape drive storage has been so prevalent in the industry that one of the commands used for archiving, `tar`, is derived from Tape ARchive. Well supported in Linux, tape drives are far from extinct and are still considered to be (in their cartridge incarnation) a standard for commercial systems. Auto-loading machines can accommodate archives that exceed the capacity of the tape and handle large backups automatically. Older tape equipment is often available in the used equipment market and might be useful for smaller operations that have outgrown more limited backup device options.

Commonly used forms are *DLT (Digital Linear Tape)*, a tape manufactured by Quantum and used in their line of tape drives and *DDS (Digital Data Storage)*, also known as *DAT (Digital Audio Tape)* when used for audio purposes. There is also an 8mm tape manufactured by Exabyte. Plenty of other formats are available.

Many businesses use the DLT, 8mm, or 4mm tapes. Large data storage facilities tend to use SD-3, 9840, 9820, and other tapes suited to their needs. The average home user and small business might well be using Travan and similar consumer-grade tape drives. Capacities and durability vary from type to type and range from a few gigabytes to hundreds of gigabytes with commensurate increases in cost for the equipment and media.

It is important to note that the failure to clean, align, and maintain tape drives puts your data at risk. The tapes themselves are also susceptible to mechanical wear and degradation as well. Hardware maintenance is part of a good backup policy. Don't ever forget that it's not a question of *if* hardware will fail, but only *when* it will fail.

Making the Big Decision

By now you should have determined that some kind of plan is needed to safeguard your data, and, like most people, you are overwhelmed by the prospect. Entire books as well as countless articles and white papers have been written on the subject of backing up and restoring data. What makes the topic so complex is that each solution is truly individual.

Yet, the proper approach to making the decision is really pretty straightforward. You start the process by asking

- What data must be safeguarded?
- How often does the data change?

The answers to these two questions determine how important the data is, determine the volume of the data, and determine the frequency of the backups. This in turn will determine the backup medium. Only then can the software be selected that will accommodate all these considerations.

Finally, the proposed solution can be examined in the context of budget, time, and personnel constraints, and the decision-making cycle can be run through again, if necessary, eventually resolving to the optimum solution for you. If you aren't willing or capable of making this decision, there exists a legion of consultants, hardware vendors, and software vendors who would love to assist you.

Although backups are really nothing more or less than insurance for your data and backup schemes and hardware can be elaborate or simple, they are nothing without a workable plan. Even the best backup plan is useless if the process isn't carried out, data isn't verified, and data restoration isn't practiced on a regular basis. Red Hat 7.2 provides many useful tools for backup, and good commercial products are available as well.

Using Backup Software

Because there are thousands of unique situations requiring as many unique backup solutions, it comes as no surprise that Linux offers many backup tools. What are the tools available in the Red Hat 7.2 distribution?

tar

The `tar` tool, the bewhiskered old man of archiving utilities, is great for saving entire directories full of files. For example, here's the command:

```
# tar cvf etc.tar /etc
```

Here, the options makes `tar` create an archive, be verbose in the message output, and use the filename `etc.tar` as the archive name for the contents of the directory `/etc`.

Or, if the output of `tar` is sent to the standard output and redirected to a file, as follows:

```
# tar cv /etc > etc.tar
```

All the files in the `/etc` directory will be saved to a file named `etc.tar`. With an impressive array of options (see the man page), `tar` is quite flexible and powerful in combination with shell scripts. With the `-z` option, it can even create and restore compressed archives.

If you want to create a full backup,

```
# tar czvf fullbackup.tgz /
```

will create a gzipped tarball (the z option) of the entire system.

If we want to perform an incremental backup, we need to locate all the files that have been changed since the last backup. (For simplicity, we are assuming that we are doing incremental backups on a daily basis.) To locate the files, we use the `find` command:

```
# find / -newer /<name of last backup file> ! -type d -print
```

When run alone, `find` will generate a list of files systemwide and prints it to the screen. The `! -type d` eliminates directories from the list, otherwise the entire directory would be sent to `tar` even if the contents weren't all changed.

We can pipe the output of our `find` command to `tar` as follows:

```
# find / -newer /<name of last backup file> ! -type d -print | tar
czT - <backup file name or device name>
```

Here, we use the `T -` option to get the filenames from a buffer (where the `-` is the buffer).

Note

The `tar` command can back up to a raw device as well as a formatted partition, for example:

```
# tar -cvzf /dev/hdd  /boot  /etc /home
```

backs up those directories to device `hdd`.

The `tar` command can also back up over multiple floppy disks:

```
# tar -cvMf /dev/fd0 /home
```

will back up the contents of `/home` and spread the file out over multiple floppies, prompting you with this message:

```
Prepare volume #2 for `/dev/fd0' and hit return:
```

---

cpio

The `cpio` tool is great for saving a few files from here or a few files from there—you get the picture. You can generate a list of files all over your system, pipe them to `cpio`, and they become part of the archive. Interestingly, RPM files (Red Hat Package Manager) are modified `cpio` files. The `rpm2cpio` command can be used to unpack (rather than install) RPM files if needed.

For a `cpio` example, we will create a list of files from the `/etc` directory and then use that list to create the `cpio` archive:

```
# find /etc -print > filelist
# cat filelist | cpio -o > backup.cpio
```

If we want to do it all on one line,

```
# find /etc -print | cpio -o > backup.cpio
```

Note that we could concatenate several file lists together and use `fgrep` to remove files we didn't want in the archive. Such is the power of the GNU tools provided with Linux. The man page for `cpio` lists an impressive array of options for backing up and restoring files.

> **Note**
>
> You can name your backups anything you want, but sticking to the filename conventions of using extensions of .tar, .tgz, .cpio, and the like is a good idea. It's also a good idea to include the current date and time in the filename, easily done when using shell scripts and cron to perform backups.

Putting It All Back with `tar` and `cpio`

The `xp` option in `tar` and the `im` option in `cpio` will restore the file from a backup and preserve the file attributes as well. Whereas `tar` will create any subdirectories it needs, the `-d` option needs to be explicitly added to `cpio` for the same result. Also, the backups might have been created with relative or absolute paths; use the `-tvf` option with `tar` and `-otv` with `cpio` to list the files in the archive before extracting them.

`dump` and `restore`

One of the older commands available is the `dump` command. `dump` will examine files on an ext2 and ext3 filesystem and determine which files need to be backed up. It can span multiple media. The amount of data to be backed up is determined by the `dump` level. Although the man page gives much more detail, here is a brief synopsis of the `dump` levels that span from 0 to 9.

0—Full backup

1–9—Incremental backups; there can be eight levels of incremental backups. The default level is 9.

In other words, `dump` `0` will do a full backup, `dump` `1` will do an incremental backup since `dump` `0`, `dump` `2` will do an incremental backup since `dump` `1`, and so on. If there are no level 1–8 backups, the default level 9 does an incremental backup from the full backup done with `dump` `0`.

The `dump` archives are restored using the program `restore`. You can restore a full backup and incremental backups, and `restore` can be used across a network.

ark

Red Hat 7.2 provides you with few GUI tools for backups (and only one X application). Archiving has traditionally been a function of the system administrator and not seen as a task for the home users, so no elaborate GUI was believed necessary. Backing up has also been seen as a script driven, automated task in which a GUI is not as useful.

Under the *nom de plume* of `Archiver`, `ark` can be found under the Utilities menu tree in both KDE and GNOME. It provides a graphical interface to viewing, creating, adding to, and extracting from archived files as shown in Figure 11.1. As long as the associated command line programs are installed, it can work with `tar`, `gzip`, `bzip2`, `zip`, and `lha` files (the latter four being compression methods used to save space by compaction of the archived files); it is also linked closely with the KDE file and Web browser, Konqueror, extending the functionality of that application.

FIGURE 11.1

The opening view of Archiver presents as a simple GUI file browser.

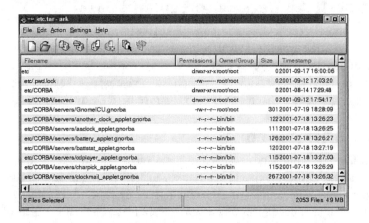

Existing archives are opened after launching the application itself, as shown in Figure 11.2. You can add files and directories to the archive or delete them from the archive. Once opened, the contents of an archive can be totally extracted, or individual files can be extracted; you can also search on patterns (all *.jpg files, for example) to select files.

Choosing New from the File menu creates new archives. You then type the name of the archive, providing the appropriate extension (.tar, .gz, and so on), and then proceed to add files and directories as you desire. When used in conjunction with Konqueror, files can be dragged to the Ark window and added automatically.

FIGURE 11.2

*Creating a new
archive is
extremely easy
and demonstrates
the benefits a
graphical inter-
face can bring to
a simple utility.*

FIGURE 11.2

*Creating a new
archive is
extremely easy
and demonstrates
the benefits a
graphical inter-
face can bring to
a simple utility.*

Taper

Yusuf Nagree wanted a user-friendly interface to `tar` and `cpio` as well as a program that
would create and maintain a database of the archive contents on his hard drive. The useful graphical interface to `tar` and `cpio` he created is taper (see Figure 11.3). The tape
device he developed taper for is a Jumbo 250 floppy tape drive, not something everyone
has handy, but it does appear to work well with most tape drives.

FIGURE 11.3

*It might appear
plain, but taper is
a powerful backup
utility once prop-
erly configured.*

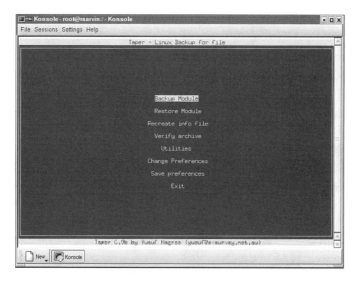

Taper is designed for tape devices and can be useful if you need a graphical interface
from a console for this purpose. It can also be used to back up to files on a hard drive,
or, in fact, anything that Linux can write to can be used.

The taper documentation is well written and extensive. Red Hat 7.2 include an ftape driver with a version greater than 3.x, so you have the advantage of the inclusion of the zftape enhanced filesystem interface.

If you understand the concepts for tar and cpio, setting the system defaults through the menus will come naturally. If you need help using taper, online help for navigation is available, but the man page is excellent.

To start taper, become root and issue the taper command followed by the -T argument for the device you will use—if you don't have a tape drive, use l (that's an L) as the device type (a regular file on the hard disk), for example,

```
# taper -T l
```

Taper can be run in unattended mode for scheduled backups via cron; the multitude of command-line options available are helpful here.

dd

Although the dd command isn't normally thought of as an archiving tool, it can be used to mirror a partition or entire disk regardless of the information contained on it. It is useful for archiving copies of floppy disks while retaining the ability to restore the data to a floppy intact. For example,

```
# dd if=/dev/fd0 of=floppyimage1.img
```

Swapping the if= and of= values reverses the process. Although best known for copying images, dd can also be used to convert data, and it is especially useful when restoring older archives or moving data between big endian and little endian systems.

> **Caution**
>
> Don't confuse the if= and of= assignments because dd will be more than happy to overwrite your valid data with garbage. Use the Carpenter's Rule: "Measure twice—Cut once."

Amanda

Amanda is a powerful, network-aware backup application created by the University of Maryland at College Park whose features include compression and encryption. It is intended for use with high-capacity tape drives, floptical, CDR, and CD-RW devices. The program's homepage is http://www.amanda.org. There, you will find information on subscribing to the mail list as well as links to Amanda-related projects and a FAQ-o-matic. The program is covered in detail by John R. Jackson in his book *UNIX Backup and Recovery*, an extract of which is available online at `http://www.backupcentral.com/amanda.html`.

Using GNUtar and dump, Amanda is intended for unattended, automated tape backups; it is not really suited for interactive or ad hoc backups. The support for tape devices is more than ample and writing special drivers is said not to be very difficult. Restoring files is easy from any backup in which the file exists. Although Amanda doesn't support Macintosh clients, it will use Samba to back up Microsoft Windows clients (as well as any UNIX client that can use GNU tools). Because Amanda runs on top of standard GNU tools, file restoration can be made using those tools on a recovery disk if the Amanda server isn't available. File compression, if done, can be done on the client or server, thus lightening the load on less powerful machines that need backing up.

> **Caution**
>
> Amanda doesn't support dump images larger than a single tape and requires a new tape for each run. If you forget to change a tape, Amanda will not back up in the way you had originally intended, but attempts to do the best it can until you insert a new tape. Don't use too small a tape or forget to change a tape.

There is no GUI interface for Amanda. Configuration is done in the time-honored UNIX tradition of editing text configuration files located in /etc/amanda. The default installation in Red Hat includes a sample cron file because it is expected that you will be using cron to run Amanda.

The man page for Amanda is well-written and useful, explaining both the configuration of Amanda as well as detailing the several programs that actually make up Amanda. The configuration files found in /etc/amanda are well-commented and provide a number of examples to assist you in configuration. As far as backup schemes, Amanda calculates an optimal scheme on-the-fly and schedule it accordingly. It can be forced to adhere to a traditional scheme, but other tools are possibly better suited for that job.

Amanda is a robust backup and restore application best suited to unattended backups with an autoloading tape drive of adequate capacity. It benefits from good user support and documentation.

Commercial Software

The Red Hat free download version doesn't provide it (the version targeted to businesses usually does), but commercial and other freeware backup products exist. Many are excellent and certain to be the answer to your prayers, but are mercifully beyond the scope of this book. Two good places to look for free backup software are Freshmeat (`http://www.freshmaet.net`) and Google (`http://www.google.com/linux`).

Here are some useful tools that aren't installed with Red Hat 7.2.

flexbackup

Although dump and restore are older programs and more modern alternatives exist, many older archives exist in the `dump` format. Besides, just because it's older doesn't mean that it's not still useful today. As a matter of fact, `flexbackup` is a large file of Perl scripts that makes `dump` and `restore` easier to use. `flexbackup`'s command syntax can be accessed by using the command with the `-help` argument. It also can use `afio`, `cpio`, and `tar` to create and restore archives locally or over a network using `rsh` or `ssh` if security is a concern. Its homepage is `http://members.home.com/flexbackup/`.

afio

The `afio` tool creates `cpio`-formatted archives, handling input data corruption better than `cpio` (which doesn't handle data input corruption very well at all). It supports multi-volume archives during interactive operation, and can make compressed archives. If you feel the need to use `cpio`, you might want to check out `afio` at `http://freshmeat.net/projects/afio/`.

cdbackup

Designed for the home or small office user, `cdbackup` will work with any backup and restore software that can read from `stdin`, write to `stdout`, and can handle linear devices such as tape drives. It just makes it easier to use CD-Rs as the storage medium. Other similar applications are available elsewhere as well; the homepage for this application is at `http://www.cableone.net/ccondit/cdbackup/`.

Copying Files

Often it makes more sense to move or copy files than to create an archive of them. We can use the `tar`, `cp` or even the `cpio` commands to do this as well as a handy file management tool known as `mc`. Using `tar` is more traditional because older versions of `cp` didn't handle symbolic links and permissions well at times. For these examples, we would like to copy (not archive) a directory tree, but this tree includes symbolic links and files that must have special file permissions.

Copy Files Using `tar`

One choice would be to use the `tar` command where you would create a tar file that would be piped to `tar` to be uncompressed in the new location. First, we change to the source directory. Then, the entire command resembles this:

```
# tar cvf - files | (cd <target directory> ; tar xpf -)
```

where `files` are the filenames you want to include; use * to include the entire current directory.

Let's examine how this works. We have already changed to the source directory and execute `tar` with the `cvf` - arguments that tell `tar` to

> c—Create an archive.
>
> v—Verbose; lists the files processed so we can see that it's working.
>
> f—The filename will be what follows. In this case, it is
>
> -—A buffer to hold our data temporarily.

Other `tar` commands that might be useful here are as follows:

> l—Stay in the local filesystem (don't include remote volumes).
>
> `atime-preserve`—Don't change access times on files, even though you're accessing them now.

The contents of the `tar` file (held in our buffer) are then piped to the second expression which will un-tar the files to the target directory. Remember from shell programming that enclosing an expression in parentheses causes it to operate in a subshell.

First we change to the target directory, and then,

> x—Extract files from a tar archive.
>
> p—Preserve permissions
>
> f—The filename will be -, that temporary buffer that holds the `tar`'ed files.

Copying Files Using `cp`

We could use `cp -a <source directory> <target directory>`.

The `-a` argument is the same as giving `-dpR`, which would be

> -d—Dereference symbolic links; never follow symbolic links; copy the files that they point to instead of copying the links.

-p—Preserve all file attributes if possible (file ownership might interfere).

-R—Copy directories recursively.

Copying Files Using `cpio`

If we want to use `cpio` instead of `tar`, we need to remember that `cpio` really works with lists of files. So we need to first create the list and feed it to `cpio`.

```
# find <source directory> -print | cpio -pudv <target directory>
```

Here, we use the `find` command on the current directory with the `-print` option to generate a list of files in that directory. We then pipe that file list to `cpio`. When `cpio` gets the file list, it

-p—Runs in copy-pass mode (we are not creating an archive file here).

-u—Replaces all files without asking (unconditional).

-d—Creates directories if needed.

-v—Lists all files copied (verbose).

Copying Files Using `mc`

There is a command line file manager that is useful for copying, moving, and archiving files and directories. The Midnight Commander has a look and feel similar to the Norton Commander of DOS fame (Figure 11.4). By executing `mc` at a shell prompt, a dual-pane view of the files is displayed. It contains pull-down menu choices and function keys to manipulate files. It also uses it own virtual file system allowing it to mount FTP directories and display the contents of `tar` files, DEB files, and RPM files as well as extract individual files from them. As if that weren't enough, it contains a File Undelete virtual filesystem for ext2/3 partitions.

Figure 11.4 shows a shot of the default dual screen display. Pressing the F9 key drops down the menu, and pressing F1 displays the Help file. The configuration files are well documented, and it would appear easy to extend the functionality of `mc` for your system.

So Many Choices...

So which should you use? For copying, I suggest `cp -a` because it's the simplest. But if that doesn't work in your case (permissions, ownerships, and timestamps don't travel well), the `tar` alternative is the next best option. `cpio` isn't as easily suited to simply copying files, unless you want to exclude a number of files; then you could filter the file list using `fgrep -v` and a premade list of excluded files before the file list is passed to `cpio`. The use of `mc` is probably the best combination of ease, power, and flexibility, but it cannot be counted on to be found on every system; you should find `tar` and `cp` everywhere.

FIGURE **11.4**
*The default view
of the Midnight
Commander, a
highly versatile
file tool.*

System Recovery

On multiuser systems, when files are deleted, their inodes are made available immediately for use by the system. In that case, recovering that data intact is very unlikely, although not impossible. The first step is to unmount the filesystem containing the deleted files and then methodically find the deleted parts of the file and reassemble them. It is a time-consuming process and should be reason enough to back up the files in the first place. On a single user system, the chances of recovery are better because fewer writes to the disk have occurred after the file deletion.

File recovery isn't something to be attempted without preparation and practice because both will improve your chances of recovering more of the data. The following approaches should work with ext3 filesystems as well as the ext2 filesystems they describe.

Before you can restore your data, you must sometimes recover your system. Although hardware failures aren't covered here (but you will certainly have them), corruption of the bootloader code, the partition table, and individual files will occur, often rendering the entire system unusable.

All too often, files are deleted and cannot be recovered from backups either because backups weren't made or were corrupted or lost. If you have failed to make adequate backups or are unable to restore them, sometimes a little system recovery magic is in order.

Backing Up and Restoring the Master Boot Record

The Master Boot Record is the first 512 bytes of a hard disk. It contains the bootloader code in the first 446 bytes and the partition table in the next 64 bytes; the last two bytes identify that sector as the MBR.

To back it up, we will use the dd command (that comes from disk to disk, although the program is much more versatile than that) as root and will back up the entire MBR. If the bootloader code changes from the time you make this image and you restore the old code, the system won't boot; it's easy enough to keep a boot floppy handy and then re-run LILO if that's what you are using.

To copy the entire MBR to a file, use this:

```
# dd if=/dev/hda of=/tmp/hdambr bs=512 count=1
```

To restore the MBR, use this:

```
# dd if=/tmp/hdambr of=/dev/hda bs=512 count=1
```

To restore only the Partition Table, skipping the bootloader code, use this:

```
# dd if=/tmp/hdambr of=/dev/hda bs=1 skip=446 count=66
```

Of course, it would be safer to move the copy of the MBR to a floppy or other storage device. You will need to be able to run dd on the system to restore it (which means that you will be using the Red Hat rescue disk or an equivalent).

Make a Hard Copy of the Partition Table

A different way of approaching the problem is to have a hard copy of the partition table that can then be restored by hand using the Red Hat rescue disk and the fdisk program.

We can also make a listing of the printout of the partition table with fdisk using the L option, as follows:

```
# fdisk /dev/hda -l > /tmp/hdaconfig.txt
```

And we can copy the file /tmp/hdaconfig.txt to the backup floppy for safekeeping as well.

Restoring the MBR Using fdisk

It is possible to restore the MBR by hand as long as you have a hard copy of the partition information as was just described (or unless the entire disk is a single partition).

Backing Up, Restoring, and Recovery

CHAPTER 11

281

11

BACKING UP,
RESTORING, AND
RECOVERY

Use the Red Hat 7.2 Rescue Disk. Simply boot from the first install CD-ROM and enter **linux rescue** at the LILO prompt.

Once logged on (you are root by default), start `fdisk` on the first drive:

```
# fdisk /dev/hda
```

Use the p command to display the partition information and compare it to the hard copy you have. If the entries are identical, you have a problem somewhere else; it's not the partition table.

if there is a problem, use the d command to delete all the partitions showing.

Now use the n command to create new partitions that will match the partition table from your hard copy. Make certain that the partition types (ext2, FAT, swap) are the same. If you have a FAT partition at /dev/hda1, make certain that you set the bootable flag for it.

If you find you have made an error somewhere along the way, just use the q command to quit `fdisk` without saving any changes and start over.

When you have it correct, write the changes to the disk with the w command; you will be kicked out of `fdisk`. Restart it to verify your handiwork, and then remove the rescue disk and reboot.

It helps to practice this on an old drive before you have to do it.

Reformatting with the -S Option

As a last ditch effort, you can run the `mke2fs` command with the -S option like this, if you are having trouble with the ext2 partition on /dev/hda1:

```
# mke2fs -S /dev/hda1
```

The -S argument writes new superblock information, but doesn't write new inodes; this might make the data salvageable. You should run `e2fsck` on the unmounted partition after using the `mke2fs` command in this manner.

Undeleting a File

If you have deleted a file by mistake, it is possible (but often not likely) that you will be able to undelete it. This has to do with the reason that the ext2/3 filesystem doesn't need to be defragmented like a FAT filesystem; deleted inodes are immediately returned to the system for use. If the system is heavily used, the old inode will likely have already been overwritten. Therefore, the first rule in undeleting a file is to stop all disk writes as soon as possible.

The Ext2fs Undeletion mini-HOWTO (`http://www.linuxdoc.org/HOWTO/mini/Ext2fs-Undeletion.html`)has been written to detail the process. It's not all that complicated, but requires some practice before you would be ready to use it in the real world. Use the information in Chapter 10, "Managing the Filesystems," to create a loopback filesystem to experiment with. With that, you can safely delete and undelete files without taking a chance on damaging your system.

> **Caution**
>
> Have you lost a file on a reiserFS partition?
>
> Hans Reiser tells us that there is no way to recover deleted files from a reiserFS filesystem.

Undeleting a Directory

Because a directory is a file as well, the same techniques for file recovery can be used to recover entire directories. The Ext2fs Undeletion of Directory Structures mini-HOWTO (`http://www.linuxdoc.org/HOWTO/mini/Ext2fs-Undeletion-Dir-Struct/index.html`) is written as a companion to the Ext2fs Undeletion mini-HOWTO, both of which should be on everyone's required reading list if you want to successfully undelete any files.

Undeleting Using MC

The Midnight Commander can make use of a virtual filesystem and includes an undelete filesystem that can be used on ext2/3 partitions. The `mc` utility is really just an interface to the ext2fs library.

To use the recovery filesystem, you must `cd` in one of the panels to the special filename formed by combining the prefix `/#undel:` with the partition name where your deleted file resides. For example, to attempt to recover a deleted file on `/dev/hda1`, do this:

```
cd /#undel:hda1
```

Be patient because it will take a while for the deleted files to be displayed. You will see is a list of inodes that you can examine with the text editor (using the F4 key); then use the F12 key to Save As and the F10 key to exit when done.

Note

If you need to know what is on an unknown drive, use

```
# dd if=/dev/hda1 count=1 bs=512 | file -
```

which produces output similar to the following:

```
1+0 records in
1+0 records out
standard input:              x86 boot sector, system MSWIN4.1, FAT (16 bit)
```

To discover what an unknown floppy disk is, use this

```
# dd if=/dev/fd0 count=1 bs=512 | file -
```

which produces output similar to the following:

```
1+0 records in
1+0 records out
standard input:              x86 boot sector, system )_3oEIHC, FAT (12 bit)
```

Booting the System from the Rescue CD

You can use the rescue CD to boot the system if the bootloader code is damaged or incorrect, but in order to do that, you must know the name of the partition on which the root filesystem resides. It might be necessary to boot into rescue mode, use fdisk to identify the partitions, and then selectively mount them until you find the root filesystem. You could use the empirical method as well and start with /dev/hda1 and, if that doesn't work, progress to /dev/hda2, and so on.

To use the Rescue CD to boot your system from /dev/hda1, first boot the CD and press the F1 key. At the LILO prompt, enter something similar to this if you have a specific partition in mind (on a dual-boot system, for example):

```
linux rescue root=/dev/hda1
```

If you aren't certain where the root partition is, the following will cause the rescue CD to attempt to find the root partition on its own:

```
linux rescue
```

Booting the System from a Generic Boot Floppy

If you failed to make a boot floppy or cannot locate the one you did make, any boot floppy can be pressed into service as long as it has a reasonably similar kernel version using the same techniques as described previously. Although you are almost guaranteed to get some error messages, you will at least be able to recover the system.

Special Drivers

In both preceding cases, it is assumed that you don't need any special filesystem or device drivers to access the root partition. If you do, add the `initrd=` argument to the LILO line. If you don't know the exact name of the initrd file, you are out of luck unless you use a GRUB boot floppy.

GRUB Boot Floppy

The *GRand Unified Bootloader (GRUB)* can be a lifesaver when attempting to boot a system from a floppy without a viable custom-made boot floppy. The image for the floppy can be downloaded from `ftp://alpha.gnu.org/gnu/grub/` `grub-0.90-i386-pc.ext2fs` and copied to a floppy using `dd` (`rawrite` would be used on a Microsoft system). Or, if you have a boot floppy from an existing system using GRUB, that one will work as well.

GRUB has its own command shell, filesystem drivers and search function (much like command completion in the bash shell). It is possible to boot using the GRUB floppy, examine the drive partitions, and search for the kernel and initrd image as well, using them to boot the system. Worthy of a chapter all its own, the GRUB documentation is extensive: In addition to info GRUB, the GRUB docs contain a tutorial that is worth reading.

Backing Up, Restoring, and Recovery

CHAPTER 11

285

11

BACKING UP,
RESTORING, AND
RECOVERY

11

BACKING UP,
RESTORING, AND
RECOVERY

FIGURE 11.5

The GRUB boot-loader gives you incredible flexibility in booting even unfamiliar systems. It can be used with the Linux, BSD, and Microsoft operating systems and is flexible enough to accommodate other operating systems if the appropriate code is written.

Using the Recovery Facility from the Installation Disk

Red Hat has provided a recovery disk built in to the installation disk. When booting from the CD (or from a floppy disk that boots the CD), a menu is displayed and Rescue is one of the options.

By typing **linux rescue** at the prompt and pressing the Enter key, you can launch a very minimal Linux system with a minimum of tools to help you attempt to repair your damaged computer.

Upon beginning the rescue mode, you get your choice of language and keyboard layouts. The minimal operating system attempts to mount your Red Hat installation at /mnt/sysimage; this step can be skipped (you might not want to mount anything yet), and it will drop you to command shell.

If you choose to mount the installation, you are asked to confirm which partition is the root partition. It does offer support for software RAID arrays (RAID 0,1,and 5) as well as IDE or SCSI partitions formatted as ext2, ext3, reiserfs, vfat, fat and msdos. After asking for input if it is unsure how to proceed, you eventually arrive at a command shell as root; there is no logon or password. Depending on your configuration, you might or might not see prompts for additional information.

If you need network connectivity, the ne2k-pci and 8390 modules are available as are the `ifconfig`, `route`, `rcp`, `rlogin`, `rsh`, and `ftp` commands. For archiving (and restoring archives), `cpio`, `uncpio`, `gzip`, `gunzip`, `dd`, `zcat`, and `md5sum` commands are there. For editors, `vi` (of course) and `pico` are present as well as other useful system commands. However, a closer look at the commands reveals that they are all links to a program called `busybox` with a homepage at `http://busybox.lineo.com/`. From their homepage, "BusyBox combines tiny versions of many common UNIX utilities into a single small executable. It provides minimalist replacements for most of the utilities you usually find in fileutils, shellutils, findutils, textutils, grep, gzip, tar, etc."

BusyBox provides a fairly complete POSIX environment for any small or embedded system. The utilities in BusyBox generally have fewer options than their full-featured GNU cousins; however, the options that are included "provide the expected functionality and behave very much like their GNU counterparts." This means that you should test the rescue mode first to see if it can restore you data and see which options are available to you.

An Alternative to the Red Hat Rescue CD

If the Red Hat rescue CD is inadequate for your intended use for it, lacking ethernet support, filesystem support or the kind of full utility functionality that you require for a successful recovery operation, an alternative exists in the SuperRescue CD created by H. Peter Anvin.

Essentially, it's a reasonably full and robust Red Hat distribution (based on Red Hat 7 at the moment) that runs completely from a bootable CD. The best thing about the SuperRescue CD is that it comes with build scripts, so it is incredibly easy to add new software (that special driver or app) and create a new CD. The homepage is at `http://freshmeat.net/projects/superrescue/`.

Reference

`http://www.linuxdoc.org/HOWTO/Filesystems-HOWTO.html`—The Filesystems HOWTO is a good place to start if you are dealing with an unfamiliar filesystem.

`http://www.linuxdoc.org/HOWTO/Bootdisk-HOWTO/index.html`—The Linux Bootdisk HOWTO covers the design and construction of boot diskettes. It contains a great deal of information about the boot process, providing background information to assist you in solving boot problems.

`http://www.linuxdoc.org/HOWTO/Bootdisk-HOWTO/a1439.html`—Here's a list of LILO Boot error codes to help you debug a cranky system that won't boot.

`http://metalab.unc.edu/pub/Linux/system/boot/lilo/lilo-u-21.ps.gz`—If it isn't installed on you system and you can't find the installation CD to load it, this is the LILO User Documentation.

`http://www.freshmeat.net`—The Freshmeat site serves up a steady stream of Linux application announcements and information as well as providing a search function for the site.

`http://www.google.com/linux/`—The Linux-specific section of Google helps eliminate a lot of less-than-useful hits.

`http://kmself.home.netcom.com/Linux/FAQs/backups.html`—The Linux Backups mini-FAQ contains some useful, although brief, comments on backup media, compression, encryption, and security.

`http://www.linuxdoc.org`—The Linux Documentation Project offers several useful HOWTO documents that discuss backups and disk recovery.

`http://www.linuxdoc.org/HOWTO/mini/Ext2fs-Undeletion.html`—If you need to undelete a file from an ext2/3 filesystem, the Linux Ext2fs Undeletion mini-HOWTO is the document for you. You will be more successful if you practice.

`http://www.linuxdoc.org/HOWTO/mini/Ext2fs-Undeletion-Dir-Struct/index.html`—The Ext2fs Undeletion of Directory Structures is a companion HOWTO to the Linux Ext2fs Undeletion mini-HOWTO, helping you cope with an errant `rm -rf *`.

`http://www.linuxdoc.org/FAQ/Ftape-FAQ.html`—This is a FAQ for the floppy tape device driver; it's a little old.

`http://www.linux-usb.org/USB-guide/x498.html`—The USB Guide for mass storage devices. If you have a USB device and need to know if it's supported, check here.

`http://www.linuxdoc.org/HOWTO/LILO-crash-rescue-HOWTO.html`—This HOWTO describes how to use floppy-based recovery disks, but the general techniques are universal. The techniques covered include checking the integrity of the target filesystem. A little thin in content, but it is notable for its related URL links.

`http://www.backupcentral.com/amanda.html`—This is the Amanda chapter of *UNIX Backup and Recovery* available online; the site features a search tool for the chapter.

System Services Administration

PART

III

IN THIS PART

Printing Services

This chapter discusses printing services for Red Hat Linux. You'll see that Linux developers have kept up with the advent and growth in popularity of the Universal Serial Bus (USB) protocol and hardware in today's laptops, desktops, and servers. Excellent support still exists for legacy parallel-port (IEEE-1284) printers, but many newer printing devices are now sold only with USB support.

Red Hat Linux provides support for more than 600 printers from more than 40 manufacturers. You'll find that it is also possible to mix and match printing hardware with newer computers. For example, if you have a legacy parallel-port printer that you'd like to attach to a USB-only computer running Linux, you're almost guaranteed success if you use a USB-to-parallel converter to attach the printer. This device (such as a D-Link DSB-P36) generally provides a cable with a Centronics parallel-port connector that is plugged into the older printer, and a USB connector on the other end that is plugged into your hub, desktop or notebook USB port. On the other hand, if you have a USB printer you'd like to attach to an older computer, it might be possible to use a USB interface card to provide support.

Many different programs, files, and directories are integral to supporting printing under Red Hat Linux, but print service can be quickly configured and new printers made available almost immediately using a variety of methods.

Overview of Red Hat Linux Printing

Red Hat's new and revised print filter system is the main engine that enables the printing of many types of documents using Linux. The heart of that engine is the GNU GPL version of Aladdin, Inc.'s Ghostscript interpreter, the gs client. The Red Hat system administrator's printer configuration tool is the printconf client.

When you use the printconf client to create, configure, and save a printer definition, the definition is saved as an entry in your system's printer capabilities database, /etc/printcap. Each definition contains a text field that points to a related and appropriately named spool directory under /var/spool/lpd, along with a pointer to /usr/share/printconf/util/mf_wrapper. This file, a shell script, in turn calls the /usr/bin/magicfilter-t utility. A sample printer description with an if: filter entry looks like this:

```
lp:\
        :sh:\
        :ml=0:\
        :mx=0:\
        :sd=/var/spool/lpd/lp:\
```

```
:af=/var/spool/lpd/lp/lp.acct:\
:lp=/dev/lp0:\
:lpd_bounce=true:\
:if=/usr/share/printconf/util/mf_wrapper:
```

In this example, the mf_wrapper filter utility is used as a printer filter. In turn, mf_wrapper calls a related utility (magicfilter-t) to first identify the file stream (a text file, document, or image) according to initial-byte headers, or *magic* values as listed in the file /usr/share/printconf/mf.magic. The stream is then converted to PostScript according to filter rules located under the /usr/share/printconf/mf_rules directory. The values returned by this logic assign proper arguments to the gs interpreter, which reads the input file stream as PostScript and then converts the stream to a proper printer format or language. The text stream is then fed (sent) to the desired printer.

Your task as a system administrator (or root operator of your workstation) is to properly define entries in /etc/printcap for local or remote printers and to ensure that printing services are enabled and running properly. Printing services and job requests are handled by the lpd daemon, started by the /etc/rc.d/init.d/lpd startup script, which looks like this (in part):

```
start () {
    echo -n $"Starting $prog: "
    # Is this a printconf system?
    if [[ -x /usr/sbin/printconf-backend ]]; then
            # run printconf-backend to rebuild printcap and spools
            if ! /usr/sbin/printconf-backend ; then
                # If the backend fails, we dont start no printers defined
                echo -n $"No Printers Defined"
                echo_success
                echo
                return 0
            fi
...
```

Note that not all the script is shown here. However, as you can see, the script first reports that the service is starting. Next, an associated command to the Red Hat printconf utility is used to check for the existence of your system's /etc/printcap database. The script then starts the lpd daemon, which runs in the background as a process, waiting for any files to appear under a defined printer's directory under the /var/spool/lpd directory.

The printconf utility is an update to the now-legacy printtool client included with previous distributions, but retains the same name. (printtool is actually a symbolic link pointing to the binary command /usr/sbin/printconf-gui, which in turn, is a six-line Python script used to launch the client.) After defining a printer, you can then use one or more traditionally named line printer spooler utilities to control printing services, manage

12

PRINTING SERVICES

printing (or print *jobs*), and enable, disable, or authorize remote printing services (see the section "Printing Tools" at the end of this chapter).

Table 12.1 contains a list of related printing commands and drivers included with Red Hat Linux.

TABLE 12.1   Print-Related Commands and Drivers

Name	Description
a2ps	Format text files for PostScript printing
dvi[lj,lj4l,lj2p,lj4]	Convert TeX DVI files to specific PCL format
escputil	Epson Stylus inkjet printer utility
grolbp	groff driver for Canon LBP-4 and LBP-8 laser printers
gs	The Ghostscript interpreter
gsbj[dj500, lp]	Ghostscript BubbleJet printer drivers
gsdj[dj500,lj,lp]	Ghostscript DeskJet printer drivers
kljettool	KDE Laserjet printer utility
klp	Comprehensive KDE printer utility
lout	Lout document printing utility
lpc	Printer control utility
lpd	Print spooling daemon
lpf	General printer filter
lprm	Print queue management utility
mpage	PostScript text formatting utility
pbm[2ppa,page,to10x,toepson, toppa,toptx]	Portable bitmap conversion utilities
pr	Text formatting command
printmail	Format mail for printing
printtool	Printer configuration utility
psmandup	Duplex printing utility for non-duplex printers
sensors	Printing sensors information
setup	Launch printer configuration tool
smbclient	SMB print spooler
smbprint	SMB print shell script
smbspool	SMB printer spooler
thinkjettopbm	Portable bitmap to ThinkJet printer conversion utility

> **Note**
>
> To display PostScript documents (including compressed documents) or images, use the gv client. To display Portable Document Format (PDF) documents, you can try gv or use the xpdf client.

You can use the Ghostscript interpreter gs to verify its built-in printer devices by using the gs interpreter with its --help command-line option like this:

```
# gs --help
```

The gs command will output many lines of help text on command-line usage and then list built-in printer and graphics devices. Another way to get this information is to start gs and then use the devicenames == command like this:

```
# gs
$ gs
GNU Ghostscript 6.51 (2001-03-28)
Copyright  2001 artofcode LLC, Benicia, CA.  All rights reserved.
This software comes with NO WARRANTY: see the file COPYING for details.
Loading NimbusRomNo9L-Regu font from \
/usr/share/fonts/default/Type1/n021003l.pfb... \
2362024 982552 1622424 328124 0 done.
Loading NimbusSanL-Regu font from /usr/share/fonts/default/Type1/n019003l.pfb...
\
2639936 1238227 1642520 335588 0 done.
GS> devicenames ==
[/hpdj /iwhi /pcx256 /md50Mono /eps9high /uniprint /fmlbp /cgmmono /ljet4 \
/pr1000_4 /bmpasep8 /bmp16 /x11cmyk4 /ap3250 /x11 /r4081 /png256 /mgrmono \
/tiff12nc /nullpage /ln03 /ppmraw /md2k /iwlo /pcx24b /md50Eco /eps9mid /bj10e \
/ml600 /cljet5pr /ljet4d /jj100 /ccr /bmp256 /x11cmyk8 /appledmp /bbox /sj48 \
/png16m /miff24
...
```

Not all the devices are listed in this example.

> **Aladdin or GNU?**
>
> At least two versions of Ghostscript are available for Linux. One version is named "AFPL Ghostscript," which went by the former name "Aladdin Ghostscript." This version is licensed under the Aladdin Free Public License, which disallows commercial distribution. The other version is called "GNU Ghostscript," which is distributed under the GNU General Public License. You'll
>
> *continues*

find this version installed with Red Hat Linux. For details about the different versions or for answers to questions regarding licensing, see the Ghostscript home page (listed in the "Reference" section at the end of this chapter).

Creating Local Printers

Creating a local printer for your Red Hat Linux system can be accomplished in six easy steps. You must have root permission to use the `printconf` client, and you might also need an active X session. To launch `printconf`, select the Printer Configuration menu item from the GNOME or KDE desktop panel's System menu, or use the command line of an X terminal window like this:

```
# printtool &
```

After you press Enter, `printconf`'s main window will appear. Next, click the New toolbar button and you'll see a configuration dialog box as shown in Figure 12.1.

FIGURE 12.1

Click the New toolbar button to start configuration of a new printer for your system; then click the Next button to begin.

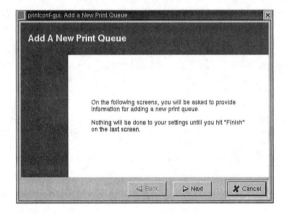

Click the Next button, and you'll be asked to select a type of printer. as shown in Figure 12.2. Using this dialog box, you'll be able to configure a local, remote, Windows, Netware, or HP JetDirect print server (an intelligent, remotely managed network appliance supporting print spooling and multiple printer queues).

Type in a name of printer you'd like to define for your system, and then click a type of printer. When finished, click the Next button to continue, and you'll see a list of printer devices, as shown in Figure 12.3.

FIGURE 12.2

Enter the desired name of your new printer; then click to select a type of printer for your system and click the Next button.

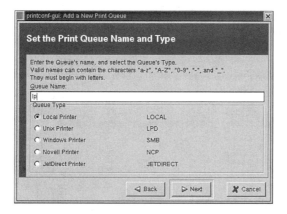

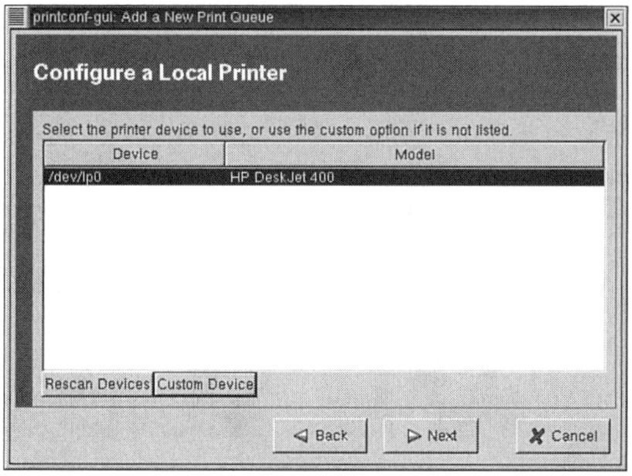

FIGURE 12.3

Click to select the desired printer device you'd like to configure for your system.

In the example in Figure 12.3, a parallel-port printer device, /dev/lp0, is shown. If you have a USB printer, you should see the device /dev/usb/lp0 listed. Double-click on the device you'd like to configure, and you'll then be able to choose the printer and its driver, as shown in Figure 12.4.

> **Note**
>
> Even if your printer's device isn't shown (perhaps because the desired printer isn't attached to your computer), you can still enter a device by clicking the Custom Device button and typing in the device name. This is also useful for creating a serial printer entry.

FIGURE 12.4

Scroll through the list of manufacturers to select a printer and driver.

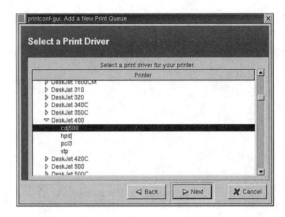

Look through the list manufacturers; then choose a printer model and a driver for your printer. Note that you shouldn't worry if you don't see your model listed; it is possible to use a driver for a closely related printer. You might also find multiple drivers listed for your printer; if so, you can experiment to see which driver performs best. If you select a somewhat-compatible driver, you might not be able to use all the features of your printer, but you will be able to set up printing service. When finished, click the Next button to confirm your choices, as shown in Figure 12.5.

FIGURE 12.5

Before configuring printer settings, double-check your settings before you commit to creating a new printer entry in /etc/printcap.

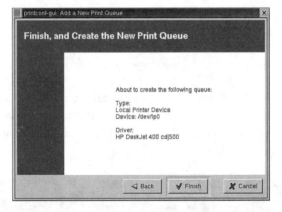

Check to make sure that the definition (perhaps as shown in Figure 12.5) is correct before proceeding. Note that you can use the Back button at any time during the process to correct an error or choice. When verified, click the Next button and you'll see the new printer defined in the printconf main window as shown in Figure 12.6.

FIGURE 12.6

New printer entries created in /etc/printcap *will be displayed in* printconf's *main window.*

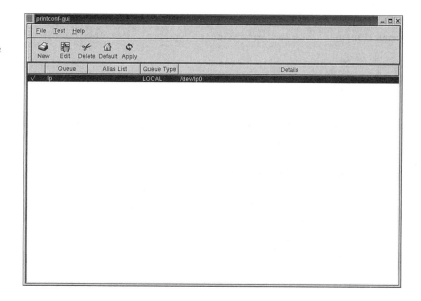

To edit the printer settings, click on the toolbar's Edit button after selecting (highlighting) the printer definition as shown in Figure 12.6. A dialog box will appear, as shown in Figure 12.7.

FIGURE 12.7

Edit a new printer's settings by using tabs in printconf's *Edit Queue window.*

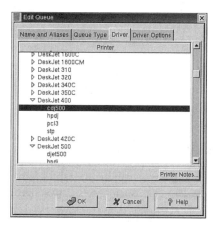

Click on a desired tab, and you can assign an *alias* or synonym for the name of the new printer, change the definition to a new type of printer, select or update the driver, or choose available driver options for the printer, as shown in Figure 12.8. Printer aliases can also be entered manually into /etc/printcap entries, but using a graphical user

12

PRINTING SERVICES

interface (GUI) might appeal to many administrators. Aliases are found along with the printer queue's name in the /etc/printcap entry, and might look like this:

```
gigilp|sammie:\
        :sh:\
        :ml=0:\
...
```

In this example, the printer (queue) has the name gigilp or sammie; either one can be used for printing.

FIGURE 12.8

A printer's driver settings can be changed in print-conf*'s Edit Queue window.*

When you have finished creating your new printer definition (or *queue*), click the OK button, and then use the File menu to first save the definition and then restart the lpd daemon. This is extremely important because you need to update /etc/printcap and restart the daemon to force it to re-read your new settings. You can then use the Test menu to print a PostScript or ASCII text file on your printer.

Creating Network Printers

Setting up remote printing service requires work on the local and remote computer hosting the printer. This section introduces a quick method of enabling printing from one Linux workstation to another Linux computer on a LAN. You'll need root permission and access to both computers, but the process is simple and easy to perform.

First, go to (or ssh or telnet to) a remote computer and note its hostname or IP address (such as *green.home.org* or *192.168.2.37*). Use root access and ensure that the printer is configured and working on the remote system, or use printconf on the remote computer to create a local printer entry. Note the printer's name (queue name, such as lp, not the printer's device name, such as /dev/usb/lp0), and the name of the printer's driver.

Next, as root on the remote computer, use a favorite text editor and create or edit the file named /etc/hosts.lpd. In the file, enter the hostnames or IP addresses of remote computers you want to allow to use the local printer, such as:

```
192.168.2.35
thinkpad.home.org
```

Save the file, and then restart the lpd daemon. This will allow incoming print requests with the proper queue name from the remote hosts to be routed to the printer. After you have finished, log out and return to a remote computer without an attached printer.

Again, use the printconf client to create a new print queue. Enter a name for the remote printer, and then click the UNIX printer type in the dialog box shown in Figure 12.2. When finished, click the Next button. You'll be asked to enter the hostname of the remote computer with a printer, along with the printer's (queue) name, as shown in Figure 12.9.

FIGURE 12.9

Enter the host-name or IP address of the remote computer with a printer, along with the remote printer's queue name.

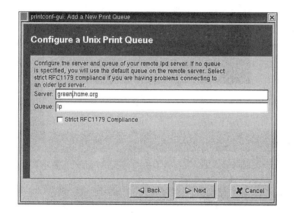

Click the Next button after entering this information; then continue to configure the new entry as if the remote printer were attached locally. When finished, don't forget to save the changes and restart the lpd daemon! The new remote printer entry /etc/printcap might look something like this:

```
remote:\
        :sh:\
        :ml=0:\
        :mx=0:\
        :sd=/var/spool/lpd/remote:\
        :af=/var/spool/lpd/remote/remote.acct:\
        :rm=green.home.org:\
        :rp=green:\
        :lpd_bounce=true:\
        :if=/usr/share/printconf/util/mf_wrapper:
```

In this example, the :rm entry defines the remote host, whereas the :rp entry defines the remote queue. As before, test the new remote printer by clicking the Tests menu item and using the ASCII or PostScript test pages. The ASCII test page will print a page of text, whereas the PostScript test page will print a page of text with outlined borders, the Red Hat logo, and a multicolored box (if you use a color printer).

Session Message Block Printing

Printing to an SMB printer requires Samba, along with its utilities such as the smbclient and associated smbprint printing filter. Using this software requires connection to a Windows network if you want to print to a shared printer. You must also have printer sharing enabled on the remote Windows computer hosting the printer and access to the printer share.

This is usually accomplished under Windows operating systems through configuration settings using the Control Panel's Network device. After enabling print sharing (and rebooting), right-click the desired printer to share and select the Sharing menu item. Set the Shared As item; then enter a shared name and a password. This information is required in order to configure the printer when running Linux. You'll also need to know the printer's workgroup name, IP address, printer name, and have the username and password on hand.

You can get this information from the shared printer's Properties menu. As before, create a new printer queue locally using a name, and then select Windows Printer. Click the Next button, and then enter the required information, as shown in Figure 12.10.

FIGURE 12.10
Create a shared remote printer using required information for Windows.

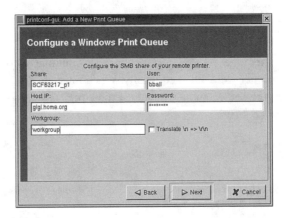

Again, create a printer queue with characteristics that match the remote printer. (For example, if the remote printer is an HP400, select the proper HP400 driver in your configuration.) Don't forget to save and restart `lpd` after creating or editing a local or remote printer queue. The new entry in `/etc/printcap` might look like this:

```
gigilp:\
        :sh:\
        :ml=0:\
        :mx=0:\
        :sd=/var/spool/lpd/gigilp:\
        :af=/var/spool/lpd/gigilp/gigilp.acct:\
        :lp=|/usr/share/printconf/util/smbprint:\
        :lpd_bounce=true:\
        :if=/usr/share/printconf/util/mf_wrapper:
```

In this example you can see that an SMB printing filter is used, but that Red Hat's printing filter system is still an active part of the process. Using remote printers requires an active network connection, but Red Hat's print setup and printer queue naming makes the process of printing fairly painless and easy, without resorting to complex command lines with a lot of required options. Printing various documents from the command line using the `lpr` command and other Red Hat Linux print utilities is discussed next.

Printing Tools

Older versions of Red Hat Linux used the 4.3BSD line-printer spooling system and its suite of printing utilities. Newer versions of these utilities (with the same names) are used today in the latest Red Hat Linux distribution. The commands support the launching of print jobs in the background (as a background process), printing of multiple documents, the ability to specify specific local and networked printers, control of the printers, and management of the queued documents waiting in the printer's spool queue.

The main commands used for printing from the command line are as follows:

- `lpr`—The line printer spooling command, used to print documents using a specific printer
- `lpq`—The line printer queue display command, used to view the existing list of documents waiting to be printed
- `lprm`—The line printer queue management command, used to remove print jobs from a printer's queue
- `lpc`—The line printer control program, used by the root operator to manage print spooling, the `lpd` daemon, and printer activity

These commands provide all the basic features needed to start and control printers and print queues from the command line. Red Hat Linux uses Patrick Powell's LPRng print spooler software, an improved and totally revised version of the 4.3BSD UNIX printing system. Configure this printing system by editing the /etc/lpd.conf file; by default no options are enabled in Red Hat Linux. You can get a status check of the print spooling system by using LPRng's checkpc command like this:

```
# checkpc -V
LPRng-3.7.4, Kerberos5, Copyright 1988-2000 Patrick Powell, <papowell@lprng.com>
Checking for configuration files '/etc/lpd.conf'
  found '/etc/lpd.conf', mod 0100644
Checking for printcap files '/etc/printcap'
  found '/etc/printcap', mod 0100644
Checking for lpd only printcap files '/etc/lpd_printcap'
 DaemonUID 4, DaemonGID 7
Using Config file '/etc/lpd.conf'
LPD lockfile '/var/run/lpd.printer'

.names
 :gigilp=gigilp
 :lp=lp
 :remote=remote
 :sammie=gigilp
...
```

Note that not all the information output from this command is displayed here. In this example, the program reports important configuration files, permissions, and names of printers. Other information in the output includes /etc/printcap definitions, diagnostics regarding each printer's spool directory (under /var/spool/lpd/*printername*), and the permissions of all print filters.

Files (documents or images) are printed using the lpr command, along with a designed printer and filename. For example, to print the file mydoc.txt using the printer named lp, use the lpr command like this:

```
# lpr -Plp mydoc.txt
```

You can also print multiple documents. For example, to print a number of files at once to the lp printer, use lpr like so:

```
# lpr -Plp *.txt
```

> **Note**
>
> As with earlier versions, there is a limit of only printing of 52 files at once. To print more files than 52, split up the print job. As the system administrator, you should also be aware that some spooled print jobs can take up a lot of hard drive space.

Use the lpq command to view the printer's queue like so:

```
# lpq
Printer: lp@thinkpad
 Queue: 1 printable job
 Server: pid 9531 active
 Unspooler: pid 9532 active
 Status: IF filter 'mf_wrapper' filter msg - \
'<</HWResolution[300 300]>>setpagedevice' at 10:29:03.569
 Rank   Owner/ID                Class Job Files           Size Time
1      root@thinkpad+530         A    530 CHANGES         251703 10:29:02
```

The lpq reports on the printer, number of jobs, the lpd PID, information from the print filter (such as dots per inch, or *dpi*), and a formatted list of print jobs, each with a job *number* (530 in this example), owner, name of file, its size, and the time the job was started. To stop the example print job, use the lprm command, followed by the job number, like this:

```
# lprm 530
Printer lp@thinkpad:
  checking perms 'root@thinkpad+530'
  dequeued 'root@thinkpad+530'
```

The lprm command will remove the spooled files from the printer's queue and kill the job. Print job owners, such as regular users, can only remove spooled jobs that are owned. As the root operator, you can kill any job.

Only the root operator can use the lpc command. This command is used for printer and queue control. The order of print jobs can be rearranged, and you can get a display of the status of any system printer. Start lpc on the command line like this:

```
# lpc
```

The lpc command has built-in help on command keywords and syntax. Use the help keyword or press ? like so:

```
lpc> help
```

Several pages of help text will echo back to your display. Another helpful command is lpstat, which can be used like this:

```
# lpstat
Printer: lp@thinkpad
 Queue: no printable jobs in queue
 Status: subserver pid 9532 exit status 'JFAIL' at 10:34:43.338
```

Waiting print jobs will be listed along with information similar to that returned by lprm.

12

PRINTING SERVICES

Reference

`http://www.redhat.com/cgi-bin/htsearch`—Enter a phrase such as **"printing"**, and then click the Search button to view all related documents in Red Hat, Inc.'s knowledge base regarding printers and printing with Red Hat Linux.

`http://www.linuxprinting.org/`—Browse here for specific drivers and information about USB printers.

`http://www.hp.com/cposupport/printers/support_doc/bpd06898.html`—Short, but definitive information from HP regarding printing product support under Linux.

`http://www.linuxdoc.org/HOWTO/Printing-HOWTO/`—Grant Taylor's Printing-HOWTO, with information on using various print services under Linux.

`http://www.linuxprinting.org/cups-doc.html`—Information about the Common UNIX Printing System (CUPS).

`http://www.cs.wisc.edu/~ghost/`—Home page for the Ghostscript interpreter.

`http://www.samba.org/`—Base entry point for getting more information about Samba and using the SMB protocol with Linux, UNIX, MacOS, and other operating systems.

Network Connectivity

One of Linux's strongest features is its networking. Linux can emulate or share files with almost every operating system. Linux can talk to BeOS, MacOS, Netware, ALL flavors of UNIX, and even Windows (with the help of SAMBA). I know of companies whose system administrators have installed Linux servers in homogeneous networks for weeks, even months before anyone noticed the change. It's that kind of flexibility that can account for Linux's increased presence in the workplace and in homes.

The basic building block for any heterogeneous network as well as any network based on UNIX hosts is the Transport Control Protocol/Internet Protocol (TCP/IP) suite of three protocols. The TCP/IP suite is *packet* based, which means that data is broken into little chunks on the transmit end for transmission to the receiving end. Breaking data up into manageable packets allows for faster and more accurate transfers. The suite consists of the Internet Protocol (IP), Transport Control Protocol (TCP), and Universal Datagram Protocol (UDP). IP is the base protocol. All data travels via IP packets, which is why addresses are referred to as IP addresses. It is the lowest level of the suite. TCP is a connection based protocol. Before data is transmitted, a connection is established between the two machines communicating. Once a connection is made, a stream of data is sent to the Internet Protocol to be broken into the packets that are then transmitted. At the receiving end, the packets are put back in order and sent to the proper application port. UDP is connectionless protocol. Applications using this protocol just chose their destination and start sending. Usually UDP is used for small amounts of data or on networks that are fast and reliable. If you're interested in the internals of TCP/IP, see the reference section at the end of this chapter for places to look for more information.

TCP/IP

A large number of books are published that cover TCP/IP in great detail. We only have enough space here to cover the basics dealing mostly with TCP/IP addressing. A TCP/IP address is four sets of numbers ranging from zero to 255 (known as octets) separated by dots (.). The first set of numbers usually determine what class the network belongs to. There are three classes of networks. The classes are

> **Class A**—Consists of networks with the first octet ranging from 1 to 127. Notice that zero isn't included. This because the zero address is used for network to network broadcasts. The "10." network is reserved for local network use, and the "127." network is reserved for the *loopback* address of 127.0.0.1. Loopback addressing is mostly used to check a hosts network setting without using network bandwidth. There are only 126 Class A networks each comprising of up to

16,777,214 hosts. (If you're doing the math, there are potentially 16,777,216 addresses but no host portion of an address can be all zeros or 255s.)

Class B—Consists of networks with the first octet ranging from 128 to 191. The "128." network is also reserved for local network use. There are 16,382 Class B networks each with 65,534 possible hosts.

Class C—Consists of a network with the first octet ranging from 192 to 223. The "192." network is another that is reserved for local network use. There are a possible 2,097,150 Class C networks of up to 254 hosts each.

Class D—Have a first octet ranging from 224 to 239. Class D networks are reserved for multicast addresses and not for use by network hosts.

Class E—Have a first octet from 240 through 255. Class E addresses are deemed as experimental and thus are not open for public addressing.

As noted with the Class A network, no host portion of an IP address can be all zeros or 255s. These addresses are reserved for broadcast addresses. IP addresses with all zeros in the host portion are reserved for network to network broadcast addresses. IP addresses with all 255s in the host portion are reserved for local network broadcasts. Broadcast messages are not typically seen by users.

These classes are the standard, but the real key to what class your network is in is determined by the netmask. The netmask determines what part of an IP address represents the network and what part represents the host. Common netmasks for the different classes are

Class A—255.0.0.0

Class B—255.255.0.0

Class C—255.255.255.0

You can mix and match class IP addresses and netmasks (that is, a Class A network address 10.1.1.10 with a netmask of 255.255.255.0 becomes a Class C subnet), but it's best to downgrade a class than attempt to upgrade a class.

Currently, it is virtually impossible to get a Class A network, nearly impossible to get a Class B network (all the addresses have been given out but some companies are said to be willing to sell theirs), and Class C network availability is dropping rapidly with the current growth of Internet use worldwide.

You probably noticed that one octet (10., 128., and 192.) in Class A, B, and C networks has been reserved for local use. When building a network for your business or home, you should choose one of these octets whether or not your network connects to the Internet. If your network connects to the Internet, it can sometimes be best to keep the class of your local network the same class as the Internet network your network connects to. If your network doesn't connect to the Internet, you should still use these octets in case you do at a later date.

Ports

Most servers on your network have more than one task. Web servers have to serve both standard pages and possibly secure pages. For this reason, applications are provided ports to use to make "direct" connections. These ports help TCP/IP distinguish services so data can get to the correct application. If you check the file /etc/services, you will see the common ports and their usage.

Networking

Setting up your network addressing properly can range in difficulty from trivial for a Class C network with less than 254 devices to horrendous for a large, worldwide company with a Class A network and many different subnets. If your company has less than 254 hosts (hosts refers to any device that requires an IP address, including computers, printers, routers, switches among other devices) and all your workgroups can share information, a Class C network will be sufficient (unless you can see your network growing in the near future). Otherwise, a Class A of B network is a better choice.

Subnets

Within Class A and B networks, there can be separate networks called subnets. Subnets are considered part of the host portion of an address for network class definitions. For example, in the 128. Class B network, you can have one computer with an address of 128.10.10.10 and another with an address of 128.10.200.20 that are on the same network (128.10.) but different subnets (128.10.10. and 128.10.200.). Because of this, communication between the two computers requires either a router or a switch (both are discussed later in the Network Devices section). Subnets can be helpful for separating workgroups within your company.

Often subnets are used to separate workgroups that have no real need to interact. For example, if your company is large enough to have its own HR department and payroll section, it might be a good idea to put those departments hosts on their own subnet and use your router configuration to limit the hosts that can connect to this subnet. This will keep the average worker on your network from being able to view some of the confidential information the HR and payroll personnel work with. Having subnets also allows your network to grow beyond 254 hosts. With proper routing configuration, users might not even know they are on a different subnet from their co-workers. Another common use for subnetting is with networks that cover a wide geographic area. It's not practical for a company with offices in Chicago and London to have both offices on the same subnet, so using a separate subnet for each office is the best solution.

Subnet Masks

Subnet masks are usually referred to netmasks. They are used by TCP/IP to show which part of an IP address is the network portion and which part is the host. For a pure Class A network the netmask would be 255.0.0.0, for a Class B network the netmask would be 255.255.0.0, and for a Class C network the netmask would be 255.255.255.0. Netmasks can also be used to deviate from the standard classes. By using customized netmasks, you can subnet your network to fit your needs. For example, your network has a single Class C address assigned to it. You have a need to subnet your network. Although this isn't possible with a normal Class C subnet mask, you can change the mask to break your network into subnets. By changing the last octet to a number greater than zero, you can break the network into as many subnets as you need. For more information on how to create customized subnet masks, see Chapter 6 of *Teach Yourself TCP\IP Network Administration in 21 Days*. This chapter goes into great detail on how to create custom netmasks and explains how to create an addressing cheat sheet for hosts on each subnet.

Addressing

Information can get to systems in three ways: Unicast, Multicast, and Broadcast. Each type of address depends on the purpose of the information being sent. Each of the three is explained here:

> **Unicast**—A unicast address, as the name implies, will send the information to one specific host. This is used for telnet, FTP, SSH, or any other information that needs to be shared in a one-to-one type situation. Although it is possible that any host on the subnet/network can see the information being passed, only one host is the intended recipient and that's the only host that will take action on the information being received.

> **Multicasting**—As mentioned previously, Class D networks are reserved for multicast addresses. Multicast addresses are a means to broadcast to groups of computers sharing an application. The most common use of multicasting is probably a video conference. All the machines require the same information at precisely the same time for a video conference to be effective.

Broadcasting—Broadcasting is used to transmit information to all the hosts on a network or subnet. *Dynamic Host Configuration Protocol (DHCP)* uses broadcast messages when the DHCP client looks for a DHCP server to get its network settings and *Reverse Address Resolution Protocol (RARP)* use broadcast messages too for hardware address to IP address resolution. Broadcast messages use .255 in all the host octets of the network IP address (10.255.255.255 will broadcast to every host in your Class A network).

Network Devices

As stated in the beginning of this chapter, networking is one of the strong points of the Linux operating system. This section covers the devices that are required for basic networking.

Network Interface Cards

Any computer wanting to connect to a network will need a Network Interface Card (NIC). Currently, there are several topologies (See definition) for network connections ranging from the old and mostly outdated 10Base2 to the much newer wireless networking that is gaining popularity. Each NIC has a unique address (the hardware address) which identifies that NIC. This address is six pairs of hexadecimal bits separated by colons (:). It looks similar to this: 00:60:08:8F:5A:D9. The hardware address is used by DHCP (see DHCP later in this chapter) to identify a specific host. It is also used by the Address Resolution Protocol (ARP) and Reverse Address Resolution Protocol (RARP) to map hosts to IP addresses. This section covers some of the different types of NIC used to connect to your network.

10Base2

Networks based on 10Base2 are rarely seen these days. There are a few reasons for its decline. First, there is a distance limitation that isn't very practical in most places where hosts are spread out over distanced. 10Base2 uses coaxial cable that has a limit of 185 meters between hosts. This wouldn't work too well if your network had to cover more than one building or floor. Second, 10Base2 uses a bus architecture, which is sort of like a bus route; it has a starting point and an end point with stops along the way. Each computer connects to the computer next to it. At each end of the network, you must have a terminator. If one machine goes down, the whole network is down.

The nature of the bus architecture also causes a high rate of collisions. (Two packets of data traveling toward each other "collide," requiring both packets to be resent.) This also creates a troubleshooting nightmare for a network administrator who has to find the broken link by trial and error. The third reason is that coaxial cable is rather thick and not very flexible. If you have a large network, this can get very bulky.

You can tell a 10Base2 NIC because of the BNC (British Naval Connector) which sticks out of the back of the card. It's a 1/2 to 3/4 inch cylinder that has two knobs about half way down. Red Hat Linux can detect most standard 10Base2 NICs automatically.

10Base5

10Base5 never really caught on. It allowed for a 500 meter distance between hosts, but it also used coaxial cable, which subjected it to the same problems as 10Base2. Again, most 10Base5 NICs are automatically detected. 10Base5 quickly gave way to 10BaseT.

Token Ring

Token ring was developed by IBM. As the name implies, the network is set up in a ring. A single "token" is passed from host to host, indicating the receiving hosts "permission" to transmit data. This alleviated the collisions inherent to the bus architecture, but it hurts the speed in which the data can travel from host to host and still has the same troubleshooting problems as bus architecture. Token ring has a maximum transfer rate of 16Mbps (16 million bits per second). Unlike 10Base2 and 10Base5, token ring uses what is called unshielded twisted pair (UTP) cable. This looks a lot like the cable that connects your phone to the wall. Almost all token ring NICs are recognized by Red Hat Linux.

13

NETWORK
CONNECTIVITY

10BaseT

10BaseT was the standard for a long time. A large number of networks still use it. 10BaseT also uses UTP cable. Instead of being configured in a ring, 10BaseT mostly uses a star architecture. In this architecture, the hosts all connect to a central location (usually a hub). All the data is sent to all hosts, but only the destination host takes action on individual packets. 10BaseT has a transfer rate of 10Mbps, but is easier to troubleshoot than any of the previous architectures.

10BaseT has a maximum segment length of 100 meters, which makes the location of your hubs important. The use of hubs also allows your network to grow easily by just adding new hubs when you need to. Each hub can connect to the other hubs on the network. If one host goes down, none of the other hosts are affected (depending on the purpose of the downed host). There are many manufacturers of 10BaseT NICs and most are recognized by Red Hat, however your chances of recognition of generic 10BaseT NICs aren't guaranteed.

100BaseT

100BaseT is quickly becoming the most popular network. It has a speed of 100Mbps and the ease of administration equal to 10BaseT. For most networks, the step from 10BaseT to 100BaseT is as simple as replacing NICs and hubs. Most 100BaseT NICs and hubs can also handle 10BaseT and can automatically detect which is in use. This allows for a gradual network upgrade and usually doesn't require rewiring your whole network. Pretty much all brand name NICs and most generic NICs are compatible with Red Hat Linux. 100BaseT requires category 5 unshielded twisted pair cabling. Unshielded twisted pair cables are covered in more detail later.

Fiber Optic

Fiber optic isn't used much because of the cost of upgrading. Fiber optics are used on Fiber Distributed Data Interface (FDDI) networks. This is similar to token ring in structure except that there are two rings. One is primary, whereas the other is secondary. The primary ring is used exclusively, and the secondary sits idle until there is a break in the primary ring. At this point, the secondary ring takes over keeping the network alive. FDDI has a speed of 100Mbps and has a maximum ring length of 62 miles. FDDI uses several tokens at the same time that, along with the faster speed of fiber optics, account for the drastic increase in network speed. As stated, the cost of switching to a fiber optic network can be very costly. To make the upgrade, the whole network has to be rewired (as much as $150 U.S. per network connection), and all NICs must be replaced at the same time. Most all FDDI NICs are recognized by Red Hat.

Wireless

Wireless has really taken off in the past year or two. One of the reasons for this includes the fact that wireless networking, as the name states, doesn't require any network cables. Upgrading is as easy as replacing network cards and equipment such as routers and switches. Wireless networking equipment can also work along with the traditional wired networking using existing equipment. Wireless technology is used mostly for users with either laptop or handheld computers. It's not really practical to upgrade a desktop or large server to wireless if the wiring is already in place since wireless networking is slower than the traditional wired network. As of this writing, the price for wireless networking equipment is low enough that many home users are using wireless networking to eliminate the need to run cable throughout their houses. With each new version of Red Hat Linux, more and more wireless NICs are being made compatible (it's usually better to get brand name wireless NICs, you have a better chance of compatibility). Check the linuxhardware.net Web page for more specific hardware compatibility information. More on wireless networking is discussed later in this chapter.

Loopback

As mentioned previously in the TCP/IP section, the IP address 127.0.0.1 is reserved for the loopback address. This isn't an actual hardware component attached to your computer but, rather, a software device and therefore doesn't have a hardware address. The primary use for the loopback address is to test a host's internal networking. If you can ping the loopback address, your host should have the correct networking packages installed.

Network Cable

There are currently three types of network cable—coaxial, unshielded twisted pair (UTP), and fiber. Coaxial cable looks a lot like the coaxial cable used to connect your television to the cable jack or antenna. UTP looks a lot like the cable that runs from your phone to the wall jack. Fiber cable looks sort of like the RCA cables used on your stereo or like the cable used on your electrical appliances in your house (two separate segments connected together).

Coaxial Cable

There are two types of coaxial network cable—thin Ethernet and thick Ethernet. Thin Ethernet, as the name suggests, is physically the thinner of the two. It is used on 10Base2 networks. Each segment has a limit of 185 meters (about 600 feet) before the signal becomes too degraded to be considered reliable.

Thick Ethernet provides a stronger signal, allowing 500 meter (about 1,600 feet) segments. Because it is thicker and thus more difficult to handle, it isn't widely used even with the signal improvement over thin Ethernet. Thick Ethernet is used for 10Base5 networks, and its bulkiness is probably the reason that 10Base5 never really caught on.

Unshielded Twisted Pair

Unshielded twisted pair (UTP) uses color coded pairs of thin copper wire to transmit data. There are five categories of UTP, each one serving a different purpose.

> **Category 1 (Cat1)**—Used for voice transmissions such as your phone. Only one pair is used per line—one wire to transmit and one to receive. An RJ-11 plug is used to connect the cable to your phone and the wall.

> **Category 2 (Cat2)**—Used in early token ring networks. Has a transmission rate of 4Mbps (million bits per second) and has the slowest data transfer rate. An RJ-11 plug is also used for cable connections.

13

NETWORK
CONNECTIVITY

Category 3 (Cat3)—Used for 10BaseT networks. It has a transmission rate of 10Mbps. Three pairs of cables are used to send and receive signals. RJ-11 or RJ-45 plugs can be used for Cat3 cables, usually deferring to the smaller RJ-11. RJ-45 plugs are similar in design to RJ-11, but are larger to handle up to four pairs of wire and are used more commonly on Cat5 cables.

Category 4 (Cat4)—Used in modern token ring networks. It has a transmission rate of 16Mbps and is less and less common as companies are switching to better alternatives. RJ-45 plugs are used for cable connections.

Category 5 (Cat5)—The fastest of the UTP categories with a transmission rate of up to 100 Mbps. It is used in both 10BaseT and 100BaseT networks and uses four pairs of wire. Cat5 cable came out just as 10BaseT networks were becoming popular and isn't much more expensive than Cat 3 cable. As a result, most 10BaseT networks use cat5 UTP instead of cat3. Cat5 cable uses RJ-45 plugs.

Fiber Optic Cable

Fiber optic cable (fiber) is usually orange or red in color. The transmission rate is 100Mbps and has a maximum length of 62 miles. Fiber uses a two pronged plug to connect to devices. A couple of advantages to fiber are that because it uses light instead of electricity to transmit its signal, it is free from the possibility of electromagnetic interference and is also more difficult to tap into and eavesdrop.

Hubs

Hubs are used to connect several hosts together on a star architecture network. Hubs can have any number of connections to it. The common sizes are 4, 8, 16, 24, and 48 connections (ports)—each port has a light that comes on once a network connection is made (link light). As stated previously, hubs can be connected together to allow for network growth. Usually this is done through a port on the hub called an *uplink* port. This allows two hubs, connected by their uplink ports, to act as one hub. Having a central location where all the hosts on your network can connect allows for easier troubleshooting of problems.

If a user complains that he has lost his network connection, the hub is a good place to start. If the link light for the user's port is lit, chances are the problem is with the users network configuration and not the network outside of the host that is down. If the link light isn't on, either the host's NIC is bad or the cable has gone bad for some reason. Because hubs aren't directly involved with Linux operating system, Red Hat compatibility isn't an issue.

Routers and Switches

Routers and switches are used to connect different networks to your network and to connect different subnets within your network. They both serve almost the same purpose, so you should pick whichever one suits your needs.

Bridges

Bridges are used within a network to connect different subnets. A bridge will blindly relay all information from one subnet to another without any filtering and is often referred to as a dumb gateway. This can be helpful if one subnet in your network is becoming overburdened and you need to lighten the load. A bridge isn't all that good for connecting to the Internet for the same reason. Your network really doesn't want all traffic traveling the Internet to be able to get through to your network.

Routers

Routers are best suited to connect your network to an outside network, such as the Internet. Routers can pass data from one network to another, and they allow for filtering of data. This way, if you have a Web server for an internal intranet that you don't want people to access from the Internet, you can use a filter to block port 80 from your network. These filters can be used to block specific hosts from accessing the Internet as well. For these reasons, routers are also called smart gateways. Routers range in complexity and price from a Cisco brand router that can cost thousands of dollars to almost generic brands that can be less than two hundred dollars. Routers are also often referred to as gateways.

Configuration Tools

All the initial network configuration for Red Hat Linux is normally done during installation. There are times, however, when a host needs to be moved to a different subnet or a different network altogether. This is where knowing how to configure a system can come in handy. There are two basic types of configuration, command line and graphical. To configure a host by command line, you can use a combination of commands or editing specific files. The other configuration method is to use the graphical tool called `linux-conf`. `linuxconf` can be used to configure a number of services on your machine but for our purposes we'll stick to network configuration. Both of these methods require root access to work. If you don't have root access, get it before trying any of these actions. Normally, any user can view current configurations through any of these tools/files except `linuxconf`, which must be run as root.

> **Note**
>
> This network configuration is for client hosts. Any server network configuration such as Domain Name System (DNS)(see Chapter 14, "Managing DNS," for more information) and DHCP (see the "DHCP" section later for more information) cannot be done during installation.

Command Line Configuration

Configuring your networking using the command line can be done two ways. The first way uses commands to change your current settings. The second way is to edit up to seven different files. Two commands are used for network configuration, `ifconfig` and `route`. There is also a command to display information about the network connections, `netstat`.

/sbin/ifconfig

`ifconfig` is used to configure your network interface. You can use it to create an IP alias to allow more than one IP address on your NIC. You can change your machine's IP address, netmask, or broadcast address. You can activate or deactivate your NIC or change your NIC's mode—`ifconfig` can be used to set a destination address for a point-to-point connection, as well as other obscure options that you can read about in the man page. You can change as many or as few of these as needed in a single command. The basic structure for the command is as follows:

```
/sbin/ifconfig [network device] options
```

The man page shows a family type option that allows your machine to interface with a number of network types such as AppleTalk, Novell, IPv6, and others. Again, read the man page for details on these network types.

Table 13.1 shows the `ifconfig` options and examples of their use.

TABLE 13.1 `ifconfig` Options

Use	Option	Example
Create alias	[network device] :[number]	ifconfig eth0:0 10.10.10.10
Change IP address		ifconfig eth0 10.10.10.12
Change the netmask 255.255.255.0	netmask [netmask]	ifconfig eth0 netmask

TABLE 13.1 continued

Use	*Option*	*Example*
Change the broadcast	`broadcast [address]`	`ifconfig eth0 broadcast` `10.10.10.255`
Take interface down	`down`	`ifconfig eth0 down`
Bring interface up	`up (add IP address)`	`ifconfig eth0 up (ifconfig` `eth0 10.10.10.10)`

Set NIC promiscuous mode on [off]	`[-]promisc`	`ifconfig eth0`
		`  promisc`
		
		`[ifconfig eth0 -promisc]`

Set multicasting mode on [off]	`[-]allmulti`	`ifconfig eth0`
		`  allmulti`
		
		`[ifconfig eth0 -allmulti]`

Enable [disable] point-to-point address	`[-]pointopoint`
	`[address]`
		`ifconfig`
		`eth0`
		`pointopoint`
		`10.10.10.20`
		
		`[ifconfig eth0`
		`-pointopoint`
		`10.10.10.20]`

13

NETWORK CONNECTIVITY

> **Note**
>
> Promiscuous mode causes the NIC to receive all packets on the network. It is often used to sniff a network. Multicasting mode allows the NIC to receive all multicast traffic on the network.

If no argument is given, `ifconfig` displays the status of active interfaces. With an argument of `-a` (`ifconfig -a`), `ifconfig` displays the status of all devices on the network. The output of `ifconfig` without arguments looks similar to this:

```
# /sbin/ifconfig
lo        Link encap:Local Loopback
          inet addr:127.0.0.1  Mask:255.0.0.0
          UP LOOPBACK RUNNING  MTU:16436  Metric:1
          RX packets:716 errors:0 dropped:0 overruns:0 frame:0
          TX packets:716 errors:0 dropped:0 overruns:0 carrier:0
          collisions:0
          RX bytes:51255 (50.0 Kb)  TX bytes:51255 (50.0 Kb)
```

`ifconfig` with a -a looks similar to this with the eth0 interface down:

```
# /sbin/ifconfig -a
eth0      Link encap:Ethernet  HWaddr 00:60:08:8F:5A:D9
          inet addr:216.164.58.120  Bcast:255.255.255.255  Mask:255.255.255.0
          BROADCAST MTU:1500  Metric:1
          RX packets:37937 errors:0 dropped:0 overruns:1 frame:0
          TX packets:45767 errors:0 dropped:0 overruns:0 carrier:0
          collisions:892
          RX bytes:30519779 (29.1 Mb)  TX bytes:14805768 (14.1 Mb)

lo        Link encap:Local Loopback
          inet addr:127.0.0.1  Mask:255.0.0.0
          UP LOOPBACK RUNNING  MTU:16436  Metric:1
          RX packets:716 errors:0 dropped:0 overruns:0 frame:0
          TX packets:716 errors:0 dropped:0 overruns:0 carrier:0
          collisions:0
          RX bytes:51255 (50.0 Kb)  TX bytes:51255 (50.0 Kb)
```

With the eth0 interface up, the interface looks like the following:

```
# /sbin/ifconfig -a
eth0      Link encap:Ethernet  HWaddr 00:60:08:8F:5A:D9
          inet addr:216.164.58.120  Bcast:255.255.255.255  Mask:255.255.255.0
          UP BROADCAST RUNNING  MTU:1500  Metric:1
          RX packets:37937 errors:0 dropped:0 overruns:1 frame:0
          TX packets:45767 errors:0 dropped:0 overruns:0 carrier:0
          collisions:892
          RX bytes:30519779 (29.1 Mb)  TX bytes:14805768 (14.1 Mb)

lo        Link encap:Local Loopback
          inet addr:127.0.0.1  Mask:255.0.0.0
          UP LOOPBACK RUNNING  MTU:16436  Metric:1
          RX packets:716 errors:0 dropped:0 overruns:0 frame:0
          TX packets:716 errors:0 dropped:0 overruns:0 carrier:0
          collisions:0
          RX bytes:51255 (50.0 Kb)  TX bytes:51255 (50.0 Kb)
```

The only difference between the two is the UP and RUNNING in the third line.

The output is pretty self explanatory. The `inet` entry displays the IP address for the interface. UP signifies that the interface is ready for use, BROADCAST denotes that the interface is connected to a network that supports broadcast messaging (`ethernet`), RUNNING means that the interface is operating, and LOOPBACK shows which device (`lo`) is the loopback address. The Maximum Transmission Unit (MTU) on eth0 is 1500 bytes. This determines the size of the largest packet that can be transmitted over this interface. `Metric` is a number from zero to three that relates to how much information from the interface is placed in the routing table. The lower the number, the smaller the amount of information.

/sbin/route

The second command used to configure your network is the route command. route is used to build the routing tables used for routing messages as well as displaying the routing information. It is used after ifconfig has initialized the interface. route is normally used to set up static routes to other networks via the gateway or to other hosts. The command configuration is like this:

/sbin/route [*options*] [*commands*] [*parameters*]

To display the routing table, use the route command with no options. The display will look similar to this:

```
# /sbin/route
Kernel IP routing table
Destination     Gateway        Genmask          Flags Metric Ref   Use Iface
149.112.50.64   *              255.255.255.192  U     0      0     0   eth0
208.59.243.0    *              255.255.255.0    U     0      0     0   eth0
127.0.0.0       *              255.0.0.0        U     0      0     0   lo
default         149.112.50.65  0.0.0.0          UG    0      0     0   eth0
```

The first column, Destination is the IP address (or, if the host is in /etc/hosts or /etc/networks, the hostname) of the receiving host. The default entry is the default gateway for this machine. The Gateway column lists the gateway that the packets must go through to reach their destination. An asterisk (*) means that packets go directly to the host. Genmask is the netmask. The Flags column can have several possible entries. In our example, the U verifies that the route is enabled and the G specifies that the Destination requires the use of a gateway. The Metric column displays the distance to the Destination. Some daemons use this to figure the easiest route to the Destination. The Ref column is used by some UNIX flavors to convey the references to the route. It isn't used by Linux. The Use column indicates the number of times this entry has been looked up. Finally, the Iface column is the name of the interface for the corresponding entry.

Using the -n option to the route command will give the same information substituting IP addresses for names and asterisks (*) and looks like this:

```
# /sbin/route -n
Kernel IP routing table
Destination     Gateway        Genmask          Flags Metric Ref   Use Iface
149.112.50.64   0.0.0.0        255.255.255.192  U     0      0     0   eth0
208.59.243.0    0.0.0.0        255.255.255.0    U     0      0     0   eth0
127.0.0.0       0.0.0.0        255.0.0.0        U     0      0     0   lo
0.0.0.0         149.112.50.65  0.0.0.0          UG    0      0     0   eth0
```

The route command can add to the table using the add option. With the add option, you can specify a host (-host) or a network (-net) as the destination. If no option is used,

13

NETWORK
CONNECTIVITY

the `route` command assumes that you are configuring the host issuing the command. The most common uses for the `route` command is to add the default gateway for a host that has either lost its routing table or the gateway address has changed. The command for that would be the following:

`/sbin/route add default gw 149.112.50.65`

Another common use is to add the network to the routing table right after using the `ifconfig` command to configure the interface. Assuming that the 208.59.243.0 entry from the previous examples was missing, to replace it use the following command:

`/sbin/route add -net 208.59.243.0 netmask 255.255.255.0 dev eth0`

A third use would be to configure a specific host for a direct (point-to-point) connection. For example, say that you have a home network of two computers. One of the computers has a modem while you are sitting at the other one. The computer with the modem is connected through the modem to your business. You can use the `route` command to establish a connection using the following command:

`/sbin/route add -host 198.135.62.25 gw 149.112.50.65`

The preceding example makes the computer with the modem the gateway for the computer you are using.

There are many more uses for the `route` command that are rarely used. See the man page for those uses.

/bin/netstat

The `netstat` command is used to display the status of your network. It has several parameters that can display as much or as little information as you prefer. The services are listed by sockets. (Sockets are application-to-application connections between two computers.) You can use `netstat` to display the information in Table 13.2.

TABLE 13.2 `netstat` Options

Option	Output
-g	Displays the multicast groups configured
-i	Displays the interfaces configured by `ifconfig`
-s	Lists a summary of activity for each protocol
-v	Gives verbose output, listing both active and inactive sockets
-c	Will update output every second (good for testing and troubleshooting)

TABLE 13.2 continued

Option	Output
-e	Gives verbose output for active connections only
-C	Displays information from the route cache and is good for looking at past connections

Several other options aren't used nearly as often. As with the /sbin/route command, the man page can give you details about those options and parameters.

Configuration Files

As previously stated, seven network configuration files can be modified to make your changes. The files are

    /etc/hosts

    /etc/services

    /etc/nsswitch.conf

    /etc/resolv.conf

    /etc/host.conf

    /etc/HOSTNAME

    /etc/sysconfig/network

Once the first six of these files are modified, the changes are active. As with most configuration files, comments can be added with a hash mark (#) preceding the comment. The last file (/etc/sysconfig/network) requires the networking daemons to be restarted before the file is used. All seven of these files have a man page written about them for more information.

/etc/hosts

The /etc/hosts file is a map of IP to hostnames. If you're not using DNS or another naming service, and you are connected to a large network, this file can get quite large and can be a real headache to manage. A small /etc/hosts file can look something like this:

```
127.0.0.1       localhost.localdomain   localhost
128.112.50.69   myhost.mydomain.com     myhost
128.112.50.169  yourhost.mydomain.com   yourhost
```

The first entry is for the loopback entry. The second is for the name of the machine. The third is another machine on the network. If no naming service is in use on the network,

13

NETWORK
CONNECTIVITY

the only host that myhost will recognize by name is yourhost (IP addresses on the network can still be used).

If your network is using a naming service, the last line isn't needed and can be deleted. However, if myhost connects to yourhost frequently, it might be good to leave the entry so that myhost doesn't need to consult the naming service each time. This can save time and reduce the strain on the network or the name service server. Edit this file if you need to change your hostname or IP address or if you aren't using a naming service and a host has been added to your network.

/etc/services

The /etc/services file maps port numbers to services. The first few lines look similar to this (the /etc/services file can be quite long, more than 500 lines):

```
# Each line describes one service, and is of the form:
#
# service-name  port/protocol  [aliases ...]   [# comment]

tcpmux          1/tcp                           # TCP port service multiplexer
tcpmux          1/udp                           # TCP port service multiplexer
rje             5/tcp                           # Remote Job Entry
rje             5/udp                           # Remote Job Entry
echo            7/tcp
echo            7/udp
discard         9/tcp           sink null
discard         9/udp           sink null
systat          11/tcp          users
```

Typically, there are two entries for each service because most services can use either TCP or UDP for their transmissions. Usually once /etc/services is initially configured, you will not need to change it except for security. (Network security is briefly discussed in the "Security" section, later in this chapter.)

/etc/nsswitch.conf

This file was initially developed by Sun Microsystems to specify the order that services are accessed on the system. A number of services are listed in the /etc/nsswitch.conf file, but the most commonly modified entry is the hosts entry. A portion of the file can look like this:

```
passwd:     files
shadow:     files
group:      files

#hosts:     db files nisplus nis dns
hosts:      files dns
```

This tells services that they should consult standard UNIX/Linux files for passwd, shadow, and group (/etc/passwd, /etc/shadow, /etc/group, respectively) lookups. For host lookups, the system will check /etc/hosts and if there is no entry, it will check DNS. The commented hosts entry lists the possible values for hosts. Only edit this file if your naming service has changed.

/etc/resolv.conf

/etc/resolv.conf is used by DNS. DNS is covered in detail in Chapter 14. The following is an example of resolv.conf:

```
domain mydomain.com
nameserver 192.172.3.8
nameserver 192.172.3.9
search mydomain.com
```

This sets the domain, the nameservers, and the order of domains for DNS to use. This file would only be changed if any of the listed information has changed for the host.

/etc/host.conf

The /etc/host.conf file lists the order in which your machine will search for hostname resolution. The following is the default /etc/host.conf file:

```
order hosts, bind
```

In this example, the host will check the /etc/hosts file first and then perform a DNS lookup. A couple more options control how the name service is used. The only reason to modify this file is if you use NIS for your name service or your want one of the optional services. The nospoof option can be a good option for system security. It will compare a standard DNS lookup to a reverse lookup (host-to-IP then IP-to-host) and fail if the two don't match. The drawback is that often when proxy services are used, the lookup will fail, so you will want to use this with caution.

/etc/HOSTNAME

This file contains a single word, your hostname. It is initially created from the /etc/sysconfig/network file. Modify this if your hostname changes. The /etc/HOSTNAME file is no longer used by Red Hat Linux; however to avoid confusion, it is best to include this file when making changes.

/etc/sysconfig/network

/etc/sysconfig/network is the only file that might require action once it is modified. If you make all the modifications listed previously, you can modify this file and leave it until you have to restart the networking daemons or you reboot the system. The file looks like this:

13

NETWORK
CONNECTIVITY

```
NETWORKING=yes
HOSTNAME="myhost.mydomain.com"
GATEWAY="192.112.50.99"
GATEWAYDEV=""
FORWARD_IPV4="no"
```

The only additional entry is for NIS domain machines and would look like this:

```
NISDOMAIN=rebel
```

The `FORWARD_IPV4` value determines whether the host forwards IP packets. This would be yes for routers. This file is modified when any of the listed information changes.

Graphical Configuration Tools

Using the command line tools can be difficult and really shouldn't be attempted unless you are comfortable making the changes. If you are new to networking, the `linuxconf` graphical tool would be the way to go. `linuxconf` is normally run as root.

Like most graphical tools, `linuxconf` allows you to fill in the blanks, and the tool will modify the required files and issue the proper commands. The trickiest thing is remembering to click the Accept button after each modification, but then `linuxconf` will remind you when you exit.

As stated previously, you must be root to run `linuxconf`. There are two ways to start `linuxconf`. The most reliable way is from the command line with the command `/sbin/linuxconf` or `/sbin/linuxconf-auth`. There are ways to start `linuxconf` graphically through KDE or GNOME, but the menus vary from distribution to distribution if it appears on the menu at all.

Once started, `linuxconf` looks like this Figure 13.1.

FIGURE 13.1

Initial linuxconf *networking screen.*

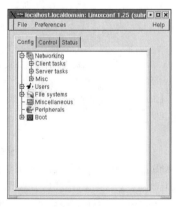

To get to the preceding screen, start linuxconf, click on Networking and then on Client Tasks. Once you click on Host Name and IP Network Devices, you will be taken to the screen that will allow you to set up your hostname and configure up to five NICs. Figure 13.2 reveals how to fill in your hostname on the space provided to add or change your hostname.

FIGURE 13.2

Adding hostname myhost.example. com.

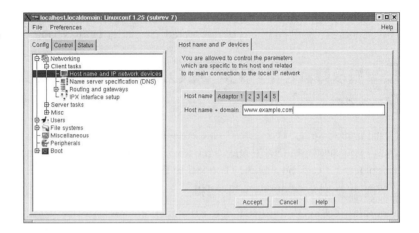

To configure your NIC, click on the Adapter 1 tab (see Figure 13.3). From here, you are allowed to choose how your card will get its configuration, manually, from DHCP, or from Bootp. Just fill in the blanks as needed.

FIGURE 13.3

Adapter 1 configured.

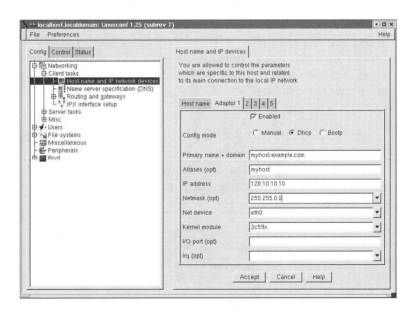

13

NETWORK CONNECTIVITY

> **Note**
>
> Bootp is the initial protocol that DHCP was built on and it has mostly been replaced by DHCP.

Obviously using manual configuration will require more information than using DHCP. The meaning of each entry has been covered previously in this chapter.

Dynamic Host Configuration Protocol

As the name implies, Dynamic Host Configuration Protocol configures hosts for connection to your network. DHCP allows a network administrator to configure all TCP/IP parameters for each host as they connect to the network. DHCP is covered by RFC2131 "Dynamic Host Configuration Protocol."

According to RFC2131, DHCP has two main purposes. The first is to "provide persistent storage of network parameters for network clients." This is achieved by holding some form of identifying information for each client that could potentially connect to the network. The three most common pairs of identifying information are network subnet/host address for hosts to connect to the network at will, subnet/hostname allows the specified host to connect to the subnet, subnet/hardware address allows a specific client to connect to the network getting the hostname from DHCP.

The second purpose of DHCP is the "allocation of temporary or permanent network (IP) addresses to clients." Once a lease has elapsed, the client can request to have the lease extended, or, if the address is no longer needed, the client can relinquish the address. For hosts that will be permanently connected to a network with adequate addresses available, infinite leases are also allowed.

A couple of advantages to DHCP are that (1) responsibility for assigning IP addresses shift from the network administrator (who can accidentally assign duplicate IP addresses) to the DHCP server, and (2) DHCP makes better use of limited IP addresses. If a user is away from the office for whatever reason, the user's host can release its IP address for use by other hosts.

Like most things in life, DHCP is not perfect. Servers cannot be configured through DHCP alone because DNS doesn't know what addresses that DHCP assigns to a host. This means that DNS look-ups aren't possible on machines configured through DHCP alone, and therefore services cannot be provided. DHCP however can make assignments based on DNS entries when using subnet/hostname or subnet/hardware address identifiers. This issue is being addressed by Dynamic DNS which, when fully developed, will allow DHCP to register IP addresses with DNS. The largest hurdle to overcome is the security implication of allowing each host connecting to the system to update DNS. A few companies are already offering Dynamic DNS services.

If you install the DHCP RPMs or activate DHCP at install time, it will create a directory called /etc/dhcpc, which has two files:

```
# ll
total 8
-rw-------   1 root     root          124 Sep 15 18:03 dhcpcd-eth0.cache
-rw-r--r--   1 root     root          359 Sep 15 18:03 dhcpcd-eth0.info
```

If you check the file type with the file command, you'll find that dhcpcd-eth0.cache is a data file that lists the Linux kernel that you are running. dhcpcd-eth0.info is an interesting file containing network information for your current DHCP lease and will look something like this:

```
# more dhcpcd-eth0.info
IPADDR=192.122.60.235
NETMASK=255.255.255.0
NETWORK=192.122.60.0
BROADCAST=255.255.255.255
GATEWAY=192.122.60.1
HOSTNAME=dhcp-422-13
DOMAIN=domain.com
DNS=192.172.3.8,192.172.3.9
DHCPSID=192.122.64.45
DHCPGIADDR=0.0.0.0
DHCPSIADDR=0.0.0.0
DHCPCHADDR=00:60:08:8F:5A:D9
DHCPSHADDR=00:01:03:A4:21:09
DHCPSNAME=
LEASETIME=3600
RENEWALTIME=1800
REBINDTIME=3150
```

13

NETWORK CONNECTIVITY

The first eight lines consist of the TCP/IP configuration information required to connect this system to the domain.com network. The IP address is 193.122.60.235, the netmask shows that this is a class C network, the network address is 192.122.60.0. The broadcast address is set at 255.255.255.255 because the client is initially unaware where the DHCP server is, so the request must travel every network until a server replies. The gateway shows this network's router or switch, the hostname assigned by the DHCP server is dhcp-422-13, and the domain is the domainname of the network. Finally, the DNS servers are at the IP addresses 192.172.3.8 and 192.172.3.9.

The last nine lines display the DHCP specific information for this client. DHCPSID is the DHCP servers IP address: DHCPGIADDR, DHCPSIADDR, and DHCPSNAME are not used. DHCPCHADDR is the hardware address of the client, DHCPSHADDR is the hardware address of the DHCP server, and LEASETIME is 3600 seconds (one hour) and represents the length of time that the lease is valid. RENEWAL TIME is the time in seconds until the client tried to renew the lease, REBINDTIME is the time in seconds (57 minutes, 30 seconds) when the client gives up on renewing the current lease and starts to look for a whole new lease. If the LEASETIME reaches zero before the client's lease is renewed or a new lease is issued, the client's connection is cut due to the lack of a valid IP address. If the network capacity is planned correctly, no client should ever lose or be refused a lease.

Installation

Installation for the DHCP client and Server is easy whether you use RPMs or download the source code and build it yourself. The RPMs are already compiled and are good if your machine is small and the time to compile is a concern. If you do download the source and compile yourself, you have a bit more flexibility. The ISC version of the source code includes the DHCP client and server in the distribution.

Client

As with most things in Linux, DHCP is much easier to install when installing Red Hat on your host. As you saw during installation (as read in Chapter 3, "Installing Red Hat Linux"), when you are doing the network step you can chose to have DHCP initiated at boot time. If you choose to do this (and choose to install the DHCP client package), the DHCP client will send a broadcast message that the DHCP server will reply to with networking information for your host. That's it; you're done.

If you choose to install from source, you will have to download and install the server packages that include the DHCP client with later releases. Unpack your tar file, run ./configure from the root of the source directory, run make, and then run make install. This should put the DHCP client binaries where they will start at the correct time in the boot process.

Server

Again, the easiest way to install the DHCP server on your computer is to include the RPMs at install time or to use RPMs if you've installed your machine without installing the DHCP server RPMs. If you are so inclined, you can go to the Internet Software Consortium (ISC) Web site and download the source code and build it yourself.

If you decide to install from source downloaded from the ISC Web site, the installation is very straightforward. Just unpack your tar file, run `./configure` from the root of the source directory, run `make`, and finally, if there are no errors, run `make install`. This will put all the files used by the DHCP daemon in the correct places. If you have the disk space, it's best to leave the source files in place until you are sure that DHCP is running correctly, otherwise you can delete the source tree.

> **Note**
>
> For whichever installation method you choose, be sure that a file called `/etc/dhcpd.leases` is created. The file can be empty, but it does need to exist in order for `dhcpd` to start properly.

Configuration

As with most services, the configuration is the hardest part. Configuring the client is easy. Configuring the server takes a bit of work. How much work depends on how complex your network is and how much you want DHCP to do.

Client

If you install DHCP client software from RPM, there is no configuration needed; DHCP will be ready to run. All the configuration is done on the server side. If you install from source, you will need to include a startup script in your `rc2.d` through your `rc5.d` start up directories (`/etc/rc2.d/`, `/etc/rc3.d/`, and so on). This is done by creating a link from the `rcX.d` directories (where *X* is a number from two to five) to the `/etc/init.c/dhcpc` script. Now reboot your system, run the command `ifconfig -a`, and you should see your shiny new IP address. (The `ifconfig` command is discussed earlier in the chapter in the "Command Line Configuration" section.)

Server

Configuring the server does take some work. Luckily the work only involves setting up your startup script (as discussed previously) and building a single configuration file, `/etc/dhcpd.conf`. This file will contain all the information needed to run `dhcpd`.

The DHCP server source files contain an example of the `dhcpd.conf` file. That file is a great starting point for configuring your DHCP server. The RPMs do contain a sample `dhcpd.conf` file, but the file that comes with the RPM isn't as detailed as the one that comes with the source. It might be worth the effort to download the less than 900KB source file just for this file.

The /etc/dhcpd.conf file can be looked at as a three-part file. The. first part contains configurations for DHCP itself. The configurations include setting the domain name (option domain-name "example.org"), setting DNS servers (option domain-name-servers ns1.example.org, ns2.example.org), setting the default and maximum lease times (default-lease-time 3600 and max-lease-time 14400), whether the server is the primary (authoritative) server, and what type of logging DHCP should use. These settings are considered default and can be overridden by the subnet and host portion of the configuration. Each of these are self explanatory and don't need discussion here.

Note

The dhcpd.conf file requires semicolons (;) after each line. If your configuration file has errors or runs improperly, check for this.

The next part of the dhcpd.conf deals with the different subnets that your DHCP server serves. The subnet section is pretty straightforward. Each subnet is defined separately and can look like this:

```
subnet 10.5.5.0 netmask 255.255.255.224 {
   range 10.5.5.26 10.5.5.30;
   option domain-name-servers ns1.internal.example.org;
   option domain-name "internal.example.org";
   option routers 10.5.5.1;
   option broadcast-address 10.5.5.31;
   default-lease-time 600;
   max-lease-time 7200;
}
```

This defines the IP addressing for the 10.5.5.0 subnet. It defines the IP address range 10.5.5.26 through 10.5.5.30 to be dynamically assigned to hosts that reside on that subnet. This example shows that any TCP/IP option can be set from the subnet portion of the configuration file. It shows which DNS server the subnet will connect to, which can be good for DNS server load balancing or can be used to limit the hosts that can be reached through DNS. It defines the domain name, so you can have more than one domain on your network. It can also change the default and maximum lease time.

If you want your server to ignore a specific subnet, the following entry can be used to accomplish this:

```
subnet 10.152.187.0 netmask 255.255.255.0 {
}
```

This defines no options for the 10.152.187.0 subnet, and, therefore, the DHCP server ignores it.

The last part is the host part. This can be good if you want hosts to have a specific IP address or any other information specific to that host. The key to the host section is knowing the hardware address of the host. Hardware addresses are discussed in the "Network Devices" section earlier in this chapter. The hardware address is used to differentiate the host for configuration. Your hardware address can be obtained by using the `ifconfig -a` command as described previously. The hardware address is on the eth0 line labeled "`Hwaddr`".

```
host fantasia {
  hardware ethernet 08:00:07:26:c0:a5;
  fixed-address fantasia.fugue.com;
}
```

This example takes the host with the hardware address 08:00:07:26:c0:a5 and does a DNS lookup to assign the IP address for fantasia.fugue.com to the host.

DHCP can also define and configure booting for diskless clients like this:

```
host passacaglia {
  hardware ethernet 0:0:c0:5d:bd:95;
  filename "vmunix.passacaglia";
  server-name "toccata.fugue.com";
}
```

The diskless host passacaglia will get its boot information from server toccata.fugue.com and use vmunix.passacaglia kernel. All other TCP/IP configuration can also be included.

A whole host of other options can be used in `dhcpd.conf`: Entire books are dedicated to DHCP. The most comprehensive book is *The DHCP Handbook*. You can define NIS domains, configure NETBIOS, set subnet masks, and define time servers, or most any other type of server to name a few. The preceding example will get your DHCP server and client up and running. The DHCP server distribution contains an example of the `dhcpd.conf` file that you can use as a template for your network. The file shows a basic configuration that can get you started with explanations for the options used. If you need a more complex configuration, check out *The DHCP Handbook*.

Here's one last note. You might find that you have done everything possible to configure your DHCP server correctly, and for some reason it just isn't working. Often Windows NT servers will have the Windows DHCP server install by default. Because there is no configuration file for NT to sort through, that DHCP server will configure your host before the Linux server. Check your NT servers for this, disable DHCP on the NT server, and your host should configure correctly.

13

NETWORK CONNECTIVITY

Network File System

The Network File System (NFS) was developed by Sun Microsystems as a way for computers to share files as if they were local to the remote machine. NFS is commonly used to share home directories between hosts within a network. This reduces the need to have a home directory on every computer and ensures that no matter which computer you log in to, your home directory will be consistent. The other popular use is to share binary files between similar computers. In this way if you have a new version of a package that you want all machines to have, you only have to do the upgrade on the NFS server, and all hosts running the same version of Red Hat will have the same upgraded package.

Installing NFS

NFS installs by default on Red Hat Linux and consists of three programs that work together to provide the NFS server service. The first is `rpc.portmapper`, which maps NFS requests to the correct daemon. The second is `rpc.nfsd`, which is the NFS daemon. The third one is `rpc.mountd`, which controls the mounts and unmounts of filesystems.

The client requires no special software to run. However, rpc.portmapper is a helpful program to have for NFS and other programs.

> **Note**
>
> The portmapper program maps *Remote Procedure Call (RPC)* programs to ports and is required to be running for any RPC program to run.

To check if your host can act as an NFS server, try the following command

```
rpcinfo -p
```

or

```
rpminfo -p hostname
```

to check another host on the network. The resulting output should look similar to this:

```
# rpcinfo -p
program  vers  proto  port
100000   2     tcp    111     portmapper
100000   2     udp    111     portmapper
100005   2     tcp    821     mountd
100005   2     udp    823     mountd
100003   2     tcp    2049    nfs
100003   2     udp    2049    nfs
```

In this example, all three services are running so the server can now be configured. The mountd daemon is not configured in the /etc/services file by default. To include it, add the following two lines where the port numbers are numerically:

```
nfs    821/tcp    mountd    # mountd daemon
nfs    823/udp    mountd    # mountd daemon
```

NFS Server Configuration

The NFS server is configured using the /etc/exports file. This file is similar to the /etc/fstab file in that it is used to set the permissions for the filesystems being exported. The entries look like this:

```
/file/system   yourhost(options) *.yourdomain.com(options)
192.15.69.0/24(options)
```

This shows three common clients to share /file/system to. The first, yourhost, shares /file/system to just one host. The second, .yourdomain.com, uses the asterisk (*) as a wildcard to allow all hosts in yourdomain.com to access /file/system. The third share allows all hosts of the Class C network, 192.15.69.0, to access /file/share. For security, it is best not to use shares like the last two across the Internet because all data will be readable by any network the data passes by.

Some common options are shown in Table 13.3.

TABLE 13.3 /etc/fstab Options

Option	Purpose
rw	Gives read and write access.
ro	Gives read only access.
async	Writes data when the server feels the need, not the client.
sync	Writes data as it is received.

The following is an example of an /etc/exports file:

```
# /etc/exports file for myhost.mydomain.com
/usr/local        yourhost(ro,show)
/home/jkennedy    *.yourdomain.com(rw,hide,sync)
```

This file exports /usr/local to yourhost. The mount is read-only (which is good for a directory of binary files that don't get written to). It also allows users on yourhost to see the contents of filesystems that might be mounted on /usr/local. The second export mounts /home/jkennedy to any host in yourdomain.com. It doesn't allow subsidiary filesystems to be viewed, but you can read and write to the filesystem.

13

NETWORK
CONNECTIVITY

Once you have finished with the /etc/exports file, the following command

```
/usr/sbin/exportfs -r
```

will export all the filesystems in the /etc/exports file.

The -r option to the command reads the whole /etc/exports file and mounts all the entries. The exportfs command can also be used to export specific files temporarily. An example using exportfs to export a file system would be

```
/usr/sbin/exportfs  -o async yourhost:/usr/tmp
```

This command will export /usr/tmp to yourhost with the async option.

NFS Client Configuration

To configure your host as an NFS client, edit the /etc/fstab file as you would to mount any internal files system except that instead of listing the device to be mounted, you list the host and exported filesystem. The entry will be similar to

```
# Device            Mount Point   Type   Options        Freq  Pass
yourhost:/usr/local  /usr/local   nfs    nfsvers=3,ro    0     0
```

The options column uses the same options as standard fstab file entries with some additional entries such as nfsvers=3, which specifies the third version of NFS. If you recompile the kernel, be sure to include the NFS 3 option to be sure NFS 3 shares work.

NFS and `linuxconf`

For simple NFS configuration, linuxconf is an easy, convenient way to configure NFS shares. Like everything else configured with linuxconf, just fill in the blanks and linuxconf will do the rest. It's not nearly as flexible as editing the files, but it will get the job done for easy configurations. linuxconf must be run as root and, as mentioned earlier, is easiest if run from the command line with the command:

```
/sbin/linuxconf
```

The NFS configuration screen is shown in Figure 13.4.

The configuration from Figure 13.4 will write the following to the /etc/exports file:

```
# more exports
/usr/local yourhost(ro)
```

It exports /usr/local to yourhost as a read-only filesystem. To make the filesystem read/write, just check the May write check box. To give yourhost root privileges, just check the Root privileges check box. With the pictured configuration, clicking the Accept button will result in the screen shown in Figure 13.5.

FIGURE **13.4**

Exporting
/usr/local *to*
yourhost.

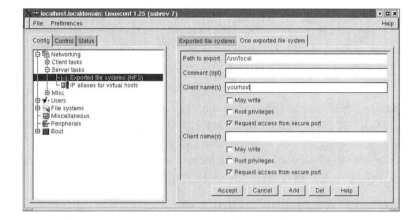

FIGURE **13.5**

/usr/local *suc-*
cessfully exported.

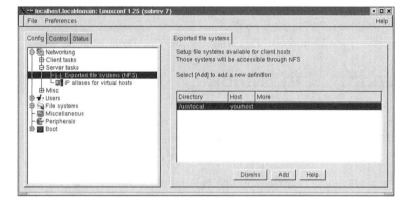

It's simple, but it can be effective.

Samba

Samba uses Microsoft Corporation's SMB protocol to allow the Windows operating system to access Linux files. Using Samba you can make your Red Hat Linux machine look just like a Windows computer to other Windows computers on your network.

Samba is a very complex program. So much so that the book *Samba Unleashed* (Sams, 2000, ISBN 0-672-31862-8) is more than 1200 pages long. The Samba man page (when converted to text) for just the configuration file is 330KB and 7013 lines long! Although Samba is complex, it doesn't have to be difficult. There are many options that account for Samba's complexity. Depending on what you want, Samba can be as easy or as difficult as you'd like it to be.

Like most of the software that comes with Red Hat Linux, Samba is written under the GPL and free. It comes as both an RPM and as source code. In both cases, installation is very straightforward. Just install the RPMs that fit your needs. The Samba RPMs should be on your second Red Hat install disk, or the latest version can be downloaded from the Internet.

Installing from source code can be a bit more time-consuming but a bit more configurable if you don't want to install to the default location. Just download the source and unpack the files. Change into the source directory and run the command `./configure` along with any changes from the defaults and then run `make`, `make test` (if you want), followed by `make install` to install Samba in the specified locations.

One big advantage to installing from source is the amount of documentation that is easily found in the source directory tree starting at `~/samba-2.2.1a/docs` and come in several formats including PDF, HTML, and text among others. Altogether there's almost 7MB of documentation included with the source code. This documentation includes HTML and PDF versions of the book *Using Samba* by O'Reilly.

Configuring Samba

Once Samba is installed, you can either create the file `/etc/smb.conf` or use the `smb.conf` file supplied with Samba. If installing from source, it can be found in `~/samba-2.2.1a/packaging/RedHat,`: If installing from RPM, it will be in the /etc/samba directory. This configuration file controls most all of Samba's functionality.

Depending on your needs, this can be a simple file of less than 20 lines to a huge file spanning many pages of text. If your needs are complex, I would suggest picking up a copy of *Samba Unleashed* at your favorite bookstore.

/etc/smb.conf

The `/etc/smb.conf` file is broken into sections. Each section is a description of the resource shared (share) and should be titled appropriately. There are three special sections, `[global]`, which establishes the global configuration settings; `[homes]`, which shares users' home directories; and `[printers]`, which, as the name gives away, handles printing.

Typical Sections

Each section should be named for the resource being shared. For example, if the resource `/usr/local/programs` is being shared, you could call the section `[programs]`. When Windows sees the share, it will be called by whatever you name the section (programs in this example). The easiest and fastest way to set up this share is with the following sample from `smb.conf`:

```
[programs]
path = /usr/local/programs
writeable = true
```

This bit will share the /usr/local/programs directory with any valid user who asks for it and make that directory writeable. It is the most basic share because it sets no limits on the directory.

Some of the things you can set are requiring a user to enter a password before accessing the directory, limiting the hosts allowed to access the directory, permissions users are allowed to have on the directory, and even the time of day that the directory is accessible. The possibilities are almost endless. Any parameters set in the individual sections override the parameters set in the [global] section. The following section adds a few restrictions to the [programs] section.

```
[programs]
path = /usr/local/programs
writeable = true
valid users = jkennedy
browseable = yes        .
create mode = 0700
```

The valid users entry limits userid to just jkennedy. All other users can browse the directory because of the browseable = yes entry but only jkennedy can write to the directory. Any files created by jkennedy in the directory will give jkennedy full permissions but no one else will have access to the file. This is exactly the same as setting permissions with the chmod command. Again, there are numerous options so you can be as creative as you want to when developing sections.

[global] Section

The [global] section set parameters for all of Samba. The section sets the defaults and if a parameter isn't specifically set in a specific section Samba will use the setting in the [global] section. The [global] section also sets the general security configuration for Samba. The [global] section is the only section that doesn't require the name in brackets.

It is assumed that anything before the first bracketed section is part of the global configuration. (Using the bracketed heading will make the file a little more readable though.)

[homes] Section

The [homes] section shares out home directories for the users. This happens automatically when a user's Windows computer connects to the Linux server holding the home directory. The one problem with using the default configuration is that the user will see all the configuration files (such as `.profile`) that they normally wouldn't see when logging on through Linux. One quick way to avoid this would be to include a path option in the `[homes]` section. To do this would require that each user requiring a Samba share of their home directory will need a separate "home directory" to act as their Windows home directory.

If you have a `[homes]` section, the share shows up in the user's Network Neighborhood as the user's name. When the user connects, the existing sections in `smb.conf` are scanned for a specific instance of the user's home directory. If there isn't one, the username is looked up in `/etc/passwd`. If the correct username and password have been given, the home directory listed in `/etc/passwd` is shared out at the user's home directory. Typically the `[homes]` section will look like this (the `browseable = no` entry will prevent other users from being able to browse your home directory and is a good security practice):

```
[homes]
browseable = no
writable = yes
```

This will share out the home directory and make it writable to the user. To specify a separate Windows home directory for each user, it would look like:

```
[homes]
browseable = no
writable = yes
path = /path/to/windows/directories
```

`[printers]` Section

The `[printers]` section works much like the `[homes]` section but for printers. If the section exists, users will have access to any printer listed in your Red Hat `/etc/printcap` file.

Like the `[homes]` section, when a print request is received, all the sections are scanned for the printer. If no share is found (with careful naming there should not be unless you create a section for a specific printer), the `/etc/printcap` file is scanned for the printer name that is then used to send the print request.

For printing to work properly, printing services *must* be set up correctly on your Red Hat computer. (See Chapter 12, "Printing Services," for more information.) A typical `[printers]` section will look like the following:

```
[printers]
comment = Red Hat Printers
browseable = no
```

```
printable = yes
path = /var/spool/samba
```

The `/var/spool/samba` is a spool path set just for Samba printing.

`testparm` Command

Once you have created your `/etc/smb.conf` file, you can check it for correctness. This is done with the `testparm` command. This command will parse through your `/etc/smb.conf` file and check for any syntax errors. If none are found, it's a good bet that your configuration file will work correctly. It does not, however, guarantee that the services specified in the file will work. It is merely making sure that the file is correctly written.

As with all configuration files, if you are modifying an existing, working file, it is *always* prudent to copy the working file to a different location and modify that file. Once done, you can check the file with the `testparm` utility. The command syntax is as follows:

```
# testparm /path/to/smb.conf.back-up
Load smb config files from smb.conf.back-up
Processing section "[homes]"
Processing section "[printers]"
Loaded services file OK.
```

This shows that the Samba configuration file is correct and as long as all the services are running correctly on your Red Hat machine, Samba should be correct. Now copy your old `smb.conf` file to a new location, put the new one in its place, and restart Samba with the command `/etc/init.d/smb restart`. Your new or modified Samba configuration should now be in place.

13

NETWORK
CONNECTIVITY

The `smbd` Daemon

Now that your `smb.conf` file is correctly configured, you can start your Samba server daemon. This is done with the `/usr/sbin/smbd` command. `/usr/sbin/smbd` with no options will start the Samba server with all the defaults. The most common option that you will change is the location of the `smb.conf` file. The `-s` option allows you to change the `smb.conf` file used and is a good option for testing whether your `smb.conf` file actually works. Another good option is the `-l` option, which specifies the log file that Samba uses to store information.

`smbstatus` Command

The `smbstatus` command will report on the current status of your Samba connections. The syntax is

```
/usr/bin/smbstatus [options]
```

Some of the available options are shown in Table 13.4.

TABLE 13.4 smbstatus Options

Option	Result
-b	Brief output.
-d	Verbose output.
-s /path/to/config	Used if the configuration file used at startup is not the standard one.
-u *username*	Shows the status of a specific user's connection.
-p	Lists current smb processes. This can be useful in scripts.

smbclient Command

The smbclient command allows users on other Linux hosts to access your smb shares. You can't mount the share on your host, but you can use it in a way that's very similar to an FTP client. There are several options you can use with the smbclient command. The most used will be -I followed by the IP address of the computer you are connecting to. The smbclient command does not require root access to run.

```
smbclient -I 10.10.10.20 -Uusername%password
```

Will give you the following prompt:

```
smb: <current directory on share>
```

From here, the commands are almost identical to the standard UNIX/Linux FTP commands.

Samba Mounts

There are two ways to mount Samba shares to your host. The first is to use the standard Linux mount command:

```
mount -t smbfs //10.10.10.20/homes /mount/point -o username=jkennedy,dmask=777,\
 fmask=777
```

> **Note**
>
> The hostname can be substituted for an IP address if your name service is running or the host is in your /etc/hosts file.

This command will mount jkennedy's home directory on your host and will give all users full permissions to the mount. The permissions are equal to the permissions on the chmod command.

The same results will occur using the smbmount command as follows:

```
smbmount //10.10.10.20/homes /mount/point -o username=jkennedy,dmask-777,\
 fmask=777
```

To unmount the share, use the standard

```
umount /mount/point
```

These mount commands can also be used to mount true Windows client shares to your Red Hat host.

Using Samba, you can configure your Red Hat Linux host to provide any service that Windows can serve, and no one but your would ever know.

Wireless Networking

As stated earlier, Linux has had support for wireless networking since the standard was developed in the early 90s. With computers getting smaller and smaller, the uses for wireless networking increased. There are several different ways to create a wireless network and the transmission speeds are increasing all the time. One of the oldest methods has been in use by Amateur Radio operators for quite some time. It is an excellent way to get Internet access to remote locations cheaply. Its use is quite specialized and won't be covered in detail.

Wireless networking is also a great way to provide networking to a location that doesn't have the resources to maintain a standard wired network. An excellent article about this can be found on the Internet (See the "Reference" section at the end of this chapter). Considering that the network referred to in the article was built in early 1996, the technology used to build the network is outdated. Not much will be said here about it, but the concept is still very true today.

With the 2.4 kernel, which ships with Red Hat now, support for wireless networking is now included in the kernel.

Cellular Networking

The ads are starting to crop up on TV: This cellular service will allow you to check your e-mail anywhere your cellular phone can reach; that cellular company will provide news and other information via the Internet to your phone. Personal Digital Assistants have cellular add-ons or even built in.

13

NETWORK
CONNECTIVITY

More importantly to this book, your laptop has a cellular modem that you can use to dial in to your network. This isn't truly wireless networking if the network dialed in to is wired, but it does illustrate how far reaching wireless networks can go. You could be on a trip to anywhere in the world, and as long as your cellular service follows you (at a substantial cost), your can dial in to any network you have access to (be it home or office) and check your e-mail, submit reports that could possibly be due, or even submit your book to be published. As with most devices, the majority of brand-name PCMCIA cards will work with Red Hat Linux. A lot of generic equipment should work, but you are taking a chance.

Wireless

The advantage to wireless networking is the mobility and the potential range. If you have a large enough antenna network, your network can stretch many miles. This would be an expensive network, but one that would easily break out of the brick and mortar confines of the office.

Wireless networking would also be a great advantage to college campuses to eliminate the need to tear through walls to install cabling because more and more students expect to have a network connection in their dorm rooms. Wireless networking cards are becoming more reasonable in price and can easily be issued to each student as he requires them.

Home networkers can also benefit from wireless networking. For those who cannot do modifications to their homes, wireless networking removes the unsightly wires running along baseboards and ceilings that are required to connect computers in different rooms. With a wireless home network, you aren't even confined to inside the house. Depending on the transmit power of your router, you can sit out in your back yard and watch passing clouds as you type away. Wireless routers are coming down in price with each passing day.

IEEE 802.11 Standard

The Institute of Electrical and Electronics Engineers (IEEE) started to look seriously at wireless networking in 1990. This is when the 802.11 Standard was first introduced by the Wireless Local Area Networks Standards Working Group. The group based the standard roughly around the architecture used in cellular phone networks. The wireless network is controlled by a Base Station, which can be just a transmitter attached to the network or, more commonly these days, a router. For larger networks, more than one base station can be used. Networks with more than one base station are usually referred to as distribution systems. Use of a distribution system not only increases the number of hosts, but can also be used to increase the coverage space.

Frequencies

The 802.11 standard specifies that wireless devices use a frequency range of 2400-2483.5 MHz. This is the standard used in North America and Europe. In Japan however, wireless networks are limited to a frequency range of 2471–2479MHz because of Japanese regulations. Within these ranges, each network is given up to 79 non-overlapping frequency channels to use. This reduces the chance of two closely located wireless networks of using the same channel at the same time. It also allows for channel hopping, which can be used for security.

Power

In North America, the maximum power that a wireless network can use to transmit is one watt. In Europe and Japan, regulations set the limit at 100 milliwatts and 10 milliwatts per MHz. If you consider that radio stations in the United States can transmit up to 100,000 watts, these signals are rather weak.

Wireless Security

Because of the nature of wireless networking, its security needs will be discussed here, rather than the main "Security" section in this chapter.

Wireless, although convenient, can be very insecure. Extra care must be used to protect the actual frequency used by your network. Great progress has been made in the past couple of years, but the possibility of a security breech is increased once the attacker is in the area and knows the frequency to listen on. It should also be noted that the encryption method used by more wireless NICs has long been broken and should not be considered as part of your security plan.

The better the physical security is around your network, the more secure it will probably be. Keep wireless transmitters (routers, switches, and so on) as close to the center of your building as possible and if it can be done, build a fence around your building to keep intruders too far away to be able to pick up the transmitted signals. An occasional walk around your building not only can give you a break from work, but it can also give you a chance to notice any people or equipment that should not be in the area.

Security

The only way to make sure that your system is secure is to lock the system in a room and never even turn it on. This isn't very practical, but it's true.

As long as there is access to your system, whether physical or over a network, there is the threat that information can be compromised. The more access given, the higher the

13

NETWORK
CONNECTIVITY

threat. If your network is connected to the Internet, the threat of someone breaking into your computer is very real.

Not even a home computer that uses a cable modem, regular modem, or DSL to access the Internet is safe. As DSL and cable modems become more common, the home computer has become a favorite target for script kiddies to use as stepping stones to get to larger corporate networks. This not only means that the private information on your computer can be accessed at will, but also, if a script kiddie uses your computer to launch a cyber attack or a virus, your computer can be taken as evidence.

If this causes concern, it should. Although there is no way to stop a serious cracker who is intent on getting into your computer or network, there are ways to make it harder for him and to warn you when he does. Tripwire is a good program for detecting computer break-ins. There are several others as well.

First and foremost, use secure passwords on your network and ensure that users use them as well, especially the root password. If the root password on just one machine is cracked, the whole network is in trouble.

Also, keep in mind that some studies show that as much as 90% of network break-ins are by current or former employees. If a person no longer requires access to your network, lock and, if possible, remove his account immediately. Even if he has left on good terms, people are fickle and can change for the smallest of reasons.

Second, if you don't need a service, don't start it. Although NFS can be very helpful, it isn't overly secure. Just the concept of sharing a whole filesystem over a network is insecure. Some other potentially vulnerable services are Web services, telnet, ftp, especially anonymous ftp, finger, and remote services such as rlogin, rcp, and rwho.

Third, be aware of physical security. If a potential attacker can get physical access to your system, getting full access becomes trivial. Keep all servers in a locked room, and ensure that only authorized personnel are given access to clients.

TCP/IP and Networking

There isn't much you can do to change TCP/IP and make it more, or less, secure. It is the standard. Just be sure that no user can access parts of the network that he is not supposed to by using good subnetting practices. Use tools like nmap to scan your network for potential weaknesses such as unused ports being open. Many network administrators (with permission, of course) will try and break into their business network from their home PC to test security, which isn't a bad idea.

PortSentry will monitor your network for port scans and respond to the scan in real time to help prevent break-ins. Upon detecting a scan, PortSentry will block the system doing the scanning. PortSentry will also log the scan to syslog for later investigation. Combine PortSentry with logcheck for nearly real-time notification of scan attempts.

TripWire is another security tool. TripWire will check the integrity of normal system binaries and report any changes to syslog or by e-mail. This is a good tool for ensuring that your binaries have not been replaced by Trojan Horse programs.

Devices

Do not ever advertise that you have set an NIC to promiscuous mode. Promiscuous mode is good for monitoring traffic across the network and can often allow you to monitor the actions of someone who might have broken into your network. Keep in mind that this is one way that a cracker will use to monitor your network to gain the ever so important root password.

Use the right tool for the right job. Although a bridge can be used to connect your network to the Internet, it wouldn't be a good idea. Bridges have become almost obsolete because they will forward any packet that comes their way. That isn't good when it is connected to the Internet. A router will allow you to filter which packets are relayed.

DHCP

DHCP so far appears to be fairly secure on UNIX/Linux servers. Be sure that only root can modify the `dhcpd.conf` file, and you should have no DHCP related security issues.

Configuration Tools

As with all root tasks, you should be careful who has access to the `ifconfig` command. `ifconfig` allows you to set the NIC in promiscuous mode. In the wrong hands, this could lead to disastrous results. A few years ago, `linuxconf` had a security hole, but that has been fixed in recent releases. Although `linuxconf` is powerful, one wouldn't look at it as a potential security threat.

NFS

As mentioned previously, even the concept of what NFS does is a potential security nightmare. If your use your favorite Internet search engine and search for "NFS exploits," you will be given many, many different listings. If you don't need a service, be sure that it is disabled.

Samba

Samba is well written. There aren't too many exploits. Like DHCP, you need to protect your configuration file (/etc/smb.conf). The biggest security holes are the ones created by improper configuration. Be careful giving privileges with Samba, and you should be safe.

Keeping Up to Date

There are a multitude of Web sites relating to security. One in particular hosts an excellent mailing list. The site is called Security Focus and the mailing list is called BugTraq. BugTraq is well known for its unbiased discussion of security flaws. It receives a relatively large amount of traffic (20–100+ messages daily, depending on the amount of exploits being discussed).

Often security holes are discussed on BugTraq before the software makers have even released the fix. The Security Focus site has other mailing lists and sections on its Web site dedicated to Linux in general and is an excellent resource.

Patches/Upgrades

One of the keys to security not mentioned previously is to keep up-to-date with at least the latest stable versions of your software. Each time a new version of a software package comes out, it corrects any known security holes found in the previous release. Also be sure to keep your operating systems patched to the latest patch level. Your network security is only as strong as the weakest host.

With effort, your system can be secure enough to keep most intruders out. Just keep your software up-to-date, keep yourself informed of potential security threats to your software, and you should be fine.

Reference

The following Web sites and books are great resources for more information on the topics covered in this chapter. Networking is complex. The more you take the time to learn, the easier setting up and maintaining your network will be.

General

http://www.ietf.org/rfc.html—Go here to search for, or get a list of, Request for Comments (RFC).

http://www.linuxhardware.net—For information on Linux hardware compatibility.

DHCP

`http://www.oth.net/dyndns.html`—For a list of Dynamic DSN service providers, go to this site.

`http://www.isc.org/products/DHCP/dhcpv3-README.html`—The DHCP README is available at this site.

Wireless

`http://www.ieee.org`—The Institute of Electrical and Electronics Engineers (IEEE) Web site.

`http://www.ictp.trieste.it/~radionet/papers`—Wireless case study

Security

`http://www.insecure.org/nmap/`—This site contains information on `nmap`.

`http://www.securityfocus.com/`—The Security Focus Web site.

`http://www.psionic.com/abacus/portsentry/`—Has information on PortSentry.

`http://www.tripwire.com`—Has information on TripWire.

Books

Sams Teach Yourself TCP/IP Network Administration in 21 Days, Sams Publishing, ISBN: 0-672-31250-6

TCP/IP Network Administration, O'Reilly Publishing, ISBN: 1-56592-322-7

Practical Networking, Que Publishing, ISBN: 0-7897-2252-6

Samba Unleashed, Sams Publishing, ISBN: 0-672-31862-8

The DHCP Handbook, Macmillan Technical Publishing, ISBN: 1-57870-137-6

Managing DNS

by Abhijit Menon-Sen

CHAPTER 14

It is often convenient to refer to networked computers by name rather than by IP address, and various translation mechanisms have been devised to make this possible. The *DNS (Domain Name System)* is one such method, now used almost universally on the Internet. This chapter introduces DNS concepts and practice using *BIND (Berkeley Internet Name Domain)*, the de facto standard DNS software for UNIX.

Hostnames are merely a convenience for users. Communication with other computers still requires knowledge of their IP addresses, and to allow hosts to be referred to by name, it must be possible to translate a name into an equivalent IP address. This process is called *name resolution*, and is usually performed by software known as a resolver. Because it is a very common operation, whatever translation method we use must be very fast and reliable.

Hostname to address mappings were once maintained by the SRI (Stanford Research Institute) in the hosts.txt file, each line of which contained the name and address of a host. Anyone could obtain a copy of this file via FTP and let their resolver use it locally. This scheme worked well when there were only a few machines, but it quickly grew impractical as more and more people began connecting to the Internet.

A lot of bandwidth was wasted in keeping the ever-growing hosts.txt file synchronized between the increasing number of hosts. Name resolution was progressively slowed down because the resolver took longer to search the list of hosts each time. Changes to the database took forever to make and propagate because the SRI was inundated by requests for additions and changes.

DNS is designed to address these problems and provide a consistent, portable namespace for network resources. Its database is maintained in a distributed fashion to accommodate its size and the need for frequent updates. Performance and bandwidth utilization is improved by the extensive use of local caches. Authority over portions of the database is delegated to people who are able and willing to maintain them in a timely manner so that updates are no longer constrained by the schedules of a central authority.

DNS is a simple but delicate system that is vital to today's Internet. Errors might manifest themselves in far from obvious ways, long after the changes that caused them were made, often leading to unacceptable and embarrassing service disruptions. An understanding of the concepts and processes involved will help to make sure that your experiences as a DNS admin are pleasant ones.

DNS Concepts

We begin with a look at the ideas behind DNS, independent of the details of the software used to implement it. An understanding at this level is invaluable in avoiding the majority

of problems, and in diagnosing and quickly solving the ones that do occur. In the following overview, I avoid several small details in the protocol because they aren't very relevant to the everyday tasks of a DNS administrator. If you need more information, consult
the DNS standards, especially RFC 1034. (The RFCs related to DNS are distributed with
BIND. Red Hat 7.2 installs them in /usr/share/doc/bind-9.1.3/rfc/.)

The domain namespace is structured as a tree. Each domain is a node in the tree, and has
a name. For every node, there are *resource records (RRs)*, each of which stores a single
fact about the domain (Who owns it? What is its IP address?). Domains can have any
number of children, or subdomains. The root of the tree is a domain named " . " (similar
to the " / " root directory in a filesystem).

The resource records belonging to a domain each store a different type of information.
For example, A (Address) records store the IP address associated with a name. NS
(Name Server) records name an authoritative name server for a domain. Some other
common RRs are MX (Mail Exchanger), SOA (Start of Authority), and PTR (Pointer).
They are discussed later.

Every node has a unique name that specifies its position in the tree, just as every file has
a unique path from the root directory to itself. That is, one starts with the root domain
" . ", and prepends to it each name in the path, using a dot to separate the names. The
root domain has children named com., org., net., de., and so on. They, in turn, have
children named ibm.com, wiw.org., and gmx.de. In general, a fully-qualified domain
name (FQDN) such as foo.example.com. is similar to the path /com/example/foo.
(Notice how the trailing dot in an FQDN is often omitted.)

Information about the structure of the tree, and the associated resource records, is stored
by programs called *name servers*. Every domain has an authoritative name server that
holds a complete local copy of the data for the domain (and its administrators are responsible for maintaining the data). A name server can also cache information about parts of
the tree for which they have no authority. For administrative convenience, name servers
can delegate authority over certain subdomains to other, independently maintained, name
servers.

The authoritative name server for a zone knows about the name servers to which author
ity over subdomains has been delegated. It might refer queries about the delegated zones
to those name servers. So, we can always find authoritative data for a domain by following the chain of delegations of authority from " . " (the root domain) until we reach an
authoritative name server for the domain. This is what gives DNS its distributed tree
structure.

14

MANAGING DNS

Users of DNS need not be aware of these details. To them, the namespace is just a single tree, any part of which they can request information about. The task of finding the requested RRs from the resource set for a domain is left to programs called resolvers. Resolvers are aware of the distributed structure of the database. They know how to contact the root name servers (which are authoritative for the root domain), and how to follow the chain of delegations until they find an authoritative name server that can give them the information they are looking for.

At the risk of stretching the analogy too far, you can think of domains as directories in a filesystem and resource records as files in these directories. The delegation of authority over subdomains is similar to having an NFS filesystem mounted under a subdirectory: Requests for files under that directory would go to the NFS server, rather than this filesystem. The resolver's job is to start from the root directory and walk down the directory tree (following mount points) until they reach the directory that contains the files they are interested in. (For efficiency, they can then cache the information they find for some time.) This process is examined in detail next.

In practice, there are several authoritative name servers for a domain. One of them is the *master* (or primary) name server, where the domain's data is held. The others are known as *slave* (or secondary) name servers, and they hold automatically updated copies of the master data. Both the master and the slaves serve the same information, so it doesn't matter which one a resolver asks. The distinction between master and slave is made purely for reasons of reliability, to ensure that the failure of a single name server doesn't result in the loss of authoritative data for the domain. As a bonus, this redundancy also distributes the network load between several hosts so that no one name server is overwhelmed with requests for authoritative information.

(As a DNS administrator, it is your responsibility to ensure that your name servers provide sufficient redundancy for your zones. Your slaves should be far away from the master so that power failures, network outages, and other catastrophes don't affect your name service.)

Despite these precautions, the load on DNS servers would be crushing without the extensive use of local caches. As mentioned before, name servers are allowed to cache the results of queries and intermediate referrals for some time so that they can serve repeated requests for data without referring to the source each time. If they didn't do this, root name servers, and the name servers for other popular zones, would be contacted by clients all over the world for every name lookup, wasting a huge amount of resources.

Name Resolution in Practice

Letus see what happens behind the scenes when a Web browser issues a request for the IP address of www.ibm.com. Usually, the request is sent to a local name server, which resolves the name, stores the result in its cache, and returns the IP address. We will mimic the actions of our resolver by using the incredibly useful dig utility to follow the chain of delegations between zones until we find the A record we are looking for. (Because most name servers would follow the delegations for us, we use the +norec dig parameter to turn off recursion. That is, if the name server doesn't know how to answer our query, it will not issue further queries on its own.)

We randomly select one of the thirteen root name servers (ranging from a.root-servers.net to m.root-servers.net; we picked e), and ask what it knows about an A record for www.ibm.com:

```
$ dig @e.root-servers.net www.ibm.com A +norec

; <<>> DiG 9.1.3 <<>> @e.root-servers.net www.ibm.com A +norec
;; global options:  printcmd
;; Got answer:
;; ->>HEADER<<- opcode: QUERY, status: NOERROR, id: 52356
;; flags: qr; QUERY: 1, ANSWER: 0, AUTHORITY: 13, ADDITIONAL: 13

;; QUESTION SECTION:
;www.ibm.com.                   IN      A

;; AUTHORITY SECTION:
com.                   172800  IN      NS      A.GTLD-SERVERS.NET.
com.                   172800  IN      NS      G.GTLD-SERVERS.NET.
com.                   172800  IN      NS      H.GTLD-SERVERS.NET.
com.                   172800  IN      NS      C.GTLD-SERVERS.NET.
com.                   172800  IN      NS      I.GTLD-SERVERS.NET.
com.                   172800  IN      NS      B.GTLD-SERVERS.NET.
com.                   172800  IN      NS      D.GTLD-SERVERS.NET.
com.                   172800  IN      NS      L.GTLD-SERVERS.NET.
com.                   172800  IN      NS      F.GTLD-SERVERS.NET.
com.                   172800  IN      NS      J.GTLD-SERVERS.NET.
com.                   172800  IN      NS      K.GTLD-SERVERS.NET.
com.                   172800  IN      NS      E.GTLD-SERVERS.NET.
com.                   172800  IN      NS      M.GTLD-SERVERS.NET.

;; ADDITIONAL SECTION:
A.GTLD-SERVERS.NET.    172800  IN      A       192.5.6.30
G.GTLD-SERVERS.NET.    172800  IN      A       192.42.93.30
H.GTLD-SERVERS.NET.    172800  IN      A       192.54.112.30
C.GTLD-SERVERS.NET.    172800  IN      A       192.26.92.30
```

14

MANAGING DNS

```
I.GTLD-SERVERS.NET.      172800  IN      A       192.36.144.133
B.GTLD-SERVERS.NET.      172800  IN      A       192.33.14.30
D.GTLD-SERVERS.NET.      172800  IN      A       192.31.80.30
L.GTLD-SERVERS.NET.      172800  IN      A       192.41.162.30
F.GTLD-SERVERS.NET.      172800  IN      A       192.35.51.30
J.GTLD-SERVERS.NET.      172800  IN      A       210.132.100.101
K.GTLD-SERVERS.NET.      172800  IN      A       213.177.194.5
E.GTLD-SERVERS.NET.      172800  IN      A       192.12.94.30
M.GTLD-SERVERS.NET.      172800  IN      A       202.153.114.101

;; Query time: 819 msec
;; SERVER: 192.203.230.10#53(e.root-servers.net)
;; WHEN: Wed Sep 26 10:05:08 2001
;; MSG SIZE  rcvd: 461
```

The QUERY: 1, ANSWER: 0 in the response means that e.root-servers.net didn't
know the answer to our question. It does know the authoritative name servers for the com
TLD, and it refers our query to them in the AUTHORITY section. (Not too long ago, all the
root-servers.net name servers were themselves authoritative for the com TLD, but
additional delegations were recently introduced.)

The resolver's next step would be to select one of these listed servers at random, to use
the IP addresses mentioned in the ADDITIONAL section of the response to connect to the
server, and to repeat the question. This is what we do now, having chosen i.gtld-
servers.net:

```
; <<>> DiG 9.1.3 <<>> @i.gtld-servers.net www.ibm.com A +norec
;; global options:  printcmd
;; Got answer:
;; ->>HEADER<<- opcode: QUERY, status: NOERROR, id: 61562
;; flags: qr; QUERY: 1, ANSWER: 0, AUTHORITY: 5, ADDITIONAL: 5

;; QUESTION SECTION:
;www.ibm.com.                    IN      A

;; AUTHORITY SECTION:
ibm.com.                172800  IN      NS
➥INTERNET-SERVER.ZURICH.ibm.com.
ibm.com.                172800  IN      NS      NS.WATSON.ibm.com.
ibm.com.                172800  IN      NS      NS.ERS.ibm.com.
ibm.com.                172800  IN      NS      NS.ALMADEN.ibm.com.
ibm.com.                172800  IN      NS      NS.AUSTIN.ibm.com.

;; ADDITIONAL SECTION:
INTERNET-SERVER.ZURICH.ibm.com. 172800 IN A     195.212.119.252
```

```
NS.WATSON.ibm.com.        172800  IN      A       198.81.209.2
NS.ERS.ibm.com.           172800  IN      A       204.146.173.35
NS.ALMADEN.ibm.com.       172800  IN      A       198.4.83.35
NS.AUSTIN.ibm.com.        172800  IN      A       192.35.232.34

;; Query time: 8337 msec
;; SERVER: 192.36.144.133#53(i.gtld-servers.net)
;; WHEN: Wed Sep 26 10:06:46 2001
;; MSG SIZE  rcvd: 240
```

We still have 0 ANSWERs, but we are clearly getting closer. The response lists the names and IP addresses of five authoritative name servers for the ibm.com domain. (Notice the abnormally large query time. This tells us that our choice of i.gtld-servers.net was, for some reason, a poor one. Intelligent resolvers remember this fact, and would pick a different server in future. BIND only does this for the root servers, though.)

We choose NS.WATSON.ibm.com, and repeat our question:

```
$ dig @NS.WATSON.ibm.com www.ibm.com A +norec

; <<>> DiG 9.1.3 <<>> @NS.WATSON.ibm.com www.ibm.com A +norec
;; global options:  printcmd
;; Got answer:
;; ->>HEADER<<- opcode: QUERY, status: NOERROR, id: 32287
;; flags: qr aa ra; QUERY: 1, ANSWER: 4, AUTHORITY: 5, ADDITIONAL: 5

;; QUESTION SECTION:
;www.ibm.com.                    IN      A

;; ANSWER SECTION:
www.ibm.com.            1800    IN      A       129.42.18.99
www.ibm.com.            1800    IN      A       129.42.19.99
www.ibm.com.            1800    IN      A       129.42.16.99
www.ibm.com.            1800    IN      A       129.42.17.99

;; AUTHORITY SECTION:
ibm.com.                600     IN      NS      ns.watson.ibm.com.
ibm.com.                600     IN      NS      ns.austin.ibm.com.
ibm.com.                600     IN      NS      ns.almaden.ibm.com.
ibm.com.                600     IN      NS      ns.ers.ibm.com.
ibm.com.                600     IN      NS
➥internet-server.zurich.ibm.com.

;; ADDITIONAL SECTION:
ns.watson.ibm.com.      600     IN      A       198.81.209.2
ns.austin.ibm.com.      86400   IN      A       192.35.232.34
```

```
ns.almaden.ibm.com.       86400   IN     A      198.4.83.35
ns.ers.ibm.com.           259200  IN     A      204.146.173.35
internet-server.zurich.ibm.com. 1800 IN A      195.212.119.252

;; Query time: 441 msec
;; SERVER: 198.81.209.2#53(NS.WATSON.ibm.com)
;; WHEN: Wed Sep 26 10:08:21 2001
;; MSG SIZE  rcvd: 304
```

NS.WATSON.ibm.com knew the answer to our question, and for the first time, the response contains an ANSWER section that lists four A records for www.ibm.com. Most resolvers pick one at random and return it to the program that initiated the name resolution. This concludes our search.

Reverse Resolution

Given an IP address, it is often necessary to find the name associated with it (while writing Web server logs, for example). This process is known as *reverse resolution*, and is accomplished with the help of an elegant subterfuge. The problem is that IP addresses (similar to filenames) are "backward" from the DNS point of view. Because we can only associate RRs with DNS names, we must find a way to write an IP address, with its left-to-right hierarchy (129.42.18.99 belongs to 129.*), as a DNS name with a right-to-left hierarchy (ibm.com belongs to com).

We do this by reversing the order of the octets in the address, and then appending .in-addr.arpa (a domain used exclusively to support reverse lookups) to the result. For example, 129.42.18.99 would be written as 99.18.32.129.in-addr.arpa. PTR (Pointer) records associated with this special name would then tell us the real name of the host to which the IP belongs.

We can look for PTR records in the usual fashion, by following a chain of delegations from a root server. We examine this process briefly by resolving 203.200.109.66 (which is one of the dial-up IP addresses that my ISP assigns to its customers). We ask a root name server about 66.109.200.203.in-addr.arpa:

```
$ dig @a.root-servers.net 66.109.200.203.in-addr.arpa PTR +norec

; <<>> DiG 8.2 <<>> @a.root-servers.net
➥66.109.200.203.in-addr.arpa PTR +norec
; (1 server found)
;; res options: init defnam dnsrch
;; got answer:
```

```
;; ->>HEADER<<- opcode: QUERY, status: NOERROR, id: 17284
;; flags: qr; QUERY: 1, ANSWER: 0, AUTHORITY: 4, ADDITIONAL: 3
;; QUERY SECTION:
;;      66.109.200.203.in-addr.arpa, type = PTR, class = IN

;; AUTHORITY SECTION:
203.in-addr.arpa.         1D IN NS      SVC00.APNIC.NET.
203.in-addr.arpa.         1D IN NS      NS.APNIC.NET.
203.in-addr.arpa.         1D IN NS      NS.TELSTRA.NET.
203.in-addr.arpa.         1D IN NS      NS.RIPE.NET.

;; ADDITIONAL SECTION:
SVC00.APNIC.NET.          2D IN A       202.12.28.131
NS.APNIC.NET.             2D IN A       203.37.255.97
NS.RIPE.NET.              2D IN A       193.0.0.193

;; Total query time: 432 msec
;; FROM: lustre to SERVER: a.root-servers.net  198.41.0.4
;; WHEN: Sun Sep 23 02:10:19 2001
;; MSG SIZE  sent: 45  rcvd: 186
```

Notice that this output is from an old version of dig (one shipped with BIND 8) that I happened to have installed. There are minor differences in output format, notably that the QUESTION section is missing and time intervals are specified in days and hours rather than seconds. Continuing with NS.TELSTRA.NET, we have

```
$ dig @NS.TELSTRA.NET 66.109.200.203.in-addr.arpa PTR +norec

; <<>> DiG 8.2 <<>> @NS.TELSTRA.NET 66.109.200.203.in-addr.arpa PTR
+norec
; (1 server found)
;; res options: init defnam dnsrch
;; got answer:
;; ->>HEADER<<- opcode: QUERY, status: NOERROR, id: 11519
;; flags: qr ra; QUERY: 1, ANSWER: 0, AUTHORITY: 2, ADDITIONAL: 2
;; QUERY SECTION:
;;      66.109.200.203.in-addr.arpa, type = PTR, class = IN

;; AUTHORITY SECTION:
200.203.in-addr.arpa.    4D IN NS      ns3.vsnl.com.
200.203.in-addr.arpa.    4D IN NS      dns.vsnl.net.in.

;; ADDITIONAL SECTION:
ns3.vsnl.com.            19h48m53s IN A  203.197.12.42
dns.vsnl.net.in.         3h30m22s IN A   202.54.1.30
```

14

MANAGING DNS

```
;; Total query time: 723 msec
;; FROM: lustre to SERVER: NS.TELSTRA.NET  203.50.0.137
;; WHEN: Sun Sep 23 02:11:51 2001
;; MSG SIZE  sent: 45  rcvd: 132
```

And then,

```
$ dig @ns3.vsnl.com 66.109.200.203.in-addr.arpa PTR +norec

; <<>> DiG 8.2 <<>> @ns3.vsnl.com 66.109.200.203.in-addr.arpa PTR +norec
; (1 server found)       ;; res options: init defnam dnsrch
;; got answer:
;; ->>HEADER<<- opcode: QUERY, status: NXDOMAIN, id: 65340
;; flags: qr aa ra; QUERY: 1, ANSWER: 0, AUTHORITY: 1, ADDITIONAL: 0
;; QUERY SECTION:
;;      66.109.200.203.in-addr.arpa, type = PTR, class = IN

;; AUTHORITY SECTION:
200.203.in-addr.arpa.    1D IN SOA     dns.vsnl.net.in.
                                       helpdesk.giasbm01.vsnl.net.in. (
                                       200001053        ; serial
                                       1D               ; refresh
                                       2H               ; retry
                                       4w2d             ; expiry
                                       4D )             ; minimum


;; Total query time: 233 msec
;; FROM: lustre to SERVER: ns3.vsnl.com  203.197.12.42
;; WHEN: Sun Sep 23 02:15:07 2001
;; MSG SIZE  sent: 45  rcvd: 114
```

What happened here? If you've been reading the responses carefully so far, you would have noticed that the status has always been NOERROR, but this one has a status of NXDO-MAIN (Nonexistent Domain), and the flags section has the aa (Authoritative Answer) flag. This means that the name we are looking for is known not to exist. Notice the difference between this and earlier responses. The response from the root name servers didn't have the aa flag set, and said "We don't know about this name: Ask somebody else." The authoritative answer from ns3.vsnl.com says "I know that this name doesn't exist, and you might as well stop looking."

The administrators at vsnl.net.in clearly haven't bothered to set up PTR records for their dial-up IP address pool. If they had, the response would have looked like the ones we've seen before, and included a PTR record. As it is, the response lists the SOA record for zone (including the e-mail address of the domain contact, `helpdesk@giasbm01.vsnl.net.in`, should we choose to complain about broken reverse resolution).

What Did the Resolver Learn?

We have a list of names and addresses of the authoritative name servers for the `com` TLD. In future, if we are asked to resolve, say `www.mcp.com`, we can direct our query to `gtld-servers.net` from the start, instead of wasting one query on a root server. However, the NS records have an expiry time of `2D`, so we must throw away the information once it is older than two days.

Similarly, we know the authoritative name servers for ibm.com, which are for use in queries involving ibm.com during the next two days. For instance, a Web browser might ask for the IP address of `commerce.ibm.com` when a user clicks on a link on the IBM Web page. We can save two queries by asking `NS.WATSON.ibm.com` again. Of course, we also have the four A records for `www.ibm.com` in our cache, and we can return one of them if the browser asks us to resolve the name again.

All this information (including that gleaned from the reverse resolution process) can be cached until expiry and used to speed up further queries.

We have also learned some things that a resolver cannot remember or make use of. We can guess from the names, for instance, that the DNS administrators at IBM have, as recommended, delegated their DNS service to servers that are distant both geographically and network-wise. We can see that IBM runs four Web servers on the same network, perhaps to gracefully handle the load. We know that the DNS administrators at VSNL (a large ISP) aren't as conscientious as they could be because they have only two name servers for their entire domain and don't have correct reverse mappings.

DNS is endlessly fascinating, and a few hours of playing with `dig` is well rewarded—both in terms of learning interesting things and because familiarity with `dig` queries and responses is very useful in debugging problems with your own DNS setup.

BIND

BIND is the de facto standard DNS software suite for UNIX. It contains a nameserver daemon (named) that answers DNS queries, a resolver library that allows programs to make such queries, and some utility programs. It is maintained by the ISC (Internet Software Consortium), whose Web site is at `http://www.isc.org/bind/`.

Three major versions of BIND are in common use today: 4, 8, and 9. The use of BIND 4 is now strongly discouraged (due to numerous security vulnerabilities and other bugs), and won't be discussed here. BIND 8, with many new features and bug fixes, is now quite widely deployed. It is actively maintained, but still vulnerable to a variety of attacks.

In this chapter, we discuss the use of BIND 9, which is now shipped with Red Hat Linux. BIND 9 was rewritten from scratch in an attempt to make the code more robust and leave behind the problems inherent in the old code. It is compliant with new DNS standards, and is claimed to represent a substantial improvement in features, performance, and security.

BIND has often been criticized for its recurrent security problems, but few alternatives exist. djbdns (http://cr.yp.to/djbdns.html) is the only one that seems ready for production at the moment. Its use is not discussed here.

At the time of writing, BIND 9.1.3 is the latest version. Installing it is just a matter of installing the bind and bind-utils RPMs shipped with the Red Hat 7.2 distribution. The former contains named and a wealth of BIND documentation, whereas the latter contains, among other things, the invaluable dig(1) utility. Of course, you might choose to compile BIND yourself, in which case you can download the source distribution from the ISC's Web site and follow the build instructions therein.

Once you install the RPMs, the following directories are of special interest. (If you installed from source, the files will be in the locations you specified at configure time, with the default being directories under /usr/local/.)

```
/etc/                      Configuration files.
/usr/bin/                  dig, host, nslookup, nsupdate.
/usr/sbin/                 named, rndc, and various support programs.
/usr/share/doc/bind-9.1.3/ BIND documentation.
/usr/share/man/            Manual pages.
/var/named/*               Zone files.
```

Basic Configuration

We develop a minimal name server configuration next, and then expand it as necessary to provide useful DNS service. The components that must be configured are named (the nameserver daemon) and rndc (a control utility that permits various interactions with a running named); often, it is also necessary to configure the resolver software, as discussed later.

rndc.conf

rndc uses a TCP connection (on port 953) to communicate with named; for authentication, it uses cryptographic keys to digitally sign commands before sending them over the network to named. The configuration file, /etc/rndc.conf by default, must specify a server to talk to, and the corresponding key (which must be recognized by named) to use while talking to it.

The only authentication mechanism currently supported is the use of a secret, encrypted with the HMAC-MD5 algorithm, and shared between rndc and named. The easiest way to generate a key is to use the dnssec-keygen utility. Here, we are asking it to generate a 128-bit HMAC-MD5 user key named rndc:

```
$ dnssec-keygen -a hmac-md5 -b 128 -n user rndc
Krndc.+157+14529

$ cat Krndc.+157+14529.private
Private-key-format: v1.2
Algorithm: 157 (HMAC_MD5)
Key: mKKd2FiHMFe1JqXl/z4cfw==
```

Two files are created, with .key and .private extensions, respectively. The Key: line in the .private file tells us the secret that rndc and named need to share (mKKd2FiHMFe1JqXl/z4cfw==). Once we have this, we can proceed to set up the very simple /etc/rndc.conf:

```
# Use the key named "rndc" when talking to the name server "localhost."
server localhost {
    key                 rndc;
};

# Here are the details about the key named "rndc."
key rndc {
    algorithm           HMAC-MD5;
    secret              "mKKd2FiHMFe1JqXl/z4cfw==";
};

# Defaults.
options {
    default-server      localhost;
    default-key         rndc;
};
```

14

MANAGING DNS

The file needs to have three sections. The first is a `server` section that defines a name server (`localhost`) and specifies a key (`rndc`) to be used while communicating with it. Next, the corresponding `key` section contains some details about the key, as generated by `dnssec-keygen`. When we set up `named`, we need to tell it the same information about the key so that it can authenticate requests made by `rndc`. The third section, `options`, just sets up reasonable defaults (because the file might list multiple servers and keys). Should you need it, the `rndc(8)` and `rndc.conf(5)` manual pages contain more information.

named.conf

Our next task is to configure `named` itself. Its single configuration file (`/etc/named.conf`) has syntax very similar to `rndc.conf`, but only a small subset of its many available configuration directives, essential to the configuration of a functional name server, are described here. For a more exhaustive reference, consult the BIND 9 ARM (Administrator Reference Manual; it is distributed with BIND, and Red Hat 7.2 installs it under /usr/share/doc/bind-9.1.3/arm/).

Only two sections are absolutely necessary: the `options` section must tell `named` where the zone files are kept, and `named` must know where to find the root zone (`"."`). We also set up a `controls` section to allow suitably authenticated commands from `rndc` to be accepted. Because clients (notably `nslookup`) often depend on resolving the name server's IP, we set up the `0.0.127.in-addr.arpa` reverse zone as well.

We start with a configuration file similar to this:

/etc/named.conf

```
options {
    # This is where zone files are kept.
    directory            "/var/named";
};

# Allow rndc running on localhost to send us commands.
controls {
    inet 127.0.0.1
        allow { 127.0.0.1; }
        keys { rndc; };
};

# The same information as specified in rndc.conf
key rndc {
    algorithm           hmac-md5;
    secret              "mKKd2FiHMFe1JqXl/z4cfw==";
};

# Information about the root zone.
zone "." {
```

```
    type            hint;
    file            "root.hints";
};

# Lots of software depends on being able to resolve 127.0.0.1
zone "0.0.127.in-addr.arpa" {
    type            master;
    file            "rev/127.0.0";
};
```

The options section is where most of the interesting directives go. For now, we will content ourselves with specifying the directory in which named should look for zone files (as named in other sections of the file). Other options will be introduced as required along the way.

Next, we instruct named to accept commands from an authenticated rndc. We add a key section, identical to the one from rndc.conf, and the controls section saying that rndc will be connecting from localhost and using the specified key. (You can specify more than one IP address in the allow list, or use an access control list as described in the section "Security.")

The "." zone tells named about the root name servers, whose names and addresses are contained in the root.hints file. This information is used to decide which root name server to consult initially. (The decision is frequently revised based on the server's response time.) Although the hints file can be obtained via FTP, the recommended, network-friendly way to keep it synchronized is to use dig. We ask a root name server (it doesn't matter which one) for the NS records of ".", and use the dig output directly:

/var/named/root.hints

```
# dig @j.root-servers.net. . ns > /var/named/root.hints
# cat /var/named/root.hints
; <<>> DiG 8.2 <<>> @j.root-servers.net . ns
; (1 server found)
;; res options: init recurs defnam dnsrch
;; got answer:
;; ->>HEADER<<- opcode: QUERY, status: NOERROR, id: 6
;; flags: qr aa rd; QUERY: 1, ANSWER: 13, AUTHORITY: 0, ADDITIONAL: 13
;; QUERY SECTION:      ;; ., type = NS, class = IN

;; ANSWER SECTION:
.                       6D IN NS        H.ROOT-SERVERS.NET.
.                       6D IN NS        C.ROOT-SERVERS.NET.
.                       6D IN NS        G.ROOT-SERVERS.NET.
.                       6D IN NS        F.ROOT-SERVERS.NET.
.                       6D IN NS        B.ROOT-SERVERS.NET.
```

14

MANAGING DNS

```
   .                       6D IN NS        J.ROOT-SERVERS.NET.
   .                       6D IN NS        K.ROOT-SERVERS.NET.
   .                       6D IN NS        L.ROOT-SERVERS.NET.
   .                       6D IN NS    /   M.ROOT-SERVERS.NET.
   .                       6D IN NS        I.ROOT-SERVERS.NET.
   .                       6D IN NS        E.ROOT-SERVERS.NET.
   .                       6D IN NS        D.ROOT-SERVERS.NET.
   .                       6D IN NS        A.ROOT-SERVERS.NET.

   ;; ADDITIONAL SECTION:
   H.ROOT-SERVERS.NET.     5w6d16h IN A    128.63.2.53
   C.ROOT-SERVERS.NET.     5w6d16h IN A    192.33.4.12
   G.ROOT-SERVERS.NET.     5w6d16h IN A    192.112.36.4
   F.ROOT-SERVERS.NET.     5w6d16h IN A    192.5.5.241
   B.ROOT-SERVERS.NET.     5w6d16h IN A    128.9.0.107
   J.ROOT-SERVERS.NET.     5w6d16h IN A    198.41.0.10
   K.ROOT-SERVERS.NET.     5w6d16h IN A    193.0.14.129
   L.ROOT-SERVERS.NET.     5w6d16h IN A    198.32.64.12
   M.ROOT-SERVERS.NET.     5w6d16h IN A    202.12.27.33
   I.ROOT-SERVERS.NET.     5w6d16h IN A    192.36.148.17
   E.ROOT-SERVERS.NET.     5w6d16h IN A    192.203.230.10
   D.ROOT-SERVERS.NET.     5w6d16h IN A    128.8.10.90
   A.ROOT-SERVERS.NET.     5w6d16h IN A    198.41.0.4

   ;; Total query time: 4489 msec
   ;; FROM: lustre to SERVER: j.root-servers.net  198.41.0.10
   ;; WHEN: Mon Sep 10 04:18:26 2001
   ;; MSG SIZE  sent: 17  rcvd: 436
```

The Zone File

The zone `0.0.127.in-addr.arpa` section in named.conf says that we are a master name server for that zone, and that the zone data is in the file 127.0.0. Before we examine our first real zone file in detail, let us look at the general format of a resource record specification:

```
   name        TTL     class   type    data
```

Here, `name` is the DNS name with which this record is associated. In a zone file, names ending with a `"."` are fully qualified, whereas others are relative to the name of the zone. In the zone example.com, `foo` refers to the fully-qualified name `foo.example.com.`. The special name `@` is a short form for the name of the zone itself. If the name is omitted, the last specified name is used again.

The *TTL (Time To Live)* field is a number that specifies the time for which the record can be cached. This is explained in greater detail in the discussion of the SOA record in the next section. If it is omitted, the default TTL for the zone is assumed. TTL values are usually in seconds, but (since BIND 8) you can append an *m* for minutes, *h* for hours, or *d* for days.

BIND supports different record classes, but for all practical purposes, the only important class is IN, for Internet. If no class is explicitly specified, a default value of IN is assumed; to save a little typing, we don't mention the class in any of the zone files we write here.

The type field is mandatory, and names the RR in use, such as A, NS, MX, or SOA. (We will only use a few of the existing RRs here. Consult the DNS standards for a complete list.) The data field (or fields) contains data specific to this type of record. The appropriate syntax will be introduced as we examine the use of each RR in turn.

Here is the zone file for the `0.0.127.in-addr.arpa` zone:

/var/named/rev/127.0.0

```
$TTL 2D
@       SOA     localhost. hostmaster.example.com. (
                        2001090101  ; Serial
                        24h         ; Refresh
                        2h          ; Retry
                        3600000     ; Expire (1000h)
                        1h)         ; Minimum TTL
        NS      localhost.

    PTR     localhost.
```

The `$TTL` directive, which should begin every zone file, sets the default minimum time-to-live for the zone to 2 days. This is discussed further in the next section.

The SOA Record

The second line uses the special @ name that you saw earlier. Here, it stands for `0.0.127.in-addr.arpa`, to which the SOA (Start of Authority) record belongs. The rest of the fields (continued on the next few lines, until the closing parenthesis) contain SOA-specific data.

The first data field in the SOA record is the fully-qualified name of the master name server for the domain. The second field is the e-mail address of the contact person for the zone. It is written as a DNS name by replacing the @ sign with a ".";`foo@example.com` would be written as `foo.example.com.`. (Note the trailing `.`.) Don't use an address such as `a.b@example.com` because it is written as `a.b.example.com.`, and will later be misinterpreted as `a@b.example.com`. It is important to ensure that mail to this address is

14

MANAGING DNS

frequently read because it is used to report DNS setup problems and other potentially useful information.

The next several numeric fields specify various characteristics of this zone. It is important to configure these values correctly, and hence to understand them all. As shown in the comments (note that zone file comments aren't the same syntax as `named.conf` comments), the fields are serial number, refresh interval, retry time, expire period, and minimum TTL.

Serial numbers are 32-bit quantities that can hold values between `0` and `4,294,967,295` (`2^32-1`). Every time the zone data is changed, the serial number must be incremented. This change serves as a signal to slaves that they need to transfer the contents of the zone again. It is conventional to assign serial numbers in the format *YYYYMMDDnn*; that is, the date of the change and a two-digit revision number (for example, `2001090101`). For changes made on the same day, you increment only the revision (this reasonably assumes that you don't make more than 99 changes to a zone in one day). For changes on the next day, the date is changed and the revision number starts from 01 again.

The refresh interval specifies how often a slave server should check whether the master data has been updated. It has been set to 24 hours here, but if the zone changes often, the value should be lower. (Slaves can reload the zone much sooner if they and the master both support the DNS `NOTIFY` mechanism. Most DNS software does.) The retry time is relevant only when a slave fails to contact the master after the refresh time has elapsed. It specifies how long it should wait before trying again. (It is set to two hours here.)

If the slave is consistently unable to contact the master for the length of the expire period (usually because of some catastrophic failure), it discards the zone data it already has and stops answering queries for the zone. Thus, the expire period should be long enough to allow for the recovery of the master name server. It has repeatedly been shown that a value of one or two weeks is too short. 1,000 hours (about six weeks) is accepted as a good default.

The TTL fields deserve more explanation. Every RR has a TTL, which specifies how long it can be cached before the origin of the data must be consulted again. If the RR definition doesn't specify a TTL explicitly, the default TTL (set by the `$TTL` directive) is used instead. This allows individual RRs to override the default TTL as required.

The SOA TTL, the last numeric field in the SOA record, is now used to determine how long negative responses (`NXDOMAIN`) should be cached. (That is, if a query results in an `NXDOMAIN` response, that fact is cached for as long as indicated by the SOA TTL.) Older versions of BIND used the SOA minimum TTL to set the default TTL, but BIND 9 no longer does so. The default TTL of 2 days and SOA TTL of 1 hour is recommended for cache friendliness.

The values used previously are good defaults for zones that do not change often. You might have to adjust them a bit for zones with very different requirements; in which case, the Web site `http://www.ripe.net/docs/ripe-203.html` is recommended reading.

Other Records

The next two lines in the zone file create NS and PTR records. The NS record has no explicit name specified, so it uses the last one, which is the @ of the SOA record. Thus, the name server for `0.0.127.in-addr.arpa` is defined to be `localhost`. The PTR record has the name `1`, which becomes `1.0.0.127.in-addr.arpa` (which is how you write the address `127.0.0.1` as a DNS name) and the name `localhost` when qualified. (You will see some of the numerous other RR types when we later configure our name server to be authoritative for a real domain.)

Logging

We now have all the elements of a minimal functioning DNS server, but before we experiment further, some extra logging will allow us to see exactly what `named` is doing. Log options are configured in a `logging` section in `named.conf`, and the various options are described in detail in the BIND 9 ARM.

All log messages go to one or more channels, each of which can write messages to the syslog, to an ordinary file, to stderr, or to `null` (that is, discard the message). Categories of messages exist, such as those generated while parsing configuration files, those caused by OS errors, and so on. Your logging statement must define some channels and associate them with the categories of messages that you want to see.

BIND logging is very flexible, but complicated, so we'll only examine a simple log configuration here. If you need anything significantly more complicated, refer to the ARM. The following addition to your `named.conf` will set up a channel called `custom`, which writes timestamped messages to a file and send messages in the listed categories to it.

14

MANAGING DNS

```
logging {
    channel custom {
        file "/tmp/named.log";   # Where to send messages.
        print-time yes;          # Print timestamps?
        print-category yes;      # Print message category?
    };

    category config      { custom; };     # Configuration files
    category notify      { custom; };     # NOTIFY messages
    category dnssec      { custom; };     # TSIG messages
    category general     { custom; };     # Miscellaneous
    category security    { custom; };     # Security messages
```

```
        category xfer-out    { custom; };    # Zone transfers
        category lame-servers { custom; };
    };
```

Keeping track of logs is especially important because syntax errors often cause BIND to reject a zone and not answer queries for it, causing your server to become *lame* (that is, not authoritative for a zone for which it is supposed to be).

Resolver Configuration

The last thing we need to do before running BIND is to set up the local resolver software. This involves configuring three files: /etc/hosts, /etc/resolv.conf, and /etc/nsswitch.conf.

To avoid gratuitous network traffic, most UNIX resolvers still use a hosts.txt-like file named /etc/hosts to store the names and addresses of commonly used hosts. Each line in this file contains an IP address and a list of names for the host. Add entries to this file for any hosts you want to be able to resolve independent of DNS.

/etc/resolv.conf specifies the addresses of preferred name servers and a list of domains relative to which unqualified names will be resolved. A name server is specified with a line of the form *nameserver 1.2.3.4* (where *1.2.3.4* is the address of the name server). You can use multiple nameserver lines (usually up to three). You can also use a search line to specify a list of domains to search for unqualified names. A search line such as search example.com example.net would cause the resolver to attempt to resolve the unqualified name xyz, first as xyz.example.com, and, if that fails, as xyz. example.net. Don't use too many domains in the search list because it slows down resolution.

A hosts: files dns line in /etc/nsswitch.conf will cause the resolver to consult /etc/hosts before using the DNS during the course of a name lookup. This allows you to override the DNS by making temporary changes to /etc/hosts, which is especially useful during network testing. (Older resolvers might require an order hosts, bind line in the /etc/host.conf file instead.)

Running named

Finally! You can now start named with /etc/rc.d/init.d/named start. You should see messages similar to the ones that follow in the syslog (or according to the logging configuration you have set up).

```
Sep 26 09:47:12 ns1 named[30507]: starting BIND 9.1.3
Sep 26 09:47:12 ns1 named[30507]: using 1 CPU
Sep 26 09:47:12 ns1 named[30509]: loading configuration from
➥'/etc/named.conf'
Sep 26 09:47:12 ns1 named[30509]: listening on IPv4 interface lo,
➥ 127.0.0.1#53
Sep 26 09:47:12 ns1 named[30509]: command channel listening on
➥127.0.0.1#953
Sep 26 09:47:12 ns1 named[30509]: running
```

You can interact with this instance of named with rndc. Running rndc without arguments displays a list of available commands, including the ability to reload or refresh zones, dump statistics and the database to disk, toggle query logging, and stop the server. (Unfortunately, rndc does not yet implement all the commands that were supported by ndc, the control program shipped with earlier versions of BIND.)

You should now be able to resolve 1.0.0.127.in-addr.arpa locally (try dig @localhost 1.0.0.127.in-addr.arpa PTR +norec), and other names via recursive resolution. If you cannot, there is something wrong, and you should read the "Troubleshooting" section later to diagnose and correct your problem before proceeding further. Remember to read the logs!

A Real Domain

Let us expand this minimal configuration into one that performs useful name service for a real domain. Suppose that we own (that is, our ISP has assigned to us) the IP addresses in the 192.0.2.0/29 range (which has six usable addresses: 192.0.2.1-6), and that we want to serve authoritative data for the domain example.com. A friend has agreed to configure her name server (192.0.2.96) to be a slave for the domain, as well as a backup mail server. In return, she wants the foo.example.com subdomain delegated to her own name servers.

Forward Zone

First, we must introduce the zone to named.conf

```
zone "example.com" {
    type master;
    file "example.com";
};
```

14

MANAGING DNS

and create the zone file:

```
$TTL 2D
@        SOA     ns1.example.com. hostmaster.example.com. (
                        2001090101  ; Serial
                        24h         ; Refresh
                        2h          ; Retry
                        3600000     ; Expire (1000h)
                        1h)         ; Minimum TTL
         NS      ns1.example.com.
         NS      ns2.example.com.
         MX 5    mx1.example.com.
         MX 10   mx2.example.com.
         A       192.0.2.1

; Addresses
ns1      A       192.0.2.1           ; Name servers
ns2      A       192.0.2.96
mx1      A       192.0.2.2           ; Mail servers
mx2      A       192.0.2.96
www      A       192.0.2.3           ; Web servers
dev      A       192.0.2.4
work     A       192.0.2.5           ; Workstations
play     A       192.0.2.6

; Delegations
foo      NS      dns1.foo.example.com.
foo      NS      dns2.foo.example.com.
dns1.foo A       192.0.2.96
dns2.foo A       192.0.2.1
```

The SOA record is similar to the one you saw before. (Note that the next five records all use the implicit name @, short for `example.com`.)

The two NS records define `ns1.example.com` (our own server, `192.0.2.1`) and `ns2.example.com` (our friend's server, `192.0.2.96`) as authoritative name servers for `example.com`.

The MX (Mail Exchanger) records each specify a mail server for the zone. An MX RR takes two arguments: a priority number and the name of a host. In delivering mail addressed to `example.com`, the listed MXes are tried in increasing order of priority. In this case, `mx1.example.com` (our own machine, `192.0.2.2`) has the lowest priority, and is always tried first. If the attempt to deliver mail to mx1 fails (for whatever reason), the next listed MX, `mx2.example.com` (our friend's server) is tried.

The A record says that the address of example.com is 192.0.2.1, and the next few lines specify addresses for other hosts in the zone: our name servers ns1 and ns2, mail servers mx1 and mx2, two Web servers, and two workstations.

Next, we add NS records to delegate authority over the foo.example.com domain to dns1 and dns2.foo.example.com. The A records for dns1 and dns2 are known as glue records, and they enable resolvers to find the address of the authoritative name servers so that they can continue the query. (If we were using dig, the NS records for dns1 and dns2 would be listed in the AUTHORITY section of the response, whereas the ADDITIONAL section would contain their addresses.)

Notice that dns2.foo.example.com is 192.0.2.1, our own name server. We are acting as a slave for the foo.example.com zone, and must configure named accordingly. We introduce the zone as a slave in named.conf and specify the address of the master name server:

```
zone "foo.example.com" {
    type slave;
    file "foo.example.com";
    masters {
        192.0.2.96;
    };
};
```

Similarly, our friend must configure 192.0.2.96, which is a master for foo.example. com, and a slave for example.com. (She must also configure her server to accept mail addressed to example.com. Usually, mx2 would just queue the mail until it could be delivered to mx1.)

Reverse Zone

Let us pretend that we live in a perfect world, our highly competent ISP has successfully delegated authority of our reverse zone to us, and we must set up named to handle reverse resolution as well. Nothing is particularly different between this and the reverse zone we set up for 0.0.127.in-addr.arpa. There is, however, one new issue we must address. What is our zone named?

DNS can only delegate authority at the "." in domain names. This means that you can set up reverse zones for the whole of a class A, B, or C network because they are divided at octet boundaries in the IP address. This is clearly unsuitable for classless subnets such as ours because the divisions aren't at octet boundaries, but in the middle of an octet. In

other words, our network can't be described as x.* (class A), x.y.* (class B), or
x.y.z.* (class C). The latter comes closest, but includes several addresses (such as
192.0.2.22) that don't belong to our tiny 192.0.2.0/29 network. To set up a reverse
zone for our network, we must resort to the use of classless delegation (described in RFC
2317).

The ISP, which is authoritative for the 2.0.192.in-addr.arpa zone, must either maintain your reverse zone for you, or add the following records into its zone file:

```
1           CNAME    1.1-6
2           CNAME    2.1-6
3           CNAME    3.1-6
4           CNAME    4.1-6
5           CNAME    5.1-6
6           CNAME    6.1-6

1-6         NS       192.0.2.1
1-6         NS       192.0.2.96
```

The first CNAME record says that 1.2.0.192.in-addr.arpa is an alias for 1.1-6.2.0.
192.in-addr.arpa. (The others are similar. We don't have CNAME records for network
and broadcast addresses 0 and 7 because they don't need to resolve.) Resolvers already
know how to follow CNAME aliases while resolving names. When they ask about the 1-6
domain, they find the NS records defined previously, and continue with their query by
asking our name server about 1.1-6.2.0.192.in-addr.arpa.

So, we must set up a zone file for 1-6.2.0.192.in-addr.arpa. Apart from the peculiar
name, this zone file is similar in every respect to the reverse zone we set up earlier, and
should contain six PTR records (apart from the SOA and NS records). Note that we
make 192.0.2.96 (ns2) a slave for the reverse zone as well, so the administrator must
add a suitable zone statement to named.conf for it.

In the real world, however, you might have to wait for months for your ISP to get the
reverse delegation right, and your reverse zone will remain broken until it does.

Registering the Domain

You now have a working DNS setup, but external resolvers cannot see it because there is
no chain of delegations from the root name servers to yours. You need to create this
chain by *registering* the domain; that is, by paying the appropriate registration fees to an
authority known as a registrar, who then delegates authority over the chosen zone to your
name servers.

There is nothing magical about what a registrar does. It has authority over a certain portion of the DNS database (say, the `com.` TLD), and, for a fee, it delegates authority over a subdomain (`example.com`) to you. This delegation is accomplished by the same mechanisms that were explained earlier in our delegation of `foo.example.com`.

The site `http://www.iana.org/domain-names.htm` contains a list of all the TLDs and the corresponding registrars (of which there are now several). The procedure and fees for registering a domain vary wildly between them. Visit the Web site of the registrar in question and follow the procedures outlined there. After wading through the required amounts of red tape, your domain should be visible to the rest of the world.

Congratulations! Your job as a DNS administrator has just begun.

Troubleshooting

A lot of good material exists about finding and fixing DNS errors. The DNSRD Tricks and Tips page at `http://www.dns.net/dnsrd/trick.html` and the `comp.protocols.tcp-ip.domains` FAQ (an HTML version is at `http://www.intac.com/~cdp/cptd-faq/`) are good places to start. This section discusses some of the more common errors and their cures. I strongly recommend reading RFC 1912, entitled "Common DNS Operational and Configuration Errors," which discusses a number of these problems at length. It's available at `http://www.isi.edu/in-notes/rfc1912.txt`.

Delegation Problems

Your zone must be delegated to the name servers authoritative for them, either by the root name servers or the parents of the zone in question. The lack of proper delegation can lead to problems ranging from the name service for your domain being entirely dysfunctional to some networks being unable to use it. These are usually a problem only in the initial stages of setting up a domain, when the delegations have not propagated widely yet. As discussed at length earlier, you can use `dig` to follow delegation chains and find the point at which problems occur. Tools such as `dnswalk` might also be useful.

The opposite situation is also problematic. When a name server is listed as being authoritative for a zone, but in fact isn't authoritative (it has not been configured to be a master for the zone), it is called a *lame server*, and the situation is a *lame delegation*. Unfortunately, lame delegations are very common on the Internet, either temporarily because of moving domains around, or (especially in the case of reverse zones) more permanent configuration errors that are never detected because of a lack of attention to detail.

14

MANAGING DNS

If your registrar's bills for your domain aren't promptly paid, they might discontinue the delegation of authority for your zone. If this happens (and the whois record for your domain will usually mention this), the best thing to do is quickly pay the registrar and ask him to renew the delegation. It's better not to let it happen, though, because such changes can take a relatively long time to make and propagate.

Reverse Lookup Problems

Reverse lookup problems are often very hard to diagnose because they manifest themselves as failures in systems other than DNS. Many security sensitive services perform reverse lookups on the originating host for all incoming connections and deny the connection if the query fails.

Even if reverse resolution succeeds, many servers might reject connections from your host if your A and PTR records do not match (that is, the PTR record for a particular IP address refers to a name, and the A record for that name refers to a different IP address). They perform a double lookup to verify that the PTR and A records match to eliminate spoofing attacks. Maintain your reverse zones carefully at all times.

Delegation problems are a frequent source of woe. Unfortunately, many ISPs appear unable to understand, configure or delegate reverse zones. In such cases, you often have little choice but to try and tell them what to do to fix the problem, and if they refuse to listen, find a new ISP (or live with broken DNS).

Another typical symptom of failing reverse lookups is an abnormally long delay on connection attempts. This happens when the server's query for a PTR record isn't answered and times out (often due to network problems or the name server being down). This can be baffling to diagnose, but you should suspect DNS problems whenever you hear questions such as "Hey! Why is telnet taking so long to connect?"

Serial Numbers

Serial numbers are very important to the correct operation of slave servers. An increase in the serial number of a zone causes slaves to reload the zone and update their local cache. A very common mistake is forgetting to increment the serial number after a change to the zone data. Secondary name servers won't reload the zone, and will continue to serve old data. If you suspect that the data on the master and slave servers are out of sync, you can use dig to view the SOA record for the zone on each server (dig @master domain SOA and dig @slave domain SOA) and compare the serial numbers in the responses.

Another common problem is setting the serial number to an incorrect value, either too small or too large. A too small serial number causes slaves to think that they possess a more up-to-date copy of the zone data, but this is easily corrected by increasing the serial number as necessary. A too large serial number is more problematic, and needs more elaborate measures to fix.

Serial number comparisons are defined in such a way that if a serial number, when subtracted from another with no overflow correction, results in a positive number, the second number is newer than the first, and a zone transfer is required. (See RFC 1982 "Serial Number Arithmetic" for details.) You can exploit this property by temporarily setting the serial number to 2^32 (`4,294,967,296`), waiting for all the slaves to reload the zone, and then setting it to the correct number.

Zone Files

The most common error in zone data is to forget that names in a zone file are relative, not to the root, but to the origin of the zone. Writing `www.example.com` in the zone file for `example.com`, and expecting it to be fully qualified, causes names such as `www.example.com.example.com` to show up in the DNS. You should either write `www`, which is qualified to the correct `www.example.com`, or write `www.example.com.` with the trailing period, to indicate that the name is fully qualified.

The SOA record should be treated with care. It should contain (as the first field) the domain name of the master server (not a CNAME), and a contact address (with the `@` replaced by a "`.`") to report problems to. Mail sent to this address should be read frequently. The other fields should contain sensible values for your zone, and the serial number should be correctly incremented after each change.

As discussed earlier, A and PTR records should always match; that is, the A record pointed to by a PTR should point back to the address of the PTR record. Remember to quote the two arguments of HINFO records if they contain any whitespace. Avoid the use of CNAME records for MX, NS, and SOA records.

In general, after making changes to zone data, it is a good idea to reload `named` and examine the logs for any errors that cause `named` to complain or reject the zone. Even better, you could use one of the verification tools such as `dnswalk`, discussed briefly next.

Tools

The Web site `http://www.dns.net/dnsrd/tools.html` maintains an extensive list of programs that can help you debug and prevent DNS problems. BIND itself includes the

14

MANAGING DNS

always useful `dig` program, as well as named-checkconf (to check `/etc/named.conf` for syntax errors) and named-checkzone (to do the same for zone files).

I also specially recommend `dnswalk` and `nslint`. `dnswalk` is a Perl script that scans the DNS setup of a given domain for problems. It should be used in conjunction with RFC 1912, which explains most of the problems it detects. `nslint`, like the analogous `lint` utility for C programs, searches for common BIND and zone file configuration errors.

The occasional use of these programs, especially after non-trivial zone changes, helps to keep your DNS configuration healthy and trouble free.

Security

Security considerations are of vital importance to DNS administrators because DNS isn't a very secure protocol and a number of successful attacks against BIND have been found over the years. The most important defense is to keep abreast of developments in security circles and act on them promptly. The BugTraq mailing list, hosted at `http://www.securityfocus.com`, and the SANS Institute at `http://www.sans.org` are good places to start.

DNS is especially vulnerable to attacks known as poisoning and spoofing. *Poisoning* refers to placing incorrect data into the DNS database, which then spreads to clients and caches across the world, potentially causing hundreds of thousands of people to unwittingly use the bad data. Although DNS poisoning can occur because of carelessness, it has serious implications when performed deliberately. What if someone set up a clone of a common Web site, redirected users to it by DNS poisoning, and then asked them for their credit card numbers? *Spoofing* is the practice of forging network packets, and making name servers believe that they are receiving a valid answer to a query is one of the ways malicious poisoning can be performed.

BIND has often been criticized as being very insecure, and although the recent versions are greatly improved in this regard, DNS administrators today must take several precautions to ensure that its use is adequately protected from attacks. Of course, it is important to always run the latest recommended version of BIND.

UNIX Security Considerations

The very first thing to do is to configure the environment BIND runs in to use all the security mechanisms available to it through the operating system to its advantage. `named` should run with as few privileges as it needs to function. Even if an attacker manages to exploit a security hole in BIND, the effects of the break-in can be minimized if `named` is running as nobody rather than root. Of course, named needs to be started as root (because it needs to bind to port 53), but it can be instructed to switch to a given user and group with the -u and -g command line options.

Starting named with a command such as named -u nobody -g nogroup is highly recommended. Remember, however, that if you run multiple services as nobody, the risks of a compromise are no longer negligible. In such a situation, it is best to create separate accounts for each service and use them for nothing else.

You can also use the chroot feature of UNIX to isolate named into its own part of the filesystem. If correctly configured, such a jail will restrict attackers—if they manage to break in—to a part of the filesystem that contains little of value. It is important to remember that a chroot jail isn't a panacea, and it doesn't eliminate the need for other defensive measures. (Programs that use chroot but don't take other precautions as well have been shown to be insecure. BIND does, however, take such precautions.)

In order for a chroot environment to work properly, you need to set up a directory that contains everything which BIND needs to run. It is recommended that you start with a working configuration of BIND, create a directory, say /usr/local/bind, and copy over the files it needs into subdirectories under that one. For instance, you will need to copy the binaries, some system libraries, the configuration files, and so on. Consult the BIND documentation for details about exactly which files you need.

Once your chroot environment is set up, you can start named with the -t /usr/local/bind option (combined with the -u and -g options) to instruct it to chroot to the directory you have set up.

You might also want to keep track of resource usage. named manages a cache of DNS data that can potentially grow very large; it will also happily hog CPU and bandwidth, making your server unusable. This is something that can be exploited by clever attackers, but you can configure BIND to set resource limits. Several such options in the named. conf file are available, including datasize, which limits the maximum size of the data segment (and thus the cache). One downside of this approach is that named might be killed by the kernel if it exceeds these limits, which means that you have to run it in a loop, which restarts it if it dies (or run it from /etc/inittab).

DNS Security Considerations

Several configuration options exist for named that can make it more resistant to various potential attacks. The most common ones are briefly described next. For more detailed discussions of the syntax and use of these options, refer to the BIND 9 documentation.

14

MANAGING DNS

ACLs (Access Control Lists)

Specifying network and IP addresses multiple times in a configuration file is tedious and error prone. BIND allows you to define *ACLs (Access Control Lists)*, which are named collections of network and IP addresses, to ease the task of assigning permissions.

Four predefined ACLs exist: any, which matches anything; none, which matches nothing; localhost, which matches all the network interfaces local to your name server, and localnets, which matches any network directly attached to a local interface. In addition, you can define your own lists in named.conf, containing as many network and IP addresses as you prefer, using the acl command as shown:

```
acl trusted {
    192.0.2.0/29;         // Our own network is OK.
    localhost;            // And so is localhost.
    !192.0.2.33/29;       // But not this range.
};
```

As shown, you can use a ! to negate members in an ACL. Once defined, you can use these ACLs in allow-query, allow-transfer, allow-recursion and similar options, as discussed next.

Queries

As mentioned before, most name servers will perform recursive resolution for any queries they receive unless specifically configured not to do so. (We suppressed this behavior by using the dig +norec.) It so happens that explicitly denying recursion is a good idea because, by repeatedly fetching data from a number of unknown and untrusted name servers, it makes your installation vulnerable to DNS poisoning.

Recursive queries can be disabled by adding a recursion no statement to the options section of named.conf. It might still be desirable to allow recursive queries from some trusted hosts, however, and this can be accomplished by the use of an allow-recursion statement. This excerpt would configure named to disallow recursion for all but the listed hosts:

```
options {
    ...

    recursion no;
    allow-recursion {
```

```
            192.0.2.0/29;
            localnets;          // Trust our local networks.
            localhost;          // And ourselves.
        };
    };
```

You can choose to be still more restrictive and allow only selected hosts to query your name server by using the `allow-query` statement (with syntax similar to `allow-recursion`, as described previously). Of course, this is not desirable if your server is authoritative for a zone. In that case, you will have to explicitly `allow-query { all; }` in the configuration section of each zone for which you want to serve authoritative data.

Allow only known slave servers to perform zone transfers from your server. Not only do zone transfers consume a lot of resources (they require a `named-xfer` process to be forked each time) and provide an avenue for denial of service attacks, but also there have been remote exploits via buffer overflows in `named-xfer` that allow attackers to gain root privileges on the compromised system. To prevent this, add sections such as the following to all your zone definitions:

```
    zone "example.com" {
        ...

        allow-transfer {
            192.0.2.96;         // Known slave.
            localhost;          // Often required for testing.
        };
    };
```

Despite all this, it might be necessary to single out a few troublesome hosts for special treatment. The `server` and `blackhole` statements in named.conf can be used to tell named about known sources of poisoned information or attack attempts. For instance, if the host `203.122.154.1` is repeatedly trying to attack the server, the following addition to the `options` section of named.conf will cause our server to ignore traffic from that address. Of course, you can specify multiple addresses and networks in the blackhole list.

```
    options {
        ...
```

14

MANAGING DNS

```
blackhole {
            203.122.154.1;
        };
    };
```

For a known source of bad data, you can do something such as the following to cause your name server to simply stop asking the listed server any questions. This is different from adding a host to the blackhole list. A server marked as bogus will never be sent queries, but it can still ask us questions. A blackholed host is simply ignored altogether.

```
server bogus.info.example.com {
    bogus yes;
};
```

The AUS-CERT advisory AL-1999.004, which discusses denial of service attacks against DNS servers, also discusses various ways of restricting access to name servers, and is a highly recommended read. A copy is at ftp://ftp.auscert.org.au/pub/auscert/ advisory/AL-1999.004.dns_dos. Among other things, it recommends the most restrictive configuration possible and the permanent blackholing of some addresses known to be popular sources of spoofed requests and answers. It is a good idea to add the following ACL to the blackhole list of all your servers:

```
/* These are known fake source addresses. */
acl "bogon" {
    0.0.0.0/8;      # Null address
    1.0.0.0/8;      # IANA reserved, popular fakes
    2.0.0.0/8;
    192.0.2.0/24;   # Test address
    224.0.0.0/3;    # Multicast addresses

    /* RFC 1918 addresses may be fake too. Don't list these if you
       use them internally. */
    10.0.0.0/8;
    172.16.0.0/12;
    192.168.0.0/16;
};
```

DNSSEC

DNSSEC, a set of security extensions to the DNS protocol, provides data integrity and authentication by using cryptographic digital signatures. It provides for the storage of public keys in the DNS and their use for verifying transactions. DNSSEC still isn't widely deployed, but BIND 9 does support it for inter-server transactions (zone transfers, NOTIFY, recursive queries, dynamic updates). It is worth configuring the *TSIG (Transaction Signature)* mechanism if your slaves also run BIND 9. I briefly discuss using TSIG for authenticated zone transfers here.

The first thing to do is to use dnssec-keygen, as we did with rndc, to generate a shared secret key. This key is stored on both the master and slave servers. As before, we extract the Key: data from the .private file. The following command creates a 512-bit host key named transfer:

```
$ dnssec-keygen -a hmac-md5 -b 512 -n host transfer
```

Next, we set up matching key statements in the named.conf for both the master and slave servers (exactly as we did for rndc and named earlier). Remember not to transfer the secret key from one machine to the other over an insecure channel. Use ssh, secure FTP, or something similar. Remember also that the shared secrets shouldn't be stored in world readable files. The statements, identical on both machines, would look something similar to this:

```
key transfer {
    algorithm "hmac-md5";
    secret "...";          # Key from .private file
};
```

Finally, we set up a server statement on the master, to instruct it to use the key we just created when communicating with the slave, and enable authenticated zone transfers with the appropriate allow-transfer directives:

```
server 192.0.2.96 {
    key { transfer; };
};
```

14

MANAGING DNS

The BIND 9 ARM contains more information on TSIG configuration and DNSSEC support in BIND.

Split DNS

BIND is often run on firewalls, both to act as a proxy for resolvers inside the network and to serve authoritative data for some zones. In such situations, many people prefer to avoid exposing more details of their private network configuration via DNS than is unavoidable (although there is some debate about whether this is actually useful). The outside world should only see information they are explicitly allowed access to, whereas internal hosts are allowed access to other data. This kind of setup is called *split DNS*.

The best way to do this was to run two separately configured instances of named on internal and external interfaces and forward selected traffic from the former to the latter. BIND 9 provides an elegant and convenient solution to the problem with its support for views. Suppose you have a set of zones that you want to expose to the outside world and another set that you want to allow hosts on your network to see. You can accomplish this with a configuration such as the following:

```
acl private {
    localhost;
    192.168.0.0/24;      # Define your internal network suitably.
};

view private_zones {
    match { private; };
    recursion yes;      # Recursive resolution for internal hosts.

    zone internal.zone {
        # Zone statements;
    };

    # More internal zones.
};

view public_zones {
    match { any; }
    recursion no;

    zone external.zone {
        # Zone statements;
    };
```

```
       # More external zones.
    };
```

On a somewhat related note, you might want to configure internal hosts running `named` to forward all queries to the firewall and never try to resolve queries themselves. The `forward only` and `forwarders` options in `named.conf` do this. (`forwarders` specifies a list of IP addresses of the name servers to forward queries to.)

The BIND 9 ARM discusses several details of running BIND in a secure split-DNS configuration.

Reference

`http://www.dns.net/dnsrd/`—The DNS Resources Database.

`http://www.isc.org/bind/`—The ISC's BIND Web page.

`http://www.nominum.com/resources/documentation/Bv9ARM.pdf`—The BIND 9 Administrator Reference Manual.

I recommend the book *The Concise Guide to DNS and BIND*, by Nicolai Langfeldt, for an in-depth discussion of both theoretical and operational aspects of DNS administration.

Internet Connectivity

Red Hat Linux supports Internet connections and the use of Internet resources in many different ways. You'll find a wealth of Internet-related software included with this book's version of Red Hat Linux, and you can download hundreds of additional free utilities from a variety of sources.

Many Red Hat Linux home users (and even businesses) connect to the Internet using a modem and Point-to-Point Protocol (PPP), but there are other means to connect, such as a newer Digital Subscriber Linux (DSL) service. This chapter covers configuring and connecting using both these services. After successfully configuring and connecting, additional clients can be used for sending and receiving electronic mail, Web surfing, FTP file transfers, and other Internet activities.

Red Hat Linux provides tools to easily set up a system to use PPP. Although many experienced Red Hat Linux users continue to use manual scripts to establish connections, new users and system administrators will find Red Hat's graphical PPP configuration interface, rp3-config, much easier to set up and use. Red Hat Linux can also be quickly configured to provide dial-in PPP support, and DSL users will be pleased to learn that Red Hat Linux also includes Roaring Penguin's DSL utilities, such as adsl-start.

Configuring the `localhost` Interface

One necessary task that must be performed prior to connecting to the Internet is to create a dummy or localhost interface for a computer. This interface is used by the TCP/IP protocol to assign an IP address to your machine, and is required for establishing a PPP interface. This interface, known as lo, is also used by many network-aware applications and is easy to set up.

The localhost interface's Internet Protocol (IP) address is defined in a text file that can be used by Red Hat Linux to store network IP address information. This file is called /etc/hosts and should exist on a system even if empty. The file provides IP addresses and associated hostnames to the Linux kernel and other network-related utilities. Prior to configuring network interfaces, you might find that the /etc/hosts file only contains a single line:

```
127.0.0.1       localhost.localdomain          localhost
```

This line defines the special localhost interface and assigns it an IP address of 127.0.0.1. You might hear or read about terms such as *localhost*, *loopback*, and *dummy interface*; all these terms refer to the use of the IP address 127.0.0.1. The term *loopback interface* indicates that to Linux networking drivers, it looks as though the machine is talking to a network that consists of only one machine; the kernel sends network traffic out one port and back in to another on the same machine. *Dummy interface* indicates that the interface doesn't really exist to the outside world, only to the local machine.

Each networked Red Hat Linux machine on a LAN will use this IP address for its localhost. If for some reason a Red Hat Linux computer does not have this interface, edit the /etc/hosts file to add the localhost entry, and then use the ifconfig and route commands as root to create the interface like this:

```
# ifconfig lo 127.0.0.1
# route add 127.0.0.1 lo
```

These commands will create the localhost interface in memory (all interfaces, such as eth0 or ppp0 are created in memory when using Linux), and then add the IP address 127.0.0.1 to an internal (in-memory) table so that the Linux kernel's networking code can keep track of routes to different addresses.

Use the ifconfig command with the name of the interface (lo for localhost) to test the interface like this:

```
# ifconfig lo
lo        Link encap:Local Loopback
          inet addr:127.0.0.1  Mask:255.0.0.0
          UP LOOPBACK RUNNING  MTU:16436  Metric:1
          RX packets:1062 errors:0 dropped:0 overruns:0 frame:0
          TX packets:1062 errors:0 dropped:0 overruns:0 carrier:0
          collisions:0
          RX bytes:75098 (73.3 Kb)  TX bytes:75098 (73.3 Kb)
```

The example output shows that the loopback interface is active and running, that it has been assigned the IP address 127.0.0.1, that the broadcast mask of 255.0.0.0 is used, and that the interface hasn't had much traffic. You should also be able to use the ping command to check that the interface is responding properly like this (using either local-host or its IP address):

```
# ping -c 3 localhost
PING localhost.localdomain (127.0.0.1) from 127.0.0.1 : 56(84) bytes of data.
64 bytes from localhost.localdomain (127.0.0.1): icmp_seq=0 ttl=255 time=212 \
usec
64 bytes from localhost.localdomain (127.0.0.1): icmp_seq=1 ttl=255 time=80 usec
64 bytes from localhost.localdomain (127.0.0.1): icmp_seq=2 ttl=255 time=50 usec

--- localhost.localdomain ping statistics ---
3 packets transmitted, 3 packets received, 0% packet loss
round-trip min/avg/max/mdev = 0.050/0.114/0.212/0.070 ms
```

15

INTERNET
CONNECTIVITY

The -c option is used to set the number of pings, and the command, if successful (as it was previously) will return information regarding the round-trip speed of sending a test packet to the (local) or remote host.

Configuring Red Hat Linux to Use PPP

Most dial-up Internet service providers (ISPs) provide connections sporting PPP because it is a fast and efficient protocol for using TCP/IP over serial lines. PPP is designed for two-way networking; TCP/IP provides the transport protocol for data. One hurdle faced by new Red Hat Linux users is how to set up PPP and connect to the Internet. It isn't necessary to understand the details of the PPP protocol in order to use it, and setting up a PPP connection is easy.

PPP connections can be configured manually by a system administrator using the command line, or graphically during an X session using Red Hat's rp3-config client. Each approach produces the same results. PPP uses two components on your system. The first is a daemon called pppd, which controls the use of PPP. The second is a driver called the high-level data link control (HDLC), which controls the flow of information between two machines. A third component of PPP is a routine called chat that dials the other end of the connection for you when you want it to. Although PPP has many "tunable" parameters, default settings usually work.

If for some reason PPP isn't installed on your system, use Red Hat's rpm command to install the PPP package from the first Red Hat Linux CD-ROM. Red Hat Linux includes version 2.4.1 of PPP.

Manual Dial-Up PPP Connection: Using pppd and the chat Command

If you have a Red Hat Linux system connected to a modem and telephone line, you can quickly create dial-up PPP service. This section outlines one way to do this. The first step is to log in as root in order to copy and edit the necessary files. This approach will require the chat command, the pppd daemon, and several files:

/etc/ppp/ppp-on—Used to start a PPP connection. This file contains the ISP's phone number, your username and password, and various options such as IP address options, the modem device and its settings (such as baudrate) for the connection.

/etc/ppp/ppp-off—Used to terminate a PPP connection.

`/etc/ppp/ppp-on-dialer`—Used to perform dialing and connection with the `chat` command; this script contains error-handling and negotiation responses between the remote system and the `chat` command script.

First, copy the scripts from the `/usr/share/doc/ppp*/scripts` directory to the `/etc/ppp` directory like so:

```
# cp /usr/share/doc/ppp*/scripts/ppp-o* /etc/ppp
```

Edit the `ppp-on` script (making sure to disable line wrapping), and change the first four entries to reflect your ISP's phone number and your username and password, like this:

```
TELEPHONE=555-1212      # The telephone number for the connection
ACCOUNT=george          # The account name for logon (as in 'George Burns')
PASSWORD=gracie         # The password for this account (and 'Gracie Allen')
LOCAL_IP=0.0.0.0        # Local IP address if known. Dynamic = 0.0.0.0
```

Change the values for `TELEPHONE`, `ACCOUNT`, and `PASSWORD`, substituting your ISP's phone number and your username and password. The `LOCAL_IP` entry should be changed to an IP addressed only if your ISP provides one for use; otherwise leave the entry blank. Next, scroll through the script until you find the dialing setup, which can look like this:

```
exec /usr/sbin/pppd debug lock modem crtscts /dev/ttyS0 38400 \
        asyncmap 20A0000 escape FF kdebug 0 $LOCAL_IP:$REMOTE_IP \
        noipdefault netmask $NETMASK defaultroute connect $DIALER_SCRIPT
```

These lines (actually a single script line) contain modem options for the `chat` script used in the `ppp-on-dialer` script, and will start the `pppd` daemon on your computer after establishing a connection. Change the modem device (`/dev/ttyS0` in this example) to `/dev/modem` if the Red Hat Linux `kudzu` utility has recognized and configured the computer's modem. (If `/dev/modem` does not exist, use the `ln` command to create the file as a symbolic link pointing to the correct serial port.) Set the baud rate (38,400 in this case) to the desired connection speed, most likely 115200 or 57600. When finished, save the files.

Next, use the `chmod` command to make these scripts executable like this:

```
# chmod +x /etc/ppp/ppp-o*
```

To debug or check the progress of your modem connection, dialing, and connection to your ISP, use the `tail` command with its `-f` "loop forever" option like this:

```
# tail -f /var/log/messages
```

To connect to your ISP, run the `ppp-on` script:

```
# /etc/ppp/ppp-on
```

Use the ppp-off script to stop the PPP connection like so:

```
# /etc/ppp/ppp-off
```

You can also move the ppp-on and ppp-off scripts to a recognized $PATH, such as /usr/local/bin. Enabling use of these scripts by normal users will entail changing permissions of the serial port and other files (which can be a security problem).

Graphical Dial-Up PPP Connection Using rp3-config

The rp3-config client can be used to set up a PPP connection quickly and easily. This client provides a number of advantageous features, such as the ability to define multiple ISP account logins, use different modems, and manage multiple users. Launch the command from the GNOME desktop panel Programs, Internet menu and select the Dialup Configuration menu item. You can also launch a configuration session by using the rp3-config command at the command line of an X11 terminal window like this:

```
# rp3-config &
```

The rp3-config slash dialog box will appear. Click the Next button to start the configuration. If this is the first time the client has been used, you'll be prompted to click the Next button to configure a modem (even if the modem has been recognized and configured by kudzu). After you click the Next button, the program will search for an installed and usable modem. If a modem is found, it will be displayed in a dialog box as shown in Figure 15.1.

FIGURE 15.1

The rp3-config
*client will display
any found
modems.*

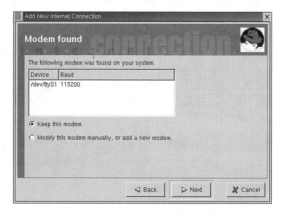

Click on a desired modem in the list. You can then keep the modem configuration or modify the modem's settings. When finished, click the Next button to continue. You'll then be asked to designate a name for the service and to enter your ISP's phone number, as shown in Figure 15.2.

FIGURE 15.2

Enter a name for your ISP's service, along with the phone number of the service's modem.

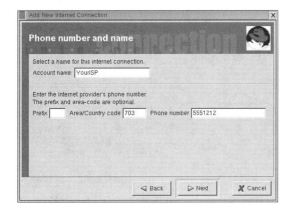

The phone number to enter is the number of your ISP's remote computer's modem. Enter a country code if needed, along with an area code and phone number. Note that some areas require a 10-digit number for local telephone service. When finished, click the Next button. You'll then be asked to enter your username and password, as shown in Figure 15.3.

FIGURE 15.3

Enter the username and password assigned by your ISP.

Enter your username and password. Note that this is the username and password assigned by your ISP, not your Red Hat Linux username and password. Click the Next button to continue, and you will then be asked to select an ISP type, as shown in Figure 15.4.

FIGURE 15.4

Select a type of ISP PPP dial-in service.

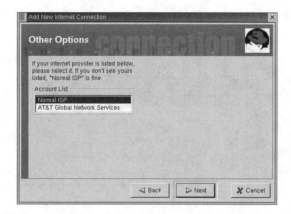

Scroll to select a type of service. Fortunately, most ISPs will use a standard login process that only requires a username and password before initiating PPP, so most users will select the Normal ISP option. When finished, click the Next button to continue, and you will then be asked to confirm your settings as shown in Figure 15.5.

FIGURE 15.5

Confirm your PPP account settings.

Confirm that the entries are correct to this point. Note that you can use the Back button to backtrack and correct any errors. Click the Finish button to complete your entry. You'll then see an account dialog box labeled Internet Connections, as shown in Figure 15.6.

Click to select an account in the dialog box. You can then add, edit, delete, or copy an account. If you click on an account and then click the Edit button, you'll see a new dialog box, as shown in Figure 15.7.

FIGURE **15.6**

You can use rp3-config *to manage numerous Internet connection accounts.*

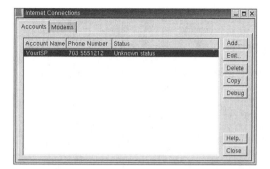

FIGURE **15.7**

Edit a specific dial-up service account using rp3-config.

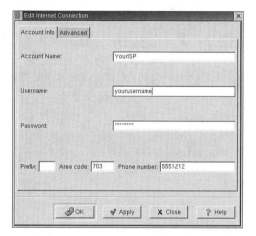

Click on the Account Info tab in the dialog box. You can then change the account name, username, password, and phone number of the account. Click the Apply and then the OK buttons to save your changes. If you click the dialog box's Advanced tab, you'll see another setup dialog box as shown in Figure 15.8.

This dialog box allows you to set numerous features and parameters for the account's PPP session. If you haven't created nameserver entries in the system's /etc/resolv.conf file (used for Domain Name Server lookups), you can enter the DNS IP addresses for your ISP in this dialog box. This is probably a good idea because it might help to increase the speed of hostname lookups while Web browsing (or performing other functions) during PPP sessions with the ISP. When finished, click the Apply and then OK buttons to save any changes. Then click the Close button in the Internet Connections dialog box (shown earlier in Figure 15.6).

FIGURE **15.8**

Edit advanced
PPP settings
using rp3-config.

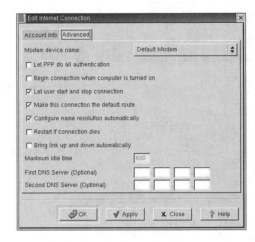

These settings are saved in the file /etc/wvdial.conf and look like this:

```
[Modem0]
Modem = /dev/ttyS1
Baud = 115200
Init1 = ATZ
Init2 = ATQ0 V1 E1 S0=0 &C1 &D2 S11=55 +FCLASS=0

[Dialer Defaults]
Modem = /dev/ttyS1
Baud = 115200
Init1 = ATZ
Init2 = ATQ0 V1 E1 S0=0 &C1 &D2 S11=55 +FCLASS=0

[Dialer YourISP]
Username = yourusername
Password = yourpassword
Phone = 5551212
Area Code = 703
Inherits = Dialer Defaults
Stupid mode = 0
```

As a system administrator, you can manually edit this file to create additional accounts or use the rp3-config client.

Note

KDE users can also use the kppp client to graphically set up a dial-up PPP account and connect to the Internet. Start the client by using the command line of a terminal and typing **kppp &**.

Starting a PPP Connection Using rp3

To start your PPP connection, you can click the GNOME desktop panel, select Programs, click Internet, and then click the RH PPP Dialer menu item to launch the rp3 client, which is shown in Figure 15.9.

FIGURE 15.9

Use the rp3 client to start a dial-up PPP connection.

If you're not using GNOME, you can launch this client by typing its name, **rp3**, from the command line of an X11 terminal window, like this:

```
# rp3 &
```

When the client's small dialog box appears, select a desired dial-up service account, and then click the OK button to begin your PPP connection.

Select the ppp0 interface, and then click the OK button. You'll be asked if you want to start the connection. Click OK to connect. Note that the applet will dock into your GNOME desktop's panel if you are using a GNOME-aware window manager. You can use the applet to control your session and to keep track of your connect time (important if you pay by the minute for a connection).

> **Tip**
>
> Another way to start your PPP connection is to use the usernet client by launching it from the command line of an X11 terminal window like this:
> usernet &.

Setting Up a DSL PPPOE Connection

Red Hat Linux also supports the use of a Digital Subscriber Line, (DSL) service. This service generally provides 256Kbps–768Kbps or 4.5Mbps–7.1Mbps download speeds,

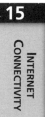

and presently uses copper telephone lines from a central office to the home. DSL service is an "always on" type of Internet service, although you can turn the connection on or off under Red Hat Linux using included software tools. A DSL connection requires an Ethernet network interface card in your computer or notebook, and many users also configure a gateway, firewall, or other computer with at least two network interface cards in order to share a connection with a LAN.

Establishing a DSL connection with an ISP providing a static IP addresses is fairly easy. Unfortunately, most DSL providers use a type of PPP protocol named PPPOE, or Point-to-Point Protocol over Ethernet that provides dynamic IP address assignment and authentication by encapsulating PPP information inside Ethernet frames. Fortunately, Roaring Penguin's rp-pppoe clients are included with Red Hat Linux, but you can download and install newer versions (see the Roaring Penguin link in the "Reference" section at the end of this chapter).

Setting Up a PPPOE Connection

The basic steps involved in setting up a DSL connection using Red Hat Linux involve connecting the proper hardware, and then running a simple configuration script if you install rp-pppoe from Roaring Penguin. First, connect your DSL modem to your phone line, and then plug in your Ethernet cable from the modem to your computer's network interface card. If you plan to share your DSL connection with the rest of your LAN, you'll need at least two network cards, designated eth0 (for your LAN) and eth1 (for the DSL connection).

You'll also need your username and password, along with the IP addresses of your provider's DNS servers. The following example assumes that you have more than one computer and will share your DSL connection on a LAN. First, log in as root, and ensure that your first eth0 device is enabled and up (perhaps using the ifconfig command). Next, bring up the other interface, but assign a null IP address like this:

```
# ifconfig eth1 0.0.0.0 up
```

Now use the adsl-setup command to set up your system. Type the command like this:

```
# adsl-setup
```

You'll be asked to enter your username and the Ethernet interface used for the connection (such as eth1). You'll then be asked to use "on demand" service or have the connection stay up all the time (until brought down by the root operator). You can also set a timeout in seconds, if desired. You'll then be asked to enter the IP addresses of your ISP's DNS servers if you haven't configured the system's /etc/resolv.conf file.

After that, you'll be prompted to enter your password two times, and will then have to choose firewall and IP masquerading rules. Using a firewall is essential nowadays, so you should choose this option unless you intend to craft your own set of firewall rules. After you have chosen your firewall and IP masquerading setup, you'll be asked to confirm, save, and implement your settings.

Changes will be made to your system's `/etc/ppp/pppoe.conf`, `/etc/resolv.conf`, `/etc/ppp/pap-secrets`, and `/etc/ppp/chap-secrets` files.

After configuration has finished, use the `adsl-start` command to start a connection and DSL session like this:

```
# adsl-start
```

The DSL connection should be nearly instantaneous, but if problems occur check to make sure that your DSL modem is synched with the phone company's central office, that all cables are properly attached, that your interfaces are properly configured, and that you have entered the correct information to the setup script.

If IP masquerading is enabled, other computers on your LAN on the same subnet address (such as 192.168.2) can use the Internet, but must have the same `/etc/resolv.conf` nameserver entries and a routing entry with the DSL-connected computer as a gateway. For example, if the host computer with the DSL connection has an IP address of 192.168.2.32, and other computers on your LAN use addresses in the 192.168.2.XXX range, use the `route` command on each computer like this:

```
# route add default gw 192.168.2.32
```

Note that you can also use a hostname instead if each computer has an `/etc/hosts` file with hostname and IP address entries for your LAN. To stop your connection, use the `adsl-stop` command like this:

```
# adsl-stop
```

Setting Up a Dial-In PPP Server

Simple dial-up PPP service can be quickly configured on your Red Hat Linux system by configuring Linux to answer a remote modem and start PPP. You'll need a phone line, serial port, and attached modem. The modem must be set to answer incoming calls using AT commands, with the configuration saved using AT&W. A line-monitoring application such as `agetty`, `getty`, or `mgetty` is then used to watch the serial port by editing an entry in the system's initialization table `/etc/inittab`. Then by creating a special user account and script, Red Hat Linux can be configured to automatically start the `pppd` daemon and PPP service after a user logs in.

Many modems can use a modem string such ATE1Q0V1&C1&S0S0=1&W to autoanswer calls. Some terminal monitors, such as uugetty have configuration files that automatically set up the modem for a particular serial port and use an entry in /etc/inittab that looks like this:

```
3:2345:respawn:/sbin/uugetty ttyS1 38400 vt100
```

This entry assumes that a modem is attached to /dev/ttyS1.

Other commands, such as agetty can directly configure a modem port and might use an /etc/inittab like this:

```
3:2345:respawn:/usr/local/bin/agetty -w -I 'ATE0Q1&D2&C1S0=1\015' \
115200 ttyS2 vt100
```

The next step is to create a user named ppp and to then assign a password. Although it is possible to allow remote users to log in and start pppd from the command line (assuming that you've set pppd to SUID), you can have the pppd daemon started automatically by creating a short shell script and then assigning the shell script in the user's /etc/passwd entry like this:

```
ppp:x:501:501::/home/ppp:/usr/local/bin/doppp
```

In this instance, the script doppp (made executable with chmod +x) would contain the following:

```
exec /usr/sbin/pppd -detach
```

Using this approach, pppd will start automatically after the ppp dial-in user connects and logs in (perhaps using the ppp-on scripts or other clients on the remote computer). The file options under the /etc/ppp directory should include general dial-in options for PPP service on your system, and specific options files (such as options.ttyS1 for this example) should be created for each enabled dial-in port. For example, /etc/ppp/options could contain

```
asyncmap 0
netmask 255.255.255.0
proxyarp
lock
crtscts
modem
```

There are many approaches to providing PPP service. IP addresses can be assigned dynamically, or a static IP address can be doled out for a user. For example, /etc/ppp/options.ttyS1 could contain

```
IPofPPPserver:assignedIPofdialinuser
```

In this example, the first IP address is for the host computer, whereas the second IP address will be assigned to the remote user. For details about configuring PPP for Linux, read the pppd manual page or documentation under the /usr/share/doc/pppd* directory. If you're a Linux developer, browse the files ppp_async.c, ppp_deflate.c, ppp_generic.c, and ppp_synctty.c under the /usr/src/linux/drivers/net directory.

Red Hat Linux provides flexibility in the available approaches to connecting to the Internet. Many additional related software packages and utilities could be used to establish connections over dial-up phone lines or over a network, even a simple network between two computers.

Reference

http://www.roaringpenguin.com/pppoe/—Home page for the fabulous rp-pppoe software package that enables DSL users to connect to the Internet using Linux. This is a "must-have" software package for Red Hat Linux and DSL users.

http://devel-home.kde.org/~kppp/—Home page for KDE's kppp PPP Internet dialer.

http://www.redhat.com/support/resources/web_ftp/ppp.html—Definitive links to using PPP with Red Hat Linux.

http://www.redhat.com/support/resources/tips/Dialup-Tips/Dialup-Tips.html—How to dial up and connect with an ISP using Red Hat Linux.

http://www.redhat.com/support/resources/tips/Dialup-Tips/ppp_server_tips.html—How to set up a dial-in server using Red Hat Linux and the mgetty+sendfax software package.

http://axion.physics.ubc.ca/ppp-linux.html—W.G. Unruh's extensive Web page describing how to use PPP and Linux to connect to an ISP.

http://www.linuxdoc.org/HOWTO/PPP-HOWTO/—A great place to start reading about PPP and Linux; includes directions on configuring various clients, linking LANs, and setting up a PPP server.

http://www.linuxdoc.org/HOWTO/DSL-HOWTO—The latest information about using DSL and Linux, with details about DSL hardware, setting up a network, using USB modems, DSL use and security, and other helpful tips. Highly recommended reading for any Red Hat Linux user contemplating use of DSL service.

http://www.redhat.com/mirrors/LDP/HOWTO/PPP-HOWTO/—A copy of the PPP-HOWTO via Red Hat, Inc.'s Linux Documentation Project mirror site.

15

INTERNET
CONNECTIVITY

Apache Web Server Management

CHAPTER 16

This chapter covers the installation, configuration, and management of the Apache Web server.

Apache is the most widely used Web server on the Internet today, according to the NetCraft survey of Web sites, which is shown in Table 16.1.

TABLE 16.1   Results of September 2001 NetCraft Survey

Web Server	Number	Percentage*
Apache	19279109	59.51%
Microsoft IIS	8895343	27.46%
iPlanet	1319271	4.07%
Zeus	783261	2.42%

Of 32,398,046 sites surveyed

What is more revealing in these statistics is growth rate of the Apache server versus the other server platforms. Between August and September of 2001, Apache gained 1.43 percent of the total market share, while IIS only gained 0.99 percent.

The name "Apache" appeared during the early development of the software because it was "a patchy" server, made out of patches for the freely available source code of the NCSA HTTPd Web server. For a while after the NCSA HTTPd project was discontinued, a number of people wrote a variety of patches for the code, either to fix bugs or to add features that they wanted. There was a lot of this code floating around and people were freely sharing it, but it was completely unmanaged.

After a while, Bob Behlendorf and Cliff Skolnick set up a centralized repository of these patches, and the Apache project was born. The project is still composed of a rather small core group of programmers, but anyone is welcome to submit patches to the group for possible inclusion in the code.

In the last couple of years, there has been a surge of interest in the Apache project, partially buoyed by the new interest in Open Source. It's also due, in part, to IBM's commitment to support and use Apache as the basis for the company's Web offerings. They have dedicated substantial resources to the project because it made more sense to use an established, proven Web server than to try to write their own. The consequences of this interest have been a stable version for the Windows NT operating system and an accelerated release schedule.

In mid-1999 The Apache Software Foundation was incorporated as a not-for-profit company. A board of directors, who are elected on an annual basis by the ASF members, oversees the company. This company provides a foundation for several different Open Source Software development projects—including the Apache Web Server project.

The best places to find out about Apache are the Apache Group's Web site, `http://www.apache.org/`, and the *Apache Week* Web site, `http://www.apacheweek.com/`, where you can subscribe to receive *Apache Week* by e-mail to keep up on the latest developments in the project.

> **Tip**
>
> In addition to the extensive online documentation, you will also find the complete documentation for Apache in the HTML directory of your Apache server. You can access this documentation by looking at `http://localhost/manual/` on your new Red Hat system, with one of the Web browsers included on your system.

Red Hat ships with as recent a version of Apache as possible, but it quickly gets dated because of Apache's rapid release schedule. You can obtain Apache as an RPM (Red Hat Package Manager) installation file in the `/pub/redhat/linux/7.2/en/os/i386/RedHat/RPMs` area of Red Hat's FTP server, or you can get the source code from the Apache Web site and, in true Linux tradition, build it for yourself.

This chapter covers version 1.3.20, which ships with Red Hat 7.2.

Server Installation

You can install Apache from RPMs or by building the source code yourself. The Apache source builds on just about any UNIX-like operating system, and also on Win32.

If you are about to install a new version of Apache, it is probably a good idea to shut down the old server. Even if it is unlikely that the old server will interfere with the installation procedure, shutting it down ensures that there will be no problems. If you don't know how to stop Apache, look at the section "Starting and Stopping the Server" later in this chapter.

Installing from the RPM

You can find the Apache RPM either on the Red Hat Linux installation media, on the Red Hat FTP server, or one of its many mirror sites. You will want to check the `updates.redhat.com` FTP site (or one of the mirrors) as often as possible. In the directory corresponding to your Red Hat version, you will, from time to time, find updates for Apache. These can be important updates that fix bugs or security breaches. When an updated version comes out, you will want to install it as quickly as possible in order to be secure.

Note

If you want as recent a version as possible, you might want to look into Red Hat's Rawhide distribution, also available on their FTP server (`ftp://ftp.redhat.com/pub/redhat/linux/rawhide/`). This distribution is experimental and always contains the latest versions of all RPMs. However, do note that the Apache package might depend on new functionality available in other RPMs in the Rawhide distribution. Therefore, you might need to install many new RPMs to be able to use packages from Rawhide. If you want to use an Apache version from the Rawhide distribution, it might be a better option to download the source code RPM, or SRPM as they are called, and compile it yourself—that way you should be able to avoid dependencies on other, new packages.

Caution

You should be wary of installing experimental packages, especially on servers that are used in "real life." Very carefully test the packages beforehand!

After you have obtained an Apache RPM, you can install it with the command-line `rpm` tool by typing the following

```
rpm -Uvh latest_apache.rpm
```

where `latest_apache.rpm` is the name of the latest Apache RPM.

For more information on installing packages with RPM, see Chapter 8, "Managing Software and System Resources."

The Apache RPM installs files in the following directories:

- `/etc/httpd/conf`—This directory contains all the Apache configuration files, which include `access.conf`, `httpd.conf`, and `srm.conf`. See the section on configuration files later in this chapter.

Apache Web Server Management

CHAPTER 16

407

16

APACHE WEB
SERVER
MANAGEMENT

- `/etc/rc.d/`—The tree under this directory contains the system startup scripts. The Apache RPM installs a complete set for the Web server. These scripts, which you can use to start and stop the server from the command line, will also automatically start and stop the server when the computer is halted, started, or rebooted.

- `/var/www`—The RPM installs the default server icons, CGI programs, and HTML files in this location. If you want to keep Web content elsewhere, you can do so by making the appropriate changes in the server configuration files.

- `/var/www/html/manual/`—If you have installed the apache-manual RPM, you will find a copy of the Apache documentation in HTML format here. You can access it with a Web browser by going to `http://localhost/manual/`.

- `/usr/share/man`—The RPM contains manual pages, which are placed in this directory.

- `/usr/sbin`—The executable programs are placed in this directory. This includes the server executable itself, as well as various utilities.

- `/usr/bin`—Some of the utilities from the Apache package are placed here—for example, the `htpasswd` program, which is used for generating authentication password files.

- `/var/log/httpd`—The server log files are placed in this directory. By default, there are two important log files (among several others)—`access_log` and `error_log`—but you can define any number of custom logs containing a variety of information. See the section on logging later in this chapter.

- `/usr/src/redhat/SOURCES/`—This directory contains a `tar` archive containing the source code for Apache, and in some cases patches for the source. You must have installed the Apache SRPM for these files to be created.

When Apache is being run, it will also create files in the following directories:

- `/var/lock/subsys`—The startup script adds a lock file, called `httpd`.

- `/var/run`—Apache will create a file, `httpd.pid`, containing the process ID of Apache's parent process.

Note

If you are upgrading to a newer version of Apache, RPM will not write over your current configuration files. RPM moves your current files and appends the extension `.rpmnew` to them. For example, `srm.conf` becomes `srm.conf.rpmnew`.

Building the Source Yourself

There are several ways in which you can obtain the source code for Apache. The Red Hat distribution has SRPMs containing the source of Apache, which sometimes include patches to make it work better with Red Hat's distribution. The most up-to-date versions are found at `ftp://updates.redhat.com`. When you install one of these SRPMs, a tar archive containing the Apache source will be created in `/usr/src/redhat/SOURCES/`. You can also download the source directly from `http://www.apache.org/`.

Once you have a `tar` file, you will need to unroll it in a temporary directory somewhere nice, like `/tmp`. This will create a directory called apache_*version_number*, where *version_number* is the version that you have downloaded (for example, apache_1.3.20).

There are two ways to compile the source—the old, familiar way (at least, to those of us who have been using Apache for many years) and the new, easy way.

The Easy Way

To build Apache the easy way, just run the `./configure` in the directory just created. You can provide it with a `--prefix` argument to install in a directory other than the default, which is `/usr/local/apache/`.

```
./configure --prefix=/preferred/directory/
```

This will create a file called `Configuration` in the `/usr/src/` subdirectory. It also generates the `Makefile` that will be used to compile the server code.

Once this step is done, type **make** to compile the server code. After the compilation is completed, type **make install** to install the server. You can now configure the server via the configuration files. See the section "Runtime Server Configuration Settings" for more information.

> **Note**
>
> The Apache Autoconf-style interface (APACI), described here, is only available in version 1.3 and later.

The Advanced Way

If you want to do things the old-fashioned way, or you just want more control over the way that your server is built, follow these steps:

Apache Web Server Management
CHAPTER 16

409

16

APACHE WEB
SERVER
MANAGEMENT

1. In the source directory, copy the file `Configuration.tmpl` to `Configuration` and open up `Configuration` with your favorite editor.

2. Modify the compiler flags if, and only if, you know what you're doing. Uncomment those modules that you would like included, comment out modules that you don't want, or add lines for custom modules that you have written or acquired elsewhere.

3. Run the `Configure` script to create the `Makefile`.

4. Finally, compile and install the server with `make` and `make install`.

Tip

You might want to symlink, using the `ln` command, the existing file locations (listed in the RPM installation section earlier in this chapter) to the new locations of the files because the default install locations aren't the same as when the RPM installs the files. Failure to do this could result in your Web server process not being started automatically at system startup.

It is strongly recommended that you stick with the RPM version of Apache until you really know your way around what happens at system startup.

File Locations After Manual Installation

As of version 1.3.4, all the files are placed in various subdirectories of `/usr/local/apache` (or whatever directory you specified with the `--prefix` parameter). Before version 1.3.4, files were placed in `/usr/local/etc/httpd`.

The following is a list of those directories used by Apache, as well as brief comments on their usage.

- `/usr/local/apache/conf`—This directory contains all the Apache configuration files, which include `access.conf`, `httpd.conf`, and `srm.conf`. See the section on configuration files later in this chapter.

- `/usr/local/apache`—The `cgi-bin`, `icons`, and `htdocs` subdirectories contain the CGI programs, standard icons, and default HTML documents, respectively.

- `/usr/local/apache/bin`—The executable programs are placed in this directory.

- `/usr/local/apache/logs`—The server log files are placed in this directory. By default, there are two log files—`access_log` and `error_log`—but you can define any number of custom logs containing a variety of information. See the section on logging later in this chapter.

Runtime Server Configuration Settings

At this point, you have successfully installed the Apache server one way or another. It will run, but perhaps not quite the way that you want it to. This section talks about configuring the server so that it works exactly how you want it to work.

Traditionally, Apache had the runtime configurations in three files: `httpd.conf`, `access.conf`, and `srm.conf`. This was mainly because that's how the config files were written for NCSA, and Apache grew out of NCSA. Although there was some logic behind the original decision to split configuration options into three files, this made less and less sense over time—especially because you could put any configuration option in any file and it would work.

So, starting with Apache 1.3.4, the runtime configurations are stored in just one file—`httpd.conf`. The other files are still there, but they contain only a comment telling you that the files are there for purely historical reasons and that you should really put all of your configuration files in `httpd.conf`.

> **Note**
>
> You can still use the three-configuration-file approach if you really want to. It makes sense to some people. However, the distinction between what should go in one file or another has become increasingly blurred over the years.
>
> If you want to keep using the three-file system, I've noted when these files appeared in `srm.conf` or `access.conf` prior to version 1.3.4.

Apache reads the data from the configuration file(s) when the parent process is started (or restarted). You can also cause the Apache process to reload configuration information with the command `/etc/rc.d/init.d/httpd reload`. This is discussed later in the section, "Starting and Stopping the Server."

You perform runtime configuration of your server with *configuration directives*, which are commands that set some option. You use them to tell the server about various options that you want to enable, such as the location of files important to the server configuration and operation. Configuration directives follow this syntax:

```
directive option option...
```

You specify one directive per line. Some directives only set a value such as a filename, whereas others let you specify various options. Some special directives, called *sections*, look like HTML tags. Section directives are surrounded by angle brackets, such as *<directive>*. Sections usually enclose a group of directives that apply only to the directory specified in the section:

```
<Directory somedir/in/your/tree>
  directive option option
  directive option option
</Directory>
```

All sections are closed with a matching section tag that looks like *</directive>*. Note that section tags, like any other directives, are specified one per line.

Editing `httpd.conf`

Most of the default settings in the config files are okay to keep, particularly if you have installed the server in a default location and aren't doing anything unusual on your server. In general, if you don't understand what a particular directive is for, you should leave it set to the default value.

Table 16.2 lists some of the settings that you *might* want to change.

TABLE 16.2   Some Commonly Used Configuration Directives

Directive	*Description*
ServerType	This is mentioned more as a curiosity than anything else. The two server types are standalone and inetd. You will want this to be standalone in almost every imaginable case. Setting the ServerType to inetd will cause a new server to be spawned to handle every incoming HTTP request. That server will then die off immediately when the request has been served. This is presumably useful for testing configuration changes because the configuration files will be reloaded each time a new server process is spawned. Of course, this is extremely slow because you have the overhead of server startup with every request.
ServerRoot	This directive sets the absolute path to your server directory. This directive tells the server where to find all the resources and configuration files. Many of these resources are specified in the configuration files relative to the ServerRoot directory.

TABLE 16.2 continued

Directive	Description
	Your `ServerRoot` directive should be set to `/etc/httpd` if you installed the RPM or `/usr/local/apache` (or whatever directory you chose when you compiled Apache) if you installed from the source.
Port	The `Port` directive indicates which port you want your server to run on. By default, this is set to 80, which is the standard HTTP port number. You might want to run your server on another port, such as for running a test server that you don't want people to find by accident. Don't confuse this with real security! See the section "Authentication and Access Control" for more information on how to secure parts of your Web server.
User and Group	The `User` and `Group` directives should be set to the UID and group ID (GID) that the server will use to process requests. There are generally two ways to set this up. The most common way is to set user to `nobody` and group to `nobody`. The other way, which is used in Red Hat, is to set them to a user with few or no privileges. In this case, they are set to user `apache` and group `apache`. As you can imagine, this is a user defined specifically to run Apache. If you want to use a different UID or GID, you need to be aware that the server will run with the permissions of the user and group set here. This means that in the event of a security breach, whether on the server or (more likely) in your own CGI programs, those programs will run with the assigned UID. If the server runs as `root` or some other privileged user, someone can exploit the security holes and do nasty things to your site. Always think in terms of the specified user running a command like `rm -rf /` because that would wipe all files from your system. That should convince you that leaving this as a user with no privileges is probably a good thing.
	Instead of specifying the `User` and `Group` directives using names, you can specify them using the UID and GID numbers. If you use numbers, be sure that the numbers you specify correspond to the user and group you want and that they are preceded by the pound (#) symbol.

TABLE 16.2   continued

Directive	Description
	Here's how these directives look if specified by name:
	`User nobody`
	`Group nogroup`
	Here's the same specification by UID and GID:
	`User #-1`
	`Group #-1`
ServerAdmin	The `ServerAdmin` directive should be set to the address of the Webmaster managing the server. It should be a valid e-mail address or alias, such as *webmaster@gnulix.org*. Setting this value to a valid address is important because this address will be returned to a visitor when a problem occurs on the server.
ServerName	The `ServerName` directive sets the hostname the server will return. Set it to a fully qualified domain name (FQDN). For example, set it to *www.your.domain* rather than simply *www*. This is particularly important if this machine will be accessible from the Internet rather than just on your local network. You really do not need to set this unless you want a different name returned than the machine's canonical name. If this value isn't set, the server will figure out the name by itself and set it to its canonical name. However, you might want the server to return a friendlier address, such as *www.your.domain*. Whatever you do, `ServerName` should be a real Domain Name System (DNS) name for your network. If you are administering your own DNS, remember to add an alias for your host. If someone else manages the DNS for you, ask that person to set this name for you.
DocumentRoot	Set this directive to the absolute path of your document tree, which is the top directory from which Apache will serve files. By default, it is set to `/var/www/html` or, if you built the source code yourself, `/usr/local/apache/htdocs` (if you didn't choose another directory when you compiled Apache.) Prior to version 1.3.4, this directive appears in `srm.conf`.

TABLE 16.2 continued

Directive	Description
UserDir	This directive defines the directory relative to a local user's home directory where that user can put public HTML documents. It's relative because each user will have her own HTML directory. The default setting for this directive is `public_html`. So, each user will be able to create a directory called `public_html` under her home directory, and HTML documents placed in that directory will be available as `http://servername/~username`, where *username* is the username of the particular user. Prior to version 1.3.4, this directive appears in `srm.conf`.
DirectoryIndex	The `DirectoryIndex` directive indicates which file should be served as the index for a directory, such as which file should be served if the URL `http://gnulix.org/SomeDirectory/` is requested. It is often useful to put a list of files here so that, in the event that `index.html` (the default values) isn't found, another file can be served instead. The most useful application of this is to have a CGI program run as the default action in a directory. If you also have users who make their Web pages on Windows, you might want to add `index.htm` as well. In this case, the directive would look like `DirectoryIndex index.html index.cgi index.htm`. Prior to version 1.3.4, this directive appears in `srm.conf`.

Caution

Allowing individual users to put Web content on your server poses several important security considerations. If you are operating a Web server on the Internet rather than on a private network, you should read the WWW Security FAQ by Lincoln Stein and John Stewart. You can find a copy at `http://www.w3.org/Security/Faq/www-security-faq.html`.

.htaccess Files

Almost any directive that appears in the configuration files can appear in an `.htaccess` file. This file, specified in the `AccessFileName` directive in `httpd.conf` (or `srm.conf` prior to version 1.3.4) sets configurations on a per-directory basis. As the system

Apache Web Server Management

CHAPTER 16

415

16

APACHE WEB
SERVER
MANAGEMENT

administrator, you can specify both the name of this file and which of the server configurations may be overridden by the contents of this file. This is especially useful for sites in which there are multiple content providers and you want to control what these people can do with their space.

To limit what .htaccess files can override, you need to use the AllowOverride directive. This can be set globally or per directory. To configure which options are available by default, you need to use the Options directive.

Note

Prior to version 1.3.4, these directives appear in the access.conf file.

For example, in your httpd.conf file, you will see the following:

```
# Each directory to which Apache has access can be configured with respect
# to which services and features are allowed and/or disabled in that
# directory (and its subdirectories).
#
# First, we configure the "default" to be a very restrictive set of
# permissions.
#
<Directory />
    Options FollowSymLinks
    AllowOverride None
</Directory>
```

Options Directives

Options can be None, All, or any combination of Indexes, Includes, FollowSymLinks, ExecCGI, or MultiViews. MultiViews isn't included in All and must be specified explicitly. These options are explained in Table 16.3.

TABLE 16.3 Switches Used by the Options Directive

Switch	Description
None	None of the available options are enabled for this directory.
All	All the available options, except for MultiViews, are enabled for this directory.
Indexes	In the absence of an index.html file or another DirectoryIndex file, a listing of the files in the directory will be generated as an HTML page for display to the user.

TABLE 16.3 continued

Switch	Description
Includes	Server-Side Includes (SSIs) are permitted in this directory. This can also be written as IncludesNoExec if you want to allow includes, but don't want to allow the exec option in these includes. For security reasons, this is usually a good idea in directories over which you do not have complete control, such as UserDir directories.
FollowSymLinks	Allows access to directories that are symbolically linked to a document directory. This is usually a bad idea, and you shouldn't set this globally for the whole server. You might want to set this for individual directories, but only if you have a really good reason to do so. This option is a potential security risk because it allows Web users to escape from the document directory, and it could potentially allow them access to portions of your filesystem where you really don't want people poking around.
ExecCGI	CGI programs are permitted in this directory, even if it isn't a ScriptAlias-ed directory.
MultiViews	This is part of the mod_negotiation module. When the document that the client requests isn't found, the server tries to figure out which document best suits the client's requirements. See http://localhost/manuals/mod/mod_negotiation.html for your local copy of the Apache documentation.

Note

These directives also affect all subdirectories of the specified directory.

AllowOverrides Directives

The AllowOverrides directives specify which options .htaccess files can override. You can set this per directory. For example, you can have different standards about what can be overridden in the main document root and in UserDir directories.

This capability is particularly useful for user directories, where the user doesn't have access to the main server configuration files.

AllowOverrides can be set to All or any combination of Options, FileInfo, AuthConfig, and Limit. These options are explained in Table 16.4.

TABLE 16.4 Switches Used by the AllowOverrides Directive

Switch	*Description*
Options	The .htaccess file can add options not listed in the Options directive for this directory.
FileInfo	The .htaccess file can include directives for modifying document type information.
AuthConfig	The .htaccess file might contain authorization directives.
Limit	The .htaccess file might contain allow, deny, and order directives.

Authentication and Access Control

There will be times when you have material on your Web site that isn't supposed to be available for the general public. You need to be able to lock out these areas somehow and only provide the means to unlock them to the right users. There are several ways in which you can accomplish this type of access, authentication, and authorization with Apache. You can use different criteria to control access to these sections, from simply checking the client's IP address or hostname to asking for a username and password. This section briefly covers some of these methods.

Access Restrictions with allow and deny

One of the simplest ways to provide access to a specific group of users is to restrict accesses based on IP addresses or hostnames. Apache uses the allow and deny directives to accomplish this. Both of these directives take an address expression as a parameter. See the following list for possible values and usage of the address expression:

- all can be used to affect all hosts.

- A host or domain name, which can either be a partially or a fully qualified domain name. For example, test.gnulix.org or gnulix.org.

- An IP address, which can be either full or partial. For example, 212.85.67 or 212.85.67.66.

- A network/netmask pair, such as `212.85.67.0/255.255.255.0`.
- A network address specified in CIDR format. For example, `212.85.67.0/24`. This is the CIDR notation for the same network and netmask that was used in the previous example.

If you have the choice, it is preferable to base your access control on IP addresses, rather than hostnames. This is faster because no name lookups are necessary—the IP address of the client is included with each request.

There is also another way to use `allow` and `deny`. Apart from specifying a hostname or an IP address, you can also check for the existence of a specific environment variable. For example, the following statement will deny access to a request with a context that contains an environment variable named NOACCESS:

```
deny from env=NOACCESS
```

The default behavior of Apache is to apply all the `deny` directives first and then check the `allow` directives. If you want to change this order, you can use the `order` statement. There are three different ways in which Apache might interpret this statement:

- `Order deny,allow`—The deny directives are evaluated before `allow`. If a host isn't specifically denied access, it will be allowed to access the resource. This is the default ordering if nothing else is specified.
- `Order allow,deny`—All `allow` directives are evaluated before `deny`. If a host isn't specifically allowed access, it will be denied access to the resource.
- `Order mutual-failure`—Only hosts that are specified in an `allow` directive and at the same time do not appear in a `deny` directive will be allowed access. If a host doesn't appear in either directive, it will not be granted access.

Consider this example. Suppose that you only wanted to allow persons from within your own domain to access the `server-status` resource on your Web. If your domain were named `gnulix.org`, you would add something along these lines in your configuration file:

```
<Location /server-status>
    SetHandler server-status
    Order deny,allow
    Deny from all
    Allow from gnulix.org
</Location>
```

Authentication

Authentication is the process of ensuring that visitors really are who they claim to be. By specifying that only certain users are allowed to access an area, Apache will request that the client authenticate itself before granting access.

There are several methods of authentication in Apache. We will cover the most common method: basic authentication. Using this method, a user will be required to supply a username and a password to access the protected resources. Apache will then verify that the user is allowed to access the resource in question. Should this be the case, the password will be verified. If this also checks out, the user will have been authorized and the request will be served.

HTTP is a stateless protocol, therefore the authentication information must be included with each request. This means that each request to a password-protected area will be larger and therefore somewhat slower. Taking this into account, it is a good idea to protect only those areas that absolutely need it.

In order to use Basic authentication, you will need a file that lists which users are allowed to access the resources. This list will consist of a plain text file containing name and password pairs. It looks very much like the user file of your Linux system—that is, /etc/passwd. In fact, you could actually use this as a user list for authentication. But this is a very bad idea!

> ### Caution
>
> When you are using Basic authentication, passwords and usernames are sent as base64-encoded text from the client to the server—which is just as readable as plain text. The username and password are included in each request that is sent to the server. So anyone who might be snooping on Net traffic could be able to get hold of this information!

To create a user file for Apache, use the htpasswd command. This is included with the Apache package, and if you installed using the RPMs it will be found in /usr/bin. Running htpasswd without any options will produce the following output:

```
Usage:
        htpasswd [-cmdps] passwordfile username
        htpasswd -b[cmdps] passwordfile username password

  -c  Create a new file.
  -m  Force MD5 encryption of the password.
```

```
-d  Force CRYPT encryption of the password (default).
-p  Do not encrypt the password (plaintext).
-s  Force SHA encryption of the password.
-b  Use the password from the command line rather than prompting for it.
On Windows and TPF systems the '-m' flag is used by default.
On all other systems, the '-p' flag will probably not work.
```

As you can see, it isn't a very difficult command to use. For example, to create a new user file named `gnulixusers` with a user named `wsb`, you would need do something like this:

```
htpasswd -c gnulixusers wsb
```

You would then be prompted for a password for the user. To add more users, you would repeat the same procedure, only omitting the `-c` flag.

You can also create user group files. The format of these files is more or less like the `/etc/groups`. The first entry on a line is the group name. A colon follows this and then a list of all users is specified, separated by spaces. For example, an entry might look like this:

```
gnulickers: wsb pgj jp ajje nadia rkr hak
```

Now that you know how to create a user file, it is time to look at how Apache might use this to protect Web resources. First of all, you will want to point Apache to the user file. You do this with the `AuthUserFile` directive. As its parameter the directive takes the file path to the user file. If it isn't absolute—that is, beginning with a /—it will be assumed that it is relative to the `ServerRoot`. Using the `AuthGroupFile` directive, you can specify a group file in the same manner.

The next directive you need to use is `AuthType`. This sets the type of authentication to be used for this resource. Because this section is looking at how to use Basic authentication, this will be set to `Basic`.

Now you need to decide which realm the resource is to belong to. This is used to group different resources that will share the same users for authorization. The realm can consist of just about any string. The realm will be shown in the Authentication dialog box on the user's Web browser. Therefore, it is best to set the realm string to something informative. The realm is defined with the `AuthName` directive.

Finally, you need to state what type of users are required for the resource. You do this with the `require` directive. There are three ways to use this directive:

- If you specify `valid-user` as an option, any user in the user file will be allowed to access the resource (that is, provided she also entered the correct password).

- You can specify a list of users who are allowed access with the `users` option.
- You can specify a list of groups with the `group` option. Entries in the group list as well as the user list are separated by a space.

Returning to the `server-status` example from earlier, instead of letting users access the `server-status` resource based on hostname, change it to require that they be authenticated. You can do this with the following entry in the configuration file:

```
<Location /server-status>
    SetHandler server-status
    AuthType Basic
    AuthName "Server status"
    AuthUserFile "gnulixusers"
    Require valid-user
</Location>
```

Final Words on Access Control

If you have host-based as well as user-based protection on a resource, the default behavior of Apache is to require that the requester satisfy both controls. But you want to mix host-based and user-based protection and allow access to a resource if either method succeeds. You can do this using the `satisfy` directive. This can either be set to `All` (this is the default) or `Any`. When set to `All`, all access control methods must be satisfied before the resource is served. If it is set to `Any`, the resource is served if any of the access conditions are met.

Here's another example. Once again using the previous `server-status` example, this time combine access methods so that all users from the `Gnulix` domain are allowed access and those from outside the domain must identify themselves before gaining access. You can do this with the following:

```
<Location /server-status>
    SetHandler server-status
    Order deny,allow
    Deny from all
    Allow from gnulix.org
    AuthType Basic
    AuthName "Server status"
    AuthUserFile "gnulixusers"
    Require valid-user
    Satisfy Any
</Location>
```

There are more ways to protect material on you Web server, but the methods discussed here should get you started and will probably be more than adequate for most circumstances. Look to Apache's online documentation for more examples of how to secure areas of your site.

Apache Modules

Apache is built upon a modular concept. At its core there is little functionality. Modules are added in order to implement more advanced features and functionality. Each module solves a well-defined problem by adding the extra features that are needed. Using this concept, you can more or less tailor Apache server to suit your exact needs.

Forty modules are included with the basic Apache server. Many more are available from other developers. There is a repository for add-on modules for Apache called The Apache Module Registry, and it can be found at `http://modules.apache.org/`.

Each module adds new directives that can be used in your configuration files. As you might guess, there are far too many extra commands, switches, and options to describe them all in this chapter. Therefore, this section will only briefly describe those modules that are available with Red Hat's Apache installation. If you need further information on how to use a module, refer to the online documentation for the server that is included with the Red Hat distribution or look at the Apache Groups Web site. Local copies of this documentation are located at `http://localhost/manual/`.

Following is an alphabetical list of those modules that are included with Red Hat's Apache RPM.

mod_access

This module gives you the ability to control access to areas on your Web server based on IP addresses, hostnames, or environment variables. You will be able to grant or deny access to any part of your Web server depending on those criteria. It is possible to use partial hostnames or subsets of IP addresses as access qualifiers. For example, you might want to allow anyone from within your own domain to access certain areas of your Web. See the section "Authentication and Access Control" for more information.

mod_actions

This module provides the ability to dynamically execute scripts based on the type of HTTP request. You will be able to map the execution of CGI scripts to MIME content types or request methods.

mod_alias

There are times when you need to manipulate the URLs of incoming HTTP requests. You might want to redirect the client's request to another URL, or you might want to map a part of the filesystem into your Web hierarchy. For example,

```
Alias /images/ /home/wsb/graphics/
```

would fetch contents from the /home/wsb/graphics directory for any URL that starts with /images/. This will be done without the client knowing anything about it. If you use a redirection, the client will be instructed to go to another URL to find the requested content.

For more advanced URL manipulation, look at mod_rewrite also.

mod_asis

Using this module, you will be able to specify in fine detail all information that is to be included in a response. This will completely bypass any headers that Apache might otherwise have added to the response. All files with an .asis extension will be sent straight through to the client without any changes.

As a short example, assume that you have moved the contents from one location to another on your site. Now you need to inform people who try to access this resource that it has moved, as well as redirect them to the new location automatically. To do this you might add something like the following code into a file with an .asis extension.

```
Status: 301 No more old stuff!
Location: http://gnulix.org/newstuff/
Content-type: text/html

<HTML>
 <HEAD>
  <TITLE>We've moved...</TITLE>
 </HEAD>
 <BODY>
   <P>We've moved the old stuff and now you'll find it at:</P>
   <A HREF="http://gnulix.org/newstuff/">New stuff</A>!.
 </DODY>
</HTML>
```

mod_auth

This is the simplest of all user authentication schemes available for Apache, and as such it is often referred to as Basic authentication. This scheme is based on storing usernames and encrypted passwords in a text file. This file looks very much like UNIX's

/etc/passwd file. These files are created with the htpasswd command. See the section "Authentication and Access Control" for more information about this subject.

mod_auth_anon

This module provides anonymous authentication similar to that of anonymous FTP. The module will allow you to define user IDs of those who are to be handled as guest users. When such a user tries to log on, she will be prompted for her e-mail address as her password. It is possible to have Apache check the password to ensure that it is a (more or less) proper e-mail address. Basically it ensures that there is an @ character and at least one . character in the password.

mod_auth_db

This module is very much like the mod_auth module. Rather than keeping the user data in a plain text file it uses Berkeley DB files.

mod_auth_digest

This is an extension of the basic mod_auth module. Instead of sending the user information in plain text, it will be sent via the MD5 Digest Authentication process. This authentication scheme is defined in RFC 2617. This is a much more secure way of sending user data over the Internet compared to using Basic authentication. Unfortunately, not all Web browsers support this authentication scheme.

To create password files for use with mod_auth_dbm, you will need to use the htdigest utility. It has more or less the same functionality as the htpasswd utility. See the man page of htdigest for further information.

mod_autoindex

If you haven't provided a default HTML file for a directory and have enabled directory indexing, this module will dynamically create a file list for the directory in question. This list will be rendered in a user-friendly manner similar to those lists that FTP provides. There are many options that will provide you with the ability to fine-tune every aspect of the look and feel of the directory listing.

mod_bandwidth

This module provides bandwidth usage limitation. It enables basic traffic shaping for replies so that the server will not become overloaded when there are too many requests. This can be applied either to parts of the server or the whole server. You can apply the module based on file size, location, or domain of the client, and the location or directory of the requested material.

This is one of the third-party modules that Red Hat has added that are generally not part of the Apache distribution.

mod_cern_meta

This module gives you the ability to add additional HTTP headers to each HTTP response. You can configure Apache so that the contents of files with certain extensions, usually .meta, will be included together with any other HTTP headers that Apache generates.

mod_cgi

This module allows you to execute CGI scripts on you server. See the section on dynamic content for more information about how to use CGIs.

mod_digest

This module is being deprecated and will be replaced by mod_auth_digest. Therefore, you are probably better off using that module instead.

mod_dir

This is used to determine which files are returned automatically when a user tries to access a directory. The default is index.html. If you have users who create Web pages on Windows systems, you will probably want to include index.htm as well like this:

```
DirectoryIndex index.html index.htm
```

mod_env

This module allows you to control how environment variables are passed to CGI and SSI scripts.

mod_example

This is only a demo module. Its main purpose is for people to study its source code and learn how to code new modules for Apache.

mod_expires

Use this module if you want to add an expire date to content on your site. This is accomplished by adding an Expires header to the HTTP response. Content that has expired will not be cached by Web browsers or cache servers.

mod_headers

This is a very useful module that allows you to manipulate the HTTP headers of your server's responses. You can replace, add, merge, or delete headers as you see fit. The module supplies a directive for this called Header. Ordering of the Header directive is important. A set followed by an unset for the same HTTP header will remove the header altogether. You can place Header directives almost anywhere within your configuration files. These directives are then processed in the following order:

1. Core Server
2. Virtual Host
3. *<Directory>* and .htaccess files
4. *<Location>*
5. *<Files>*

mod_imap

This module provides for server-side handling of image map files. Clickable regions are defined in a .map file. Six directives are available for use in the .map file. These are used to describe the layout of the clickable regions as well as which URLs they lead to.

mod_include

This enables the use of Server-Side Includes on your server. See the section "Dynamic Content" later in the chapter for more information about how to use SSI.

mod_info

The mod_info module provides comprehensive information about your server's configuration. For example, it will display all the modules that are installed, as well as all the directives that are used in its configuration files.

mod_log_agent

This enables you to log the content of the UserAgent header from HTTP requests. Using this information allows you to see which Web browsers visitors to your site are using.

mod_log_config

This module allows you to define how your log files should look. See the section "Logging" for further information about this subject.

mod_log_referer

This enables you to log the referer part of an HTTP request.

mod_mime

This module tries to determine the MIME type of files from their extensions.

mod_mime_magic

This module tries to determine the MIME type of files by examining portions of their content.

mod_mmap_static

This module uses the mmap() function to map static pages into system memory. This is used to reduce the server latency introduced by disk access. Because these pages are cached within system memory, the server will need to be restarted if the pages are updated on disk.

mod_negotiation

Using this module, it is possible to select one of several document versions that best suits the client's capabilities. There are several options to select which criteria to use in the negotiation process. You can, for example, choose among different languages, graphics file formats, and compression methods.

mod_proxy

This module implements proxy and caching capabilities for an Apache server. It can proxy and cache FTP, CONNECT, HTTP/0.9, and HTTP/1.0 requests. This isn't an ideal solution for sites that have a large number of users and therefore have very high proxy and cache requirements. However, it is more than adequate for a small number of users.

mod_put

This module implements the PUT and DELETE methods from the HTTP/1.1 protocol.

> **Caution**
>
> Because this module grants people write access, you will have to ensure that write access is limited only to trusted users!

This is one of the third-party modules that Red Hat has added. These are generally not part of the Apache distribution.

mod_rewrite

This is the Swiss army knife of URL manipulation. It allows you to perform any imaginable manipulation of URLs using powerful regular expressions. It provides rewrites, redirection, proxying, and so on. There is very little that you cannot accomplish using this module.

See `http://localhost/manual/misc/rewriteguide.html` for a cookbook, which will give you a very good overview of what this module is capable of.

mod_setenvif

This module allows you to manipulate environment variables. Using regular expressions, it is possible to conditionally change the content of environment variables. The order in which `SetEnvIf` directives appear in the configuration files is important. It is possible that each `SetEnvIf` directive might reset an earlier `SetEnvIf` directive when used on the same environment variable. Be sure to keep that in mind when using the directives from this module.

mod_so

This module, which replaces the old `mod_dld` module found on Apache 1.2 and prior (and `so_dll` on the Windows platform), provides support for loading .shared-object files on UNIX-based machines at runtime. For Windows, this module will load .dlls at runtime.

Classifies as an experimental module, this module only has two directives: `LoadFile` and `LoadModule`. For more information, see `http://httpd.apache.org/docs/mod/mod_so.html`.

mod_speling

This module automatically corrects minor typos in URLs. If no file matches the requested URL, this module will build a list of the files in the requested directory and will extract those files that are the closest matches. It will try to correct only one spelling mistake.

mod_status

This module creates a Web page containing a plethora of information about a running Apache server. The page will contain information about the internal status as well as statistics about the running Apache processes. This can be a great aid when you are trying to configure your server for maximum performance. It is also a good indicator when something is amiss with your Apache server.

mod_throttle

This module provides you with the possibility to throttle incoming requests so that the server will not become overloaded when there are too many requests. You can throttle requests directed either to a certain user's material or to a specific virtual host.

You can access the documentation for this module at `http://www.snert.com/Software/Throttle/`.

This is one of the third-party modules that Red Hat has added. These are generally not part of the Apache distribution.

mod_unique_id

This module generates a unique request identifier for every incoming request. This ID will be put into the UNIQUE_ID environment variable.

mod_userdir

This module enables you to map a subdirectory in each user's home directory into your Web tree. The module provides several different ways to accomplish this.

mod_usertrack

This module generates a cookie for each user session. This can be used to track the user's click stream within your Web tree. You will need to enable a custom log that logs this cookie into a log file.

mod_vhost_alias

This module provides excellent support for dynamically configured mass virtual hosting. It is especially useful for ISPs with very many virtual hosts. However, for the average user, Apache's ordinary virtual hosting support should prove to be more than sufficient.

There are two ways to host virtual hosts on an Apache server. You can either have one IP address with multiple CNAMEs, or you can have multiple IP addresses with one name per address. Apache has different sets of directives to handle each of these options.

Virtual Hosting

One of the more popular services to provide with a Web server is to host a virtual domain, also known as a virtual host. This is a complete Web site with its own domain name, as if it were a standalone machine, but it's hosted on the same machine as other Web sites. Apache implements this capability in a simple way with directives in the httpd.conf configuration file.

A new way to dynamically host virtual servers was recently added. This is enabled using the mod_vhost_alias module. The module is primarily intended for ISPs and similar large sites that host a large number of virtual sites. This is a module for more advanced use, and as such it goes outside the scope of this introductory chapter. Instead, this section concentrates on the traditional ways of hosting virtual servers.

Address-Based Virtual Hosts

Once you have configured your Linux machine with multiple IP addresses, setting up Apache to serve them as different Web sites is quite simple. You need only put a VirtualHost directive in your httpd.conf file for each of the addresses that you want to make an independent Web site:

```
<VirtualHost 212.85.67.67>
ServerName gnulix.org
DocumentRoot /home/virtual/gnulix/public_html
TransferLog /home/virtual/gnulix/logs/access_log
ErrorLog /home/virtual/gnulix/logs/error_log
</VirtualHost>
```

It is recommended that you use the IP address, rather than the hostname, in the VirtualHost tag.

You can specify any configuration directives within the <VirtualHost> tags. For example, you might want to set AllowOverrides directives differently for virtual hosts than you do for your main server. Any directives that aren't specified default to the settings for the main server.

The directives that cannot be set in `VirtualHost` sections are `ServerType`, `StartServers`, `MaxSpareServers`, `MinSpareServers`, `MaxRequestsPerChild`, `BindAddress`, `Listen`, `PidFile`, `TypesConfig`, `ServerRoot`, and `NameVirtualHost`.

Name-Based Virtual Hosts

Name-based virtual hosts allow you to run more than one host on the same IP address. You need to add the additional names to your DNS as CNAMEs of the machine in question. When an HTTP client (Web browser) requests a document from your server, it sends with the request a variable indicating the server name from which it is requesting the document. Based on this variable, the server determines from which of the virtual hosts it should serve content.

> **Note**
>
> Some older browsers are unable to see name-based virtual hosts because this is a feature of HTTP 1.1, and those older browsers are strictly HTTP 1.0-compliant. However, many other older browsers are partially HTTP 1.1-compliant, and this is one of the parts of HTTP 1.1 that most browsers have supported for a while.

Name-based virtual hosts require just one step more than IP address-based virtual hosts. You first need to indicate which IP address has the multiple DNS names on it. This is done with the `NameVirtualHost` directive:

```
NameVirtualHost 212.85.67.67
```

You then need to have a section for each name on that address, setting the configuration for that name. As with IP-based virtual hosts, you only need to set those configurations that need to be different for the host. You must set the `ServerName` directive because that is the only thing that distinguishes one host from another:

```
<VirtualHost 212.85.67.67>
ServerName bugserver.gnulix.org
ServerAlias bugserver
DocumentRoot /home/bugserver/htdocs
ScriptAlias /home/bugserver/cgi-bin
TransferLog /home/bugserver/logs/access_log
</VirtualHost>
```

```
<VirtualHost 212.85.67.67>
ServerName pts.gnulix.org
ServerAlias pts
DocumentRoot /home/pts/htdocs
ScriptAlias /home/pts/cgi-bin
TransferLog /home/pts/logs/access_log
ErrorLog /home/pts/logs/error_log
</VirtualHost>
```

Tip

If you are hosting Web sites on an intranet or internal network, there is often a chance that users will use the shortened name of the machine rather than the fully qualified domain name. For example, they might type `http://bugserver/index.html` in their browser location field rather than `http://bugserver.gnulix.org/index.html`. In that case, Apache will not recognize that those two addresses should go to the same virtual host. You could get around this by setting up `VirtualHost` directives for both `bugserver` and `bugserver.gnulix.org`, but the easy way around this is to use the `ServerAlias` directive, which lists all valid aliases for the machine:

```
ServerAlias bugserver
```

For more information on `VirtualHost`, refer to the help system on `http://localhost/manual`.

Logging

Apache provides for logging just about any information you might be interested in from Web accesses. Two standard log files are generated when you run your Apache server—`access_log` and `error_log`. All logs except for the `error_log` (by default, this is just the `access_log`) are generated in a format specified by the `CustomLog` and `LogFormat` directives. These directives appear in your `httpd.conf` file.

A new log format can be defined with the `LogFormat` directive:

```
LogFormat "%h %l %u %t \"%r\" %>s %b" common
```

The `common` log format is a good starting place for creating your own custom log formats. Note that most of the log analysis tools available will assume that you are using the `common` log format or the `combined` log format, both of which are defined in the default configuration files.

The following variables are available for LogFormat statements:

%a	Remote IP address.
%A	Local IP address.
%b	Bytes sent, excluding HTTP headers. This is shown in CLF format. For a request without any data content, a - will be shown instead of 0.
%B	Bytes sent, excluding HTTP headers.
%{VARIABLE}e	The contents of the environment variable VARIABLE.
%f	Filename.
%h	Remote host.
%H	Request protocol.
%{HEADER}i	The contents of HEADER; header line(s) in the request sent to the server.
%l	Remote logname (from identd, if supplied).
%m	Request method.
%{NOTE}n	The contents of note NOTE from another module.
%{HEADER}o	The contents of HEADER; header line(s) in the reply.
%p	The canonical port of the server serving the request.
%P	The process ID of the child that serviced the request.
%q	The contents of the query string, prepended with a ? character. If there is no query string, this will evaluate to an empty string.
%r	First line of request.
%s	Status. For requests that were internally redirected, this is the status of the *original* request—%>s for the last.
%t	Time, in common log format time format.
%{format}t	The time, in the form given by format, which should be in strftime(3) format. See the section "Basic SSI Directives" for a complete list of available formatting options.
%T	The time taken to serve the request, in seconds.
%u	Remote user from auth; might be bogus if return status (%s) is 401.
%U	The URL path requested.

%V	The server name according to the `UseCanonicalName` directive.
%v	The canonical `ServerName` of the server serving the request.

In each variable, you can put a conditional in front of the variable that will determine whether the variable is displayed. If it isn't displayed, - will be displayed instead. These conditionals are in the form of a list of numerical return values. For example, `%!401u` will display the value of `REMOTE_USER` unless the return code is 401.

You can then specify the location and format of a log file using the `CustomLog` directive:

```
CustomLog logs/access_log common
```

If it isn't specified as an absolute path, the location of the log file is assumed to be relative to the `ServerRoot`.

Dynamic Content

The most common way to provide dynamic content on Web sites is with CGI (common gateway interface) programs. The CGI is a specification of communication between server processes (such as programs that generate dynamic documents) and the server itself. Server-Side Includes (SSIs) allow output from CGI programs, or other programs, to be inserted into existing HTML pages.

Another way to add dynamic content to your Web site is to use PHP. This is an HTML-embedded scripting language that was designed specifically for Web usage. The PHP module for Apache is one of the most popular third-party modules available.

CGI

By default, you can put any CGI program in the `ScriptAlias` directory on your server. These programs must be executable by the user as to which server is running. This usually means that you will need to change the mode of the files to 555 so that the user whom Apache is running as can execute them. The default in Red Hat is that Apache runs as a user named `apache`.

```
chmod 555 program.cgi
```

In order to execute CGI programs outside of the `ScriptAlias` directory, you will need to enable the `ExecCGI` option for that directory. This is done either in your `httpd.conf` file (`access.conf` prior to version 1.3.4) or in an `.htaccess` file in the directory.

Apache Web Server Management

CHAPTER 16

435

16

APACHE WEB
SERVER
MANAGEMENT

CGI programs can be written in any language. The most popular languages for CGI programming are Perl and C. You might want to pick up a good book on CGI programming, such as *CGI Programming With Perl, Second Edition*, because this isn't intended to be a CGI book. You can also see Chapter 23, "Using Perl," for more information on the Perl scripting language.

To test whether you have CGI configured correctly, try the CGI program in Listing 16.1, written in Perl, which displays the values of the HTTP environment variables.

LISTING 16.1 environment.pl

```perl
#!/usr/bin/perl -w

print <<EOF;
"Content-type: text/html"

<HTML>
 <HEAD>
  <TITLE>Simple CGI program</TITLE>
 </HEAD>
 <BODY>
EOF
for (keys %ENV)    {
    print "  $_ = $ENV{$_}<BR>\n";
}
print <<EOF;
 </BODY>
</HTML>
EOF
```

If you are going to be writing CGI programs in Perl, you might want to look at the CGI modules that come bundled with Perl. There is also an extensive module library for Perl, which contains many modules designed to be used when writing CGIs. The archive can be accessed at http://www.cpan.org.

If you are using many CGIs written in Perl, you might want to look into the mod_perl module. It embeds a Perl interpreter within the Apache server. This will result in faster execution times for your CGIs because there will be no need to start up a new Perl interpreter for each request. However, this will make the memory footprint of each Apache process much larger.

SSI

Server-Side Includes (SSIs) are directives written directly into an HTML page, which the server parses when the page is served to the Web client. They can be used to include other files, the output from programs, or environment variables.

The most common way to enable SSI is to indicate that files with a certain filename extension (typically .shtml) are to be parsed by the server when they are served. This is accomplished with the following lines in your httpd.conf file (srm.conf prior to version 1.3.4):

```
# To use server-parsed HTML files
#
#AddType text/html .shtml
#AddHandler server-parsed .shtml
```

If you uncomment the AddType and AddHandler lines, you will tell the server to parse all .shtml files for SSI directives.

The less commonly used, but in my opinion much better, way of enabling SSI is with the XBitHack directive. XBitHack can be set to a value of on or off, and can be set in either your configuration file or in .htaccess files. If the XBitHack directive is on, it indicates that all files with the user execute bit set should be parsed for SSI directives. This has two main advantages. One is that you don't need to rename a file, and change all links to that file, simply because you want to add a little dynamic content to it. The other reason is more cosmetic—users looking at your Web content cannot tell by looking at the filename that you are generating a page dynamically, so your wizardry is just a tiny bit more impressive.

Another positive side effect of using XBitHack is that it enables you to control how clients should cache your page. Usually pages containing SSI statements will not contain a Last-modified HTTP header. Therefore they will not be cached by proxies nor Web browsers. If you enable XBitHack, the group-execute bit for files will control whether a Last-modified header should be generated. It will be set to the same value as the last modified time of the file. Be sure to use this only on files that really are supposed to be cached.

In addition to these directives, the following directive must be specified for directories in which you want to permit SSI:

```
Options Includes
```

This can be set in the server configuration file or in a .htaccess file.

Basic SSI Directives

SSI directives look rather like HTML comment tags. The syntax is as follows:

```
<!--#element attribute=value attribute=value ... -->
```

The *element* can be one of the following:

config
> This lets you set various configuration options regarding how the document parsing is handled. Because the page is parsed from top to bottom, `config` directives should appear at the top of the HTML document. Three configurations can be set with this command:
>
> errmsg
>> Sets the error message that is returned to the client if something goes wrong while parsing the document. This is usually [an error occurred while processing this directive], but it can be set to anything with this directive.
>
> Example: `<!--#config errmsg="[It's broken,`
> `➥dude]"-->`
>
> sizefmt
>> Sets the format used to display file sizes. You can set the value to `bytes` to display the exact file size in bytes, or `abbrev` to display the size in KB or MB.
>
> Example: `<!--#config sizefmt="bytes" -->`
>
> timefmt
>> Sets the format used to display times. The format of the value is the same as is used in the `strftime` function used by C (and Perl) to display dates, shown in the following table.
>
> %%
>> PERCENT
>
> %a
>> Day of the week abbr.
>
> %A
>> Day of the week
>
> %b
>> Month abbr.
>
> %B
>> Month
>
> %c
>> `ctime` format: `Sat Nov 19 21:05:57 1994`
>
> %d
>> Numeric day of the month
>
> %e
>> DD
>
> %D
>> MM/DD/YY

%h	Month abbr.
%H	Hour, 24-hour clock, leading 0's
%I	Hour, 12-hour clock, leading 0's
%j	Day of the year
%k	Hour
%l	Hour, 12-hour clock
%m	Month number, starting with 1
%M	Minute, leading 0's
%n	NEWLINE
%o	Ornate day of month—1st, 2nd, 25th, and so on
%p	AM or PM
%r	Time format: `09:05:57 PM`
%R	Time format: `21:05`
%S	Seconds, leading 0's
%t	Tab
%T	Time format: `21:05:57`
%U	Week number; Sunday as first day of week
%w	Day of the week, numerically; Sunday == 0
%W	Week number; Monday as first day of week
%x	Date format: `11/19/94`
%X	Time format: `21:05:57`
%y	Year (2 digits)
%Y	Year (4 digits)
%Z	Time zone in ASCII, such as PST

echo   Displays any one of the include variables, listed below. Times are displayed in the time format specified by `timefmt`. The variable to be displayed is indicated with the `var` attribute.

DATE_GMT   The current date in Greenwich Mean Time.

	DATE_LOCAL	The current date in the local time zone.
	DOCUMENT_NAME	The filename (excluding directories) of the document requested by the user.
	DOCUMENT_URI	The (%-decoded) URL path of the document requested by the user. Note hat in the case of nested include files, this is not the URL for the current document.
	LAST_MODIFIED	The last modification date of the document requested by the user.
exec		Executes a shell command or a CGI program, depending on the parameters provided. Valid attributes are cgi and cmd.
	cgi	The URL of a CGI program to be executed. The URL needs to be a local CGI, not one located on another machine. The CGI program is passed the QUERY_STRING and PATH_INFO that were originally passed to the requested document, so the URL specified cannot contain this information. You should really use include virtual instead of this directive.
	cmd	A shell command to be executed. The results will be displayed on the HTML page.
fsize		Displays the size of a file specified by either the file or virtual attribute. Size is displayed as specified with the sizefmt directive.
	file	The path (filesystem path) to a file, either relative to the root if the value starts with /, or relative to the current directory if not.
	virtual	The relative URL path to a file.

`flastmod`	Displays the last modified date of a file. The desired file is specified as with the `fsize` directive.
`include`	Includes the contents of a file. The file is specified with the `file` and `virtual` attributes, as with `fsize` and `flastmod`. If the file specified is a CGI program and `IncludesNOEXEC` is not set, the program will be executed and the results displayed. This is to be used in preference to the `exec` directive. You can pass a `QUERY_STRING` with this directive, which you cannot do with the `exec` directive.
`printenv`	Displays all existing variables. There are no attributes. Example: `<!--#printenv -->`
`set`	Sets the value of a variable. Attributes are `var` and `value`. Example: `<!--#set var="animal" value="cow" -->`

> **Note**
>
> All defined CGI environment variables are also allowed as `include` variables.

> **Note**
>
> In your configuration files (or in `.htaccess`), you can specify `Options IncludesNOEXEC` to disallow the `exec` directive because this is the least secure of the SSI directives. Be especially cautious when Web users are able to create content (like a guest book or discussion board) and these options are enabled!

These variables can be used elsewhere with some of the following directives.

Flow Control

Using the variables set with the `set` directive and the various environment variables and include variables, there is a limited flow control syntax that can be used to generate a certain amount of dynamic content on server-parsed pages.

Apache Web Server Management

CHAPTER 16

441

16

APACHE WEB
SERVER
MANAGEMENT

The syntax of the if/else functions is as follows:

```
<!--#if expr="test_condition" -->
<!--#elif expr="test_condition" -->
<!--#else -->
<!--#endif -->
```

expr can be a string, which is considered true if non-empty, or a variety of comparisons between two strings. Available comparison operators are =, !=, <, <=, >, and >=. If the second string has the format /string/, the strings are compared with regular expressions. Multiple comparisons can be strung together with && (AND) and || (OR). Any text appearing between the if/elif/else directives will be displayed on the resulting page. An example of such a flow structure follows:

```
<!--#set var="agent" value="$HTTP_USER_AGENT" -->
<!--#if expr="$agent = /Mozilla/" -->
Mozilla!
<!--#else -->
Something else!
<!--#endif -->
```

This code will display Mozilla! if you are using a browser that passes Mozilla as part of its USER_AGENT string, and Something else! otherwise.

PHP

PHP can to some extent be seen as a mixture of the CGI and SSI. It is embedded in HTML as is SSI, but it provides full and rich language features. The syntax of PHP is largely inspired by C and Perl. There are also several PHP-specific features. It allows developers to rapidly design and write applications for usage on the Web.

You can use PHP with Apache in two ways. The first approach is to use it as a script engine that is run as a CGI program—much the same way as Perl is commonly used for CGIs. The other, and far superior, way is to use the mod_php approach. This will embed PHP within Apache. Therefore, there will be no overhead to start up PHP when an application is run. It will, however, add to the memory footprint of the Apache processes.

The mod_php module is included in the Red Hat distribution, but it is not initially enabled by Apache in Red Hat 7.2. After activating the module, you can test if it has been installed properly on your system by using this code snippet in your Web site.

```
<HTML>
 <HEAD>
 <TITLE>Testing PHP</TITLE>
 </HEAD>
 <BODY>
  <H1>Testing PHP</H1>
```

```
   <P>If you have PHP installed, you'll get a greeting;</P>
   <?php print "Hello world!"; ?>
  </BODY>
</HTML>
```

PHP has far too many features to go into it in this chapter, especially because this isn't a chapter on programming. However, there are several excellent PHP resources available online. The best place to start is http://www.php.net.

Starting and Stopping the Server

At this point, you have your Apache server installed and configured the way you want it. It's time to start it up for the first time.

Starting the Server Manually

The Apache server, httpd, has a few command-line options you can use to set some defaults specifying where httpd will read its configuration directives. The Apache httpd executable understands the following options:

```
httpd [-D name][-d directory] [-f file]
          [-C "directive"] [-c "directive"]
          [-v] [-V] [-h] [-l] [-L] [-S] [-t] [-T]
```

The -D option defines a name for use with <IfDefine name> directives in your configuration files. This allows you to conditionally include or exclude sections of your configuration when starting the server.

The -d option overrides the location of the *ServerRoot* directory. It sets the initial value of the *ServerRoot* variable (the directory where the Apache server is installed) to whichever path you specify. This default is usually read from the ServerRoot directive in httpd.conf.

The -f flag specifies the location of the main configuration file, conf/httpd.conf. It reads and executes the configuration commands found in *ConfigurationFile* on startup. If the *ConfigurationFile* isn't an absolute path (it doesn't begin with a /), its location is assumed to be relative to the path specified in the *ServerRoot* directive in httpd.conf. By default, this value is set to *ServerRoot*/conf/httpd.conf.

The -v option prints the development version of the Apache server and terminates the process.

The -V option shows all the settings that were in effect when the server was compiled.

The -h option prints the following usage information for the server:

```
Usage: httpd [-D name] [-d directory] [-f file]
             [-C "directive"] [-c "directive"]
             [-v] [-V] [-h] [-l] [-L] [-S] [-t] [-T]
Options:
  -D name          : define a name for use in <IfDefine name> directives
  -d directory     : specify an alternate initial ServerRoot
  -f file          : specify an alternate ServerConfigFile
  -C "directive"   : process directive before reading config files
  -c "directive"   : process directive after  reading config files
  -v               : show version number
  -V               : show compile settings
  -h               : list available command line options (this page)
  -l               : list compiled-in modules
  -L               : list available configuration directives
  -S               : show parsed settings (currently only vhost settings)
  -t               : run syntax check for config files (with docroot check)
  -T               : run syntax check for config files (without docroot check)
```

The -l option lists those modules that are compiled into your Apache server.

The -L option lists all the configuration directives that are available with the modules that are compiled into your Apache server.

The -S option lists the virtual host settings for the server.

The -t option is extremely useful. It runs a syntax check on your configuration files. It's a good idea to run this check before restarting your server, once you have made changes to your configuration files. Performing such a test is especially important because an error in the configuration file might result in your server shutting down when you try to restart it.

The -T option is the same as the -t option, but it doesn't check the configured document roots.

Note

When you start the server manually from the command line, you need to do so as root. There are two main reasons for this:

- If your standalone server uses the default HTTP port (port 80), only the superuser can bind to Internet ports that are lower than 1024.
- Only processes owned by root can change their UID and GID as specified by the User and Group directives. If you start the server under another UID, it will run with the permissions of the user starting the process.

The /etc/rc.d httpd Scripts

Red Hat Linux uses scripts in the /etc/rc.d directory to control the startup and shutdown of various services, including the Apache Web server. The main script installed for the Apache Web server is /etc/rc.d/init.d/httpd.

> **Note**
>
> /etc/rc.d/init.d/httpd is a shell script and isn't the same as the Apache server located in /usr/sbin. That is, /usr/sbin/httpd is the program executable file, and /etc/rc.d/init.d/httpd is a shell script that helps control that program.

You can use the following options to control the Web server:

- start—The system uses this option to start the Web server during boot up. You, as root, can also use this script to start the server.
- stop—The system uses this option to stop the server gracefully. You should use this script, rather than the kill command, to stop the server.
- reload—You can use this option to send the HUP signal to the httpd server to have it reread the configuration files after modification.
- restart—This option is a convenient way to stop and then immediately start the Web server. If the httpd server wasn't running, it will be started.
- condrestart—The same as the restart parameter, except that it will only restart the httpd server if it is actually running.
- status—This option indicates whether the server is running, and if it is, it provides the various PIDs for each instance of the server.

For example, to check on the current status, use the command

/etc/rc.d/init.d/httpd status

which prints the following for me:

httpd (pid 8643 8642 6510 6102 6101 6100 6099 6323 6322 6098 6097 6096
➡ 6095 362 6094 6093) is running...

This indicates that the Web server is running; in fact, there are 16 instances of the server currently running in this configuration.

> **Tip**
>
> Use the `reload` option if you are making many changes to the various server configuration files. This saves time when you're stopping and starting the server by having the system simply reread the configuration files.

Graphic Interface Configuration

None of the 1.3.X versions of Apache include a direct graphical configuration tool. Although many people can work with the command line interface for Apache, many others prefer the ease of a GUI tool.

Recently, Red Hat Linux has included `apacheconf`, which is euphemistically called Comanche. With Comanche, you can do most of the same configurations that you can by manually editing the configuration files.

The thing to remember is that the Comanche tool is not the be-all end-all of working on the `httpd.conf` file.

> **Caution**
>
> Red Hat advises that if you use the apacheconf tool, you shouldn't try and edit the httpd.conf file by hand.

Once started by the `/usr/bin/apacheconf` command, you will see the screen shown in Figure 16.1.

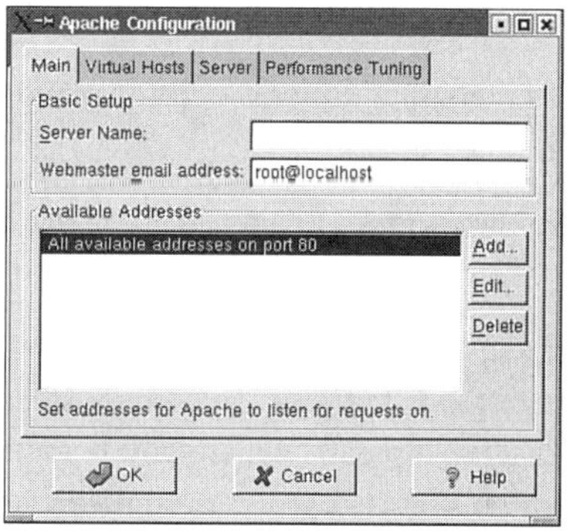

FIGURE 16.1

The Comanche main configuration screen.

In the Main tab, you can set the server name, decide where to send e-mail addressed to the Webmaster, and decide which port Apache will use. If you want, you can also configure specific virtual hosts to listen on different ports.

If you click on the Virtual Hosts tab, you can configure each individual virtual host to behave differently. Once there you can open the Virtual Hosts Properties dialog box by highlighting the virtual host entry and clicking the Edit button.

In this dialog box, there are several options to choose from. You can use the Site Configuration section to set defaults such as which files contain the different error messages; you can also set which files get loaded by default when no files are specified (the default is index.*) in the URL.

The Logging section (shown in Figure 16.2) configures where the error messages get logged to as well as where the transfer log file is kept and how much information is put in it.

FIGURE 16.2

*Comanche's
Virtual Host
Properties
dialog box.*

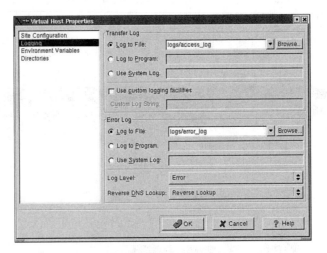

The Environment Variables section, as the name implies, configures some of the different environment directives not covered in other sections.

The Directories section configures the directory options as well as the order entries mentioned in the httpd.conf section.

Back in the primary Comanche interface, the Server tab allows you to configure things such as where the lock file is and where the PID file is. In both these cases, it's best to use the defaults. You can also configure the directory where any potential core dumps will be placed. Finally, you can set which user and group to run Apache as. For security reasons, it is best not to run Apache as the root. On the occasions in which Apache can

be exploited, it is better to not give root access to those people trying to break into your system (see Figure 16.3).

FIGURE 16.3

Comanche's Server configuration tab.

Finally, the last apacheconf tab is the Performance Tuning tab. This sets the maximum number of people who can connect to your server at one time.

When setting this number, keep in mind that for each connection to your server another instance of the httpd program is run, taking resources such as CPU time and memory. You can also configure details about each connection such as how long, in seconds, before a connection times out and how many requests each connection can make to the server.

Other Web Servers

There are, of course, other Web servers out there that can be used with Red Hat Linux. Apache is by far the most popular, but this doesn't rule out using something else.

There are the needs of the Web site you are managing to consider. Will it need heavy security (for e-commerce), multimedia (music, video, and pictures), or the ability to download files easily? How much are you willing to spend for the software? Do you need software that is easy to, or includes, support? The answers to these questions might steer you to something other than Apache.

In this section, some of the more popular alternatives are listed to give you a better idea of what's out there.

thttpd

It isn't entirely clear what the *t* in thttpd stands for. Meanings alternate between *tiny*, *turbo*, and *throttling*, depending on who you ask. Whatever meaning you opt for, it is clear that thttpd is *not* big and slow.

thttpd is, on the surface, a simple little HTTP server that can handle a fair amount of traffic with little strain. Although not as robust as Apache, it does feature something that Apache doesn't have readily available: a throttling control.

Throttling, in the context of thttpd, is a process in which incoming URL calls are kept under control for a certain page or collection of pages on the Web site. If traffic to these pages hits a defined limit, the requesters for the page are sent a try again code until the traffic returns to a more manageable level.

thttpd is available as freeware from the thttpd Web site (`http://www.acme.com/software/thttpd`).

iPlanet

Despite the NetCraft numbers shown in Table 16.1, there is evidence that iPlanet might be even more popular than Apache in strictly corporate arenas. According to the Gartner Group, iPlanet ranks the highest among Web servers found at Fortune 100 Web sites.

And with good reason. iPlanet got its start as the Netscape Enterprise Server—one of the first powerful Web servers ever to hit the market. Microsoft's Internet Information Server (IIS) was launched long after iPlanet was on the shelves. Apache has passed them both, but Netscape continues to hold a strong presence on the Web.

Certainly America Online was eyeing the Netscape Enterprise Server when it purchased the company in 1998 and spun the server division off into an alliance with Sun Microsystems to form iPlanet.

iPlanet comes in many different flavors—all of them big. Besides the enterprise-level Web server that can be run on Red Hat, iPlanet features application, messaging, calendar, and directory servers... just to name a few.

iPlanet is for handling big Web needs, and it comes with an appropriately big price tag: $1495 (U.S.) for the basic enterprise server package. Definitely not something to run the school Web site, unless your school happens to be a major state university with several regional campuses. For more information on iPlanet, you can visit its Web site (`http://www.iplanet.com/`).

Stronghold

If you are looking for something a little more secure than Apache, but still don't want to lose the Apache functionality, you can purchase Stronghold from Red Hat Software.

Although not a Web server *per se*, Stronghold is a server add-on that provides 128-bit cryptography and security certificates to the Apache Web server (which is included in your purchase of Stronghold).

Stronghold supports SSL and TLS security standards, as well as many of the certificate standards that are out on the market today.

The price for this kind of security isn't particularly light. The software, which can be previewed at `http://www.c2.net/products/sh3/index.php3`, runs for $995 (U.S.). Still, security is a useful premium, particularly in today's troubling times.

Zope

Zope is another Open Source Web server. Although it is still relatively young and might not have as much flexibility as Apache, it is making strong inroads in the Web server market.

What makes Zope unique from Apache is the fact that it is managed through a completely Web-based graphic interface. This has broad appeal for those who aren't enthused about a command-line only interface.

Zope is a product of the Zope Corporation (formerly Digital Creations), the same firm that made the Python programming language. And, like all things Open Source, it's free. Information on Zope can be found at both `http://www.zope.com` and `http://www.zope.org`.

Reference

There are still some things that you can do to further customize your Web server, but by this point you should at least have a functional server.

There is a plethora of Apache documentation online. For more information about Apache and the subjects discussed in this chapter, look at some of the following resources:

`http://www.apache.org/`—Extensive documentation and information about Apache are available at The Apache Project Web site.

`http://www.apacheweek.com/`—You can obtain breaking news about Apache and great technical articles at the ApacheWeek site.

`http://apachetoday.com/`—Another good Apache site, with original content as well as links to Apache-related stories on other sites can be found at Apache Today's site.

`http://www.hwg.org/`—HTML, CGI, and related subjects are available at The HTML Writers Guild site.

`http://modules.apache.org/`—Available add-on modules for Apache can be found at The Apache Module Registry Web site.

There are also several good books about Apache. For example, *Apache Server Unleashed*, ISBN 0-672-31808-3.

For more information on Zope, see *The Zope Book*, (New Riders) ISBN 0-7357-11372.

Database Services

Data… It's everywhere. Virtually all animals deal with data in one form or another, and humans are certainly no exception. Everywhere you go, your senses are bombarded with various forms of data—so much data that your brain can only take in a fraction of the data flowing into your senses at any given time. In a business or scientific setting, the amount of data you have to deal with just to do your job could number in the gigabyte, or even the terabyte range. How do you keep track of, sort, and find information in a mountain of data this large? Sure, you could write it down and keep it in filing cabinets. But that method has severe limitations. For one thing, it takes a long time to find anything. Another problem is that only one person can be viewing any given record at any given time. And also of course, if someone in a branch office needs access to that data, he has to call you and have you find what he needs, and then you have to either mail the record to him or fax it to him. If he then makes changes to that data and forgets to notify you, you could end up with a mess really quick. The other major problem with paper records is that if you want to look for trends in your data or generate useful reports, this can take months or possibly even years of work if you have an extremely large amount of data with complex relationships. This is work that could be done by a computer in hours, or possibly even minutes. Enter the computerized database.

Types of Databases

Databases generally come in two basic forms: flat file and relational. This section looks briefly at each one, starting with flat file databases.

Flat File Databases

A flat file database can be as simple as a text file with a space, tab, or some other character delimiting different parts of the information. One example of a simple flat file database is the Red Hat `/etc/passwd` file. Another example could be a simple address book that might look something like this:

```
Doe~John~505 Some Street~Anytown~NY~12345~555-555-1212
```

You could then of course, use standard UNIX tools like `grep`, `awk`, or `perl` to search for and extract information from this primitive database. Although this might work fine for a small database such as an address book that only one person uses, flat file databases of this sort do have several limitations:

- They don't scale well. Flat file databases such as this cannot perform random access on data. They can only perform sequential access. This means that they have to scan each line in the file, one by one to look for the requested information. As the size of the database grows, access times get longer and performance decreases.

- It is difficult to look for data relationships. This will be covered in more detail when we look at relational databases, but basically, flat file databases make it difficult to search for relationships between one piece of data and another.

- Depending on how the database is set up, it will either lock the entire database file when one user is accessing it, preventing any other user from writing to any part of it, or it will allow two users to make changes that could end up overwriting each other and cause data loss. Because of this, flat file databases such as this are unsuitable for multiuser environments.

The preceding limitations obviously make the flat file database unsuitable for any kind of serious work in even a small business much less an enterprise environment. This is where the relational database comes in.

Relational Databases

Most of the workhorse databases available today are relational databases—commonly referred to as an *RDBMS*, which stands for *relational database management system*. Oracle, DB2, Microsoft SQL Server, and the freely available PostgreSQL and MySQL are all examples of RDBMSs. Why are they called relational? Because as we will see in the section "An Introduction to Relational Database Theory," they are very good at finding relationships between different pieces of related data. RDBMSs don't have the limitations of flat file databases, and as such, are much more versatile for a wider variety of tasks. Because of this, the RDBMS is the type of database that this chapter focuses on.

Overview of DBA Responsibilities

If you are reading this chapter, chances are you have been designated as a database administrator (DBA) for your organization. The DBA has several responsibilities. Depending on the size of your organization and the delegation of responsibility among your IT staff, your responsibilities will include some (and possibly all) of the following:

- Database server installation and maintenance. This involves installing and maintaining the database server software. Maintenance can involve such tasks such as installing patches that fix bugs and security issues, as well as upgrading the software when the time comes.

- Database client installation and maintenance. The database client is the program that your users use to access the database (more on that in the section "Database Clients"). Your responsibilities might include installing and maintaining these client programs on your users' systems.

17

DATABASE SERVICES

- Managing accounts and users. This includes adding and deleting users from the database, as well as dealing with users who have forgotten their database passwords and such.

- Database security. This involves things such as access control, which ensures that only authorized people can access the database, as well as permissions, which ensures that people who can access the database cannot do things they shouldn't do. Should John be able to create and destroy databases? Or should he only be able to use existing databases? Should Jane be able to add records to the database and modify existing records? Or should she have read-only access to the database? And what about the rest of the world? Should the general public have any kind of access to your database through the Internet? For example, should they be able to check your Web site to see if you have a part in stock that they want to order? In today's Internet connected world, database security is one of your most important responsibilities. **You don't want someone stealing your customers' credit card information do you?**

- Ensuring data integrity. Of all the information stored on your server's hard disk storage, chances are the information in the database is the most critical. Imagine the disaster and millions or even billions of dollars that could be lost if a company suddenly lost all records of its half a million customers. Ensuring that your organization's database is properly backed up is another one of your most important responsibilities. Restoring data from backups might also be important (for example, if a user accidentally deletes a customer record and you need to get it back).

An Introduction to Relational Database Theory

In order to effectively set up and administer an RDBMS, it is necessary to learn a little bit about relational database theory. We aren't going to go into a lot of detail here, but we will give you enough information to get you started if you are unfamiliar with how an RDBMS works.

An RDBMS stores data in tables. The table itself has a name that you will use to refer to that table when you want to get data out of it or put data into it. Each column in the table is a field. For example, a column might contain a name or an address. Each row in the table is an individual record. Tables can best be visualized as spreadsheets. Figure 17.1 shows an example.

Figure 17.1

A visualization of how an RDBMS stores data.

last_name	first_name	address	city	state	zip	phone
Doe	John	501 Somestreet	Anytown	NY	55011	555-555-1212
Doe	Jane	501 Somestreet	Anytown	NY	55011	555-555-1212
Palmer	John	205 Anystreet	Sometown	NY	55055	123-456-7890
Johnson	Robert	100 Easystreet	Easytown	CT	12345	111-222-3333

In this example, the database contains only a single table. Most RDBMS setups are much more complex, however, and contain multiple tables in a single database. Figure 17.2 shows an example of a database that contains more than one table.

Figure 17.2

A single database that contains two tables.

sample_database

phonebook

last_name	first_name	phone
Doe	John	555-555-1212
Doe	Jane	555-555-1212
Palmer	John	123-456-7890
Johnson	Richard	111-222-3333

serengeti_mammal

common_name	order	family	genus	species	sub-species
African Lion	Carnivora	Felidae	Panthera	leo	
African Elephant	Proboscidea	Elephantidae	Loxodonta	africana	
Meercat	Carnivora	Viverridae	Suricata	suricatta	
Hyena	Carnivora	Hyaenidae	Crocuta	croucuta	
Reticulated Giraffe	Artiodactyla	Giraffidae	Giraffa	cameloparalis	retciculata
Grant's Zebra	Perissodactyla	Equidae	Equus	burchelli	bohmi
Cheetah	Carnivora	Felidae	Acinonyx	jubatus	
Thompson's Gazelle	Artiodactyla	Bovidae	Gazella	thomsoni	
Hippopotamus	Artiodactyla	Hippopotamidae	Hippopotamus	amphibius	

If you are thinking that there is absolutely no logical relationship between the phonebook table and the serengeti_mammal table, you would be absolutely correct. In this case, there isn't a relationship. What this example shows is that you, as a DBA, can grant a user permission to create tables in a single database, and the user can create multiple "virtual databases" within that single database by creating multiple, unrelated tables. This way, a user can store multiple different types of data and still only have access to one database.

Related Tables

As the preceding example shows, it is possible to have a single database that contains multiple tables that have no relation to each other. However, the power of an RDBMS really begins to show when you have multiple tables that are somehow related to each other. For example, suppose you run a small company that sells widgets, and you have a

computerized database of customers. In addition to simply being able to store your customer's name, address, and phone number, you want to be able to look up how many
outstanding orders that customer has, as well as any outstanding invoices that the customer has. (You don't want to allow customers to place orders if they have outstanding
invoices that are more than 30 days overdue.) Figure 17.3 shows an example of how you
could use three related tables in an RDBMS to accomplish this.

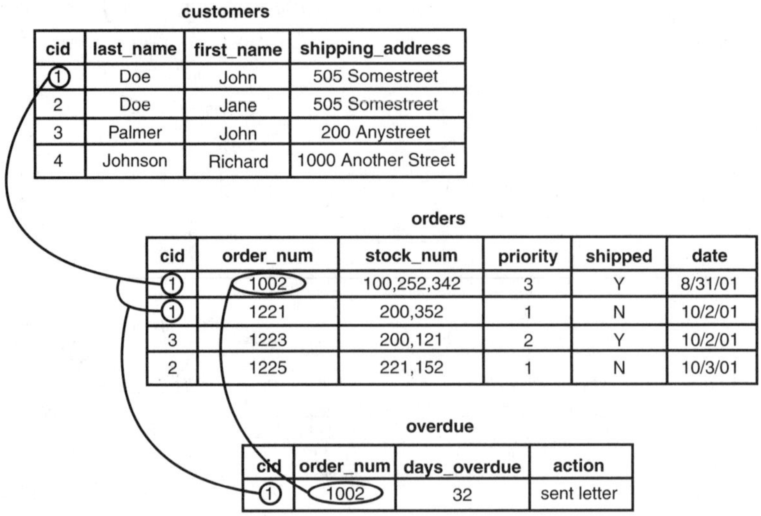

FIGURE 17.3

An example of using three related tables to track customers, orders, and outstanding invoices.

customers

cid	last_name	first_name	shipping_address
1	Doe	John	505 Somestreet
2	Doe	Jane	505 Somestreet
3	Palmer	John	200 Anystreet
4	Johnson	Richard	1000 Another Street

orders

cid	order_num	stock_num	priority	shipped	date
1	1002	100,252,342	3	Y	8/31/01
1	1221	200,352	1	N	10/2/01
3	1223	200,121	2	Y	10/2/01
2	1225	221,152	1	N	10/3/01

overdue

cid	order_num	days_overdue	action
1	1002	32	sent letter

In this example, we have added a customer ID number to each customer. This customer
ID number is the common link that can be used to link orders and invoices to that customer because each table uses the customer ID number. So why use a customer ID number as a link? Wouldn't it be simpler to just use the customer's name? Possibly, but there
is one major problem with this approach. It isn't inconceivable that you could end up
with two customers that have the same first and last name. If this happened, neither the
orders table or the outstanding table would have any way of knowing which invoices
belonged to which customer if two of them had the same name. Sure, you could include
the address or the phone number in the orders and outstanding table to eliminate this
problem, but now when you want to run a search, you need to search with multiple keys.
These searches have more overhead than a search using just a single key. Because the
customer ID number is often automatically generated by the database, it is transparent to
the person doing the search. Because of this, the customer ID number is probably the
best way to organize and link data in different tables for our purposes with this example.

So now that we have an idea of how data is stored in an RDBMS, we need a way to actually get data in to and out of the database. This is where SQL comes in.

An Introduction to SQL

SQL (which can be pronounced as "es-qu-el," or "sequel," either form is accepted) is an acronym for *structured query language*. You use SQL statements to get data in to, as well as retrieve data from, a database. Virtually all RDBMSs available today understand SQL. As a general rule, the SQL logic will be programmed into a front-end database application (or into a middlewear application), thus isolating the application's end user from the underlying SQL. Thus, the end user of the application doesn't even have to know that SQL exists. The user can just ask a question about the data he is looking for, and the database programmer worries about the actual SQL statements required to get the user the answer for that question. However, as a database administrator, you should understand the basics of SQL, even if you won't be doing any of the actual programming yourself. Fortunately, SQL is very similar to standard English, and learning the basics is very simple.

> **Tip**
>
> The following sections aren't intended to be a tutorial on SQL. They are simply intended to introduce you to the basics of the language. If you want to follow along on your computer, you will need to have a database already set up and you will also need permissions to create and modify tables in that database. The procedures for doing this vary between databases. Read the sections on choosing a database and also the sections on administering your chosen database if you want to follow along on your computer for this section. After you have installed and configured your database, return to this section. If you need a full tutorial on SQL programming, several books are available on this topic including *MySQL (by New Riders)*, *Teach Yourself MySQL in 21 Days*, and *PostgreSQL (both by Sams Publishing)*.

Creating Tables

As mentioned previously, an RDBMS stores data in tables that look similar to spreadsheets. Of course, before you can store any data in your database, you will need to create the necessary tables and columns to store the data. This is done with the CREATE statement. Because I am a biology major with a fascination for African mammals, we are going to use the serengeti_mammal table from Figure 17.2 for this example.

In this table, we have six columns, or fields. The columns are common_name, order, family, genus, species, and sub_species. Of course, this doesn't include columns for the entire hierarchy of classification. However, because the table will only contain data on mammals, the remaining groups in the hierarchy will be constant, so we don't need an entry in the database for them. (For the curious, this would be kingdom: Animalia, phylum: Chordata, and class: Mammalia. This is somewhat over-simplified because it doesn't make allowances for sub-phylums and such. For our purposes, we will leave things as they are. After all, this is a computer book and not a zoology textbook.)

SQL provides several different column types for data that define what kind of data will be stored in that column. Some of the available types include INT, FLOAT, CHAR, and VARCHAR. (The difference between CHAR and VARCHAR is that CHAR holds a fixed length string, whereas VARCHAR holds a variable length string.) There are also special column types such as DATE that take only data in a date format, and ENUM, which can be used to specify that only certain values are allowed. (If for example, we wanted to record the sex of an animal in our database, we could use an ENUM column that only accepted the values of M or F. We shall look more at this later.)

Looking at our serengeti_mammal table, we can see that all our columns hold character string data. In addition, these character strings are of variable length. Based on this information, we determine that the best type to use for all of our columns is type VARCHAR. Notice something else about our table. All the columns in the table, with the exception of the last one (sub-species), require a value. Not all the animals in our table have a sub-species classification however, so the last column can be left empty. These two facts will also be important when we set up our table.

Using the CREATE Statement to Set Up the Table

We are now ready to create our table. As mentioned before, this is done with the CREATE statement. The CREATE statement uses the following syntax:

```
CREATE TABLE table_name (column_name column_type(parameters) options, ...);
```

The ellipsis (...) indicates that everything starting from column_name is simply repeated for each column you want to create, and each column is separated by a comma.

The following things should be pointed out about this:

- The SQL commands are not case sensitive. For example, CREATE TABLE, create table, and Create Table are all valid. I suggest that you get in the habit of using all uppercase, however. Later on, when you start writing front ends to your databases in C, Perl, and so on, using all uppercase will make it easier to pick out the SQL code. (Keywords in C, Perl, and so on are almost always in lowercase.)

- Whitespace is generally ignored. This will be shown in the next example in which we create the table for our `serengeti_mammal` database.

The following example shows how we can create the table for our `serengeti_mammal` database:

```
CREATE TABLE serengeti_mammal
(
    commonname VARCHAR(25) NOT NULL,
    torder VARCHAR(20) NOT NULL,
    family VARCHAR(20) NOT NULL,
    genus VARCHAR(20) NOT NULL,
    species VARCHAR(20) NOT NULL,
    subspecies VARCHAR(20) NULL
);
```

Notice that the statement terminates with a semicolon. This is how SQL knows that you are finished with all the entries in the statement. (In some cases, the semicolon can be omitted. We will point out these cases when we come to them.) In MySQL and PostgreSQL, the preceding example could be entered directly into the command line clients (which will be discussed later in this chapter). However, this introduces a lot of opportunity for error. If you make a mistake, you would have to type all of it over again from the beginning. Fortunately, both MySQL and PostgreSQL can read a list of SQL statements from a plain text file. For example, you could enter the preceding text into a text editor and save the file as `mammal.sql`. The extension `.sql` isn't required, but including it is helpful because it would be easy to see that this file contains SQL statements when doing a directory listing. If the preceding statements are saved into a text file, they can be imported into the database with the following commands in MySQL and PostgreSQL, respectively:

```
$ mysql database_name < mammal.sql
$ psql database_name < mammal.sql
```

Of course, in order for this to work, `mysql` or `psql` must be invoked as a user who has permission to create tables in the database represented by *database_name*.

> **Tip**
>
> You might be wondering why we used "torder" instead of just "order" for the column that contains the order information. This is because "order" is a reserved keyword in PostgreSQL that cannot be used as a column name (it isn't reserved in MySQL however, and would work in MySQL). Because "order" is a reserved word, we simply but a "t" on the front. ("t" being an abbreviation for "taxonomy", which is the system of classification we are dealing with.)

17

DATABASE SERVICES

Inserting Data into the Tables

Once the tables have been created, we will, of course, want to put some data into them. Manual insertion of data is done with the INSERT statement. The INSERT statement uses the following syntax:

```
INSERT INTO table_name VALUES('value1', 'value2', 'value3', ...);
```

The preceding statement will insert *value1, value2,* and so on into the table *table_name.* The values inserted will constitute one row, or record, in the database. Unless specified otherwise, values will be inserted in the order in which the columns are listed in the database table. If, for whatever reason, you want to insert values in a different order (or if you only want to insert a few values and they aren't in sequential order), you can specify which columns you want the data to go in using the following syntax:

```
INSERT INTO table_name (column1,column4) VALUES('value1', 'value2');
```

You can also fill multiple rows with a single INSERT statement using a syntax such as the following:

```
INSERT INTO table_name VALUES('value1', 'value2'),('value3', 'value4');
```

In the previous example, *value1* and *value2* will be inserted into the first row, and *value3* and *value4* will be inserted into the second row.

The following example shows how we would insert the African lion entry into our database:

```
INSERT INTO serengeti_mammal VALUES('African Lion', 'Carnivora', 'Felidae',
➡ 'Panthera', 'leo', NULL);
```

MySQL requires the NULL value for the last column (subspecies) if you do not want to include a subspecies, PostgreSQL will let you get away with just omitting the last column. Of course, if you had columns in the middle that were NULL, you would need to explicitly state NULL in the INSERT statement.

Normally, the INSERT statements would be coded into a front end program so that users adding data to the database wouldn't have to worry about the SQL statements involved.

Of course, if you have a lot of data to enter that is already stored in a file (a spreadsheet for example), manually adding each entry in this fashion would get very tedious. Fortunately, both MySQL and PostgreSQL have ways to import data from a text file. However, the method for doing this is different for each database, so it will be covered later on when we discuss each database specifically.

Retrieving Data from the Database

Of course, the main reason for storing data in a database is so that you can later look up, sort, and generate reports on that data. Basic data retrieval is done with the SELECT statement. The syntax of the SELECT statement looks like this:

```
SELECT column(s) FROM table_name WHERE search_criteria;
```

The first two parts of the statement are required. The WHERE portion of the statement is optional. If it is omitted, all rows in the table *table_name* will be returned.

columns(s) indicates the name of the columns that you want to see. If you want to see multiple columns, you can list them separated by commas. If you want to see all columns, you can also use the wildcard * to show all the columns that match the search criteria. For example, the following statement would display all columns of all records in the serengeti_mammal table:

```
SELECT * FROM serengeti_mammal;
```

If we only wanted to see the common names of all the animals in our database, we could use a statement such as the following:

```
SELECT common_name FROM serengeti_mammal;
```

To select the genus and species of an animal, we could use the following:

```
SELECT genus,species FROM serengeti_mammal;
```

However, this won't produce output in the format we prefer. When stating the scientific name of an animal, the genus and species are always listed together. They make up the full species name. Both MySQL and PostgreSQL provide string concatenation functions to handle problems such as this. However, the syntax is different in the two systems.

In MySQL, you can use the CONCAT function to combine the columns genus, and species into one column. The following statement is an example:

```
SELECT CONCAT(genus," ",species) AS Scientific_Name FROM serengeti_mammal;
```

This will list both the genus and species under one column that has the label Scientific_Name. The blank quoted space between genus and species inserts a space between the genus and species names. Without it, the two would be run together, and this isn't what we want.

In PostgreSQL, the string concatenation function is simply a double pipe (||). The following command is the PostgreSQL equivalent of the command given previously:

```
SELECT (genus||' '||species) AS Scientific_Name FROM serengeti_mammal;
```

Note that the parenthesis are optional, but they make the statement easier to read. Once again, the single quotes in the middle (note the space between the quotes) is used to insert a space between the genus name and species name. Without them, the two values would be run together as one word, and that isn't what we want.

Of course, more often then not, you won't want a list of every single row in the database. Rather, you will only want to find rows that match certain characteristics. For this, we add the WHERE statement to the SELECT statement. For example, suppose that we want to find all the animals in our table that are carnivores. We could use a statement like the following:

```
SELECT * FROM serengeti_mammal WHERE torder="Carnivora";
```

Using the table from Figure 17.2, we can see that this query would return the rows for the African lion, the meercat, the hyena, and the cheetah. This is a very simple query, and SQL is capable of handling queries that are much more complex than this. Complex queries can be written using logical AND and logical OR statements. For example, suppose we want to refine our query so that it lists only those carnivores that don't belong to the family "Hyaenidae". We can use a query like the following:

```
SELECT * FROM serengeti_mammal WHERE torder="Carnivora" AND family!="Hyaenidae";
```

As you might or might not know, in computer programming, != means "is not equal to." So once again, looking at our table from Figure 17.2, we can see that this query will return the rows for the African lion, the meercat, and the cheetah, but it won't return the row for the hyena because the hyena belongs to the family Hyaenidae.

So what if we want to list all the carnivores and all the artiodactyls except for those animals that belong to the family "Hyaenidae" or the family "Hippopotamidae"? This time, we combine logical AND and logical OR statements:

```
SELECT * FROM serengeti_mammal WHERE torder="Carnivora" OR
➥torder="Artiodactyla" AND family!="Hyaenidae" AND family!="Hippopotamidae";
```

This query would return entries for the African lion, the meercat, the cheetah, the reticulated giraffe, and Thompson's gazelle. However, it wouldn't return entries for the hyena or the hippopotamus.

> **Tip**
>
> One of the most common errors among new database programmers is confusing logical AND and logical OR. For example, in every day speech, we might say "Find me all records with genus Panthera and Acinonyx." At first glance, you might think that if you fed this statement to the database in SQL format, it would return the rows for the African lion and the cheetah. In fact however, it would return no rows at all. This is because the database interprets the statement as "Find all rows in which the animal belongs to both the genus Panthera and the genus Acinonyx." It is, of course, impossible for an animal to belong to more than one genus, so this statement would never return any rows no matter how many animals we had stored in our table. The correct way to form this statement is with an OR statement instead of an AND statement.

Of course, SQL is capable of far more than what we have demonstrated here. But as mentioned before, this section wasn't intended to teach you all there is to know about SQL programming, but rather to teach you the basics so that you will be a more effective database administrator. The first step is deciding which database will serve your needs best.

Choosing a Database

Many different databases are available for Red Hat that range in cost from free to hundreds of thousands of dollars. The expensive commercial databases are beyond the scope of this book. Instead, we will focus on two freely available ones—MySQL and PostgreSQL. Both of these are high quality SQL databases that are available free. But, just because they are free doesn't mean that they lack power. Both of these databases (and PostgreSQL in particular) can handle very complex projects. They are being used in commercial organizations, government agencies (NASA uses MySQL), research institutions (we use PostgreSQL at the Lion Research Center), and educational institutions. The next section compares both of these databases and helps you make the decision about which one is right for your project.

MySQL Versus PostgreSQL

Both of these databases are quite capable, and either one could probably serve your needs. However, there are certain features which might be present in one database and not in the other that will allow it to serve your needs better or make developing database applications easier. (You won't have to resort to client-side programming tricks to make up for the lack of features in your database.) The following sections look at some of the key features and discuss how those features are implemented in each database.

Speed

Until recently, this category was quite simple. If the speed of performing queries was paramount to your application, you used MySQL. MySQL has a reputation for being an extremely fast database. PostgreSQL on the other hand, was quite slow by comparison. However, when the PostgreSQL folks released version 7.1, the benchmarks surprised a lot of people. Not only had PostgreSQL caught up to MySQL in speed, but it had actually surpassed it. These days, PostgreSQL seems to be slightly faster than MySQL. (And in very busy environments, it can be significantly faster. We will see why in the next section.) However, the fact that PostgreSQL has surpassed MySQL in speed does not mean that MySQL is now considered slow. MySQL is still extremely fast when compared to many other databases.

Data Locking

In order to prevent data corruption, the database will put a lock on data while it is being accessed. As long as the lock is on, no other process can access the data until the first process has released the lock. This means that any other processes trying to access the data will have to wait until the current process completes. The next process in line will then lock the data, until it is finished, and the remaining processes will have to wait for their turn, and so on. Of course, operations on the database generally complete quite quickly, so in environments with a small number of users simultaneously accessing the database, the locks are usually of such short duration that they don't cause any significant delays. However, in environments in which a lot of people are accessing the database simultaneously, locking can begin to create performance problems as different people wait their turn to access the database. There are some fundamental differences in the ways that MySQL and PostgreSQL lock data that we need to consider.

Table Versus Row Level Locking

MySQL locks data at the table level. This means that when someone accesses a row of data in the table, the entire table is locked so that no one else can access it. If your table has 500,000 rows (or records if you prefer) in it, all 500,000 rows are locked any time a row is accessed. Once again, in environments with a relatively small number of simultaneous users, this doesn't cause serious performance problems because most operations complete so quickly that the lock time is extremely short. However in environments in which a lot of people are accessing the data simultaneously, MySQL's table level locking can be a significant performance bottleneck.

PostgreSQL, on the other hand, locks data at the row level. In PostgreSQL, only the row that is currently being accessed is locked. The rest of the table can be accessed by other users. This row level locking significantly reduces the performance impact of locking in environments with a high number of simultaneous users. Because of this, as a general rule, PostgreSQL is better suited for high load environments than MySQL.

ACID Compliance

Another way in which MySQL and PostgreSQL differ is in the amount of protection they provide for keeping your data from becoming corrupted. The acronym ACID is commonly used to describe several aspects of data protection. They are *Atomicity*, *Consistency*, *Isolation*, and *Durability*. We will look at each of these traits in the following sections.

Atomicity

This term is derived from the word *atom*, which as you might know, means "indivisible." In the database world, this means that several database operations will be treated as an atomic unit, often called a *transaction*. In a transaction, either all the operations in the unit are carried out, or none of them are carried out. In other words, if any operation in the atomic unit fails, the entire atomic unit will be canceled. Why is this important? Because for example, sometimes, operations involve deleting a record, and then replacing it with an updated one. What happens if you have a power failure or server crash after the original record has been deleted but before the updated one has been added? You would end up losing that record. Atomic transactions ensure that this cannot happen because the original record wouldn't be deleted if the update portion of the atomic unit failed.

Consistency

As its name suggests, consistency ensures that no transaction can cause the database to be left in an inconsistent state. Consistency rules can vary between different databases, and can be determined by the database programmer. For example, suppose we are designing a database that will keep track of wild animals that we are tracking. Consistency rules we might want to implement could include the following:

- No two animals should be allowed to be assigned the same ID number.
- The database shouldn't allow the deletion of physiological data on any animal that has open tracking information in other tables because this would leave orphaned information in the tables. If the physiological information on an animal is deleted, the related entries in the tracking tables should also be deleted.

Inconsistent states can be caused by database client crashes, network failures, and any number of other problems. Consistency ensures that any transaction or partially completed transaction that would cause the database to be left in an inconsistent state will be *rolled back*, or undone.

Isolation

Isolation ensures that multiple transactions operating on the same data are completely isolated from each other. This prevents data corruption if two different users try to write to the same record at the same time. The way isolation is handled can generally be configured by the database programmer. One way that isolation can be handled is through locking as we discussed previously.

Durability

Durability ensures that once a transaction has been committed to the database, it cannot be lost in the event of a system crash, network failure, and so on. This is usually accomplished through transaction logs. This way, for example, if the server crashes, the database can examine the logs when it comes back up and commit any transactions that were not yet complete into the database.

PostgreSQL is ACID compliant, whereas MySQL isn't. MySQL doesn't support transactions, which means that you are more likely to lose data in MySQL if you have a server crash or network failure than you are in PostgreSQL. Because of this, PostgreSQL is probably better suited for environments with a lot of users or a large amount of information being added and changed on a regular basis.

SQL Features and Other Enhanced Features

Another consideration when choosing a database is the SQL features and other features that it supports. This is another area in which PostgreSQL has quite a few more features than MySQL. Some of these features are discussed next.

Subqueries

Subqueries allow you to combine several operations into one atomic unit, as well as allowing those operations to access each others data. This can allow you to perform some extremely complex operations on your database. In addition, it eliminates the potential problem of data changing between two operations as a result of another user performing some operation on the same set of data. PostgreSQL has support for subqueries. MySQL doesn't, although some workarounds are available in MySQL to simulate subqueries.

Procedural Languages and Triggers

A *procedural language* is an external programming language that can be used to write functions and procedures. This allows you to do things that aren't supported by simple SQL. A *trigger* allows you to define an event that will invoke the external function or procedure that you have written. A trigger for example, can be used to throw an exception if an INSERT statement is given that contains an unexpected or out of range value for a column. For example, in our animal tracking database, we could use a trigger to throw an exception if a user entered coordinate data that didn't make sense. PostgreSQL has a procedural language called PL/pgSQL. Although MySQL has support for a limited number of built in procedures and triggers, it doesn't have any procedural language. This means that you cannot create custom procedures or triggers in MySQL, although the same effects can often be achieved through creative client side programming.

At this point, you might be getting the impression that there is no reason to even consider using MySQL because PostgreSQL has so many more features. Actually, there is one primary reason to consider MySQL—the number of pre-made applications available for it. For example, if you want to create an online discussion forum, a program called Phorum is available that uses MySQL. This saves you the work of having to do all the SQL programming yourself. If you plan to start from scratch, however, you are probably better off going with PostgreSQL.

After you have decided which database you want to use, you will need to install and configure it. Because the configuration procedures are different for MySQL and PostgreSQL, they will be covered separately in the following sections.

> **Note**
>
> Although many of the previously mentioned features aren't available in the standard version of MySQL, they are available in a product called MySQL-Max. At the time of this writing, however, MySQL-Max is considered beta quality because it hasn't been extensively tested. For this reason, MySQL-Max isn't suitable for production environments. It's possible that MySQL-Max will be production quality by the time this book is published. In this case, many of the disadvantages of MySQL talked about previously will be reduced or eliminated.

Installing and Configuring MySQL

The latest version of MySQL is available from the Web site www.mysql.com. It is available in both source versions and in a binary RPM format for Red Hat. This section only covers installing the binary RPM. If, for whatever reason, you want to install from source code, see the MySQL documentation for instructions on how to do this.

If you install from the RPM, the necessary user and groups for MySQL will be created automatically. Otherwise, you will want to create a user and group for MySQL to run as. The group and the user should both be named mysql. These accounts should be configured so that they cannot be logged into because their only purpose is to run the MySQL server daemon. See Chapter 9, "Managing Users," for more information on how to create accounts.

> **Caution**
>
> The reason you create these accounts is so that MySQL can run as a non-privileged user. Do not run MySQL as the root user. There is no reason to do so, and running MySQL as root opens up a major security hole.

There are two binaries you will want to download. The first one is for the MySQL server, and the second one is for the MySQL command line client. (If you want the GUI client, you can grab that as well. The GUI client is discussed later on in this chapter.)

Once you've downloaded the RPM files, you can install them with the rpm -i command. This will install the MySQL binaries and libraries into their standard locations.

By default, the RPM file places the data directory in /var/lib/mysql, and also installs a startup script in /etc/re.d/init.d to automatically start the server at each system boot.

Initializing the Data Directory

Once you have MySQL installed, you need to initialize the grant tables. This is done with the mysql_install_db command. It should be issued from the scripts directory of the same directory in which MySQL was installed. Unless you changed the defaults, this directory will be /usr/local/mysql. If you installed MySQL from the CD included with the book, it will be /usr/bin. This command will initialize the grant tables and create a MySQL root user.

> **Caution**
>
> The MySQL data directory needs to be owned by the user that MySQL will run as. In addition, only this user should have any permissions on this directory. (In other words, the permissions should be 700.). Setting up the data directory any other way will create a security hole.

> **Caution**
>
> By default, the MySQL root user is created with no password. This will be one of the first things that you will want to change because the MySQL root user has access to all aspects of the database. The following section explains how to change the password of the user.

Setting a Password for the MySQL Root User

Hopefully, that last caution box got your attention. Here is how to set a password for the root MySQL user.

First, connect to the MySQL server as the root MySQL user. This can be done with the command `mysql -u root`. This will connect you to the MySQL client (which will be discussed in more detail later in the chapter). Once you have the MySQL command prompt, issue a command like the following to set a password for the root user:

```
mysql> SET PASSWORD FOR root = PASSWORD("secretword");
```

secretword should be replaced by whatever you want the password for the root user to be. You can use this same command with other usernames to set or change passwords for other database users.

Once you have entered a password, you can exit the MySQL client by typing **exit** at the command prompt.

> **Caution**
>
> Do not confuse the root MySQL user with the Red Hat system administration account that is also called root. The two accounts aren't the same.

Creating a Database

Creating a database in MySQL is done with the CREATE DATABASE statement. To create a database, connect to the server by typing `mysql -u root -p` and pressing Enter. This will connect you to the database as the MySQL root user as well as prompt you for a password. After you enter the password, you will be placed at the MySQL command prompt. Then use the CREATE DATABASE command. For example, the following command will create a database called `sampledata`:

```
CREATE DATABASE sampledata;
```

Granting and Revoking Privileges from Users

You will also probably want to grant yourself some privileges on a database, and eventually grant privileges to other users. To add a user account, connect to the database by typing **`mysql -u root -p`** and pressing Enter. This will connect you as the root user and prompt you for a password. (You did set a password for the root user as instructed in the last section, right?). Once you have entered the root password, you will be placed at the MySQL command prompt.

To grant privileges to a user, use the GRANT statement. The GRANT statement takes the following syntax:

```
grant what_to_grant ON where_to_grant TO user_name IDENTIFIED BY 'password';
```

The first option is what privileges to grant. A list of privileges is beyond the scope of this chapter. See the MySQL documentation or a book on MySQL for more information. The second option is what resources the privileges should be granted on. The third option is the username that you want to grant the Privileges to. Finally, the forth option is a password that should be assigned to this user. If this is an existing user who already has a password and you are modifying permissions, you can omit the IDENTIFIED BY portion of the statement.

> **Caution**
>
> MySQL will allow you to omit the IDENTIFIED BY option, in which case the user won't be given a password. This is security hole, so never omit the IDENTIFIED BY portion of the GRANT statement.

For example, to grant all privileges on a database named `sampledata` to a user named `foobar`, we could use the following command:

```
GRANT ALL ON sampledata.* TO foobar IDENTIFIED BY 'secretword';
```

The user `foobar` can now connect to the database `sampledata` using the password `secretword`, and has all privileges on the database, including the ability to create and destroy tables.

Later on, if we need to revoke privileges from `foobar`, we can use the REVOKE statement. For example, the following statement revokes all privileges from the user `foobar`.

```
REVOKE ALL ON sampledata FROM foobar;
```

Of course, advanced database administration, privileges, and security are very complex topics that are beyond the scope of this book. For more information on administering MySQL, check out a good book on MySQL such as *MySQL* from New Riders Publishing.

Installing and Configuring PostgreSQL

The latest PostgreSQL binaries and source are available at `http://www.postgresql.org`. The PostgreSQL RPMs are distributed as several files. At a minimum, you will probably want the `postgresql`, `postgresql-server`, and `postgresql-libs` RPMs. See the `README.rpm-dist` file in the FTP directory to determine whether you need any other packages.

If you are installing from the Red Hat RPM files, the necessary user account will be created automatically for you. Otherwise, you will want to create a user called `postgres` during the installation. This user shouldn't have login privileges because only root will `su` to this user, and no one will ever log in as the user directly. See Chapter 9 for more information on how to add users to your Red Hat system. Once you have added the user, you can install each of the PostgreSQL RPMs that you downloaded using the standard `rpm -i` command for a default install.

Initializing the Data Directory

Once the RPMs have been installed, you will need to initialize the data directory. To do so, you must first create the data directory. In this example, the data directory will be `/usr/local/pgsql/data`. You will need to be the root user to create these directories. Once you have created the directory, change the ownership of the

/usr/local/pgsql/data directory so that it is owned by the user postgres. Now su to the user postgres, and issue the following command:

```
initdb -D /usr/local/pgsql/data
```

This will initialize the database and also set the permissions on the data directory to their correct values.

> **Caution**
>
> The initdb program will set the permissions on the data directory to 700. You should not change these permissions to anything else because this will create a security hole.

You can then start the postmaster program with the following command (make sure that you are still the user postgres):

```
postmaster -D /usr/local/pgsql/data
```

If you decided to use a directory other then /usr/local/pgsql/data as the data directory, you should replace the directory in the postmaster command line with whatever directory you used.

> **Tip**
>
> By default, Red Hat will make the PostgreSQL data directory /var/lib/pgsql/data. This isn't a very good place to store the data however because most people will not have the necessary space in the /var partition for any kind of serious data storage. Note that if you do change the data directory to something else (such as /usr/local/pgsql/data as in our examples), you will need to edit the PostgreSQL startup file located in /etc/rc.d/init.d to reflect the change.

Creating a Database

Creating a database in PostgreSQL is very straightforward. As a user sho has permissions to create databasesin PostgresSQL, simply issue the following command from the shell prompt (not the PSQL client prompt, but a normal Red Hat shell prompt):

```
createdb database
```

where *database* is the name of the database that you want to create.

The `createdb` program is actually a wrapper that makes it easier to create databases without having to log in to to `psql`. However, you can also create databases from within `psql` with the `CREATE DATABASE` statement. For example,

```
CREATE DATABASE database;
```

You will need to create at least one database before you will be able to start the pgsql client program. This database should be created while logged in as the user `postgres`. To log in as this user, you will need to `su` to root, and then `su` to the user `postgres`. To connect to the new database, start the `psql` client program with the name of the new database as a command line argument. For example,

```
psql sampledata
```

If you don't specify the name of a database when invoking `psql`, it will attempt to connect to a database with the same name as the user that you invoke `psql` as.

Setting a Password for the `postgres` User

By default, the `postgres` user will not have a password. This is insecure because it allows anyone to connect as the `postgres` user. To set a password for the `postgres` user, use the `ALTER USER` command from within the `psql` client. For example,

```
ALTER USER postgres WITH password 'secretword';
```

Creating Database Users

To create a database user, `su` to the user `postgres` from the Red Hat root account; you can then start the PostgreSQL command line client by typing **psql**. (You can also invoke `psql with the` -U option and specify the `postgres` user as the user to connect with). You can now use the `CREATE USER` command to create a new user. Here is an example:

```
CREATE USER foobar WITH PASSWORD 'secretword';
```

> **Caution**
>
> PostgreSQL allows you to eliminate the `WITH PASSWORD` portion of the statement. However, doing so causes the user to be created with no password. This is a security hole, so the `WITH PASSWORD` option should always be used when creating users.

If you want the new user to have permissions to create databases, you should create the new user with the CREATEDB option. For example,

```
CREATE USER foobar WITH PASSWORD 'secretword' CREATEDB;
```

Note that this will also give the user foobar the permission to destroy any databases that he creates. However, foobar won't be able to destroy databases created by other users.

> **Tip**
>
> When you are finished working in the psql command line client, type \q to get out of it and return to the Red Hat shell prompt.

Granting and Revoking Privileges

As in MySQL, granting and revoking privileges in PostgreSQL is done with the GRANT and REVOKE statements. The syntax is the same except that PostgreSQL doesn't use the INDENTIFIED BY portion of the statement because with PostgreSQL, passwords are assigned when you create the user with the CREATE USER statement discussed previously. Here is the syntax of the GRANT statement:

```
GRANT what_to_grant ON where_to_grant TO user_name;
```

For example, the following command will grant all privileges to the user foobar on the database sampledata:

```
GRANT ALL ON sampledata TO foobar;
```

To revoke privileges, use the REVOKE statement. For example,

```
REVOKE ALL ON sampledata FROM foobar;
```

This command will remove all privileges from user foobar on the database sampledata.

Advanced administration and user configuration are complex topics. This section cannot begin to cover all the aspects of PostgreSQL administration or of privileges and users. For more information on administering PostgreSQL, see the PostgreSQL documentation, or consult a book on PostgreSQL such as *PostgreSQL* from Sams Publishing.

Database Clients

Both MySQL and PostgreSQL use a client/server type system of accessing the database. In the database world, the server is sometimes called the *back end,* and the client is sometimes called the *front end.* (Actually, the part that the user interacts with is called the front end. Sometimes this is the same as the client, but other times it isn't. You will see how this works later on in this section.)

Basically, you never talk directly to the database server, even if it happens to be located on the same machine that you are using. All requests to the database server are handled by a database client, which might or might not be running on the same machine as the database server. You are probably somewhat familiar with the term *client/server*, but it can sometimes be a source of confusion for new database administrators. In the simplest terms, the database server handles the requests that come into the database, and the database client handles getting the requests to the server, as well as getting the output from the server to the user. The following sections give some examples of different types of clients, and where the client is running.

Telnet or SSH Access to the Database

There are two possible scenarios here. In the first, the user logs directly in to the database server through Telnet or SSH, and then starts a program on the server to access the database. In this case, the database client is running on the database server itself. Figure 17.4 shows an example.

FIGURE 17.4

The user logs in to the database server located on host simba from the workstation (host cheetah). The database client is running on simba.

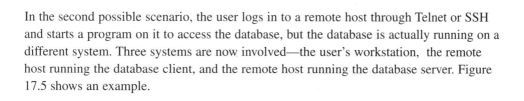

In the second possible scenario, the user logs in to a remote host through Telnet or SSH and starts a program on it to access the database, but the database is actually running on a different system. Three systems are now involved—the user's workstation, the remote host running the database client, and the remote host running the database server. Figure 17.5 shows an example.

FIGURE 17.5

The user logs into the remote host leopard from the workstation (host cheetah) and starts a database client on leopard. The client on leopard then connects to the database server running on host simba. The database client is running on leopard.

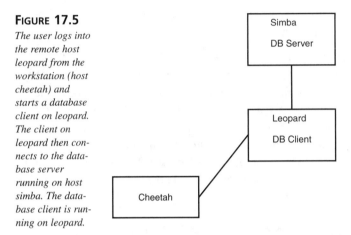

The important thing to note in Figure 17.5 is the middleman system leopard. Although the client is no longer running on the database server itself, it isn't running on the user's local workstation either.

Local GUI Client Access to the Database

In this scenario, a user logs in to the database server using a graphical client (which could be running on Windows, Macintosh, or a UNIX workstation). The graphical client then connects to the database server. In this case, the client is running on the user's workstation. Figure 17.6 shows an example.

FIGURE 17.6

The user starts a GUI database program on his workstation (hostname cheetah). This program, which is the database client, then connects to the database server running on the host lion.

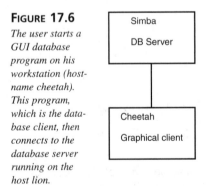

Web Access to Database

We will look at two examples of Web access to the database server. In the first example, a user accesses the database through a form located on the World Wide Web. At first glance, it might appear that the client is running on the user's workstation. In fact though, it isn't. It is actually running on the Web server. The Web browser on the user's workstation simply provides a way for the user to enter the data that he wants to send to the database, and also a way for the results sent from the database to be displayed to the user. The software that actually handles sending the request to the database is running on the Web server in the form of a CGI script, Java servlet, or embedded scripting such as PHP or JSP. This is an example in which the client and the front end aren't the same thing. The front end is the form displayed in the user's Web browser. In cases such as this, the client is sometimes referred to as *middlewear*. Figure 17.7 shows an example.

FIGURE 17.7

The user accesses the database through the World Wide Web. The front end is the user's Web browser, the client is running on leopard, and the server is running on lion.

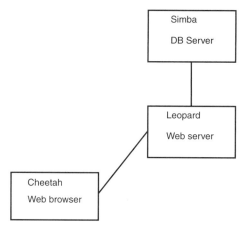

In another possible Web access scenario, it could be said that the client is a two-piece application in which part of it is running on the user's workstation, and the other part is running on the Web server. For example, the database programmer can use JavaScript in the Web form to make sure that the user has entered a valid query. In this case, the user's query is partially processed on his own workstation, and partially on the Web server. (Error checking is done on the user's own workstation. This helps reduce the load on the server, and also helps reduce network traffic because the query is checked for errors before being sent across the network to the server.)

Command Line Clients

Both MySQL and PostgreSQL come with a command line client. The command line client is a very primitive way of interfacing with the database, and generally won't be used by end users. However, the command line client is handy because it allows you to test new queries and such interactively without having to write front end program first. Because the various options and such available for the two clients varies, we will discuss them separately.

The MySQL Command Line Client

The MySQL command line client is simply called `mysql`. It is invoked with the following syntax:

```
mysql [options] [database]
```

Some of the available options are discussed in Table 17.1. `database` is optional, and if given, should be the name of the database that you want to connect to.

TABLE 17.1   Command Line Options to Use When Invoking `mysql`

Option	Action
-h *hostname*	Connects to the remote host *hostname* (if the database server isn't located on the local system).
-u *username*	Connects to the database as the user *username*.
-p	Prompts for a password. This option is required if the user you are connecting as needs a password to access the database. Note that this is a lowercase p.
-P *n*	Where *n* is the number of the port that the client should connect to. Note that this is an uppercase P.
-?	Displays a help message.

More options are available than those listed here, but these are the most common options. See the man page for `mysql` for more information on the available options.

> **Caution**
>
> Although `mysql` will allow you to specify the password on the command line after the -p option, and thus allow you to avoid having to type the password at the prompt, you should never invoke the client this way. Doing so will cause your password to display in the process list, which can be accessed by any user on the system. This is a major security hole, so never give your password on the `mysql` command line.

The PostgreSQL Command Line Client

The PostgreSQL command line client is invoked with the command psql. Like mysql, it can be invoked with the name of a database on the command line that should be made active. Also, like mysql, it can take several options. These options are listed in Table 17.2.

TABLE 17.2 Command Line Options to Use When Invoking psql

Option	Action
-h *hostname*	Connects to the remote host *hostname* (if the database server isn't located on the local system).
-p *n*	Where *n* is the number of the port that the client should connect to. Note that this is a lowercase p.
-U *username*	Connects to the database as the user *username*.
-W	Prompts for a password after connecting to the database. In PostgreSQL 7 and later, password prompting will be automatic if the server requests a password after a connection has been established.
-?	Displays a help message.

Several more options are available than are listed here. Please see the man page for psql for details on all the available options.

Graphical Clients

If you'd rather interact with the database using a graphical database client rather than the command line clients discussed in the previous section, there are a few options available.

MySQL has an official graphical client available called MySQLGUI. It is available in both source and binary formats from the MySQL Web site at http://www.mysql.com.

Web based administration interfaces are also available for MySQL and PostgreSQL. phpMyAdmin and phpPgAdmin are two such products. Both of these products are based around the PHP embedded scripting language and as such will require you to have PHP installed. Of course, you will also need to have a Web server installed.

Reference

The following are references for the databases mentioned in this chapter.

www.mysql.com—This is the official Web site of the MySQL database server. Here you will be able to find the latest versions as well as up-to-date information and online documentation for MySQL. You can also purchase support contracts here. You might want to look into this if you will be using MySQL in a corporate setting. (Many corporations balk at the idea of using software for which the company has no support contract in place.)

www.postgresql.org—The official Web site of the PostgreSQL database server. You will be asked to select a mirror once you arrive at this site. After you have selected a mirror, you will be taken to the main site. From here, you can find information on the latest versions of PostgreSQL, as well as read the online documentation.

www.pgsql.com—This is a commercial company that provides fee based support contracts for the PostgreSQL database.

File Transfer Protocol

CHAPTER 18

File Transfer Protocol (FTP) is the primary method used to transfer files over a network from computer to computer. Around since the TCP/IP protocol was developed, FTP is still heavily used today, although not in the original text-based interface. As computers have evolved, so has FTP, going from the original text-based interface to the more popular *graphical user interface (GUI)*.

There are two ways to use FTP: as a client accessing other servers to download files or as a server providing access to files for download. Just about every computer platform available has software written to allow that machine to act as a FTP server. Red Hat Linux provides the average user the ability to do this without paying hefty licensing fees, whether for personal or public usage.

FTP Servers

There are two types of FTP servers: anonymous and standard. A standard FTP server requires that an account name and password be given to access the server. Anonymous servers allow anyone to connect to the server to retrieve files. Anonymous servers provide the most flexibility for anyone to retrieve files; however they can also present a security risk.

It is vital to ensure that an anonymous FTP server is properly installed and configured to retain a relatively secure environment. Generally, sites that host anonymous FTP servers place them outside of the firewall on a dedicated machine. Typically, this machine only contains the FTP server and doesn't contain any data that cannot be restored quickly. This prevents malicious users from obtaining critical or sensitive data should the security of the server be compromised.

Red Hat Linux includes the wu-ftp server developed by the University of Washington under the General Public License (GPL). This license states that anyone is free to use the software, whether for personal or business purposes. Although there are several FTP servers available for Linux, wu-ftp is what comes bundled with Red Hat. This FTP server will be covered in this chapter.

Although wu-ftp is a respectable FTP server, it isn't the optimal FTP server to use if a site needs to provide access to a high number of concurrent users. NcFTPd, www.ncftp.com, operates independently of xinetd, providing its own optimized daemon. Additionally, NCFTPd has the ability to cache directory listings of the FTP server in memory, thereby increasing the speed at which users can obtain a list of available files and directories. Although NcFTPd has many advantages over wu-ftpd, NcFTPd isn't GPL licensed software. Because it has been optimized for speed and business usage, NcFTPd isn't free software. The license fee is $199 for 50 or more concurrent users and

$99 for up to 50 concurrent users. Because of this licensing, Red Hat doesn't package the NcFTPd with its distribution of Linux.

> **Note**
>
> Do not confuse nc-ftp with ncftpd. The package ncftp-3.0.3-6.i386.rpm on the CD-ROM is the client software, a replacement for ftp-0.17-12. Ncftpd is the FTP server, which can be downloaded from `www.ncftpd.com`.

Installing the Software

As part of the Workstation installation, the client software for FTP is already installed. This can be verified by the following query:

```
[root@pheniox RPMS]$ rpm -qa|grep ftp
ftp-0.17-12
gftp-2.0.8-2
anonftp-4.0-7
```

The package ftp-0.17-12 provides the ftp binary `/usr/bin/pftp` symbolically linked to `/usr/bin/ftp` as well as the corresponding man pages.

> **Note**
>
> Always check the Red Hat Errata page, `http://www.redhat.com/support/errata/`, for up-to-date security and bug fixes for all RPM packages.

> **Note**
>
> The Computer Emergency Response Team (`http://www.cert.org`) provides security advisories about current attacks and vulnerabilities on multiple platforms. Checking this site regularly for updates is a must for any site administrator.

Installation of the server, or daemon in the UNIX/Linux world, requires the user to have selected the Server or Custom installation during the installation of Red Hat Linux. To ensure that FTP is installed, the *Red Hat Package Manager (RPM)* database can provide the necessary information:

18

FILE TRANSFER PROTOCOL

```
[tdc@pheniox tdc]$ rpm -qa|grep ftp
wu-ftpd-2.6.1-18
ftp-0.17-12
anonftp-4.0-7
```

If these packages aren't installed, install them from the installation CD as root with the rpm -Uhv command:

```
[root@pheniox RPMS]# rpm -Uhv anonftp-4.0-7.i386.rpm wu-ftpd-2.6.1-18.i386.rpm
Preparing...              ######################################### [100%]
   1:wu-ftpd             ######################################### [ 50%]
   2:anonftp             ######################################### [100%]
```

This will create the /var/ftp directory and place necessary libraries and binaries in this directory structure used by the FTP server.

The FTP User

During the rpm installation, an FTP user was added to the /etc/passwd file:

```
ftp:x:14:50:FTP User:/var/ftp:/sbin/nologin
```

> **Note**
>
> The FTP user as is discussed here only applies to anonymous FTP configurations. If the anonftp package isn't installed, an entry for the FTP user will be created, but a default shell won't be set, nor will the /var/ftp directory be created.

This entry follows the standard /etc/passwd entry—username, password, user id, group id, comment field, home directory, and shell—separated by colons. From this entry, it is possible to determine that the server has the shadow-utils package installed, hence the x in the password field. It is important that this be done during the installation of Red Hat Linux to ensure the maximum amount of security for the accounts on the server.

The FTP server software uses this account to assign permissions to users connecting to the server. Notice that the default shell is /sbin/nologin versus /bin/bash or some other standard, interactive shell. /sbin/nologin isn't a shell, but a program usually assigned to an account that has been locked. As root inspection of the /etc/shadow file, as seen in Listing 18.1, shows, it isn't possible to log into this account, denoted by the * as the password.

LISTING 18.1 Shadow Passwords File

```
[root@pheniox root]# cat /etc/shadow
root:$1$FaMr0FTe$vEn.rPK1mj1sP7SoRlTU./:11560:0:99999:7:::
bin:*:11560:0:99999:7:::
daemon:*:11560:0:99999:7:::
adm:*:11560:0:99999:7:::
lp:*:11560:0:99999:7:::
sync:*:11560:0:99999:7:::
shutdown:*:11560:0:99999:7:::
halt:*:11560:0:99999:7:::
mail:*:11560:0:99999:7:::
news:*:11560:0:99999:7:::
uucp:*:11560:0:99999:7:::
operator:*:11560:0:99999:7:::
games:*:11560:0:99999:7:::
gopher:*:11560:0:99999:7:::
ftp:*:11560:0:99999:7:::
nobody:*:11560:0:99999:7:::
nscd:!!:11560:0:99999:7:::
mailnull:!!:11560:0:99999:7:::
rpm:!!:11560:0:99999:7:::
ident:!!:11560:0:99999:7:::
rpc:!!:11560:0:99999:7:::
rpcuser:!!:11560:0:99999:7:::
xfs:!!:11560:0:99999:7:::
gdm:!!:11560:0:99999:7:::
pcap:!!:11560:0:99999:7:::
bb:$1$x5KpPxOY$FR8TUf54jdirIpozu.qJL.:11560:0:99999:7:::
tdc:$1$tRz88qIl$QzVVw2AWN2Q0goLrbKDSv/:11560:0:99999:7:::
test:$1$CyGL4/9k$s5zy07r6RelLAqP5Tli0B1:11563::5:1:10:11572:
oracle:$1$o3CGaAYK$6dXzrwI8oKZ6jXeBWnEH81:11566::99999::::
shaun:$1$4aIy046p$.9ozGClAg1slXBIt1Skhj.:11584::99999::::
```

The shadow file contains additional information not found in the standard /etc/passwd file, such as account expiration, password expiration, whether the account is locked, and the encrypted password. The ! in the password field indicates that the account isn't a standard login account, thus it doesn't have a password.

Although shadow passwords are in use on the system, this doesn't mean that the password is transmitted in a secure manner. Because FTP was written before the necessity of encryption and security, it doesn't provide the mechanics necessary to send the password encrypted. Anyone with enough knowledge and a network sniffer can find the password for the account you connect to on an FTP server because it is sent in plain text. This is another reason why many sites will employ the use of an anonymous FTP server: to prevent normal account passwords from being transmitted over the Internet.

Figure 18.1 shows an ethereal capture of an FTP session displaying the actual password for the anonymous user.

FIGURE **18.1**

Sniffing an FTP session with ethereal.

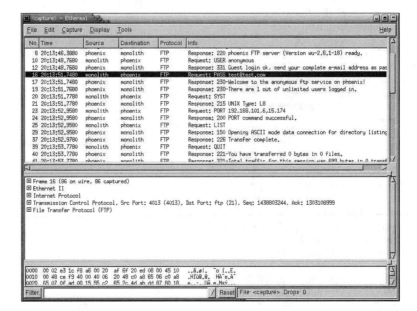

Cleaning Up the Installation

After installation, some cleanup is necessary to ensure that the most secure permissions are assigned to the files the server will use during a session. Execute the following commands as root to do this:

```
cd /var/ftp/bin
rm cpio zcat
cd /var/ftp/etc/
cd /var/ftp/lib/
```

Finally, add the proper locked-down permissions.

```
chmod 111 /var/ftp/bin/* /var/ftp/bin /var/ftp/etc /var/ftp/lib
chmod 444 /var/ftp/etc/*
chmod 555 /var/ftp /var/ftp/lib/* /var/ftp/pub
```

Files that are placed in /var/ftp/pub are for users to get during their FTP sessions. These files should have the read permission only for the FTP user.

```
chmod 444 file_name
```

Additionally, any subdirectories that are created in /var/ftp/pub need to be restricted to read and execute permissions.

chmod 555 subdirectory_name

Once these commands are executed, the result should be as seen in Listing 18.2.

LISTING 18.2   Files and Permissions for Anonymous FTP Server Installation

```
[root@pheniox ftp]# ls -alR /var/ftp/
/var/ftp/:
total 24
dr-xr-xr-x    6 root     root         4096 Aug 30 23:44 .
drwxr-xr-x   20 root     root         4096 Aug 30 23:44 ..
d--x--x--x    2 root     root         4096 Aug 31 02:15 bin
d--x--x--x    2 root     root         4096 Aug 31 02:15 etc
d--x--x--x    2 root     root         4096 Aug 30 23:44 lib
dr-xr-xr-x    2 root     ftp          4096 Aug 31 02:09 pub
/var/ftp/bin:
total 288
d--x--x--x    2 root     root         4096 Aug 31 02:15 .
dr-xr-xr-x    6 root     root         4096 Aug 30 23:44 ..
---x--x--x    1 root     root          313 Aug 30 23:44 bin.md5
---x--x--x    2 root     root        17276 Jun 25 03:14 compress
---x--x--x    4 root     root        51228 Jun 25 09:22 gzip
---x--x--x    2 root     root        45724 Jun 26 11:28 ls
---x--x--x    2 root     root       150812 Jun 25 01:45 tar
/var/ftp/etc:
total 16
d--x--x--x    2 root     root         4096 Aug 31 02:15 .
dr-xr-xr-x    6 root     root         4096 Aug 30 23:44 ..
-r--r--r--    1 root     root           53 Aug  7 09:46 group
-r--r--r--    1 root     root            0 Aug 30 23:44 ld.so.conf
-r--r--r--    1 root     root           79 Aug  7 09:46 passwd
/var/ftp/lib:
total 2440
d--x--x--x    2 root     root         4096 Aug 30 23:44 .
dr-xr-xr-x    6 root     root         4096 Aug 30 23:44 ..
-r-xr-xr-x    2 root     root       475913 Jul 26 17:44 ld-2.2.3.so
lrwxrwxrwx    1 root     root           11 Aug 30 23:44 ld-
linux.so.2  &gt; ld-2.2.3.so
-r-xr-xr-x    2 root     root      1276360 Jul 26 18:10 libc-2.2.3.so
lrwxrwxrwx    1 root     root           13 Aug 30 23:44 libc.so.6
-&gt; libc-2.2.3.so
-r-xr-xr-x    2 root     root       437128 Jul 26 17:44 libnsl-2.2.3.so
lrwxrwxrwx    1 root     root           15 Aug 30 23:44
libnsl.so.1 -&gt; libnsl-2.2.3.so
-r-xr-xr-x    2 root     root       261588 Jul 26 17:44 libnss_files-2.2.3.so
lrwxrwxrwx    1 root     root           21 Aug 30 23:44
libnss_files.so.2 -&gt; libnss_files-2.2.3.so
```

LISTING 18.2 continued

```
-r-xr-xr-x    1 root      root           260 Aug 30 23:44 libs.md5
lrwxrwxrwx    1 root      root            19 Aug 30 23:44
libtermcap.so.2 -&gt; libtermcap.so.2.0.8
-r-xr-xr-x    2 root      root         11832 Jul  9 19:57 libtermcap.so.2.0.8
/var/ftp/pub:
total 8
dr-xr-xr-x    2 root      ftp           4096 Aug 31 02:09 .
dr-xr-xr-x    6 root      root          4096 Aug 30 23:44 .
```

Note

A good reference for locking down FTP can be found at http://www.redhat.com/support/docs/tips/FTP-Setup-Tips/FTP-Setup-Tips.html.

Xinetd Configuration

Xinetd is the Red Hat 7.0 and higher replacement for inetd. Xinetd works similarly to inetd, handling incoming connections for network services. However, in addition to several other improvements, Xinetd allows individual access policies to be applied to different requests. When installing wu-ftp, the rpm package contains an xinetd configuration file, /etc/xinetd.d/wu-ftp, as seen in Listing 18.3. Although the file is included in the rpm package, it still needs to be edited because the default is to disable incoming FTP requests.

LISTING 18.3 Xinetd Configuration File for FTP

```
# default: on
# description: The wu-ftpd FTP server serves FTP connections. It uses \
#    normal, unencrypted usernames and passwords for authentication.
service ftp
{
    socket_type        = stream
    wait            = no
    user            = root
    server          = /usr/sbin/in.ftpd
    server_args        = -l -a
    log_on_success        += DURATION USERID
    log_on_failure        += USERID
    nice            = 10
    disable          = yes
}
```

Using an editor, change the disable line to no. Save the file and exit the editor. Xinetd needs to be restarted because configuration files are only parsed at startup. To restart xinetd as root, issue the command /etc/rc.d/init.d/xinetd restart. This makes a call to the same shell script that is called at system startup and shutdown for any runlevel to start or stop the xinet daemon. Xinetd should report its status as

```
[root@pheniox root]# /etc/rc.d/init.d/xinetd restart
Stopping xinetd:                                        [  OK  ]
Starting xinetd:                                        [  OK  ]
```

Once restarted, the FTP server is accessible to all incoming requests. Because a user can now connect to the FTP server, it should be configured to ensure security and usability.

Configuring the Server

Wu-FTP uses the following four files to control how it operates:

- ftpusers
- ftpaccess
- ftpconversions
- ftphosts

These files are installed in the /etc directory by the RPM package.

18

Caution

When configuring an anonymous FTP server, it is extremely important to ensure that all security precautions are taken to prevent malicious users from gaining privileged level access to the server. Although this chapter provides the necessary configuration to ensure a secure configuration, all machines connected to the Internet are potential targets for malicious attacks. It is important to note that even though the FTP server is secure, the rest of the system is still vulnerable to attacks.

Tip

Whenever editing the FTP server files, it is always a good idea to comment out what is changed instead of deleting or overwriting entries. Follow these comments with a brief description why the change was made. This leaves a nice

continues

audit trail of what was done, by who, when, and why. Thus, when trying to troubleshoot what might be an incorrect configuration, there is a point of reference to a valid entry as well as when something has changed.

Note

It is always a good idea to back up the FTP server configuration files to another machine, should the working copy become corrupt. There might be a need to replicate server configurations across multiple hosts or revert back to an original copy of the defaults at some point in time. By making regular backups before changing a file, the administrator will guarantee that the changes can be undone and a working server restored with minimal down time.

/etc/ftpaccess

The ftpaccess file is where most of the configuration of the server is specified. Each line contains a definition or parameter that is passed to the server to specify how the server is to operate. The directives can be broken down into the following categories, which are discussed in the next several sections.

Tip

Many more options can be specified for the FTP server in the ftpaccess file. The most common commands have been covered here. A full list of configuration options can be found in the man page.

- Access Control
- Information
- Logging
- Permission Control
- Miscellaneous

Access Control

Controlling who and how users can access the FTP server is a critical part of security. The following commands in the ftpaccess file allow the administration to specify which group the user access the server is assigned to.

autogroup <groupname> <class> [<class>]

This command provides more stringent security for the anonymous user. If the anonymous user is a member of a group, he will only be allowed access to files and directories of which he is the owner or group member. The group must be a valid group from /etc/groups or /var/ftp/etc/groups.

class <class> <typelist> <addrglob> [<addrglob>]

This defines a class of users by the address to which the user is connected. There might be multiple members for a class of users, as well as multiple class statements to designate multiple classes. In the case of multiple classes applying to one user, the first class that applies will be applied.

The typelist field is a comma separated list of the keywords anonymous, guest, real. Real defines those users that have a valid entry in the /etc/passwd file. Anonymous applies to the anonymous user, and guest applies to the guest access account, as specified in the guestgroup directive.

The addrglob field is a regular expression that specifics addresses to which the class is to be applied. The (*) entry specifies all hosts.

deny <addrglob> <message_file>

Sometimes it is necessary to block access to the server to entire hosts. deny will always deny access to hosts that match a given address.

The addr_glob is a regular expression field that contains a list of addresses, either numeric or a DNS name. This field can also be a file reference, which contains a listing of addresses. If the address is a file reference, it must be an absolute file reference, that is, starting with a /. To ensure that IP addresses can be mapped to a valid domain name, use the !nameserver parameter.

A sample deny line looks as follows:

```
deny *.exodous.net /home/ftp/.message_exodous_deny
```

This entry will deny access to the FTP server from all users who are coming from the exodous.net domain, and will display the message contained in the file `.message_exodous_deny` in the `/home/ftp` directory.

guestgroup <groupname> [<groupname>]

The `guestgroup` line assigns a given groupname or groupnames to behave exactly like the anonymous user. The user will be confined to a specific directory structure, such as `/var/ftp` for the anonymous user, and will only have permission to see files that group has permissions for.

The `groupname` parameter can be the name of a group or that group's corresponding gid. If a gid is given, a `%` needs to be placed in front of it. Ranges of groups are valid; thus an entry such as the following is valid:

```
guestgroup %500-550
```

This would restrict all users with the group IDs 500–550 to be treated as a guest group instead of a regular user. In order for `guestgroup` to work, the user's home directories need to be set up with the correct permissions, exactly like the anonymous FTP user.

guestuser <username> [<username>]

The `guestuser` line works exactly like the `guestgroup` line, except it uses the user ID, uid, instead of the groupid. Thus, this limits the guest user to files that the user has privileges. Generally, a user will have more privileges than a group, thus this type of assignment can be viewed as less restrictive than the `guestgroup` line.

limit <class> <n> <times> <message_file>

`limit` restricts the number of users in a class during given times. If the number is exceeded, the user will see the contents of the file given in the `message_file` parameter.

The `times` parameter is somewhat terse and not inherent. The format for this is a comma delimited string in the form of days, hours. Valid day strings are Su, Mo, Tu, We, Th, Fr, Sa, and Any. The hours are formatted in a 24-hour format. A sample is as follows:

```
limit anonymous 10 MoTuWeThFr,Sa0000-2300 /home/ftp/.message_limit_anon_class
```

This line will limit the anonymous class to 10 concurrent connections on Monday through Friday, and on Saturday from midnight to 11:00 p.m. If the number of concurrent connections is exceeded or at 11:00 p.m. on Saturday, the users will see the contents of the file `/home/ftp/.message_limit_anon_class`.

Syntax for finer control over limiting user connections can be found in the ftpaccess man page.

`loginfails <number>`

This line allows control over how many times an invalid password will be accepted before the FTP server terminates the session. The default for `loginfails` is set to 5.

Information

Providing users some information about the server is considered good practice for any public FTP server. The following commands allow messages to be displayed to users when logging into the server or when an action is preformed. Giving information or guidance to users in this manner is an excellent way to document how the server should be used.

`banner <path>`

This is a reference to a file that is displayed before the user receives a login prompt from the FTP server. Generally, this file contains information to identify the server. The path is an absolute pathname, relative to the system root (`/`), not the base of the anonymous FTP user's home.

> **Note**
>
> Not all FTP clients can handle multiline responses from the FTP server. This is how the banner line passes the file contents to the client. If a client cannot interrupt multiline responses, the FTP server will be useless to them.

`email <name>`

This line sets the e-mail address for the FTP administrator. This string will be printed whenever the `%E` magic cookie is specified. This magic cookie is used in the messages line or in the shutdown file. It is good practice to show this string to users in the login banner message so that users know who to contact in case of problems. It is also recommended that this not be a live address, but an alias so that real e-mail addresses aren't hard-coded into the configuration of the server. In addition to good practice, an e-mail alias allows multiple users to see messages sent to this address.

message <path> {<when> {<class> ...}}

This line specifies a file to be displayed to the user during login as well as when the cd command is issued by the user. The optional when clause can be LOGIN or CWD=(dir), where dir is the name of a directory that is current. The optional class parameter allows messages to be shown only to a given class or classes of users.

When displaying messages, symbolic constants that are replaced by system information, called *magic cookies*, that can breathe life into messages. Table 18.1 lists valid magic cookies for the message command and their representation.

TABLE 18.1 Magic Cookies and Their Descriptions

Cookie	Description
%T	Local time (form Thu Nov 15 17:12:42 1990)
%F	Free space in partition of CWD (kbytes)
	[Not supported on all systems]
%C	Current working directory
%E	The maintainer's e-mail address as defined in ftpaccess
%R	Remote hostname
%L	Local hostname
%u	Username as determined via RFC931 authentication
%U	Username given at login time
%M	Maximum allowed number of users in this class
%N	Current number of users in this class
%B	Absolute limit on disk blocks allocated
%b	Preferred limit on disk blocks
%Q	Current block count
%I	Maximum number of allocated inodes (+1)
%i	Preferred inode limit
%q	Current number of allocated inodes
%H	Time limit for excessive disk use
%h	Time limit for excessive files

Table 18.1 continued

Ratios	*Description*
%xu	Uploaded bytes
%xd	Downloaded bytes
%xR	Upload/Download ratio (1:n)
%xc	Credit bytes
%xT	Time limit (minutes)
%xE	Elapsed time since login (minutes)
%xL	Time left
%xU	Upload limit
%xD	Download limit

For anonymous users, when using the CWD=(dir) directive, it is necessary to specific the path from the anonymous FTP user home, not the full path.

By default, no message file is given. An entry of

```
message /home/ftp/welcome.msg    login
message /welcome.msg             login
```

will show the contents of the welcome.msg file to all real users who log in to the server. The second entry will show the same message for the anonymous user.

As this file isn't created with the installation of the RPM using a text editor, type the following:

```
Welcome to the anonymous ftp service on %L!

There are %N out of %M users logged in.

Current system time is %T

Please send email to %E if there are
any problems with this service.

Your current working directory is %C
```

Save this file as /var/ftp/welcome.msg. Verify that it works by connecting to the FTP server:

```
Connected to localhost (127.0.0.1).
220 pheniox FTP server (Version wu-2.6.1-18) ready.
Name (localhost:tdc): anonymous
331 Guest login ok, send your complete e-mail address as password.
```

18

File Transfer Protocol

```
Password:
230-Welcome to the anonymous ftp service on pheniox!
230-
230-There are 1 out of unlimited users logged in.
230-
230-Current system time is Tue Sep  4 10:26:25 2001
230-
230-Please send email to root@localhost if there are
230-any problems with this service.
230-
230-Your current working directory is /
```

Using messages is a good way to give information about where things are on your site as well as information that is system dependant.

readme <path> {<when {<class>}}

The readme line tells the server if a notification should be displayed to the user when a specific file was last modified. The path parameter is any valid path for the user. The optional when parameter is exactly as seen in the message line. class can be one or more classes as defined in the class file. The path is absolute for real users. For the anonymous user, the path is relative to the anonymous home directory, which is /var/ftp by default.

Logging

Part of any system administration involves reviewing log files for what the server is doing, who accessed it, what files were transferred, and other pieces of important information.

```
log <syslog>{+<xferlog>}
```

This line allows the administrator to redirect where logging information from the FTP server will be recorded. By default, the information for commands is stored in /var/log/messages, although the man pages packaged in the Red Hat RPM states that this information will be written to /var/log/xferlog. Information regarding what files were transferred and received are written to /var/xferlog.

log commands [<typelist>]

This line enables logging for all commands issued by the user. typelist is a comma separated list of anonymous, guest, and real. If no typelist is given, commands are logged for all users. The wu-ftpd RPM packaged with Red Hat 7.2 by default writes these messages to /var/log/messages, . which is the default syslog file. This default behavior is different from what is described in the man page for ftpaccess. Here is an example of a sample log file for commands:

```
Sep  4 05:51:05 pheniox ftpd[27438]: USER anonymous
Sep  4 05:51:09 pheniox ftpd[27438]: PASS testing@test.com
Sep  4 05:51:09 pheniox ftpd[27438]: ANONYMOUS FTP LOGIN FROM
localhost.localdomain [127.0.0.1], testing@test.com
Sep  4 05:51:09 pheniox ftpd[27438]: SYST
Sep  4 05:51:10 pheniox ftpd[27438]: TYPE Image
Sep  4 05:51:13 pheniox ftpd[27438]: TYPE ASCII
Sep  4 05:51:13 pheniox ftpd[27438]: PASV
Sep  4 05:51:13 pheniox ftpd[27438]: LIST
Sep  4 05:51:19 pheniox ftpd[27438]: QUIT
Sep  4 05:51:19 pheniox ftpd[27438]: FTP session close
```

A date/time stamp is given with the host that the user came from, what service and process ID performed the action, and what commands the user entered as interpreted by the FTP daemon. These aren't necessarily the same syntax as the user typed in, but the corresponding system calls the FTP server received. For example, the LIST entry is actually the ls command, and the TYPE Image is the command bin.

log security [<typelist>]

This line enables the logging of security violations for anonymous, guest, and real users, as specified in the typelist, as in log commands. If no typelist is given, security violations for all users will be logged.

log transfers [<typelist> [<directions>]]

This line writes a log of all files transferred to and from the server. typelist is the same as seen in log commands and log security lines. directions is a comma-separated list of the keywords inbound for uploaded files and outbound for downloaded files. If no directions are given, both uploaded and downloaded files will be logged. Inbound and outbound logging is turned on by default.

Permission Control

Knowing what users can and cannot execute is one of many steps is setting up security for the server. The following lines in the ftpaccess file allow the administrator to have greater control over what users can and cannot do during an FTP session. By default, for all of these lines, anonymous users aren't allowed and all other users are allowed.

18

FILE TRANSFER PROTOCOL

chmod <yes|no> <typelist>

The chmod line determines if a user has the ability to change a file's permissions. This command acts the same as the standard chmod command. An exhaustive description of its purpose and parameters can be found in the man page. The yes|no parameter designates whether the command can be executed, and typelist is a comma delimited string of the keywords anonymous, guest, and real. Not specifying a typelist string will result in the command being applied to all users.

delete<yes|no> <typelist>

The delete line determines whether the user can delete files with the rm command. The yes|no parameter is to turn this permission on or off, and typelist is the same as the chmod command.

overwrite <yes|no> <typelist>

This line allows or denies the user the ability to overwrite a file that currently exists. This line is specific to an upload to the server because the FTP client will determine whether the user can overwrite files on his own local machine. The yes|no parameter toggles the permission on or off, and typelist is the same as seen in the chmod line.

rename <yes|no> <typelist>

Allow or disable the user from renaming files. The yes|no parameter toggles the permission on of off, and typelist is the same comma-delimited string as seen in chmod.

umask <yes|no> <typelist>

This line is a bit different from the other commands in the permission control section. The umask command determines what permissions a user will create new files with. The yes|no parameter toggles based on whether a user is allowed to create a file with his default permissions when uploading a file. This line is specific to uploaded files because the client machine will determine how new files are created from a download.

Miscellaneous

These commands allow miscellaneous configuration options to be specified to the server. Most of these deal with the user experience, which allows the administrator to tune the server.

alias <string> <dir>

This line allows the administrator to provide another name for a directory other than its standard name. The alias line only applies to the `cd` command. This line is particularly useful if a popular directory is buried deep within the anonymous FTP user's directory tree. A sample entry is the following:

```
alias linux-386 /pub/redhat/7.1/en/i386/
```

This line would allow the user to type `cd linux-386` and be automatically taken to the `/pub/redhat/7.1/en/i386` directory.

cdpath <dir>

This line specifies in what order the `cd` command will look for a given string the user enters. The search path is done in the order in which the `cdpath` lines are entered in the ftpacess file.

For example, if the following `cdpath` entries are in the ftpaccess file,

```
cdpath /pub/redhat/
cdpath /pub/linux/
```

And the user types `cd i386`, the server will search for an entry in any defined aliases first in the `/pub/redhat` directory and then in the `/pub/linux` directory. If a large number of aliases are defined, it is recommended that symbolic links to the directories be created instead of aliases. This will reduce the amount of work on the FTP server and decrease wait time for the user.

18

FILE TRANSFER PROTOCOL

compress <yes|no> [<classglob> ...]

This line determines whether the user will be able to use the `compress` command on files. The yes|no parameter toggles the permission on or off, and `classglob` is a regular express string that specifies one or more defined classes of users. The actual conversions from the use of this command is specified in the ftpconversions file.

tar <yes|no> [<classglob> ...]

This line determines whether the user will be able to use the `tar` command on files. The yes|no parameter toggles the permission on or off, and `classglob` is a regular express string that specifies one or more defined classes of users. The actual conversions from the use of this command is specified in the ftpconversions file.

shutdown <path>

This line tells the server where to look for the shutdown message generated by the `ftp-shut` command or by the user. If this file exists, the server will check the file to see when the server should shut down. The syntax of this file is as follows:

```
<year> <month> <day> <hour> <minute> <deny_offset> <disc_offset> <text>
```

`year` can be any year after 1970 (called the epoch), `month` is from 0–11, `hour` is 0–23, `minute` is 0–59, `deny_offset` is a number in minutes before shutdown in which the server will disable new connections, `disc_offset` is the number of minutes before connected users will be disconnected, and `text` is a message that will be displayed to the users at login. In addition to valid magic cookies defined in the messages section, those listed in Table 18.2 are also available.

TABLE 18.2   Magic Cookies for the Shutdown File

Cookie	Description
%s	The time the system will be shut down.
%r	The time new connections will be denied.
%d	The time current connections will be dropped.

/etc/ftpconversions

The FTP server can convert files during transfer to compress and uncompress files automatically. Suppose that the user is transferring a file to his Microsoft Windows machine that was tared and gziped on a Linux machine. The user doesn't have an archive utility installed to uncompress these files, so they are essentially useless. The FTP server administrator can configure the FTP server to automatically unarchive these files before download, should the site support users who have this particular problem. Additionally, if an upload area is configured for the users, the FTP server can be configured to automatically compress any files transferred to the server.

> **Tip**
>
> Allowing users to upload files to the FTP server is highly dangerous unless restricted to authorized local users. Anonymous upload areas have often been the breeding ground for viruses, unlicensed software, and cracking software used by system crackers for malicious usage. Should an anonymous upload area be allowed, be sure to check it regularly.

The format of the ftpconversions file is

```
1:2:3:4:5:6:7:8
```

where 1 is the strip prefix, 2 is the strip postfix, 3 is the add-on prefix, 4 is the add-on postfix, 5 is the external command, 6 is the types, 7 is the options, and 8 is the description.

Strip Prefix

The strip prefix is one or more characters at the beginning of a filename that should be automatically removed by the server when the file is requested. By specifying a given prefix to strip in a conversions rule, such as devel_, the user can request the file devel_procman.tar.gz by the command get procman.tar.gz, and the FTP server will perform any other rules that apply to that file and retrieve it from the server. Although this feature is documented, as of version 2.6.1, it has yet to be implemented.

Strip Postfix

The strip postfix works much the same as strip prefix, except one or more characters are taken from the end of the filename. Typically, this feature is used to strip the .gz extension from files that have been tared and gziped when the server is performing automatic decompression before sending the file to the client.

Add-On Prefix

The add-on prefix conversion instructs the server to insert one or more characters to a filename before it is transferred to the server or client. For example, a user requests the file procman.tar.gz. The server has a conversion rule to add a prefix of gnome_ to all .tar.gz files; thus the server would append this string to the file before sending it to the client. The user would receive a file called gnome_procman.tar.gz. Keywords such as uppercase and lowercase can be used in this function to change the case of the filename for those operating systems in which case makes a difference. Similar to the strip prefix conversion, this feature is not yet implemented in version 2.6.1.

Add-On Postfix

An add-on postfix instructs the server to append one or more characters to the end of a filename during the transfer or reception of a file. A server can contain tared packages of applications that are uncompressed. If an add-on postfix conversion was configured on the server, the server could compress the file, append a .gz extension once the file was compressed, and then send that file to the client. The server could also do the same

18

FILE TRANSFER PROTOCOL

action for uncompressed files that are sent to the server. This would have the effect of conserving disk space on the server.

External Command

The external command is where the bulk of the conversion rules happen. This entry will tell the server what should be done with a file once it is transferred to the server. This can be any command on the server, although generally it is a compression utility. As the file is sent, the server passes the file through the external command. If the file is being uploaded to the server, the command needs to send the result to standard in, whereas a download will send the command to standard out.

Types

It is necessary to tell the server what types of files the conversion rules apply to. The types is where the server is told what types of files this should be done on. These types are all separated by the (|) character and have a value of T_REG, T_ASCII, and T_DIR. T_REG signifies a regular file, T_ASCII an ASCII file, and T_DIR a directory. A typical entry is T_REG | T_ASCII, which signifies a regular ASCII file.

Options

The options field informs the server what action is being done to the file. Similar to the types file, options are separated by the (|) character and have a valid range of O_COMPRESS to compress the file, O_UNCOMPRESS to uncompress the file, and O_TAR to tar the file. An example of this would be O_COMPRESS | O_TAR for files that are both compressed and tared.

Description

This field allows an administrator to quickly understand what the rule is doing. This field does not have any syntax restriction, although it is usually a one word entry, enough to get the concept across.

An Example of Conversions in Action

Although this might mean something to the Linux/UNIX expert, the average person has no idea what to do. It's not really that difficult, so let's examine and decode an example:

```
:.Z:  :  :/bin/compress -d -c %s:T_REG|T_ASCII:O_UNCOMPRESS:UNCOMPRESS
```

In this example, the strip prefix (field 1) is null because it isn't yet implemented, so this rule doesn't apply to prefixes. The second field of this rule contains the .Z postfix, thus it deals with files that have been compressed with the compress utility. The rule doesn't address the add-on prefix or postfix, so fields 3 an 4 are `null`. Field 5, the external command field, tells the server to run the `compress` utility to decompress all files that have the `.Z` extension, as the `-d` parameter signifies. The `-c` options tells compress to write the output of the `compress` utility to the standard out, which is the server in this case. The `%s` is the name of the file that the rule was applied against. Field 6 specifies that this file is a regular file in ASCII format. Field 7, the options field, tells the server that this command uncompresses the file. Finally, the last field is a comment that gives the administrator a quick decode of what the conversion rule is doing, that is, uncompressing the file.

> **Examples**
>
> Several conversion rules are already specified in the ftpconversions file that is part of the RPM package on the Red Hat CD or in `/usr/share/doc/wu-ftpd.2.6.1/examples/ftpconversions`. Special conversions for Sun's Solaris are also provided in this directory.

18

FILE TRANSFER PROTOCOL

/etc/ftpusers

Certain accounts are created during the installation of Linux that are for the system to segment and separate tasks with specific permissions. The ftpusers file is where accounts that are for system purposes are listed. The version of wu-ftp that comes with Red Hat Linux has depreciated the usage of this file, implementing the specific functionality of this file in the ftpaccess file with the commands of `deny-uid/deny-gid`.

/etc/ftphosts

The purpose of the ftphosts file is to allow or deny specific users or addresses from connection to the FTP server. The format of the file is the word `allow` or `deny` optionally followed by a username, followed by an IP or a DNS address.

```
allow username address
deny username address
```

Listing 18.4 shows a sample configuration of this file.

LISTING 18.4   ftphosts Configuration File for Allowing or Denying Users

```
# Example host access file
#
# Everything after a '#' is treated as comment,
# empty lines are ignored
```

LISTING 18.4 continued

```
allow tdc 128.0.0.1
allow tdc 192.168.101.*
allow tdc insanepenguin.net
allow tdc *.exodous.net
deny anonymous 201.*
deny anonymous *.pilot.net
```

The * is a wildcard that will match any combination of that address. For example, `allow tdc *.exodous.net` will allow the user `tdc` to log in to the FTP server from any address that contains the domain name exodous.net. Similarly, the anonymous user will not be allowed to access the FTP if he is coming from a 201 public class C IP address because configuration files are only parsed at startup. To restart `xinetd` as root, issue the command `/etc/rc.d/init.d/xinetd` restart. This makes a call to the same shell script that is called at system startup and shutdown for any runlevel to start or stop the xinet daemon. Xinetd should report its status as

```
[root@pheniox root]# /etc/rc.d/init.d/xinetd restart
Stopping xinetd:                                        [  OK  ]
Starting xinetd:                                        [  OK  ]
```

Once restarted, the FTP server is accessible to all incoming requests.

Server Administration

Wu-ftp provides a few commands to aid in the administration of the server. These commands are

- `ftpwho`
- `ftpcount`
- `ftpshut`
- `ftprestart`

Each of these commands must be executed with superuser privileges because they reference the ftpaccess configuration file to obtain information about the FTP server.

/usr/bin/ftpwho

This command provides information about users who are currently connected to the FTP server. Listing 18.5 shows a typical output of this command. It lists the process ID for the `ftp` daemon handling requests, the class that the particular user belongs to, the total time connected, what username the user is connected as, and the status of his session. In addition to the information given about each connected user, ftpwho will also display the total number of users connected out of any maximum that might have been set in the ftpaccess file.

As most programs in Linux do, ftpwho has parameters that can be passed to it. Finding them is done by the typical *ftpwho --help* command. For ftpwho, there is only one parameter, -V. This prints out version and licensing information for wu-ftp, as seen in Listing 18.5. The output is shown in Listing 18.6. Table 18.3 shows the format ftpwho displays.

TABLE 18.3 ftpwho Fields

Name	Description
Process ID	The process ID of the FTP server process.
TTY	The terminal ID of the process. This will always be a ? because the FTP daemon isn't an interactive login.
Status	Status of the FTP process. The values are
	S: sleeping.
	Z: zombie, indicating a crash.
	R: running.
	N: normal process.
Time	The elapsed processor time the process has used in minutes and seconds.
Details	Tells what host the process is connecting from, the user who connected, and the current command that is executing.

18

FILE TRANSFER PROTOCOL

LISTING 18.5 The ftpwho Command

```
Service class all:

17324 ?       SN     0:00 ftpd: localhost.localdomain: tdc: IDLE
17288 ?       SN     0:00 ftpd: monolith:
➥ anonymous/testing@test.com: IDLE
17281 ?       SN     0:00 ftpd: helios:
➥ anonymous/tigechastain@yahoo.com: IDLE
17275 ?       SN     0:00 ftpd: darkstar:
➥ anonymous/name@somewhere.com: IDLE
   -   4 users (no maximum)
```

LISTING 18.6   `ftpwho -V` Command Output

```
Copyright  1999,2000,2001 WU-FTPD Development Group.
All rights reserved.

Portions Copyright  1980, 1985, 1988, 1989, 1990, 1991, 1993, 1994
  The Regents of the University of California.
Portions Copyright  1993, 1994 Washington University in Saint Louis.
Portions Copyright  1996, 1998 Berkeley Software Design, Inc.
Portions Copyright  1989 Massachusetts Institute of Technology.
Portions Copyright  1998 Sendmail, Inc.
Portions Copyright  1983, 1995, 1996, 1997 Eric P.  Allman.
Portions Copyright  1997 by Stan Barber.
Portions Copyright  1997 by Kent Landfield.
Portions Copyright  1991, 1992, 1993, 1994, 1995, 1996, 1997
  Free Software Foundation, Inc.

Use and distribution of this software and its source code are governed
by the terms and conditions of the WU-FTPD Software License ("LICENSE").

If you did not receive a copy of the license, it may be obtained online
at http://www.wu-ftpd.org/license.html.

Version wu-2.6.1-18
```

/usr/bin/ftpcount

`ftpcount` will count the number of connected users to the FTP server and the maximum number of users allowed. This same information is found at the end of the output for the `ftpwho` command. This command only takes one parameter, `-V`, which displays the same output as in Listing 18.6.

```
[root@pheniox bin]# ftpcount
Service class all              -    4 users (no maximum)
```

/usr/sbin/ftpshut

The `ftpshut` command allows the administrator to take the FTP server down at a specific time based on some parameters passed to it. The format of the command is as follows and is documented in the `ftpshut` man page:

```
ftpshut [ -V ] [ -l min] [ -d min] time [ warning-message ... ]
```

The `-V` parameter displays the version information of the command, with output similar to that of Listing 18.6. The `time` parameter is the time when the ftpshut command will stop the FTP servers. This parameter will take either a + number for the number of min-utes from the current time, or a specific hour and minute in 24-hour clock format with the syntax of *HH:MM*.

The -l parameter allows the FTP server administrator to specify how long, in minutes, before shutdown the server will disable new connections. The default for this is 10 min-utes. If the time given to shut down the servers is less than 10 minutes, new connections will be disabled immediately.

The -d parameter is similar to the -l parameter, but controls when the FTP server will terminate the current connections. By default this will occur 5 minutes before the server shuts down. If the shut down time is less than 5 minutes, the server will terminate the connections immediately.

When shutting down an FTP server, it is always good practice to notify the users when the server will be going down. Table 18.4 lists all the available magic cookies that are valid in the ftpshut command with a description of their meaning. This information can also be found in ftpshut's man page.

TABLE 18.4   Magic Cookies for the ftpshut Command

Cookie	Description
%s	Time the system will be shut down
%r	Time new connections will be denied
%d	Time the current connections will be dropped
%C	Current working directory
%E	Server administrators e-mail address as specified in the ftpaccess file
%F	Available free space in the current working directories par-tition in kilobytes
%L	Local host time
%M	Maximum number of allowed connections in this user class
%N	Current number of connections for this user class
%R	Remote hostname
%T	Local time, in the form of Fri Aug 31 21:04:00 2001
%U	Username given at login

18

FILE TRANSFER
PROTOCOL

As with any public server administration, it is always good practice to let users of the server know about upcoming outages, when the server will be updated, and other relevant site information. The ftpshut command allows the administrator to let the FTP server do much of this automatically. Once executed, the FTP server will create a file containing the shutdown information in the location as specified in the ftpaccess file under the shutdown section. The default configuration for this file is /etc/shutmsg. If the ftpshut command has been executed with any warning messages, these will be displayed when the user logs in to the server.

```
Name (pheniox:tdc): anonymous
331 Guest login ok, send your complete e-mail address as password.
Password: testing@test.com
230-system doing down at Mon Sep  3 06:23:00 2001
230-0 users of unlimited on pheniox.
230 Guest login ok, access restrictions apply.
Remote system type is UNIX.
Using binary mode to transfer files.
```

A sample ftpshut command would be

```
ftpshut -l 5 -d 5 +10 "system going down at %s %N users of %M on %R"
```

This tells the FTP server to disconnect new connections in 5 minutes, drop all current connections in 5 minutes, shut down the server in 10 minutes, and display a warning message to the users at login. The message can be a mixture of text and magic cookies, defined in Table 18.4. It is important to keep in mind that the message can only be 75 characters in length. Additionally, it isn't important to know how many characters the magic cookies will take because the system knows this information and will truncate the message at 75 characters.

/usr/sbin/ftprestart

When ftpshut is issued to the system, it creates a file that stores the necessary information. The ftprestart command removes this file for all servers, either canceling the impending shutdown or removing the shutdown file and restarting the FTP server. The ftprestart only takes one argument, -V; the output of which is found in Listing 18.6.

/var/log/xferlog

The xferlog file gives a log of what transactions have occurred with the FTP server. Depending on the settings in the /etc/ftpaccess file, the contents of this file can contain the files sent or received by who with a date stamp. Table 18.5 lists the fields of this file. The same information can also be found in the corresponding man page included in the wu-ftp RPM.

TABLE 18.5 `/var/log/xferlog` Fields

Field	Description
current-time	Current local time in the form of *DDD MMM dd hh:mm:ss YYYY*. Where *DDD* is the day of the week, *MMM* is the month, *dd* is the day of the month, *hh* is the hour, *mm* is the minutes, *ss* is the seconds, and *YYYY* is the year.
transfer-time	Total time in seconds for the transfer.
remote-host	Remote host name.
file-size	Size of the transferred file in bytes.
filename	Name of the file.
transfer-type	A single character indicating the transfer type. The types are
	a for ascii transfers.
	b for binary transfers.
special-action-flag	One or more character flags indicating any special action taken by the server. The values are
	C for compressed files.
	U for uncompressed files.
	T for tared files.
	- for no special action taken.
direction	Indicates whether the file was sent from the server or received by the server.
access-mode	The way in which the user logged in to the server. The values are
	a anonymous guest user.
	g guest user, corresponding to the `guestgroup` command in the `/etc/ftpaccess` file.
	r real user on the local machine.
username	If logged in as a real user, the username.
	If the access mode was `guest`, the password is given.
service-name	The name of the service used, usually FTP.
authentication-method	Type of authentication used. The values are
	0: none
	1: RFC931 Authentication (a properly formed e-mail address).

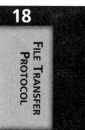

18

FILE TRANSFER
PROTOCOL

Table 18.5   continued

Field	Description
authenticated-user-id	This is the user ID returned to the server based on the authentication method used to access the server. A * is used when an authenticated user ID cannot be found.
completion-status	A single character field indicating the status of the transfer. The values are
	c: completed transfer.
	i: incomplete transfer.

A sample of this file is seen in Listing 18.7

Listing 18.7   Sample `/var/log/xferlog` File with Inbound and Outbound Logging

```
Mon Sep  3 07:13:05 2001 1 localhost.localdomain 100
 /var/ftp/pub/README b _ o a testing@test.com ftp 0 * c
Mon Sep  3 02:35:35 2001 1 helios 8 /var/ftp/pub/configuration a
 _ o a testing@test.com ftp 0 * c
Mon Sep  3 02:35:35 2001 1 helios 8 /var/ftp/pub/temp.txt a _ o a
testing@test.com ftp 0 * c
Mon Sep  3 02:35:35 2001 1 helios 8 /var/ftp/pub/tftp-server-
0.17-14.i386.rpm a _ o a testing@test.com ftp 0 * c
Mon Sep  3 02:35:35 2001 1 helios 8 /var/ftp/pub/wu-ftpd-2.6.1-
18.i386.rpm a _ o a testing@test.com ftp 0 * c
```

Using FTP

FTP is a client/server system, thus a client must be used to connect to the server. The following sections discuss the different types of interfaces to FTP and their usage.

Text Interface

There are two basic interfaces for FTP: text or graphical. There are many graphical clients available for FTP, however the tried and true method on Linux machines is the text interface. Once a user understands how to use the FTP client on the text level, he has a better understanding of what each action in a graphical interface does. This is particularly handy when the graphic client doesn't automatically detect the file type that is being transferred. This will result in a binary file being transferred as an ASCII file, thus rending it useless. Conversely, an ASCII file transferred as a binary will print the ^M control character at the end of each line. This is usually only seen when transferring a file from Microsoft Windows to Linux.

Common Commands

Because Linux is a text-based operating system, some of the following common commands are used in a typical FTP session:

- `ascii`
- `bin`
- `bye`
- `hash`
- `mget`
- `mput`
- `prompt`
- `put`
- `quit`
- `send`
- `tick`

The `bin` and `ascii` commands set the type of transfer. `hash` and `tick` will show the user some feedback during a transfer. This is particularly helpful over a slower transfer to confirm that something is indeed happening.

`send` and `put` are essentially the same command, initiating a transfer from the local machine that the user is on to the FTP server. `send` or `put` cannot handle sending multiple files, however. Sending multiple files must be done with the `mput` command.

Similar to `send` or `put`, `get` or `mget` will receive files from the FTP server. Just as `mput` will send multiple files, `mget` receives multiple files.

The `prompt` command is an interactive command, asking the user for input on whether to get a specific file when the `mput` or `mget` command is issued. If the user initiates an `mget` *, with prompting on, the FTP client will prompt the user to transfer each file that the * wildcard matches. This can be particularly useful when several files in a directory need to be transferred, with one or two files that are unwanted. By default, prompting is turned on.

These are just some of the commands available during an FTP session. By typing **help**, the user can see a full list of valid commands that. Typing **help command-name** will give a brief description of what that command does. Listing 18.8 shows the `help` output.

LISTING 18.8 The Commands Listed by help in an FTP Session

```
Commands may be abbreviated.  Commands are:

!            debug        mdir        sendport     site
$            dir          mget        put          size
account      disconnect   mkdir       pwd          status
append       exit         mls         quit         struct
ascii        form         mode        quote        system
bell         get          modtime     recv         sunique
binary       glob         mput        reget        tenex
bye          hash         newer       rstatus      tick
case         help         nmap        rhelp        trace
cd           idle         nlist       rename       type
cdup         image        ntrans      reset        user
chmod        lcd          open        restart      umask
close        ls           prompt      rmdir        verbose
cr           macdef       passive     runique      ?
delete       mdelete      proxy       send
```

A Typical FTP Session

Now that the server is configured, it is time to test it. First, initiate a connection to a server.

```
[tdc@pheniox tdc]$ ssh -l tdc darkstar
tdc@darkstar's password:
Last login: Mon Sep  3 04:17:50 2001 from pheniox
[tdc@darkstar tdc]$ ftp pheniox
Connected to pheniox.
220 pheniox FTP server (Version wu-2.6.1-18) ready.
Name (pheniox:tdc): anonymous
331 Guest login ok, send your complete e-mail address as password.
Password: testing@test.com
230 Guest login ok, access restrictions apply.
Remote system type is UNIX.
Using binary mode to transfer files.
ftp>
```

Now that a connection has been established and authenticated to the server, it is necessary to set up the FTP client to operate as desired.

```
ftp> hash
Hash mark printing on (1024 bytes/hash mark).
ftp> prompt
Interactive mode off.
ftp> bin
200 Type set to I.
```

We have told `ftp` to print a hash (#) character for every 1024 bytes that are transferred, turn off prompting, and set the transfer type to binary. Next, we will want the server to show us a listing of what directories and files are available on the server.

```
ftp> ls
200 PORT command successful.
150 Opening ASCII mode data connection for directory listing.
total 32
d--x--x--x   2 root     root         4096 Aug 31 07:15 bin
d--x--x--x   2 root     root         4096 Aug 31 07:15 etc
d--x--x---   2 root     root         4096 Aug 31 04:44 lib
d-x-x---x    2 root     50           4096 Sep  3 07:34 pub
226 Transfer complete.
```

If the permissions were set correctly, the `pub` directory should be the only directory that will show any files under it. To verify this, change directories to `etc` and list the contents.

```
ftp> cd etc
250 CWD command successful.
ftp> ls
200 PORT command successful.
150 Opening ASCII mode data connection for directory listing.
total 0
226 Transfer complete.
```

By setting the permissions to execute only on the directories `bin`, `lib`, and `etc`, we cannot see any files in that directory. If the permissions were set to read or read/write access, it would be possible to see the passwd file in the `/etc` directory, thus allowing a user to get a copy of the encrypted password file. Although this file doesn't contain passwords, it still gives the user information about the system that could aid in hacking attempts.

Now that we have verified the server is relatively secure, change directories to `/pub` and list the contents of that directory.

```
ftp> cd pub
250-Please read the file README
250-  it was last modified on Sun Sep  2 19:25:47 2001 - 1 day ago
250 CWD command successful.
ftp> ls
200 PORT command successful.
150 Opening ASCII mode data connection for directory listing.
total 552
-rw-r--r--   1 root     50            100 Sep  2 19:25 README
-rw-r--r--   1 root     50              8 Sep  3 07:33 configuration
-rw-r--r--   1 root     50              8 Sep  3 07:33 temp.txt
-rw-r--r--   1 root     50          15798 Sep  3 10:29 tftp-0.17-14.i386.rpm
-rw-r--r--   1 root     50          26011 Sep  3 10:30 tftp-
server-0.17-14.i386.rpm
-rw-r--r--   1 root     50         219332 Sep  3 10:29 wu-ftpd-
2.6.1-18.i386.rpm226 Transfer complete.
```

To transfer all the RPM files to our local machine, issue the `mget *.rpm` command.

```
ftp> mget *.rpm
local: tftp-0.17-14.i386.rpm remote: tftp-0.17-14.i386.rpm
200 PORT command successful.
150 Opening BINARY mode data connection for tftp-0.17-14.i386.rpm
 (15798 bytes).##############
226 Transfer complete.
15798 bytes received in 0.974 secs (16 Kbytes/sec)
local: tftp-server-0.17-14.i386.rpm remote: tftp-server-0.17-
14.i386.rpm
200 PORT command successful.
150 Opening BINARY mode data connection for tftp-server-0.17-
14.i386.rpm (26011 bytes).
########################
226 Transfer complete.
26011 bytes received in 2.5 secs (10 Kbytes/sec)
local: wu-ftpd-2.6.1-18.i386.rpm remote: wu-ftpd-2.6.1-
18.i386.rpm
200 PORT command successful.
150 Opening BINARY mode data connection for wu-ftpd-2.6.1-
18.i386.rpm (219332 bytes).
##############################################################
##############################################################
##############################################################
##################
226 Transfer complete.
219332 bytes received in 50.3 secs (4.3 Kbytes/sec)
```

As described before, the `mget` command transferred all files with the `.rpm` extension to our local machine. The `ftp` client printed a # for each 1024 bytes transferred to our machine. This is helpful when transferring over a slow connection to ensure that the connection hasn't timed out.

> **Tip**
>
> After every action, the FTP server will return a status code and brief message showing the result of the command issued. A listing of all status codes and their corresponding messages can be found in Request For Comment 959. A copy of this can be found at `http://www.ietf.org/rfc/rfc959.txt`.

Because we are done with this session, issuing the command `quit` or `bye` will end our session. Additionally, the FTP server will inform us of how many bytes our session transfers, how many files, and the total transferred data in bytes between our local machine and the server.

```
ftp> bye
221-You have transferred 503818 bytes in 5 files.
221-Total traffic for this session was 506422 bytes in 7 transfers.
221 Thank you for using the FTP service on pheniox.
```

Also this is a simple example: Average FTP sessions are about this trivial. Several other commands are available during an FTP session, however they generally go unused for the typical user. Although this session and many like it are simplistic, FTP has the ability to take scripted input and define macros that allow for a much more complicated session. Should you need to use these advanced commands, see the info text on `ftp` by issuing the command

```
info ftp
```

The info pages are much like the man (manual) pages almost every command in Linux ships with, but generally contain much more detailed information.

Although the standard `ftp` client has been covered in this example, other text-based FTP clients are available for Linux. Nc-FTP, which is included on the Red Hat CD-ROM or from www.ncftp.com, provides extra functionality, such as the ability to get multiple directories at one time, thus eliminating the need to perform recursive `mgets` on the user's part as well as reconstructing the directory structure on their local machine. The Web site for this product has a list of all features this client offers to the user—in addition to the standard set of actions descriptor in the example.

Graphical FTP Clients

Many graphical FTP clients are available for Linux. Red Hat has packages gFTP for the GNOME desktop. The KDE desktop includes the KDE File Manager, kfm, thus ensuring FTP functionality in all versions of the K Desktop Environment. These two applications provide the necessary functionality most users will require, regardless of their graphic desktop of choice.

gFTP

For the GNOME graphic environment, gFTP is the standard FTP application. It contains all the typical features of FTP, including the ability to save profiles of common connections. Figure 18.2 shows a typical gFTP session in action. On the left panel is the local host, and on the right panel is the remote server. A connection is initiated by typing the address of the host into the host field, a specific port if not the standard FTP port (21), a valid username for the server, and a password. Once the information has been entered, clicking the icon that looks like a monitor will start the connection to the server. The bottom panel displays session information, such as changing directories, as seen in Figure 18.2.

FIGURE 18.2

*A typical gFTP
session.*

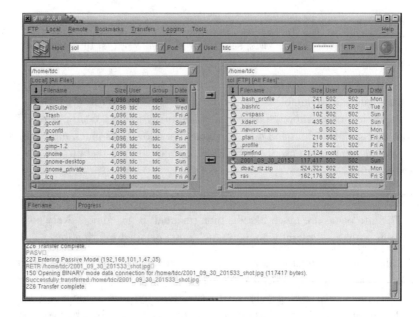

gFTP sets the file type as binary by default, which can be changed by clicking on ASCII in the FTP drop-down menu. To upload a file to the server, the user clicks on a filename in the left panel and clicks on the right arrow icon. The file is then transferred to the server, and the right panel will be updated to reflect this new file being added to the server. Similarly, to download a file from the server, the user selects the correct file type from the drop-down menu, selects the file to be downloaded, and clicks the left arrow icon. The left panel will then be updated to show the result of the transfer, with logging information shown in the bottom panel.

Once all files are uploaded or downloaded, the session must be closed. This is done by clicking the red button on the top right of the application window. This performs the quit command, and the session summary information will be displayed in the log panel at the bottom of the application.

Although graphical, the user still needs to understand the basic functionality of FTP to use gFTP. Not knowing the file type that needs to be set can result in wasted time downloading a binary file in ASCII format, thus rendering the file unusable. In it's defense, gFTP defaults to a binary file type, but detects the file type during the transfer. When using other operating systems, it is critical to ensure that the file type is correct, or the preceding situation can occur. gFTP is a robust application, providing all the necessary actions typical of an FTP session, in a pretty, easy-to-use format.

kfm

The *K Desktop Environment (KDE)* has integrated FTP functionality into kfm. To start an FTP session, the user launches kfm from the K start menu by clicking on the Home Directory entry on the K start menu. By typing `ftp://` followed by the server name in to the location field and pressing the Enter key, kfm will start an anonymous FTP session with the password `kfm-session@nowhere.org`. If the server doesn't allow anonymous FTP logins, kfm will fail to log in to the server.

KDE version 2.1 uses drag-and-drop functionality, allowing the user to select a file on the server and drag it to the desired location on the left navigation panel. Figure 18.3 shows a typical FTP session in kfm for KDE 2.1. By clicking on the README file and dragging it to the Home Directory listing on the navigation panel, the file is downloaded from the server to the client. One advantage kfm has over gFTP is the ability to automatically determine the file type that is being transferred and set it. By doing this, kfm excludes users from understanding some details of how FTP works.

FIGURE 18.3

The KDE file manager in an FTP session.

18

FILE TRANSFER PROTOCOL

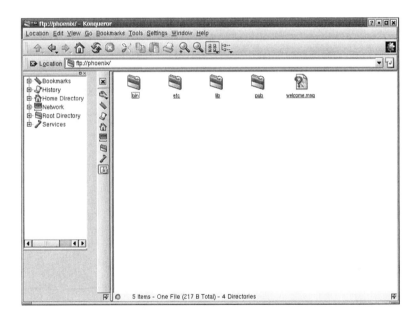

Reference

`http://www.wu-ftpd.org/`—WU-FTP official Web site

`http://www.redhat.com/`—Red Hat official Web site

`http://www.redhat.com/support/docs/tips/FTP-Setup-Tips/FTP-Setup-Tips.`
`html`—FTP Setup Tips Documentation from Red Hat

`http://www.cert.org/`—Computer Emergency Response Team

`http://www.cert.org/tech_tips/anonymous_ftp_config.html`—CERT Anonymous
FTP Configuration Guidelines

Handling Electronic Mail

Although electronic mail, or e-mail is one of the oldest applications of the Internet, it is still one of the most important. Indeed, for some people, e-mail is the only thing that they use the Internet for. This chapter looks both at configuring Red Hat to act as an e-mail server, as well as using various e-mail clients that are available for Red Hat. We will start with a basic overview of how e-mail works.

An Introduction to E-mail

At least two components are involved in electronic mail. These are MTAs and MUAs. MTA stands for *Mail Transfer Agent,* and MUA stands for *Mail User Agent.*

The MTA is the server application that handles sending and receiving e-mail. Whenever you send an e-mail message to someone from your e-mail program, it is handled by your Internet provider's MTA (or your office MTA) after you press the Send button. Likewise, any incoming mail for you is handled by the MTA. The MTA's responsibilities include things such as the following:

- Accepting and delivering mail sent from clients.
- Queuing outgoing mail so that clients don't have to wait for the mail to actually be sent.
- Accepting mail for clients and placing that mail in a holding area until the user connects to pick up the mail.
- Selectively relaying and denying relaying of messages received that are intended for a different host.

Each of these roles of the MTA will be discussed in more detail later on when we discuss configuring an MTA for Red Hat.

Main transfer is done with a protocol called SMTP, which stands for *Simple Mail Transfer Protocol.* As the name suggests, the protocol is really quite simple. It can send and receive only plain text, and it uses relatively simple commands to communicate with other mail servers. Figure 19.1 shows an example of how mail is transferred between two servers. The numbered callouts in the figure correspond to the explanations that follow.

1. user1@lion.org composes and sends an e-mail message to user2@cheetah.org.
2. MTA at lion.org receives user1's e-mail message and queues it for delivery behind any other messages that are also waiting to go out.
3. MTA at lion.org contacts the MTA at cheetah.org on port 25. After cheetah.org acknowledges the connection, the MTA at lion.org sends the mail message. After cheetah.org accepts and acknowledges receipt of the message, the connection is closed.

4. The MTA at cheetah.org places the mail message into user2's holding directory. user2 is notified that she has new mail the next time she logs on.

FIGURE **19.1**

An simplified example of how e-mail is processed and sent to its destination.

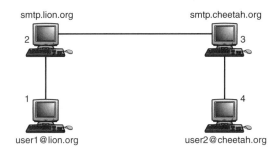

Of course, several things can go wrong during this process. For example, what if user2 doesn't exist at cheetah.org? In this case, the MTA at cheetah.org will reject the e-mail and notify the MTA at lion.org of what the problem is. The MTA at lion.org will then generate an e-mail message and send it to `user1@lion.org`, informing her that no user2 exists at cheetah.org (or perhaps just silently discard the message and give the sender no indication of the problem, depending on how the email server is configured.) What happens if cheetah.org doesn't respond to lion.org's connection attempts (maybe the server is down for maintenance or something)? In this case, the MTA at lion.org will leave the mail in the queue and will attempt to contact cheetah.org at regular intervals (defined by the e-mail administrator) for a certain period of time (also defined by the server administrator). The MTA at lion.org will keep the message in the queue for several days, and will try to deliver it to cheetah.org for several days before giving up and removing the message from the queue. In this case, `user1@lion.org` will be informed of the status of her message at least twice—once after the initial delivery attempt has failed, and again after the MTA has given up and stopped trying to deliver the message.

The other necessary part of the e-mail system is the MUA, or *Mail User Agent*. The MUA is the client that the user actually interacts with. Common MUAs with which you might be familiar are Microsoft Outlook, Eudora, or Netscape Messenger. In UNIX, some common text mode MUAs include the venerable `mail`, as well as more user-friendly, menu driven MUAs such as `elm` and `pine`.

The main difference between Windows and Macintosh MUAs and UNIX MUAs is that Windows and Macintosh often include some MTA functionality in the MUA. For example, Microsoft Outlook can connect to your Internet provider's mail server to send messages. UNIX MUAs on the other hand, generally don't include any MTA functionality, but rely on an external MTA. This might seem like a needlessly complicated way to do things, but actually it allows you much greater flexibility because a great number of

19

HANDLING
ELECTRONIC MAIL

external programs that work with each other can be used in dealing with e-mail. For example, you could use `pine` to read and send mail, `xbiff` to place a little mailbox icon on your desktop that checks for and notifies you when you have new mail, and `procmail` to automatically sort your incoming mail based on sender, subject, or many other variables.

One more part of a mail system is often present. It is sometimes known as the *mail delivery agent*, or MDA. The basic problem is that SMTP was designed to deliver mail to systems that are always connected to the Internet. Dial up systems of course, don't fit in this category. Because of this, a different method was needed to transfer mail to systems without permanent Internet connections. Two methods are commonly used for this. The first is POP3, and the second is IMAP.

Choosing an MTA

Several different MTAs are available for Red Hat, and each one has various strengths and weaknesses. For example, some are extremely powerful, but very difficult to configure and somewhat slow. Others are very fast and easy to configure, but do not contain as many features. We will look at some of the more common ones here.

Sendmail

The vast majority of e-mail traffic on the Internet is handled by an MTA called Sendmail. Sendmail is one of the oldest MTAs in existence, and it is still one of the most powerful. Sendmail also ships as the default MTA with the vast majority of UNIX distributions out there, including Red Hat Linux. Because of this, one of the advantages of Sendmail is of course, that it is already installed.

However, Sendmail also has a few disadvantages. The first is that it is somewhat slow. In a high load environment, there are several other MTAs out there that will run circles around Sendmail as far as the sheer volume of messages that can be handled per second. The second major disadvantage of Sendmail is that it is notoriously convoluted. Sendmail configuration files are extremely cryptic. (In fact, the bestselling book on Sendmail is more than 1,000 pages in length.)

Fortunately, the default configuration of Sendmail works fine for most basic installations, and only minor changes are needed to configure it for a basic e-mail server installation. However, because of the complexity of Sendmail, many administrators choose to replace it with one of the alternative MTAs that we will look at next.

Postfix

Postfix is a popular Sendmail alternative written by Witese Venema. It was originally released in 1998 as IBM Secure Mailer. The goals of Postfix are to be fast, secure, and easy to administer. Postfix seems to have succeeded in all these areas. Postfix is quite fast and also secure. In addition, it is much easier to administer than Sendmail. Postfix is a drop-in replacement for Sendmail. In fact, it uses a Sendmail wrapper so that MUAs and such can communicate with it just as if they were communicating with Sendmail. Because of the drop-in nature of Postfix, it is relatively easy to migrate an existing Sendmail installation to Postfix without breaking things.

Qmail

Qmail is a direct competitor to Postfix. Like Postfix, qmail aims to be easier to use than Sendmail, as well as faster and more secure. However, qmail isn't as much as a drop-in replacement as Postfix, so migrating an existing Sendmail installation to qmail isn't quite as simple as migrating from Sendmail to Postfix.

Like Postfix, qmail is fast and secure. It is also relatively easy to administer. Qmail also introduced `maildir`, which is an alternative method to the standard UNIX way of storing incoming mail. `maildir` is a more versatile system of handling incoming e-mail, but it does require your e-mail clients to be reconfigured and it isn't compatible with the traditional UNIX way of storing incoming mail. One other benefit of qmail is the large amount of add-on software designed to integrate with it. Some of the available software includes Web mail systems and POP3 servers.

A few other alternative MTAs are available for Red Hat, but these two are the most popular. So which one should you choose? It depends on what you need to do. Sendmail's main strengths are that it is already installed and it can do things that most other MTAs cannot. However, if ease of use or speed is a concern to you, you might want to consider replacing Sendmail with Postfix or qmail.

Basic Sendmail Configuration and Operation

Because Sendmail is the default MTA that is included with Red Hat, it is the one we are going to cover here. However, as mentioned previously, Sendmail is an extremely complex program with a very convoluted configuration. As such, we only have space to cover some of the very basics. For more information on Sendmail, as well as other MTAs, see the "Reference" section at the end of this chapter.

19

HANDLING ELECTRONIC MAIL

Sendmail configuration is handled by files in the directory /etc/, with much of the configuration being handled by the file sendmail.cf. Although it is possible to edit this file direction, it is extremely cryptic and difficult to understand. Because of this, Sendmail also precedes the /etc/sendmail.mc. The sendmail.mc file is somewhat easier to work with than the sendmail.cf file (although even this file is still rather cryptic.) However, sendmail.mc isn't a configuration file that Sendmail reads. Rather, it is simply a file that makes it easier for you to build a sendmail.cf file, which Sendmail does read. You will use the m4 macro processor to convert your sendmail.mc file into the sendmail.cf format that Sendmail can read. We will cover that later on in this section after we have covered some of the basic configuration you might want to do with Sendmail.

> **Note**
>
> The strange syntax of this configuration file is because of the requirements of the m4 macro processor. We aren't going to go into detail about m4 here, but note the quoting system. The starting quote is a backtick and the ending quote is simply a single quote. Also, the dnl sequence basically means "delete to new line," and causes anything from the sequence up to and including the new line character to be deleted in the output.

Masquerading

Sometimes you might want to have Sendmail masquerade as a host other than the actual hostname of your system. An example would be if you have a dial-up connection to the Internet, and your ISP handles all your mail for you. In this case, you will want Sendmail to masquerade as the domain name of your ISP. For example,

```
MASQURADE_AS(`samplenet.org')dnl
```

Smart Hosts

If you don't have a full-time connection to the Internet, you will probably want to have Sendmail send your messages to your ISP's mail server and let it handle delivery for you. Without a full-time Internet connection, you could find it difficult to deliver messages to some locations (such as some underdeveloped areas of the world where e-mail services are unreliable and sporadic). You can use a line such as the following in the sendmail.mc file to enable a smart host:

```
define(`SMART_HOST', `smtp.samplenet.org')
```

This will cause Sendmail to simply pass any mail it receives to the server `smtp.samplenet.org` rather than attempt to deliver it directly.

Building the `sendmail.cf` File

Once you have made all your changes to `sendmail.mc`, you need to rebuild the `sendmail.cf` file. As we mentioned previously, Sendmail cannot read the `sendmail.mc` file directly. You must run `sendmail.mc` through the `m4` macro processor in order to generate a usable configuration file. A command like the following is used to do this:

```
m4 /etc/mail/m4/cf.m4 sendmail.mc > ../sendmail.cf
```

This command loads the `cf.m4` macro file from /usr/share/sendmail-cf/m4/cf.m4 and then uses it to process the `sendmail.mc file`. The output, (which would normally be sent to STDOUT) is then redirected to the file `sendmail.cf`, and your new configuration file is ready. You will need to restart Sendmail before the changes will take effect.

Considerations for Dial-Up Systems

As mentioned previously in the chapter, normally Sendmail will attempt to deliver messages as soon as it receives them, and again at regular intervals after that. Sometimes however, this behavior is undesirable. For example, you might have a dial-up connection to the Internet, or be on a laptop and currently have no Internet connection available. In this case, you might want to have Sendmail hold all messages in the queue and not attempt to deliver them immediately. This can be done by adding the following line to `sendmail.mc`:

```
define(`confDELIVERY_MODE', `d')dnl
```

This line will cause Sendmail to only attempt to deliver mail at regularly scheduled queue processing intervals (which by default are usually somewhere between 20 and 30 minutes).

However, this still creates a problem because Sendmail will still attempt to deliver mail in the queue on a regular basis. If you are on a 15 hour trans-oceanic flight and you have Sendmail running on your laptop, this is obviously not a desirable situation. You can change this behavior by invoking Sendmail with no queue processing time. For example, by default, Sendmail might start with the following command:

```
sendmail -bd -q30m
```

This tells Sendmail that it should process the mail queue every 30 minutes, and thus attempt to deliver any messages in it every 30 minutes. You can, of course, simply

19

HANDLING ELECTRONIC MAIL

change 30 to any other number to have Sendmail process the queue at a different interval. If you don't want Sendmail to ever process the queue automatically, you can invoke Sendmail with no queue time, such as the following:

```
sendmail -bd -q
```

If Sendmail is invoked this way, it will process the queue once when it is started, and then it will never process the queue again until it is manually directed to do so. To manually tell Sendmail to process the queue, you can use a command like the following:

```
sendmail -q
```

> **Tip**
>
> There is a configuration file for pppd called `ppp.linkup`, which is located in `/etc/ppp`. Any commands in this file will automatically be run each time the PPP daemon is started. You can add the line `sendmail -q` to this file to have your mail queue automatically processed each time you dial your Internet connection.

Mail Relaying

By default, Sendmail won't relay mail that didn't originate from the local domain. This means for example, that if a Sendmail installation running at lion.org receives mail intended for cheetah.org, and that mail didn't originate from lion.org, the mail will be rejected and won't be sent. If you want to allow selected domains to relay through you, add an entry for the domain to the file `/etc/relay-domains`. If the file doesn't exist, simply create it in your favorite text editor and add a line containing the name of the domain that you want to allow to relay through you. Sendmail will need to be restarted for this change to take effect.

> **Caution**
>
> Be extremely careful with mail relaying. For example, simply allowing all domains to relay through you will make you a SPAM magnet (as in spammers will use your mail server to send SPAM). This will quickly get you black listed as a site that allows SPAM relaying. Many sites don't accept mail from other sites that are black listed. The result is that you could end up with a lot of sites that won't accept mail from you or your users, even if the mail is legitimate.

Aliases

An alias tells Sendmail that any e-mail it receives that is addressed to a certain account, should be forwarded to another account. The alias does not have to be a real account. For example, a very common alias is "postmaster", even though this isn't usually a real system account. Aliases are configured in the file /etc/aliases. Here is an example of an alias entry:

```
postmaster: root
```

This entry forwards any mail received for "postmaster" to the root user. By default, almost all the aliases listed here forward to root.

> **Caution**
>
> Reading e-mail as root is a security hazard because there are various ways in which a malicious e-mail message might be able to exploit an e-mail client and cause it to execute arbitrary code as the user running the client. Because of this, you will probably want to forward all of root's mail to another account and read it from there. This can be done in one of two ways. The first way is by adding an entry to the /etc/mail/aliases file that sends root's mail to a different account. For example root: foobar would forward all mail intended for root to the account "foobar". The other way is to create a file called .forward in root's home directory that contains the address that the mail should forward to.

Anytime you make a change to the /etc/aliases file, you will need to rebuild the aliases database before that change will take effect. This is done with the command newaliases.

Sendmail Access Control

In the section on mail relaying, we mentioned how important it is that you be careful with mail relaying so that you don't become a spam magnet. We also mentioned that many e-mail services will not accept e-mail from sites that are known to allow spam. So what do you do if you are having problems with a certain site sending you spam? You can use the /etc/access file to automatically reject mail from certain sites.

There are several rules that you can use in the access file. Table 19.1 gives a list of these rules.

TABLE 19.1 The Various Possible Options for Access Rules

Option	Action
OK	Accepts mail from this site, overriding any rules that would reject mail from this site.
RELAY	Allows this domain to relay through the server.
REJECT	Rejects mail from this site and sends a canned error message.
DISCARD	Simply discards any message received from the site.
ERROR:"*n message*"	Where *n* is an RFC821 compliant error code number and *message* can be any message that you would like to send back to the originating server.

The following is an example of three rules that would reject messages from spam.com, and also reject message from lamer.com with an error message. However, mail from the host `user5.lamer.com` is specifically allowed and will override the fact that there is a rule that rejects mail from `lamer.com`.

```
spam.com          REJECT
lamer.com          ERROR:"550 Mail from spammers is not accepted at this site."
user5.lamer.com    OK
```

You will need to restart Sendmail before changes you make to the `access` file will take effect.

Retrieving Mail from Remote Mail Servers

As we mentioned previously, SMTP is designed to work with systems that have a full-time connection to the Internet. But what if you are on a dial-up account? Or if you have another system store your e-mail for you and then you log in to pick it up once in awhile? (Most users who aren't setting up servers will be in this situation.) In this case, you cannot receive e-mail using SMTP, and need to use a protocol such as POP3 or IMAP instead. However, MTAs don't know anything about POP3 or IMAP. So how do you retrieve your mail under these conditions? This is where a program called fetchmail, written by Eric Raymond, comes in to the picture. Fetchmail is designed to contact mail servers using POP3 or IMAP, download mail off the servers, and then inject those messages into the local MTA just as if they had come from a standard SMTP server.

Installing and Configuring Fetchmail

The latest version of fetchmail can be obtained at `http://tuxedo.org/~esr/fetchmail`. It is available in both source and RPM binary formats. Building and installing fetchmail from source is beyond the scope of this chapter, and we will only cover installing the RPM binary version of fetchmail.

Similar to other RPM files, fetchmail can be installed with the `rpm -i` command. This will install all files to their default locations. If, for whatever reason, you need to perform a custom installation, see Chapter 8, "Managing Software and System Resources," for more information on changing the default options or `rpm`.

Once you've installed fetchmail, you will need to configure it to fetch your email. Fetchmail configuration is handled by the file `.fetchmailrc`, which you should create in your home directory.

There are two ways to create the `.fetchmailrc` file. The first is by simply creating and editing the file by hand with any text editor. The second is by using the graphical `fetchmailconf` program. Because the configuration file is straightforward and quite easy to create, we are going to cover the manual method here.

The `.fetchmailrc` file is divided into three different sections. We will cover each of these sections next.

It is very important that these sections appear in the order listed. Once you have switched to an option for a different section, **DO NOT** add options below it from a previous section. Putting options in the wrong place is one of the most common problems that new users make with fetchmail configuration files.

We aren't going to cover all the options available in the `.fetchmailrc` file, but we will cover the most common ones needed to get a basic fetchmail installation up and running. For advanced configuration, see the man page for fetchmail. It is extremely well written and documents all the configuration options in great detail.

The first section of the `.fetchmailrc` contains the global options. These options will affect all the mail servers and user accounts that will be listed later on in the configuration file. Some of these global options can be overridden with local configuration options, but we will discuss these later on in this section. Here is an example of the options that might appear in the global section of the `.fetchmailrc` file.

```
set daemon 600
set postmaster foobar
set logfile ./.fetchmail.log
```

The first line in this example tells fetchmail that it should start in daemon mode, and that it should check the mail servers for new mail every 600 seconds, or 10 minutes. Daemon mode means that after `fetchmail` starts, it will move itself into the background and continue running. Without this line, `fetchmail` would check for mail once when it started, and would then terminate and never check again.

The second option tells `fetchmail` that it should use the local account "foobar" as a last resort address. In other words, any e-mail that it receives and cannot deliver to a specified account should be sent to foobar.

The third line tells `fetchmail` that it should log its activity to the file `./.fetchmail.log`. Alternatively, you can use the line `set syslog`, in which case `fetchmail` will log through the syslog facility.

The second section of the `.fetchmailrc` file contains information on the servers. It contains the information for each of the mail servers that should be checked for new mail. Here is a sample of what the mail section might look like:

```
poll mail.samplenet.org
proto pop3
no dns
```

The first line tells `fetchmail` that it should check the mail server `mail.samplenet.org` at each poll interval that was set in the global options section (which was 600 seconds in our example). The alternative is `skip`. If a mail server line begins with `skip`, it will not be polled as the poll interval, but will only be polled when it is specifically specified on the `fetchmail` command line.

The second line specifies the protocol that should be used when contacting the mail server. In this case, we are using the POP3 protocol. Other legal options are IMAP, APOP, and KPOP. You can also use AUTO here, in which case `fetchmail` will attempt to automatically determine the correct protocol to use with the mail server.

The third line tells `fetchmail` that it shouldn't attempt to do a DNS lookup on multi-drop. You will probably want to include this option if you are running over a dial-up connection.

The third and final section of `.fetchmailrc` contains information about the user account on the server specified in the previous section. Here is a sample:

```
user foobar
pass secretword
fetchall
flush
```

The first line, of course, simply specifies the username that is used to log into the e-mail server, and the second line, of course, specifies the password for that user.

The third line tells `fetchmail` that it should fetch all messages from the server, even if they have already been read.

The fourth line tells `fetchmail` that it should delete the messages from the mail server after it has completed downloading them. This is the default, so we wouldn't really have to specify this option. If you wanted to leave the messages on the server after downloading them, use the option `no flush`.

To summarize, here is what our entire `.fetchmailrc` file looks like:

```
set daemon 600
set postmaster foobar
set logfile ./.fetchmail.log

poll mail.samplenet.org
proto pop3
no dns

user foobar
pass secretword
fetchall
flush
```

What this file basically tells `fetchmail` is to check the POP3 server `mail.samplenet.org` for new mail every 600 seconds, to log in using the username `foobar` and the password `secretword`, to download all messages off the server, to delete the messages from the server after it has finished downloading them, and that any mail it receives that it cannot deliver to a local user should be sent to the account `foobar`.

As mentioned before, many more options can be included in the `.fetchmailrc` file than are listed here. However, these options will get you up and running with a basic configuration. For more advanced options, see the `fetchmail` man page, which is very well written and documents all options in great detail.

19

HANDLING
ELECTRONIC MAIL

Caution

Because the `.fetchmailrc` file contains your mail server password, it should be readable only by you. This means that it should be owned by you and should have permissions no greater than 600. `fetchmail` will complain and refuse to start if the `.fetchmailrc` file has permissions greater than this.

Console Mail Clients

Several console mail clients are available for Red Hat. These clients range from very primitive and arcane command line clients to easy-to-use menu driven clients. We will look at a few of these clients here, starting with the venerable mail program.

`mail`

`mail` is a standard UNIX utility that is included with all UNIX distributions. Because it has a very Spartan interface, it isn't commonly used interactively. However, it is still an extremely useful program to use in shell scripting because it can take all the information it needs to send mail from the command line. No user interaction is required. It is also useful for sending quick notes because it starts up quickly and doesn't require going through menus to send a message.

To begin sending a message in `mail`, simply type **mail** at the shell prompt, followed by the e-mail address that you want to send mail to; for example, `mail john@cheetah.org`. `mail` will then prompt you for the subject of the message. Enter the subject and press Enter. The cursor will then move down to the next blank line. You can now start entering the body of your message. When you have finished, press `Ctrl+D` on a blank line to exit the `mail` program and send the message. (You might be prompted for Cc:. If you do not want to send carbon copies to anyone, simply press Enter here.) The shell prompt will return, and the message will be sent. To abandon a message you are currently writing, press `Ctrl+C`.

If you want to retrieve your e-mail using the `mail` program, simply type **mail** at the shell prompt. The system will respond with something similar to the following:

```
Mail version 8.1 6/6/93.  Type ? for help.
"/var/mail/user1": 1 message 1 unread
>U  1 user2@cheetah.org   Tue Sep 25 07:15   18/551   "Meeting tomorrow"
>N  2 spam@lamer.com      Tue Sep 25 08:25   18/542   "A large and
➥obnoxious spam message"
>N  3 user2@cheetah.org   Tue Sep 25 09:21   17/524   "Meeting has
➥been rescheduled"
>N  4 user5@lion.org      Tue Sep 25 09:24   17/528   "Issues regarding
➥software build"
&
```

The & prompt is `mail`'s way of prompting you for input.

The first column in the list of messages is a flag that indicates the status of the message. For example, `U` means that the message is unread. `N` means that the message is new. The rest of the columns are pretty self explanatory.

To read one of these messages, simply type the message number and press Enter. For example,

```
& 4
Message 4

From user5@lion.org  Tue Sep 25 09:24:35 2001
Date: Tue, 25 Sep 2001 09:24:34 -0500
From: user5@lion.org
To: user1@lion.org
Subject: Issues regarding software build

Hey guy,

The software build of the project appears to be broken.
➥It is blowing up with all kinds of errors. Any ideas?

Thanks

&
```

If you want to respond to this message, you can type **respond** and press Enter. You can also simply type **r** and press Enter. By default, the command will be applied to the currently active message, which is indicated in the message list by a > (and will be the last message that you read). If you want to have the command applied to a different message, you can simply specify the message number after the command. For example r 2 will respond to message number 2.

A complete list of commands is available within mail by typing **?** at the prompt. Note that you can abbreviate all commands to the shortest abbreviation that isn't ambiguous.

Shell Scripting with `mail`

As mentioned previously, mail's most useful application is in shell scripting. This is because it can take all the options it needs to send a message on the command line. For example, suppose we have a shell script that generates a report and stores it as a text file. Now we want to e-mail that text file to a user at the end of the script. With mail, we could use a command such as the following:

```
mail user1@lion.org -s "Report from shell script" < report.txt
```

As you probably guessed, the -s specifies a subject line on the command line, and then we use simple shell redirection to use the file report.txt as the body for the message. It's simple, clean, and requires no user interaction to send the message.

For other options available on the mail command line, see the man page for mail.

Pine

Pine is a menu driven e-mail client developed by the University of Washington that was designed to be easy for new users to work with. It is similar to another client called Elm, but is easier to use. (Pine is a recursive acronym that stands for *Pine is not Elm*). Figure 19.2 shows the Pine interface.

FIGURE 19.2

The Pine e-mail client. It has an easy-to-use, menu driven interface.

Because of its ease of use, Pine is one of the most popular UNIX e-mail clients available.

> **Caution**
>
> Pine has a history of security problems. Although all of these problems have been fixed at the time of this writing, it is likely that many more have not yet been discovered because Pine is written in a very insecure fashion. If you decide to use Pine or make it available to your users, make sure that you keep up with the latest versions of Pine. News and information regarding Pine can be found on the Pine Web site located at http://www.washington.edu/pine.

Mutt

Mutt is a relatively new mail client that is rapidly becoming popular with users. It is called Mutt because it is known as "the mongrel of e-mail clients," in that it attempts to combine the best features of several other clients such as Elm and Pine. Mutt is an extremely feature rich e-mail client, although it isn't as easy to use as Pine. It is however, more secure than Pine. Figure 19.3 shows the Mutt interface.

FIGURE 19.3

Mutt is a powerful and versatile email client that is designed to combine the best features of Elm and Pine.

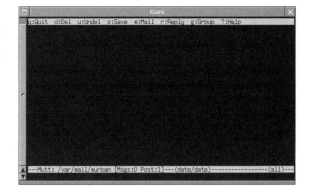

The latest versions of Mutt, as well as news and information about it, are available at `http://www.mutt.org`.

Graphical E-mail Clients

For those who prefer to work with a graphical interface, several graphical e-mail clients are available for Red Hat. We will look at some of these here.

Netscape Messenger

Netscape Communicator comes with Netscape Messenger. The Red Hat version is virtually identical to the Windows version, so we are not going to cover it in depth here.

One of the things you might like about Netscape Messenger is that it has limited MTA functionality built into it. This means that you don't have to configure a separate MTA, and possibly another third-party program to retrieve your e-mail, if you are using a dial-up Internet connection, or some other non-server setup. Of course, as mentioned previously in this chapter, setting up e-mail this way does limit your flexibility somewhat.

Balsa

Balsa is an e-mail client that was designed to work with Gnome. Although several Gnome e-mail clients are available, Balsa is one of the more mature ones. Figure 19.4 shows a screenshot of the Balsa interface.

The latest version of Balsa, as well as news and information about it, is available at `http://www.balsa.net`.

19

HANDLING ELECTRONIC MAIL

FIGURE 19.4

The Balsa e-mail client. It shouldn't take long for users of Outlook Express or Netscape Messenger to get comfortable with the interface.

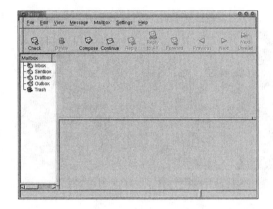

Kmail

If you are using the KDE Desktop Environment rather than the Red Hat default Gnome desktop, you will also have Kmail installed. Similar to Balsa, it won't take users of Outlook Express or Netscape Messenger very long to get used to the Kmail interface. Figure 19.5 shows the Kmail e-mail program.

FIGURE 19.5

The Kmail e-mail client, which is part of the KDE Desktop Environment.

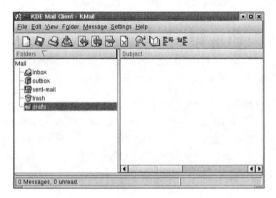

E-mail Forwarding

If you want to have your e-mail forwarded to a different account, it is quite simple to configure this. Simply create a file in your home directory called .forward, and in it, place the e-mail address that you prefer your e-mail to be forwarded to. As long as this file exists, any e-mail for the account will be forwarded to the address in the .forward file.

uuencode and uudecode

As we mentioned at the beginning of the chapter, the SMTP protocol can only transfer plain text. So how do we send images and binary files through e-mail? This is handled by a program called uuencode. Basically, uuencode encodes a binary file as plain text so that it can be transferred across e-mail with SMTP. At the destination, a companion program called uudecode decodes the text file back into its original binary form. Many times, the uuencoding and uudecoding of binary files is handled automatically by the e-mail client, but sometimes it isn't. If you receive a uuencoded file and your e-mail program doesn't recognize it, you will receive something that at first glance appears to be several hundred or even a thousand lines of garbage text. However, the block of text will begin with a special line. Here is an example of what the first few lines of a uuencoded file might look like:

```
begin 644 lion_in_tree.jpg
M_]C_X``02D9)1@`!`0$`8`!@``#_VP!#``(!`0(!`0("`@("`@("`P4#`P,#
M`````!!`0$!`0$`0$``0``
M!`Q`#$Q`Q'Q$``1``!`$$``"
M$;34F2!@``SE5`CW\`A
```

As you probably deduced, the first line of the block gives the permissions that the file should have when it is decoded (644) and the name of the file that should be created when the file is decoded. So how do you decode this file? Simply save the e-mail message as a text file. For example, lion_in_tree.txt. Next, use the uudecode program to decode it:

```
uudecode lion_in_tree.txt
```

This will create a new file, which in this case would be called lion_in_tree.jpg.

So what if you have a binary file that you want to encode so that you can e-mail it to someone? This is of course, done with the uuencode program. Its syntax however, is a little different from the uudecode program. uuencode uses the following syntax:

```
uuencode local_file remote_file
```

local_file is the name of the binary file that is stored on your hard disk. *remote_file* is the name that you want the file to decode as later on when you or someone else uses uudecode on it. Normally, you will probably want to use the same name for *local_file* and *remote_file*.

By default, this will send output to STDOUT, which is normally the screen. However, this isn't very useful, so normally you will use redirection with the uuencode command. Here is an example:

```
uuencode lion_in_tree.jpg lion_in_tree.jpg > lion_in_tree.txt
```

19

HANDLING ELECTRONIC MAIL

This command line will encode the file `lion_in_tree.jpg` into a plain text file that will decode as a file with the same name (`lion_in_tree.jpg`) and store the encoded file in the file `lion_in_tree.txt`. This text file is suitable for e-mailing.

Of course, you can also use pipes to pipe the output of `uuencode` to another application. For example, you could pipe the results to the standard `mail` program and have it mailed to another user directly. For example,

```
uuencode lion_in_tree.jpg lion_in_tree.jpg | mail -s "Lion photograph"
➥user1@lion.org
```

Reference

The following references are recommended reading for e-mail configuration. Of course, not all references will apply to you. Select the ones that apply to the e-mail server that you are using.

Web Resources

`http://www.sendmail.org`—This is the Sendmail home page. Here you will find configuration information and FAQs regarding the Sendmail MTA.

`http://www.postfix.org`—This is the Postfix home page. If you are using the Postfix MTA, documentation and sample configurations can be found at this site.

`http://www.qmail.org`—This is the home page for the qmail MTA. It contains documentation and links to other resources on qmail.

Books

Sendmail from O'Reilly Publishing. This is the de facto standard guide for everything Sendmail. It is loaded with more than 1,000 pages, which gives you an idea of how complicated Sendmail really is.

Postfix from Sams Publishing. This is a new book from Sams Publishing that covers the Postfix MTA.

Running qmail from Sams Publishing. This is similar to the Postfix book from Sams Publishing except that it covers the qmail MTA.

News Server
Management

One of the oldest applications on the Internet is the Usenet network news system. Usenet started out as a network of hosts connected via modems, allowing users to share information on a wide range of topics.

The Usenet newsgroups are still a popular medium for people to exchange ideas. Many sites require a news server to either connect to the Usenet newsgroups, or host private local news groups for local customers. A Red Hat Linux server can provide this functionality.

This chapter describes the software included with Red Hat Linux that can be used to connect your Linux server to Usenet news servers to receive newsfeeds, or to act as a standalone local news server for other news clients.

Overview of Network News

The concept of newsgroups revolutionized the way information was exchanged between people across a network. The Usenet network news system created a method for people to electronically communicate with large groups of people with similar interests.

This section describes the Usenet network newsgroups format, and how newsgroup information is transmitted between hosts.

Newsgroups

Usenet network newsgroups act as a form of bulletin board system. Users can subscribe to individual newsgroups and post messages that are sent to the newsgroup, where all the other subscribers of the newsgroup can read them. Some newsgroups include an administrator, who must approve each message before it is posted. These are called *moderated* newsgroups. Others are open, allowing any subscribed member to post a message.

Usenet Network newsgroups are divided into a hierarchy to make it easier to find individual newsgroups. The hierarchies are based on topics—computers, science, recreation, social issues, and others. Each newsgroup is named as a subset of the higher level topic. For example, the newsgroup `comp` relates to all computer topics. The newsgroup `comp.laptops` relates only to laptop computer issues. Often the hierarchy goes several layers deep. The newsgroup `comp.databases.oracle.server` relates to Oracle server database issues.

Within the newsgroup, each individual message sent is referred to as an *article*. The act of sending an article to a newsgroup is called *posting*. When the article is posted to the newsgroup, it is transferred to all the other hosts in the news network.

The format of articles follows strict guidelines defined in the Internet standards document *Request for Comments (RFC)* 1036. Each article must contain two distinct parts—header lines and a message body. The header lines identify information about when and from whom the article was posted. Many different header lines are defined in RFC 1036 that can be used in article messages. The required header lines are

- FROM:—Whom the message is from
- DATE—When the message was sent
- Newsgroups—What newsgroups the message belongs to
- Subject—The subject of the message
- Message-ID—A unique message ID
- Path—The path the message took to reach the current news system

The body of the message should contain only standard ASCII text characters. No binary characters or files should be posted within news articles. To get around this restriction, binary files are converted to text data using either the standard UNIX uuencode program, or the newer *Multipurpose Internet Mail Extensions (MIME)* protocol. The resulting text file is then posted to the newsgroup. Newsgroup readers can then decode the posted text file back into its original binary form.

A collection of articles posted in response to a common topic is called a *thread*. A thread can contain many different articles as users post messages in response to other posted messages. Some newsreader programs allow the user to track articles based on the thread they belong to. This helps simplify the organization of articles in the newsgroup.

The NNTP Protocol

The method used to transfer newsgroup articles from one host to another is the *Network News Transfer Protocol (NNTP)*, defined in RFC 977. It was designed as a simple client/server protocol that allows two hosts to exchange newsgroup articles in an efficient manner. This section describes the basic parts of NNTP.

NNTP Commands

NNTP behaves similar to the *Simple Mail Transfer Protocol (SMTP)* used for transmitting e-mail between hosts. After the client initiates the NNTP connection, it controls the session by sending plain text commands to the server. The server must respond with either the requested information, or an error code explaining why the information couldn't be returned.

NNTP is composed of several text commands that perform separate functions in transfer-ring news between the hosts. The following sections describe the valid NNTP commands defined in RFC 977.

The ARTICLE Command

The ARTICLE command is used to display a specific article from the news server. The for-mat of the ARTICLE command is as follows

```
ARTICLE ident
```

The *ident* parameter identifies the ARTICLE to retrieve from the news server. Two meth-ods are used to identify individual articles:

- A globally unique message ID
- A newsgroup sequence number

Each article is identified by a message ID value unique for each article, no matter what newsgroup it is located in. The news server that first receives the posting assigns the message ID to the article. Because the message ID must be unique, the news server host-name is often incorporated within the message ID.

Each article is also numbered sequentially within its newsgroup. This number is assigned within the article list on an individual news server, and might vary from news server to news server. (One news server might receive new postings before another news server, and thus assign different sequence numbers). This isn't a problem because the sequence number is only used to identify the articles on the local news server.

Either number can be used to identify an individual article with the ARTICLE command. If the message ID is used, it must be entered within angle brackets(<>). If the numeric sequence is used, you must ensure that the NNTP session is pointing to the proper news-group that the article is in (see the GROUP command described later).

When the news server receives an ARTICLE command, it should return the article header fields, a blank line, and the complete body of the article. If the article message ID or numeric sequence number is invalid, the server will return an error code to the client (see NNTP return codes described later).

The BODY Command

The BODY command is used to display only the body of a posted article in a newsgroup. As with the ARTICLE command, each article is identified by either its message ID or its numerical sequence within the newsgroup. The news server should return the complete text body of the message requested, or an appropriate error code if the article requested was invalid.

The HEAD Command

The HEAD command is used to display only the header lines of a posted article. Again, as with the ARTICLE command, each article is identified by either its message ID or its numerical sequence within the newsgroup. The news server should return all header lines associated with the requested article.

The STAT Command

The STAT command is similar to the ARTICLE command except that no text is returned from the news server. When the STAT command is used with a numerical sequence value, it sets a current article pointer to the specific article within the newsgroup, without returning any text of the article. Using the STAT command with a message ID value does not result in any action.

The GROUP Command

The GROUP command is used to select a specific group to retrieve messages from, and to relate article sequence numbers to. The format of the GROUP command is as follows:

```
GROUP groupname
```

The *groupname* parameter is used to identify the specific group to select articles from. The group name is presented using the standard newsgroup notation (such as comp.laptops).

If the newsgroup requested is valid, the news server returns a text message using the following format:

```
211 num first last groupname
```

The 211 number is the command return code used by the news server. The *num* parameter specifies the total number of articles in the newsgroup. The *first* and *last* parameters are used to specify the sequence numbers of the first and last articles in the newsgroup. The first article in a newsgroup isn't always 1 because old articles are often expired and removed from the news server. And of course, *groupname* specifies the newsgroup name. The news server also sets a current article pointer to the first article in the specified newsgroup.

If the newsgroup is invalid, the news server returns an appropriate error code.

The HELP Command

The HELP command is used to retrieve a list of all valid NNTP commands recognized by the news server. The text returned from the remote news server includes multiple lines of command text, ending with a single period alone on a separate line to indicate the end of the list.

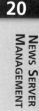

20

NEWS SERVER
MANAGEMENT

The IHAVE Command

The IHAVE command is used to identify what articles the client host already has on hand in its news files. If the server doesn't have that article, it might return a response requesting the client to forward the complete article to the server. The IHAVE command uses the article message ID value as its sole parameter.

The LAST Command

The LAST command instructs the news server to set the current article pointer to the previous article in the current newsgroup. If the article pointer is set to the first article in the newsgroup, the news server returns an error message and keeps the pointer at the first article.

The LIST Command

The LIST command returns a list of the valid newsgroups contained on the news server. The news server responds with a list of all the newsgroups contained on the server, including any local newsgroups. Each newsgroup is listed on a separate line with additional information about the newsgroup. The format of each newsgroup line sent by the news server is as follows

```
group last first post
```

where,

- *group* is the name of the newsgroup on the server.
- *last* is the sequence number of the last article in the newsgroup.
- *first* is the sequence number of the first article currently in the newsgroup.
- *post* is a *y* or *n* character denoting whether posting new articles to the newsgroup is allowed.

The client can use the *first* and *last* information to determine whether any new articles have been posted to a newsgroup since the last time it downloaded articles. The *post* parameter is equally important because the client can determine which newsgroups it can post messages to through the news server.

The NEWSGROUPS Command

The NEWSGROUPS command is similar to the LIST command in that the server will return a list of newsgroups, using the same format as the LIST command. The NEWSGROUPS command differs from the LIST command in that it uses parameters to define a date and time. Only newsgroups created since the date and time supplied are returned in the list. The format of the NEWSGROUPS command is as follows:

```
NEWSGROUPS date time [GMT] [<distributions>]
```

The *date* value is in *YYMMDD* format, whereas the *time* value is in *HHMMSS* format, using the 24-hour clock format. The time is assumed to be relative to the news server's time zone unless the optional GMT parameter is included.

Using the default NEWSGROUPS command, a client can retrieve a list of all newsgroups held on the news server that were created since a specific time. Alternatively, the client can use the optional *distributions* parameter to list what newsgroups to limit the search to. For example, specifying comp in the distributions parameter limits the returned newsgroups to the comp.* hierarchy of newsgroups. Multiple newsgroups can be listed, separated by a comma.

The NEWNEWS Command

The NEWNEWS command is used to retrieve a list of message IDs of articles posted to a specific newsgroup since a specific date. The format of the NEWNEWS command is as follows:

```
NEWNEWS newsgroup date time [GMT] [<distributions>]
```

The *newsgroup* parameter specifies the newsgroups to list the message IDs from. You can use wildcard characters for this parameter (such as comp.*) to list more than one newsgroup. The *date* and *time* parameters define the specific time, using the same format as the NEWSGROUPS command earlier. Also, the *distributions* parameter can be used to limit the search to a specific newsgroup subset. This can be trickier than with the NEWSGROUPS command shown earlier, as both the *newsgroup* and *distributions* parameters can use wildcard characters to list the available newsgroups.

The NEXT Command

The NEXT command is used to advance the current article pointer to the next article in the newsgroup. If the pointer is at the last article in the newsgroup, an error is returned and the pointer is set to the last article in the newsgroup.

The POST Command

The POST command is used to post new articles to the current newsgroup. After the POST command is sent, and the server responds to send the article, the complete article is sent, using the standard message format specified in RFC 1036.

The QUIT Command

The QUIT command is used to terminate the NNTP session.

The SLAVE Command

The SLAVE command is used to indicate to the remote news server that the connecting server is a client NNTP host that servers other clients. This allows the news server the option to give the connecting host a higher priority in transferring articles.

NNTP Response Codes

For each command received from the remote client, the news server must send a return code to indicate whether the command was accepted. Similar to the SMTP format, NNTP return codes are composed of two parts:

- A numeric code indicating the status of the command
- A text message detailing specific results for the command

The numeric code is used by the NNTP software to determine whether the command was successful. Each return code is a three-digit number. The first digit represents the overall status of the submitted command:

- 1—information message
- 2—command OK
- 3—command OK so far, send the rest of it
- 4—command was correct, but couldn't be performed for some reason
- 5—command unimplemented, or incorrect, or a serious program error occurred.

The second digit in the return code represents the function response category:

- 0—connection, setup, and miscellaneous messages
- 1—newsgroup selection
- 2—article selection
- 3—distribution functions
- 4—posting
- 8—nonstandard extensions
- 9—debugging output

The third digit represents the specific command status. Table 20.1 lists some of the more common return codes and their text messages returned to the client.

TABLE 20.1 NNTP Response Codes and Messages

Code	Message
200	server ready—posting allowed
201	server ready—no posting allowed
202	slave status noted
205	closing connection—goodbye!
211	group selected
215	list of newsgroups follows
220	article retrieved—head and body follow
221	article retrieved—head follows
222	article retrieved—body follows
223	article retrieved—request text separately
230	list of new articles by message-id follows
231	list of new newsgroups follows
235	article transferred ok
240	article posted ok
335	send article to be transferred. End with <CR-LF>.<CR-LF>
340	send article to be posted. End with <CR-LF>.<CR-LF>
400	service discontinued
411	no such news group
412	no newsgroup has been selected
420	no current article has been selected
421	no next article in this group
422	no previous article in this group
423	no such article number in this group
430	no such article found
435	article not wanted—do not send it
436	transfer failed—try again later
437	article rejected—do not try again.
440	posting not allowed
441	posting failed
500	command not recognized
501	command syntax error

20

NEWS SERVER MANAGEMENT

TABLE 20.1 continued

Code	Message
502	access restriction or permission denied
503	program fault—command not performed

Sample NNTP Session

Often the easiest way to understand a new protocol is to see it in action. You can manually use NNTP by initiating a `telnet` session with the news server on TCP port 119. This is the port that the NNTP protocol uses to communicate with remote news servers and newsreaders. Because NNTP is ASCII text based, you can manually enter commands and see what responses the news server generates. Listing 20.1 shows a sample NNTP session.

LISTING 20.1 Sample NNTP Session

```
$ telnet localhost 119
Trying 127.0.0.1...
Connected to localhost.localdomain.
Escape character is '^]'.
200 shadrach.isp.net InterNetNews server INN 2.3.2 ready
mode reader
200 shadrach.isp.net InterNetNews NNRP server INN 2.3.2 ready (posting ok).
list
215 Newsgroups in form "group high low flags".
control 0000000000 0000000001 n
control.cancel 0000000000 0000000001 n
control.checkgroups 0000000000 0000000001 n
control.newgroup 0000000000 0000000001 n
control.rmgroup 0000000000 0000000001 n
junk 0000000000 0000000001 n
local.test 0000000006 0000000001 y
.
group local.test
211 4 3 6 local.test
stat 3
223 3 <3B954114.2977714B@isp.net> status
article 3
220 3 <3B954114.2977714B@isp.net> article
Path: shadrach.isp.net!not-for-mail
From: "BLUM,RICHARD" <richard.blum@isp.net>
Newsgroups: local.test
Subject: Test posting
Date: Tue, 04 Sep 2001 16:01:08 -0500
Organization: Rich's test news site
```

LISTING 20.1 continued

```
Lines: 1
Message-ID: <3B954114.2977714B@isp.net>
Reply-To: richard.blum@isp.net
NNTP-Posting-Host: 192.168.1.15
Mime-Version: 1.0
Content-Type: text/plain; charset=us-ascii
Content-Transfer-Encoding: 7bit
X-Trace: shadrach.isp.net 999637147 8917 192.168.1.15 (4 Sep 2001
➥ 20:59:07 GMT)
X-Complaints-To: news@shadrach.isp.net
NNTP-Posting-Date: Tue, 4 Sep 2001 20:59:07 +0000 (UTC)
X-Mailer: Mozilla 4.75 [en]C-CCK-MCD   (WinNT; U)
X-Accept-Language: en
Xref: shadrach.isp.net local.test:3

This is a test posting to the local.test newsgroup.
.
quit
205 .
Connection closed by foreign host.
$
```

The sample session shown in Listing 20.1 demonstrates how a simple NNTP session behaves. The first command entered, mode reader, isn't an NNTP command, but is used by the INN news server software to differentiate a remote newsreader from a remote news server. After the mode reader command is entered, the newsreader can use standard NNTP commands to retrieve articles from various newsgroups. In this example, the GROUP command is used to select a local newsgroup (local.test) to read articles from, and an individual article is displayed.

Types of News Servers

Many different methods can be used when implementing a news server on your network. How the news server will be used determines how you need to configure it. This section describes three of the more popular methods of using news servers on local networks.

Full Newsfeed Server

A full newsfeed news server receives all the available Usenet newsgroup postings from an upstream news server. Because it receives all the newsgroups, it can serve as an upstream news server for other sites, providing newsfeeds to other servers. The other servers themselves might or might not subscribe to all the newsgroups. Besides providing newsfeeds for other sites, the news server can also support newsreader clients that

20

NEWS SERVER MANAGEMENT

connect to the news server to read and post articles to newsgroups. This is shown in Figure 20.1.

FIGURE 20.1

A full newsfeed news server.

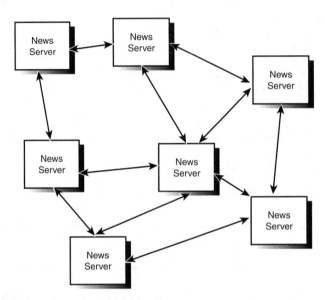

Each news server receives newsfeeds and forwards postings to one or more remote news servers. The full newsfeed server must have enough storage capacity to maintain the newsfeeds for all the newsgroups it services. You might also have to determine how long to maintain articles on the news server. If the remote news servers don't connect to download their newsfeeds on a daily basis, the news server must be able to maintain all the newsfeeds for those days. This can require a large amount of data storage capability.

Leaf Node

A *leaf node* news server only receives newsfeeds from upstream news servers: It doesn't feed other news servers. This is the most common configuration for corporate news servers. Because it doesn't have to feed other news servers, it doesn't have to retrieve all the newsgroups from its upstream newsfeed. You can pick and choose which newsgroups the news server retrieves from the newsfeed. The main role of the leaf node news server is to provide news service to newsreader clients. Figure 20.2 demonstrates how a leaf node fits into the news server system.

FIGURE 20.2

A leaf node news server.

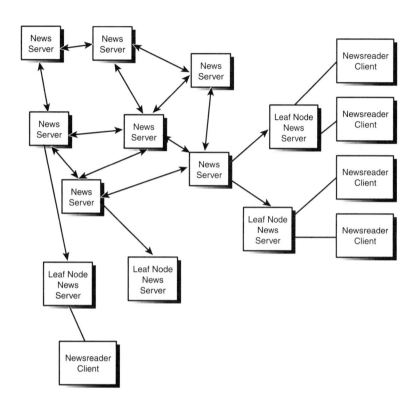

The leaf node does however have to maintain a system for users to connect to the news server to read and post messages. This is often done using UNIX, Microsoft Windows, or Apple Macintosh workstation software. Each client must connect to the leaf node to download articles from specific newsgroups, and upload postings made to the newsgroups. The leaf node must be able to forward new postings from customers to the newsfeed server.

Local News Server

Although many organizations don't want to participate in the worldwide Usenet newsgroups, they often want to use the newsgroup software to create their own news server to handle internal communications within the organization. Usually these communications need to remain private to the organization and don't need to be sent to all the Usenet newsfeed hosts around the world.

Two methods are used to accomplish this. Many organizations create a standalone news server that doesn't receive any newsfeeds from Usenet servers. The server only contains local newsgroups that are used for internal corporate communications. Alternatively, you can create local newsgroups on a Usenet news server that aren't forwarded through any newsfeeds in the Usenet system. This allows organizations to create their own local newsgroups that their employees can participate in without sharing their information with the rest of the world.

Thus, local newsgroups can be created on news servers that either aren't connected to the Usenet network, or that are connected to the Usenet network, but do not forward the local groups to their upstream newsfeeds. Any postings to the local newsgroups appear only on the local news server. Figure 20.3 demonstrates both news servers that contain both Usenet and local newsgroups and a standalone local news server.

FIGURE 20.3

A news server servicing both local and Usenet newsgroups.

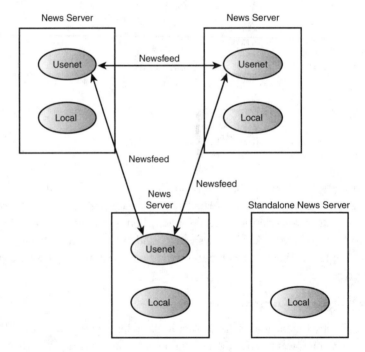

The Usenet news servers allow clients to post articles to both the local and Usenet newsgroups. However, only the articles posted to Usenet newsgroups are forwarded to the upstream news server. The local articles remain on only the local news server.

The INN News Server

The *InterNet News Package (INN)* is the most popular news server software used on UNIX servers. The *Internet Software Consortium (ISC)* currently maintains it, along with the INN Web site (`http://www.isc.org/products/INN/`). The Red Hat Linux distribution includes the INN package as a standard RPM file.

This section describes how the INN package works, how to install it, and how to configure it for the different types of network news servers.

The Innd Programs

The INN package contains many different executable programs and configuration files that allow the Red Hat Linux server to work as a network news server. The standard INN RPM package contains all the files necessary for the installation. Table 20.2 describes some of the INN programs included in the distribution.

TABLE 20.2   INN Program Files

File	Description
ctlinnd	Manually sends control messages to the innd program.
getlist	Obtains a list of newsgroups from a news server.
grephistory	Queries the history database files for a specific message ID value and returns the record information.
inncheck	Examines INN configuration files and databases.
innconfval	Prints the values of parameters specified in the innd command line.
innd	The INN daemon program that handles all incoming newsfeeds and spawns INN programs as needed.
inndstart	Starts the innd daemon from the news user ID.
innreport	Summarizes INN log files into readable reports.
innstat	Prints a snapshot of the current status of the INN system.
innwatch	Monitors the running INN system, and if necessary throttles the newsfeeds to help reduce the load on the news server.
mailpost	Manually sends a mail message into a specified newsgroup.
makedbz	Creates binary indexed database files from the history file.
makehistory	Creates a text history file of message IDs seen by the news server.

20

NEWS SERVER MANAGEMENT

TABLE 20.2 continued

File	Description
news.daily	Script file often run as a cron job to perform daily maintenance of the news server.
nnrpd	Used by the innd daemon to communicate with newsreaders.
nntpget	Connects to a remote news server and retrieves articles specified on the standard input.
nntpsend	Connects to a remote news server and posts articles to newsgroups.
ovdb_recover	Attempts to repair a damaged INN database file.
ovdb_upgrade	Attempts to upgrade an existing INN database file.
prunehistory	Removes specific filenames from the history file.
pullnews	Retrieves newsgroup articles from one news server and forwards them to another news server.
rnews	Receives newsgroup articles from a news server using a UUCP connection.
scanlogs	Summarizes information in the INN logs files, and performs general cleaning and rotating of the log files.
sm	Provides a command-line interface to the article storage manager.

As you can see, lots of programs are used to help the news process on the server. Besides all the program files, the INN package uses lots of configuration files to define how articles are handled. Table 20.3 shows the different configuration files that are used.

TABLE 20.3 INN Configuration Files

File	Description
control.ctl	Specifies how control messages are handled.
expire.ctl	Specifies how articles are expired.
incoming.conf	Specifies addresses and authentication information for servers that send newsfeeds to your news server.
inn.conf	The primary general configuration file for the innd program.
innfeed.conf	Specifies parameters for the incoming newsfeed handler.

TABLE 20.3   continued

File	Description
innwatch.ctl	Determines how the innwatch program monitors the INN system.
moderators	Specifies e-mail addresses for moderators of moderated newsgroups.
motd.news	Specifies information posted to newsreaders if they send a list motd command.
newsfeeds	Specifies which newsgroups are fed to other news servers from this news server.
nnrpd.track	Specifies newsreaders or servers that should have their activity recorded during an NNTP session.
nntpsend.ctl	Specifies remote news servers that your news server will feed articles to in batch mode.
passwd.nntp	Specifies passwords used to connect to remote news servers.
readers.conf	Specifies authorized remote newsreader addresses, along with newsgroup permissions.
sasl.conf	Specifies file locations for the encryption keys used for the SASL configuration.
storage.conf	Specifies the storage method used for specific newsgroup articles.
subscriptions	Specifies a list of newsgroups that newsreaders can subscribe to.

As you can see, there are also lots of configuration files that are required for INN to work. But don't get worried: Most of the parameters defined in the configuration files will work fine with their default settings straight from the Red Hat RPM package. There are usually only a few changes that you need to make for the INN news server to work in your particular network news environment.

Installing Innd

The Red Hat Linux distribution uses two separate RPM files to install the INN package. The first package, simply called inn, installs the necessary configuration and application files needed for the INN package to work on the system. The second package, called inn-devel, is used to install INN header files that some external newsreader programs use to work with inn. You don't need to install the inn-devel package for INN, but if you are using other newsreader packages on the server, it might not be a bad idea to install it.

You can check to see whether the INN package is already installed on your Red Hat Linux server by using the rpm command with the -qa option, and piping the output to the grep command:

```
$ rpm -qa | grep inn
inn-2.3.2-5
$
```

This example shows the inn-2.3.2-5 package installed on the system. If no packages are returned, you must install the RPM package. As with other RPM packages, you can install the INN packages using the rpm command-line program with the -ivh option to show a status line as the package installs.

Configuring the Innd Package

After all the INN files are installed, you must begin the task of setting the proper parameters in the configuration files before you attempt to start the innd program. When you modify the INN configuration files, you must ensure that you are logged in as the news user (or use the su command to become the news user). If the ownership or permissions of any of the INN configuration files changes, the innd package won't start.

Although there are lots of configuration files, there are just a handful of files that need to be modified for a simple news server. This section describes common changes that must be made to the configuration files to get your news server operational.

The Innd.conf File

The innd.conf file is the heart of the innd configuration process. It defines the core features of the news server operation. Each parameter is listed on a separate line, using the following format:

```
parameter:    value
```

Lots of parameters are defined in the innd.conf file, but fortunately most of them will work just fine with their default values. Table 20.4 shows the parameters that should be changed in the innd.conf file to represent your news server environment.

TABLE 20.4 The Innd.conf Configuration Parameters

Parameter	Description
domain	The complete domain name of your Internet domain.
mailcmd	The command innd uses to send mail messages. Usually this should be the innmail program.
mta	The command used to invoke the system MTA mailer. The %s variable is included to replace the recipient address in the command line. If you have installed the default Red Hat sendmail package, this should be set OK.
pathhost	The name of the host to place in the Path: article header line. This should represent your news server hostname.
server	The name of a default NNTP server.
maxconnections	The maximum number of incoming NNTP connections your news server will support.
ovmethod	The storage method used for the article indexes. The default of tradindexed is usually fine for small sites. Large sites might want to use faster methods.
fromhost	The domain used to construct e-mail addresses by the INN system. Should be set to your local system address.
moderatormailer	The e-mail address where messages posted to moderated newsgroups is sent if there is no corresponding entry in the moderators file.
organization	A text description of your organization. This value is used in the article header lines for all articles posted from your site, so be careful!
status	How frequently (in seconds) innd should create a status report. A value of 0 disables this feature (not recommended).
timer	How frequently (in seconds) innd should report performance statistics to the logfiles. A value of 0 disables this feature (not recommended).

The inn.conf file is a text file that can be modified using a standard text editor, such as the vi editor. For a minimum configuration, you should ensure that the organization, domain, mailcmd, mta, server, and fromhost parameters are specified. Listing 20.2 shows sample inn.conf file entries for a test server.

20

NEWS SERVER MANAGEMENT

LISTING 20.2 Sample inn.conf Configuration File Entries

```
mta:                /usr/sbin/sendmail -oi -oem %s
organization:       Rich's test news site
ovmethod:           tradindexed
domain:             isp.net
mailcmd:            /usr/bin/innmail
status:             3600
timer:              3600
```

The sample configuration uses the standard sendmail MTA for the mailer, the traditional indexed method for overview databases, and creates new status reports every hour.

The Incoming.conf File

The incoming.conf file is used to define from where the news server receives its newsfeeds. If you are building a standalone news server that doesn't receive newsfeeds, this file is still important because it also specifies the local address of the news server.

The incoming.conf file contains three types of data:

- Peer news server definitions
- Groups of news server definitions
- Parameter value definitions

Parameters can be defined globally, within peer definitions, and within group definitions. As expected, parameters defined globally apply to all peers and groups defined in the configuration file. Parameters defined within group definitions apply to all peers within the group definition and override any global definitions of the same parameter. Finally, parameters defined within peer definitions apply only to the peer, and they override any group or global definitions of the same parameter.

Ten parameters can be used to define the connection with a remote news server. Table 20.5 describes these parameters.

TABLE 20.5 Incoming.conf Parameters

Parameter	Description
hostname	The address of the remote host in either a fully qualified domain name format or as an IP address.
streaming	Whether NNTP streaming commands can be used with the remote news server. (default = True)
max-connections	Defines the maximum number of simultaneous NNTP connections allowed with the remote news server. A value of 0 defines an unlimited number of connections. (default = 0)

TABLE 20.5   continued

Parameter	Description
hold-time	Defines the time (in seconds) to hold the connection before closing. A value of 0 defines an immediate close. (default = 0)
password	Defines a password that must be used to connect with the remote news server. (default = no password)
patterns	A list of newsgroups accepted from this host. (default = *)
email	Reserved for future use. (Default = empty)
comment	Reserved for future use. (default = empty)
skip	Causes the peer definition to be skipped. (default = False)
noresendid	Defines whether innd should send a response for the remote news server to stop sending articles already received from another peer. (default = False)

Each remote news server that sends newsfeeds to your server must be defined in a peer definition. The peer definition contains parameter values that define how the news server should communicate with the remote news server. The format of the peer definitions is as follows:

```
peer name {
          parameter:    value
}
```

The *name* value identifies a name that the remote news server will be identified by within the configuration. A simple peer definition looks like this:

```
peer mainfeed {
          hostname:         news.mainisp.net
          max-connections:  10
}
```

This defines a newsfeed that will provide all newsgroups to the news server. It defines a max-connections value of 10, which would override any globally defined max-connections value.

One special peer definition must be defined for all news servers. The ME peer definition must point to the localhost address of the server for it to be able to receive articles posted by newsreaders. The definition should look like this:

```
peer ME {
          hostname:       "localhost, 127.0.0.1"
}
```

Note that the ME peer definition uses two separate hostnames. A comma must separate them, and they must be enclosed in quotes. The standard Red Hat inn distribution already has the ME peer definition defined in the incoming.conf file.

Group definitions can be used to create groups of news servers with common parameters. An example of this is shown in Listing 20.3.

LISTING 20.3 Sample Incoming.conf Group Definition

```
max-connections:     5

peer normalhost {
                hostname:     news.ispmain.net
                max-connections:     10
}

group altsites {
    patterns:          alt.*
    peer altsite1 {
                    hostname:     news.site1.net
    }
    peer altsite2 {
                    hostname:     news.site2.net
                    max-connections:     20
    }
}

peer ME {
        hostname:     "localhost, 127.0.0.1"
}
```

The normalhost peer definition defines a news server that feeds all newsgroups to the news server. The alsites group defines two separate sites that feed only the alt. hierarchy newsgroups to the news server. The altsite2 entry also overrides the global max-connections parameter and allows up to 20 simultaneous NNTP connections with the news.site2.net host to help speed things along. The last peer definition defines the standard ME peer to allow newsreaders to post messages to the news server.

The Newsfeeds File

Although the incoming.conf file controls how the news server receives newsfeeds, the newsfeeds file controls how the news server sends newsfeeds to any downstream news servers. Each server that uses your news server as a newsfeed must be entered into the newsfeeds file. Even if you aren't being a newsfeed for any other sites, you must have a newsfeed file with the special ME definition.

The format of an entry in the newsfeeds file is as follows:

```
sitename[/exclude,exclude,...]\
                :pattern,pattern...[/distrib,distrib...]\
                :flag,flag...\
                :param
```

The *sitename* value is the hostname of the site that is receiving newsfeeds from your news server. Any articles that contain the *sitename* value in their path header line won't be forwarded (because they originated from that server). The *exclude* values define newsgroups that you don't want to forward to the downstream news servers. This must include the `local.*` newsgroup hierarchy. The *pattern* value(s) specify newsgroups that will be forwarded to the downstream news server. You can specify more than one pattern within the entry. The *flag* and *param* values specify special behaviors that control how the newsfeeds are established and how articles are sent.

The newsfeeds configuration file is possibly the most complicated to configure. For a standalone news server that is only serving local newsgroups, you can use the default newsfeeds file supplied with the Red Hat Linux distribution. It contains a single ME entry that defines how the local news server will feed itself:

```
ME:!*/!local,!collabra-internal::
```

This entry rejects all newsgroups from the local and collabra-internal newsgroups, and accepts all other newsgroups. If you are planning on feeding newsgroups to other news servers, you should consult the INN documentation because there are lots of specific parameter settings that you must set.

The Storage.conf File

Another important configuration file used by innd is the /etc/news/storage.conf file. It tells the innd program how to store newsgroup articles on the news server. Currently, four different methods can be used for storing articles on the news server:

- Traditional spool
- Time hashed spool
- Time hashed buffered spool
- Cyclic buffer spool

The *traditional spool* method (tradspool) was the method used in the original versions of INN. Originally, innd created a text file for each article received, placed in a specific directory for each newsgroup. Although this method is simple to implement, it creates problems for high-volume news servers. As individual newsgroups receive lots of

20

NEWS SERVER MANAGEMENT

articles, retrieving the articles from directories with hundreds of files becomes a bottle-neck for the news server.

The *time hashed spool* method (`timehash`) attempts to solve this problem by creating directories based on the arrival time of the articles. This creates more directories with fewer articles in each directory, but adds an additional overhead for reading articles in that it is more difficult for the news server to find an individual article.

The *time hashed buffered spool* method (`timecaf`) improves on the time hashed spool method by concatenating multiple articles into a single text file. This saves processing time by causing fewer file creations, but again increases reading time by causing the server to search for individual articles.

The last method, *cyclic buffer spool* (`cnfs`) attempts to use a preconfigured file buffer to speed things up. As articles are received, they are placed in a preconfigured file of a set size. This greatly speeds up processing because no new files are created as articles are received. The catch to the `CNFS` method is that the buffer files are created at a set size. When the articles fill up a buffer file, the file is overwritten starting from the beginning. This method forces an automatic expiration of articles on the news server. Although this prevents the server from running out of disk space, it can cause premature article expiration—depending on the size of the buffer file. Most news administrators who use this method learn by trial and error the buffer file size necessary to handle the standard news traffic load at their site.

Each storage method is configured in a separate section of the configuration file. The format of each section is as follows:

```
method methodname {
                class: storage_class
                newsgroups: wildmat
                size: minsize[,maxsize]
                expires: mintime[,maxtime]
                options: options
        }
```

The *methodname* value identifies the storage method defined in the file, `tradspool`, `timehash`, `timecaf`, or `cnfs`. Each method requires parameters to define how it will operate:

- `class`—An identifying number unique for each storage method
- `newsgroups`—A list of which newsgroups were stored using the defined method
- `size`—A range of article sizes (in bytes) that should be stored using the defined method

- `expires`—A range of article expiration times that should be stored using the defined method
- `options`—Used for passing special options to the `cnfs` storage method

Listing 20.4 shows a sample storage.conf file that uses the `timehash` storage method for the local newsgroups, and the `cnfs` storage method for all other newsgroups.

LISTING 20.4 Sample Storage.conf File

```
method timehash {
        newsgroups: local.*
        class: 0
}

method cnfs {
        newsgroups: *
        class: 1
        size: 0,3999
        expires: 0s,4d
}
```

If a newsgroup isn't covered by a specific storage method, INN will produce an error message for each article received for that newsgroup, as well as not store the article. This can have a devastating effect on the news server. For a simple news server, it is best to select a single method of storage and configure the storage.conf file to use that method for all the newsgroups. By default, the Red Hat storage.conf file doesn't define any storage methods. You must define at least one method to use for INN to work properly.

The Readers.conf File

In version 2.3 and later of the INN package, the readers.conf configuration file is used to define permissions for newsreaders to your news server. Older versions of the INN package used the nnrp.access file to set permissions. If you are allowing users to connect to your news server to read articles, you must configure the readers.conf file to support them.

The readers.conf file consists of the following three types of data.

- An authentication definition
- An access definition
- Parameters and values

The authentication definition defines categories of users who will be accessing your news server. You can create several different categories of users based on various factors, such

20

NEWS SERVER
MANAGEMENT

as remote address, newsgroups accessed, or type of authentication method used. The authentication section format is as follows:

```
auth name {
                hosts: host-wildmat
                auth: auth-program
                res: res-program
                default: defuser
                default-domain: defdomain
        }
```

The *name* value is used as a label to uniquely identify the authentication definition. The authentication definition uses parameters and values to identify its actions. The `hosts` parameter uses the *host-wildmat* value to identify individual remote hosts that are covered by the authentication definition. These can be listed using either hostnames or numeric IP addresses, along with matching wildcard characters.

The `res` parameter specifies an authentication program used to authenticate the connection based on its network information. Alternatively, you can use the `auth` parameter to specify an authentication program that can authenticate the connection using a user ID/password pair. If you are interested in authenticating remote news servers, consult the INN documentation because it is a somewhat complicated process.

The access definition defines categories of access restrictions and permissions for groups of newsreaders. The format of the access definition is as follows:

```
access name {
                users: identity-wildmat
                newsgroups: group-wildmat
                access: permissions
}
```

The *name* value must match a corresponding authentication definition. The parameters defined in the access definition only apply to the hosts defined in the corresponding authentication definition. The `users` parameter limits the access rules to the specific set of users listed in the value. If the `users` parameter isn't present, all users apply. The `newsgroups` parameter defines which newsgroups the group has access to, and the *access* parameter defines what access privileges they have. The privileges are defined as follows:

- R—Read-only access.
- P—Posting articles is allowed.
- A—Posting approved articles is allowed (using a moderator).
- N—The NEWNEWS command is allowed.
- L—Allowed to post to newsgroups that are set to disallow local posting.

A sample readers.conf file that allows all local newsreaders to read and post articles to all newsgroups is shown in Listing 20.5.

LISTING 20.5   Sample Readers.conf Configuration File

```
auth "localhost" {
    hosts: "localhost, 127.0.0.1, 192.168.1.1, stdin"
    default: "<localhost>"
}

access "localhost" {
    users: "<localhost>"
    newsgroups: "*"
    access: RPA
}
auth "localnet" {
        hosts: "192.168.*"
        default: "<user>"
        default-domain: "isp.net"
        }

access "localnet" {
        users: "*@isp.net"
        newsgroups: "*"
        access: "RP"
}
```

The sample readers.conf file shown in Listing 20.5 defines two separate groups of users. The first group, called localhost, allows the localhost, address 127.0.0.1, address 192.168.1.1 (the local host's network address), and any connection using the standard input to connect to the news server.

The second group defines any client located on the 192.168. network. It allows both reading and posting of all newsgroups to any client on the network.

The Active and Newsgroups Files

The active and newsgroups files, although not specifically configuration files, are crucial to the operation of the news server. These files control what newsgroups your news server will handle. Each newsgroup handled by the news server must have an entry in both the active and newsgroups files. Both of these files are located in the /var/lib/news directory when installed using the Red Hat RPM package.

The format of the active file is as follows:

```
newsgroup first last post
```

20

NEWS SERVER
MANAGEMENT

Each newsgroup handled by the news server is defined on a separate line in the active file. The default Red Hat Linux INN configuration supplies a skeleton active file that defines several special newsgroups:

```
control 0000000000 0000000001 n
control.cancel 0000000000 0000000001 n
control.checkgroups 0000000000 0000000001 n
control.newgroup 0000000000 0000000001 n
control.rmgroup 0000000000 0000000001 n
junk 0000000000 0000000001 n
```

The first field defines the newsgroup name. The second and third fields define the first and last article sequence numbers. The final field defines whether posting is allowed for the newsgroup on the news server. The default newsgroups are set to 'n' to prevent posting.

The control and control.cancel newsgroups are used to receive NNTP control articles for performing maintenance on the news server. As remote sites create new newsgroups, and delete old newsgroups, control articles are sent to the news servers to perform these tasks. The `control` series of newsgroups handle these articles. Also, the `junk` newsgroup is created to handle articles that have been misposted and have no place to go.

The preceding sample article file is fine if you are running a standalone news server. If you plan on running a news server that receives newsfeeds from Usenet, you must create an active file that lists all the newsgroups your news server will carry. You can obtain a complete active file containing all the current newsgroups from the ISC FTP server using the URL `ftp://ftp.isc.org/pub/usenet/CONFIG/active.gz`.

After you download and uncompress the current complete active file, you can remove any newsgroups that you don't want your news server to carry.

Along with the active file is the newsgroups file. It must contain the same newsgroup definitions as the active file. Again, you can either use the default newsgroup file supplied by the default installation, or you can download a complete current newsgroup file from the ISC FTP server shown previously and remove the newsgroups you don't want to carry. The default newsgroups file looks like this:

```
control                 Various control messages (no posting).
control.cancel          Cancel messages (no posting).
control.checkgroups     Hierarchy check control messages (no posting).
control.newgroup        Newsgroup creation control messages (no posting).
control.rmgroup         Newsgroup removal control messages (no posting).
junk                    Unfiled articles (no posting).
```

The History Files

Also in the /var/lib/news directory are the INN history files. These files are used to keep a running index of each article posted to each newsgroup. It is crucial that these files are not tampered with because if they get out of sync with the actual newsgroup articles, the news server will have problems retrieving articles.

There are two separate parts to the history files—a text history file and a set of binary index files created using a database program such as the common Berkely db package. You must create both sets of files before you can start the innd daemon.

The makehistory command is used to create the text history file based on the current newsgroup articles on the server (which should be none).

After the text history file is created, the binary index files must be created. The makedbz program is used to convert the text history file into the binary index files. The makedbz -i command creates the following three separate binary files:

- history.n.dir
- history.n.index
- history.n.hash

These files must be renamed to the standard history filenames (history.dir and history.pag) before the innd program will recognize them. After the history files have been created, you are finally ready to start the news server.

Running Innd

The inndstart program is the best way to start the innd daemon, which in turn starts other INN package programs. The inndstart program must be run from the news user ID. It starts the innd program as well as the controlchan program in background mode. The innd program listens for newsfeeds and newsreader requests on the NNTP TCP port. If a remote newsreader establishes a connection, the innd program spawns the active program to authenticate the remote connection and handle the newsreader requests. If the incoming articles are control articles, they are passed to the controlchan program for processing.

After the innd program is running, you can control it by using the ctlinnd program. The format of the ctlinnd program is as follows:

```
ctlinnd [ -h ] [ -s ] [ -t timeout ] command [ argument...]
```

The -s option suppresses any output from the ctlinnd command. This option is often used in batch programs. The -t option specifies how long to wait for a response from the server (in seconds). If you are connecting to a server across a slow link or to a slow server, you can increase the value of *timeout*.

The *command* parameters define what actions the ctlinnd program should take with the innd news server. The -h command line option prints a summary of all the available *command* parameters that can be used with ctlinnd. For now, you can use the newgroup command to create a new local newsgroup that newsreaders can use to read and post messages:

```
$ctlinnd newgroup local.book.club y rich@ispnet1.net
```

The newgroup command uses three parameters:

- The name of the new newsgroup
- A flag to define what type of newsgroup to create (y stands for regular open group, and m stands for a moderated group)
- An e-mail address for the maintainer of the new newsgroup

The ctlinnd program should be run from the news user ID. If the command is successful, it will return a simple OK message. You can use the getlist command to check whether the new newsgroup has been added to the news server.

The Cleanfeed Package

One problem that has plagued the Usenet newsgroup system is the proliferation of spam mail messages. Spam providers often attempt to post their messages to newsgroups to force messages to a large captive audience.

Several methods have been used to help minimize spam on the newsgroups. One of the most effective methods is the cleanfeed package. It consists of a Perl script that scans incoming newsfeed articles and posted articles from newsreaders, searching for common spam phrases and addresses, as well as any newsgroup abnormalities. This helps block spam messages before they enter the news server.

The Red Hat Linux distribution includes the cleanfeed RPM package. You can install it using the rpm package installer program as normal. Once installed, you must modify the cleanfeed configuration files to meet your news environment requirements.

The cleanfeed package consists of two files used for the program:

- A Perl script—/usr/bin/filter/filter_innd.pl
- A configuration file—/etc/news/cleanfeed.conf

The Perl script is added to the Perl script files that are run by the innd daemon. The configuration file contains many parameters that can be turned on or off to control what types of messages the `filter_innd.pl` script will block. Many default parameters are set that are useful in blocking simple spam, such as catching binary files sent to text newsgroups.

After you have set the parameters in the configuration file, you must tell the innd daemon to use the new Perl script. This is done using the ctlinnd program:

```
$ctlinnd reload filter.perl starting cleanfeed
```

The reload command uses two parameters—the name of the script to load and the reason for loading it. The reason is logged in the log files. Once innd recognizes the new cleanfeed Perl script, you can turn the filtering capabilities on by using the following command:

```
$ctlinnd perl y
```

and turn the filtering capabilities off by using the following command:

```
$ctlinnd perl n
```

News Readers

Whether or not your Red Hat server is set up as a news server, you can use a newsreader program to read newsgroup articles. The newsreader programs just require a connection to a news server. It doesn't matter if the news server is on the same machine or a remote news server on the other side of the world.

Several programs are available for UNIX systems to connect to news servers to read and post articles in newsgroups. This section describes the newsreaders available with the Red Hat Linux distribution.

The Slrn Program

The slrn program is a text-based newsreader program included with the Red Hat distribution. It uses the ncurses package to paint text-based windows on the terminal screen. It can be used to both read and post articles to newsgroups on a configured news server.

The slrn program is included in the slrn RPM package and can be installed using the standard rpm package installer. Once installed, the only configuration required is to create an environment variable NNTPSERVER that points to the desired news server you want to retrieve articles from. This can be done either from the command line before you start slrn, or can be entered into the .bash_profile file in your $HOME directory. To manually enter it, you can type the following:

```
$ NNTPSERVER=192.168.1.1 ; export NNTPSERVER ; slrn
```

This single command line sets the NNTPSERVER variable to the IP address of the news server. You could also use the domain name of the news server, or the localhost name if the same machine also is running the innd program.

When the slrn program starts, it displays a list of the groups available on the news server. You can select which group you want to read articles from, and then select the individual articles to read. Figure 20.4 shows a sample slrn screen.

FIGURE 20.4

A sample slrn article display.

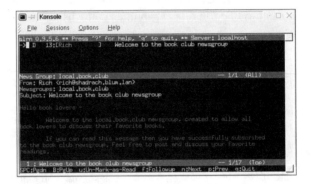

Pine

Although the *Program for Internet News and Email (Pine)* package has gained popularity as a standard UNIX mail reader package, as its name suggests, it also has the capability of reading and posting articles to newsgroups. The Pine package is installed by default in the Red Hat Linux distribution.

You must configure the news server address in the Pine setup screen. You can do this by first selecting the S option from the main Pine menu, and then selecting the C (configure) option from the setup options. Figure 20.5 demonstrates where this is done.

You can enter either the IP or domain name address of the news server. After you enter the news server address, you can select it from the folders list using the F option from the main menu. After selecting the news server, Pine displays a list of all newsgroups available on the news server. You must then select the newsgroup you want to see articles from.

FIGURE 20.5

The Pine configuration screen.

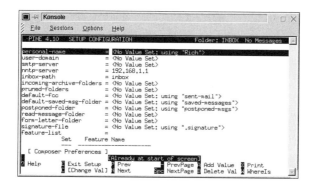

The Xrn Program

One of the first attempts at creating a graphical newsreader program was the XRN program. It uses standard X Window graphics to list newsgroups and display articles. Figure 20.6 shows a sample XRN display.

FIGURE 20.6

The XRN newsreader display.

Similar to the slrn program, the XRN program uses the NNTPSERVER environment variable to define the news server address. Ensure that you set that value before starting the XRN program.

The Knode Program

The KNode program is part of the *K Desktop Environment (KDE)* networks package, which is included in the Red Hat distribution as the kdenetwork RPM package. This is usually installed by default if you select the KDE windows manager option in the Red Hat installation.

The KNode program is an excellent graphical program that allows you to connect to news servers (again, either the local server or a remote server) and select newsgroups to read and post articles to. Before you can begin though, you must configure the address of your news server into KNode.

This is accomplished from the Settings menu item on the main KNode window. From the Settings drop-down menu, select the Configure KNode item. The KNode configuration window appears. Under the Accounts item, you can select the News item. A list of configured news servers appears in the window. To add a new news server, click the New button. Figure 20.7 shows the news server edit window where you can enter the new news server information.

FIGURE 20.7

The KNode news server configuration window.

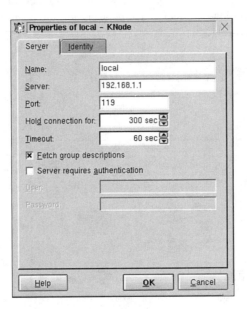

The Pan Program

Never to be outdone by the KDE group, the GNOME windows manager group has also created its own graphical newsreader program. The Pan program is normally installed if you select the GNOME windows manager option, but can also be manually installed using the Pan RPM package file included with the distribution.

The Pan program is another excellent graphical program that allows you to connect to news servers and select newsgroups to read and post articles to. Similar to the KNode program, you must configure the news servers that you want to connect to in the Pan program.

This is accomplished by selecting the Online/Offline Settings option from the drop-down menu of the Online menu item. The Pan Preferences window is displayed, showing various different options that can be configured for the Pan system. Select the News Servers option, and the list of configured news servers appears in the window. Click the New button, and the New/Edit Server window appears, where you can enter the information for the new news server. Figure 20.8 shows a sample of this.

FIGURE 20.8

The Pan news server configuration window.

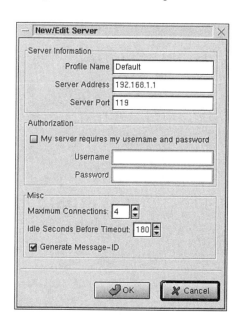

Reference

http://www.faqs.org/rfcs/rfc977.html—RFC 977

http://www.faqs.org/rfcs/rfc1036.html—RFC 1036

http://www.isc.org/products/INN/—The INN package

http://www.slrn.org—The slrn program

http://www.washington.edu/pine/—The Pine program

`http://www.mit.edu/people/jik/software/xrn.html`—The XRN program

`http://apps.kde.com/`—The KNode program

`http://pan.rebelbase.com/`—The Pan program

Programming and Productivity

PART

IV

Introduction to C/C++ Programming Tools

When you think about putting lines of code together in Linux, the first thing you're likely to think of is scripting. And why not? Linux shells support a wide range of commands that can be combined, in the form of scripts, into reusable programs. Command scripts for shell programs (and utilities such as gawk and Perl) are all the programming that many users need in order to customize their computing environments.

Many users find it fairly easy to learn a scripted, interpreted language because the commands usually can be tried out one at a time, with clearly visible results. You can learn more about scripting in Chapter 22, "Shell Scripting."

Script languages have several shortcomings, however. To begin with, the commands a user types into a script are read and evaluated only when the script is being executed. Interpreted languages are flexible and easy to use, but they are inefficient because the commands must be reinterpreted each time the script is executed. Interpreted languages are also ill suited to manipulating the computer's memory and I/O devices directly. Therefore, programs that process scripts (such as the various Linux shells, the awk utility, and the Perl interpreter) are themselves written in the C and C++ languages, as is the Linux kernel.

Learning a language such as C or C++ is more complex and difficult because you must learn to think in terms of machine resources and the way actions are accomplished within the computer, rather than in terms of user-oriented commands.

Linux comes with many tools that support program development. Not only are there the C and C++ compilers, but there are also debuggers, project organizing tools, and code management tools. This chapter introduces you to the commands used to compile C and C++ programs along with some of the other tools in the programming environment. Additional resources are listed at the end of the chapter.

Background on the C Language

C is the programming language most frequently associated with UNIX. Since the 1970s, the bulk of the UNIX operating system and its applications have been written in C. Because the C language doesn't directly rely on any specific hardware architecture, UNIX was one of the first portable operating systems. In other words, the majority of the code that makes up UNIX doesn't know and doesn't care which computer it is actually running on. Machine-specific features are isolated in a few modules within the UNIX kernel, which makes it easy for you to modify them when you are porting to different hardware architectures.

C was first designed by Dennis Ritchie for use with UNIX on DEC PDP-11 computers. The language evolved from Martin Richard's BCPL, and one of its earlier forms was the B language, which was written by Ken Thompson for the DEC PDP-7. The first book on C was *The C Programming Language* by Brian Kernighan and Dennis Ritchie, published in 1978.

In 1983, the American National Standards Institute (ANSI) established a committee to standardize the definition of C. The resulting standard is known as *ANSI C*, and it is the recognized standard for the language, grammar, and a core set of libraries. The syntax is slightly different from the original C language, which is frequently called K&R for Kernighan and Ritchie. There is also an ISO (International Standards Organization) standard that is very similar to the ANSI standard.

Programming in C—Basic Concepts

C is a compiled, third-generation procedural language. *Compiled* means that C code is analyzed, interpreted, and translated into machine instructions at some time prior to the execution of the C program. These steps are carried out by the C compiler and, depending on the complexity of the C program, by the make utility. After the program is compiled, it can be executed over and over without recompilation.

The phrase *third-generation procedural* describes computer languages that clearly distinguish the data used in a program from the actions performed on that data. Programs written in third-generation languages take the form of a series of explicit processing steps, or procedures. These procedures manipulate the contents of data structures by means of explicit references to their locations in memory and manipulate the computer's hardware in response to hardware interrupts.

Elements of the C++ Language

If C is the language most associated with UNIX, C++ is the language that underlies most graphical user interfaces available today.

C++ was originally developed by Dr. Bjarne Stroustrup at the Computer Science Research Center of AT&T's Bell Laboratories (Murray Hill, NJ), also the source of UNIX itself. Dr. Stroustrup's original goal was an object-oriented simulation language. The availability of C compilers for many hardware architectures convinced him to design the language as an extension of C, allowing a preprocessor to translate C++ programs into C for compilation.

After the C language was standardized by a joint committee of the American National Standards Institute and the International Standards Organization in 1989: A new joint committee began the effort to formalize C++ as well. This effort has produced several new features and has significantly refined the interpretation of other language features.

Programming in C++—Basic Concepts

C++ is an object-oriented extension to C. Because C++ is a superset of C, C++ compilers will compile C programs correctly, and it is possible to write non–object-oriented code in C++.

The distinction between an object-oriented language and a procedural one can be subtle and hard to grasp, especially with regard to C++, which retains all of C's characteristics and concepts. One way to describe the difference is to say that when programmers code in a procedural language, they specify actions that process the data, whereas when they write object-oriented code, they create data objects that can be requested to perform actions on or with regard to themselves.

Thus, a C function receives one or more values as input, transforms or acts on them in some way, and returns a result. If the values that are passed include pointers, the contents of data variables can be modified by the function. As the standard library routines show, it is likely that the code calling a function will not know, and will not need to know, what steps the function takes when it is invoked. However, such matters as the datatype of the input parameters and the result code are specified when the function is defined and remain invariable throughout program execution.

Functions are associated with C++ objects as well. But the actions performed when an object's function is invoked can automatically differ, perhaps substantially, depending on the specific type of the data structure with which it is associated. This is known as *overloading* function names. Overloading is related to a second characteristic of C++—the fact that functions can be defined as belonging to C++ data structures, an aspect of the wider language feature known as *encapsulation*.

In addition to overloading and encapsulation, object-oriented languages allow programmers to define new abstract data types (including associated functions) and then derive subsequent data types from them. The notion of a new class of data objects, in addition to the built-in classes such as integer, floating-point number, and character, goes beyond the familiar capability to define complex data objects in C. Just as a C data structure that includes an integer element inherits the properties and functions applicable to integers, a C++ class that is derived from another class *inherits* the parent class's functions and properties. When a specific variable or structure (instance) of that class's type is defined, the class (parent or child) is said to be *instantiated*.

Introduction to C+/C++ Programming Tools

CHAPTER 21

581

21

C+/C++
PROGRAMMING
TOOLS

File Naming

Most C programs will compile with a C++ compiler if you follow strict ANSI rules. For example, you can compile the standard `hello.c` program (everyone's first program) with the GNU C++ compiler. Typically, you will name the file something like `hello.cc`, `hello.C`, `hello.c++`, or `hello.cxx`. The GNU C++ compiler will accept any of these names.

Project Management Tools

This section introduces some of the programming and project management tools included with Red Hat Linux. On this book's CD-ROM, you will find these tools that you can use to help automate your software development projects. If you have some previous UNIX experience, you will be familiar with most of these programs because they are traditional complements to a programmer's suite of software.

If you have programming experience on other software platforms, you will find that these programs are easy to learn. However, mastery will come with experience!

Building Programs with `make`

The `make` command is only one of several programming automation utilities included with Red Hat Linux. You will find others, such as `pmake` (a parallel make), `imake` (a dependency-drive Makefile generator, usually for building X11 applications), `automake`, and one of the newer tools, `autoconf` (which builds shell scripts used to configure program source code packages). Check the man pages for more information.

The `make` command's roots stem from an early version of System V UNIX. The version included with Red Hat Linux is part of the GNU utilities distribution. `Make` is used to automatically handle the building and install of a program, which can be as simple as

```
# make install
```

The magic of `make` is that it will automatically update and build applications. You create this magic through a default file named `Makefile`. However, if you use `make`'s `-f` option, you can specify any Makefile, such as `MyMakeFile`, like this:

```
# make -f MyMakeFile
```

A Makefile is a text file that can contain instructions about which options to pass on to the compiler preprocessor, the compiler, and the linker. The Makefile can also specify which source code files need to be compiled (and the compiler command line) for a particular code module, and which code modules are needed to build the program—a mechanism called *dependency checking*.

Using make can also aid in the portability of your program through the use of macros. This allows users of other operating systems to easily configure a program build by specifying local values, such as the names and locations, or *pathnames* of any required software tools. In the following example, macros define the name of the compiler (CC), the installer program (INS), where the program should be installed (INSDIR), where the linker should look for required libraries (LIBDIR), the names of required libraries (LIBS), a source code file (SRC), the intermediate object code file (OBS), and the name of the final program (PROG):

```
# a sample Makefile for a skeleton program
CC= gcc
INS= install
INSDIR = /usr/local/bin
LIBDIR= -L/usr/X11R6/lib
LIBS= -lXm -lSM -lICE -lXt -lX11
SRC= skel.c
OBJS= skel.o
PROG= skel

skel:   ${OBJS}
        ${CC} -o ${PROG} ${SRC} ${LIBDIR} ${LIBS}

install: ${PROG}
        ${INS} -g root -o root ${PROG} ${INSDIR}
```

> **Note**
>
> The indented lines in the previous example are indented with tabs, not spaces. This is very important to remember. Visually, it is difficult to see the difference but make can tell. When I first started out, I tried spaces and had a tough time figuring out why make kept giving me errors.

Using this approach, you can build the program with

`# make`

To build a specified component of your Makefile, use a *target* definition on the command line. To build just the program, use make with the skel target like this:

`# make skel`

If you make any changes to any element of a target object, such as a source code file, make will rebuild the target. To build and install the program in one step (using the example), specify the install target like this:

`# make install`

Larger software projects might have any number of traditional targets in the Makefile, such as

- `test`—To run specific tests on the final software.
- `man`—To process an include `troff` document with the `-man` macros.
- `clean`—To delete any remaining object files.
- `archive`—To clean up, archive, and compress the entire source code tree.
- `bugreport`—To automatically collect and then mail build or error logs.

The beauty of the `make` command is in its flexibility. You can use `make` with a simple Makefile, or write complex Makefiles containing numerous macros, rules, or commands that work in a single directory or traverse your filesystem recursively to build programs, update your system, and even function as a document management system. The `make` command will work with nearly any program, including text processing systems such as TeX!

Building Large Applications

C programs can be broken into any number of files, as long as no single function spans more than one file. To compile this program, you compile each source file into an intermediate object before you link all the objects into a single executable. The `-c` flag tells the compiler to stop at this stage. During the link stage, all the object files should be listed on the command line. Object files are identified by the `.o` suffix.

Making Libraries with `ar`

If several different programs use the same functions, they can be combined into a single library archive. The `ar` command is used to build a library. When this library is included on the compile line, the archive is searched to resolve any external symbols. Listing 22.1 shows an example of building and using a library.

LISTING 22.1 Building a Large Application

```
$ gcc -c sine.c
$ gcc -c cosine.c
$ gcc -c tangent.c
$ ar c libtrig.a sine.o cosine.o tangent.o

$ gcc -c mainprog.c
$ gcc -o mainprog mainprog.o libtrig.a
```

gcc is the command used to invoke the GNU C Compiler. The "GNU C Compiler Command-Line Switches" section will explain what -c and -o mean.

Large applications can require hundreds of source code files. Compiling and linking these applications can be a complex and error-prone task of its own. The make utility, described previously, is a tool that helps developers organize the process of building the executable form of complex applications from many source files.

Managing Software Projects with RCS and CVS

Although make can be used to manage a software project, larger software projects requiring document management, source code controls, security, and tracking usually use the Revision Control System (RCS) or the Concurrent Versions System (CVS). You will find both of these source code version control utilities in RPM packages on your Red Hat Linux CD-ROM.

The RCS and CVS systems are used to track changes to multiple versions of files, and they can be used to backtrack or branch off versions of documents inside the scope of a project. The systems are also used to prevent or resolve conflicting entries or (sometimes simultaneously) changes to source code files by numerous developers.

Although RCS and CVS aim to provide similar features, the main difference between the two systems is that RCS uses a locking and unlocking scheme for access, whereas CVS provides a modification and merging approach to working on older, current, or new versions of software. Whereas RCS uses different programs to check in or out of a revision under a directory, CVS uses a number of administrative files in a software *repository* of source code *modules* to merge and resolve change conflicts.

RCS uses at least eight separate programs, including the following:

- ci—Checks in revisions.
- co—Checks out revisions.
- ident—Starts keyword utility for source files.
- rcs—Changes file attributes.
- rcsclean—Cleans up working files.
- rcsdiff—Starts revision comparison utility.
- rcsmerge—Merges revisions.
- rlog—Activates logging and information utility.

Source code control with CVS requires the use of at least six command options on the `cvs` command line. Some of these commands require additional fields, such as the names of files:

- `checkout`—Checks out revisions.
- `update`—Updates your sources with changes by other developers.
- `add`—Adds new files in `cvs` records.
- `import`—Adds new sources into the repository.
- `remove`—Eliminates files from the repository.
- `commit`—Publishes changes to other repository developers.

RCS and CVS can be used for more than software development projects. These tools can also be used for document preparation and workgroup editing of documents, and will work with any text files. Both systems use registration and control files to accomplish revision management. Both systems also offer the opportunity to revisit any step or branch in a revision *history*, and to restore previous versions of a project. This mechanism is extremely important in cross-platform development or for software maintenance.

Tracking information is usually contained in separate control files, and each document within a project might contain information automatically updated with each change to a project using a process called *keyword substitution*. CVS can use keywords similar to RCS, which are usually included inside C comment strings (`/* */`) near the top of a document. A sample of the available keywords includes

- `$Author$`—Username of person performing last check-in.
- `$Date$`—Date and time of last check-in.
- `$Header$`—The pathname of the document's RCS file, revision number, date and time, author, and state gets inserted.
- `$Id$`—Same as `$Header$`, but without full pathname.
- `$Name$`—A symbolic name (see the `co` man page).
- `$Revision$`—The assigned revision number (such as 1.1).
- `$Source$`—RCS file's full pathname.
- `$State$`—The state of the document, such as `Exp` for experimental, `Rel` for released, or `Stab` for stable.

These keywords can also be used to insert version information into compiled programs by using character strings in program source code. For example, given an extremely short C program named `foo.c`:

```
/* $Header$ */
#include <stdio.h>
static char rsrcid{} = "$Header$";
main() {
    printf("Hello, Linus!\n");
}
```

The resulting $Header$ keyword might expand (in an RCS document) to

`$Header: /home/bball/sw/RCS/foo.c,v 1.1 1999/04/20 15:01:07 root Exp Root $`

Getting started with RCS is as simple as creating a project directory and an RCS directory under the project directory, and then creating or copying initial source files in the project directory. You then use the `ci` command to check in documents. Getting started with CVS requires you to initialize a repository by first setting the `$CVSROOT` environment variable with the full pathname of the repository and then using the `init` command option with the `cvs` command, like this:

 # cvs init

You will find documentation for RCS and CVS in various man pages, under the `/usr/doc` directories for each of them, and in GNU info documents.

Many organizations use CVS and RCS to manage the source for their projects. Commercial code-management (version control) tools also exist that include fancy interfaces, homogenous platform support, and greater flexibility. But those tools require dedicated administrators and significant licensing costs—major disadvantages when compared to RCS or CVS.

Debugging Tools

Debugging is a science and an art unto itself. Sometimes, the simplest tool—the code listing—is best. At other times, however, you need to use other tools. Three of these tools are `lint`, `gprof`, and `gdb`. Other available tools include `escape`, `cxref`, and `cb`. Many UNIX commands have debugging uses.

`lint` is a traditional UNIX command that examines source code for possible problems, but it is not included with Red Hat Linux. The code might meet the standards for C and compile cleanly, but it might not execute correctly. `lint` checks type mismatches and incorrect argument counts on function calls. `lint` also uses the C preprocessor, so you can use command-like options similar to those you would use for `gcc`. The GNU C compiler supports extensive warnings (through the `-Wall` and `-pedantic` options) that might eliminate the need for a separate `lint` command.

21

> **Note**
>
> If you would like to explore various C syntax-checking programs, navigate to `http://www.ibiblio.org/pub/Linux/devel/lang/c/`. One program that closely resembles the traditional `lint` program is `lclint`, found in the `lclint-2.2a-src.tar.gz` file.

The `gprof` command is used to study how a program is spending its time. If a program is compiled and linked with `-p` as a flag, a `mon.out` file is created when it executes, with data on how often each function is called and how much time is spent in each function. `gprof` parses and displays this data. An analysis of the output generated by `gprof` helps you determine where performance bottlenecks occur. Whereas using an optimizing compiler can speed up your program, taking the time to use `gprof`'s analysis and revising bottleneck functions will significantly improve program performance.

The third tool is `gdb`—a symbolic debugger. When a program is compiled with `-g`, the symbol tables are retained and a symbolic debugger can be used to track program bugs. The basic technique is to invoke `gdb` after a core dump and get a stack trace. This indicates the source line where the core dump occurred and the functions that were called to reach that line. Often, this is enough to identify the problem. It isn't the limit of `gdb`, though.

`gdb` also provides an environment for debugging programs interactively. Invoking `gdb` with a program enables you to set breakpoints, examine variable values, and monitor variables. If you suspect a problem near a line of code, you can set a breakpoint at that line and run the program. When the line is reached, execution is interrupted. You can check variable values, examine the stack trace, and observe the program's environment. You can single-step through the program, checking values. You can resume execution at any point. By using breakpoints, you can discover many of the bugs in your code that you have missed.

There is an X Window version of `gdb` called `xxgdb`.

> **Note**
>
> If you browse to `http://www.ibiblio.org/pub/Linux/devel/debuggers/`, you will find at least a dozen different debuggers, including the Data Display Debugger, or `ddd`, an interface to `gdb`.

cpp is another tool that can be used to debug programs. It performs macro replacements, includes headers, and parses the code. The output is the actual module to be compiled. Normally, though, cpp is never executed by the programmer directly. Instead, it is invoked through gcc with either an -E or -P option. -E sends the output directly to the terminal; -P makes a file with an .i suffix.

GNU C Compiler Command-Line Switches

If you loaded the development tools when you installed Linux (or later using RPM), you should have the GNU C compiler (gcc). Many different options are available for the GNU C compiler, and many of them match the C and C++ compilers available on other UNIX systems. Table 22.1 shows the important switches. Look at the man page or info file for gcc for a full list of options and descriptions.

TABLE 22.1   GNU C Compiler Switches

Switch	Description
-x *language*	Specifies the language (C, C++, Java, and assembler are valid values).
-c	Compiles and assembles only (does not link).
-S	Compiles (does not assemble or link); generates an assembler code (.s) file.
-E	Preprocesses only (does not compile, assemble, or link).
-o *file*	Specifies the output filename (a.out is the default).
-l *library*	Specifies the libraries to use.
-I *directory*	Searches the specified directory for include files.
-w	Inhibits warning messages.
-pedantic	Requires strict ANSI compliance.
-Wall	Prints additional warning messages.
-g	Produces debugging information (for use with gdb).
-ggdb	Generates native-format debugging info (and gdb extensions).
-p	Produces information required by gprof.
-pg	Produces information for use by gprof.
-O	Optimizes the compilation.

> **Note**
>
> Some controversy has been stirred up by Red Hat's decision to release an unofficial version of gcc, 2.96, with its 7.1 release. Version 2.96 of gcc isn't sanctioned by the GNU C Compiler steering committee, and led to some problems getting certain applications to compile correctly in Red Hat. The gcc Committee has pushed ahead and released a new gcc 3.0.1, which is included in Red Hat 7.2. Version 2.96 of gcc is also included for the sake of backward compatibility.

The compilation process takes place in several steps:

1. First, the C preprocessor parses the file. To do so, it sequentially reads the lines, includes header files, and performs macro replacement.

2. The compiler parses the modified code for correct syntax. This builds a symbol table and creates an intermediate object format. Most symbols have specific memory addresses assigned, although symbols defined in other modules, such as external variables, do not.

3. The last compilation stage, linking, ties together different files and libraries and then links the files by resolving the symbols that had not previously been resolved.

New Features of the GNU egcs Compiler System

The egcs (pronounced "eggs") program suite originally was an experimental version of the gcc compiler whose development was first hosted by Cygnus Support (which is now part of Red Hat). Starting with Red Hat 5.1 for Intel, egcs was made available for installation as part of your Red Hat Linux system.

When first being developed, Cygnus described egcs as an experimental step in the development of gcc. Since its first release in late summer 1997, egcs has incorporated many of the latest developments and features from *parallel* development of gcc with many new developments of its own, such as a built-in Fortran 77, Java, and Objective C front ends. Some people have suggested that the name be changed from "Experimental GNU Compiler System" to "Enhanced GNU Compiler System."

> **Note**
>
> You will need to use the `gcj` front end to the `egcs` compiler to compile Java language classes.
>
> Intrepid Linux developers can jump right to the source code tree for the latest `egcs` and Java support software via the Red Hat Web site.

Although some Linux developers might have felt that development of `egcs` represented a fork (or split) in gcc compiler development, Cygnus stated that cooperation between the developers of gcc and `egcs` would prevent this. The hope, according to Cygnus, was that the new compiler architecture and features of `egcs` would help gcc be the best compiler in the world.

In April 1999, `egcs` officially became part of future GNU gcc software, and according to Cygnus, the `egcs` team will be responsible for rolling out future GCC releases. We can only hope that Red Hat will live up to that commitment.

Problems might occur when you are using `egcs` if you try to build a software package written in C++ that references gcc in its Makefile.

The Makefile script might contain names and locations of programs and files used during the build process. The `wmx Makefile` contained the following two definitions:

```
CC    = gcc
CCC   = gcc
```

Although this will work if you have only gcc installed, if you install the `egcs` suite, you will need to change the name of the designated C++ compiler in your Makefile to g++, like this:

```
CC    = gcc
CCC   = g++
```

Just be aware that if you use `egcs` to compile C++ source files (files ending in `.C`, `.cc`, or `.cxx`), you might have to fix the software's Makefile first.

Additional Resources

UNIX and, later, Linux was built on the C language. C is a platform-independent, compiled, procedural language based on functions and the capability to derive new, programmer-defined data structures.

C++ extends the capabilities of C by providing the necessary features for object-oriented design and code. C++ compilers such as gcc correctly compile ANSI C code. C++ also provides some features, such as the capability to associate functions with data structures, that do not require the use of full, class-based, object-oriented techniques. For these reasons, the C++ language allows existing UNIX programs to migrate toward the adoption of object orientation over time.

Red Hat Linux 7.2 is full of tools that make your life as a C/C++ programmer easier. There are tools to create your program (editors), compile it (gcc and egcs), create libraries (ar), control the source (RCS and CVS), build your code (make), debug it (gdb and xxgdb), and finally, determine where inefficiencies lie (gprof). Take advantage of the environment!

If you are interested in learning more about C and C++, you should look for the following books:

- *Sams Teach Yourself C in 21 Days*, by Peter Aitken and Bradley Jones, Sams Publishing.
- *Sams Teach Yourself C++ for Linux in 21 Days*, by Jesse Liberty and David B. Horvath, CCP, Sams Publishing.
- *C How to Program* and *C++ How to Program*, by H. M. Deitel and P. J. Deitel.
- *The C Programming Language*, by Brian Kernighan and Dennis Ritchie.
- *The Annotated C++ Reference Manual*, by Margaret Ellis and Bjarne Stroustrup.
- *Programming in ANSI C*, by Stephen G. Kochan.

Reference

http://gcc.gnu.org/java/compile.html—Browse here for more information about egcs Java support.

http://www.gnu.org/software/gcc/gcc.html—This site is about egcs and has information about the latest updates, versions, or feature news about egcs

Shell Scripting

CHAPTER

22

When you enter commands from the command line, you are entering commands one at a time and getting a response from the system. From time to time, you will need to execute more than one command, one after the other, and get the final result. You can do so with a *shell program* or *shell script*. A shell program is a series of Linux commands and utilities that have been put into a file by using a text editor. When you execute a shell program, the commands are interpreted and executed by Linux one after the other.

You can write shell programs and execute them like any other command under Linux. You can also execute other shell programs from within a shell program if they are in the search path. A shell program is like any other programming language and has its own syntax. You can define variables, assign various values, and so on. These functions are discussed in this chapter.

The Red Hat Linux 7.2 CD-ROM that accompanies this book comes with a rich assortment of capable, flexible, and powerful shells. These shells have numerous built-in commands, configurable command-line prompts, and features such as command-line history and editing. Table 22.1 lists each shell, along with its description and location in your Red Hat Linux filesystem.

TABLE 22.1 Shells with Red Hat Linux

Name	*Description*	*Location*
ash	A small shell (sh-like)	/bin/ash
ash.static	A version of ash not dependent on software libraries	/bin/ash.static
bash	The Bourne Again SHell	/bin/bash
bsh	A symbolic link to ash	/bin/bsh
csh	The C shell, a symbolic link to tcsh	/bin/csh
ksh Korn shell	The public-domain	/bin/ksh, /usr/bin/ksh
pdksh	A symbolic link to ksh	/usr/bin/pdksh
rsh	The restricted shell (for network operation)	/usr/bin/rsh
sh	A symbolic link to bash	/bin/sh
tcsh	A csh-compatible shell	/bin/tcsh
zsh	A compatible csh, ksh, and sh shell	/bin/zsh

Creating and Executing a Shell Program

Say you want to set up a number of aliases whenever you log on. Instead of typing all the aliases every time you log on, you can put them in a file by using a text editor, such as vi, and then execute the file.

Here is what is contained in myenv, a sample file created for this purpose (for bash):

```
#!/bin/sh
alias ll='ls -l'
alias dir='ls'
alias copy='cp'
```

myenv can be executed in a variety of ways under Linux.

You can make myenv executable by using the chmod command, as follows, and then execute it as you would any other native Linux command:

```
# chmod +x myenv
```

This turns on the executable permission of myenv. You need to ensure one more thing before you can execute myenv—it must be in the search path. You can get the search path by executing

```
# echo $PATH
```

If the directory where the file myenv is located is not in the current search path, you must add the directory name in the search path.

Now you can execute the file myenv from the command line as if it were a Linux command:

```
# myenv
```

22

SHELL SCRIPTING

> **Note**
>
> The first line in your shell program should start with a pound sign (#), which tells the shell that the line is a comment. Following the pound sign, you must have an exclamation point (!), which tells the shell to run the command following the exclamation point and to use the rest of the file as input for that command. This is common practice for all shell scripting. For example, if you write a shell script for bash, the first line of your script will contain #!/bin/bash.

A second way to execute `myenv` under a particular shell, such as `pdksh`, is as follows:

```
# pdksh myenv
```

This invokes a new `pdksh` shell and passes the filename `myenv` as a parameter to execute the file.

> **Note**
>
> The `pdksh` shell, originally created by Eric Gisin, is a public domain version of the `ksh` shell and is found under the `/usr/bin` directory as a symbolic link. In Red Hat Linux, `pdksh` is named `ksh`. Two symbolic links, `/usr/bin/pdksh` and `/usr/bin/ksh`, point to the `pdksh` shell. For more information about `pdksh`, see the `/usr/doc/pdksh` directory or the `ksh` man page.

You can also execute `myenv` from the command line as follows:

Command Line	Environment
`# . myenv`	`pdksh and bash`
`# source myenv`	`tcsh`

The dot (`.`) is a way of telling the shell to execute the file `myenv`. In this case, you do not have to ensure that the execute permission of the file has been set. Under `tcsh`, you have to use the `source` command instead of the dot (`.`) command.

After you execute the command `myenv`, you should be able to use `dir` from the command line to get a list of files under the current directory and `ll` to get a list of files with various attributes displayed. However, the best way to use the new commands in `myenv` is to put them into your shell's login or profile file. For Red Hat Linux users, the default shell is `bash`, so make these commands available for everyone on your system by putting them in the `/etc/profile.d` directory. Copy in a `tcsh` version with the file extension `.csh` and the `bash/pdksh` version with a `.sh` file extension.

> **Note**
>
> If you find you'd prefer to use a shell other than `bash` after logging in to Red Hat Linux, use the `chsh` command. You'll be asked for your password and the location and name of the new shell (see Table 22.1). The new shell will become your default shell (but only if its name is in the list of acceptable system shells in `/etc/shells`).

In some instances, you might need to modify how your shell scripts are executed. For example, the majority of shell scripts use a *hash-bang* line at the beginning, like this:

```
#!/bin/sh
```

One of the reasons for this is to control the type of shell used to run the script (in this case, an sh-incantation of bash). Other shells, such as ksh, might respond differently depending on how they're called from a script (hence the reason for symbolic links to different shells).

You might also find different or new environment variables available to your scripts by using different shells. For example, if you launch csh from the bash command line, you'll find at least several new variables, or variables with slightly occluded definitions, such as

 # env
```
...
VENDOR=intel
MACHTYPE=i386
HOSTTYPE=i386-linux
HOST=thinkpad.home.org
```

On the other hand, bash might provide these variables, or variables of the same name with a slightly different definition, such as

 # env
```
...
HOSTTYPE=i386
HOSTNAME=thinkpad.home.org
```

Although the behavior of a bang line isn't defined by POSIX, variations of its incantation can be helpful when you're writing shell scripts. As described in the wish man page, you can use a shell to help execute programs called within a shell script without needing to hard-code pathnames of programs. This increases shell script portability.

For example, if you want to use the wish command (a windowing tcl interpreter), your first inclination might be to write

```
#!/usr/local/bin/wish
```

Although this will work on many other operating systems, the script will fail under Linux. However, if you use

```
#!/bin/sh
exec wish "$@"
```

the wish command (as a binary or itself a shell script) can be used. There are other advantages to using this approach. See the wish man page for more information.

22

SHELL SCRIPTING

Variables

Linux shell programming is a full-fledged programming language and, as such, supports various types of variables. Variables have three major types: environment, built-in, and user.

- *Environment variables* are part of the system environment, and you do not have to define them. You can use them in your shell program. Some of them, such as PATH, can also be modified within a shell program.
- *Built-in variables* are provided by the system. Unlike environment variables, you cannot modify them.
- *User variables* are defined by you when you write a shell script. You can use and modify them at will within the shell program.

A major difference between shell programming and other programming languages is that in shell programming, variables are not typecast. That is, you do not have to specify whether a variable is a number or a string, and so on.

Assigning a Value to a Variable

Say you want to use a variable called lcount to count the number of iterations in a loop within a shell program. You can declare and initialize this variable as follows:

Command	Environment
lcount=0	pdksh and bash
set lcount = 0	tcsh

> **Note**
>
> Under pdksh and bash, you must ensure that the equals sign (=) does not have spaces before and after it.

Shell programming languages don't use typed variables, so the same variable can be used to store an integer value one time and a string another time. This isn't recommended, however, and you should be careful not to do this.

To store a string in a variable, you can use the following:

Command	Environment
`myname=Sanjiv`	`pdksh` and `bash`
`set myname = Sanjiv`	`tcsh`

The preceding can be used if the string doesn't have embedded spaces. If a string has embedded spaces, you can do the assignment as follows:

Command	Environment
`myname='Sanjiv Guha'`	`pdksh` and `bash`
`set myname = 'Sanjiv Guha'`	`tcsh`

Accessing Variable Values

You can access the value of a variable by prefixing the variable name with a $ (dollar sign). That is, if the variable name is var, you can access the variable by using $var.

If you want to assign the value of var to the variable lcount, you can do so as follows:

Command	Environment
`lcount=$var`	`pdksh` and `bash`
`set lcount = $var`	`tcsh`

Positional Parameters

It is possible to write a shell script that takes a number of parameters at the time you invoke it from the command line or from another shell script. These options are supplied to the shell program by Linux as *positional parameters*, which have special names provided by the system. The first parameter is stored in a variable called 1 (number 1) and can be accessed by using $1 within the program. The second parameter is stored in a variable called 2 and can be accessed by using $2 within the program, and so on. One or more of the higher numbered positional parameters can be omitted while you're invoking a shell program.

For example, if a shell program mypgm expects two parameters—such as a first name and a last name—you can invoke the shell program with only one parameter, the first name. However, you cannot invoke it with only the second parameter, the last name.

Here's a shell program called mypgm1, which takes only one parameter (a name) and displays it on the screen:

```
#!/bin/sh
#Name display program
if [ $# -eq 0 ]
then
    echo "Name not provided"
else
    echo "Your name is "$1
fi
```

If you execute mypgm1 in pdksh and bash as follows

 # . mypgm1

you get the following output:

```
Name not provided
```

However, if you execute mypgm1 as follows

 # . mypgm1 Sanjiv

you get the following output:

```
Your name is Sanjiv
```

The shell program mypgm1 also illustrates another aspect of shell programming: the built-in variables. In mypgm1, the variable $# is a built-in variable and provides the number of positional parameters passed to the shell program.

Built-In Variables

Built-in variables are special variables that Linux provides to you that can be used to make decisions within a program. You cannot modify the values of these variables within the shell program.

Some of these variables are

$#—Number of positional parameters passed to the shell program

$?—Completion code of the last command or shell program executed within the shell program (returned value)

$0—The name of the shell program

$*—A single string of all arguments passed at the time of invocation of the shell program

To show these built-in variables in use, here is a sample program called `mypgm2`:

```
#!/bin/sh
#my test program
echo "Number of parameters is "$#
echo "Program name is "$0
echo "Parameters as a single string is "$*
```

If you execute `mypgm2` from the command line in `pdksh` and `bash` as follows

```
# . mypgm2 Sanjiv Guha
```

you get the following result:

```
Number of parameters is 2
Program name is mypgm2
Parameters as a single string is Sanjiv Guha
```

Special Characters

Some characters have special meaning to Linux shells, so using them as part of variable names or strings causes your program to behave incorrectly. If a string contains such characters, you also have to use escape characters (backslashes) to indicate that the special characters should not be treated as special characters. Some of these characters are shown in Table 22.2.

TABLE 22.2 Special Shell Characters

Character	Explanation
$	Indicates the beginning of a shell variable name
|	Pipes standard output to next command
#	Starts a comment
&	Executes a process in the background
?	Matches one character
*	Matches one or more characters
>	Output redirection operator
<	Input redirection operator
`	Command substitution (the backquote or backtick—the key above the Tab key on most keyboards)
>>	Output redirection operator (to append to a file)
<<	Wait until following end-of-input string (HERE operator)
[ ]	Range of characters

TABLE 22.2 continued

Character	Explanation
[a-z]	All characters a through z
[a,z]	Characters a or z
. *filename*	Execute ("source") the file *filename*
Space	Delimiter between two words

A few characters deserve special note. They are the double quotes ("), the single quotes ('), the backslash (\), and the backtick (`), all discussed in the following sections. Also note that you can use input and output redirection from inside your shell scripts. Be sure to use output redirection with care when you're testing your shell programs because you can easily overwrite files!

Double Quotes

If a string contains embedded spaces, you can enclose the string in double quotes (") so the shell interprets the whole string as one entity instead of more than one. For example, if you assigned the value of abc def (abc followed by one space followed by def) to a variable called x in a shell program as follows, you would get an error because the shell would try to execute def as a separate command.

Command	Environment
x=abc def	pdksh and bash
set x = abc def	tcsh

What you need to do is surround the string in double quotes:

Command	Environment
x="abc def"	pdksh and bash
set x = "abc def"	tcsh

The double quotes resolve all variables within the string. Here is an example for pdksh and bash:

```
var="test string"
newvar="Value of var is $var"
echo $newvar
```

Here is the same example for `tcsh`:

```
set var = "test string"
set newvar = "Value of var is $var"
echo $newvar
```

If you execute a shell program containing these three lines, you get the following result:

```
Value of var is test string
```

Single Quotes

You can surround a string with single quotes (`'`) to stop the shell from resolving a variable. In the following examples, the double quotes in the preceding examples have been changed to single quotes.

`pdksh` and `bash`:

```
var='test string'
newvar='Value of var is $var'
echo $newvar
```

`tcsh`:

```
set var = 'test string'
set newvar = 'Value of var is $var'
echo $newvar
```

If you execute a shell program containing these three lines, you get the following result:

```
Value of var is $var
```

As you can see, the variable `var` did not get interpolated.

Backslash

You can use a backslash (`\`) before a character to stop the shell from interpreting the succeeding character as a special character. Say you want to assign a value of `$test` to a variable called `var`. If you use the following command, a null value is stored in `var`:

Command	Environment
`var=$test`	`pdksh` and `bash`
`set var = $test`	`tcsh`

This happens because the shell interprets `$test` as the value of the variable `test`. No value has been assigned to `test`, so `var` contains null. You should use the following command to correctly store `$test` in `var`:

Command	Environment
var=\$test	pdksh and bash
set var = \$test	tcsh

The backslash (\) before the dollar sign ($) signals the shell to interpret the $ as any other ordinary character and not to associate any special meaning to it.

Backtick

You can use the backtick (`) character to signal the shell to execute the string delimited by the backtick. This can be used in shell programs when you want the result of the execution of a command to be stored in a variable. For example, if you want to count the number of lines in a file called test.txt in the current directory and store the result in a variable called var, you can use the following command:

Command	Environment
var=`wc -l test.txt`	pdksh and bash
set var = `wc -l test.txt`	tcsh

Comparison of Expressions

The way the logical comparison of two operators (numeric or string) is done varies slightly in different shells. In pdksh and bash, a command called test can be used to achieve comparisons of expressions. In tcsh, you can write an expression to accomplish the same thing.

pdksh and bash

This section covers comparisons using the pdksh or bash shells. Later in the chapter, the section "tcsh" contains a similar discussion for the tcsh shell.

The syntax of the test command is as follows

test *expression*

or

[*expression*]

Both forms of test commands are processed the same way by pdksh and bash. The test commands support the following types of comparisons:

- String comparison
- Numeric comparison
- File operators
- Logical operators

String Comparison

The following operators can be used to compare two string expressions:

> =—To compare whether two strings are equal
>
> !=—To compare whether two strings are not equal
>
> -n—To evaluate whether the string length is greater than zero
>
> -z—To evaluate whether the string length is equal to zero

Next are some examples comparing two strings, string1 and string2, in a shell program called compare1:

```
#!/bin/sh
string1="abc"
string2="abd"
if [ $string1 = $string2 ]; then
   echo "string1 equal to string2"
else
   echo "string1 not equal to string2"
fi

if [ $string2 != string1 ]; then
   echo "string2 not equal to string1"
else
   echo "string2 equal to string2"
fi

if [ $string1 ]; then
   echo "string1 is not empty"
else
   echo "string1 is empty"
fi

if [ -n $string2 ]; then
   echo "string2 has a length greater than zero"
else
   echo "string2 has length equal to zero"
fi
```

```
if [ -z $string1 ]; then
   echo "string1 has a length equal to zero"
else
  echo "string1 has a length greater than zero"
fi
```

If you execute compare1, you get the following result:

```
string1 not equal to string2
string2 not equal to string1
string1 is not empty
string2 has a length greater than zero
string1 has a length greater than zero
```

If two strings are not equal in size, the system pads out the shorter string with trailing spaces for comparison. That is, if the value of string1 is abc and that of string2 is ab, string2 will be padded with a trailing space for comparison purposes—it will have a value of ab.

Number Comparison

The following operators can be used to compare two numbers:

-eq—To compare whether two numbers are equal

-ge—To compare whether one number is greater than or equal to the other number

-le—To compare whether one number is less than or equal to the other number

-ne—To compare whether two numbers are not equal

-gt—To compare whether one number is greater than the other number

-lt—To compare whether one number is less than the other number

The following examples compare two numbers, number1 and number2, in a shell program called compare2:

```
#!/bin/sh
number1=5
number2=10
number3=5

if [ $number1 -eq $number3 ]; then
   echo "number1 is equal to number3"
else
    echo "number1 is not equal to number3"
fi

if [ $number1 -ne $number2 ]; then
   echo "number1 is not equal to number2"
else
    echo "number1 is equal to number2"
```

```
fi

if [ $number1 -gt $number2 ]; then
    echo "number1 is greater than number2"
else
    echo "number1 is not greater than number2"
fi

if [ $number1 -ge $number3 ]; then
    echo "number1 is greater than or equal to number3"
else
    echo "number1 is not greater than or equal to number3"
fi

if [ $number1 -lt $number2 ]; then
    echo "number1 is less than number2"
else
    echo "number1 is not less than number2"
fi

if [ $number1 -le $number3 ]; then
    echo "number1 is less than or equal to number3"
else
    echo "number1 is not less than or equal to number3"
fi
```

When you execute the shell program compare2, you get the following results:

```
number1 is equal to number3
number1 is not equal to number2
number1 is not greater than number2
number1 is greater than or equal to number3
number1 is less than number2
number1 is less than or equal to number3
```

File Operators

The following operators can be used as file comparison operators:

- -d—To ascertain whether a file is a directory

- -f—To ascertain whether a file is a regular file

- -r—To ascertain whether read permission is set for a file

- -s—To ascertain whether the name of a file has a length greater than zero

- -w—To ascertain whether write permission is set for a file

- -x—To ascertain whether execute permission is set for a file

Assume that a shell program called compare3 is in a directory with a file called file1 and a subdirectory dir1 under the current directory. Assume that file1 has a permission of r-x (read and execute permission) and dir1 has a permission of rwx (read, write, and execute permission). The code for compare3 would look like this:

```
#!/bin/sh
if [ -d $dir1 ]; then
    echo "dir1 is a directory"
else
    echo "dir1 is not a directory"
fi

if [ -f $dir1 ]; then
    echo "file1 is a regular file"
else
    echo "file1 is not a regular file"
fi

if [ -r $file1 ]; then
    echo "file1 has read permission"
else
    echo "file1 does not have read permission"
fi

if [ -w $file1 ]; then
    echo "file1 has write permission"
else
    echo "file1 does not have write permission"
fi

if [ -x $dir1 ]; then
    echo "dir1 has execute permission"
else
    echo "dir1 does not have execute permission"
fi
```

If you execute the file compare3, you get the following results:

```
dir1 is a directory
file1 is a regular file
file1 has read permission
file1 does not have write permission
dir1 has execute permission
```

Logical Operators

Logical operators are used to compare expressions using the rules of logic. The characters represent NOT, AND, and OR.

> !—To negate a logical expression
>
> -a—To logically AND two logical expressions
>
> -o—To logically OR two logical expressions

This example named `logic` uses the file and directory mentioned in the previous `compare3` example.

```
#!/bin/sh
if [ -x file1 -a -x dir1 ]; then
    echo file1 and dir1 are executable
else
    echo at least one of file1 or dir1 are not executable
fi

if [ -w file1 -o -w dir1 ]; then
    echo file1 or dir1 are writable
else
    echo neither file1 or dir1 are executable
fi

if [ ! -w file1 ]; then
    echo file1 is not writable
else
    echo file1 is writable
fi
```

If you execute `logic`, it will yield the following result:

```
file1 and dir1 are executable
file1 or dir1 are writable
file1 is not writable
```

tcsh

As stated earlier, the comparisons are different under `tcsh` from what they are under `pdksh` and `bash`. This section explains the same concepts as the section "pdksh and bash," but it uses the syntax necessary for the `tcsh` shell environment.

String Comparison

The following operators can be used to compare two string expressions:

> `==`—To compare whether two strings are equal
>
> `!=`—To compare whether two strings are not equal

The following examples compare two strings, `string1` and `string2`, in the shell program `compare1`:

```
#!/bin/tcsh
set string1 = "abc"
set string2 = "abd"

if  (string1 == string2)  then
    echo "string1 equal to string2"
```

```
else
    echo "string1 not equal to string2"
endif

if  (string2 != string1)  then
    echo "string2 not equal to string1"
else
    echo "string2 equal to string1"
endif
```

If you execute compare1, you get the following results:

```
string1 not equal to string2
string2 not equal to string1
```

Number Comparison

These operators can be used to compare two numbers:

>=—To compare whether one number is greater than or equal to the other number

<=—To compare whether one number is less than or equal to the other number

>—To compare whether one number is greater than the other number

<—To compare whether one number is less than the other number

The next examples compare two numbers, number1 and number2, in a shell program called compare2:

```
#!/bin/tcsh
set number1 = 5
set number2 = 10
set number3 = 5

if  ($number1 > $number2)  then
    echo "number1 is greater than number2"
else
    echo "number1 is not greater than number2"
endif

if  ($number1 >= $number3) then
    echo "number1 is greater than or equal to number3"
else
    echo "number1 is not greater than or equal to number3"
endif

if  ($number1 < $number2)  then
    echo "number1 is less than number2"
else
    echo "number1 is not less than number2"
endif
```

```
if  ($number1 <= $number3) then
   echo "number1 is less than or equal to number3"
else
   echo "number1 is not less than or equal to number3"
endif
```

When executing the shell program `compare2`, you get the following results:

```
number1 is not greater than number2
number1 is greater than or equal to number3
number1 is less than number2
number1 is less than or equal to number3
```

File Operators

These operators can be used as file comparison operators:

> -d—To ascertain whether a file is a directory
>
> -e—To ascertain whether a file exists
>
> -f—To ascertain whether a file is a regular file
>
> -o—To ascertain whether a user is the owner of a file
>
> -r—To ascertain whether read permission is set for a file
>
> -w—To ascertain whether write permission is set for a file
>
> -x—To ascertain whether execute permission is set for a file
>
> -z—To ascertain whether the file size is zero

The following examples are based on a shell program called `compare3`, which is in a directory with a file called `file1` and a subdirectory `dir1` under the current directory. Assume that `file1` has a permission of `r-x` (read and execute permission) and `dir1` has a permission of `rwx` (read, write, and execute permission).

The following is the code for the `compare3` shell program:

```
#!/bin/tcsh
if  (-d dir1) then
   echo "dir1 is a directory"
else
   echo "dir1 is not a directory"
endif

if (-f dir1)  then
   echo "file1 is a regular file"
else
   echo "file1 is not a regular file"
endif
```

```
if (-r file1) then
    echo "file1 has read permission"
else
    echo "file1 does not have read permission"
endif

if (-w file1) then
    echo "file1 has write permission"
else
    echo "file1 does not have write permission"
endif

if (-x dir1) then
    echo "dir1 has execute permission"
else
    echo "dir1 does not have execute permission"
endif

if (-z file1) then
    echo "file1 has zero length"
else
    echo "file1 has greater than zero length"
endif
```

If you execute the file compare3, you get the following results:

```
dir1 is a directory
file1 is a regular file
file1 has read permission
file1 does not have write permission
dir1 has execute permission
file1 has greater than zero length
```

Logical Operators

Logical operators are used with conditional statements. These operators are used to negate a logical expression or to perform logical ANDs and ORs.

> !—To negate a logical expression
>
> &&—To logically AND two logical expressions
>
> ||—To logically OR two logical expressions

This example named logic uses the file and directory mentioned in the previous com-pare3 example.

```
#!/bin/tcsh
if ( -x file1 && -x dir1 ) then
    echo file1 and dir1 are executable
else
```

```
      echo at least one of file1 or dir1 are not executable
endif

if ( -w file1 || -w dir1 ) then
   echo file1 or dir1 are writable
else
   echo neither file1 or dir1 are executable
endif

if ( ! -w file1 ) then
   echo file1 is not writable
else
   echo file1 is writable
endif
```

If you execute `logic`, it will yield the following result:

```
file1 and dir1 are executable
file1 or dir1 are writable
file1 is not writable
```

Iteration Statements

Iteration statements are used to repeat a series of commands contained within the iteration statement.

The for Statement

The `for` statement has a number of formats. The first format is as follows:

```
for curvar in list
do
    statements
done
```

This form should be used if you want to execute *statements* once for each value in
list. For each iteration, the current value of the list is assigned to `vcurvar`. *list* can be
a variable containing a number of items or a list of values separated by spaces. This format of the `for` statement is used by `pdksh` and `bash`.

The second format is as follows:

```
for curvar
do
    statements
done
```

In this form, the `statements` are executed once for each of the positional parameters passed to the shell program. For each iteration, the current value of the positional parameter is assigned to the variable `curvar`.

This form can also be written as follows:

```
for curvar in "$@"
do
    statements
done
```

Remember that `$@` gives you a list of positional parameters passed to the shell program, all strung together.

Under `tcsh`, the `for` statement is called `foreach`. The format is as follows:

```
foreach curvar (list)
    statements
end
```

In this form, `statements` are executed once for each value in `list` and, for each iteration, the current value of `list` is assigned to `curvar`.

Suppose that you want to create a backup version of each file in a directory to a subdirectory called `backup`. You can do the following in `pdksh` and `bash`:

```
#!/bin/sh
for filename in `ls`
do
    cp $filename backup/$filename
    if [ $? -ne 0 ]; then
        echo "copy for $filename failed"
    fi
done
```

In the preceding example, a backup copy of each file is created. If the copy fails, a message is generated.

The same example in `tcsh` is as follows:

```
#!/bin/tcsh
foreach filename (`/bin/ls`)
    cp $filename backup/$filename
    if ($? != 0) then
        echo "copy for $filename failed"
    endif
end
```

The while Statement

The while statement can be used to execute a series of commands while a specified condition is true. The loop terminates as soon as the specified condition evaluates to false. It is possible that the loop will not execute at all if the specified condition evaluates to false right at the beginning. You should be careful with the while command because the loop will never terminate if the specified condition never evaluates to false.

In pdksh and bash, the following format is used:

```
while expression
do
     statements
done
```

In tcsh, the following format is used:

```
while (expression)
    Statements
end
```

If you want to add the first five even numbers, you can use the following shell program in pdksh and bash:

```
#!/bin/bash
loopcount=0
result=0
while [ $loopcount -lt 5 ]
do
    loopcount=`expr $loopcount + 1`
    increment=`expr $loopcount \* 2`
    result=`expr $result + $increment`
done

echo "result is $result"
```

In tcsh, this program can be written as follows:

```
#!/bin/tcsh
set loopcount = 0
set result = 0
while ($loopcount < 5)
    set loopcount = `expr $loopcount + 1`
    set increment = `expr $loopcount \* 2`
    set result = `expr $result + $increment`

end

echo "result is $result"
```

The `until` Statement

The `until` statement can be used to execute a series of commands until a specified condition is true. The loop terminates as soon as the specified condition evaluates to true.

In `pdksh` and `bash`, the following format is used:

```
until expression
do
    statements
done
```

As you can see, the format is similar to the `while` statement.

If you want to add the first five even numbers, you can use the following shell program in `pdksh` and `bash`:

```
#!/bin/bash
loopcount=0
result=0
until [ $loopcount -ge 5 ]
do
    loopcount=`expr $loopcount + 1`
    increment=`expr $loopcount \* 2`
    result=`expr $result + $increment`
done

echo "result is $result"
```

The example here is identical to the example for the `while` statement, except the condition being tested is just the opposite of the condition specified in the `while` statement.

The `tcsh` command does not support the `until` statement.

The `repeat` Statement (`tcsh`)

The `repeat` statement is used to execute only one command a fixed number of times.

If you want to print a hyphen (-) 80 times on the screen, you can use the following command:

```
repeat  80 echo '-'
```

The `select` Statement (`pdksh`)

The `select` statement is used to generate a menu list if you are writing a shell program that expects input from the user online. The format of the `select` statement is as follows:

```
select  item in itemlist
do
    Statements
done
```

itemlist is optional. If it's not provided, the system iterates through the entries in item one at a time. If itemlist is provided, however, the system iterates for each entry in itemlist and the current value of itemlist is assigned to item for each iteration, which then can be used as part of the statements being executed.

If you want to write a menu that gives the user a choice of picking a Continue or a Finish, you can write the following shell program:

```
#!/bin/bash
select  item in Continue Finish
do
   if [ $item = "Finish" ]; then
      break
   fi
done
```

When the select command is executed, the system displays a menu with numeric choices to the user—in this case, 1 for Continue, and 2 for Finish. If the user chooses 1, the variable item contains a value of Continue; if the user chooses 2, the variable item contains a value of Finish. When the user chooses 2, the if statement is executed and the loop terminates.

The shift Statement

The shift statement is used to process the positional parameters, one at a time, from left to right. As you'll remember, the positional parameters are identified as $1, $2, $3, and so on. The effect of the shift command is that each positional parameter is moved one position to the left and the current $1 parameter is lost.

The format of the shift command is as follows:

```
shift   number
```

The parameter *number* is the number of places to be shifted and is optional. If not specified, the default is 1; that is, the parameters are shifted one position to the left. If specified, the parameters are shifted *number* positions to the left.

The shift command is useful when you are writing shell programs in which a user can pass various options. Depending on the specified option, the parameters that follow can mean different things or might not be there at all.

Conditional Statements

Conditional statements are used in shell programs to decide which part of the program to execute depending on specified conditions.

The `if` Statement

The `if` statement evaluates a logical expression to make a decision. An `if` condition has the following format in `pdksh` and `bash`:

```
if [ expression ]; then
    Statements
elif [expression ]; then
    Statements
else
    Statements
fi
```

The `if` conditions can be nested. That is, an `if` condition can contain another `if` condition within it. It isn't necessary for an `if` condition to have an `elif` or `else` part. The `else` part is executed if none of the expressions that are specified in the `if` statement and are optional in subsequent `elif` statements are true. The word `fi` is used to indicate the end of the `if` statements, which is very useful if you have nested `if` conditions. In such a case, you should be able to match `fi` to `if` to ensure that all `if` statements are properly coded.

In the following example, a variable `var` can have either of two values: `Yes` or `No`. Any other value is an invalid value. This can be coded as follows:

```
if [ $var = "Yes" ]; then
   echo "Value is Yes"
elif [ $var = "No" ]; then
   echo "Value is No"
else
   echo "Invalid value"
fi
```

In `tcsh`, the `if` statement has two forms. The first form, similar to the one for `pdksh` and `bash`, is as follows:

```
if (expression) then
    Statements
else if (expression) then
    Statements
else
    Statements
endif
```

The `if` conditions can be nested—that is, an `if` condition can contain another `if` condition within it. It isn't necessary for an `if` condition to have an `else` part. The `else` part is executed if none of the expressions specified in any of the `if` statements are true. The optional `if` part of the statement (`else if (expression) then`) is executed if the condition following it is true and the previous `if` statement is not true. The word `endif` is used to indicate the end of the `if` statements, which is very useful if you have nested `if` conditions. In such a case, you should be able to match `endif` to `if` to ensure that all `if` statements are properly coded.

Remember the example of the variable `var` having only two values, `Yes` and `No`, for `pdksh` and `bash`? Here is how it would be coded with `tcsh`:

```
if ($var == "Yes") then
    echo "Value is Yes"
else if ($var == "No" ) then
    echo "Value is No"
else
    echo "Invalid value"
endif
```

The second form of the `if` condition for `tcsh` is as follows:

```
if (expression) command
```

In this format, only a single command can be executed if the expression evaluates to true.

The case Statement

The `case` statement is used to execute statements depending on a discrete value or a range of values matching the specified variable. In most cases, you can use a `case` statement instead of an `if` statement if you have a large number of conditions.

The format of a `case` statement for `pdksh` and `bash` is as follows:

```
case str in
    str1 | str2)
        Statements;;
    str3|str4)
        Statements;;
    *)
        Statements;;
esac
```

You can specify a number of discrete values—such as `str1`, `str2`, and so on—for each condition, or you can specify a value with a wildcard. The last condition should be `*` (asterisk) and is executed if none of the other conditions are met. For each of the specified conditions, all the associated statements until the double semicolon (`;;`) are executed.

You can write a script that will echo the name of the month if you provide the month number as a parameter. If you provide a number that isn't between 1 and 12, you will get an error message. The script is as follows:

```
#!/bin/sh

case $1 in
    01 | 1) echo "Month is January";;
    02 | 2) echo "Month is February";;
    03 | 3) echo "Month is March";;
    04 | 4) echo "Month is April";;
    05 | 5) echo "Month is May";;
    06 | 6) echo "Month is June";;
    07 | 7) echo "Month is July";;
    08 | 8) echo "Month is August";;
    09 | 9) echo "Month is September";;
    10) echo "Month is October";;
    11) echo "Month is November";;
    12) echo "Month is December";;
    *) echo "Invalid parameter";;
esac
```

You need to end the statements under each condition with a double semicolon(;;). If you do not, the statements under the next condition will also be executed.

The format for a `case` statement for `tcsh` is as follows:

```
switch (str)
    case str1|str2:
        Statements
        breaksw
    case str3|str4:
        Statements
        breaksw
    default:
        Statements
        breaksw
endsw
```

You can specify a number of discrete values—such as `str1`, `str2`, and so on—for each condition, or you can specify a value with a wildcard. The last condition should be `default` and is executed if none of the other conditions are met. For each of the specified conditions, all the associated statements until `breaksw` are executed.

The example that echoes the month when a number is given, shown earlier for `pdksh` and `bash`, can be written in `tcsh` as follows:

```
#!/bin/tcsh

set month = 5
switch ( $month )
```

```
    case 1:
       echo "Month is January"
       breaksw
    case 2:
       echo "Month is February"
       breaksw
    case 3:
       echo "Month is March"
       breaksw
    case 4:
       echo "Month is April"
       breaksw
    case 5:
       echo "Month is May"
       breaksw
    case 6:
       echo "Month is June"
       breaksw
    case 7:
       echo "Month is July";;
       breaksw
    case 8:
       echo "Month is August";;
       breaksw
    case 9:
       echo "Month is September"
       breaksw
    case 10:
       echo "Month is October"
       breaksw
    case 11:
       echo "Month is November"
       breaksw
    case 12:
       echo "Month is December"
       breaksw
    default:
       echo "Oops! Month is Octember!"
       breaksw
endsw
```

You need to end the statements under each condition with breaksw. If you do not, the statements under the next condition will also be executed.

Miscellaneous Statements

You should be aware of two other statements: the break statement and the exit statement.

The break Statement

The break statement can be used to terminate an iteration loop, such as a for, until, or repeat command.

The exit Statement

exit statements can be used to exit a shell program. You can optionally use a number after exit. If the current shell program has been called by another shell program, the calling program can check for the code and make a decision accordingly.

Functions

As with other programming languages, shell programs also support *functions*. A function is a piece of a shell program that performs a particular process that can be used more than once in the shell program. Writing a function helps you write shell programs without duplication of code.

The following is the format of a function in pdksh and bash for function definition:

```
func(){
    Statements
}
```

You can call a function as follows:

```
func param1 param2 param3
```

The parameters *param1*, *param2*, and so on are optional. You can also pass the parameters as a single string—for example, $@. A function can parse the parameters as if they were positional parameters passed to a shell program.

The following example is a function that displays the name of the month or an error message if you pass a month number. Here is the example, in pdksh and bash:

```
#!/bin/sh
Displaymonth() {
    case $1 in
        01 | 1) echo "Month is January";;
        02 | 2) echo "Month is February";;
        03 | 3) echo "Month is March";;
        04 | 4) echo "Month is April";;
        05 | 5) echo "Month is May";;
        06 | 6) echo "Month is June";;
        07 | 7) echo "Month is July";;
        08 | 8) echo "Month is August";;
        09 | 9) echo "Month is September";;
```

```
      10) echo "Month is October";;
      11) echo "Month is November";;
      12) echo "Month is December";;
      *) echo "Invalid parameter";;
   esac
}
```

```
Displaymonth 8
```

The preceding program displays the following:

```
Month is August
```

Reference

http://www.linuxnewbie.org/nhf/intel/shells/basic.html—Learn basic shell commands at this site.

http://web.cs.mun.ca/~michael/pdksh/—The pdksh home page.

http://www.tcsh.org/—Find out more about tcsh here.

http://www.zsh.org/—Examine zsh in more detail here.

22

SHELL SCRIPTING

Using Perl

CHAPTER 23

Larry Wall, who was already responsible for a number of rather important UNIX utilities, developed Perl (Practical Extraction and Report Language) in the mid-1980s. Larry claims that Perl really stands for "Pathologically Eclectic Rubbish Lister." With the birth of the WWW in the early 1990s, Perl took off as the language of choice for CGI programming. With the recent burst of interest in the Open Source movement, Perl has gotten almost as much press as Linux.

Perl, according to Larry, is all about "making easy things easy, and hard things possible." So many programming languages make you spend an undue amount of time doing stuff to keep the language happy before you ever get around to making it do what you want. Perl lets you get your work done without worrying about things like memory allocation and variable typing.

Perl contains the best features of C, Basic, and a variety of other programming languages, with a hearty dollop of awk, sed, and shell scripting thrown in. One advantage of Perl over the other UNIX tools is that it can process binary files (those without line terminators or that contain binary data), whereas sed and awk cannot.

In Perl, "there is more than one way to do it." This is the unofficial motto of Perl, and it comes up so often that it is usually abbreviated as TIMTOWTDI. If you are familiar with some other programming language, chances are you can write functional Perl code.

A version of Perl comes with most Linux distributions, but it is typically several versions out of date. This makes sense when you consider the time required to produce a distribution and actually distribute it. As of this writing, the current production version of Perl is 5.6.1 (which is Perl version 5 point 6, patch level 1). Version 5.7.2 is available as a developer release (generally considered experimental). You can determine what version of Perl you have installed by typing **perl -v** at a shell prompt.

This chapter focuses on version 5. Many of the examples shown will fail if you try them with version 4 of Perl. If you have version 4, you should get one of the newer versions. If you are installing the latest Red Hat distribution, you should have version 5.6.0.

Perl is an interpreted language. The interpreter has been ported to just about every operating system that known. For UNIX and UNIX-like (Linux, for example) operating systems, you can just download the code from `http://www.perl.com/` and build it yourself.

A Simple Perl Program

To introduce you to the absolute basics of Perl programming, Listing 23.1 illustrates a trivial Perl program.

LISTING 23.1 A Trivial Perl Program

```
#!/usr/bin/perl
print "Look at all the camels!\n";
```

That is the whole program. Type that in, save it to a file called **trivial.pl**, **chmod +x** it, and execute it by typing the filename at the command prompt.

> **NOTE**
>
> If you get the message bash: trivial.pl: command not found, it means that you either typed the command name incorrectly, forgot to make it executable (with the **chmod** command), or do not have the current directory in your path.
>
> You have two choices. You can force the command to execute in the current directory as follows:
>
>   ./trivial.pl
>
> Or you can add the current directory to the path as follows:
>
>   export PATH=$PATH:.

The #! line is technically not part of the Perl code at all (the # character is the comment character in Perl), but is instead a message to the shell, telling it where it should go for the executable to run this program. That is standard practice in shell programming.

> **NOTE**
>
> #! is often pronounced *she-bang*, which is short for *sharp* (the musical name for the # character), and *bang*, which is another name for the exclamation point.
>
> Another pronunciation is *pound-bang* because most people refer to the # character on a telephone keypad as *pound*.

If for some reason Perl isn't located at /usr/bin/perl on your system, you can locate the correct location of Perl by using the which command:

```
which perl
```

If you do not have Perl installed, you might want to skip to "Reference" in this chapter to find out where you can obtain the Perl interpreter. Because a version of Perl comes with most Linux distributions, this shouldn't be the case.

The second line does precisely what you would expect—it prints the text enclosed in quotation marks. \n is the escape sequence for a newline character.

Perl statements are terminated with a semicolon. A Perl statement can extend over several actual screen lines. Alternatively, you can have Perl statements in one line. Perl isn't particularly concerned about whitespace.

The # character indicates that the rest of the screen line is a comment. That is, there is a comment from the # character until the next newline, and it is ignored by the interpreter. Exceptions to this include when the # character is in a quoted string and when it is being used as the delimiter in a regular expression.

A block of code, such as what might appear inside a loop or a branch of a conditional statement, is indicated with curly braces ({}).

Included with the Perl installation is a document called *perlfunc*, which lists all the available Perl functions and their usage. You can view this document by typing **perldoc perlfunc** at the command line. You can also find this document online at http://www.cpan.org/doc/manual/html/pod/perlfunc.html.

Tip

You can use the perldoc and man commands to get more information on the version of Perl installed on your system.

To get information on the perldoc command, enter the following:

```
perldoc perldoc
```

To get introductory information on Perl, you have a choice of two different commands:

```
perldoc perl
man perl
```

The documentation is extensive and is well organized to help you find what you need.

Perl Variables and Data Structures

Perl is a *weakly typed* language, meaning that it doesn't require that you specify what datatype will be stored in a particular variable. C, for example, makes you declare that a particular variable is an integer, a character, a pointer, or whatever the case may be. Perl variables are whatever type they need to be, and can change type when you need them to.

Perl Variable Types

There are three variable types in Perl—scalars, arrays, and hashes. In an attempt to make each data type visually distinct, a different character is used to signify each variable type.

Scalar Variables

Scalar variables are indicated with the $ character, as in $penguin. Scalars can be numerical and can be strings, and they can change type from one to the other as needed. If you treat a number like a string, it's a string. If you treat a string like a number, it will be translated into a number if it makes sense to do so; otherwise, it will probably evaluate as 0. For example, the string "76trombones" will evaluate as the number 76 if used in a numerical calculation, but the string "polar bear" will evaluate to 0.

Arrays

Arrays are indicated with the @ character, as in @fish. An *array* is a list of values that are referenced by index number, starting with the first element numbered 0, just like C and awk. Each element in the array is a scalar value. Because scalar values are indicated with the $ character, a single element in an array is also indicated with a $ character. For example, $fish[2] refers to the third element in the @fish array. This tends to throw some people off, but is completely consistent.

Hashes

Hashes are indicated with the % character, as in %employee. A *hash*, which used to go by the cumbersome name *associative arrays*, is a list of name, value pairs. Individual elements in the hash are referenced by name, rather than by index. Again, because the values are scalars, the $ character is used for individual elements. For example, $employee{name} gives you one value from the hash. Two rather useful functions for dealing with hashes are *keys* and *values*. The keys function returns an array containing all of the keys of the hash, and values returns an array of the values of the hash. The code in Listing 23.2 displays all the values in your environment, much like typing the env command.

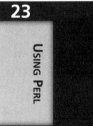

23

USING PERL

LISTING 23.2 Displaying the Contents of the *env* Hash

```
foreach $key (keys %ENV)  {
    print "$key = $ENV{$key}\n";
}
```

Special Variables

Perl has a wide variety of special variables. These usually look like punctuation—such as $_, $!, and $]—and are extremely useful for shorthand code. ($_ is the default variable, $! is the error message returned by the operating system, and $] is the Perl version number.)

$_ is perhaps the most useful of these, and you use that some more within this chapter. $_ is the Perl default variable, which is used when no argument is specified. For example, the following two statements are equivalent:

```
chomp;
```

```
chomp($_);
```

The following loops are equivalent:

```
for $cow (@cattle) {
        print "$cow says moo.\n";
}
for (@cattle)      {
        print "$_ says moo.\n";
}
```

For a complete listing of these special variables, you should see the `perlvar` document that comes with your Perl distribution, or you can go online to `http://www.cpan.org/doc/manual/html/pod/perlvar.html`.

Operators

Perl supports a number of operators to perform various operations. There are comparison operators (used, as the name implies, to compare values), compound operators (used to combine operations or multiple comparisons), arithmetic operators (to perform math), and special string constants.

Comparison Operators

The comparison operators used by Perl are similar to those used by C, awk, and the shells. They are the notation used to specify and compare values (including strings). Most frequently, a comparison operator is used within an `if` statement or loop.

Perl has comparison operators for numbers and strings.

Table 23.1 shows the numeric comparison operators and their behavior.

TABLE 23.1 Numeric Comparison Operators in Perl

Operator	*Meaning*
==	Is equal to
<	Less than
>	Greater than
<=	Less than or equal to
>=	Greater than or equal to
!=	Not equal to
..	Range of >= first operand to <= second operand
<=>	Return -1 if less than, 0 if equal, and 1 if greater than

Table 23.2 shows the string comparison operators and their behaviors.

TABLE 23.2 String Comparison Operators in Perl

Operator	*Meaning*
eq	Is equal to
lt	Less than
gt	Greater than
le	Less than or equal to
ge	Greater than or equal to
ne	Not equal to
cmp	Return -1 if less than, 0 if equal, and 1 if greater than
=~	Matched by regular expression
!~	Not matched by regular expression

23

USING PERL

Compound Operators

The compound operators used by Perl are similar to those used by C, awk, and the shells. They are the notations used to combine other operations into a complex form of logic.

Table 23.3 shows the compound pattern operators and their behavior.

TABLE 23.3 Compound Pattern Operators in Perl

Operator	Meaning
&&	Logical AND
||	Logical OR
!	Logical NOT
()	Parentheses; used to group compound statements

Arithmetic Operators

Perl supports a wide variety of math operations. Table 23.4 summarizes these operators.

Table 23.4   Perl Arithmetic Operators

Operator	Purpose
x**y	Raises x to the y power (same as x^y)
x%y	Calculates the remainder of x/y
x+y	Adds x to y
x-y	Subtracts y from x
x*y	Multiplies x times y
x/y	Divides x by y
-y	Negates y (switches the sign of y); also known as the *unary minus*
++y	Increments y by 1 and uses value (prefix increment)
y++	Uses value of y and then increments by 1 (postfix increment)
−y	Decrements y by 1 and uses value (prefix decrement)
y−	Uses value of y and then decrements by 1 (postfix decrement)
x=y	Assigns value of y to x. Perl also supports operator-assignment operators (+=, -=, *=, /=, %=, **=, and others)

You can also use comparison operators (like == or <) and compound pattern operators (&&, \|\|, and !) in arithmetic statements. They evaluate to the value 0 for false and 1 for true.

Other Operators

Perl supports a number of operators that don't fit any of the prior categories. Table 23.5 summarizes these operators.

TABLE 23.5   Other Perl Operators

Operator	Purpose
~x	Bitwise not (changes 0 bits to 1 and 1 bits to 0).
x & y	Bitwise and.
x | y	Bitwise or.
x ^ y	Bitwise exclusive or (XOR).
x << y	Bitwise shift left (shift x by y bits).
x >> y	Bitwise shift right (shift x by y bits).
x . y	Concatenate y onto x.
a x b	Repeat string a for b number of times.
x , y	Comma operator—evaluate x and then y.
x ? y : z	Conditional expression—if x is true, y is evaluated, otherwise z is evaluated. Provides the capability of an if statement anywhere you want (in the middle of a print, for instance).

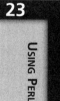

Except for the comma operator and conditional expression, these operators can also be used with the assignment operator (similar to the way addition (+) can be combined with assignment (=), giving +=).

Special String Constants

Perl supports string constants that have special meaning or cannot be entered from the keyboard.

Table 23.6 shows most of the constants supported by Perl.

TABLE 23.6   Perl Special String Constants

Expression	Meaning
\\	The means of including a backslash
\a	The alert or bell character
\b	Backspace

TABLE 23.6 Perl Special String Constants

Expression	Meaning
\cC	Control character (like holding the Ctrl key down and pressing the C character).
\e	Escape
\f	Formfeed
\n	Newline
\r	Carriage return
\t	Tab
\v	Vertical tab
\xNN	Indicates that NN is a hexadecimal number
\0NNN	Indicates that NNN is an octal (base 8) number

Conditional Statements: if/else and unless

Perl offers two conditional statements, if and unless, which function opposite one another. if allows you to execute a block of code only if certain conditions are met so that you can control the flow of logic through your program. Conversely, unless performs the statements when certain conditions are not met.

if

The syntax of the Perl if/else structure is as follows:

```
if (condition) {
    statement or block of code
    }
elsif (condition) {
    statement or block of code
    }
else {
    statement or block of code
    }
```

condition can be a statement that returns a true or false value.

> **Note**
>
> Truth is defined in Perl in a way that might be unfamiliar to you, so be careful. Everything in Perl is true except `0` (the digit zero), `"0"` (the string containing the number `0`), `""` (the empty string), and an undefined value. Note that even the string `"00"` is a true value because it is not one of those four cases.

The `statement or block of code` is executed if the test condition returns a true value.

For example, Listing 23.3 uses the `if/else` structure.

LISTING 23.3 *if/elsif/else*

```
if  ($favorite eq "chocolate") {
     print "I like chocolate too.\n";
} elsif ($favorite eq "spinach") {
     print "Oh, I don't like spinach.\n";
} else {
     print "Your favorite food is $favorite.\n";
}
```

> **Note**
>
> Larry is a linguist, so Perl contains a lot of idiomatic ways of saying things that correspond with spoken English. The `if` statement is one good example. For example, you can say the following:
>
> ```
> if ($name eq "Rich") {
>   print "Hello, Rich!\n";
> }
> ```
>
> Alternatively, you can write it as you would more likely say it:
>
> ```
> print "Hello Rich!\n" if $name eq "Rich";
> ```
>
> Larry designed Perl as a natural language. In this respect, it is rather different from most other programming languages. The traditional computer science way of doing things is to have a minimal set of keywords from which all other concepts are built. Perl, on the other hand, provides you with more than one way to say the same thing (TIMTOWTDI) like a human language would.
>
> Also like human language, Perl evolved as it was used. If people saw a need for a particular function or new syntax, Larry threw it into the next version. If nobody used a particular feature, or everyone hated a particular construct, it was thrown out. As Larry put it, "I picked the feature set of Perl because I thought they were cool features. I left the other ones behind because I thought they sucked."

unless

unless works just like `if`, only backward. `unless` performs a statement or block if a condition is false.

```
unless ($name eq "Rich")          {
        print "Go away, you're not allowed in here!\n";
}
```

> ### Note
>
> You can restate the preceding example in more natural language, like you did in the `if` example.
>
> ```
> print "Go away!\n" unless $name eq "Rich";
> ```
>
> Although it isn't a rule, you should try to put the more important part of the statement (think of it as a sentence) on the left so that it is easier to read.

Looping

A *loop* is a way to do something multiple times. A very simple example is a countdown timer that performs a task (waiting for one second) 300 times before telling you that your egg is done boiling.

Looping constructs can either perform a block of code as long as certain conditions apply, or while they step through a list of values, perhaps using that list as arguments.

Perl has four looping constructs: `for`, `foreach`, `while`, and `until`.

for

The `for` construct performs a *statement* (block of code) for a set of conditions defined as follows:

```
for (start condition; end condition; increment function) {
    statement(s)
}
```

The start condition is set at the beginning of the loop. Each time the loop is executed, the increment function is performed until the end condition is achieved. This looks much like the traditional `for/next` loop. The following code is an example of a `for` loop:

```
for ($i=1; $i<=10; $i++) {
        print "$i\n"
}
```

foreach

The foreach construct performs a statement block for each element in a list or array:

```
foreach $name (@names) {
    print "$name\n"
}
```

The loop variable ($name in the example) is not merely set to the value of the array elements; it is aliased to that element. This means that if you modify the loop variable, you are actually modifying the array.

If no loop array is specified, as in the following example, the Perl default variable $_ is used:

```
for (@names)        {
        print "$_ was here\n";
}
```

This syntax can be very convenient, but can also lead to unreadable code. Give a thought to the poor person who will be maintaining your code. It will probably be you.

> **Note**
>
> foreach is frequently abbreviated as for.

while

while performs a block of statements as long as a particular condition is true:

```
while ($x<10) {
    print "$x\n";
    $x++;
}
```

Remember that the condition can be anything that returns a true or false value. For example, it could be a function call:

```
while ( InvalidPassword($user, $password) )        {
        print "You've entered an invalid password. Please try again.\n";
        $password = GetPassword;
}
```

until

until is the exact opposite of the while statement. It performs a block of statements as long as a particular condition is false—or, rather, until it becomes true:

```
until (ValidPassword($user, $password)) {
        print "You've entered an invalid password. Please try again.\n";
        $password = GetPassword;
}
```

last and next

You can force Perl to end a loop early by using the last statement. last is similar to the C break command—the loop is exited. If you decide you need to skip the remaining contents of a loop without ending the loop itself, you can use next, which is similar to the C continue command. Unfortunately, these do not work with do_..._while.

do ... while and do ... until

The while and until loops evaluate the conditional first. The behavior is changed by applying a do block before the conditional. With the do block, the condition is evaluated last, which results in the contents of the block always executing at least once (even if the condition is false). This is similar to the C language do ... while (*conditional*) statement.

Regular Expressions

Perl's greatest strength is in text and file manipulation, which is accomplished by using the regular expression (regex) library. Regexes allow complicated pattern matching and replacement to be done efficiently and easily.

For example, the following line of code replaces every occurrence of the string bob or the string mary with fred in a line of text:

```
$string =~ s/bob|mary/fred/gi;
```

Without going into too many of the details, Table 23.7 explains what the preceding line says.

TABLE 23.7   Explanation of *$string =~ s/bob|mary/fred/gi;*

Element	Explanation
$string =~	Performs this pattern match on the text found in the variable called $string.

TABLE 23.7 continued

Element	Explanation
s	Substitute.
/	Begins the text to be matched.
bob|mary	Matches the text bob or mary. You should remember that it is looking for the text mary, not the word mary; that is, it will also match the text mary in the word maryland.
/	Ends text to be matched; begins text to replace it.
fred	Replaces anything that was matched with the text fred.
/	Ends replace text.
g	Does this substitution globally; that is, replaces the match text wherever in the string you match it (and any number of times).
i	The search text is not case sensitive. It matches bob, Bob, or bOB.
;	Indicates the end of the line of code.

If you are interested in the details, you can get more information using the regex (5) section of the manual.

Although replacing one string with another might seem a rather trivial task, the code required to do the same thing in another language (for example, C) is rather daunting.

Access to the Shell

Perl is useful for administrative functions because, for one thing, it has access to the shell. This means that Perl can perform for you any process you might ordinarily perform by typing commands to the shell. You do this with the `` syntax. For example, the code in Listing 23.4 prints a directory listing.

LISTING 23.4 Using Backticks to Access the Shell

```
$curr_dir = `pwd`;
@listing = `ls -la`;
print "Listing for $curr_dir\n";
foreach $file (@listing) {
    print "$file";
}
```

> **Note**
>
> The `` notation uses the backtick found above the Tab key (on most keyboards), not the single quotation mark.

You can also use the `Shell` module to access the shell. `Shell` is one of the standard modules that comes with Perl. It gives an even more transparent access to the shell. Look at the following code for an example:

```
use Shell qw(cp);
cp ("/home/httpd/logs/access.log", "/tmp/httpd.log");
```

It almost looks like it is importing the command-line functions directly into Perl, and although that isn't really happening, you can pretend that it is and use it accordingly.

A third method of accessing the shell is via the `system` function call:

```
$rc = 0xffff & system('cp /home/httpd/logs/access.log /tmp/httpd.log');
if ($rc == 0) {
        print "system cp succeeded \n";
}
else {
        print "system cp failed $rc";
}
```

The call can also be used with the `or die` clause:

```
system('cp /home/httpd/logs/access.log /tmp/httpd.log') == 0
        or die "system cp failed: $?"
```

However, you cannot capture the output of a command executed through the `system` function.

Access to the command line is fairly common in shell scripting languages, but is less common in higher-level programming languages.

Switches

Perl has a variety of command-line options (*switches*) that subtly change Perl's behavior. These switches can appear on the command line, or can be placed on the `#!` line at the beginning of the Perl program.

The following lists all the available command-line switches.

Note

Several command-line switches can be stacked together, so `-pie` is the same as `-p -i -e`.

`-0[digits]`—Specifies the input record separator (`$/`) as an octal number. `$/` is usually a newline, so you get one line per record. For example, if you read a file into an array, this gives you one line per array element. The value `00` is a special case and causes Perl to read in your file one paragraph per record.

`-a`—Turns on Autosplit mode when used with a `-n` or `-p`. That means that each line of input is automatically split into the `@F` array.

`-C`—Enables native support and system interfaces for wide characters (multibyte character sets).

`-c`—Tells Perl to perform syntax checking on the specified Perl program without executing it. This is invaluable, and the error messages given are informative, readable, and tell you where to begin looking for the problem, which is a rarity in error messages.

`-Dflags`—Sets debugging flags. See `perlrun` for more details.

`-d`—Runs the script under the Perl debugger. See `perldebug` for more information.

23

USING PERL

Note

The Perl documentation is referred to a few times in this section. `perldebug`, `perlrun`, `perlmod`, and `perlmodlib`, for example, are documents from the Perl documentation. To see these documents, just type **perldoc perlmodlib** at the shell prompt. You can also see all the Perl documents online at `http://www.cpan.org/doc/index.html` or on any CPAN site. (CPAN is the Comprehensive Perl Archive Network. See "Modules and CPAN" later in this chapter.)

Perl documentation is written in POD (Plain Old Documentation) format and can be converted into any other format, such as tex, ASCII, or HTML, with the pod2* tools that ship with Perl. For example, to produce HTML documentation on the Fubar module, you would type **pod2html Fubar.pm > Fubar.html**.

`-d:foo`—Runs the script under the control of a debugging or tracing module installed as `Devel::foo`. For example, `-d:Dprof` executes the script using the `Devel::DProf` profiler. See `perldebug` for additional information on the Perl debugger.

`-e commandline`—Indicates that what follows is Perl code. This allows you to enter Perl code directly on the command line, rather than running code contained in a file.

```
perl -e 'print join " ", keys %ENV;'
```

`-Fpattern`—Specifies the pattern to split on if `-a` is also in effect. This is `" "` by default, and `-F` allows you to set it to whatever works for you, such as `','` or `';'`. The pattern can be surrounded by `//`, `""`, or `''`.

`-h`—Typing `perl -h` lists all available command-line switches.

`-Idirectory`—Directories specified by `-I` are prepended to the search path for modules (`@INC`).

`-i[extension]`—This indicates that files are to be edited in place. If the extension is provided, the original is backed up with that extension. Otherwise, the original file is overwritten.

`-l[octnum]`—Enables automatic line-ending processing, which means that end-of-line characters are automatically removed from input and put back on to output. If the optional octal number is unspecified, this is just the newline character.

`-m[-]module` or `-M[-]module`—Loads the specified module before running your script. There is a subtle difference between `m` and `M`. See `perlrun` for more details.

`-n`—Causes Perl to loop around your script for each file provided to the command line. Does not print the output. The following example, from `perlrun`, deletes all files older than a week:

```
find . -mtime +7 -print | perl -nle 'unlink;'
```

`-P`—This causes your script to be run through the C preprocessor before compilation by Perl.

`-p`—This is just like `-n`, except that that each line is printed.

`-S`—This searches for the script using the `PATH` environment variable.

`-s`—This performs some command-line switch parsing and puts the switch into the corresponding variable in the Perl script. For example, the following script prints `'1'` if run with the `-fubar` switch. Your Perl code might look like this:

```
#!/usr/bin/perl -s
print $fubar;
```

When you execute it, you would enter

```
myperl -fubar
```

`-T`—This enables *taint* checking. In this mode, Perl assumes that all user input is tainted, or insecure, until the programmer tells it otherwise. This helps protect you from people trying to exploit security holes in your code and is especially important when writing CGI programs.

-U—This allows you to do unsafe things in your Perl program, such as unlinking directories while running as superuser.

-u—This tells Perl to dump core after compiling this script. You could presumably, with much time and patience, use this to create an executable file.

-V—This prints a summary of the major Perl configuration values and the current value of @INC.

```
-V:names
```

This parameter displays the value of the names configuration variable.

-v—This prints the version and patchlevel of your Perl executable.

```
% perl -v
This is perl, version 5.6.0 built for i386-linux

Copyright 1987-2000, Larry Wall

Perl may be copied only under the terms of either the
Artistic License or the GNU General Public License,
which may be found in the Perl 5.0 source kit.

Complete documentation for Perl, including FAQ lists,
should be found on this system using `man perl' or
`perldoc perl'.  If you have access to the Internet,
point your browser at http://www.perl.com/, the Perl
Home Page.
```

-W—This tells Perl to display all warning messages.

-w—This tells Perl to display warning messages about potential problems in the program, such as variables used only once (might be a typo), using = instead of == in a comparison, and the like. This is often used in conjunction with the -c flag to do a thorough program check.

```
perl -cw finalassignment.pl
```

-X—This tells Perl to disable all warning messages.

-x directory—This tells Perl that the script is embedded in something larger, such as an e-mail message. Perl throws away everything before a line starting with #!, containing the string 'perl', and everything after __END__. If a directory is specified, Perl changes to the directory before executing the script.

Modules and CPAN

A great strength of the Perl community (and the Linux community) is the fact that it is an Open Source community. Perl expresses this via CPAN (Comprehensive Perl Archive Network), which is a network of mirrors of a repository of code—Perl code, to be more precise.

Most of CPAN is made up of *modules*, which are reusable chunks of code that do useful things so that you do not have to reinvent the wheel every time you try to build a bicycle.

There are thousands of Perl modules that do everything from sending e-mail to maintain your Cisco router access lists to telling you whether a name is masculine or feminine to printing the time in some fancy format. Modules for CGI programming and modules access the socket libraries and modules that post to Usenet for you. If you can think of doing something, chances are pretty good that a module exists to help you. If there is no module that helps, you are encouraged to write one and share it with the rest of the community.

At `http://www.perl.com/CPAN/`, you will find the CPAN Multiplex Dispatcher, which will attempt to direct you to the CPAN site closest to you.

Perl comes with a set of standard modules installed. Those modules contain much of the function that you will want. You can use the CPAN module (which is one of the standard modules) to download and install other modules onto your system. Typing the following command will put you into an interactive shell that gives you access to CPAN. You can type **help** at the prompt to get more information on how to use the CPAN program.

```
perl -MCPAN -e shell
```

Once you have installed a module from CPAN (or written one of your own), you can load that module into memory where you can use it with the use function.

```
use Time::CTime;
```

use looks in the directories listed in the variable @INC for the module. In this example, use looks for a directory called Time, which contains a file called CTime.pm, which in turn is assumed to contain a package called Time::CTime. The distribution of each module should contain documentation on using that module.

For a list of all the standard Perl modules (those that come with Perl when you install it), see perlmodlib in the Perl documentation. You can read this document by typing **perl-doc perlmodlib** at the command prompt.

Code Examples

Over the last few years, a lot of people have picked up the notion that Perl is a CGI language, as though it isn't good for anything else. Nothing could be further from the truth. You can use Perl in every aspect of your system administration and as a building block in whatever applications you are planning to run on your shiny new Linux system.

The following sections contain a few examples of things you might want to do with Perl. Perl is versatile enough that you can make it do about anything.

Sending Mail

There are several ways to get Perl to send e-mail. One method that you see frequently is opening a pipe to sendmail and sending data to it (shown in Listing 23.5). Another method is using the `Mail::Sendmail` module, which uses socket connections directly to send mail (shown in Listing 23.6). The latter method is faster because it doesn't have to launch an external process.

LISTING 23.5   Sending Mail Using Sendmail

```
open (MAIL, "| /usr/sbin/sendmail -t"); # Use -t to protect from users
print MAIL <<EndMail;
To: dpitts\@mk.net
From: rbowen\@mk.net
Subject: Email notification

David,
 Sending email from Perl is easy!
Rich
..
EndMail
close MAIL;
```

> ### Note
>
> Note that the @ sign in the e-mail addresses needs to be escaped so that Perl doesn't try to evaluate an array of that name.
>
> The syntax used to print the mail message is called a *here document*. The syntax is as follows:
>
> ```
>     print <<EndText;
>     .....
>     EndText
> ```
>
> The `EndText` value must be identical at the beginning and at the end of the block, including any whitespace.

LISTING 23.6   Sending Mail Using the `Mail::Sendmail` Module

```
use Mail::Sendmail;
%mail = ('To' => 'dpitts@mk.net',
         'From' => 'rbowen@mk.net'
         'Subject' => 'Email notification',
```

23

USING PERL

LISTING 23.6   continued

```
        'Message' => 'Sending email from Perl is easy!',
        );
sendmail(%mail);
```

Perl ignores the comma after the last element in the hash. It is convenient to leave it there; if you want to add items to the hash, you do not need to add the comma. This is purely a style decision.

Note also that the @ sign did not need to be escaped within single quotation marks (' '). Perl does not *interpolate* (evaluate variables) within single quotation marks, but does within double quotation marks and here documents.

Purging Logs

Many programs maintain some variety of logs. Often, much of the information in the logs is redundant or just useless. The program shown in Listing 23.7 removes all lines from a file that contain a particular word or phrase, so lines that you know are not important can be purged. For example, you might want to remove all the lines in the Apache error log that originate with your test client machine because you know that these error messages were produced during testing.

LISTING 23.7   Purging Log Files

```perl
#!/usr/bin/perl
#       Be careful using this program!!
#       This will remove all lines that contain a given word
#       Usage:  remove <word> <file>
$word=@ARGV[0];
$file=@ARGV[1];
if ($file) {
    # Open file for reading
    open (FILE, "$file") or die "Could not open file: $!";       @lines=<FILE>;
    close FILE;
    # Open file for writing
    open (FILE, ">$file") or die "Could not open file for writing: $!";
    for (@lines) {
        print FILE unless /$word/;
    } # End for
    close FILE;
} else {
    print "Usage:  remove <word> <file>\n";
} # End if...else
```

The code uses a few idiomatic Perl expressions to keep the code brief. It reads the file into an array using the <FILE> notation; it then writes the lines back out to the file unless they match the pattern given on the command line.

The die function kills program operation and displays an error message if the open statements fail. $! in the error message, as mentioned in the section on special variables, is the error message returned by the operating system. It will likely be something like 'file not found' or 'permission denied'.

Posting to Usenet

If some portion of your job requires periodic postings to Usenet—a FAQ listing, for example—the following Perl program can automate the process for you. In the sample code, the posted text is read in from a text file, but your input can come from anywhere.

The program shown in Listing 23.8 uses the Net::NNTP module, which is a standard part of the Perl distribution. You can find more documentation on the Net::NNTP module by typing 'perldoc Net::NNTP' at the command line.

LISTING 23.8 Posting an Article to Usenet

```perl
#!/usr/bin/perl
open (POST, "post.file");
@post = <POST>;
close POST;
use Net::NNTP;
$NNTPhost = 'news';
$nntp = Net::NNTP->new($NNTPhost)
        or die "Cannot contact $NNTPhost: $!";
# $nntp->debug(1);
$nntp->post()
   or die "Could not post article: $!";
$nntp->datasend("Newsgroups: news.announce\n");
$nntp->datasend("Subject: FAQ - Frequently Asked Questions\n");
$nntp->datasend("From: ADMIN <root\@rcbowen.com>\n");
$nntp->datasend("\n\n");
for (@post)     {
     $nntp->datasend($_);
} # End for
$nntp->quit;
```

One-Liners

Perl has the rather undeserved reputation of being unreadable. The fact is that you can write unreadable code in any language. Perl allows for more than one way to do something, and this leads rather naturally to people trying to find the most arcane way to do things.

One medium in which Perl excels is the one-liner. Folks go to great lengths to reduce tasks to one line of Perl code. Some examples of one-liners that might make your life easier follow.

> **Tip**
>
> Just because you can do something is not a particularly good reason for doing it. I will frequently write somewhat more lengthy pieces of code for something that could be done in just one line, just for the sake of readability. It is very irritating to go back to a piece of code in which I reduced something to one line for efficiency, or just because I could, and have to spend 30 minutes trying to figure out what it does.
>
> Also remember to document your Perl scripts. It will help you in the future (or your co-workers who get to maintain your code).

The Schwartzian Transform

Named for Randal Schwartz, the *Schwartzian transform* is a way of sorting an array by something that is not obvious. The sort function sorts arrays alphabetically; that's pretty obvious. What if you want to sort an array of strings alphabetically by the third word? Perhaps you want something more useful, such as sorting a list of files by file size? The Schwartzian transform creates a new list that contains the information that you want to sort by, referencing the first list. You then sort the new list and use it to figure out the order that the first list should be in. Here's a simple example that sorts a list of strings by length:

```
@sorted_by_length =
  map { $_ => [0] }          # Extract original list
  sort { $a=>[1] <=> $b=>[1] } # Sort by the transformed value
  map { [$_, length($_)] }    # Map to a list of element lengths
  @list;
```

Because each operator acts on the thing immediately to the right of it, it helps to read this from right to left (or bottom to top, the way it is written here).

The first thing that acts on the list is the map operator. It transforms the list into a hash in which the keys are the list elements and the values are the lengths of each element. This is where you put in your code that does the transformation by which you want to sort.

The next operator is the sort function, which sorts the list by the values.

Finally, the hash is transformed back into an array by extracting its keys. The array is now in the desired order.

Command Line Processing

Perl is great at parsing the output of various programs. This is a task for which a lot of people use tools such as awk and sed. Perl gives you a larger vocabulary for performing these tasks. The following example is very simple, but illustrates how you might use Perl to chop up some output and do something with it. In the example, Perl is used to list only those files that are larger than 10KB.

```
ls -la | perl -nae 'print "$F[8] is $F[4]\n" if $F[4] > 10000;'
```

The -n switch indicates that I want the Perl code run for each line of the output. The -a switch automatically splits the output into the @F array. The -e switch indicates that the Perl code is going to follow on the command line. (See "Switches" earlier in this chapter.)

Perl-Related Tools

A number of tools are related to Perl or are included with the Perl distribution. The most common of these are as follows:

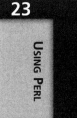

- perldoc—Displays Perl documentation.
- pod2html—Converts Perl documentation to HTML format.
- pod2man—Converts Perl documentation to man (nroff/troff) format.
- a2p—Converts awk scripts to Perl.
- s2p—Converts sed commands to Perl.

Reference

The first place to look is in the Perl documentation and Linux man pages.

Perl, all of its documentation, and millions of lines of Perl programs are all available free on the Internet. A number of Usenet newsgroups are also devoted to Perl, as well as shelves of books, and a quarterly journal.

Books

Although your local bookstore might have dozens of titles on Perl, the following are some of the more highly recommended of these. You might also look at the *Camel Critiques* (Tom Christiansen; `http://language.perl.com/critiques/index.html`) for reviews of other available Perl books.

- *Programming Perl*, Second Edition, by Larry Wall, Randall Schwartz, and Tom Christiansen. O'Reilly & Associates.
- *Effective Perl Programming: Writing Better Programs with Perl*, by Joseph Hall. Addison-Wesley Publishing Company.
- *Mastering Regular Expressions*, by Jeffrey Friedl. O'Reilly & Associates.

Usenet

Check out the following on Usenet:

- `comp.lang.perl.misc`—Discusses various aspects of the Perl programming language. Make sure that your questions are Perl-specific, not generic CGI programming questions. The regulars tend to flame folks who do not know the difference.
- `comp.infosystems.www.authoring.cgi`—Discusses authoring of CGI programs, so much of the discussion is Perl-specific. Make sure your questions are related to CGI programming, not just Perl. The regulars are very particular about staying on-topic.

WWW

Check these sites on the World Wide Web:

- `http://www.perl.com/`—Tom Christiansen maintains the Perl language home page. This is the place to find all sorts of information about Perl, from its history and culture to helpful tips. This is also the place to download the Perl interpreter for your system.
- `http://www.perl.com/CPAN/`—This is part of the site just mentioned, but it merits its own mention. CPAN (Comprehensive Perl Archive Network) is the place for you to find modules and programs in Perl. If you end up writing something in Perl that you think is particularly useful, you can make it available to the Perl community here.
- `http://www.perlmonth.com/`—A monthly e-zine dedicated to Perl. This is a fairly new venture, but already has an impressive line-up of contributors.

- `http://www.hwg.org/`—The HTML Writers Guild is a non-profit organization dedicated to assisting Web developers. One of their services is a plethora of mailing lists. The hwg-servers mailing list and the hwg-languages mailing list, are great places for asking Perl-related questions.

- `http://www.pm.org/`—The Perl Mongers are local Perl users groups. There might be one in your area.

Other

A valuable resource not falling into any of the preceding categories is as follows:

- *The Perl Journal* (`http://www.tpj.com/`)

  The Perl Journal is a quarterly publication devoted to the Perl programming language. Orchestrated by Jon Orwant, *TPJ* is always full of excellent, amusing, and informative articles, and is an invaluable resource to the new, and experienced, Perl programmer.

23

USING PERL

Kernel and Module Management

CHAPTER 24

The Linux kernel is a highly complex piece of software. The result of years of work by numerous people around the world, the Linux kernel is rapidly becoming a full-featured kernel, with all the features found in commercial software operating systems.

Most users will find the stock Red Hat Linux kernel to suit their needs, although it is sometimes necessary to recompile the kernel to support a specific piece of hardware or add a new feature that was developed recently. Although some will say that recompiling the kernel isn't something for the average user, it doesn't take a rocket scientist to recompile the Linux kernel. Although it's true that not understanding all the available options when recompiling leads to a bloated kernel, not much harm will come from tinkering with the kernel. Aside from a few critical snags, there is no reason that an average person cannot follow the instructions in this chapter and successfully make their own customized Linux kernel.

> **NOTE**
>
> It is always a good idea to keep the existing kernel in place in case something goes wrong with the new kernel.

This chapter walks the user though the following situations:

- What is a kernel?
- Areas of the Linux kernel.
- When to compile a new kernel.
- When to compile drivers as modules or inline.
- How to compile the kernel.
- How to modify Grub.
- How to modify LILO.

After reading this chapter, a user should have a better understanding of what the Linux kernel is, its function, the subsystems that make up its composition, and how to recompile it. Additionally, tuning the system with runtime parameters should eliminate the need for most users to tackle the task of recompiling the stock Red Hat kernel.

The Linux Kernel

In 1991, Linus Torvalds released unto the world the version .99 of the Linux kernel. Steaming from his want of a powerful, UNIX like operating system for his personal computer, Linus put together the footsteps necessary to create what is now know as the Linux kernel. Since then, Linux has had thousands of contributors add their talents and time to the Linux project. Linus still maintains the kernel, deciding on what will and will not make it into the kernel as official releases.

The Linux kernel is only the brain of the operating system many people call Linux. Although many people think an entire distribution is Linux, the only piece that can rightly be called Linux is the kernel maintained by Linus. Anything else packaged with the kernel is add-on software that interacts with the kernel, allowing the user to interface with the system in a meaningful manner. With just a stock kernel and no other tools, a computer would just sit waiting for something interesting to happen. However because the user wouldn't have any way to interface with the system, nothing would happen. It is the system utilities and user programs that allow computers to become valuable tools to a user. The same argument holds true for user applications and utilities without a kernel. Now that you know what a kernel is, let's look at some of the reasons why you might want to recompile the kernel.

> **NOTE**
>
> It is always a good idea to keep the existing kernel in place in case something goes wrong with the new kernel.

> **CAUTION**
>
> Before making any changes to your current, working kernel, make sure that you have a backup copy on a floppy disk. This will allow you to boot into your system with a known working kernel should something go wrong during configuration. The command to do this is the following:
>
> ```
> mkbootdisk --device /dev/fd0 `uname -r`
> ```
>
> This assumes that your floppy drive is /dev/fd0 and name is the current version of your kernel. The ` character tells the shell to execute what is inside the ` first and then return that output as part of the input of the mkbootdisk command. Thus the result on my machine is the following:
>
> ```
> mkbootdisk --device /dev/fd0 2.4.6-3.1
> ```
>
> This command won't be echoed to your screen, but this is what the system will execute.

When to Recompile

Red Hat systems use a special kernel, with special packaging such as additional drivers compiled into it that were not part of the stock Linux kernel and modules compiled to provide specific compatibility with hardware common to the PC. Red Hat has quite an intensive testing period for all distribution kernels, of which Arjan van de Ven is the maintainer. Although Red Hat does use the Linux kernel, it isn't the de facto kernel maintained by Linus Torvalds. Most users will find that the Red Hat Linux kernel does everything they need it to, thus rarely does the kernel need to be recompiled. With many parameters available to be tuned in real time using sysctl, the reasons to recompile dwindle to compiling modules for an esoteric driver or just to keep up on kernel updates.

The Linux Source Tree

The Linux kernel is a large modular system, the result of multiple developers around the world, with Linus Torvalds holding the ultimate decision as to what will and will not be included in the final release. Many kernel developers specialize in a given area of the kernel, thus limiting the amount of code they work with on a day-to-day basis. As a result of this, the Linux kernel can be categorized into several subsystems, although organized as directories. Listing 24.1 shows the major sections of the 2.4 Linux.

LISTING 24.1   Areas of the Kernel

```
Architecture
Drviers
File Systems
Init
Interprocess Communications
Kernel
Memory Management
Networking
```

Architecture

Originally written for the Intel 80386 Microprocessor, Linux now supports several different architectures. The arch directory contains all the platform specific code necessary to implementation low-level system interfaces with the multitude of processors supported by Linux. Table 24.1 provides a name and description for the architecture types supported by Linux.

TABLE 24.1 Linux supported Architectures

Name	Description
ARM	Intel ARM processor. An embedded microprocessor, commonly used in dedicated systems.
Alpha	Digital Equipment Corporation's 64-bit microprocessor known for its high performance, heat, and cost.
Athlon	Advanced Micro Devices (AMD) main microprocessor.
CRIS	Axis Communications ETRAX 100LX embedded CPU.
IA64	Intel's new 64-bit microprocessor. This processor is currently in development, with Intel working closely with Linux kernel developers to ensure Linux support.
i386	Intel's third generation 32 bit microprocessor. The main feature of the 80386 was the ability to utilize real and protected modes of operation.
i486	Intel's fourth generation 32 bit microprocessor. Featured an integrated floating point processor, FPU, thus eliminating the need for a math co-processor.
i586	Not a true Intel chip, but a general classification of microprocessor, that was based on the design of the x86 architecture, but with some additions.
i686	General term for Intel's Pentium II, and AMD's K6 32 bit microprocessors.
M68K	Motorola 68000's series of 32 bit microprocessors, commonly found in the Apple Macintosh and Commodore's Amiga.
MIPS	MIPS microprocessor used for embedded functions as well as a main microprocessor.
MIPS64	MIPS 64-bit RISC microprocessor commonly found in SGI machines.
PaRISC	Hewlett Packard's 64-bit RISC microprocessor.
PPC	IBM's 32-bit Power PC microprocessor. Commonly found in IBM PCs and Apple PowerPCs.
S390	IBM mainframe architecture.
SPARC	Sun Microsystems 32-bit RISC processor.
SPARC64	Sun Microsystems 64-bit RISC processor.

24

KERNEL AND MODULE MANAGEMENT

Drivers

This interaction and controlling of hardware is a small piece of the kernel called *drivers*. The drivers tell the computer how to interact with a modem, SCSI card, keyboard, mouse, and so on when the user does something. Listing 24.2 shows the major subsections under the drivers subsystem.

LISTING 24.2   Subsections of the Linux Kernel Drivers Subsystem

acorn	cdrom	i2o	macintosh	misc	pci	scsi	usb
acpi	char	ide mtd	pcmci	sgi	video		
atm	dio	ieee1394	md	net	pnp	sound	zorro
block	fc4	input	media	nubus	s390	tc	
bluetooth	i2c	isdn	message	parport	sbus	telephony	

These different directories are the containers for the source code of the drivers. As you can see, the drivers subsections are broken down by a major technology (that is, ieee1394 for firewire) or by general grouping (that is, net). Under each of these directory structures is the source code for those driver types, with each driver having at least one file of its own. Unless you are hacking the kernel, recompiling the kernel generally doesn't require inspection of the source code. That is, unless you are the curious type and what to see what a device driver looks like.

Filesystem

Just about every type of operating system provides the user with the ability to create, store, and modify files. The system must have a structured method of creating and storing these files in such a way as to know where files are located, when they were created and last updated, the size of the file, and other statistics that are important to system administration. The filesystem is the method that provides this information. Each operating system generally has its own method of doing this.

In order for the kernel to know how to interact with the filesystem, it must know the structure of it. The default file system of most Linux machines is the Second Extended File System, or ext2. Red Hat Linux 7.2 makes the Third Extended File System, ext3, the default filesystem.

One of the main features that has been missing from Linux that is found in other Unix system is a journaling filesystem. Ext3 has this capability, as well as backward compatibility with the ext2 filesystem. In addition to the standard filesystem, Linux provides the capability of reading files systems of other platforms. As a result of this capability, Linux is often used as a server, providing access to hosts in a mixed operating system environment.

For the Linux kernel to be able to work with different filesystems, the Virtual File System was created that provides a special interface for filesystem code to manipulate. This is done by creating a memory structure for the filesystem and registering it with the `register_filesystem()` function. By providing this abstraction, filesystem code can be compiled into the kernel directly, or as a loadable module without programmers having to convert the existing filesystem into something compatible with the default filesystem.

Table 24.2 lists the filesystems that are currently readable by Linux.

TABLE 24.2 Linux Supported Filesystems

Name	Description
BFS	Filesystem used by SCO UnixWare for the /stand partition, which contains the kernel and other files necessary during the boot of UnixWare.
CMS	IBM Mainframe filesystem. Support is for basic functionality only at this time.
CramFS	CramFS is a file system for writing small compressed images to memory. Generally this is used to create ROM images for embedded processors. CramFS cannot be updated directly, but recreated, one memory page at a time with the mkcramfs utility.
DevFS	Device Filesystem. A filesystem to handle the assignment of character device files to device drivers in the kernel. This replaces the standard method of allowing the underlying filesystem to store these as files. DevFS handles major and minor number assignments in a separate namespace, rather than in the underlying filesystem.
EFS	Extent Filesystem. Filesystem found on SGI IRIX systems that preceded XFS. Currently, SGI only uses this filesystem for its CD-ROMs because XFS is the standard filesystem for IRIX.
ext2	Linux filesystem; the second release of the extended filesystem.
ext3	Third release of the extended filesystem. A journalized filesystem that is backward compatible with ext2. As of 7.2, this is the default file system for Red Hat.
FAT	File Allocation Tables filesystem. Default Microsoft Windows filesystem for DOS and Windows 3.1X.
vFAT	Extended FAT filesystem. Filesystem used by Microsoft Windows 95, Windows 98, and Windows ME to address long filenames.

24

KERNEL AND MODULE MANAGEMENT

TABLE 24.2 continued

Name	Description
FreeVXFS	Free implementation of the VERITAS journaling filesystem by Christoph Hellwig. The current Linux implementation of this file system is read-only.
HPFS	High Performance Filesystem. Default filesystem of IBM's OS/2 operating system.
ISOFS	ISO filesystem. Standard filesystem of CD-ROMs.
JFF	Journaling Flash File System. A file system for writing to flash devices that provides journaling functionality. Developed by Axis Communications AB.
JFF2	Updated version of Journaling Flash File System developed by Red Hat. It improves on JFFS by added.
NCPFS	NetWare Core Protocol filesystem. Network Filesystem designed by Novell for NetWare. This filesystem is akin to NFS over TCP/IP, although NCPFS uses the Network Core Protocol and the IPX/SPX protocol suite.
NFS	Network filesystem. A distributed filesystem, created by Sun Microsystems. Used for mounting filesystems in a distributed, network environment. This filesystem only provides the mechanisms to allow remote hosts to mount a specific mount point.
NLS	Natural Language Support filesystem. This is used to translated the language of the locale that is set on the specific host.
NTFS	Microsoft NT Filesystem. Default filesystem for Windows NT Workstation and Server. Currently Linux can only read file systems of this type.
proc	Not a true filesystem, but a virtual filesystem of files created by the Linux kernel that provides runtime information about the kernel and its parameters.
QNX4	Filesystem for the QNX4 Operation System. This file system is for both floppy and hard disks.
reiserfs	Journaling filesystem created by Hans Reiser to address performance issues on Linux for large files, increased speed, and efficiency in storage.
ROMFS	ROM filesystem. A read-only filesystem, created in memory. This is generally used in the initial boot up of a Linux system, commonly used to link kernel modules during startup of the system.

TABLE 24.2 continued

Name	Description
SMBFS	Service Message Box filesystem. Default filesystem used by Microsoft Windows for network filesystems.
SysV-FS	UNIX System V filesystem. Filesystem used in the UNIX System V and Xenix operating systems.
UDF	A newer filesystem for CD-ROMs that is meant to replace the ISO9660 format, but currently is used in DVD-ROM and CD-RW discs.
UFS	Universal Filesystem. Default filesystem of UNIX, although the implementation details are different for each vendor. Linux currently supports the original UFS, as found in System V, 4.4 BSD, NetBSD, OpenBSD, FreeBSD, SunOs (Solaris), SunOS for Intel, NeXTStep, and OpenStep.
umsdos	Not a true filesystem, but a modification of the FAT file system to make it usable as a Linux partition. It supports the necessary long files names, user and group permissions, hard and symbolic links, and special files such as pipes, sockets, and devices.

> **NOTE**
>
> A complete description and detailed instructions on each filesystem can be found in the Documentation/filesystems directory of the kernel source code.

24

KERNEL AND MODULE MANAGEMENT

Init

Init is the initial process of the Linux kernel. All initialization of the kernel is handled in this area, from defining all devices to parsing parameters from other processes to relay to the kernel. Init is the main process on any UNIX system, and Linux is no exception.

Interprocess Control

Interprocess Control (IPC) is a method for the kernel to manage processes and allow them to communication with each other. The Linux kernel uses signals, pipes, and sockets to do this. For sockets, Linux uses the UNIX System V method of providing communication across processes: message queues, shared memory, and semaphores.

This is a large subsystem of the kernel because it must interface with the memory management subsystem, the filesystem, and the core structures of the kernel. The details of these topics are out of scope of this chapter. A list of resources for the detailed information on the structure, function, and purpose can be found in the kernel-docs.txt file in the Documentation/ directory of the Linux kernel source.

Kernel

The kernel directory contains the code to provide the other areas of the kernel with ways to communicate. Several functions that are used thought the other subsystems of the kernel reside here, such as panic, fork, printk, softirq, dma, and exit, to name a few. Fork provides the kernel with the ability to create subprocesses from their parents. The printk function provides the functionality of providing text messages for user reading. Generally, printk is used to provide some debugging or status message from the kernel.

These functions are the part of the core code of the Linux kernel and vital to it's function. Although a short description of a few functions has been provided, the author invites the curious to read the source code to get a more detailed, meaningful understanding of this subsystem's true value and function.

Memory Management

Memory is the critical subsystem of any operating system. Without memory, the kernel cannot function because all the operations waiting to do work must be stored in some form of memory. The memory management subsystem is responsible for keeping track of all system memory and its usage by the kernel.

Networking

One of the areas that Linux is known for is its networking capabilities. Linux supports several protocol suites in the kernel. This wide range of protocol coverage is what allows Linux to be at home in almost any networked environment. A list of all the protocols supported by the Linux kernel is found in Table 24.3.

TABLE 24.3 Linux Supported Network Protocols

Name	Description
802	IEEE 802.X protocol specifications. These include the specifications for Logical Link Control (LLC) (802.2), Ethernet (802.3), and Token Ring (802.4).

TABLE 24.3 continued

Name	Description
Appletalk	Apple Computer's network protocol. Designed as a client/server protocol for local area networks to allow peripheral sharing. There are two version of Appletalk, Phase I for small workgroups, and Phase II for larger intranetworks. The Linux kernel provides support for both of these versions.
ATM	Asynchronous Transfer Mode. High speed networking protocol that uses fixed frames instead of variable packet lengths.
AX25	Amateur packet radio protocol. This protocol uses the amateur radio spectrum to transmit and receive other network protocols in a digital fashion.
BGP	Border Gateway Protocol. A path vector protocol for communicating routing information between autonomous systems. This protocol is used by *Internet service providers (ISPs)* to maintain routing information for the Internet.
Bluetooth	Wireless protocol specification that can be used by a multitude of devices. Because Bluetooth uses radio communication, data and voice can be sent in real time. The design of the protocol addresses security issues as well as handling interference.
DECnet	Digital Equipment Corporation Network protocol suite. The most recent version, DECnet/OSI is backward compatible with earlier versions, but also supports proprietary and open protocols. DECnet support in Linux allows an Ethernet network card to communicate using DECnet protocols.
Econet	Acorn Computer's proprietary network protocol for local area networks used to connect Acorn's BBC microcomputers. This protocol is aging and is not maintained in the 2.4 kernel.
Ethernet	Common Local Area Network protocol that utilizes Carrier Sense Mutli-Access with Collision Detection (CSMA/CD) for communication. There are a variety of Ethernet implementations as well as speeds, with the most common being 10 or 100 MBPS.
IPV4	Internet Protocol Version 4. This is the current version of IP used on the Internet. Connection-less protocol that uses variable packet width to transfer data.
IPV6	Internet Protocol Version 6. Provides 64-bit address range, thus making the number of available host addresses above all conceivable needs for hosts on the Internet. Provides the ability to provide quality of service (QOS) prioritization, thus making it a good candidate for multimedia.
Irda	Infrared Data Association protocol. Provides support for Infrared devices such as keyboards, mice, trackballs, and other input devices. Although the Linux kernel is a part of the Irda association, the kernel implementation has yet to become certified compliant.

TABLE 24.3   continued

Name	Description
IPX/SPX	Internetwork Packet eXchange/Sequence Packet eXchange. One drawback of IPX/SPX is the inability to route packets past 16 hops. This limitation renders it unusable for routing Internet traffic.
PPP	Point to Point Protocol. Protocol used for dial-up connections between two hosts that is 8 bits, versus the older SLIP protocol.
RIP	Routing Information Protocol. Distance vector routing protocol for routing traffic over small networks.
RIP2	Routing Information Protocol version 2, which adds support for *Variable Length Subnet Masking (VLSM)* and *Classless Interdomain Routing (CIDR)*. These additions allow RIP to provide routing in larger networks, but don't address the deficiencies of distance vector protocols.
SLIP	Serial Line Internet Protocol. Used to transmit Internet Protocol (IP) over serial lines or telephone lines. This protocol has since been replaced by many provides with PPP.
TCP/IP	Transmission Control Protocol/Internet Protocol. The main two protocols used over the Internet. TCP provides connection-oriented communication, whereas IP provides connection-less communication. TCP packets are generally embedded within IP packets for upper layer communication.
Token Ring	Token Ring (IEEE 802.5) is IBMís Local Area Network (LAN) protocol for host to host communication. Utilizes token passing for communication.
X.25	*International Telecommunication Union Telecommunication Standardization Sector (ITU-T)* protocol standard for wide area network communications that governs communication between user devices and network devices that are handled. X.25 is implemented as a suite of protocols that map to the first three layers of the OSI model.

Several modified versions of the Linux kernel are available to allow a PC to function as a dedicated router or bridge. With the inclusion of IPTables in the 2.4 kernel, it is now possible to do all firewalling and routing functions with the Linux kernel by itself. This eliminates the need to purchase proprietary networking hardware because Linux on an older PC can provide the same functionality with a standard UNIX-like interface. Many older machines are pulled out of the junk pile and loaded with a restricted Linux distribution and function as a router, firewall, proxy, gateway, or bridge with minimal hardware or cost.

Types of Kernels

There are two general types of kernels that Linux can be configured to operate as: modular and monolithic. The operation of each type of kernel is functionally the same, although there might be some performance gain of modular over monolithic.

> **Note**
>
> It is important to keep in mind that although these two classifications are mutually exclusive, most kernels are a mixture of both—compiled inline drivers and modules.

Modular Kernels

A modular kernel is a very basic kernel that includes code only necessary to allow the system to provide major functionality such as memory management and module support. The rest of the kernel is compiled as modules, code that can be loaded at runtime to handle the communication between kernel and hardware. When a device needs to be used, the user can instruct the kernel to load that code into memory. Once loaded, the hardware can then be accessed and used.

Thus main advantages of using this type of kernel are reduced memory overhead and flexibility. By compiling all drivers as modules, it isn't necessary to recompile the kernel every time a new piece of hardware is installed in the host. The disadvantage is the load time of the driver and the requirement of making an initial RAM driver image for the kernel to use during boot to automatically load all modules needed by a specific configuration.

Monolithic Kernels

Monolithic kernels include all the necessary drivers for every piece of hardware that will be installed in the host. Thus, if a new piece of hardware is installed in the future, it is necessary to either plan for this addition at compile time by selecting the driver or recompiling the kernel. The advantage of a monolithic kernel is reduced compile time for the entire kernel, making bootable kernels for diskless workstations and the lack of an initial RAM device at boot time.

24

KERNEL AND
MODULE
MANAGEMENT

Kernel Versions

The Linux kernel is in a constant state of development. As new features are added, bugs fixed, and new technology incorporated into the code base, it becomes necessary to provide stable releases of the kernel for use in a production environment, but it's also important to have releases that contain the newest code for developers to test. To address these issues, the Linux kernel always has the two most recent kernel versions available.

To distinguish between these two versions, a numbering schema was developed. Typing **uname -r** at the command prompt displays the current kernel version.

```
[root@phoenix net]# uname -r
2.4.7-10enterprise
```

The kernel version can be broken down into four sections:

- major version
- minor version
- sublevel number
- extraversion level

In the case of the stock Red Hat 7.2 kernel, it is the 2 major version, the fourth patch-level, the 7th sublevel, and an extra version level of 10. The extra version level indicates a Red Hat specific implementation of the 2.4.7 kernel, which generally addresses some code issues in the stock kernel that are necessary for special applications or hardware support. As described by Alan Cox, they "are workarounds for problems but not generalized or clean enough to feed into the main tree without further work."

Even numbered minor versions are stable kernels, whereas odd numbered versions are development releases. Version 2.2.X was the stable production kernel of version 2.2, whereas version 2.3.X was the development of the new Linux kernel. On January 4, 2001, Linus decided that the 2.3.X code base was sufficiently finished enough to be called Linux 2.4. All new development for the current design is being addressed in the 2.4.x kernel version. As yet, there is no 2.5.x release. However when a new version of the kernel is started, it will be labeled linux-2.5.x.

AC Patches

Since the release of Linux 2.4, there have been some changes to the procedure for releasing new kernel versions. Prior to Linux 2.4, everything was submitted to Linus, and he chose what would be applied. With the increasing popularity of Linux, it was necessary to distribute some of the workload. Alan Cox, an accomplished English kernel developer, became Linus' right hand man, releasing a new kernel every couple of days. The purpose of the Alan Cox patches is to include new code being tested by developers. After sufficient testing, Alan sends patches to Linus, where a decision will be made to either reject the patches or apply them to the main code tree. Alan's releases are distinguishable by the -ac at the end of the kernel version. Hence, linux-2.4.9-ac10, is the ninth release of the 2.4 Linux kernel, with the 10th Alan Cox patch.

Getting the Kernel

The Linux kernel has always been freely available to anyone who wants to play with it. To get the latest version, open an FTP connection to `ftp.kernel.org`. Log in as anonymous. Because the 2.4 kernel is what we are interested in, change directories to /pub/l inux/kernel/v2.4. The latest kernel as of this writing is 2.4.9, so list everything for this version.

NOTE

`ftp.kernel.org` receives more than its share of requests for download. It is considered a courtesy to use a mirror site to reduce the traffic that `ftp.kernel.org` bears. `http://www.kernel.org/mirrors/` has a list of all mirrors around the world. Find one close to your geographic location and substitute that address for `ftp.kernel.org`.

```
Connected to kernel.nitco.com (216.176.132.235).
220 ProFTPD 1.2.2rc3 Server (NetNITCO's Red Hat, Kernel.org, Mandrake & CPAN
Mirrors) [216.176.132.235]
Name (kernel.nitco.com:root): anonymous
331 Anonymous login ok, send your complete email address as your password.
Password:
230 Anonymous access granted, restrictions apply.
Remote system type is UNIX.
Using binary mode to transfer files.
ftp> cd pub/linux/kernel/v2.4/
250 CWD command successful.
ftp> ls *2.4.9*
227 Entering Passive Mode (216,176,132,235,13,243).
150 Opening ASCII mode data connection for file list
-rw-r--r--   1 root     ftp          1872 Aug 16 18:32 ChangeLog-2.4.9
-rw-r--r--   1 root     ftp             0 Aug 16 18:33 LATEST-IS-2.4.9
-rw-r--r--   1 root     ftp      22232256 Aug 16 18:32 linux-2.4.9.tar.bz2
-rw-r--r--   1 root     ftp           248 Aug 16 18:32 linux-2.4.9.tar.bz2.sign
-rw-r--r--   1 root     ftp      27474071 Aug 16 18:32 linux-2.4.9.tar.gz
-rw-r--r--   1 root     ftp           248 Aug 16 18:32 linux-2.4.9.tar.gz.sign
```

```
-rw-r--r--   1 root      ftp          607194 Aug 16 18:32 patch-2.4.9.bz2
-rw-r--r--   1 root      ftp             248 Aug 16 18:32 patch-2.4.9.bz2.sign
-rw-r--r--   1 root      ftp          722077 Aug 16 18:32 patch-2.4.9.gz
-rw-r--r--   1 root      ftp             248 Aug 16 18:32 patch-2.4.9.gz.sign
226 Transfer complete.
```

There are several entries for 2.4.9, but because we are only interested in the full kernel for 2.4.9, it is necessary to get the full package of source code. There are two of these:

```
-rw-r--r--   1 root      ftp        22232256 Aug 16 18:32 linux-2.4.9.tar.bz2
-rw-r--r--   1 root      ftp        27474071 Aug 16 18:32 linux-2.4.9.tar.gz
```

At first examination, it appears as if these two are totally different packages, and they are. The difference is in the compression utility used to package the source. The .gz extension is the gzip package, found on almost every Linux system available. The .bz2 extension is the BZip2 utility, which has a bit better compression than gzip, as is apparent from the file size. Either one of these packages will work because they contain the same contents.

Once downloaded, move the package to a directory other than /usr/src and unpack it. If you downloaded the gzip package, the command is tar -xzvf linux-2.4.9.tar.gz. Else, the BZip2 unpack command is tar -xIvf linux-2.4.9.tar.bz2. Once unpacked, the package will create a new directory, linux, and place all the files in it. Rename this directory to linux-2.4.9 and either copy it to /usr/src or move it there. Once moved, create a symbolic link of linux-2.4 to linux-2.4.9.

> **NOTE**
>
> Some kernels may extract to a linux-2.4.x directory. In this case, all that needs to be done is the symbolic linking of the kernel directory to the unpacked version.

```
[root@phoenix src]# ln -s linux-2.4 linux-2.4.9
```

By creating a symbolic link to linux-2.4, it is possible to allow multiple kernels to be compiled and tailored for different functions.

Patching the Kernel

It is possible to patch a kernel to the newest version verses a download of the entire code. This can be beneficial for those who aren't using a high-speed broadband connection. Patching the kernel isn't a mindless task, requiring the user to retrieve all patches from her current version to the version she wants to upgrade to. For example, if I am currently running 2.4.7 and I want to upgrade to 2.4.9, I must retrieve the 2.4.8, and 2.4.9 patch sets. Once downloaded, these patches must be applied in succession to upgrade to 2.4.9. This is a little more tedious than downloading the entire source, but useful for those who keep up with kernel hacking and constantly need to be on the edge of kernel hacking.

For those who need to patch the kernel up multiple revisions or don't want to deal with the intricacies of patch, there is a ready-to-run script, located in the scripts/ directory, called `patch-kernel`. It takes the form of the following:

```
patch-kernel <source_dir> <patch_dir> <stopversion>
```

The source directory defaults to /usr/src/linux if none is given, and the `patch_dir` defaults to the current working directory if one isn't supplied.

For example, we have a 2.4.7 kernel code tree that needs to be patched to the latest kernel, 2.4.9. The 2.4.8 and 2.4.9 patch files have been downloaded from `ftp.kernel.org` and are placed in the patch/ directory in the source tree. We issue the following command:

```
[root@phoenix linux-2.4.7]# scripts/patch-kernel /usr/src/linux-
2.4.7 /usr/src/linux-2.4.7/patch
```

Each successive patch file will be applied, thus creating a 2.4.9 code tree. If any errors occurred, files named *xxx#* or *xxx*.rej will be created, where *xxx* is the version of patch that failed. These failed patches will have to be resolved manually. Because this was a stock 2.4.7 code tree, the patches were all successfully applied without errors. Now we can run make clean on this code tree and proceed with configuring the kernel as if we started with a stock 2.4.9 kernel tree.

Compiling the Kernel

In order to make a new kernel, it must be compiled, translated from human-readable code to binary form. The process of compiling the kernel the kernel is mostly automated by the make utility. By providing the necessary arguments and following the steps covered below, the average user should be able to recompile a kernel that contains only the features the user feels necessary to include.

Initial Steps

Now that we have the new code and unarchived it, it's time to do the configuration. The first thing to do during a kernel compile is verify that your system has the necessary version of tools the kernel requires to compile and run. This has been automated into a script that is found in the scripts/ directory. The script is called `ver_linux` and is found in the Documentation/scripts directory.

Change the permissions on this file to executable by issuing the command `chmod 755` `ver_linux` from the scripts/ directory. Before running the script, you might want to look at the script to get an idea of what it is doing. Generally speaking, just about every version of operating systems tools used to compile the kernel has a version argument. The script calls all the commands that the kernel relies on with that version argument and formats it into a nice output to compare against the Documentation/Changes file.

If some fields are empty or look unusual, you might have an old version. Compare to the current minimal requirements in Documentation/Changes.

```
Linux phoenix 2.4.7-10enterprise
#1 SMP Thu Sep 6 16:48:20 EDT 2001 i686 unknown

Gnu C                    2.96
Gnu make                 3.79.1
binutils                 2.11.90.0.8
util-linux               2.11f
mount                    2.11g
modutils                 2.4.6
e2fsprogs                tune2fs
reiserfsprogs            3.x.0j
pcmcia-cs                3.1.22
PPP                      2.4.1
isdn4k-utils             3.1pre1
Linux C Library          2.2.4
Dynamic linker (ldd)     2.2.4
Procps                   2.0.7
Net-tools                1.60
Console-tools            0.3.3
Sh-utils                 2.0.11
Modules Loaded           ide-cd cdrom via82cxxx_audio uart401
ac97_codec sound soundcore tuner tvaudio bttv i2c-algo-bit
i2c-core videodev iscsi nfsd lockd sunrpc autofs natsemi
appletalk ipx usb-uhci usbcore ext3 jbd raid0 BusLogic
sd_mod scsi_mod
```

The output shown here is from a default Red Hat 7.2 installation. Comparing the versions to those in the Changes file, it is apparent that all version requirements have been met. If any utilities are older than what is required, download the latest version from the sites listed in the Changes file, and you should be ready to get started compiling the kernel.

Preparing to Compile

It is important to ensure that the code tree you are compiling from is clean and ready for a new configuration. The process of compiling the kernel is done with the command `make`, which processes `Makefiles` across the kernel code tree. `Makefiles` set up the environment and send the necessary parameters to the pre-compiler, the compiler, and the linker that are necessary to successfully compile the kernel. Because the Linux kernel is extremely complex, `Makefiles` are used to hold all these flags. The `make` command can take several arguments, one of which is know as a directive. *Directives* are names for a series of routines that should be performed. Several directives are used to make the kernel, depending on what needs to be done to the source tree. The most common ones will be covered when we compile the kernel.

> **NOTE**
>
> The make utility is a very diverse program. Complete documentation on the structure of make files as well as the arguments that it can accept can be found at `http://www.gnu.org/manuals/make/index.html`

First, make sure that all old object files, those ending in .o, or old configurations don't exist in the code tree. This is done by the `make` directive `mrproper`. Looking at the `Makefile`, we see that this directive does quite a bit:

```
mrproper: clean archmrproper
        find . \( -size 0 -o -name .depend \) -type f -print |
 xargs rm -f
        rm -f $(MRPROPER_FILES)
        rm -rf $(MRPROPER_DIRS)
        $(MAKE) -C Documentation/DocBook mrproper
```

Line 1 is the name of the directive, `mrproper`, with a listing of any other directives that are called by this directive. `archmrproper` is a directive found in the architecture `make` files that has corresponding instructions to clean up any files that are architecture dependant before compiling. Line 2 finds all files that use 0 blocks of disk space or files that are named .depend and removes them. Line 3 removes the contents of the variable `MRPROPER_FILES`. Similarly, line 4 removes the contents of `MRPROPER_DIRS`. The last line tells `make` to change directories to the Documentation/DocBook directory and to perform the `mrproper` directive found in the `Makefile` in that directory. This is quite a bit of work for just one word!

> **Caution**
>
> If you have a previous verification of the kernel in the code tree, the `mrproper` directive will erase the .config file. To preserve this configuration, follow the Red Hat example and create a configs/ directory in the root of the kernel code tree and rename the .config file to something meaningful. By doing so, it is possible to go back to previous configurations without going through the entire routine of selecting all the configuration options.

Listing 24.4 is an expansion of the `MRPROPER_FILES` and `MRPROPER_DIRS` variables called in the clean directive declaration.

LISTING 24.4 Files and Directories Removed with the Clean Directive

```
MRPROPER_FILES = \
        include/linux/autoconf.h include/linux/version.h \
        drivers/net/hamradio/soundmodem/sm_tbl_{afsk1200,afsk2666,fsk9600}.h \
        drivers/net/hamradio/soundmodem/sm_tbl_{hapn4800,psk4800}.h \
        drivers/net/hamradio/soundmodem/sm_tbl_{afsk2400_7,afsk2400_8}.h \
 \
        drivers/net/hamradio/soundmodem/gentbl \
        drivers/sound/*_boot.h drivers/sound/.*.boot \
        drivers/sound/msndinit.c \
        drivers/sound/msndperm.c \
        drivers/sound/pndsperm.c \
        drivers/sound/pndspini.c \
        drivers/atm/fore200e_*_fw.c drivers/atm/.fore200e_*.fw \
        .version .config* config.in config.old \
        scripts/tkparse scripts/kconfig.tk scripts/kconfig.tmp \
        scripts/lxdialog/*.o scripts/lxdialog/lxdialog \
        .menuconfig.log \
        include/asm \
        .hdepend scripts/mkdep scripts/split-include scripts/docproc \
        $(TOPDIR)/include/linux/modversions.h
MRPROPER_DIRS = \
        include/config \
        $(TOPDIR)/include/linux/modules
```

Now that we are sure we have a fresh, clean installation of the kernel tree, it's time to configure what we want in the kernel.

Different Configuration Interfaces

Over time, the configuration of the Linux kernel has changed. Originally, the kernel was configured with a series of prompts to the user for each configuration parameter that is possible in the Linux kernel. Although still functional, anyone but kernel hackers probably find this type of configuration confusing in the least. Figure 24.1 is a screen shot of the `make config` utility.

As each question is asked, the user either responds with a Y, N, M, or ?. These responses can be in either upper or lower case. The M response is to select the option be compiled as a loadable module. A response of ? will show the user context help for that specific options, if available.

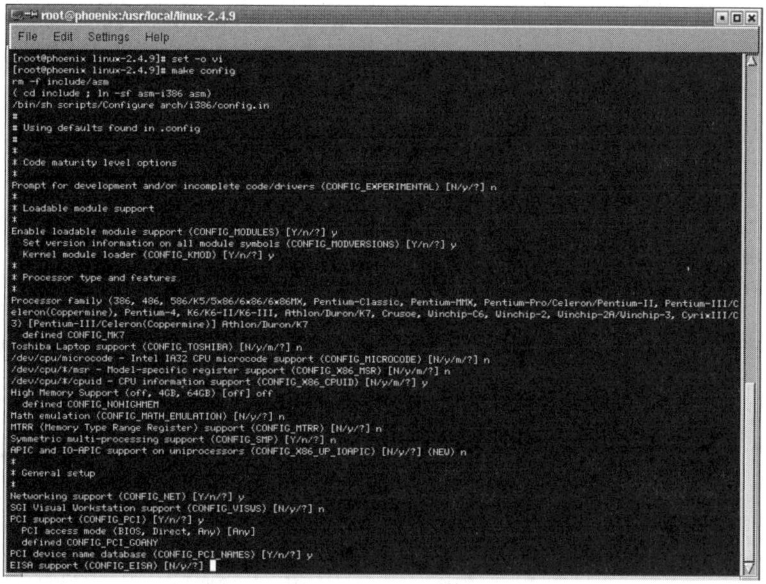

FIGURE 24.1

The make
config *utility.*

For many people, the command line isn't the most intuitive interface. Another directive for configuring the Linux kernel is make menuconfig. Menuconfig provides a graphical wrapper around a text interface. Although it isn't as raw as make config, menuconfig isn't a buttoned interface that allows use of the mouse to configure the kernel. Figure 24.2 shows a typical make menuconfig session.

menuconfig used the arrow keys to move the selector up and down and the spacebar to toggle a selection. The Tab key moves the focus at the bottom of the screen to either select, exit, or help.

Both of these utilities provide the user an interface for configuring the kernel other than directly editing a .config file. However, for the true GUI interface, with mouse support and clickable buttons, make xconfig is what most users will want to use. To use this utility, it is necessary to have a working version of the X Windows System running. xconfig is really nothing but a TCL/TK interface used to wrap around data files that are parsed at execution time. Figure 24.3 is the main menu of xconfig for the 2.4.9 kernel.

Once loaded, the user clicks on each of the buttons that list the configuration options. Each button clicked on will create another window that has the detail configuration options for that subsection. In the subsection window, three buttons are at the bottom; Main Menu, Next, and Prev. Clicking the Main Menu button will close the current window and display the main window. Clicking Next will take the user to the next configuration section. When configuring a kernel from scratch, the general path is to click on the

24

KERNEL AND
MODULE
MANAGEMENT

button labeled Code Maturity Level Options and continually click on the Next button to proceed through all the subsections of the kernel configuration. When all the options have been selected by the user, the main menu is displayed. The buttons on the lower right of the main menu are for saving and loading configurations. Their functions are self explanatory.

FIGURE 24.2

The make menu-config *utility.*

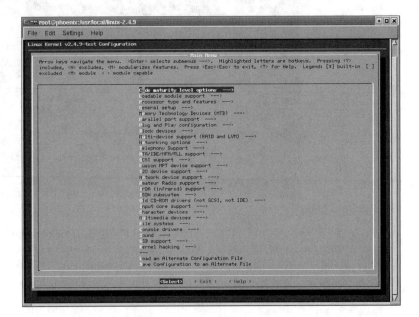

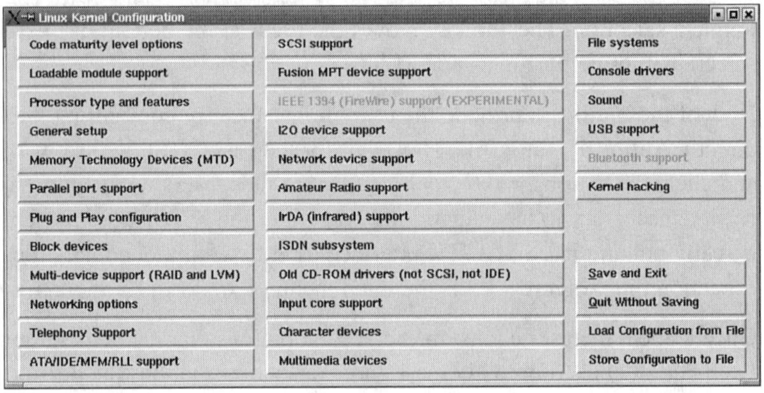

FIGURE 24.3

The make xconfig *GUI interface.*

> **NOTE**
>
> If a saved configuration is loaded for modification, it should be saved before exiting as a new configuration. This allows flexibility with the different configurations available for compiling the kernel in the future.

> **NOTE**
>
> If recompiling the Red Hat default kernel, the configs/ directory contains several versions of configuration files for different purposes. Running make xconfig, clicking on Load Configuration File, and typing in the path and filename of the desired configuration will load those options, thus allowing the user to be able to change the parameters that need alteration without configuring the entire kernel.

One more configuration should be mentioned. If upgrading kernels from a previous release, it isn't necessary to go though the entire configuration from scratch. The directive oldconfig can be used that will only prompt the user for answers to new configuration items in the new kernel.

For simplicity sake, this walk through will assume that you are using make xconfig. This directive provides the most flexibility and ease of use.

Configuring the Kernel

Once in xconfig, several subsections need to be configured. Each subsection contains specific options that can be configured for the kernel. Table 24.4 provides a brief description of each subsection.

TABLE 24.4 Kernel Subsections for Configuration

Name	Description
Code maturity level options	Allows development code to be compiled into the kernel even if it has been marked as obsolete or as testing code only. This option should only be used by kernel developers or testers because of the possible unusable state of the code during development.

24

KERNEL AND MODULE MANAGEMENT

TABLE 24.4   continued

Name	Description
Loadable module support	Whether the kernel allows drivers and other non-essential code to be compiled such that it can be loaded and unloaded at runtime. This option is generally a good idea because the smaller a kernel is, the faster it runs.
Processor type and features	Several options dealing with the architecture that will be running the kernel.
General setup	This section contains several different options covering how the kernel talks to the BIOS, should it support PCI or PCMCIA, and what kind of binaries will be supported.
Binary emulation of other systems	Contains several options for supporting kernel structures necessary to run binaries compiled for other systems directly without recompiling the program.
Memory Technology Devices (MTD)	Options for supporting flash memory devices, such as EEPROMS. Generally these devices are used in embedded systems.
Parallel port support	Several options for configuring how the kernel will support parallel port communications.
Plug and Play configuration	Options for supporting Plug and Play PCI, ISA, and plug-and-play BIOS support. Generally, it is a good idea to support plug and play for PCI and ISA devices. BIOS plug and play is still experimental in the 2.4.9 kernel.
Block devices	Section dealing with devices that communication with the kernel in blocks of characters instead of streams. This includes IDE and ATAPI devices connected via parallel ports, as well as allowing network devices to communicate as block devices.
Mutli-device support (RAID and LVM)	Options for allowing the kernel to support RAID devices in software emulation and the different levels of RAID. Also contains options for support of a logical volume manager.
Networking options	Several options for the configuration of networking in the kernel. The options are for the types of supported protocols and configurable options of those protocols.
Telephony Support	Support for devices that allow the use of regular telephone lines to support VOIP applications. This section doesn't handle the configuration of MODEMs.

TABLE 24.4   continued

Name	Description
ATA/IDE/MFM/RLL support	Large section to configure the kernel to communicate using different types of data communication protocols to talk to mass storage devices, such as hard drives. Note that this section doesn't cover SCSI.
SCSI support	Options for configuring the kernel to support Small Computer Systems Interface. This subsection covers drivers for specific cards, chipsets, and tunable parameters for the SCSI protocol.
Fusion MPT device support	Configures support for LSI's Logic Fusion Message Passing Technology. This technology is for high performance SCSI and local area network interfaces.
I20 device support	Options for supporting the Intelligent Input/Output architecture. This architecture allows the hardware driver to be split from the operating system driver, thus allowing a multitude of hardware devices to be compatible with an operating system in one implementation.
Network device support	Configuration options for network chipsets and card support. Covers AppleTalk, ArcNet, Ethernet, FDDI, HPPI, PCMCIA, and Token Ring cards.
Amateur Radio support	Options for configuring support of devices that support the AX25 protocol.
IrDA (infrared) support	Options for configuring support of the infrared Data Association suite of protocols and devices that use these protocols.
ISDN subsystem	Options to support Integrated Services Digital Networks protocols and devices. ISDN is a method of connection to a large area network digitally over conditioned phone lines, largely found to connect users to ISPs.
Old CD-ROM drivers	Configuration options to(not SCSI, not IDE) support obscure, older CD-ROM devices that don't conform to the SCSI or IDE standards. These are typically older CD-ROM drivers that are usually a proprietary type of SCSI.
Input core support	Options for configuring *Universal Serial Bus (USB) Human Interface Devices (HID)*. These include keyboards, mice, and joysticks.

24

KERNEL AND MODULE MANAGEMENT

TABLE 24.4 continued

Name	Description
Character devices	Configuration options for devices that communicate to the server in sequential characters. This is a very large subsection that contains the drivers for several motherboard chipsets.
Multimedia devices	Drivers for hardware implementations of video and sound devices such as video capture boards, TV cards, and AM/FM radio adapter cards.
File system	Configuration options for supported filesystem types. See Table 24.2 for a description of the filesystems support by the kernel.
Console drivers	Configures VGA text console, video mode selection, and support for frame buffer cards.
Sound	Large subsection to configure supported sound card drivers and chipset support for the kernel.
USB support	Universal Serial Bus configuration options. Includes configuration for USB devices, as well as vendor specific versions of USB.
Bluetooth support	Supports the Bluetooth wireless protocol. Includes options to support the BlueTooth protocols and hardware devices.
Kernel hacking	This section determines whether the kernel will contain advanced debugging options. Most users won't want to include this option in their production kernels because the kernel size is increased and performance is slow due to the extra routines that are added.

After you select all the options you want compiled into the kernel and those you want to compile as modules, save the configuration. xconfig will tell you the file has been saved and to look at the toplevel Makefile for additional configuration options and run the make dep command. If you want to keep any current version of the kernel that was compiled with the same code tree, edit the Makefile and add some unique string to the EXTRAVERSION variable. Here is a sample to append the current date to the kernel:

```
EXTRAVERSION = ".`date +%D|sed -e 's/\//\-/g'`"
```

This will create a kernel with a name of 2.4.9. with the current month, day, and year separated by the - character. Thus, if compiled on January 1, 2001, the kernel name would be linux-2.4.9.1-01-2001.

Once the `Makefile` has been edited, it's time to start compiling the kernel. We want to make sure that there are no stale binaries in the code tree, so run `make clean` to remove them.

Making Dependencies

Now that we have a clean code tree, configured all the options we want, and edited the `make` file to produce a unique name, it is necessary to compile the dependencies for all the options we have selected. The command to do this is `make dep`. During the execution of this, quite a bit of information will scroll across the screen, showing what commands are being executed and the results of those commands. Generally this isn't too important to the standard user. However, if the `make dep` command ends with an error in the last line, something isn't correct and the configuration of the dependencies is incorrect. On a stock Red Hat 7.2 install, dependencies should compile just fine.

Final Steps

Once all the dependencies have been configured, its time to make the kernel image. There are several `make` directives for this, although the most common ones are as follows:

- `zImage`
- `bzImage`
- `bzDisk`

The `zImage` directive compiles the kernel, creating an uncompressed file called zImage. Some systems require the kernel image to be under a certain size, else the BIOS won't be able to parse the image, resulting in a failure to boot the new kernel. To avoid this, the `bzImage` directive creates a compressed kernel image. The `bzDisk` directive does the same thing as `bzImage`; however, it copies the new kernel image to a floppy disk for testing purposes. This is helpful for testing new kernels without committing your hard drive.

24

KERNEL AND
MODULE
MANAGEMENT

NOTE

Before running make `bzDisk`, make sure that you have a blank floppy disk in the drive because the command won't prompt you to insert one.

After several minutes or hours, the new kernel image will finish. Now that we have a new kernel image, we could test it directly by copying it to a floppy and rebooting the machine. However, because it is highly probable that module support was configured into the kernel, we need to make all the modules in order for the kernel to use them. Because we are installing the kernel to the hard drive, copy the file arch/<platform>/boot/bzImage to /boot/vmlinuz-2.4.9 so that LILO can be configured to boot the new image.

```
[root@phoenix boot]# cp bzImage /boot/vmlinuz-2.4.9
```

> **NOTE**
>
> A make install directive is available that will do the above steps automatically. The manual method has been covered here to show what is necessary to install a new kernel image.

Building and Installing Modules

To build the modules, run make modules. This will go though the source tree and compile the necessary .c files into .o files and create symbolic links to the linux/modules directory that point to the real location of the compiled .o files. The command make modules_install copies all the necessary .o files into their respective subdirectories in /lib/modules/<kernel_version>/, where <kernel_version> is the kernel version being compiled.

Creating a RAM Device

If you configured SCSI devices as modules and you need access to them at boot time, it is necessary to create an initial RAM disk image called initrd.img. Generally speaking however, it isn't necessary to create this file. To create an initrd.img file, use the shell script /sbin/mkinitrd provided there is a loopback adapter installed on the machine and the /etc/modules.conf file contains a line for the SCSI card.

The format for the command is the following:

```
/sbin/mkinitrd <file_name> <kernel_version>
```

Where file_name is the name of the image file you want created.

If the modules have changed from your existing kernel, mkinitrd will exit with an error message. mkinitrd looks at the /etc/fstab, /etc/modules.conf and /etc/raidtab to obtain the necessary information it needs to determine which modules should be loaded during boot. If the modules that are currently in the /etc/modules.conf file are not in /lib/modules/{kernel_version}/kernel/drivers/scsi/, mkinitrd will complain and exit with an error message:

```
[root@phoenix boot]# /sbin/mkinitrd initrd-2.4.9.img 2.4.9
No module BusLogic found for kernel 2.4.9
```

The source of the problem is the /etc/modules.conf file:

```
[root@phoenix boot]# cat /etc/modules.conf
alias scsi_hostadapter BusLogic
alias eth0 natsemi
alias parport_lowlevel parport_pc
alias sound-slot-0 via82cxxx_audio
alias char-major-81 bttv
alias usb-controller usb-uhci
```

The offending line alias scsi_hostadapter BusLogic. I compiled the BusLogic drivers into the kernel, rather than as a module, so that module file does not exist in /lib/modules/2.4.9/kernel/drivers/scsi/. The eliminate the error message and make a good initrd.img file, make a backup copy of the /etc/modules.conf file, edit the original file and remove the offending line. Once the initrd.img file has been made, restore the modules.conf file from the backup you made. In addition to the errors concerning non-existent modules, if raid is found in the /etc/raidtab file, but RAID support was compiled into the kernel, it will be necessary to pass the --omit-raid-modules parameter to mkinitrd. This will prevent mkinitrd from looking at the /etc/raidtab file. An example of this would be

```
[root@phoenix boot]# mkinitrd --omit-raid-modules initrd-2.4.9.img 2.4.9
```

Once this file is created, copy it to the /boot directory so that it can be referenced by the boot loader.

Configuring Grub

The Grand Unified Boot Loader (GRUB) is now the default boot loader for Red Hat Linux 7.2. Originally designed to boot the GNU Hurd operating system, Grub addresses many shortcomings of other boot loaders, such as determining the correct hard disk geometry, loading large kernels at boot, supporting multiple binary formats, decompression support, and full dynamic RAM detection.

Grub has two different interfaces for interacting with the user: a menu interface for pre-defined options, or a command-line interface to provide optimal flexibility in specifying multiple boot parameters. The configuration file, grub.conf is located in the /boot/grub directory, when installed via RPM. This file looks much like LILO, with the basic parameters being much the same. The default `grub.conf` file that comes with Red Hat 7.2 is

```
# grub.conf generated by anaconda
#
# Note that you do not have to rerun grub after making changes to this file
# NOTICE:  You have a /boot partition.  This means that
#          all kernel and initrd paths are relative to /boot/, eg.
#          root (hd0,0)
#          kernel /vmlinuz-version ro root=/dev/hda2
#          initrd /initrd-version.img
#boot=/dev/hda
default=0
timeout=10
splashimage=(hd0,0)/grub/splash.xpm.gz
title Red Hat Linux (2.4.7-10enterprise)
    root (hd0,0)
    kernel /vmlinuz-2.4.7-10enterprise ro root=/dev/hda2
    initrd /initrd-2.4.7-10enterprise.img
```

The default configuration of grub by Red Hat will use the menu interface for booting the machine. The menu interface is graphical, thus it can display an image to the user. The image file is defined by the splashimage line. The title line is what the particular boot option will be for the user to select in the menu.

The actual configuration of grub that looks like LILO is found on lines 14-16. A dissection of each line allows us to understand how grub works:

```
root (hd0,0)
```

This entry tells grub which device on the system to use to find a file system. Grub does not use the standard Linux device naming convention, but starts device numbers at zero, regardless of the hard disk type. This entry sets the root device as the first hard disk, the first partition:

```
kernel /vmlinuz-2.4.7-10enterprise ro root=/dev/hda2
```

The output of compiling the kernel is a new bzImage or zImage file. This file was then renamed to vmlinuz-2.4.9 and copied to the /boot directory. This entry tells grub to look on the root device and find the kernel named vmlinuz-2.4.7-10enterprise and pass the kernel two parameters: ro for read-only and root=/dev/hda22 to tell the kernel which device and partition should be used once the kernel is initialized:

```
initrd /initrd-2.4.7-10enterprise.img
```

If SCSI support was compiled as modular and is needed at boot time, we need to tell grub what the initial RAM device file is. This entry tells grub the file is in the root partition and it's name.

Now that we understand how Grub is configured in the `/boot/grub/grub.conf` file, adding the configuration for the new kernel should be simple.

First, make a backup of the /boot/grub/grub.conf file and then edit the original to look something like this:

```
# grub.conf generated by anaconda
#
# Note that you do not have to rerun grub after making changes to this file
# NOTICE:  You have a /boot partition.  This means that
#          all kernel and initrd paths are relative to /boot/, eg.
#          root (hd0,0)
#          kernel /vmlinuz-version ro root=/dev/hda2
#          initrd /initrd-version.img
#boot=/dev/hda
default=0
timeout=10
splashimage=(hd0,0)/grub/splash.xpm.gz
title Red Hat Linux (2.4.7-10enterprise)
        root (hd0,0)
        kernel /vmlinuz-2.4.7-10enterprise ro root=/dev/hda2
        initrd /initrd-2.4.7-10enterprise.imgtitle Linux 2.4.9
        root (hd0,0)
        kernel /vmlinuz-2.4.9 ro root=/dev/hda2
```

All that is left to do now is reboot the machine and test the new kernel.

Configuring LILO

Because Grub is the new kid on the block for Red Hat Linux users, it is possible during the installation LILO was selected as the default boot loader. If so, it is necessary to update LILO to tell it how to boot the new kernel image. Doing so will allow us to select the kernel version that should be run at boot time.

The file `/etc/lilo.conf` contains all the configuration information for LILO. Open this file with your favorite text editor and copy the five lines that contain the current kernel configuration. Listing 24.5 shows a typical `lilo.conf` file.

LISTING 24.5   The LILO Configuration File `/etc/lilo.conf`

```
[root@phoenix etc]# cat lilo.conf
prompt
timeout=50
default=linux
boot=/dev/hda2
map=/boot/map
install=/boot/boot.b
message=/boot/message
```

24

KERNEL AND MODULE MANAGEMENT

LISTING 24.5   continued

```
linear

image=/boot/vmlinuz-2.4.7-10enterprise
    label=linux
    initrd=/boot/initrd-2.4.7-10enterprise.img
    read-only
    root=/dev/hda2
```

To install our new kernel image, copy lines 10 through 14 and paste them at the bottom of the file. Now we need to edit these lines to point to our new kernel image. Change the pasted lines to reflect the new kernel image information. One point of note is that we didn't make an initrd image file because we didn't compile a SCSI driver as a module that is needed at boot time. Thus, this line can be deleted. So our new lilo.conf file looks like this:

```
prompt
timeout=50
default=linux
boot=/dev/hda2
map=/boot/map
install=/boot/boot.b
message=/boot/message
linear

image=/boot/vmlinuz-2.4.7-10enterprise
    label=linux
    initrd=/boot/initrd-2.4.7-10enterprise.img
    read-only
    root=/dev/hda2
image=/boot/vmlinuz-2.4.9
    label=linux-2.4.9
    read-only
    root=/dev/hda2
```

> **TIP**
>
> For a detailed description of all the possible settings available in LILO, consult the lilo.conf man page.

To verify that the new lilo.conf file is correct and everything checks out, run the command lilo without any parameters. If everything goes well, LILO should return something like this:

```
[root@phoenix boot]# lilo
Added linux-2.4.6-3.1 *
Added linux-2.4.9
```

Now it's time to test the new kernel. Reboot the machine, ensuring that the floppy drive doesn't have a disk loaded in it. You should see the BIOS initialization screen and then the LILO menu is displayed. Select the kernel image that was just made and watch it load. If everything went okay, you should now have a new, working 2.4.9 kernel, configured to your specifications.

> **Caution**
>
> Before testing the new kernel image, make sure that you have a backup copy of your current working kernel. This can be done by the following command:
>
> ```
> mkbootdisk —device /dev/fd0 2.4.6-3.1
> ```

When Something Goes Wrong

Several things can possibly go wrong during a kernel compile and installation, and several key telling factors will point to the true problem that happened.

Errors During Compile

Although rare that the kernel will not compile, there is always a chance something has slipped though the regression testing.

It is possible that the kernel compile will crash and not complete successfully. Although rare, it can happen. For the 2.4.9 kernel, on a stock Red Hat 7.2 installed, selecting the compiling of the NTFS filesystem, either as a loadable module or inline, the kernel compile will fail for a special configuration.

```
gcc -D__KERNEL__ -I/usr/src/linux-2.4.9/include -Wall -Wstrict-prototypes
-Wno-trigraphs -O2 -fomit-frame-pointer -fno-strict-aliasing -fno-common
-pipe -mpreferred-stack-boundary=2 -march=athlon   -DMODULE -DMODVERSIONS
-include /usr/src/linux-2.4.9/include/linux/modversions.h -
DNTFS_VERSION=\"1.1.16\"   -c -o unistr.o unistr.c
unistr.c: In function `ntfs_collate_names':
unistr.c:99: warning: implicit declaration of function `min'
unistr.c:99: parse error before `unsigned'
unistr.c:99: parse error before `)'
unistr.c:97: warning: `c1' might be used uninitialized in this function
unistr.c: At top level:
unistr.c:118: parse error before `if'
unistr.c:123: warning: type defaults to `int' in declaration of `c1'
unistr.c:123: `name1' undeclared here (not in a function)
unistr.c:123: warning: data definition has no type or storage class
unistr.c:124: parse error before `if'
make[2]: *** [unistr.o] Error 1
make[2]: Leaving directory `/usr/src/linux-2.4.9/fs/ntfs'
```

```
make[1]: *** [_modsubdir_ntfs] Error 2
make[1]: Leaving directory `/usr/src/linux-2.4.9/fs'
make: *** [_mod_fs] Error 2
```

At this point there are a couple of options:

- Fix the errors and recompile.
- Remove the offending module or option and wait for the errors to be fixed by the kernel team.

Most users will be unable to fix the errors, due to the complexity of the kernel code, although this might not rule out this option. It is possible the same error has been discovered by someone else during testing of the kernel, and a patch for it has been supplied. Check the Linux kernel mailing list archive, as the problem might have been encountered before. If the problem is not listed there, a search on Google might turn up something.

Look in the Maintainers file in the Documentation directory of the kernel source and find the maintainer of the code. The recommended course of action is to contact the maintainer and see if they are aware of the problems you are having. If nothing has been documented for the specific error, submitting the error to the kernel mailing list is an option. There are guidelines for doing this, which can be found in the README file in the base directory of the kernel source under the section "When Something Goes Wrong." Finally, should you wish to take on the endeavor of trying to fix the specific problem(s) yourself, this is a great opportunity to get involved with the Linux kernel and make a contribution that could help many others.

The second option, removing the code, is the easiest and what most people do in cases where the offending code is not absolutely required. In the case of the NTFS module failing, it is almost expected, as NTFS support is considered experimental and subject to errors. This is primarily because the code for the filesystem is reverse engineered instead of implemented via documented standards.

Runtime Errors, Boot Loader Problems, and Kernel Oops

Excellent documentation on the Internet exists for troubleshooting just about every type of error that LILO, Grub, or the kernel could give during boot. The best way to find this documentation is to go to your favorite search engine and type in the key words of the error you received. The most common problems deal with LILO and Grub configuration problems. Diagnosis and solutions to these problems can be found in the LILO and Grub documentation.

> **TIP**
>
> For best results, go to `http://www.google.com/linux` to find all things Linux on the Internet. Google has specifically created a Linux area of its database, which should allow faster access to information on Linux than any other search engine.

Reference

`http://www.kernel.org/`—Linux Kernel Archives

The source of all development discussion for the Linux kernel.

`http://kt.zork.net/kernel-traffic/`—Linux Kernel Traffic

Summarized version and commentary of the Linux Kernel mailing list produced weekly.

`http://www.gnu.org/`—Free Software Foundation

Source of manuals and software for programs used throughout the kernel compilation process. Tools such as `make` and `gcc` have their official documentation here.

`http://slashdot.org/article.pl?sid=01/08/22/1453228&mode=thread`—AC Patches

`http://www.linuxdoc.org/LDP/tlk/`—The Linux Kernel

Online book about the 2.2 Linux kernel describing the internals of the Linux kernel.

`http://www.linuxdoc.org/`—The Linux Documentation Project

The Mecca of all Linux documentation. Excellent source of how-to documentation, as well as FAQs and online books, all about Linux.

24

KERNEL AND MODULE MANAGEMENT

CHAPTER 25

Productivity Applications

Deploying Red Hat Linux in enterprise-level operations often involves using Linux as a support platform for server hardware. Companies can save licensing costs and gain increased reliability by combining Red Hat Linux with off-the-shelf box or rack-mounted systems. Smaller businesses can also gain the same benefits when using Linux in similar situations where the operating system is used behind the scenes to provide day-in and day-out reliability. But using Red Hat Linux to support workstations, office productivity, and other more personal uses in PC desktop settings can pose problems in planning, purchasing, installation, and training of personnel.

This chapter provides some of the details about popular productivity software included with and available for Red Hat Linux. Despite so-called tech industry pundits (usually shills for the software monopoly), Red Hat Linux can be used to support desktop operations in business settings. Efficient personal computing environments can be created by carefully choosing and installing select productivity software packages. A wealth of usable, reliable, and free software is available for Red Hat Linux. Today's modern businesses are beginning to learn what experienced Red Hat Linux users have known for years—there are great cost benefits when using Linux and free productivity software. Stepping off the software licensing and upgrade treadmill immediately contributes to the bottom line.

Productivity client include free office suites and tools used for creating documents, scheduling, organizing, and calculating. Many other miscellaneous tools will be found on your set of Red Hat Linux CD-ROMs, including multimedia applications. The suite of software packages can be combined, culled, and configured to host productive desktop computing environment suited for nearly all users in a business organization. This includes management, support personnel, administration, and sales.

Commercial Office Suite Alternatives

There are also commercial software office suites and software for Linux. These packages can be acquired and put to use if support is an issue. Nearly all the office suites include other functions such as electronic mail. For example, Anywhere Desktop for Linux (formerly known as Applixware and marketed by VistaSource, Inc.) is an integrated office environment, but can also be used to create all types of documents, including databases and new applications. This package has been available in one form or another for Linux since 1997, and even longer for UNIX variants.

Other products include Corel's WordPerfect Office 2000 for Linux and the CorelDRAW drawing client. These products depend on, in part, software libraries that emulate portions of the commercial Windows operating system. Recent improvements to the installation script for Corel's suite (so that it can be installed and used on a variety of Linux distributions) might help assure a bit more adoption. But software that relies on emulation libraries might not be as desirable, powerful, or reliable.

Free software office suites providing a word processor, spreadsheet, and one or more graphics clients are very popular with Red Hat Linux users. The most popular offerings are from Sun Microsystems and GNOME and KDE developers. Nearly all productivity applications and suites discussed in this chapter support the import and export of documents from other operating systems and platforms. Companies migrating to Linux and requiring the ability to read, edit, print and save word processing documents created using Microsoft Word, spreadsheets created using Microsoft Excel, or presentations authored by Microsoft PowerPoint can use one or more free alternative packages.

Installing and Launching StarOffice

StarOffice is the premiere free office suite for Linux and several other operating systems. This office suite is available free for download, on CD-ROM for the cost of shipping, in commercial packaging available through mail order, or in selected stores. You can also download a version named OpenOffice in source code form (see the next section, "OpenOffice").

StarOffice originally was a commercial office suite for a number of computer operating systems. After Sun Microsystems acquired its host company in 1999, the suite was released free, and made available by download or on a CD-ROM for the cost of shipping. The next year, following in the footsteps of Netscape Communications, Sun released the source code, and the open source version became OpenOffice.

Like most office suites, StarOffice provides word processing, supports creation of spreadsheet documents, and hosts graphics editing. The word processing module can also function as an HTML editor, and Web browsing is supported in the applications main desktop window. The suite also includes an organizer, presentation manager, and a database manager. Built-in Internet setup dialogs also allow using of electronic mail, and current versions have expanded support for external database managers. A built-in BASIC-like language supports Java extensions.

One or more of the commercial versions of Red Hat Linux will include StarOffice in an RPM archive and can be installed. You can also download StarOffice from Sun's Web site (see the section "Reference" at the end of this chapter). After downloading the binary file, the file is executed by root like this:

```
# chmod +x so-5_2-ga-bin-linux-en.bin
# ./so-5_2-ga-bin-linux-en.bin /net
```

The /net option is used to install the 240MB StarOffice software in a central location (such as /opt/office52). This allows individual users to install StarOffice like this:

```
$ /opt/office52/program/soffice
```

This will launch a minimal install that requires less than 2MB of storage in a directory in the user's home directory. Following installation, launch to a session either through a StarOffice menu item in the KDE desktop panel or from the command line like this:

```
$ ./office52/soffice &
```

The StarOffice desktop is shown in Figure 25.1.

FIGURE 25.1

The free StarOffice office suite can be installed and used with Red Hat Linux.

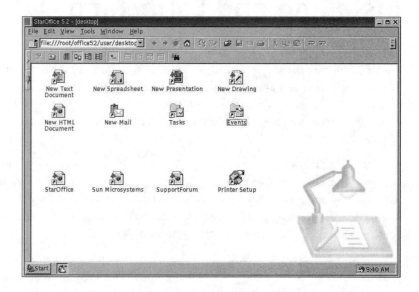

Use the StarOffice File menu, Start menu, or icons to create or open new documents. Linux users have been eagerly waiting for a new version of StarOffice. According to

Sun, a new version is slated for release sometime in late 2001 or early 2002. Check Sun's StarOffice Web site for any new developments and releases.

Breaking News—A New Star on the Horizon!

Sun Microsystems released a StarOffice 6.0 beta release for testing as this book went to print. The beta release incorporates a number of new features, such as faster launching, extensive built-in help, even better Microsoft Office document compatibility, use of XML, the separation of StarOffice components into separate modules, and the ability to install a Java interpreter. Check Sun's Web site (see the "Reference" section at the end of this chapter) to download your own copy of the new software!

OpenOffice

OpenOffice is the open source version of StarOffice. After a little more than a year, this project has developed an installable, working, and quite functional office suite supporting word processing, spreadsheets, drawing, and the creation of presentations. The latest incarnation supports printing, various automatic document-creation dialogs, known as *AutoPilot* items, and templates. The project aims to create a popular, multi-platform international office suite using XML-based file formats.

The OpenOffice Web site (see the "Reference" section at the end of this chapter) provides a link to download the source or a pre-compiled version of the latest working installation files. After downloading a pre-compiled version, decompress the 67MB compressed tarball like this:

```
$ tar xvzf install638_linux_intel.tar.gz
```

This will extract the installation files into a directory named `install` in the current directory. The installation supports either a full or minimal install exactly like StarOffice, and can be entirely installed in a home directory, or made available to users in a systemwide directory (nearly the same size as the StarOffice installed distribution). For example, to install OpenOffice for systemwide use, start the installation like this:

```
# cd install ; ./setup /net
```

After you press Enter, you'll see the first install screen, as shown in Figure 25.2

FIGURE 25.2

The OpenOffice suite is the open source version of StarOffice and has a similar installation interface.

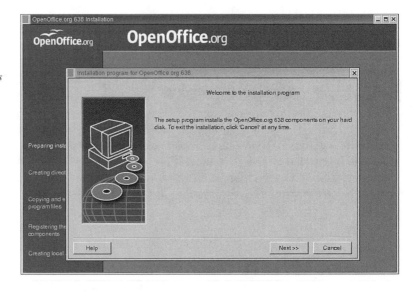

The most important installation dialog box, shown in Figure 25.3 is used to install all the software in a central directory. Individual users can then install a local, minimal OpenOffice support directory like this (using a path to the OpenOffice directory):

```
$ /opt/OpenOffice*/program/setup
```

FIGURE 25.3

Use the OpenOffice installer to create system-wide support.

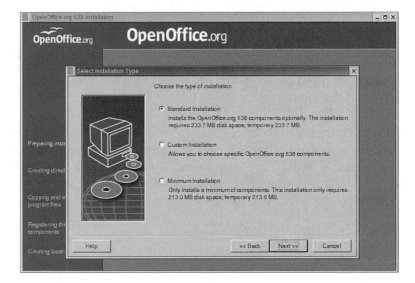

After installation, the program is launched using the `soffice` shell script like this:

$ Open*/soffice

OpenOffice will launch its Writer component and display a new, open word processing document by default, as shown in Figure 25.4 OpenOffice is purported to recognize and open nearly 120 different file formats and types of documents, ranging from popular commercial office suites to various graphics file formats. The suite is also supposed to be able to export nearly 70 types of documents.

FIGURE 25.4

The OpenOffice Writer word-processing component is launched by default.

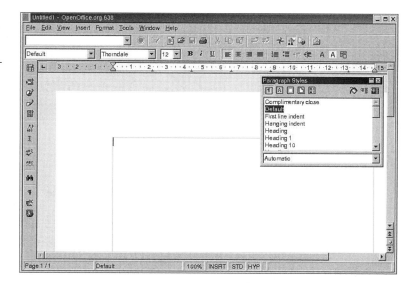

Existing documents can be opened from the command line, but the default work path must be set to the base home directory unless one wants to open documents using the full default work path. Click on Tools, Options, click the Paths list item, and then click and edit the My Documents setting, as shown in Figure 25.5.

Spell checking, the thesaurus, and built-in help aren't yet available, but should be supported by the time you read this. OpenOffice is a work in progress, but great progress has been made through the efforts of OpenOffice developers since the first source-code release. Browse to the OpenOffice Web site to get documentation, answers to frequently asked questions, and to offer feedback.

FIGURE 25.5

Edit the OpenOffice path settings to change default locations of files and directories.

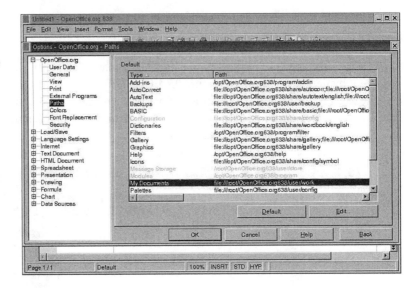

KDE's KOffice Office Suite

KOffice is a free office suite specifically designed to work with KDE (although its components can be used with any X Window manager as long as the proper KDE software libraries are installed). This office suite consists of nine different clients in an integrated package. Table 25.1 lists the various application components found in KOffice.

TABLE 25.1 KOffice Components

Name	Description
KChart	Graphing and charting editor
KFormula	Formula, equation editor
Kivio	Flow chart editor and presentation client
Kontour	Vector-based drawing editor
KPresenter	Presentation editor and display client
Krayon	Pixel-based image editor (similar to The GIMP)
KSpread	Graphing spreadsheet client
Kugar	Business report editor and presentation client
KWord	Frame-based word processor with spell check and other modern features

KOffice can be launched by selecting its menu item on the KDE desktop's panel or by using the koshell KDE client from the command line of a terminal window like this:

```
$ koshell &
```

After you press Enter, you'll see its main window as shown in Figure 25.6.

FIGURE 25.6

KDE's KOffice provides a workspace office suite environment.

Click on an icon in the left side of the main window to launch a desired component, such as the KWord word processing client. You can also launch individual clients without using the KOffice workspace by using the command line. For example, to use the KOffice editor, start KWord like this:

```
$ kword &
```

This will launch KWord, which will then ask you to select a document for your session. Like other advanced word processing clients for Red Hat Linux and X, you can specify a document to edit on the command line. The KWord client offers sophisticated editing capabilities, including rudimentary desktop publishing. For example, load a KWord document using the command line like this:

```
$ kword sample.kwd &
```

A sample document (created in only a few minutes) is shown in Figure 25.7.

25

PRODUCTIVITY APPLICATIONS

FIGURE 25.7

The KOffice KWord word processing component is a sophisticated WYSIWYG editor.

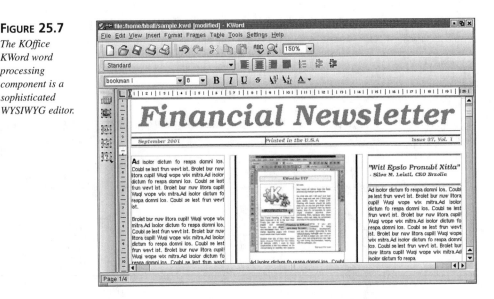

The KOffice KSpread client is a functional spreadsheet program with graphing capabilities. Like KWord, KSpread can also be launched from the command line. You'll be asked to choose a type of document, new or previous document, after using a command line like this:

```
$ kspread &
```

A simple example of kspread's graphing capabilities is shown in Figure 25.8. To create a graph, click and drag to select the data in rows and columns, and then click the Insert menu's Chart menu item. After your pointer turns into a cross-hair, click and drag on a blank area of the spreadsheet. A dialog box will appear from which you can select a graph type and then create the graph.

KDE includes other productivity clients in its collection of base and related applications. These clients provide an address book, time tracking, calculation, note taking, scheduling, and organizing. One popular client is korganizer, which provides daily, weekly, work-week, and monthly views of tasks, to-dos, and scheduled appointments with background alarms. A journal, or diary function, is also supported. You can launch this client from the KDE desktop panel's menu or from the command line like this:

```
$ korganizer &
```

A typical korganizer window is shown in Figure 25.9.

FIGURE 25.8

The KOffice KSpread spreadsheet component supports graphing of data.

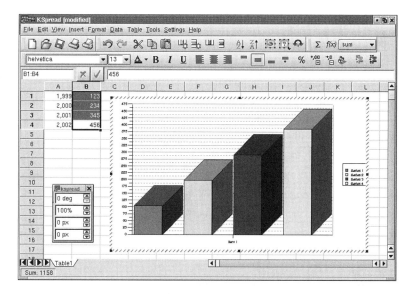

FIGURE 25.9

KDE's korganizer clients supports editing of tasks and schedules.

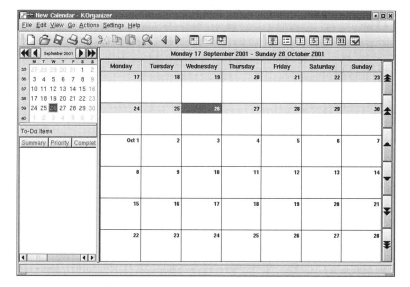

GNOME Office Suite Clients

The GNOME desktop, like KDE, includes several office productivity clients for word processing and spreadsheet editing. These clients are being developed, improved, and

25

PRODUCTIVITY APPLICATIONS

distributed by the GNOME Office Project. This project aims to create a wide range of capable and free productivity clients supported by the GNOME software libraries.

The GNOME office suite is supported by GNOME libraries that enable application data sharing and inter-client communication. This allows a word processor, for example, to share data with a spreadsheet client, and for data to be copied, pasted, or otherwise transferred easily between documents. These features, supported by the other office suites discussed so far, are the foundation or glue that makes related clients into an office suite.

Although the GNOME Office project's Web site states that "Sun is integrating their OpenOffice Suite with GNOME," the current premiere GNOME Office clients are its word processor, spreadsheet, and image editor: the AbiWord word processor; the Gnumeric spreadsheet; and the GNU Image Manipulation Program, or GIMP.

Various components of the GNOME Office project are listed in Table 25.2.

TABLE 25.2 GNOME Office Clients

Program	Description
AbiWord	Word processor with spell checking
Achtung	Presentation document client
Balsa	E-mail client
Dia	Charting, diagramming editor
Evolution	Calendaring e-mail PIM
Eye Of GNOME	Image viewer
Galeon	Web browser
Gfax	Fax-management client
GIMP	Image editor
GNOME-DB	Database connectivity
GnuCash	Personal finance management client
Gnumeric	GNOME spreadsheet client
Guppi	Plotting and graphing client
MrProject	Project management client
Sketch	Ancillary vector-based drawing client
Sodipodi	Vector-based drawing client
Toutdoux	Project management client with database features

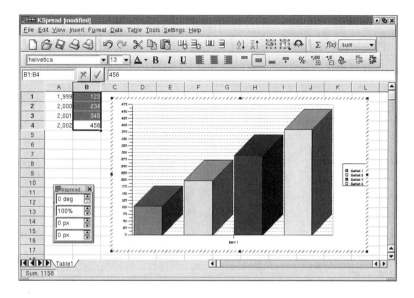

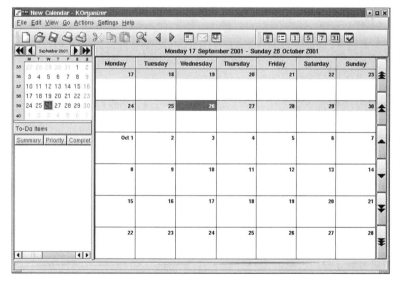

GNOME Office Suite Clients

The GNOME desktop, like KDE, includes several office productivity clients for word processing and spreadsheet editing. These clients are being developed, improved, and distributed by the GNOME Office Project. This project aims to create a wide range of capable and free productivity clients supported by the GNOME software libraries.

The GNOME office suite is supported by GNOME libraries that enable application data sharing and inter-client communication. This allows a word processor, for example, to share data with a spreadsheet client, and for data to be copied, pasted, or otherwise transferred easily between documents. These features, supported by the other office suites discussed so far, are the foundation or glue that makes related clients into an office suite.

Although the GNOME Office project's Web site states that "Sun is integrating their OpenOffice Suite with GNOME," the current premiere GNOME Office clients are its word processor, spreadsheet, and image editor: the AbiWord word processor; the Gnumeric spreadsheet; and the GNU Image Manipulation Program, or GIMP.

Various components of the GNOME Office project are listed in Table 25.2.

TABLE 25.2   GNOME Office Clients

Program	Description
AbiWord	Word processor with spell checking
Achtung	Presentation document client
Balsa	E-mail client
Dia	Charting, diagramming editor
Evolution	Calendaring e-mail PIM
Eye Of GNOME	Image viewer
Galeon	Web browser
Gfax	Fax-management client
GIMP	Image editor
GNOME-DB	Database connectivity
GnuCash	Personal finance management client
Gnumeric	GNOME spreadsheet client
Guppi	Plotting and graphing client
MrProject	Project management client
Sketch	Ancillary vector-based drawing client
Sodipodi	Vector-based drawing client
Toutdoux	Project management client with database features

These components, unlike the other suites discussed so far, aren't centrally managed and in some cases are quite disparate in appearance and behavior. However, the primary applications, AbiWord and the gnumeric spreadsheet editor are polished productivity programs. To begin editing a document, launch the AbiWord client from the GNOME desktop panel's Applications menu (or use AbiWord on the command line). The editor is shown in Figure 25.10.

FIGURE 25.10

AbiWord is a word processing program for Red Hat Linux, GNOME, and X11.

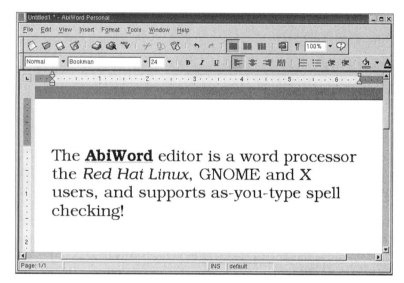

Use Gnumeric to perform financial calculations. You can launch the spreadsheet editor from the command line like this:

```
$ gnumeric &
```

After you press Enter, you'll see a blank spreadsheet document, as shown in Figure 25.11

Hopefully the GNOME Office project will work toward better integration between these applications using the inherent capabilities of the GNOME libraries. GNOME distributions also include a rich assortment of productivity clients, such as text file browsers, several calculators, checkbook managers, note-takers and time-tracking applications.

25

PRODUCTIVITY APPLICATIONS

FIGURE 25.11

GNOME's gnumeric spreadsheet is a capable financial data editor.

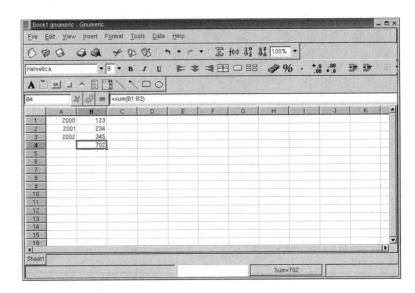

PDA Connectivity

Your Red Hat Linux distribution includes programs and clients for use with the Palm-type Personal Digital Assistants (PDAs). The most popular Palm-related software suite is the collection of utilities included with Kenneth Albanowski's `pilot-link` package.

These command-line based commands can be used to perform a variety of tasks that includes

- Extracting and uploading addresses
- Installing date book information
- Transferring text memos to and from the PDA
- Managing PDA To-do lists
- Managing user settings
- Sending and retrieving e-mail documents
- Installing new PDA programs
- Backing up the contents of a PDA
- Acquiring expense database account information.

The `pilot-xfer` command is used to perform many of these tasks, although the suite of commands includes 31 separate programs. After configuring the software, determining the proper serial port, and connecting your PDA to a desktop or notebook PC running

Red Hat Linux, you can back up the contents of your PDA with the `pilot-xfer` command like this:

```
$ pilot-xfer /dev/ttyS1 -b backupdirectory
```

This command will automatically create a directory according to the name following the `-b` option, and then download and save the contents of your PDA in the designated directory.

To interact with your PDA using a graphical interface, use Dan Pilone's `kpilot` client. This application can be used to install and retrieve text documents and back up and restore the contents of your PDA. You'll need to properly configure the software by selecting a correct serial port, speed setting, and default file location.

Another graphical PDA client, shown in Figure 25.12, is Judd Montgomery's comprehensive `jpilot` application. The `jpilot` program can be used to manage, retrieve, install, back up, and synch any information for your Palm-related PDA. Click on the date book, to-do list, address book, or memo pad buttons to perform related tasks. Use the Sync or Backup buttons to update or preserve a copy of your PDA's data.

FIGURE 25.12
The `jpilot` *PDA client supports PalmOS devices.*

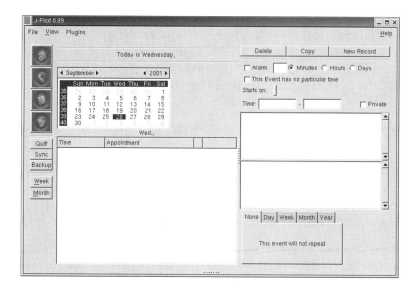

Graphics Productivity Programs

Using XFree86 in conjunction with Red Hat Linux provides a rich environment to host multimedia applications. You'll find audio, video, sound, animation, and graphics programs included in this book's Red Hat Linux distribution. One of the best graphics clients is the GIMP, a free image editor with sophisticated capabilities that can import and export more than 30 different graphics formats, including files created with Adobe Photoshop.

> **Note**
>
> Red Hat Linux includes hundreds of graphics conversion programs, and there are few if any graphics file formats that cannot be manipulated when using Linux. These commands can be used in Perl scripts, shell scripts, or command-line pipes to support many types of complex format conversion and image manipulation tasks. See the manual pages for the ppm, pbm, pnm, pgm families of commands. Also see the manual page for the convert command, part of a suite of extremely capable programs included with the ImageMagick suite.

The GIMP can be started by clicking a desktop panel menu item or by using the command line like so:

```
$ gimp &
```

You'll see an installation dialog box when the GIMP is started for the first time, and then a series of dialog boxes that display information regarding the creation and contents of a local GIMP directory. This directory can contain personal settings, preferences, external application resource files, temporary files, and symbolic links to external software tools used by the editor.

After the initial configuration has finished, the GIMP's main windows and toolboxes will appear as shown in Figure 25.13.

GIMP's main window is a toolbox with tools used for selection, drawing, movement, view enlargement or reduction, airbrushing, painting, smudging, copying, filling, and color selection. Depending on the version installed on your system, this toolbox can host more than 25 different tools.

The toolbox's File, Xtns, and Help menus are used file operations (including the ability to send the current image by electronic mail), image acquisition or manipulation, and documentation. If you right-click on an open image window, you'll see the wealth of the GIMP's menus, as shown in Figure 25.14

FIGURE 25.13

The GIMP is a sophisticated image editor for Red Hat Linux and XFree86.

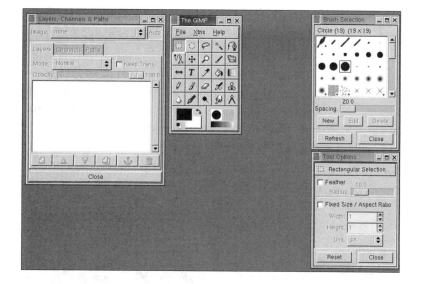

FIGURE 25.14

Right-click on an image window to access the GIMP's cascading menus.

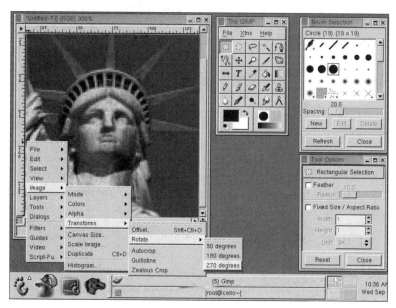

You can also use many types of image scanners with the GIMP. In the recent past, the most capable scanners required a Small Computer System Interface (SCSI) port. Today,

25

PRODUCTIVITY APPLICATIONS

however, many scanners work through a USB port. You must have scanner support enabled for Linux (usually through a loaded kernel module, such as scanner.o) before using a scanner with the GIMP.

Although some scanners can work via the command line, you'll enjoy more productive scanning sessions using a graphical interface because images manipulation tasks such as previewing and cropping can save time before actually scanning an image. Most scanners in use with Red Hat Linux use the Scanner Access Now Easy (SANE) package that supports and enables graphical scanning sessions.

SANE consists of two software components. A low-level driver enables the hardware and is specific to each scanner. Next, a graphical scanner interface X client known as xscanimage is used as a *plug-in*, or ancillary program (or script) that adds features to the GIMP.

> **Note**
>
> Although xscanimage is generally used as a GIMP plug-in, it can also be used as a standalone program. Another useful program is Joerg Schulenburg's gocr client, used for optical character recognition (OCR). Although not included with Red Hat Linux, you can download and build a copy for testing. This program works best with 300 dots-per-inch (dpi) scans in several different graphics formats. OCR is a resource-intensive task and can require hundreds of megabytes of disk storage!

Red Hat Linux also includes the GNOME gPhoto digital camera support client. This application can be launched by using the GNOME desktop panel's Programs, Multimedia menu, but must first be configured for use by selecting the type of camera and connection port shown in Figure 25.15.

After saving your configuration, you can download selected images from your camera, or download an index of thumbnail views. Desired images can then be batch retrieved from your camera by clicking on individual thumbnail images. The images will then be displayed in individual windows accessed through gPhoto's main window. Photo images can also be loaded for editing by using the File menu as shown in Figure 25.16.

FIGURE **25.15**
Configure gPhoto for your digital camera and connection before use.

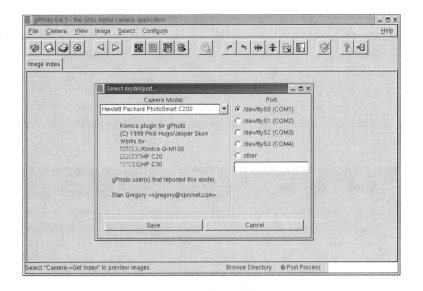

FIGURE **25.16**
gPhoto eases the job of getting, editing, and saving pictures from your digital camera.

gPhoto supports basic editing operations and can be used to rotate, flip, or scale images. Contrast, brightness, and color controls can also be used to alter each image.

25

PRODUCTIVITY
APPLICATIONS

Red Hat Linux provides software to support many additional types of productivity tasks, and the system hosts basic features such as scheduling and launching of specific clients or tasks (using the cron and at daemons). You'll also find many audio and video clients that can be used for multimedia applications. These clients include audio mixers and recorders, audio CD players, digital music players, audio conversion tools (such as the GNOME grip client used for creating compressed audio files in several formats), and video and animation playback programs (such as xanim client), and support for a variety of webcams.

> **Note**
>
> You can now easily play Digital Video Disks (DVDs) using Red Hat Linux. Browse to http://www.videolan.org, and then download, build, and install the vlc client. You'll need a fast CPU (at least 450MHz) and sound properly configured. The default Red Hat Linux kernel supports the DVD CD-ROM filesystem, so reading a DVD does not present a problem (earlier 2.2-series Linux kernels required the application of a patch and a rebuild in order to read DVDs).

Reference

http://www.sun.com/staroffice—Browse to this site to download a free copy of StarOffice for Linux and other operating systems.

http://www.kde.org/—The place to start when looking for new versions of the K Desktop Environment.

http://www.koffice.org/—Home page for KDE's premiere office suite, KOffice.

http://koffice.kde.org/—Home page for the KOffice office suite for KDE.

http://www.vistasource.com/products/axware/—The Applixware Office suite, now marketed by VistaSource, Inc.

ftp://ftp.corel.com/pub/linux/Office2000/updates/installscript/—Download site for an improved installer script to enable a less error-prone installation of Corel's WordPerfect Office 2000 suite under Red Hat Linux and other distributions.

http://www.openoffice.org—Home page for the OpenOffice project, and the latest version of OpenOffice for Linux and other operating systems. Many features of OpenOffice will appear in future versions of StarOffice.

`http://www.gnome.org/gnome-office/`—Home page for the GNOME Office project, and the place you can download the latest versions of each GNOME Office component.

`http://www.gimp.org`—Home page of the GIMP, and the location for downloading the latest version.

`http://www.mostang.com/sane/`—The SANE home page (supported by an Itanium server donated by Hewlett Packard!)

`http://altmark.nat.uni-magdeburg.de/~jschulen/ocr/`—Home page for the GOCR project.

`http://www.gphoto.org/`—The gPhoto project's home page, where you can get the latest version and more information about digital cameras with Linux.

`http://www.videolan.org`—Home page and download site for a long-awaited DVD player for Linux (available despite the monied interests of the Motion Picture Association of America).

26

CHAPTER

Emulators and Other Operating Systems

Red Hat Linux provides software you can use to manage and run foreign operating systems or the desktops of other computers running different versions of Linux or operating systems. Some of these software tools use emulation to provide system management or development environments, whereas others might be used to run virtual networks or install and then run different operating systems. System administrators new to Red Hat Linux will quickly learn that Linux "plays well" with other operating systems.

Software emulators mimic foreign CPUs in order to host foreign operating systems or computer languages. Other tools such as cross-compilers are available for Red Hat Linux and allow program development for different target CPUs and operating systems (for example the PalmOS, currently hosted by the Motorola Dragonball processor). Many developers around the world use Red Hat Linux as an inexpensive platform for acquiring and using these cross-compilers and emulators when developing, testing, and producing software for other computers.

> **Note**
>
> Browse to http://www.freelabs.com/~whitis/linux/cross.html for various links to acquire Linux cross-compilers for target operating systems such as MS-DOS, Windows 95, NT, MacOS (68K), OS/2, and the Amiga. And if you are a developer with a PalmOS PDA, browse to http://www.palmos.com/dev/tech/tools/gcc/ to download Linux development tools for building PalmOS applications free of licensing fees or royalties.

System administrators will find that they can also use a Red Hat Linux workstation to manage remote desktops, or run legacy software in a more modern environment.

Using the DOSEMU Emulator and FreeDOS Utilities

DOSEMU allows Red Hat Linux users to run a DOS session in a terminal at the console, or in an X11 terminal window. You can use this software to run many different legacy DOS applications and games, create bootable fixed or removable DOS-formatted media, or create embedded applications using development tools that require a DOS environment.

The easiest way to get started is to browse to the DOSEMU home page (see the section "Reference" at the end of this chapter), and download a "ready-to-use" binary

Emulators and Other Operating Systems

CHAPTER 26

713

26

EMULATORS AND
OTHER OPERATING
SYSTEMS

distribution. This distribution is composed of two compressed `tar` archives: the DOSEMU emulator and related files; and the FreeDos distribution of free DOS commands:

```
dosemu-1.0.2-bin.tgz
dosemu-freedos-bin.tgz
```

Note that you don't have to be the root operator to install and use this software. Download the files, and then extract the software packages using the `tar` command like this:

```
$ tar xzf dosemu-1.0.2-bin.tgz
$ tar xzf dosemu-freedos-bin.tgz
```

This will create a directory named `dosemu` in your home directory. You can then start a DOSEMU session from the console or an X11 terminal window by first navigating into the `dosemu` directory and then using the `dosemu` shell script like this:

```
$ ./dosemu
```

After you press Enter, `dosemu` will check the configuration and files in the directory and then launch the `dosemu.bin` command under the bin directory. When you run DOSEMU for the first time, the `dosemu` script will first ask for permission to start:

```
DOSEMU will run on _this_ terminal.
To exit you need to execute 'exitemu' from within DOS,
because <Ctrl>-C and 'exit' won't work!

Note, that DOS needs 25 lines and xterm per default has only 24,
so you might want to enlarge it before continuing.


Hint: if you want $HOME as DOS drive D:, use '-home' option

Now type ENTER to start DOSEMU or <Ctrl>C to cancel
```

After you press Enter again, the script will print copyright information and ask you to verify reading of copyright and disclaimer information like this:

```
The Linux DOSEMU, Copyright  2001 the 'DOSEMU-Development-Team'.
This program is  distributed  in  the  hope that it will be useful,
but  WITHOUT  ANY  WARRANTY;   without even the implied warranty of
MERCHANTABILITY  or  FITNESS FOR A PARTICULAR PURPOSE. See the file
COPYING for more details.  Use  this  programm  at  your  own risk!

By continuing execution of this programm,  you are stating that you
have read the file  COPYING  and the above liability disclaimer and
that you accept these conditions.

Enter 'yes' to confirm/continue: yes
```

Type **yes** and press Enter to start the DOSEMU session. If you are running X, you can launch a DOSEMU session in an X11 terminal window like this:

```
$ ./xdosemu
```

After you press Enter (and if you have already run DOSEMU), you'll see the DOSEMU prompt as shown in Figure 26.1.

When you run DOSEMU for the first time, it will create a directory named .dosemu in your home directory with files that can contain information about your DOSEMU session. For example, you can examine the file named boot.log, which will be created each time you boot a DOSEMU session. An example boot.log looks like this:

```
Running unpriviledged in low feature mode
kernel CPU speed is 933000049 Hz
Running on CPU=586, FPU=1
using stderr for debug-output
debug flags: -a+c
debug flags: -dARWDCvXkiTsm#pQgcwhIExMnPrSgZ
CONF: Disabling use of pentium timer
CONF: dosbanner on
CONF: timint on
CONF: CPU set to 386
CONF:  1024k bytes XMS memory
CONF: 2048k bytes EMS memory
CONF: EMS-frame = 0xe000
CONF: dosemu running on remote_xterm
CONF: Keyboard-layout keyb-user
CONF: Keyboard-layout auto
device: /dev/fd0 type 2 h: 0   s: 0    t: 0 floppy A:
CONF: DPMI-Server on
CONF: not allowing speaker port access
```

Emulators and Other Operating Systems

CHAPTER 26

715

26

EMULATORS AND
OTHER OPERATING
SYSTEMS

```
CONF: IPX support off
CONF(LPT0) f: (null)   c: lpr  o: -Plp %s  t: 20  port: 378
device: /home/bball/dosemu/freedos type 4 h: -1  s: -1   t: -1 drive C:
CONF: config variable c_system unset
CONF: not enough privilege to define config variable c_user
CONF: mostly running as USER: uid=500 (cached 500) gid=500 (cached 500)
CONF: reserving 640Kb at 0x00000 for 'd' (Base DOS memory (first 640K))
CONF: reserving 64Kb at 0xF0000 for 'r' (Dosemu reserved area)
CONF: reserving 128Kb at 0xA0000 for 'v' (Video memory)
CONF: reserving 64Kb at 0xE0000 for 'E' (EMS page frame)
TIME: using 9154 usec for updating ALRM timer
DOS termination requested
```

The DOSEMU emulator provides quite a bit of information about your DOS session. The dosemu/conf directory contains several files you can edit to change how DOSEMU runs on your computer. These files are

> dosemu.conf—Configuration of files, devices, memory, and access permissions.
>
> Dosemurc—Settings for the keyboard and other custom, computer-specific settings.
>
> global.conf—A systemwide configuration file if DOSEMU is installed by the root operator for use by all users.

Use the exitemu command to exit your DOSEMU session. DOSEMU also supports a number of command-line options you can use to enable or disable features such as enabling your home directory to appear as drive D:, enabling stdin or stdout features of the DOSEMU command line, and allowing scrollable output in the DOSEMU window (so you can see information that might have scrolled off the screen).

Configuring, Installing, and Using VMware

VMware from VMware, Inc. is a commercial software package you can use to install and run other operating systems (such as DOS, Linux and BSD, or variants of the commercial Windows operating system). The software works by using your computer's hard drive to host different virtual filesystems. Given adequate CPU horsepower and enough memory and hard drive space, system administrators or network engineers can create virtual networks on a single computer running different operating systems with separate instances of VMware sessions. Security specialists can also use this software as a safe incubator in order to study or examine how a computer virus affects an operating system.

The VMware software can be downloaded and installed using the rpm or tar command (9.3MB compressed tarballs or .rpm archives are available from VMware). You will need a license key in order to use the software after installation. To install and configure the software, you will need root permission and the gcc compiler and related software installed on your system.

If you download and extract the software using a compressed tarball, a directory name vmware-distrib will be created. You should then navigate into this directory and run a Perl script named vmware-install. Start the installation like this:

```
# ./vmware-install.pl
```

After pressing Enter, you'll be asked a series of questions regarding the installation, such as the intended location of various files:

```
Creating a new installer database using the tar2 format.

Installing the content of the package.

In which directory do you want to install the binary files?
[/usr/bin] /usr/local/bin
```

In this example, the /usr/local/bin directory is specified instead of the default /usr/bin directory. After you enter a new location and press Enter, the install script will prompt for additional file locations, such as libraries, like this:

```
In which directory do you want to install the library files?
[/usr/local/lib/vmware]
```

Note that the install script will use any leading pathname change (such as /usr/local) that deviates from the default enclosed in brackets. You'll then be asked for permission to create any required directories:

```
The path "/usr/local/lib/vmware" does not exist currently. This script is going
to create it, including needed parent directories. Is this what you want?
[yes]
```

VMware also includes documentation files and manual pages. You'll first be asked where you would like to install its manual pages like this:

```
In which directory do you want to install the manual files?
[/usr/local/share/man] /usr/local/man
```

In this example, the /usr/local/man directory has been specified instead of the default /usr/local/share/man directory. You'll then be asked to specify the location of documentation pages like this:

```
In which directory do you want to install the documentation files?
[/usr/local/share/doc/vmware]
```

Again, if the desired directory does not exist, you'll be asked for permission (as in the previous example) to create any required directories. You'll also be asked for the location of Red Hat Linux startup script directories:

```
What is the directory that contains the init directories (rc0.d/ to rc6.d/)?
[/etc/rc.d]
```

The /etc/rc.d directory contains various directories with vmware-distrib symbolically linked scripts used for each of the various Linux runlevels. VMware needs to know where these scripts are in order to properly configure and set up services when Red Hat Linux boots, restarts, or shuts down. You'll also be asked for the location of Red Hat Linux system initialization scripts (/etc/rc.d/init.d).

After confirming the location of the directories and files, you'll then be asked if you'd like to configure VMware for your system:

```
Before running VMware Workstation for the first time, you need to configure it
for your running kernel by invoking the following command:
"/usr/local/bin/vmware-config.pl". Do you want this script to invoke the command
for you now? [yes]
```

After you press Enter, the configuration script will be launched, and you'll see

```
Making sure VMware Workstation's services are stopped.

Stopping VMware services:
   Virtual machine monitor                                [  OK  ]
```

```
You must read and accept the End User License Agreement to continue.
```

Press Enter to read the license agreement. The agreement will be displayed by the default system pager (the less command). After you finish reading, type **yes** to confirm the agreement. You'll then get an acknowledgement, and will be asked the following:

```
Thank you.

Trying to find a suitable vmmon module for your running kernel.

None of VMware Workstation's pre-built vmmon modules is suitable for your
running kernel.  Do you want this script to try to build the vmmon module for
your system (you need to have a C compiler installed on your system)? [yes]
```

You'll then be asked for development header file locations, and the configuration script will build required software:

```
...
Extracting the sources of the vmmon module.

Building the vmmon module.
...
```

Note that not all the output is shown here. The software will build various kernel modules used to support VMware during operation. You'll then be asked about networking:

```
Do you want networking for your Virtual Machines? (yes/no/help) [yes]
```

In order to use any networking features of VMware (and an installed operating system), you will need to enable this feature. Note that you can type **help** to get more information about this feature, which if enabled, supports bridging of virtual systems to a hardwired LAN or a "host-only" configuration that only allows internal communication between the session and your computer. If you desire networking, you might be asked (in part):

```
What will be the IP address of your host on the private network? 192.168.2.100
```

```
What will be the netmask of your private network? 255.255.255.0
```

In this example, an IP address and netmask is assigned for network use. After you continued the setup and have finished installation, you can then start VMware as the root operator or with normal user permission. Note that you will need access permission to use adequate hard drive storage to support installation and use of a foreign operating system!

Various VMware-specific services will be started on your Red Hat Linux system, depending on how the software is configured. However, you can stop or restart VMware service by using the vmware script installed during configuration. For example, to stop VMware service in the off chance that the software interferes with other services such as networking or printing, use the script like this:

```
# /etc/rc.d/init.d/vmware stop
Stopping VMware services:
    Virtual machine monitor                          [  OK  ]
    Bridged networking on /dev/vmnet0                [  OK  ]
    DHCP server on /dev/vmnet8                       [  OK  ]
    NAT networking on /dev/vmnet8                    [  OK  ]
    Host-only networking on /dev/vmnet8              [  OK  ]
    Virtual ethernet                                 [  OK  ]
```

System administrators can examine the vmware script for more details about specific files and services, or to customize enabled or disabled services.

> **Note**
>
> Netraverse's Win4Lin software package can also be used to run many new and legacy Windows applications while using Linux. This product can be used with Red Hat Linux (and other Linux distributions), but works differently from VMware. According to Netraverse, "Win4Lin is a kernel modification to the

underlying Linux file structure while VMWare is a hardware emulator." As such, system administrators should know that each product has advantages and disadvantages in installation, system resource requirements, speed, and filesystem handling. For example, Win4Lin will require the use of a modified kernel, whereas VMware can be installed and used without kernel modification. Browse to http://www.netraverse.com for more information about Win4Lin.

Starting a VMware Session

In order to start VMware, your license key, named `license`, must reside in a directory named `.vmware` in your home directory. VMware is generally then started during an X session from the command line of a terminal like this:

```
$ vmware
```

However, the command supports several options, which you can view like this:

```
$ vmware --help
vmware: invalid option -- -
Usage: vmware [<vmx flags>] [configfile] [-- [<ui flags>]]
where <vmx flags> are:
      -s name=value          set variable NAME to VALUE
      -q                     exit at power off
      -x                     power on when program starts
      -X                     as -x, also go to full screen mode
      -v                     print program version
```

These options are useful for setting environment variables, changing power modes, and using the display. After you press Enter, the VMware window will appear and request a license number. You can then start its Configuration Wizard by selecting the File menu's Wizard menu item. A series of dialog boxes will appear that are used to prepare a filesystem on your hard drive for installation of a guest operating system. VMware supports DOS, Windows 3.1, 95, 98, Me, NT, 2000 Professional, 2000 Server, 2000 Advanced Server, XP Home Edition, XP Professional, Linux, FreeBSD, and other operating systems.

In the dialog box shown in Figure 26.2, select the type of operating system you'd like to install.

After clicking to select the desired operating system, click the Next button. You'll then be asked to name the display and specify a path for the session's configuration file and virtual disk. You'll then be asked, as shown in Figure 26.3, to choose a type of disk. You can create a new virtual disk, use an existing file, or use a physical disk (such as a network mounted or removable drive).

FIGURE 26.2

Select an operating system to install using a VMware virtual filesystem.

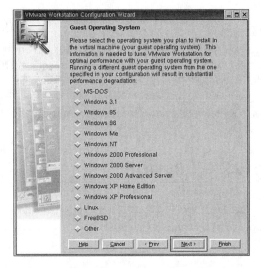

FIGURE 26.3

Select a disk type for your intended operating system's virtual filesystem.

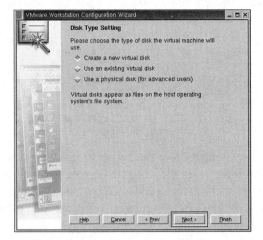

Click the Next button, and you'll be asked to enter the disk size in megabytes. This is an important step because the disk's size cannot be expanded (although you can add additional virtual disks later on if supported by the operating system in use). Take into consideration the initial requirements to install and run the intended guest operating system, and ensure that you have adequate disk space (or mount and use another volume). After entering a disk size and clicking the Next button, you'll then be asked if you'd like to use a CD-ROM, as shown in Figure 26.4.

FIGURE 26.4

Enable or disable use of a CD-ROM drive for your VMware session and guest operating system.

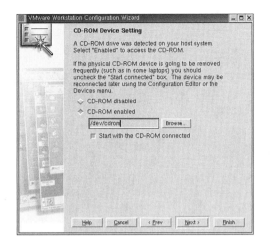

Ensure that the proper CD-ROM device is used. If you enable use of a physical CD-ROM, click the Next button to continue the same configuration for a floppy disk.

A Case of Being Too Helpful?

If you intend to install a guest operating system by booting with a CD-ROM when using VMware, you might find that Red Hat Linux will automatically mount the CD-ROM before VMware's software BIOS can use the CD! To avoid this problem, don't use the automount daemon (which mounts devices and NFS hosts "on demand") when using VMware. You can temporarily turn off this service before starting a VMware session by executing **/etc/rc.d/init.d/amd stop** as root, or disable this feature entirely by using the ntsysv or chkconfig commands. If you need to boot from a specific device, press F2 after using VMware's Power On button to change the virtual machine's BIOS settings; press the right arrow key to access the BIOS Boot menu, press the plus or minus keys to reorder the virtual machine's boot devices, and then press F10 to save and reboot using your new settings. They will be saved between VMware sessions for the current configuration file.

You'll next be asked to select a networking setting for the VMware session and operating system, as shown in Figure 26.5.

You can choose no networking, a bridged scheme in which the guest computer will can use its own addressing, or a network address translation scheme in which the physical computer's network address is used. Using the bridged scheme allows to you configure an independent computer with its own Ethernet interface.

FIGURE 26.5

Select a network scheme for your new operating system.

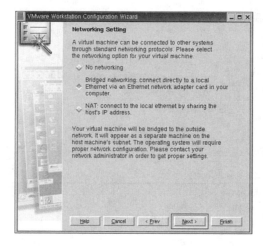

Note that unlike the virtual disk size, you can change virtual network adapters, SCSI and IDE interfaces, serial, USB, and sound devices, along with memory and power-management settings later on by using VMware's Configuration editor, shown in Figure 26.6.

FIGURE 26.6

Click Settings, Configuration Editor to change or add to the VMware virtual computer's capabilities.

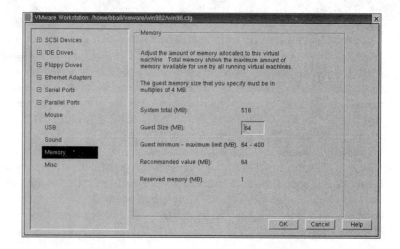

When you click Next as shown in Figure 26.5, you'll be asked to confirm the new settings, and you should then click the Done button (or use the Prev button to go back and change settings). This will complete the initial guest operating system configuration. You can then install a guest operating system by inserting a floppy diskette or CD-ROM and booting to an install by clicking the Power On button in VMware's main menu.

Use the File menu to select or change the current active guest operating system configuration. To run another operating system at the same time, simply start another instance of vmware like this:

```
$ vmware &
```

After you click the Power On button, your operating system will boot, and you can run a session in a VMware as shown in Figure 26.7.

FIGURE 26.7

You can use VMware to run outdated legacy operating systems and software while transitioning your company to Red Hat Linux.

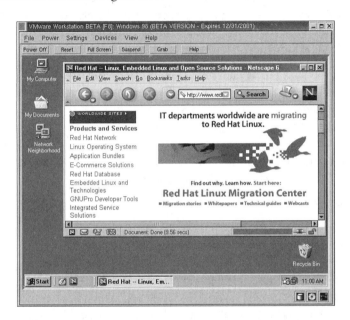

Tip

Press Ctrl+Alt+Esc to access your pointing device while running a guest operating system using VMware because the pointer might become "attached" to the VMware window during use. Press Ctrl+Alt to return your VMware session to a normal X window if you choose the View menu's Full Screen mode. You'll also want to use the Settings menu's VMware Tools Install menu item to get the most out of your virtual session, which improves display handling, screen resolution, and color depth.

You can also create a dual-boot operating system configuration and install and then use a choice of virtual systems if your computer does not have enough memory to host multiple VMware sessions, but does have enough disk space for an adequate virtual filesystem.

Windows Program Execution Using Wine

Red Hat Linux includes the Wine emulator from the Wine project. You can use Wine to run selected DOS and Windows applications. The wine command is a MB binary file, and an optional configuration file wine.conf, located under the /etc directory can be used for systemwide settings. Individual user settings (if desired) are contained in the home directory in the file config under a directory named .wine. This emulator is only useful if you have various Windows operating system files on a locally available drive.

A startup script named wine under the /etc/rc.d/init.d directory is used to enable or disable the ability to launch Windows programs using the command line (or by clicking the program's icon with the pointing device during a GNOME or KDE X session). The script creates entries in /proc/sys/fs/binfmt_misc/register that associate the wine emulator with .exe files and enable the Red Hat Linux kernel to execute these files. This means that when enabled, files such as notepad.exe can be run from the command line like this:

```
$ ./notepad.exe
```

Details about creating custom systemwide configurations for Wine will be found in the wine.conf manual page or in various files under the /usr/share/doc/wine-20010726/wine-doc/ directory. The Wine project is under active development, and new versions are released with some regularity. Check the Wine project page for the latest version. You can find out if a favorite Windows application is supported by going to http://appdb.codeweavers.com/ and browsing a database of nearly 320 Windows programs.

MacOS Emulation Using Basilisk II

Basilisk II is a free Macintosh emulator that provides pre-PowerPC CPU emulation of the MacOS in order to run selected MacOS software. A copy of earlier versions of the MacOS and a binary image of an Apple Macintosh computer's Read-Only Memory (ROM) chip are required. The emulator can use several versions of MacOS up to version 8.1. Various color displays, sound, floppy diskette, CD-ROM, and other drivers are supported. Red Hat Linux does not support the latest Extended Hierarchical File System (HFS+), but does support the earlier "regular" HFS.

Basilisk II also supports Ethernet, serial, SCSI, and Apple Desktop Bus (ADB) drivers. Settings are configured using a graphical editor, or preferences can be edited in a file named .basilisk_ii_prefs in a user's home directory. This file can be used to specify various hard drive, floppy diskette, video resolution, window geometry, color depth, sound, keyboard, mouse, network, and serial or printer-port settings, along with the location of required files, allocated memory, and boot mode.

This emulator must be downloaded and built from scratch. You'll find the source code on the Basilisk II home page (see "Reference" later) in a compressed tar archive or RPM package.

MacOS Emulation Using Executor

ARDI's Executor is a commercial software emulator that runs legacy MacOS applications under Linux. (A demonstration version can be downloaded for testing before purchase.) According to ARDI, the emulation is of a Motorola MC68040 CPU running System 6.0.7, and supports nearly 400 Macintosh applications. Some of the features and hardware not supported, however, are serial ports, LocalTalk, Control Panels, or INITs. On the other hand, Executor does not require Apple MacOS System files or binary ROM images.

The software is installed with the `rpm` command under the `/opt/executor/bin` directory with symbolic links to the `/usr/local/bin` directory. The client can be started like this:

```
$ executor &
```

After you press Enter, the main window will appear as shown in Figure 26.8.

FIGURE 26.8

Use Executor to run older MacOS programs while using Red Hat Linux.

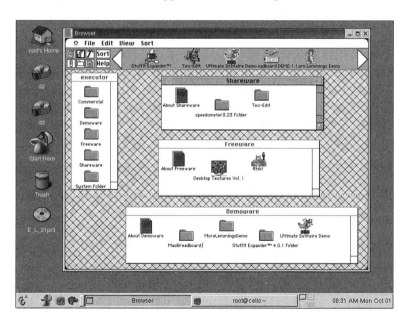

Executor has many different command-line options that can be used to configure its operation when started. The client also obeys standard X11 geometry settings. The left Alt key is used as the Apple Command key, whereas the right Alt key is used as the Apple keyboard's Option key. Press left_Alt+Shift+5 to set the program's preferences. Some MacOS System 7 features might be enabled.

Remote Computer Operating Using Xvnc

Xvnc from AT&T Laboratories in Cambridge, England provides virtual network management and graphical use of remote desktops running other operating systems under Linux (or of Linux desktops while using other operating systems on remote computers). Versions are available for more than 10 different operating systems, including PalmOS and PocketPC.

> **Note**
>
> The "official" Xvnc distribution does not include a PalmOS client for virtual networking. However, PalmOS PDA users can browse to `http://www.harakan.btinternet.co.uk/PalmVNC/` and download PalmVNC. This Xvnc-compatible PalmOS client requires less than 40KB of memory, works like the Xvnc `vncviewer` client, and comes with source code.

The Linux version of Xvnc includes a special X server named `Xvnc` used to support a background X session, a shell script named `vncserver` used to initiate a local Xvnc session, a password utility named `vncpasswd`, and an client named `vncviewer` used to view and run remote X sessions or desktops. Although you can download, build, and install new versions of the Xvnc software, you'll find nearly current copies included with Red Hat Linux.

The Xvnc server package must be running on a remote computer in order to view or manage the remote desktop. Use the `vncserver` script under Red Hat Linux to start a server instance using a specific geometry session (to offer for example, an 800x600 session) like this:

```
$ vncserver -geometry 800x600
```

You'll then be asked to assign a password. After entering the password the session will start and Xvnc will report a display number (such as `:1`). This password and display number is required when you or others access the session running under Red Hat Linux on your computer.

The first time you launch Xvnc on your Red Hat Linux system the software will create a .vnc directory in your home directory, along with a file named `xstartup`, and a log file using your computer's hostname and X display number (such as `cello.home.org:1.log`).

The Xvnc software must be installed and running on a remote computer in order to access its desktops. To access a remote desktop, use the `vncviewer` command, followed by the hostname (or IP address) of the remote computer, along with the Xvnc session number (always `0` for Windows and `1` if an X session has already been started on a Linux or UNIX computer). For example, type the following command if you're running Red Hat Linux and would like to access a remote Linux computer running Xvnc:

```
$ vncviewer cello.home.org:1
```

After entering a password, the `vncviewer` window will appear with an active image of the remote desktop, perhaps similar to that shown in Figure 26.9.

FIGURE 26.9

Use vncviewer *to manage remote Linux or other desktops running Xvnc.*

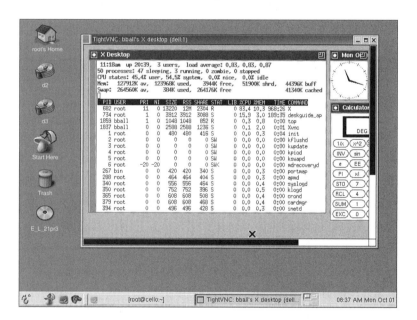

You can also use the `vncviewer` client on remote computers to view a Linux desktop, again using the assigned password and display number. And by editing a simple text file, you can also craft custom X sessions. The file `xstartup` under the .vnc directory in each user's directory contains entries somewhat similar to an .xinitrc file, and can be changed to launch a specific window manager or client.

The `xstartup` file (actually a shell script) looks like this:

```
#!/bin/sh

xrdb $HOME/.Xresources
xsetroot -solid grey
xterm -geometry 80x24+10+10 -ls -title "$VNCDESKTOP Desktop" &
twm &
```

The default window manager is `twm` with a gray root desktop and a single `xterm` terminal window. System managers can create custom desktops for remote users.

Many additional software emulators and other cross-platform tools can be used with Red Hat Linux. These tools not only demonstrate the value and power of open source software, but also extend the reach of system administrators and developers to explore and use the capabilities of Red Hat Linux to the fullest. Red Hat Linux provides a rich computing environment with superb support for legacy software and tomorrow's projects. By using these types of software tools, widely disparate computing environments can be linked to build powerful computing solutions.

Reference

`http://www.dosemu.org/`—Home page for DOSEMU, with links to pre-compiled versions, extra DOS utilities, documentation, and source code.

`http://www.freedos.org/`—Home page for the FreeDos utilities used with DOS or the DOSEMU emulator.

`http://freedos.sourceforge.net/`—Location of FreeDos development efforts.

`http://www.ardi.com`—Home page of the Executor emulator for Linux.

`http://www.uni-mainz.de/~bauec002/B2Main.html`—Support home page for the Basilisk II MacOS emulator.

`http://www.uk.research.att.com/vnc/xvnc.html`—Home page for downloading various versions of the Xvnc software package.

`http://www.vmware.com`—VMware, Inc.'s home page with links to download evaluation and beta versions of VMware for Linux and other operating systems.

`http://cygwin.com/`—Home page for the Cygwin UNIX environment for Windows.

`http://www.libsdl.org/Xmingw32/`—Home page for a build of a cross-compiler for Windows (using Cygwin tools available through the preceding link).

Reference

PART V

Internet Resources

APPENDIX A

Red Hat Linux enjoys a wealth of Internet support in the form of Web sites with technical information, specific program documentation, targeted white papers, bug fixes, user experiences, third-party commercial technical support, and even free versions of specialized, fine-tuned clone distributions (see VA Linux in the section "Commercial Support").

This appendix lists many of the supporting Web sites, FTP repositories, Usenet newsgroups, and electronic mailing lists that you can use to get more information and help with Red Hat Linux (although you can always turn to the source, Red Hat, Inc., or third-party companies, such as Linuxcare for commercial technical support on a 24/7 on-site basis, by phone, by electronic mail, or even a per-incident basis).

The appendix is divided into the following sections:

- Web sites with Linux information arranged by category
- Usenet newsgroups pertaining to Linux
- Mailing lists providing Linux user and developer discussions
- Internet Relay Chat groups for Linux information

This appendix also lists Web sites that might be of general interest when using Red Hat Linux, or specific components, such as XFree86. Every effort has been made to ensure the accuracy of the URLs, but keep in mind that the Internet is always in flux!

Web Sites and Search Engines

There are literally thousands of Web sites with information about Linux (and Red Hat Linux). The key to getting the answers you need right away involves using the best search engines and techniques. Knowing how to search can mean the difference between frustration and success when researching answers while troubleshooting problems.

Some of the basic techniques are to be specific, and use specific search terms. For example, if you simply search for "Red Hat Linux," you'll end up with too many links and too much information. But if you search for "Red Hat Linux 7.2 sound" you'll be more likely to find the information you need. Other techniques involve the use of various symbols in the search string, such as the plus sign (+) to force matches of Web pages containing both strings, searching within returned results, sorting results (usually by date to get the latest information), searching for related information, or stemming searches (such as specify returns for not only "link" but also "linking" and "linked").

Invest the time and experiment with your favorite search engine's search features—the result will be more productive searches. In addition to sharpening your search skills, also take the time to choose the best search engine for your needs.

Some of the best search engines on the Web are powered by Linux, so it makes sense to use the best available resources. Out of the myriad number of Web sites with search engines, http://google.com stands out from the crowd, with 10 million or more users per month. The site uses advanced hardware and software to bring speed and efficiency to your searches.

Why is Google so powerful? Because the site runs its search engine on an ever-growing (8,000 at last count) cluster of PCs running Red Hat Linux! Since 1998, Red Hat Linux has powered Google and provided cost-efficiency, scalability, and dependability, helping Google to create the largest database size of any search engine on the Web, with more than a billion Web pages and a petabyte (1,024TB) of storage. The database size is important because empty search results are useless to online users, and the ability to return hits on esoteric subjects can make the difference between success and failure or satisfaction and frustration.

Some of Google's features include a "GoogleScout" link to return similar pages on the results page, the ability to see the exact version of a Web page as returned to a search engine (known as a "Cached" feature), advanced searches, and more recently, a link to an active Usenet news feed!

Web Site Resources

The following lists of sites are broken up by various topics. The lists aren't comprehensive, but have been checked and were available at the time of this writing.

Certification

Linux certification courses are one of the newest developments in the Linux and computing community. The following Web sites might be of interest if you'd like to pursue a certification track for Red Hat or other Linux distributions:

- http://www.lpi.org—The Linux Professional Institute, with Linux vendor- and distribution-neutral programs.

- http://www.linuxcertification.com—Home page for the SAIR Linux and GNU certification program.

- http://www.redhat.com/training/—Entry page to Red Hat, Inc.'s Global Learning Services and information about the Red Hat Certified Engineer program.

Commercial Support

Commercial support for Linux and Red Hat Linux is an essential ingredient to the success of Linux in the corporate and business community. Although hundreds, if not thousands of consultants are well-versed in Linux and UNIX who are available on call for a fee, here is a short list of the best-known Linux support providers:

- `http://www.redhat.net/apps/support/programs.html`—Red Hat, Inc.'s main support page with links to its various support programs
- `http://www.linuxcare.com`—Home page for Linuxcare, providing local and remote technical support for many types of installations and customers
- `http://www.linux-support.net/`—One of the newer commercial Linux support companies
- `http://www.valinux.com/ps//`—A listing of the professional services offered by VA Linux with links to more information about its suite of services, including project management
- `http://e.linux-support.net/`—Enterprise-level Linux support from Linux Support Services, Inc.

In addition to service-oriented support companies, nearly every commercial distributor of Linux has some form of easily purchased commercial support. There are various ways in which to take advantage of support services (such as remote management, onsite consulting, device driver development, and so on), but needs will vary according to customer circumstances and installations.

Documentation

Every Red Hat Linux distribution includes thousands of pages of documentation in the form of manual pages, HOWTO documents (in various formats, such as text and HTML), mini-HOWTO documents, and software package documentation (usually found under the `/usr/share/doc/` directory). However, the definitive site for reading the latest versions of these documents is the Linux Documentation Project, found at: `http://www.linuxdoc.org`. You'll also find copies of

- "Advanced Bash-Scripting Guide," by Mendel Cooper; a guide to shell scripting using `bash`
- "LDP Author Guide," by Mark F. Komarinski; how to write LDP documentation
- "Linux Administration Made Easy," by Steve Frampton
- "Linux Administrator's Security Guide," by Kurt Seifried

- "Linux Consultants Guide," by Joshua Drake; a world-wide listing of commercial Linux consultants
- "Linux From Scratch," by Gerard Beekmans; creating a Linux distribution from software
- "Linux Kernel 2.4 Internals," by Tigran Aivazian; a guide to the 2.4 kernel
- "Linux Kernel Module Programming Guide," by Ori Pomerantz; a somewhat dated guide to building 2.0 and 2.2-series modules
- "Securing and Optimizing Linux," by Gerhard Mourani; specific to Red Hat Linux
- "The Bugzilla Guide," by Matthew P. Barnson; a guide to the Mozilla bug-tracking system
- "The Linux Network Administrator's Guide, Second Edition," by Olaf Kirch and Terry Dawson; a comprehensive net admin guide

Floppy-Based Linux Distributions

- `http://www.linuxrouter.org`—Home page for the Linux Router Project
- `http://www.itm.tu-clausthal.de/~perle/hal91/`—Home page of the HAL91 distribution
- `http://floppix.ccai.com/index.html`—A Debian-based floppy
- `http://www.toms.net/rb/`—Tom's root and boot disk distribution
- `http://www.trinux.org`—An ultra-secure Linux distribution on floppy
- `http://PenguinBackup.sourceforge.net/`—A unique, floppy-based distribution that allows quick backup of your Palm-type PDA

Intel-Based Distributions

- `http://www.caldera.com`—Caldera System's OpenLinux
- `http://linux.corel.com`—Corel's Debian-based Linux
- `http://www.debian.org`—The Debian Linux distribution, consisting only of software distributed under the GNU GPL license
- `http://www.independence.seul.org`—A newer Red Hat-based Linux distribution
- `http://www.libranet.com`—A Linux distribution based on Debian
- `http://www.slackware.com`—Home page for download of the newest version of one of the oldest Linux distributions, Slackware
- `http://www.suse.com`—Home page for SuSE Linux, also available for the PowerPC
- `http://www.linux-mandrake.com`—A Red Hat-based Linux distribution

PowerPC-Based Linux Distributions

- `http://www.linuxppc.org/`—Home page for the LinuxPPC distribution
- `http://www.suse.com`—SuSE PPC Linux
- `http://www.yellowdoglinux.com`—Home page for Terra Soft Solutions' Yellow Dog Linux for the PowerPC

Red Hat Linux

- `http://www.redhat.com`—Home page for Red Hat, Inc.'s distribution of Red Hat Linux for the Alpha CPU, Intel-based hardware and the new Itanium processor. Support is also provided for older, but now discontinued versions for the SPARC.
- `http://www.redhat.com/apps/support/documentation.html`—Specific Web page with links to current official Red Hat manuals and guides, FAQs, HOWTOs, white papers, free books, mailing list archives, hardware compatibility lists, and other documentation.

Linux on Laptops

One of the definitive sites for getting information about running Linux on your laptop is Kenneth Harker's Linux Laptop pages. Although not as actively updated as in the past, this site (`http://www.linux-laptop.net`) still contains the world's largest collection of Linux and laptop information, with links to user experiences and details concerning specific laptop models.

Another site to check is Werner Heuser's MobiliX—Mobile Computers and UniX Web site at `http://www.mobilix.org`. You'll find links to information such as IrDA and Linux PDAs and cell phones.

The X Window System

Although much technical information is available on the Internet regarding the X Window System, finding answers to specific questions when troubleshooting can be problematic. If you're having a problem using X, first try to determine if the problem is software or hardware related. When searching or asking for help (such as on Usenet's *comp.os.linux.x* newsgroup), try to be as specific as possible. Some critical factors or information needed to adequately assess a problem include the Linux distribution in use, the kernel version used, the version of X used, the brand, name and model of video card, name, brand and model monitor, and other related hardware.

This section lists just some of the basic resources for Red Hat Linux XFree86 users. Definitive technical information regarding X is available from `http://www.X.org`.

- `http://www.lesstif.org/`—Home page for the GPL'd OSF/Motif clone, LessTif

- `http://www.metrolink.com/`—Home page for a commercial version of X for Linux (along with many other products and services) named Metro-X

- `http://www.motifzone.net`—Site for download of the open source version of Motif for Linux, Open Motif

- `http://www.rahul.net/kenton/index.shtml`—Ken Lee's X and Motif Web site with numerous links to tutorial, development, and other information about X

- `http://www.xfree86.org`—Home page for The XFree86 Project, Inc., developers of XFree86, used with Red Hat Linux

- `http://www.xig.com/`—Home page for a commercial version of X for Linux (along with other software products)

Usenet Newsgroups

Linux-related Usenet newsgroups are another good source of information if you're having trouble using Linux. If your ISP doesn't offer a comprehensive selection of Linux newsgroups, you can browse to: `http://groups.google.com/`.

The primary Linux and Linux-related newsgroups are

- *alt.os.linux.caldera*—All about Caldera's OpenLinux
- *alt.os.linux.corel*—All about Corel's Linux
- *alt.os.linux.dial-up*—Using PPP for dial-up
- *alt.os.linux.mandrake*—All about Mandrake Linux
- *alt.os.linux.redhat*—Alternative discussions about Red Hat Linux
- *alt.os.linux.slackware*—Using Slackware Linux
- *alt.os.linux.suse*—Using SuSE Linux
- *comp.os.linux.admin*—Administering Linux
- *comp.os.linux.advocacy*—Heated discussions about Linux and other related issues
- *comp.os.linux.alpha*—Using Linux on the Alpha CPU
- *comp.os.linux.announce*—General Linux announcements
- *comp.os.linux.answers*—Releases of new Linux FAQs and other information
- *comp.os.linux.development.apps*—Using Linux development tools

- *comp.os.linux.development.system*—Building the Linux kernel
- *comp.os.linux.embedded*—Linux embedded device development
- *comp.os.linux.hardware*—Configuring Linux for various hardware devices
- *comp.os.linux.help*—Help with Linux
- *comp.os.linux.m68k*—Linux on Motorola's 68K-family CPUs
- *comp.os.linux.misc*—Miscellaneous Linux topics
- *comp.os.linux.networking*—Networking and Linux
- *comp.os.linux.portable*—Using Linux on laptops
- *comp.os.linux.powerpc*—Using PPC Linux
- *comp.os.linux.questions*—Questions about Linux
- *comp.os.linux.redhat*—All about Red Hat Linux
- *comp.os.linux.security*—Linux security issues
- *comp.os.linux.setup*—Linux installation topics
- *comp.os.linux.x*—Linux and the X Window System
- *comp.windows.x.announce*—Announcements about X11
- *comp.windows.x.apps*—Using X-based clients
- *comp.windows.x.i386unix*—X for UNIX PCs
- *comp.windows.x.intrinsics*—X Toolkit library topics
- *comp.windows.x.kde*—Using KDE and X discussions
- *comp.windows.x.motif*—All about Motif programming
- *comp.windows.x*—Discussions about X
- *linux.admin.**—Two newsgroups for Linux administrators
- *linux.debian.**—30 newsgroups about Debian
- *linux.dev.**—25 or more Linux development development newsgroups
- *linux.help*—Get help with Linux
- *linux.kernel*—The Linux kernel
- *linux.redhat.**—Red Hat-based discussions: *linux.redhat.announce, linux.redhat.list, linux.redhat.applixware, linux.redhat.misc, linux.redhat.devel, linux.redhat.pam, linux.redhat.development, linux.redhat.ppp, linux.redhat.digest, linux.redhat.rpm, linux.redhat.install, linux.redhat.sparc, linux.redhat.axp.*

Mailing Lists

Mailing lists are interactive or digest-form electronic discussions about nearly any topic. In order to use a mailing list, you must generally send an e-mail request to be subscribed to the list, and then verify the subscription with a return message from the master list mailer. After subscribing to an interactive form of list, each message sent to your list will appear in your e-mail in box. However, many lists provide a "digest" form of subscription in which a single- or half-day's traffic is condensed in a single message. This is generally preferred unless you have set up electronic mail filtering.

The main Red Hat–based mailing lists are detailed here, but there are quite a few Linux-related lists. You can search for any available online mailing list by using a typical mailing list search Web page, such as the one at: `http://paml.net/`.

> **Note**
>
> GNOME users and developers should know that more than two dozen mailing lists are available through `http://www.gnome.org/resources/mailing-lists.html`. KDE users will also benefit by perusing the KDE-related mailing lists at: `http://www.kde.org/mailinglists.html`.

Red Hat, Inc. provides a comprehensive archive and mailing list management Web page at `http://www.redhat.com/mailing-lists/`. You can use this page to subscribe to one of more than 40 mailing lists related to Red Hat Linux. Some of the more pertinent lists are

- *redhat-announce-list*—General announcements about Red Hat Linux
- *redhat-devel-list*—Information for developers using Red Hat Linux
- *redhat-install-list*—Installation issues about Red Hat Linux
- *redhat-list*—A general Red Hat Linux discussion list
- *redhat-ppp-list*—Issues regarding PPP and dialup under Red Hat Linux
- *redhat-secure-server*—Using Red Hat, Inc.'s secure server
- *redhat-watch-list*—Announcements of bug fixes, updates for Red Hat Linux
- *rpm-list*—Using the Red Hat Package Manager
- *under-the-brim*—Red Hat's helpful electronic newsletter

Internet Relay Chat

Internet Relay Chat, or IRC, is a popular form and forum of communication for many Red Hat Linux developers and users because it allows an interactive, real-time exchange of information and ideas. In order to use IRC, you'll need an IRC client and the address of a network and server hosting the desired chat channel for your discussions.

One comprehensive list of active Linux-related IRC channels can be found at `http://www.helsinki.fi/~rvaranka/Computer/Linux/IRC.shtml`. To get help with getting started with IRC, browse to `http://www.irchelp.org/`. Some of the channels of interest might be

- **#linux**—General discussions about Linux
- **#linuxhelp**—A help chat discussion for new users

Most IRC networks provide one or more Linux channels, although some providers require sign up and registration before you can access any chat channel.

RPM Package Listings

Querying the RPM Database

The Red Hat Package Manager (RPM) is an extremely powerful tool that manages packages of software for installation on a host. RPM isn't limited to a Red Hat distribution, but was developed by Red Hat as a means to distribute software via CD-ROM or the Web.

The RPM database contains information about what packages are installed on a system, what version a package is, what files it contains, any dependencies on other packages, and some summary information about the software provided by the packager. To see whether a package is installed, query the rpm database as in the following command:

```
[tdc@phoenix RedHat]$ rpm -q openssh
openssh-2.9p2-3
```

If the RPM database finds any package that matches your query, it will list the full name of that package. Usually the full name contains the version information for that particular package. From the preceding command, we can see that the installed package openssh is actually openssh-2.9p2-3, thus it is version 2.9 Preview 2-3 of OpenSSH.

Although helpful, the RPM database will only find exact matches of your query. Thus, if the database queries for a package it does not find a match for, it will return the following:

```
[tdc@phoenix RedHat]$ rpm -q gnome
package gnome is not installed
```

In this query, the database does not have a package called gnome. However, if the database was queried for gnome-core, it would have found a package by that name and returned the full name. Another easy query to perform on the RPM database is

```
rpm -qa
```

This will generate a listing of all installed packages by their full package name. Running this query and piping the output though the grep command allows the user to perform wildcard searches on the currently installed packages. As you can see, the RPM database can provide a substantial amount of information about what is installed on the system.

Table B.1 contains a listing of every RPM package available on the CD-ROMs included with this book. This table was built by querying the RPM database with the following command:

```
rpm -qa --queryformat '%{NAME}\t\t%{SUMMARY}\n'| sort
```

This query instructs RPM to query the database and list the name and summary information for each package separated by two tabs. The output was then run though the sort command, which alphabetized the listing.

TABLE B.1 RPM Package Names and Descriptions

Name	Description
4Suite	Python tools and libraries for XML processing and databases.
a2ps	Converts text and other types of files to PostScript.
abiword	A word processor.
adjtimex	A utility for adjusting kernel time variables.
alchemist	A multi-sourced configuration back end.
alchemist-devel	Files needed for developing programs that use alchemist.
alien	Install Debian, Slackware, and Stampede packages with rpm.
amanda	A network-capable tape backup solution.
amanda-client	The client component of the AMANDA tape backup system.
amanda-devel	Libraries needed for development of AMANDA applications.
amanda-server	The server side of the AMANDA tape backup system.
ami	Ami—a Korean Input Method System.
ami-gnome	Korean IMS AMI, GNOME Applet mode.
am-utils	Automount utilities including an updated version of Amd.
anaconda-runtime	Red Hat Linux installer portions needed only for fresh installs.
anaconda	The Red Hat Linux installation program.
anacron	A cron-like program that can run jobs lost during downtime.
anonftp	A fast, read-only, anonymous FTP server.
apacheconf	A configuration tool for Apache.
apache-devel	Development tools for the Apache Web server.
apache-manual	Documentation for the Apache Web server.
apache	The most widely used Web server on the Internet.
apel	A Portable Emacs Library.
apmd	Advanced Power Management (APM) BIOS utilities for laptops.
arpwatch	Network monitoring tools for tracking IP addresses on a network.
arts	A modularized sound system for KDE.

B

RPM PACKAGE
LISTINGS

TABLE B.1 continued

Name	Description
asp2php	An ASP to PHP converter.
asp2php-gtk	This package contains a GUI GTK+ interface for the asp2php file format.
aspell	A spelling checker.
aspell-ca	Catalan files for aspell.
aspell-da	Danish files for aspell.
aspell-de	German files for aspell.
aspell-devel	Static libraries and header files for aspell development.
aspell-en-ca	A Canadian English dictionary for aspell.
aspell-en-gb	A British English dictionary for aspell.
aspell-es	Spanish files for aspell.
aspell-fr	French files for aspell.
aspell-it	Italian files for aspell.
aspell-nl	Dutch files for aspell.
aspell-no	Norwegian files for aspell.
aspell-pt_BR	An aspell dictionary for Brazilian Portuguese.
aspell-pt	Portuguese files for aspell.
aspell-sv	Swedish files for aspell.
at	Job spooling tools.
atk-devel	System for layout and rendering of internationalized text.
atk	Interfaces for accessibility support.
audiofile	A library for accessing various audio file formats.
audiofile-devel	Development files for Audio File applications.
aumix	An ncurses-based audio mixer.
aumix-X11	A GTK+ GUI interface for the Aumix sound mixer.
authconfig	Text-mode tool for setting up NIS and shadow passwords.
auth_ldap	An LDAP authentication module for Apache.
autoconf	A GNU tool for automatically configuring source code.
autoconvert	Chinese HZ/GB/BIG5 encodings auto-converter.
autoconvert-xchat	Auto-convert xchat plug-ins.

TABLE B.1   continued

Name	Description
autofs	A tool for automatically mounting and unmounting filesystems.
automake	A GNU tool for automatically creating Makefiles.
autorun	A CD-ROM mounting utility.
awesfx	Utility programs for the AWE32 sound driver.
balsa	An e-mail client for basesystem The skeleton package that defines a simple Red Hat Linux system.
bash-doc	Documentation for the GNU Bourne Again shell (bash).
bash	The GNU Bourne Again shell (bash).
bc	GNU's bc (a numeric processing language) and dc (a calculator).
bcm5820	Broadcom Cryptonet BCM5820 driver for Linux.
bdflush	The daemon that starts the flushing of dirty buffers back to disk.
bg5ps	Converts Big5 encoded Chinese into printable postscript.
bind	A DNS (Domain Name System) server.
bindconf	A Red Hat DNS configuration tool.
bind-devel	Include files and libraries needed for bind DNS development.
bind-utils	Utilities for querying DNS name servers.
binutils	A GNU collection of binary utilities.
bison	A GNU general-purpose parser generator.
blas-man	Man pages for BLAS (Basic Linear Algebra Subprograms) routines.
blas	The BLAS (Basic Linear Algebra Subprograms) library.
blt	A Tk toolkit extension.
bonobo-devel	Libraries and include files for the Bonobo document model.
bonobo	Library for compound documents in GNOME.
bootparamd	A server process that provides boot information to diskless clients.

B

RPM PACKAGE
LISTINGS

TABLE B.1 continued

Name	Description
bug-buddy	A bug reporting utility for GNOME.
busybox-anaconda	Version of busybox configured for use with anaconda, the Red Hat.
busybox	Statically linked binary providing simplified versions of system.
byacc	A public domain Yacc parser generator.
bzip2	A file compression utility.
bzip2-devel	Files needed to develop applications that will use bzip2.
bzip2-libs	Libraries for applications using bzip2.
caching-nameserver	The configuration files for setting up a caching name server.
cadaver	A command-line WebDAV client.
Canna	A Japanese character set input system.
Canna-devel	Header file and library for developing programs that use Canna.
Canna-libs	The runtime library for Canna capabilities.
cdda2wav	A utility for sampling/copying .wav files from digital audio CDs.
cdecl	Encoding/decoding utilities for C/C++ function declarations.
cdlabelgen	Generates frontcards and traycards for inserting in CD jewelcases.
cdp	An interactive text-mode program for playing audio CD-ROMs.
cdparanoia	A Compact Disc Digital Audio (CDDA) extraction tool (or ripper).
cdparanoia-devel	Development tools for libcdda_paranoia (Paranoia III).
cdrdao	Writes audio CD-Rs in disk-at-once (DAO) mode.
cdrecord	A command line CD/DVD recording program.
cdrecord-devel	The libschily SCSI user level transport library.
cervisia	Graphical CVS client.

TABLE B.1   continued

Name	Description
chkconfig	A system tool for maintaining the /etc/rc*.d hierarchy.
chkfontpath	Simple utility for editing the font path for the X font server.
chromium	Chromium B.S.U. is a fast paced, arcade-style space shooter.
cipe	A kernel module and daemon for providing an encrypted IP tunnel.
cleanfeed	A spam filter for Usenet news servers commands.
compat-egcs-c++	C++ support for Red Hat 6.2 backward compatibility.
compat-egcs-g77	Fortran 77 support for Red Hat 6.2 backward compatibility.
compat-egcs-objc	Objective C support for Red Hat 6.2 backward compatibility.
compat-egcs	The GNU compiler collection for Red Hat 6.2 backward compatibility.
compat-glibc	GNU libc for Red Hat Linux 6.2 backward compatibility.
compat-libs	Runtime and development libraries for Red Hat Linux 6.2 backward compatibility.
compat-libstdc++	Standard C++ libraries for Red Hat 6.2 backward compatibility.
comsat	A mail checker client and the comsat mail-checking server.
console-tools	Tools for configuring the console.
control-center-devel	The GNOME Control Center development environment.
control-center	The GNOME Control Center.
control-panel	A Red Hat sysadmin utility program launcher for X converter.
cpio	A GNU archiving program.
cpp	The C Preprocessor.

B

RPM PACKAGE LISTINGS

TABLE B.1   continued

Name	Description
cproto	Generates function prototypes and variable declarations from C code.
cracklib	A password-checking library.
cracklib-dicts	The standard CrackLib dictionaries.
crontabs	Root crontab files used to schedule the execution of programs.
ctags	A C programming language indexing and/or cross-reference tool.
curl	A utility for getting files from remote servers (FTP, HTTP, and others).
curl-devel	Files needed for building applications with libcurl.
cvs	A version control system.
cWnn	A Chinese character input system.
cWnn-common	Common files needed by both the cWnn and tWnn Chinese input systems.
cWnn-devel	Files needed for development of cWnn and tWnn applications.
cyrus-sasl-devel	Files needed for developing applications with Cyrus SASL.
cyrus-sasl-gssapi	GSSAPI support for Cyrus SASL.
cyrus-sasl-md5	CRAM-MD5 and DIGEST-MD5 support for Cyrus SASL.
cyrus-sasl-plain	PLAIN and LOGIN support for Cyrus SASL.
cyrus-sasl	The Cyrus SASL library.
dateconfig	A graphical interface for modifying system date and time.
db1-devel	Development files for Berkeley DB (version 1) library.
db1	The BSD database library for C (version 1).
db2-devel	Development files for Berkeley DB (version 2) library.
db2	The BSD database library for C (version 2).
db31	The Berkeley DB database library for C.
db3-devel	Development files for the Berkeley DB (version 3) library.
db3	The Berkeley DB database library (version 3) for C.

TABLE B.1   continued

Name	*Description*
db3-utils	Command line tools for managing Berkeley DB (version 3) databases.
dbskkd-cdb	A dictionary server for the SKK Japanese input method system.
ddd	A GUI for several command-line debuggers.
ddskk	Daredevil SKK—Simple Kana-to-Kanji conversion program for Emacsen.
dejagnu	A front end for testing other programs.
desktop-backgrounds	Desktop background images.
dev86	A real mode 80x86 assembler and linker.
dev	The most commonly-used entries in the /dev directory.
dhcp	A DHCP (Dynamic Host Configuration Protocol) server and relay agent.
dhcpcd	A DHCP (Dynamic Host Configuration Protocol) client.
dia	A diagram drawing program.
dialog	A utility for creating TTY dialog boxes.
diffstat	A utility that provides statistics based on the output of diff.
diffutils	A GNU collection of diff utilities.
dip	Handles the connections needed for dialup IP links.
diskcheck	A hard drive space monitor.
Distutils	Python distribution utilities.
dmalloc	Memory allocation debugging routines.
docbook-dtd30-sgml	The SGML Document Type Definition for DocBook 3.0.
docbook-dtd31-sgml	The SGML Document Type Definition for DocBook 3.1.
docbook-dtd40-sgml	The SGML Document Type Definition for DocBook 4.0.
docbook-dtd412-xml	XML document type definition for DocBook 4.1.2.
docbook-dtd41-sgml	The SGML Document Type Definition for DocBook 4.1.

Table B.1 continued

Name	Description
docbook-dtd41-xml	The XML Document Type Definition for DocBook 4.1.
docbook-style-dsssl	Norman Walsh's modular stylesheets for DocBook.
docbook-utils-pdf	A script for converting DocBook documents to PDF format.
docbook-utils	Shell scripts for managing DocBook documents.
dos2unix	A text file format converter.
dosfstools	Utilities for making and checking MS-DOS FAT filesystems on Linux.
doxygen	A documentation system for C/C++.
doxygen-doxywizard	A GUI for creating and editing configuration files.
dump	Programs for backing up and restoring filesystems.
e2fsprogs-devel	Ext2 filesystem-specific static libraries and headers.
e2fsprogs	Utilities for managing the second extended (ext2) filesystem.
ed	The GNU line editor.
eel-devel	Libraries and include files for developing with Eel.
eel	Eazel Extensions Library.
ee	The Electric Eyes image viewer application.
efax	A program for faxing using a Class 1, 2, or 2.0 fax modem.
eject	A program that ejects removable media using software control.
ElectricFence	A debugger that detects memory allocation violations.
elm	The elm mail user agent.
emacs-el	The sources for elisp programs included with Emacs.
emacs-leim	Emacs Lisp code for input methods for international characters.
emacs-nox	The Emacs text editor without support for the X Window System.

TABLE B.1 continued

Name	Description
emacs	The libraries needed to run the GNU Emacs text editor.
emacs-X11	The Emacs text editor for the X Window System engine.
enlightenment	The Enlightenment window manager.
enscript	A plain ASCII to PostScript converter.
eruby	An interpreter of embedded Ruby language.
esound	Allows several audio streams to play on a single audio device.
esound-devel	Development files for EsounD applications.
ethereal-gnome	Red Hat Gnome integration for ethereal and ethereal-usermode.
ethereal	Network traffic analyzer.
ethtool	Ethernet settings tool for PCI ethernet cards.
exmh	The exmh mail handling system.
expat	A library for parsing XML.
expat-devel	Libraries and include files to develop XML applications with expat.
expect	A tcl extension for simplifying program-script interaction.
ext2ed	An ext2 filesystem editor.
extace	A GNOME sound displayer.
fam-devel	FAM, the File Alteration Monitor development files.
fam	FAM, the File Alteration Monitor.
fbset	Tools for managing a frame buffer's video mode properties.
fetchmail	A remote mail retrieval and forwarding utility.
fetchmailconf	A GUI utility for configuring your fetchmail preferences.
file	A utility for determining file types.
filesystem	The basic directory layout for a Linux system.
fileutils	The GNU versions of common file management utilities.

TABLE B.1 continued

Name	Description
findutils	The GNU versions of find utilities (find and xargs).
finger-server	The finger daemon.
finger	The finger client.
firewall-config	A configuration tool for IP firewalls and masquerading.
flex	A tool for creating scanners (text pattern recognizers).
fnlib	Color font rendering library for X11R6.
fnlib-devel	Headers, static libraries, and documentation for Fnlib.
foomatic	Foomatic printer database.
fortune-mod	A program that will display a fortune.
freecdb	A fast lookup database library and utilities.
freeciv	The Freeciv multiplayer strategy game.
freetype	A free and portable TrueType font rendering engine.
freetype-devel	Header files and static library for development with FreeType.
freetype-utils	Utilities for manipulating and examining TrueType fonts.
FreeWnn	A Japanese character set conversion system.
FreeWnn-common	Common files needed for Wnn Kana-to-Kanji conversion.
FreeWnn-devel	Development library and header files for FreeWnn.
FreeWnn-libs	A runtime library for FreeWnn.
ftpcopy	An FTP site mirroring tool.
ftp	The standard UNIX FTP (File Transfer Protocol) client.
fvwm2	An improved version of the FVWM window manager for X.
fvwm2-icons	Graphics used by the FVWM and FVWM2 window managers.
gaim	A GTK+ clone of the AOL Instant Messenger client.
gal-devel	Files for GNOME Application Library development.

TABLE B.1 continued

Name	Description
galeon	Gnome browser based on Gecko (Mozilla rendering engine).
gal	GNOME widgets and utility functions.
gated	The public release version of the GateD routing daemon.
gawk	The GNU version of the awk text processing utility.
gcc3-c++	C++ support for gcc.
gcc3-g77	Fortran 77 support for gcc version 3.
gcc3-java	Java support for gcc version 3.
gcc3-objc	Objective C support for gcc version 3.
gcc3	Various compilers (C, C++, Objective-C, Java, and so on).
gcc-c++	C++ support for the GNU gcc compiler.
gcc-chill	CHILL support for the GNU gcc compiler.
gcc-g77	Fortran 77 support for gcc.
gcc-java	Java support for gcc.
gcc-objc	Objective C support for gcc.
gcc	The GNU cc and gcc C compilers.
GConf-devel	The Gnome Config System development package.
GConf	The Gnome Config System.
gd	A graphics library for quick creation of PNG or JPEG images.
gdb	A GNU source-level debugger for C, C++ and other languages.
gdbm	A GNU set of database routines that use extensible hashing.
gdbm-devel	Development libraries and header files for the gdbm library.
gd-devel	The development libraries and header files for gd.
gdk-pixbuf	An image loading library used with GNOME.
gdk-pixbuf-devel	Files needed for developing apps to work with the GdkPixBuf library.
gdk-pixbuf-gnome	GnomeCanvas support for displaying images.
gdm	The GNOME Display Manager.

TABLE B.1 continued

Name	Description
gd-progs	Utility programs that use libgd.
gedit	A text editor for GNOME.
genromfs	Utility for creating romfs filesystems.
gettext	GNU libraries and utilities for producing multilingual messages.
gftp	A multithreaded FTP client for the X Window System.
ggv	GNOME Ghostview (ggv) is a front end for Ghostscript.
ghostscript	A PostScript interpreter and renderer.
ghostscript-fonts	Fonts for the Ghostscript PostScript interpreter.
giftrans	A program for making transparent GIFs from non-transparent GIFs.
gimp-data-extras	Extra files for the GIMP.
gimp-devel	The GIMP plug-in and extension development kit.
gimp-perl	Perl extensions and plug-ins for the GIMP.
gimp	The GNU Image Manipulation Program.
gkermit	A utility for transferring files using the Kermit protocol.
gkrellm	Multiple stacked system monitors: 1 process.
glade	A GTK+ GUI builder.
glib10	A backward compatible version of GLib.
glib2	A library of handy utility functions.
glib2-devel	The GIMP ToolKit (GTK+) and GIMP Drawing Kit (GDK) support library, beta version.
glib	A library of functions used by GDK, GTK+, and many applications.
glibc-common	Common binaries and locale data for glibc.
glibc-devel	Header and object files for development using standard C libraries.
glibc-profile	The GNU libc libraries, including support for gprof profiling.
glibc	The GNU libc libraries.

TABLE B.1 continued

Name	Description
glib-devel	GIMP ToolKit (GTK+) and GIMP Drawing Kit (GDK) support library.
glms	A GNOME hardware monitoring applet.
gmc	The GNOME version of the Midnight Commander file manager.
gmp	A GNU arbitrary precision library.
gmp-devel	Development tools for the GNU MP arbitrary precision library.
gnome-applets	Small applications for the GNOME panel.
gnome-audio-extra	Files needed for customizing GNOME event sounds.
gnome-audio	Sounds for GNOME events.
gnome-core-devel	GNOME core libraries, headers, and more.
gnome-core	The core programs for the GNOME GUI desktop environment.
gnome-games-devel	GNOME games development libraries.
gnome-games	GNOME games.
gnomeicu	An ICQ client.
gnome-kerberos	Kerberos 5 tools for GNOME.
gnome-libs-devel	Libraries and headers for GNOME application development.
gnome-libs	The main GNOME libraries.
gnome-linuxconf	The GNOME front end for linuxconf.
gnome-lokkit	A firewall configuration application for an average end user.
gnome-media	GNOME media programs.
gnome-pim-devel	GNOME PIM development files.
gnome-pim	GNOME personal productivity applications.
gnome-print-devel	Libraries and include files for developing GNOME applications.
gnome-print	Printing libraries for GNOME.
gnome-user-docs	GNOME User Documentation.
gnome-utils	GNOME utility programs.
gnome-vfs-devel	Libraries and include files for developing GNOME VFS applications.

TABLE B.1 continued

Name	Description
gnome-vfs-extras	The GNOME virtual filesystem extra modules.
gnome-vfs	The GNOME virtual filesystem libraries.
gnorpm	A graphical front end to RPM for GNOME.
gnucash	GnuCash is an application to keep track of your finances.
gnuchess	The GNU chess program.
gnumeric	A spreadsheet program for GNOME.
gnumeric-devel	Files necessary to develop gnumeric-based applications.
gnupg	A GNU utility for secure communication and data storage.
gnuplot	A program for plotting mathematical expressions and data.
gperf	A perfect hash function generator.
gphoto	Digital camera software.
gpm	A mouse server for the Linux console.
gpm-devel	Libraries and header files for developing mouse driven programs.
gq	A GUI LDAP directory browser and editor.
gqview	An image viewer.
grep	The GNU versions of grep pattern matching utilities.
grip	A GTK+ based front end for CD rippers and MP3 encoders.
groff	A document formatting system.
groff-gxditview	An X previewer for groff text processor output.
groff-perl	Parts of the groff formatting system that require Perl.
grub	GRUB—the Grand Unified Boot Loader.
gsl	The GNU Scientific Library for numerical analysis.
gsm	A GSM sound format compressor/decompressor.
gsm-devel	A development library and headers for using GSM.
gtk+10	Backward compatibility libraries linked against GTK+ and GLib 1.0.
gtk2-devel	Development tools for GTK+ applications. (Beta version).

TABLE B.1 continued

Name	Description
gtk2	The GIMP ToolKit (GTK+), a library for creating GUIs for X. (Beta version).
gtk+-devel	Development tools for GTK+ (GIMP ToolKit) applications.
gtk-doc	An API documentation generation tool for GTK+ and GNOME.
gtk-engines	Theme engines for GTK+.
gtkglarea	An OpenGL widget for the GTK+ GUI library.
gtkhtml-devel	Libraries, includes, and so on to develop gtkhtml applications.
gtkhtml	gtkhtml library.
Gtk-Perl	Perl extensions for GTK+ (the Gimp ToolKit).
gtk+	The GIMP ToolKit (GTK+), a library for creating GUIs for X.
gtoaster	A versatile CD recording package for both sound and data.
gtop	A system monitor for GNOME.
guile	A GNU implementation of Scheme for application extensibility.
guile-devel	Libraries and header files for the GUILE extensibility library.
Guppi-devel	Libraries and include files to develop Guppi-based applications.
Guppi	GNOME Data Analysis and Visualization.
gv	An X front end for the Ghostscript PostScript interpreter.
g-wrap	A tool for creating Scheme interfaces to C libraries.
g-wrap-devel	Include files and libraries needed for g-wrap development.
gzip	The GNU data compression program.
h2ps	Korean Hangul converter from text file to postscript.
hanterm-xf	Hangul Terminal for X Window System.
hdparm	A utility for displaying and/or setting hard disk parameters.

B

RPM PACKAGE
LISTINGS

TABLE B.1 continued

Name	Description
hexedit	A hexadecimal file viewer and editor.
hotplug	A helper application that loads modules for USB devices.
hotplug-gtk	GTK control interface for Hotplug PCI.
htdig	A Web indexing system.
htdig-web	Scripts and HTML code needed for using ht://Dig as a Web search.
htmlview	A script that calls an installed HTML viewer.
hwbrowser	A hardware browser.
ical	An X Window System-based calendar program.
ImageMagick	An X application for displaying and manipulating images.
ImageMagick-c++-devel	C++ bindings for the ImageMagick library.
ImageMagick-c++	ImageMagick Magick++ library (C++ bindings).
ImageMagick-devel	Static libraries and header files for ImageMagick app development.
ImageMagick-perl	ImageMagick perl bindings.
imap-devel	Development tools for programs that will use the IMAP library.
imap	Server daemons for IMAP and POP network mail protocols.
imlib	An image loading and rendering library for X11R6.
imlib-cfgeditor	A configuration editor for the Imlib library.
imlib-devel	Development tools for Imlib applications.
im	Perl scripts to replace MH, for use with the Mew mail reader.
indent	A GNU program for formatting C code.
indexhtml	The Web page you see after installing Red Hat Linux.
inews	Sends Usenet articles to a local news server for distribution.
info	A standalone TTY-based reader for GNU textinfo documentation.
initscripts	The inittab file and the /etc/init.d scripts.

TABLE B.1 continued

Name	Description
inn-devel	The INN (InterNetNews) library.
inn	The InterNetNews (INN) system, a Usenet news server.
ipchains	Tools for managing Linux kernel packet filtering capabilities.
iproute	Advanced IP routing and network device configuration tools.
iptables-ipv6	IPv6 support for iptables.
iptables	Tools for managing Linux kernel packet filtering capabilities.
iptraf	A console-based network monitoring utility.
iputils	Network monitoring tools including ping.
ipvsadm	Utility to administer the Linux Virtual Server.
ipxutils	Tools for configuring and debugging IPX interfaces and networks.
irb	The Interactive Ruby.
ircii	An Internet Relay Chat (IRC) client.
irda-utils	Utilities for infrared communication between devices.
isapnptools	Utilities for configuring ISA Plug-and-Play (PnP) devices.
iscsi	iSCSI daemon and utility programs.
isdn4k-utils	Utilities for configuring an ISDN subsystem.
isdn4k-utils-vboxgetty	ISDN voice box (getty).
isicom	Multitech Intelligent Serial Internal (ISI) support tools.
itcl	Object-oriented mega-widgets for Tcl.
jadetex	TeX macros used by Jade TeX output.
jcode.pl	A Perl library for Japanese character code conversion.
jed	A fast, compact editor based on the S-Lang screen library.
jed-common	Files needed by any Jed text editor.
jed-xjed	The X Window System version of the Jed text editor.
jikes	A Java source file to bytecode compiler.

TABLE B.1 continued

Name	Description
jisksp14	A set of Japanese fonts.
jisksp16-1990	16 dot JIS auxiliary Kanji fonts.
joe	An easy to use, modeless text editor.
joystick	Utilities for configuring most popular joysticks.
jpilot	Jpilot pilot desktop software.
junkbuster	Stops browsers from displaying ads in Web pages.
kaffe	A free virtual machine for running Java code.
kakasi	A Japanese character set conversion filter.
kakasi-devel	Files for development of applications that will use KAKASI.
kakasi-dict	The base dictionary for KAKASI.
kappa20	20 dot Japanese fonts.
kbdconfig	A text-based interface for setting and loading a keyboard map.
kcc	A Kanji code converter.
kdbg	A GUI for gdb, the GNU debugger, and KDE.
kde1-compat	Compatibility libraries for the K Desktop Environment (KDE) 1.1.x.
kde1-compat-devel	Header files and documentation for compiling KDE 1.1.2 applications.
kdeaddons-kate	Plug-ins for the Kate text editor.
kdeaddons-kicker	Plug-ins and additional applets for Kicker (the KDE panel).
kdeaddons-knewsticker	Scripts extending the functionality of KNewsTicker.
kdeaddons-konqueror	Plug-ins extending the functionality of Konqueror.
kdeaddons-noatun	Plug-ins extending the functionality of the noatun media player.
kdeadmin	Administrative tools for KDE.
kdeartwork	Additional artwork (themes, sound themes, and so on) for KDE.
kdeartwork-locolor	Low-color icons for KDE.
kdebase	Basic files needed for KDE.
kdebase-devel	Development files for kdebase.
kdebindings-devel	Development files for kdebindings.

TABLE B.1 continued

Name	Description
kdebindings	KDE bindings to non-C++ languages.
kdebindings-kmozilla	KDE bindings to Mozilla.
kdebindings-perl	Perl bindings to DCOP.
kdebindings-python	Python bindings to DCOP.
kdegames	Games for KDE.
kdegraphics-devel	Development files for kdegraphics.
kdegraphics	K Desktop Environment—Graphics Applications.
kde-i18n-British	British English support for KDE.
kde-i18n-Bulgarian	Bulgarian language support for KDE.
kde-i18n-Chinese-Big5	Chinese (Big5) language support for KDE.
kde-i18n-Chinese	Chinese (Simplified Chinese) language support for KDE.
kde-i18n-Czech	Czech language support for KDE.
kde-i18n-Danish	Danish language support for KDE.
kde-i18n-Dutch	Dutch language support for KDE.
kde-i18n-Estonian	Estonian language support for KDE.
kde-i18n-Finnish	Finnish language support for KDE.
kde-i18n-French	French language support for KDE.
kde-i18n-German	German language support for KDE.
kde-i18n-Hebrew	Hebrew language support for KDE.
kde-i18n-Hungarian	Hungarian language support for KDE.
kde-i18n-Icelandic	Icelandic language support for KDE.
kde-i18n-Italian	Italian language support for KDE.
kde-i18n-Japanese	Japanese language support for KDE.
kde-i18n-Korean	Korean language support for KDE.
kde-i18n-Lithuanian	Lithuanian language support for KDE.
kde-i18n-Norwegian	Norwegian (Bokmaal) language support for KDE.
kde-i18n-Norwegian-Nynorsk	Norwegian (Nynorsk) language support for KDE.
kde-i18n-Polish	Polish language support for KDE.
kde-i18n-Portuguese	Portuguese language support for KDE.
kde-i18n-Romanian	Romanian language support for KDE.
kde-i18n-Russian	Russian language support for KDE.
kde-i18n-Slovak	Slovak language support for KDE.

B

RPM PACKAGE
LISTINGS

Table B.1 continued

Name	Description
kde-i18n-Slovenian	Slovenian language support for KDE.
kde-i18n-Spanish	Spanish language support for KDE.
kde-i18n-Swedish	Swedish language support for KDE.
kde-i18n-Turkish	Turkish language support for KDE.
kde-i18n-Ukrainian	Ukrainian language support for KDE.
kdelibs-devel	Header files and documentation for compiling KDE applications.
kdelibs-sound-devel	Header files for compiling KDE sound applications.
kdelibs-sound	KDE libraries needed to support sound.
kdelibs	Various libraries for KDE.
kdemultimedia-devel	Development files for kdemultimedia.
kdemultimedia	Multimedia applications for the K Desktop Environment (KDE).
kdenetwork	Networking applications for KDE.
kdenetwork-ppp	PPP configuration utilities for KDE.
kdepim-cellphone	KDE support for synchronizing data with cellphones.
kdepim-devel	Development files for kdepim.
kdepim	Personal information management tools for KDE.
kdepim-pilot	KDE support for synchronizing data with a Palm or compatible PDA.
kdesdk-devel	Development files for kdesdk.
kdesdk	The KDE Software Development Kit (SDK).
kdetoys	Toys for KDE.
kdeutils	KDE utilities.
kdevelop	Integrated Development Environment for C++/C.
kdoc	Documentation for the K Desktop Environment (KDE).
kernel-BOOT	The version of the Linux kernel used on installation boot disks.
kernel-debug	The Linux Kernel compiled with options for kernel debugging
kernel-doc	Various pieces of documentation found in the kernel source.

Table B.1   continued

Name	*Description*
kernel-enterprise	Linux kernel compiled with options for a typical enterprise server.
kernel-headers	Header files for the Linux kernel.
kernel-pcmcia-cs	The daemon and device drivers for using PCMCIA adapters.
kernel-smp	The Linux kernel compiled for SMP machines.
kernel-source	The source code for the Linux kernel.
kernel	The Linux kernel (the core of the Linux operating system).
kinput2-canna-wnn6	The kinput2 input system for both Canna and Wnn6.
knm_new	The revised version of the Kaname-cho font.
koffice	A set of office applications for KDE.
koffice-devel	Development files for Koffice.
kon2	A Kanji emulator for the console.
kon2-fonts	Fonts for the KON Kanji emulator for the console.
kpppload	A PPP connection load monitor for KDE.
krb5-devel	Development files needed to compile Kerberos 5 programs.
krb5-libs	The shared libraries used by Kerberos 5.
krb5-server	The server programs for Kerberos 5.
krb5-workstation	Kerberos 5 programs for use on workstations.
krbafs	A Kerberos to AFS bridging library, built against Kerberos 5.
krbafs-devel	Development files for use with the krbafs package.
krbafs-utils	Kerberos/AFS utilities.
ksconfig	A graphical interface for making kickstart files.
ksymoops	The kernel oops and error message decoder.
kterm	A Kanji (Japanese character set) terminal emulator for X.
kudzu-devel	Development files needed for hardware probing using kudzu.
kudzu	The Red Hat Linux hardware probing tool.
kWnn	A Korean character set input system.

TABLE B.1 continued

Name	Description
kWnn-devel	Files needed for developing apps, which will use kWnn.
lam	The LAM (Local Area Multicomputer) programming environment.
lapack-man	Documentation for the LAPACK numerical linear algebra libraries.
lapack	The LAPACK libraries for numerical linear algebra.
lclint	A C code checker.
less	A text file browser similar to more, but with additional options.
lesstif	An OSF/Motif clone.
lesstif-devel	Static library and header files for LessTif/Motif development.
lftp	A sophisticated file transfer program.
lha	An archiving and compression utility for LHarc format archives.
libao	Cross Platform Audio Output Library.
libao-devel	Cross Platform Audio Output Library Development.
libcap-devel	Development files for libcap.
libcap	Library for getting and setting POSIX.1e capabilities.
libelf	An ELF object file access library.
libesmtp-devel	Headers and development libraries for libESMTP.
libesmtp	SMTP client library.
libgal7	The GNOME Application Library.
libgcc	GCC version 3.0 shared support library.
libgcj3-devel	Libraries for Java development using gcc version 3.
libgcj3	Java runtime library for gcc.
libgcj-devel	Libraries for Java development using gcc.
libgcj	The Java runtime library for gcc.
libghttp-devel	Files for development using libghttp.
libghttp	GNOME HTTP client library.
libglade-devel	The files needed for libglade application development.
libglade	The libglade library for loading user interfaces.

TABLE B.1 continued

Name	Description
libgnomeprint15	Printing libraries for GNOME.
libgtop	A library that retrieves system information.
libgtop-devel	Files needed to develop LibGTop applications.
libgtop-examples	Development examples for the LibGTop library.
libjpeg6a	A backward compatibility library for manipulating JPEGs.
libjpeg	A library for manipulating JPEG image format files.
libjpeg-devel	Development tools for programs that will use the libjpeg library.
libmng	A library that supports MNG graphics.
libmng-devel	Development files for the LibMNG library.
libmng-static	A statically linked version of the LibMNG library.
libodbc++	An ODBC class library that emulates the JDBC interface.
libodbc++-devel	Files for development using the libodbc++ library.
libodbc++-qt	Support for Qt integration into libodbc++.
libogg-devel	Files needed for development using libogg.
libogg	The Ogg bitstream file format library.
libole2-devel	Files needed for development of libole2 applications.
libole2	The Structured Storage OLE2 library.
libpcap	A system-independent interface for user-level packet capture.
libpng	A library of functions for manipulating PNG image format files.
libpng-devel	Development tools for manipulating PNG image format files.
libPropList	A utility library for storing application configuration information.
librep	A shared library that implements a Lisp dialect.
librep-devel	Include files and link libraries for librep development.
librsvg	An SVG library based on libart.
librsvg-devel	Libraries and include files for developing with librsvg.

TABLE B.1   continued

Name	Description
libsigc++-devel	Development tools for the Typesafe Signal Framework for C++.
libsigc++	The Typesafe Signal Framework for C++.
libstdc++3-devel	Header files and libraries for C++ development.
libstdc++3	GNU Standard C++ Library version 3.
libstdc++-devel	The header files and libraries needed for C++ development.
libstdc++	The GNU Standard C++ Library v3.
libtabe	Chinese lexicons library for xcin-2.5.2.
libtabe-devel	Header files and libraries for developing apps that will use libtabe.
libtermcap	A basic system library for accessing the termcap database.
libtermcap-devel	Development tools for accessing the termcap database.
libtiff	A library of functions for manipulating TIFF format image files.
libtiff-devel	Development tools for programs that will use the libtiff library.
libtool-libs13	The GNU libtool, which simplifies the use of shared libraries.
libtool-libs	Runtime libraries for GNU libtool.
libtool	The GNU libtool, which simplifies the use of shared libraries.
libungif	A library for manipulating GIF format image files.
libungif-devel	Development tools for using the libungif library.
libungif-progs	Programs for manipulating GIF format image files.
libunicode	A Unicode manipulation library.
libunicode-devel	Files for development of programs that will use libunicode.
libuser	A user account administration library.
libuser-devel	Files needed for developing applications that use libuser.
libvorbis-devel	Development tools for Vorbis applications.
libvorbis	The Vorbis General Audio Compression Codec.

TABLE B.1   continued

Name	Description
libxml10	A backward compatibility XML library.
libxml2-devel	Libraries, includes, and so on to develop XML and HTML applications.
libxml2	Library providing XML and HTML support.
libxml	An XML library.
libxml-devel	Files for developing libxml applications.
libxslt-devel	Libraries, includes, and so on to develop XML and HTML applications.
libxslt	Library providing XSLT support.
licq	An ICQ clone for online messaging.
licq-gnome	GNOME front end for licq.
licq-kde	KDE front end for licq.
licq-qt	Qt front end for licq.
licq-text	Text mode front end for licq.
lilo	The boot loader for Linux and other operating systems.
links	A text-mode Web browser.
linuxconf	A system configuration tool.
linuxconf-devel	The tools needed for developing linuxconf modules.
lm_sensors-devel	Development files for programs that will use lm_sensors.
lm_sensors	Hardware monitoring tools.
locale_config	A tool for configuring your system's locale.
lockdev	A library for locking devices.
lockdev-devel	The header files and a static library for the lockdev library.
logrotate	Rotates, compresses, removes, and mails system log files.
logwatch	A log file analysis program.
lokkit	Firewall configuration application for an average end user.
losetup	Programs for setting up and configuring loopback devices.

B

RPM PACKAGE LISTINGS

TABLE B.1 continued

Name	Description
lout-doc	The documentation for the Lout document formatting language.
lout	The Lout document formatting language.
LPRng	The LPRng print spooler.
lrzsz	The lrz and lsz modem communications programs.
lslk	A lock file lister.
lsof	A utility that lists open files on a Linux/UNIX system.
ltrace	Tracks runtime library calls from dynamically linked executables.
lv	A multilingual file viewer.
lynx	A text-based Web browser.
m2crypto	Support for using OpenSSL in python scripts.
m4	The GNU macro processor.
macutils	Utilities for manipulating Macintosh file formats.
Maelstrom	A space combat game.
magicdev	A GNOME daemon for automatically mounting/playing CDs.
MagicPoint	X based presentation software.
mailcap	Associates helper applications with particular file types.
mailman	Mailing list manager with built-in Web access.
mailx	The /bin/mail program for sending quick e-mail messages.
make	A GNU tool that simplifies the build process for users.
MAKEDEV	A program used for creating the device files in /dev.
man	A set of documentation tools: man, apropos, and whatis.
man-pages-cs	Czech man pages from the Linux Documentation Project.
man-pages-da	Danish man pages from the Linux Documentation Project.
man-pages-de	German man pages from the Linux Documentation Project.

TABLE B.1 continued

Name	Description
man-pages-es	Spanish man pages from the Linux Documentation Project.
man-pages-fr	French man pages from the Linux Documentation Project.
man-pages-it	Italian man pages from the Linux Documentation Project.
man-pages-ja	Japanese man pages from the Linux Documentation Project.
man-pages-ko	Korean man (manual) pages from the Linux Documentation Project.
man-pages	Man (manual) pages from the Linux Documentation Project.
man-pages-pl	Polish man pages from the Linux Documentation Project.
man-pages-ru	Russian man pages from the Linux Documentation Project.
mars-nwe	NetWare file and print servers that run on Linux systems.
mawk	An interpreter for the AWK programming language.
maximum-rpm	The *Maximum RPM* book.
mc	A user-friendly file manager and visual shell.
mcserv	Server for the Midnight Commander network file management system.
memprof	A tool for memory profiling and leak detection.
Mesa	A 3D graphics library similar to OpenGL.
Mesa-demos	Sample applications using the Mesa 3D graphics library.
Mesa-devel	Development files for the Mesa 3D graphics library.
metamail	A program for handling multimedia mail using the mailcap file.
mew	Mew—Messaging in the Emacs World.
mgetty	A getty replacement for use with data and fax modems.
mgetty-sendfax	Provides support for sending faxes over a modem.
mgetty-viewfax	An X Window System fax viewer.

B

RPM PACKAGE
LISTINGS

TABLE B.1 continued

Name	Description
mgetty-voice	A program for using your modem and mgetty as an answering machine.
micq	A clone of the Mirabilis ICQ online messaging program.
mikmod	A MOD music file player.
mingetty	A compact getty program for virtual consoles only.
miniChinput	A Chinese XIM server.
minicom	A text-based modem control and terminal emulation program.
mkbootdisk	Creates a boot floppy disk for booting a system.
mkinitrd	Creates an initial ramdisk image for preloading modules.
mkisofs	Creates an image of an ISO9660 filesystem.
mkkickstart	Writes a kickstart description of the current machine.
mktemp	A small utility for safely making /tmp files.
mkxauth	A utility for managing Xauthority files.
mm	A shared memory library.
mm-devel	Files needed for developing applications that use the MM library.
mod_auth_any	Basic authentication for the Apache Web server using arbitrary shell.
mod_auth_mysql	Basic authentication for the Apache Web server using a MySQL.
mod_auth_pgsql	Basic authentication for the Apache Web server using a PostgreSQL.
mod_bandwidth	A bandwidth-limiting module for use with Apache.
mod_dav	A DAV module for Apache.
modemtool	A tool for selecting the serial port for your modem.
mod_perl	An embedded Perl interpreter for the Apache Web server.
mod_put	A module that implements the PUT and DELETE methods for Apache.
mod_python	An embedded Python interpreter for the Apache Web server.

TABLE B.1 continued

Name	Description
mod_roaming	Enables Netscape Communicator roaming profiles with Apache.
mod_ssl	Cryptography support for the Apache Web server.
mod_throttle	A module that implements the bandwidth and request throttling for Apache.
modutils	Kernel module management utilities.
mount	Programs for mounting and unmounting filesystems.
mouseconfig	The Red Hat Linux mouse configuration tool.
mozilla	A Web browser.
mozilla-chat	IRC client integrated with Mozilla.
mozilla-devel	Files needed for development of Mozilla.
mozilla-mail	A Mozilla-based mail client.
mozilla-psm	SSL support for Mozilla.
mpage	A tool for printing multiple pages of text on each printed page.
mpg321	An MPEG audio player.
mrtg	Multi-Router Traffic Grapher.
mtools	Programs for accessing MS-DOS disks without mounting the disks.
mtr	A network diagnostic tool.
mtr-gtk	The GTK+ interface for mtr.
mt-st	A tool for controlling tape drives.
mtx	A SCSI media changer control program.
mutt	A text mode mail user agent.
mx	A collection of Python software tools.
MyODBC	ODBC driver for MySQL.
mysqloliont0	MySQL client and shared library shipped with Red Hat Linux 7.
mysql-devel	Files for development of MySQL applications.
mysql	MySQL client programs and shared library.
MySQL-python	An interface to MySQL.
mysql-server	The MySQL server and related files.
nasm	A portable x86 assembler that uses Intel-like syntax.

B

RPM PACKAGE LISTINGS

Table B.1   continued

Name	Description
nasm-doc	Documentation for NASM.
nasm-rdoff	Tools for the RDOFF binary format, sometimes used with NASM.
nautilus-devel	Libraries and include files for developing Nautilus components.
nautilus-mozilla	Nautilus component for use with Mozilla.
nautilus	Nautilus is a network user environment.
ncftp	An improved FTP client.
ncompress	Fast compression and decompression utilities.
ncpfs	Utilities for the ncpfs filesystem, a NetWare client for Linux.
nc	Reads and writes data across network connections using TCP or UDP.
ncurses4	A backward compatible version of ncurses.
ncurses	A CRT screen handling and optimization package.
ncurses-devel	The development files for applications that use ncurses.
nedit	A GUI text editor for systems with X and Motif.
netconfig	A text-based tool for simple configuration of ethernet devices.
netpbm	A library for handling different graphics file formats.
netpbm-devel	Development tools for programs that will use the netpbm libraries.
netpbm-progs	Tools for manipulating graphics files in netpbm supported formats.
netscape-common	Files shared by Netscape Navigator and Communicator.
netscape-communicator	The Netscape Communicator suite of tools.
netscape-navigator	The Netscape Navigator Web browser.
net-tools	Basic networking tools.
newt	A development library for text mode user interfaces.
newt-devel	Newt windowing toolkit development files.
nfs-utils	NFS utilities and supporting daemons for the kernel NFS server.

Table B.1 continued

Name	Description
nhpf	Hangul Printing Filter for a Netscape (2.0 or later) PS-saved file.
njamd	A debugger that detects memory allocation violations.
nkf	A Kanji code conversion filter.
nmap-frontend	Gtk+ front end for nmap.
nmap	Network exploration tool and security scanner.
nmh	A mail handling system with a command line interface.
nscd	A Name Service Caching Daemon (nscd).
nss_db	An NSS library for the Berkeley DB.
nss_db-compat	An NSS compatibility library for Berkeley Databases and glibc 2.0.x.
nss_ldap	NSS library and PAM module for LDAP.
ntp	Synchronizes system time using the Network Time Protocol (NTP).
ntsysv	A tool to set the stop/start of system services in a runlevel.
nut-cgi	CGI utilities for use with NUT.
nut-client	Client monitoring utilities for NUT.
nut	Tools for monitoring UPS equipment.
nvi-m17n-canna	The nvi multiligualized text editor with support for Canna.
nvi-m17n	Common files for the nvi multilingualized text editor.
nvi-m17n-nocanna	The nvi multiligualized text editor without support for Canna.
oaf-devel	Libraries and include files for OAF.
oaf	Object activation framework for GNOME.
octave	A high-level language for numerical computations.
open	A tool that will start a program on a virtual console.
openjade	A DSSSL implementation.
openldap12	Shared libraries for OpenLDAP 1.2 applications.
openldap-clients	Client programs for OpenLDAP.
openldap-devel	OpenLDAP development libraries and header files.

B

RPM PACKAGE LISTINGS

TABLE B.1   continued

Name	Description
openldap-servers	OpenLDAP servers and related files.
openldap	The configuration files, libraries, and documentation for OpenLDAP.
openssh-askpass	A passphrase dialog for OpenSSH and X.
openssh-askpass-gnome	A passphrase dialog for OpenSSH, X, and GNOME.
openssh-clients	OpenSSH clients.
openssh-server	The OpenSSH server daemon.
openssh	The OpenSSH implementation of SSH.
openssl095a	The OpenSSL toolkit.
openssl096	Secure Sockets Layer Toolkit.
openssl-devel	Files for development of applications that will use OpenSSL.
openssl-perl	Perl scripts provided with OpenSSL.
openssl	The OpenSSL toolkit.
ORBit	A high-performance CORBA Object Request Broker.
ORBit-devel	Development libraries, header files, and utilities for ORBit.
p2c	A Pascal to C translator.
pam	A security tool that provides authentication for applications.
pam-devel	Files needed for developing PAM-aware applications and modules for PAM.
pam_krb5	A Pluggable Authentication Module (PAM) for Kerberos 5.
pam_smb	A Pluggable Authentication Module (PAM) for use with SMB servers.
pan	A GNOME/GTK+ news reader for X.
pango-devel	System for layout and rendering of internationalized text.
pango	System for layout and rendering of internationalized text.
parted-devel	Files for developing apps that will manipulate disk partitions.

TABLE B.1 continued

Name	Description
parted	The GNU disk partition manipulation program.
passwd	The passwd utility for setting/changing passwords using PAM.
patch	The GNU patch command, for modifying/upgrading files.
pax	A file archiving tool.
pccts	The Purdue Compiler-Compiler Tool Set.
pciutils-devel	Linux PCI development library.
pciutils	PCI bus related utilities.
pcre-devel	Development files for pcre.
pcre	Perl-compatible regular expression library.
pdksh	A public domain clone of the Korn shell (ksh).
perl-DateManip	DateManip module for perl.
perl-DBD-MySQL	An implementation of DBI for MySQL.
perl-DBD-Pg	A PostgresSQL interface for Perl.
perl-DBI	A database access API for Perl.
perl-Digest-MD5	A perl interface to the MD5 digest algorithm.
perl-File-MMagic	A Perl5 module that guesses file types based on their contents.
perl-HTML-Parser	HTML-Parser module for perl (World_Wide_Web_HTML_HTTP_CGI/HTML).
perl-HTML-Tagset	This module contains data tables useful in dealing with HTML.
perl-libnet	Libnet module for perl (Networking_Devices_IPC/Net).
perl-libwww-perl	Libwww-perl module for perl.
perl-libxml-enno	The libxml-enno module for perl.
perl-libxml-perl	The libxml-perl module for perl.
perl-MIME-Base64	Perl module for MIME encoding/decoding (base64 and quoted-printable).
perl-NKF	A Perl extension for nkf, the Network Kanji Filter.
perl-Parse-Yapp	Parse-Yapp module for perl.
perl-SGMLSpm	A Perl library for parsing the output of nsgmls.

TABLE B.1 continued

Name	Description
perl-Storable	Storable module for perl.
perl-Text-Kakasi	A KAKASI library module for Perl.
perl	The Perl programming language.
perl-URI	URI module for perl (World_Wide_Web_HTML_HTTP_CGI/URI).
perl-XML-Dumper	Perl module for dumping Perl objects from/to XML.
perl-XML-Encoding	XML-Encoding module for perl.
perl-XML-Grove	XML-Grove module for perl.
perl-XML-Parser	A perl module for parsing XML documents.
perl-XML-Twig	XML-Twig module for perl.
php-devel	Files needed for building PHP extensions.
php-imap	An Apache module for PHP applications that use IMAP.
php-ldap	A module for PHP applications that use LDAP.
php-manual	The PHP manual, in HTML format.
php-mysql	A module for PHP applications that use MySQL databases.
php-odbc	A module for PHP applications that use ODBC databases.
php-pgsql	A PostgreSQL database module for PHP.
php	The PHP HTML-embedded scripting language.
pidentd	An implementation of the RFC1413 identification server.
pilot-link-devel	PalmPilot development header files.
pilot-link	File transfer utilities between Linux and PalmPilots.
pine	A commonly used, MIME compliant mail and news reader.
pinfo	An info file viewer.
pkgconfig	A tool for determining compilation options.
playmidi	A MIDI sound file player.
playmidi-X11	An X Window System based MIDI sound file player.
plugger	A utility that calls helper applications for Navigator.

TABLE B.1   continued

Name	Description
pmake	The BSD 4.4 version of make.
pnm2ppa	Drivers for printing to HP PPA printers.
popt	A C library for parsing command line parameters.
portmap	A program that manages RPC connections.
postgresql-contrib	Contributed source and binaries distributed with PostgreSQL.
postgresql-devel	PostgreSQL development header files and libraries.
postgresql-docs	Extra documentation for PostgreSQL.
postgresql-jdbc	Files needed for Java programs to access a PostgreSQL database.
postgresql-libs	The shared libraries required for any PostgreSQL clients.
postgresql-odbc	The ODBC driver needed for accessing a PostgreSQL DB using ODBC.
postgresql-perl	Development module needed for Perl code to access a PostgreSQL DB.
postgresql	PostgreSQL client programs and libraries.
postgresql-python	Development module for Python code to access a PostgreSQL DB.
postgresql-server	The programs needed to create and run a PostgreSQL server.
postgresql-tcl	A Tcl client library and the PL/Tcl procedural language for PostgreSQL database.
postgresql-tk	Tk shell and tk-based GUI for PostgreSQL.
ppp	The PPP (Point-to-Point Protocol) daemon.
prelink	An ELF prelinking utility.
printconf	A printer configuration back end/front end combination.
printconf-gui	A GUI front end for printconf.
procinfo	A tool for gathering and displaying system information.
procmail	The procmail mail processing program.

B

RPM PACKAGE
LISTINGS

Table B.1   continued

Name	Description
procps	System and process monitoring utilities.
procps-X11	An X-based system message monitoring utility.
psacct	Utilities for monitoring process activities.
psgml	A GNU Emacs major mode for editing SGML documents.
psmisc	Utilities for managing processes on your system.
pspell-devel	Static libraries and header files for pspell.
pspell	Portable Spell Checker Interface Library.
psutils	Utilities for use with PostScript documents.
pump	A Bootp and DHCP client for automatic IP configuration.
pump-devel	Development tools for sending DHCP and BOOTP requests.
pvm-gui	A Tcl/Tk GUI front end for monitoring and managing a PVM cluster.
pvm	Libraries for distributed computing.
pwdb	The password database library.
pxe	A Linux PXE (Preboot eXecution Environment) server.
pychecker	A python source code checking tool.
pygnome-applet	Python bindings for GNOME Panel applets.
pygnome-capplet	Python bindings for GNOME Panel applets.
pygnome-devel	Files that are useful for wrapping GNOME addon libraries.
pygnome-gtkhtml	Python bindings for GtkHTML.
pygnome-libglade	GNOME support for the libglade Python wrapper.
pygnome	Python bindings for the GNOME libraries.
pygtk-devel	Files needed to build wrappers for GTK+ addon libraries.
pygtk-glarea	A wrapper for the GtkGLArea widget for use with PyGTK.
pygtk-libglade	A wrapper for the libglade library for use with PyGTK.

TABLE B.1   continued

Name	Description
pygtk	Python bindings for the GTK+ widget set.
PyQt-devel	Files needed to build other bindings based on Qt.
PyQt-examples	Examples for PyQt.
PyQt	Python bindings for Qt.
python2	An interpreted, interactive, object-oriented programming language.
python2-devel	Development files for Python 2.
python	An interpreted, interactive, object-oriented programming language.
python-devel	The libraries and header files needed for Python development.
python-docs	Documentation for the Python programming language.
pythonlib	A library of Python code used by various Red Hat Linux programs.
python-tools	A collection of development tools included with Python.
python-xmlrpc	A set of Python modules for XML-RPC support.
PyXML	XML libraries for python.
qt1x	A backward compatible library for apps linked to Qt 1.x.
qt1x-devel	Qt 1.x development files for legacy applications.
qt1x-GL	An OpenGL (3-D graphics) add-on for the Qt GUI toolkit.
qt3-designer	Interface designer (IDE) for the Qt toolkit.
qt3-devel	Development files and documentation for the Qt GUI toolkit.
qt3	The shared library for the Qt GUI toolkit.
qt3-Xt	An Xt (X Toolkit) compatibility add-on for the Qt GUI toolkit.
qt-designer	An interface designer for the Qt toolkit.
qt-devel	Development files and documentation for the Qt GUI toolkit.

B

RPM PACKAGE LISTINGS

TABLE B.1 continued

Name	Description
qt-static	A version of the Qt GUI toolkit for static linking.
qt	The shared library for the Qt GUI toolkit.
qt-Xt	An Xt (X Toolkit) compatibility add-on for the Qt GUI toolkit.
quanta	An HTML editor for KDE.
quota	System administration tools for monitoring users' disk usage.
radvd	A Router Advertisement daemon.
raidtools	Tools for creating and maintaining software RAID devices.
rarpd	The RARP daemon.
rcs	Revision Control System (RCS) file version management tools.
rdate	Tool for getting the date/time from a remote machine.
rdist	Maintains identical copies of files on multiple machines.
readline2.2.1	A library for reading and returning lines from a terminal.
readline41	A library for editing command lines.
readline	A library for editing typed command lines.
readline-devel	Files needed to develop programs that use the readline library.
RealPlayer	Welcome to RealPlayer 8.0!
redhat-config-network	The Network Administration Tool for Red Hat Linux.
redhat-config-users	A graphical interface for administering users and groups.
redhat-logos	Red Hat-related icons and pictures.
redhat-release	The Red Hat Linux release file.
reiserfs-utils	Tools for creating, repairing, and debugging ReiserFS filesystems.
rep-gtk-gnome	GNOME bindings for the librep Lisp interpreter.
rep-gtk	GTK+ bindings for librep Lisp environment.

TABLE B.1 continued

Name	Description
rep-gtk-libglade	A librep binding of libglade for loading user interfaces.
rhmask	Generates and restores mask files.
rhn_register-gnome	A GUI client for the Red Hat Network registration program.
rhn_register	The Red Hat Network Services registration program.
rmt	Provides certain programs with access to remote tape devices.
rootfiles	The basic required files for the root user's directory.
routed	The routing daemon that maintains routing tables.
rp3	The Red Hat graphical PPP management tool.
rpm2html	Translates an RPM database and dependency information into HTML.
rpm-build	Scripts and executable programs used to build packages.
rpmdb-redhat	The entire RPM database for the Red Hat Linux distribution.
rpm-devel	Development files for manipulating RPM packages.
rpmfind	Finds and transfers RPM files for a specified program.
rpmlint	A development tool for checking the correctness of RPM packages.
rpm-perl	Native bindings to the RPM API for Perl.
rpm-python	Python bindings for apps that will manipulate RPM packages.
rpm	The RPM package management system.
rp-pppoe	A PPP over Ethernet client (for xDSL support).
rsh	Clients for remote access (rsh, rlogin, rcp).
rsh-server	Servers for remote access (rsh, rlogin, rcp).
rsync	A program for synchronizing files over a network.
ruby	An interpreter of object-oriented scripting language.
ruby-devel	A Ruby development environment.
ruby-docs	Manuals and FAQs for scripting language Ruby.

B

RPM PACKAGE
LISTINGS

TABLE B.1   continued

Name	Description
ruby-libs	Libraries necessary to run Ruby.
ruby-tcltk	Tcl/Tk interface for scripting language Ruby.
rusers	Displays the names of users logged into machines on the local network.
rusers-server	Server for the rusers protocol.
rwall	Client for sending messages to a host's logged in users.
rwall-server	Server for sending messages to a host's logged in users.
rwho	Displays who is logged in to local network machines.
rxvt	A color VT102 terminal emulator for the X Window System.
samba-client	Samba (SMB) client programs.
samba-common	Files used by both Samba servers and clients.
samba-swat	The Samba SMB server configuration program.
samba	The Samba SMB server.
sane-backends-devel	The SANE (a universal scanner interface) development toolkit.
sane-backends	Scanner access software.
sane-frontends	Graphical front end to SANE.
sash	A statically-linked shell, including some built-in basic commands.
sawfish	An extensible window manager for the X Window System.
sawfish-themer	A GUI for creating sawfish window manager themes.
screen	A screen manager that supports multiple logins on one terminal.
scrollkeeper	ScrollKeeper is a cataloging system for documentation on open systems.
SDL11	Simple DirectMedia Layer compatibility libraries.
SDL	A cross-platform multimedia library.
SDL-devel	Files needed to develop Simple DirectMedia Layer applications.

TABLE B.1 continued

Name	Description
SDL_image	A sample image loading library for SDL.
SDL_image-devel	Development files for the SDL image loading library.
SDL_mixer	A simple multi-channel audio mixer library for SDL.
SDL_mixer-devel	Development files for the SDL_mixer audio mixer library.
SDL_net-devel	Libraries and includes to develop SDL networked applications.
SDL_net	SDL portable network library.
sed	A GNU stream text editor.
semi	A library that provides MIME features for Emacs 20.
semi-xemacs	A library that provides MIME feature for XEmacs 21.
sendmail	A widely used Mail Transport Agent (MTA).
sendmail-cf	The files needed to reconfigure Sendmail.
sendmail-doc	Documentation about the Sendmail Mail Transport Agent program.
serviceconf	Serviceconf is an initscript and xinetd configuration utility.
setserial	A utility for configuring serial ports.
setup	A set of system configuration and setup files.
setuptool	A text mode system configuration tool.
sgml-common	Common SGML catalog and DTD files.
sgml-tools	A text formatting package based on SGML.
shadow-utils	Utilities for managing accounts and shadow password files.
shapecfg	A configuration tool for setting traffic bandwidth parameters.
sharutils	The GNU shar utilities for managing shell archives.
sh-utils	A set of GNU utilities commonly used in shell scripts.
sip-devel	Files needed to generate Python bindings for any C++ class library.
sip	SIP—Python/C++ Bindings Generator.

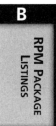

TABLE B.1 continued

Name	Description
skkdic	The SKK dictionary.
skkinput	A Japanese language input application for X.
slang-devel	The static library and header files for development using S-Lang.
slang	The shared library for the S-Lang extension language.
sliplogin	A login program for SLIP connections.
slocate	Finds files on a system via a central database.
slrn	A threaded Internet news reader.
slrn-pull	Offline news reading support for the SLRN news reader.
smpeg-devel	Development files for the SMPEG (SDL MPEG Player Library).
smpeg	The plaympeg audio/video player and the SMPEG library.
smpeg-xmms	An MPEG video plug-in for XMMS.
snavigator	Red Hat Source Navigator.
sndconfig	The Red Hat Linux sound configuration tool.
sox	A general purpose sound file conversion tool.
sox-devel	The SoX sound file format converter libraries.
specspo	Red Hat package descriptions, summaries, and groups.
squid	The Squid proxy caching server.
stat	A tool for finding out information about a specified file.
statserial	A tool that displays the status of serial port modem lines.
strace	Tracks and displays system calls associated with a running process.
stunnel	An SSL-encrypting socket wrapper.
sudo	Allows restricted root access for specified users.
swig	Connects C/C++/Objective C to some high-level programming languages.
switchdesk	A desktop environment switcher.

TABLE B.1 continued

Name	Description
switchdesk-gnome	A GNOME interface for the Desktop Switcher.
switchdesk-kde	A KDE interface for the Desktop Switcher.
sylpheed	A GTK+ based, lightweight, and fast e-mail client.
symlinks	A utility that maintains a system's symbolic links.
sysctlconfig	A configuration tool for operating system tunable parameters.
sysklogd	System logging and kernel message trapping daemons.
syslinux	A simple kernel loader that boots from a FAT filesystem.
sysreport	Gathers system hardware and configuration information.
sysstat	The sar and iostat system monitoring commands.
SysVinit	Programs that control basic system processes.
taipeifonts	Taipei Chinese Big 5 Fonts.
talk-server	The talk server for one-on-one Internet chatting.
talk	Talk client for one-on-one Internet chatting.
tamago	The Tamago multilingual input environment for Emacs.
taper	A menu-driven file backup system.
tar	A GNU file archiving program.
tcl	An embeddable scripting language.
tcllib	A library of utility modules for Tcl.
tclx	Extensions for Tcl.
tcpdump	A network traffic monitoring tool.
tcp_wrappers	A security tool that acts as a wrapper for TCP daemons.
tcsh	An enhanced version of csh, the C shell.
telnet-server	The server program for the telnet remote login protocol.
telnet	The client program for the telnet remote login protocol.

B

RPM PACKAGE
LISTINGS

TABLE B.1   continued

Name	*Description*
termcap	The terminal feature database used by certain applications.
tetex-afm	A converter for PostScript font metric files for use with TeX.
tetex-doc	The documentation files for the TeX text formatting system.
tetex-dvilj	A DVI to HP PCL (Printer Control Language) converter.
tetex-dvips	A DVI to PostScript converter for the TeX text formatting system.
tetex-fonts	The font files for the TeX text formatting system.
tetex-latex	The LaTeX front end for the TeX text formatting system.
tetex	The TeX text formatting system.
tetex-xdvi	An X viewer for DVI files.
texinfo	Tools needed to create Texinfo format documentation files.
textutils	A set of GNU text file modifying utilities.
tftp-server	The server for the Trivial File Transfer Protocol (TFTP).
tftp	The client for the Trivial File Transfer Protocol (TFTP).
time	A GNU utility for monitoring a program's use of system resources.
timeconfig	Text mode tools for setting system time parameters.
timidity++	A software wavetable MIDI synthesizer.
tix	A set of capable widgets for Tk.
tkinter	A graphical user interface for the Python scripting language.
tk	The Tk GUI toolkit for Tcl, with shared libraries.
tmake	Makefile generator.
tmpwatch	A utility for removing files based on when they were last accessed.

TABLE B.1 continued

Name	Description
traceroute	Traces the route taken by packets over a TCP/IP network.
transfig	Utilities for creating TeX documents with portable graphics.
tree	A utility that displays a tree view of the contents of directories.
tripwire	A system integrity assessment tool.
ttcp	A tool for testing TCP connections.
ttfm	True Type Font Manager.
ttfonts	A set of TrueType fonts.
ttfonts-ja	Free Japanese TrueType fonts.
ttfonts-ko	Baekmuk Korean TrueType fonts.
ttfonts-zh_CN	Arphic TrueType Font—GB ming and kai face.
ttfonts-zh_TW	Arphic TrueType Font—Big5 ming and kai face.
ttfprint	PostScript filter for Chinese.
tuxracer	Tux Racer.
tux	User-space component of TUX kernel-based threaded HTTP server.
tWnn	The tWnn Chinese character set input system.
ucd-snmp	A collection of SNMP protocol tools from UC-Davis.
ucd-snmp-devel	The development environment for the UCD-SNMP project.
ucd-snmp-utils	Network management utilities using SNMP, from the UCD-SNMP project.
umb-scheme	An implementation of the Scheme programming language.
unarj	An uncompressor for .arj format archive files.
units	A utility for converting amounts from one unit to another.
unix2dos	A UNIX to DOS text file format converter.
unixODBC	A complete ODBC driver manager for Linux.
unixODBC-devel	Development files for programs that will use the unixODBC library.

TABLE B.1   continued

Name	Description
unixODBC-kde	KDE driver manager components for ODBC.
unzip	A utility for unpacking zip files.
up2date	Determines which system packages need to be updated via RHN.
up2date-gnome	A GUI interface for Update Agent.
urw-fonts	Free versions of the 35 standard PostScript fonts.
usbview	A USB topology and device viewer.
usermode	Graphical tools for certain user account management tasks.
utempter	A privileged helper for utmp/wtmp updates.
util-linux	A collection of basic system utilities.
uucp	The uucp utility for copying files between systems.
VFlib2	A vector font library used for Japanese document processing.
VFlib2-devel	The header files and static library for VFlib v2.24.0.
VFlib2-VFjfm	Extra files and scripts for use with the VFlib library.
vim-common	The common files needed by any version of the VIM editor.
vim-enhanced	A version of the VIM editor that includes recent enhancements.
vim-minimal	A minimal version of the VIM editor.
vim-X11	The VIM version of the vi editor for the X Window System.
vixie-cron	The Vixie cron daemon for executing specified programs at set times.
vlock	A program that locks one or more virtual consoles.
vnc	A remote display system.
vnc-doc	Complete documentation for VNC.
vnc-server	A VNC server.
vorbis	The Vorbis General Audio Compression Codec libraries and tools.
w3c-libwww	An HTTP library of common code.
w3c-libwww-apps	Applications built using Libwww Web library.

TABLE B.1   continued

Name	Description
w3c-libwww-devel	Libraries and header files for programs that use libwww.
w3m	A pager with Web browsing capabilities.
w3m-el	W3m interface for emacsen.
watanabe-vf	The Watanabe font in SYOTAI CLUB format.
webalizer	A flexible Web server log file analysis program.
wget	A utility for retrieving files using the HTTP or FTP protocols.
which	Displays where a particular program in your path is located.
whois	An Internet whois client.
WindowMaker	A window manager for the X Window System.
WindowMaker-libs	Window Maker libraries.
wine	A Windows 16/32 bit emulator.
wine-devel	Wine development environment.
wireless-tools	Wireless Ethernet configuration tools.
wl	An IMAP4, POP, and NNTP client for GNU Emacs.
wl-xemacs	An IMAP4, POP, and NNTP client for XEmacs.
wmakerconf	A configuration tool for the Window Maker window manager.
Wnn6-SDK	A client library for Wnn6.
Wnn6-SDK-devel	Files needed for development of Wnn6 clients.
words	A dictionary of English words for the /usr/share/dict directory.
wu-ftpd	An FTP daemon provided by Washington University.
wvdial	A heuristic autodialer for PPP connections.
x3270	An X Window System based IBM 3278/3279 terminal emulator.
x3270-tcl	IBM 3278/3279 terminal emulator for TCL bindings.
x3270-text	An IBM 3278/3279 terminal emulator for text mode.
x3270-x11	IBM 3278/3279 terminal emulator for the X Window System.

B

RPM PACKAGE LISTINGS

TABLE B.1   continued

Name	Description
xalf	A utility to provide feedback when starting X11 applications.
Xaw3d	A version of the MIT Athena widget set for X.
Xaw3d-devel	Header files and static libraries for development using Xaw3d.
xawtv	A TV application for video4linux compliant devices.
xbill	Stop Bill from loading his OS into all the computers.
xbl	A 3D block dropping game for X.
xboard	An X Window System graphical chessboard.
xcdroast	An X Window System based tool for creating CDs.
xchat	A GTK+ IRC (chat) client.
xcin	An X Input Method Server for Chinese.
Xconfigurator	The Red Hat Linux configuration tool for the X Window System.
xcpustate	An X Window System based CPU state monitor.
xdaliclock	A clock for the X Window System.
xdelta	A binary file delta generator and an RCS replacement library.
xdelta-devel	Static library and header files for Xdelta development.
Xdialog	Xdialog in replacement for the cdialog program.
xemacs	An X Window System based version of GNU Emacs.
xemacs-el	The .el source files for XEmacs.
xemacs-info	Information files for XEmacs.
xfig	An X Window System tool for drawing basic vector graphics.
XFree86-100dpi-fonts	X Window System 100dpi fonts.
XFree86-3DLabs	The XFree86 server for 3Dlabs video cards.
XFree86-75dpi-fonts	A set of 75 dpi resolution fonts for the X Window System.
XFree86-8514	XFree86 server program for older IBM 8514 or compatible video cards.

TABLE B.1   continued

Name	Description
XFree86-AGX	The XFree86 server for AGX-based video cards.
XFree86-compat-libs	The Xv and Xxfdga shared libraries.
XFree86-compat-modules	Compatibility modules required by most XFree86 3.3.6 servers.
XFree86-cyrillic-fonts	Cyrillic fonts for X.
XFree86-devel	X11R6 static libraries, headers, and programming man pages.
XFree86-doc	Documentation on various X11 programming interfaces.
XFree86-FBDev	The X server for the generic frame buffer device on some machines.
XFree86-ISO8859-15-100dpi-fonts	ISO8859-15-100dpi-fonts.
XFree86-ISO8859-15-75dpi-fonts	ISO8859-15-75dpi-fonts.
XFree86-ISO8859-2-100dpi-fonts	ISO 8859-2 fonts in 100 dpi resolution for the X Window System.
XFree86-ISO8859-2-75dpi-fonts	A set of 75 dpi Central European language fonts for X.
XFree86-ISO8859-7-100dpi-fonts	ISO 8859-7 fonts in 100-dpi resolution for the X Window System.
XFree86-ISO8859-7-75dpi-fonts	ISO 8859-7 fonts in 75-dpi resolution for the X Window System.
XFree86-ISO8859-7	Greek language fonts for the X Window System.
XFree86-ISO8859-7-Type1-fonts	Type 1 scalable Greek (ISO 8859-7) fonts.
XFree86-ISO8859-9-100dpi-fonts	100 dpi Turkish (ISO8859-9) fonts for X.
XFree86-ISO8859-9-75dpi-fonts	75 dpi Turkish (ISO8859-9) fonts for X.
XFree86-jpfonts	Japanese fixed fonts for X11.
XFree86-KOI8-R-100dpi-fonts	KOI8-R fonts in 100-dpi resolution for the X Window System.
XFree86-KOI8-R-75dpi-fonts	A set of 75-dpi Russian and Ukrainian language fonts for X.
XFree86-KOI8-R	Russian and Ukrainian language fonts for the X Window System.
XFree86-libs	Shared libraries needed by X programs.

TABLE B.1   continued

Name	Description
XFree86-Mach32	The XFree86 server for Mach32 based video cards.
XFree86-Mach64	The XFree86 server for Mach64 based video cards.
XFree86-Mach8	The XFree86 server for Mach8 video cards.
XFree86-Mono	A generic XFree86 monochrome server for VGA cards.
XFree86-P9000	The XFree86 server for P9000 cards.
XFree86-S3	The XFree86 server for video cards based on the S3 chip.
XFree86-S3V	The XFree86 server for video cards based on the S3 ViRGE chip.
XFree86-SVGA	An XFree86 server for most simple framebuffer SVGA devices.
XFree86	The basic fonts, programs and docs for an X workstation.
XFree86-tools	Various tools for XFree86.
XFree86-twm	A simple, lightweight window manager for X.
XFree86-VGA16	A generic XFree86 server for VGA16 boards.
XFree86-W32	The XFree86 server for video cards based on ET4000/W32 chips.
XFree86-xdm	The X display manager.
XFree86-xf86cfg	A configuration tool for XFree86.
XFree86-xfs	A font server for the X Window System.
XFree86-Xnest	A nested XFree86 server.
XFree86-Xvfb	A virtual framebuffer X Windows System server for XFree86.
xinetd	A secure replacement for inetd.
xinitrc	The default startup script for the X Window System.
xisdnload	An ISDN connection load average display for the X Window System.
xloadimage	An X Window System based image viewer.
xlockmore	An X terminal locking program.
xmailbox	An X Window System utility that notifies you of new mail.

TABLE B.1 continued

Name	Description
xml-i18n-tools	This module contains some utility scripts and assorted auto* magic for internationalizing various kinds of XML files.
xmms	An MP3 player for X that resembles Winamp.
xmms-devel	Static libraries and header files for xmms plug-in development.
xmms-gnome	A GNOME panel applet for the xmms multimedia player.
xmms-skins	Skins for the xmms multimedia player.
xmorph	An X Window System tool for creating morphed images.
xosview	An X Window System utility for monitoring system resources.
xpdf	A PDF file viewer for the X Window System.
xpilot	An X Window System based multiplayer aerial combat game.
xrn	An X Window System based news reader.
xsane	An X Window System front end for the SANE scanner interface.
xsane-gimp	A GIMP plug-in that provides the SANE scanner interface.
xscreensaver	A set of X Window System screensavers.
xsnow	An X Window System based dose of Christmas cheer.
xsri	A program for displaying images on the background for X.
xsysinfo	An X Window System kernel parameter monitoring tool.
xtoolwait	A utility that aims to decrease X session startup time.
xtraceroute	An X and GTK+ based graphical display of traceroute's output.
ypbind	The NIS daemon that binds NIS clients to an NIS domain.

B

RPM PACKAGE LISTINGS

TABLE B.1   continued

Name	*Description*
ypserv	The NIS (Network Information Service) server.
yp-tools	NIS (or YP) client programs.
ytalk	A chat program for multiple users.
zebra	Routing daemon.
zip	A file compression and packaging utility compatible with PKZIP.
zlib-devel	Header files and libraries for zlib development.
zlib	The zlib compression and decompression library.
zsh	A shell similar to ksh, but with improvements.

This list should provide a quick reference to any system administrator that needs to know what a RPM package contains in general terms. The query rpm -qi *<package name>* will provide much more detail about a specific package that the administrator might require when packages are being upgraded or verified.

```
[tdc@phoenix RedHat]$ rpm -qi zlib
Name       : zlib                   Relocations: /usr
Version    : 1.1.3                  Vendor: Red Hat, Inc.
Release    : 23          Build Date: Mon 25 Jun 2001 01:18:29 AM EST
Install date: Sun 26 Aug 2001 02:11:57 PM EST
Build Host: porky.devel.redhat.com
Group      : System Environment/Libraries    Source RPM: zlib-1.1.3-23.src.rpm
Size       : 70941                    License: BSD
Packager   : Red Hat, Inc. <http://bugzilla.redhat.com/bugzilla>
URL        : http://www.gzip.org/zlib/
Summary    : The zlib compression and decompression library.
Description :
Zlib is a general-purpose, patent-free, lossless data compression
library which is used by many different programs.
```

Learning to use the RPM database via the text interface will provide any system administrator with the knowledge necessary to keep track of what is installed on the system and what version of software is currently available to the users.

Common Commands Quick Reference

Common Commands Quick Reference

APPENDIX C

This appendix contains an all-new, quick-reference guide to the most often used commands for Linux. The commands are based on a full install of Red Hat Linux and are grouped in 10 separate tables according to use. Each command is accompanied by a short description, and some files might overlap by category. For details about each command's full syntax and command-line options, see the command's GNU info file or associated man page.

File descriptions marked with '(X)' denote that the command is either generally used during an active X session or requires an active X session. (Note that this reference doesn't cover all the GNOME, KDE, and X11 clients, nor the hundreds of command-line graphics utilities included with Red Hat Linux.) The commands are grouped according to the following categories:

- Table C.1 Documentation—Tools used to display and read documentation
- Table C.2 Editing—tools used to create and edit text files
- Table C.3 Filesystem administration—Tools used to manage files and filesystems
- Table C.4 Navigation—Tools used to navigate or list directories
- Table C.5 Network administration—Tools used to manage networking and interfaces
- Table C.6 Printing—Tools used to set up, print, or manage printing
- Table C.7 Processes and resources—Tools used to monitor or manage system processes or resources
- Table C.8 Searching—Tools used to search files or file systems
- Table C.9 Software management—Tools used to manage system software
- Table C.10 User administration—Tools used to monitor or manage users

TABLE C.1 Documentation—Tools Used to Display and Read Documentation

Name	*Description*
cat	Send file to standard output
gv	Display, prints PostScript, PDF files (X)
head	Display beginning of file(s)
info	Display GNU info file(s)
less	Show, scroll text file(s)
lynx	Display HTML (text-only)
man	Display manual page(s)
more	Show, scroll text file(s)

TABLE C.1 continued

Name	Description
tail	Display end of file(s)
xpdf	Display, prints PDF file(s)
zcat	Print compress files(s)
zless	Display compressed file(s)

TABLE C.2 Editing—Tools Used to Create and Edit Text Files

Name	Description
aspell	Spell check text file(s)
cmp	Compare two files
csplit	Split a file into sections
ed	Line editor
emacs	Editing environment
enscript	Convert text file to PostScript
ex	Extended editor
fmt	Format file for printing
jed	Text editor
joe	Joe's Own Editor
gedit	GNOME text editor (X)
groff	Typeset files for printing
kwrite	KDE text editor (X)
latex	Text formatter, typesetter
look	Look up words in systemdictionary
mcedit	GUI console text editor
mpage	Multiple-page text-toPostScript utility
nedit	Motif text editor (X)
pico	Text editor included withpine
pr	Prepare text files for printing
sed	Stream text editor
sort	Sort lines in a file
strings	Show text in binary file
tac	Reverse file lister

C

COMMON
COMMANDS
QUICK REFERENCE

TABLE C.2   continued

Name	Description
tex	Text formatter, typesetter
tr	Transliterate character (sets) in text stream
uniq	Remove duplicate lines in a file
unix2dos	Convert text from UNIX to DOS
vi	Visual editor
view	Visual editor
vim	Visual editor, improved
wc	Count lines, words, characters in a file

TABLE C.3   Filesystem Administration—Tools Used to Manage Files and Filesystems

Name	Description
amanda	Back up files, directories
badblocks	Check filesystem for errors
cfdisk	GUI partition editor
chmod	Change file, directory permissions
chown	Change file, directory ownership
cp	Copy files
cpio	Create file, directory archive
dd	Copy, convert file
df	Display free disk space
du	Show disk usage
dump	Archive filesystem(s)
e2label	Label ext2 filesystem
eject	Eject, un-mount removable media
ext2ed	Filesystem editor
fdisk	Partition editor
file	Display file information
fsck	Diagnose, fix filesystem
gzip	Compress, decompress files, directories
ln	Create symbolic link
mformat	Format DOS filesystem

TABLE C.3 continued

Name	Description
mkdir	Create directories
mke2fs	Create ext2 filesystem
mkisofs	Create ISO 9660 image
mknod	Create device file
mkreiserfs	Create ReiserFS filesystem
mount	Make filesystem available
mv	Rename, move files, directories
parted	GNU partition editor
rmdir	Delete (empty) directories
shar	Create shell archive
smbmount	Make SMB filesystem available
stat	Display file information
symlinks	Check file system's symbolic links
sync	Flush disk buffers to filesystem
tar	Manage tape archives
touch	Create file, update timestamp
umount	Un-mount filesystem(s)
usermount	Mount, un-mount filesystems (X)
uudecode	Decode text file to binary
uuencode	Encode binary to text

C

COMMON
COMMANDS
QUICK REFERENCE

TABLE C.4 Navigation—Tools Used to Navigate or List Directories

Name	Description
cd	Change directory
ls	List directories or contents of directories
mc	GNU Midnight Commander, a graphical file tool
pwd	Print current working directory
tree	Show directory tree

Table C.5   Network Administration—Tools Used to Manage Networking and Interfaces

Name	Description
arpwatch	Track Ethernet IP addressing
dig	Query remote DNS servers
hostname	Display, set hostname
ifconfig	Display, configure network interfaces
ipchains	Administer firewall
ifport	Manage Ethernet interface transceiver type
iwconfig	Configure ireless network connections
linuxconf	Manage, control system (X)
netconf	Manage network interfaces (X)
netreport	Set network change notification
netstat	Display network status
nslookup	Obtain IP address of remote host
ping	Measure packet transmission times from remote host
route	Display, manage kernel routing table
ruser	Show network users logged in
tcpdump	Display network traffic
traceroute	Display packet path to remote computer

Table C.6   Printing—Tools Used to Set Up, Print, or Manage Printing

Name	Description
checkpc	Verify /etc/printcap
lpc	Manage printers
lpd	Print spooler daemon
lpq	Manage print spool queue
lpr	Print files
lprm	Delete spooled files
lpstat	Display printer status
printtool	Configure printer (X)

TABLE C.7 Processes and Resources—Tools Used to Monitor or Manage System Processes or Resources

Name	Description
at	Run command at specified time
bg	Send shell process to background
chkconfig	Check Red Hat system runlevels
crontab	Schedule regular user, systemtasks
dmesg	Display boot information
env	Display user shell environment
fg	Bring background shell process to foreground
free	Show free, shared, swap memory
jobs	Display background shell processes
kill	Kill a process by PID
killall	Kill all named processes
lsof	List all open files
nice	Assign process priority
ntsysv	Start, stop service at boot time
ps	Show processes
pstree	Show process inheritance
shutdown	Shut down or reboot system
tksysv	Runlevel editor (X)
uname	Display system, version
uptime	Show system uptime, users
vmstat	Show virtual memory statistics
w	Display uptime and who
who	Display logged in users
xload	Display system load (X)
xosview	Display system load, resources (X)

C

COMMON COMMANDS QUICK REFERENCE

TABLE C.8 Searching—Tools Used to Search Files or File Systems

Name	Description
apropos	Display related commands
find	Search filesystem(s)

TABLE C.8 continued

Name	Description
grep	Search files
locate	Display file locations
manpath	Display manual page locations
pick	Search message files
whatis	Display command
whereis	Display command locations
which	Show pathname to file
zgrep	Search compressed files
zipgrep	Search compressed archive

TABLE C.9 Software Management—Tools Used to Manage System Software

Name	Description
gnorpm	GNOME RPM client
kpackage	KDE RPM client
rpm	Red Hat Package manager
rpm2cpio	Extract cpio archive from RPM file format

TABLE C.10 User Administration—Tools Used to Monitor or Manage Users

Name	Description
ac	Show user connect times
chage	Change password expiration
chfn	Change finger information
chgrp	Change group ownership
chmod	Change file permissions
chown	Change file ownership
chsh	Change user's shell
finger	Display user information
groupadd	Create new group
groups	Display user group information
id	Display user information

TABLE C.10 continued

Name	Description
last	Display last logins
linuxconf	Manage users
logname	Display user login name
mkpasswd	Create user password
passwd	Change passwords
quota	Display user disk usage, limits
su	Run commands as other user
useradd	Create new user
userconf	Manage users (X)
userdel	Remove user from system
userinfo	GUI chfn tool (X)
w	Show uptime, who information
who	Display users logged in
whoami	Display current username

INDEX

What's on the Discs

The companion CD-ROMs contain Red Hat Linux 7.2 and the Publisher's Edition software.

Installing Red Hat Linux from the CD-ROM

1. Insert the installation disc (Disc 1) in the CD drive.
2. Restart your computer.
3. You may need to change your BIOS settings to boot from the CD-ROM. Typically, you enter your BIOS setup program with the F2 or Delete keys during the boot sequence.
4. Make your changes (if any) and exit the BIOS setup utility.
5. If your CD drive is capable of booting from CD-ROMs, you will boot into the Red Hat Linux setup program.
6. Follow the onscreen prompts to complete the installation.

Installing Red Hat Linux from Boot Floppies

1. Using DOS or Windows, format one 1.44MB floppy disk.
2. Navigate to the DOSUTILS directory on the installation disc (Disc 1).
3. Double-click on RAWRITE.EXE or type RAWRITE from a DOS prompt.
4. When prompted to do so, type in the name ..\IMAGES\BOOT.IMG and press Enter.
5. When prompted to do so, type in the drive letter of the disk(s) you are going to prepare and press Enter. Since you are going to be booting from this disk, it's typically A:.
6. If you don't already have the boot floppy in your disk drive, insert it now.
7. Restart your computer.
8. You may need to change your BIOS settings to boot from the floppy drive. Typically, you enter your BIOS setup program with the F2 or Delete keys during the boot sequence.
9. Make your changes (if any) and exit the BIOS setup utility.
10. If your computer is set up properly, you will boot into the Red Hat Linux setup program.
11. Follow the onscreen prompts to complete the installation.

License Agreement and Limited Product Warranty—Red Hat Linux 7.2

Please read this document carefully before installing Red Hat® Linux®, any of its packages, or any software included with this product, on your computer. This document contains important information about your legal rights. By installing any or all of the software included with this product, you agree to the following terms and conditions.

GENERAL

As used herein, "EULA" means an end user license agreement, and "Software Programs" means, collectively, the Linux Programs, the Third-Party Programs, the PowerTools Programs, the Loki Programs, and the Developer Programs, as each of those terms is defined herein.

Red Hat Linux is a modular operating system made up of hundreds of individual software components, each of which was written and copyrighted individually. Each component has its own applicable end user license agreement. Throughout this document the components are referred to, individually and collectively, as the "Linux Programs." Most of the Linux Programs are licensed pursuant to a Linux EULA that permits you to copy, modify, and redistribute the software, in both source code and binary code forms. However, you must review the on-line documentation that accompanies each of the Linux Programs included in this product for the applicable Linux EULA. Review these Linux EULAs carefully, in order to understand your rights under them and to realize the maximum benefits available to you with Red Hat Linux. Nothing in this license agreement limits your rights under, or grants you rights that supersede, the terms of any applicable Linux EULA.

The "Linux Applications CD—Workstation Edition"[1] and the "Linux Applications CD—Server Edition"[2] include an assortment of applications from third-party vendors. Throughout this document each of these software components are referred to, individually and collectively, as "Third-Party Programs." Generally, each of these Third-Party Programs is licensed to you by the vendor pursuant to an end user license agreement ("Third-Party EULA") that generally permits you to install each of these products on only a single computer for your own individual use. Copying, redistribution, reverse engineering, and/or modification of these components may be prohibited, and you must look to the terms and conditions of the Third-Party EULA to determine your rights and any limitations imposed on you. Any violation by you of the applicable Third-Party EULA terms shall immediately terminate your license under that Third-Party EULA. For the precise terms of the Third-Party EULAs for each of these Third-Party Programs, please check the on-line documentation that accompanies each of them. If you do not agree to abide by the applicable license terms for these Third-Party Programs, then do not install them on your computer. If you wish to install these Third-Party Programs on more than one computer, please contact the vendor of the program to purchase additional licenses.

The "PowerTools CD"[3] includes many individual software components, each of which was written and copyrighted individually. Throughout this document each of these software components are referred to, individually and collectively, as "PowerTools Programs." Each PowerTool Program has its own applicable PowerTool EULA. Most of the PowerTools Programs are licensed to you pursuant to a PowerTool EULA that permits you to copy, modify, and redistribute the software, in both source code and binary code forms. However, you must review the on-line documentation that accompanies each of the PowerTools Programs included in this product for the applicable PowerTool EULA. Review these PowerTool EULAs carefully, in order to understand your rights under them and to realize the maximum benefits available to you with these PowerTools Programs. Nothing in this license agreement limits your rights under, or grants you rights that supersede, the terms of any applicable PowerTool EULA.

The Loki Games CD[4] includes software licensed to you from Loki Corporation (the "Loki Programs"). For the precise terms of the license to you for the Loki Programs, please check the on-line documentation that accompanies them. If you do not agree to abide by the applicable Loki license terms for the Loki Programs, then do not install them on your computer. If you wish to install the Loki Programs on more than one computer, please contact Loki to purchase additional licenses.

The "Developer Modules Archive CD"[5] contains Perl, Python and Zope programs, utilities and documentation. It includes many software components (the "Developer Programs"), each of which was written and copyrighted individually. Each Developer Program has its own applicable Developer EULA. Most of these programs are licensed to you pursuant to a Developer EULA that permits you to copy, modify, and redistribute the Developer Program, in both source code and binary code forms. However, you must review the on-line documentation that accompanies each of the programs included in this product for the applicable Developer EULA. Review these Developer EULAs carefully, in order to understand your rights under them and to realize the maximum benefits available to you with these programs. Nothing in this license agreement limits your rights under, or grants you rights that supersede, the terms of any applicable Developer EULA for these Developer Programs.

BEFORE INSTALLATION

CAREFULLY READ THE FOLLOWING TERMS AND CONDITIONS BEFORE INSTALLING ANY OF THE SOFTWARE PROGRAMS. INSTALLING THE SOFTWARE PROGRAMS INDICATES YOUR ACCEPTANCE OF THE TERMS AND CONDITIONS SET FORTH IN THIS DOCUMENT AND OF THE END USER LICENSE AGREEMENT ASSOCIATED WITH THE SOFTWARE PROGRAM. IF YOU DO NOT AGREE WITH THESE TERMS AND CONDITIONS, DO NOT INSTALL THE SOFTWARE PROGRAMS.

THE SOFTWARE PROGRAMS, INCLUDING SOURCE CODE, DOCUMENTATION, APPEARANCE, STRUCTURE AND ORGANIZATION, ARE PROPRIETARY PRODUCTS OF RED HAT, INC. AND OTHERS AND ARE PROTECTED BY COPYRIGHT AND OTHER LAWS. TITLE TO THESE PROGRAMS, OR TO ANY COPY, MODIFICATION OR MERGED PORTION OF ANY OF THESE PROGRAMS, SHALL AT ALL TIMES REMAIN WITH THE AFOREMENTIONED, SUBJECT TO THE TERMS AND CONDITIONS OF THE APPLICABLE EULA RELATED TO THE SOFTWARE PROGRAMS UNDER CONSIDERATION.

THE "RED HAT" TRADEMARK AND RED HAT'S SHADOW MAN LOGO ARE REGISTERED TRADEMARKS OF RED HAT, INC. IN THE UNITED STATES AND OTHER COUNTRIES. WHILE THIS LICENSE AGREEMENT ALLOWS YOU TO COPY, MODIFY AND DISTRIBUTE THE SOFTWARE, IT DOES NOT PERMIT YOU TO DISTRIBUTE THE SOFTWARE UTILIZING RED HAT'S TRADEMARKS. YOU SHOULD READ THE INFORMATION FOUND AT `http://www.redhat.com/about/ trademark_guidelines.html` BEFORE DISTRIBUTING A COPY OF THE SOFTWARE, REGARDLESS OF WHETHER IT HAS BEEN MODIFIED.

CERTAIN LIMITED TECHNICAL SUPPORT SERVICES ACCOMPANY RED HAT LINUX. THE RIGHT TO USE THOSE TECHNICAL SUPPORT SERVICES ARE LIMITED TO THE ORIGINAL PURCHASE OF THE PRODUCT. WHILE YOU HAVE THE RIGHT TO TRANSFER YOUR COPY OF RED HAT LINUX TO ANOTHER PARTY, YOU MAY NOT TRANSFER THE RIGHT TO USE THOSE TECHNICAL SUPPORT SERVICES ONCE YOU HAVE REGISTERED FOR PRODUCT SUPPORT. ANY ATTEMPT TO TRANSFER TECHNICAL SUPPORT SERVICES FOLLOWING REGISTRATION WILL RENDER YOUR RIGHT TO THE TECHNICAL SUPPORT SERVICES NULL AND VOID.

LIMITED WARRANTY

EXCEPT AS SPECIFICALLY STATED IN THIS AGREEMENT OR IN AN EULA, THE SOFTWARE PRO-GRAMS ARE PROVIDED AND LICENSED "AS IS" WITHOUT WARRANTY OF ANY KIND, EITHER EXPRESSED OR IMPLIED, INCLUDING, BUT NOT LIMITED TO, THE IMPLIED WARRANTIES OF MERCHANTABILITY, NON-INFRINGEMENT, AND FITNESS FOR A PARTICULAR PURPOSE.

Red Hat, Inc. warrants that the media on which any of the Software Programs are furnished will be free from defects in materials and manufacture under normal use for a period of 30 days from the date of delivery to you. Red Hat, Inc. does not warrant that the functions contained in the Software Programs will meet your requirements or that the operation of the Software Programs will be entirely error free or appear precisely as described in the accompanying documentation.

ANY WARRANTY OR REMEDY PROVIDED UNDER THIS AGREEMENT EXTENDS ONLY TO THE PARTY WHO PURCHASES RED HAT LINUX FROM RED HAT OR A RED HAT AUTHORIZED DISTRIBUTOR.

LIMITATION OF REMEDIES AND LIABILITY

To the maximum extent permitted by applicable law, the remedies described below are accepted by you as your only remedies, and shall be available to you only if you or your dealer registers this product with Red Hat, Inc. in accordance with the instructions provided with this product within ten days after delivery of the Software Programs to you.

Red Hat, Inc.'s entire liability, and your exclusive remedies, shall be: if the Software Programs media are defective, you may return them within 30 days of delivery to you along with a copy of your receipt and Red Hat, Inc., at its option, will replace them or refund the money paid by you for the Software Programs. **TO THE MAXIMUM EXTENT PERMITTED BY APPLICABLE LAW, IN NO EVENT WILL RED HAT, INC. BE LIABLE TO YOU FOR ANY DAMAGES, INCLUDING LOST PROFITS, LOST SAVINGS, OR OTHER INCIDENTAL OR CONSEQUENTIAL DAMAGES, ARISING OUT OF THE USE OR INABILITY TO USE THE SOFTWARE PROGRAMS, EVEN IF RED HAT, INC. OR A DEALER AUTHORIZED BY RED HAT, INC. HAD BEEN ADVISED OF THE POSSIBILITY OF SUCH DAMAGES.**

GENERAL

If any provision of this Agreement is held to be unenforceable, that shall not effect the enforceability of the remaining provisions. This Agreement shall be governed by the laws of the State of North Carolina and of the United States, without regard to any conflict of laws provisions.

This product includes software developed by the OpenSSL Project for use in the OpenSSL Toolkit. (http://www.openssl.org/). This product includes cryptographic software written by Eric Young (eay@cryptsoft.com).

> **1** *"Linux Applications CD—Workstation Edition" is included in Deluxe Workstation and Professional Server only*
> **2** *"Linux Applications CD—Server Edition" is included in Professional Server only*
> **3** *"PowerTools" CD is included in Deluxe Workstation and Professional Server only*
> **4** *"Loki Games" CD is included in Deluxe Workstation and Professional Server only*
> **5** *"Developer Module Archive" CD is included in Professional Server only*

Read This Before Opening the Software

By opening this package, you are agreeing to be bound by the following agreement:

Individual programs and other items on the CD-ROM are copyrighted or are under an Open Source license by their various authors or other copyright holders.

This software is sold as-is without warranty of any kind, either expressed or implied, including but not limited the implied warranties of merchantability and fitness for a particular purpose. Neither the publisher nor its deal ers or distributors assumes any liability for any alleged or actual damages arising from the use of this program. (Some states do not allow for the exclusion of implied warranties, so the exclusion may not apply to you.)

This book includes a copy of the Publisher's Edition of Red Hat® Linux® from Red Hat, Inc., which you may use in accordance with the license agreement found on page 863. Official Red Hat® Linux®, which you may purchase from Red Hat, includes the complete Red Hat® Linux® distribution, Red Hat's documentation, and may include technical support for Red Hat® Linux®. You also may purchase technical support from Red Hat. You may purchase Red Hat® Linux® and technical support from Red Hat through the company's Web site (www.redhat.com) or its toll-free number 1.888.REDHAT1.

DATE DUE

OCT 12 2003			

Demco, Inc. 38-293